D1047675

CYCLING
IRELAND

Ian Connellan
Nicky Crowther
Nicola Wells

WITHDRAWN

LONELY PLANET PUBLICATIONS
Melbourne • Oakland • London • Paris

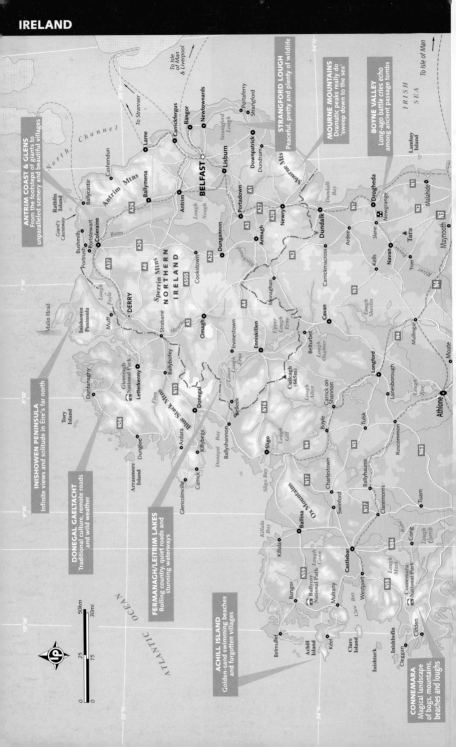

IRELAND

ANTRIM COAST & GLENS
From the footsteps of giants to
unparalleled scenery and beautiful villages

INISHOWEN PENINSULA
Infinite views and solitude in Éire's far north

DONEGAL GAELTACHT
Traditional culture, remote roads
and wild weather

FERMANAGH/LEITRIM LAKES
Rolling country, quiet roads and
stunning waterways

ACHILL ISLAND
Golden-sand swimming beaches
and forgotten villages

CONNEMARA
Magical landscape
of bogs, mountains,
beaches and loughs

STRANGFORD LOUGH
Peaceful, pretty and plenty of wildlife

MOURNE MOUNTAINS
Dramatic peaks really do
sweep down to the sea

BOYNE VALLEY
Long-ago battle cries echo
among ancient passage tombs

NORTHERN IRELAND

BELFAST

DERRY

Sperrin Mtns

Antrim Mtns

Mourne Mtns

IRISH SEA

ATLANTIC OCEAN

North Channel

To Isle of Man
& Liverpool

To Stranraer

To Isle of Man

To Isle of Man

Newtownards
Bangor
Carrickfergus
Larne
Cushendun
Ballycastle
Rathlin Island
Portstewart
Portrush
Coleraine
Bushmills
Giant's Causeway
Portrush
Malin Head
Inishowen Peninsula
Muff
Strabane
Lifford
Glenveagh National Park
Letterkenny
Ballybofey
Donegal
Ardara
Killybegs
Carrick
Glencolmcille
Dunglow
Arranmore Island
Tory Island

Portaferry
Strangford
Downpatrick
Dundrum
Lisburn
Portadown
Antrim
Lough Neagh
Ballymena
Dungannon
Cookstown
Omagh
Irvinestown
Enniskillen
Belturbet
Cavan
Monaghan
Carrickmacross
Armagh
Newry
Dundalk
Dundalk Bay
Drogheda
Newgrange
Slane
Tara
Navan
Trim
Kells
Ardee
Maynooth
Malahide
Lambay Island

Belleek
Cuilcagh (665m)
Lough Allen
Carrick on Shannon
Boyle
Tulsk
Roscommon
Longford
Lanesborough
Athlone
Moate
Mullingar
Lough Ree
Lough Sheelin
Lough Oughter

Sligo
Lough Gill
Ballyshannon
Donegal Bay
Blue Stack Mtns
Sligo Bay
Killala Bay
Killala
Ballina
Ox Mountains
Swinford
Charlestown
Ballyhaunis
Claremorris
Tuam
Ballaghaderreen

Belmullet
Achill Island
Keel
Clare Island
Inishturk
Inishbofin
Cleggan
Clifden
Connemara National Park
Cong
Lough Corrib
Lough Mask
Westport
Clew Bay
Castlebar
Mulrany
Ballycroy National Park
Bangor
Lough Conn

ATLANTIC OCEAN

A2
A26
A29
A37
A6
A5
A505
A32
A4
A1
A3
A28
A27
A24
N2
N1
N3
N4
N5
N55
N56
N15
N16
N17
N84
N59
N63

Bann
River Foyle
River Erne
Lower Lough Erne
Upper Lough Erne
River Boyne
River Moy

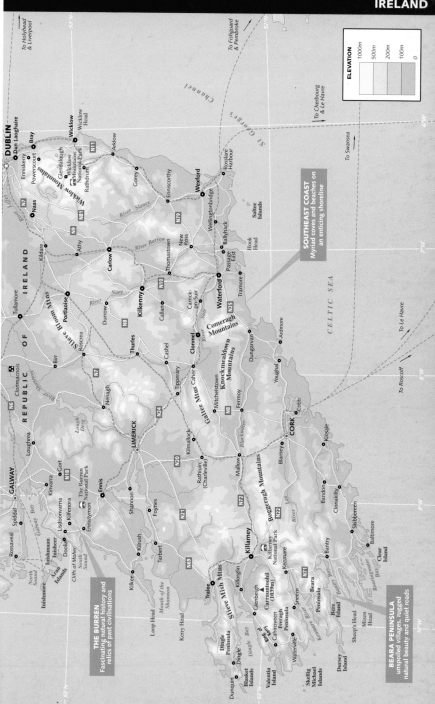

IRELAND

ELEVATION
1000m
500m
200m
100m
0

To Holyhead
& Liverpool

To Fishguard & Pembroke

To Cherbourg
& Le Havre

To Swansea

To Le Havre

To Roscoff

DUBLIN
Dun Laoghaire
Enniskerry
Powerscourt
Bray
Wicklow
Wicklow Head
Glendalough
Wicklow Mountains National Park
Rathdrum
Naas
Arklow
N7
N11
Wicklow Mountains
N81
Gorey
Enniscorthy
Wexford
Rosslare Harbour
Saltee Islands
N9
Kildare
Athy
River Slaney
N79
Carlow
N80
New Ross
Wellingtonbridge
Ballyhack
Hook Head
River Barrow
Thomastown
Passage East
Tullamore
Portlaoise
Kilkenny
N10
Durrow
River Nore
Callan
Carrick-on-Suir
Waterford
Tramore
Birr
Roscrea
Thurles
N8
Cashel
Clonmel
N25
Comeragh Mountains
Dungarvan
Ardmore
Slieve Bloom Mtns
REPUBLIC OF IRELAND
Clonmacnois
Loughrea
N6
GALWAY
Nenagh
Tipperary
Gallee Mtns
Caher
Knockmealdown Mountains
Mitchelstown
Fermoy
N8
Youghal
Cobh
River Suir
Lough Derg
River Shannon
LIMERICK
N24
Kilmallock
N20
Rathluirc (Charleville)
Mallow
Blarney
CORK
Kinsale
Blackwater River
Rosaveal
Spiddal
Kinvarra
Gort
N18
Ennis
Shannon
Foynes
N21
Boggeragh Mountains
N22
Bandon
Clonakilty
Skibbereen
Galway Bay
Inishmore
Inishmaan
Inisheer
Aran Islands
Lisdoonvarna
Kilfenora
Ennistymon
The Burren National Park
Doolin
Cliffs of Moher
South Sound
North Sound
Kilrush
Kilkee
Tarbert
N69
Killarney National Park
Killarney
Kenmare
Bantry
N71
Bere Island
Clear Island
Baltimore
Mouth of the Shannon
Loop Head
Kerry Head
Tralee
Slieve Mish Mtns
Killorglin
Carrauntoohil (1039m)
Glenbeigh
Ring of Kerry
Cahirciveen
Iveragh Peninsula
Sneem
Beara Peninsula
Kenmare River
Roughty River
Dingle Peninsula
Dingle
Dunquin
Blasket Islands
Valentia Island
Waterville
Skellig Michael Islands
Dursey Island
Sheep's Head
Mizen Head
Bantry Bay
Roaringwater Bay

St George's Channel

Irish Sea

CELTIC SEA

SOUTHEAST COAST
Myriad coves and beaches on an enticing shoreline

THE BURREN
Fascinating natural history and relics of past civilisations

BEARA PENINSULA
unspoiled villages, rugged natural beauty and quiet roads

Cycling Ireland
1st edition – July 2003

Published by
Lonely Planet Publications Pty Ltd ABN. 36 005 607 983
90 Maribyrnong St, Footscray, Victoria 3011, Australia

Lonely Planet Offices
Australia Locked Bag 1, Footscray, Victoria 3011
USA 150 Linden St, Oakland, CA 94607
UK 72-82 Rosebery Ave, London, EC1R 4RW
France 1 rue du Dahomey, 75011 Paris

Photographs
Many of the images in this guide are available for licensing from
Lonely Planet Images.
w www.lonelyplanetimages.com

Main front cover photograph
Empty roads and breathtaking views on the Ballyvoy–Cushendun scenic road (Ian Connellan)

Small front cover photograph
No bicycles allowed – P Egan's pub, Moate, County Westmeath (Richard Cummins)

ISBN 1 74059 316 2

Printed through Colorcraft Ltd, Hong Kong
Printed in China

Although the authors and Lonely Planet try to make the information as accurate as possible, we accept no responsibility for any loss, injury or inconvenience sustained by anyone using this book.

Contents

2 Contents

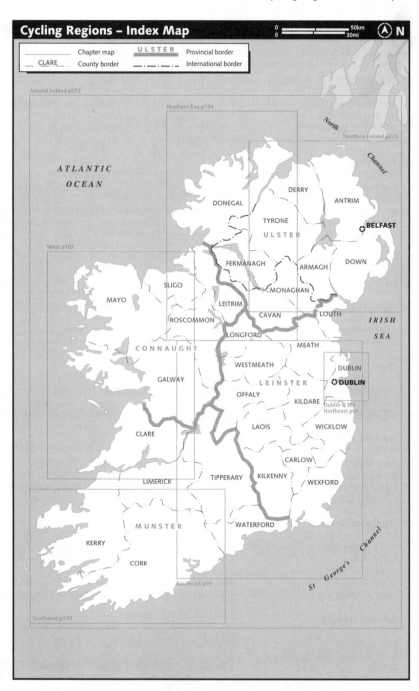

Cycling Regions – Index Map

	0	50km
	0	30mi

N

	Chapter map	ULSTER	Provincial border
CLARE	County border		International border

Around Ireland p252

Northern Éire p194

North

Northern Ireland p223

ATLANTIC
OCEAN

North Channel

DONEGAL

DERRY

ANTRIM

TYRONE

ULSTER

BELFAST

West p162

FERMANAGH

ARMAGH

DOWN

MAYO

SLIGO

MONAGHAN

LEITRIM

CAVAN

LOUTH

IRISH

ROSCOMMON

LONGFORD

MEATH

SEA

CONNAUGHT

WESTMEATH

DUBLIN

GALWAY

LEINSTER

DUBLIN

OFFALY

KILDARE

Dublin & the
Northeast p65

LAOIS

WICKLOW

CLARE

CARLOW

LIMERICK

TIPPERARY

KILKENNY

WEXFORD

MUNSTER

WATERFORD

St George's Channel

KERRY

CORK

Southeast p94

Southwest p130

The Rides	Duration	Distance	Difficulty
Dublin & the Northeast			
Cycling to/from the Airport	1–1¼ hours	11.4km	easy
Dublin Orientation	2–3 hours	11.6km	easy
Heart of Ireland Explorer	8 days	557.3km	easy–moderate
Hunting the Bog of Allen	4½–8 hours	82.9km	easy
Slieve Bloom Mountains	3–5½ hours	55.0km	hard
Westmeath Lakeland & the Fore Valley	4½–8½ hours	83.8km	easy
Southeast			
Into the Wicklow Mountains	2 days	115.7km	moderate–hard
Wicklow, Carlow & Wexford	3 days	216.3km	easy–moderate
Mt Leinster Ascent	2–3 hours	42.4km	hard
Tipperary & Waterford Highlands	4 days	304.6km	easy–moderate
Comeragh Mountains	5–9 hours	90.5km	hard
Waterford, Kilkenny & Cashel	3 days	209.3km	easy–moderate
Southeast Coast Cruise	2 days	160.5km	moderate
Southwest			
Harbour Hopping in Southwest Cork	4 days	220.0km	moderate
Ring of Beara	2 days	130.3km	hard
Ring of Kerry	4 days	221.9km	moderate–hard
Dingle Peninsula	3 days	176.6km	moderate–hard
West			
Clare Circuit	6 days	348.0km	moderate
Connemara & Inishmór	7 days	349.2km	moderate
Beaches & Bogs	4 days	303.9km	moderate–hard
Northern Éire			
Donegal to Derry	5 days	338.2km	moderate
Donegal Highlands	2 days	121.3km	moderate–hard
Inishowen Circuit	3 days	168.5km	moderate–hard
Kingfisher Country	3 days	201.5km	moderate
Northern Ireland			
Across Ulster	3 days	139.1mi/224.1km	moderate
Antrim Coast	2 days	92.0mi/148.2km	moderate–hard
Glens of Antrim	3–5 hours	25.3mi/40.7km	moderate
Down South	3 days	127.1mi/204.6km	easy–moderate
Mourne Mountains Circuit	3–5 hours	27.5mi/44.3km	moderate–hard
Around Ireland			
Around Ireland	42 days	2798.6km	hard
Totals	**124 days**	**7981.2km**	**30 rides**

Features	Page

The Authors

Ian Connellan

Sydney-born Ian spent much of the 1980s ski- and cycle- bumming in Australia, the USA and Europe before starting work as a writer and editor. Since the late 1980s, he has written for newspapers and magazines, edited magazines and books, and flirted with proper grown-up life as a book-publishing manager. Currently Ian is a part-time travel author and full-time homekeeper/father with a hard-working partner and under-10 twins; they all live amid clutter in northern Sydney. Ian has also written for Lonely Planet's *Cycling Australia* and *Cycling Britain*.

Nicky Crowther

Having grown up cycling in London, Nicky toured New Zealand, Iceland and the Rocky Mountains before returning to her home town for a second look. The result was a handbook of London cycle routes, from which she went on to contribute to Lonely Planet's *Cycling Britain*. She is former national-level mountain-bike racer, and continues to compete as an amateur, to commute by bike and to cycle tour. She nurtures a dream to one day ride the 4000km (2500mi) Great Divide route the length of the Rockies from New Mexico to Montana.

Nicola Wells

Nicola lives in Melbourne and grew up in regional Victoria. She rode a bike while living in Sweden, aged 12, and rediscovered cycling at university, where she became passionate about the environmental, social and health benefits it offers. Cycling is still her main transport, preserver of sanity and preferred mode for travel. With an honours degree in ecology, she has had various writing and research-based jobs, worked for Bicycle Victoria and done a stint in a bike shop. Her other passions include music, especially choral singing (which, she regrets, is not terribly compatible with cycle touring) and food (which is). She has a particular weakness for good coffee. Nicola has also written for Lonely Planet's *Cycling New Zealand*, *Cycling Britain* and *Cycling Australia*.

FROM THE AUTHORS

Ian Connellan Thanks to Jane, Tess and Adam for holding the fort, Nicola and Nicky for Dublin fun and general on-timeness, and Jac and James for queues, views and fun on the way home. Cyclist, Dubliner and riverside bagel–gourmand Damien O'Tuama provided Ralph Raleigh the rental bike (Mk II), advice, baggage storage and bright company – heartfelt thanks. Northern Ireland Tourist Board staff in Derry and Belfast, especially Gillian Little, were patient and helpful. Dr Peter Pyne's tips for Derry proved unerring, Joan's friendliness and unexpected bath were a godsend, and Philomena's eggs and insight were a revelation. Mourne Mountains hill-climbing partner Austin Flynn told of life in the North; Seamus O'Kane revealed some of the mysteries of *bodhrán* playing; Thomas Hughes gave a tutorial on turf cutting. Iris McCann told quiet, powerful tales about Omagh; Jeanette Zulli shared biscuits and St Patrick in Armagh. In Sligo town, Seamus Flanagan pointed out the best local roads. Leo and Mary served tea, biscuits and *craic* in Glencolmcille. Chris Perkins gave route advice and led to great trad music. For background for the introductory chapters, special thanks to the authors of Lonely Planet's *Ireland*, *Walking in Ireland* and *Dublin*.

Nicky Crowther Thanks Oonagh Sheehan for help with the Battle of the Boyne; Charles McCarthy of NorthConsult for info on the Dublin–Belfast motorway; Frank Quinn for the latest on Sean Kelly; the librarians at Wexford, Waterford, Carlow, New Ross and Tramore who hunted high and low; and Jill and Monica for timely map aid in the Victoria. For their personal backup, thanks to Mel of Brixton Cycles for her technical support, to Phil for taking on offspring duties when it was critical, and particularly to Judith, without whom I could not have done the job.

Nicola Wells I'd especially like to thank to Ian Connellan, Darren Elder, my family, Nicky Crowther and Noella Sullivan without whose encouragement and support my legs may not have made it to the airport, let alone around western Ireland. I'm indebted to those who patiently and passionately gave advice about good cycling in Ireland: Chris Perkins and Kieran Byrne in Dublin, Michael Gibbons and Richard in Clifden, Karl in Doolin, the Mountain Trail Bike Shop in Galway, and Rothar Bike Shop and Frank Donaldson in Cork. To biking buddies I met along the way: Sean, Bernard, Miriam, Paul and others, your camaraderie, tips and impressions were much appreciated. Yvonne and Mark kindly provided a warm welcome and an unexpected cultural highlight in Limerick. Speaking of cultural highlights, Luka, thanks for the show and the lowdown in Killarney. For the Keem Bay tour and a pint, I'll remember you, Shea. And to Mr and Mr Congeniality, Stuey and Paul, thanks you guys – dinner's on me, okay?

UPDATES & READER FEEDBACK

Things change – prices go up; schedules change; bad dirt roads get paved and decent ones get washed out; good places go bad and bad places go bankrupt. Nothing stays the same. So, if you find things better or worse, recently opened or long-since closed, please tell us and help make the next edition even more accurate and useful.

Lonely Planet thoroughly updates each guidebook as often as possible – usually every two years, although for some destinations the gap can be longer. Between editions, up-to-date information is available in our free, monthly email bulletin *Comet* (ⓦ www.lonelyplanet.com/newsletters). You can also check out the *Thorn Tree* bulletin board and *Postcards* section of our website, which carry unverified, but fascinating, reports from travellers.

Tell us about it! We genuinely value your feedback. A well-travelled team at Lonely Planet reads and acknowledges every email and letter we receive and ensures that every morsel of information finds its way to the relevant authors, editors and cartographers.

Everyone who writes to us will find their name listed in the next edition of the appropriate guidebook. The very best contributions will be rewarded with a free guidebook.

We may edit, reproduce and incorporate your comments in Lonely Planet products such as guidebooks, websites and digital products, so let us know if you don't want your comments reproduced or your name acknowledged.

How to contact Lonely Planet:
Online: ⓔ talk2us@lonelyplanet.com.au, ⓦ www.lonelyplanet.com
Australia: Locked Bag 1, Footscray, Victoria 3011
UK: 72-82 Rosebery Ave, London, EC1R 4RW
USA: 150 Linden St, Oakland, CA 94607

Maps & Profiles

Rides in this book have an accompanying map that shows the route, services provided in towns en route, attractions (look for the star symbol) and possible alternative routes and side trips, depending on the map scale. For greater detail, we also recommend the most suitable commercial map available in the 'Maps' section of each ride.

We provide a profile or elevation chart when there is a significant amount of climbing and/or descending on a day's ride. These charts are included with the cues for the day. Elevation profiles are approximate and should be used as a guide only.

Map Legend

Note: not all symbols displayed below appear in this book

CUE SHEET SYMBOLS

Continue Straight	Left Turn	Point of Interest	Traffic Lights
Right Turn	Veer Left	Mountain, Hill	Roundabout/Traffic Circle
Veer Right	Return Trip	Caution or Hazard	Side Trip/Alternative Route

MAP SYMBOLS

Airport/Airfield	Gallery, Museum	Point of Interest
Bike Shop	Hospital	Post Office
Church	Information	Restaurant, Pub, Café
Camping	Place to Stay	Store, Supermarket
Embassy		

POPULATION

CAPITAL .... National Capital	LARGE Medium .... City	Town .. Day Start/End Town on Ride
CAPITAL .... State Capital	Town Village .... Town	Urban Area

ROUTES & TRANSPORT

M1 .... Freeway, Tunnel	Train Line, Train Station
N7 .... Primary Road	Tramway, Bus Terminal
N76 .... Main Road	Bikepath, Track
R543 .... Secondary Road	Cable Car, Chairlift
Unsealed Road	Ferry
Lane (One-way)	

CYCLING ROUTES

Main Route
Alternative Route
Side Trip
Other Routes
Route Direction

HYDROGRAPHIC FEATURES

Coastline, River, Creek	Spring, Rapids
Canal	Swamp
Lake	Waterfalls

TOPOGRAPHIC FEATURES

Cave
Cliff
Mountain, Hill
Pass, Saddle

AREA FEATURES

Building	Beach
Cemetery	Glacier
National Park	Mall, Market

BOUNDARIES

International
County
Disputed

Cue Sheets

Route directions are given in a series of brief 'cues', which tell you at what kilometre point (mileage point in Northern Ireland) to change direction and point out features en route. You'll find the cues (some with elevation profiles) in the text near each day's description. Cues should be used in conjunction with the map recommended in each ride's Maps section. The only other thing you need is a cycle computer.

To make the cue sheets as brief and simple to understand as possible, we've developed a series of symbols (see the Map Legend on p8) and the following rule:

Once your route is following a particular road, continue on that road until the cue sheet tells you otherwise.

Follow the road first mentioned in the cues even though it may cross a highway, shrink to a lane, change name (we generally include only the first name, and sometimes the last), wind, duck and climb its way across the country. Rely on us to tell you when to turn off it.

Because the cue sheets rely on an accurate odometer reading we suggest you disconnect your cycle computer (pop it out of the housing or turn the magnet away from the fork-mounted sensor) whenever you deviate from the main route.

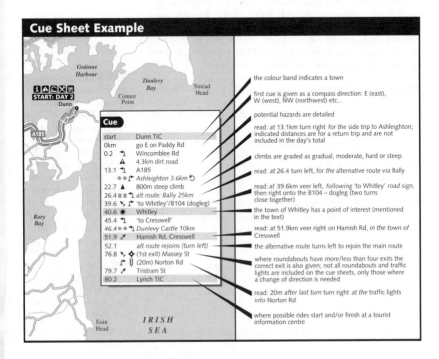

Cue Sheet Example

the colour band indicates a town

first cue is given as a compass direction: E (east), W (west), NW (northwest) etc...

potential hazards are detailed

read: *at* 13.1km turn right *for the* side trip *to* Ashleighton; indicated distances are for a return trip and are not included in the day's total

climbs are graded as gradual, moderate, hard or steep

read: *at* 26.4 turn left, *for the* alternative route *via* Bally

read: *at* 39.6km veer left, *following* 'to Whitley' *road sign*, then right onto the B104 – dogleg (two turns close together)

the town of Whitley has a point of interest (mentioned in the text)

read: *at* 51.9km veer right *on* Hamish Rd, *in the town of* Cresswell

the alternative route turns left to rejoin the main route

where roundabouts have more/less than four exits the correct exit is also given; not all roundabouts and traffic lights are included on the cue sheets, only those where a change of direction is needed

read: 20m *after last turn* turn right *at the* traffic lights *into* Norton Rd

where possible rides start and/or finish at a tourist information centre

Foreword

HOW TO USE A LONELY PLANET CYCLING GUIDE

The best way to use this Cycling Guide is any way you choose. Some people might link a few days of one ride with a few days of another; others might feel most comfortable following the cue sheets to the letter for an entire tour; or you might use the guide simply to gather ideas on the areas you'd like to explore by bike. Keep in mind that the most memorable travel experiences are often those that are unexpected, and the finest discoveries are those you make yourself.

Our approach is to detail the 'best' rides in each destination, not all possible rides, so if you intend touring for several months you should consider also packing our *Ireland* guidebook.

What's Inside Cycling Guides follow roughly the same format as regular Lonely Planet guidebooks. The Facts about the Destination chapters give background information ranging from the history of cycle touring to weather. Facts for the Cyclist deals with cycle-touring practicalities – it answers planning questions and suggests itineraries. Health & Safety covers medical advice and road rules, while basic maintenance is addressed in Your Bicycle. The Travel Facts chapter at the end of the book will help you make your travel plans and also gives handy hints on packing your bicycle. In countries where English is not the main language, we include a cyclist-specific language chapter.

What's left are the rides chapters, broken into geographical regions. Depending on the destination these chapters might cover individual states, countries or traditional provinces.

Ride Descriptions We start each ride with background information and access details. Each day's ride is summarised, and the highlights en route are noted in the cues and detailed in the text. At the end of each day our authors recommend the best places to stay and eat, and detail things to see and do out of the saddle. Where possible, each day of a ride starts and ends at a tourist information centre (TIC) or somewhere you can get a town map.

Navigating a Cycling Guide The traditional 'signposts' for Lonely Planet guidebooks are the contents (p1) and index (p275). In addition, Cycling Guides offer a comprehensive table of rides (p5), providing a quick sketch about every ride featured, as well as an index of maps (p3) showing the regional chapter break-up.

A colour map at the front of the book shows highlights; these are dealt with in greater detail in the Facts for the Cyclist chapter (p23). Each rides chapter also begins with a map showing all the rides for that region.

Lonely Planet's cycling guides are written for cyclists, by cyclists. So, if you know a quieter road than the one we've recommended or want to tell us about your favorite ride, drop us a line. Likewise, if you find a cyclist-friendly café or place to stay, or a great bike shop, we'd love to hear about it.

We plan to produce more cycling guides, but if we don't have one to the country you want to cycle in, please let us know and we'll put it on our list.

Introduction

Try as you might, it's almost impossible to find reasons *not* to enjoy cycling in Ireland. The Irish economic miracle of the 1990s transformed the nation, lifting a miasma of troubled history to reveal an energetic and welcoming people inhabiting a land of haunting beauty and intriguing mysticism. Yes, the weather can be trying; but the countryside is a washed-clean, green-tinged revelation when skies clear. It's true that there's little flat terrain – particularly near the exceptionally scenic coastline – but even the stunning mountainous areas are relatively easy riding.

The biggest bonus of all is glaringly apparent: Ireland is populated by the Irish, who might just be the most relaxed, friendly and entertainingly talkative people in the Western world. This is one place where you can tour alone and yet rarely feel lonely. In remote areas, a breezy wave at the occupants of any vehicle is *de rigueur*. You learn to stop and ask for directions only if you're not in a hurry. You enter a pub only if you're in for the long haul – leaving before the last song is sung or story spun seems a monstrous breach of etiquette.

Cycling will lead you through this land of saints and scholars, sinners and sippers at the pace that best suits Ireland's size and character. With rare exceptions, it seems absurd to cycle more than 60km or 70km a day here – there's just too much to see and do, and too much potential for pleasure, to speed past. Towns are rarely more than a short ride apart, and the terrain is rarely flat, so why hurry? An Irish cycling tour includes long, funny roadside discussions with strangers, and the occasional solid drenching with rain. There will be hours spent in blissful solitude on empty, isolated roads amid memorable views, and there will be the madness of peak-hour traffic-dodging in what appears to be only a medium-sized town.

In the Republic's main tourist-destination counties, particularly Kerry and Cork, the busy roads can be crammed with cars and tourist buses, and fellow cyclists will be a regular sight. In the Midlands, flatter terrain, and quieter roads and towns greet visitors; the relative lack of tourists makes for a more individual Irish experience here. The Republic's north, County Donegal, is different again. This was the region of Gaelic Ireland's last stand before the English invaders; today, it is a stronghold of traditional culture and harbours some of Ireland's largest Gaeltacht (Irish-speaking) areas. Northern Ireland is as beautiful, varied and surprising as any other part of the country, with the added poignancy of a troubled recent history. The cycle-touring scene in the North is small but growing, and deservedly so.

This book maps and details a connoisseur's selection of the very best rides in the country, to suit all ability levels. There is a wealth of advice to help smooth your trip: inside knowledge on the best places to eat, stay and play, as well as tips on bike transport and maintenance.

From vibrant cities to spectacular coastlines and with thousands of sites to demonstrate a long and rich contribution to human culture, Ireland presents a most tantalising cycling destination – a compact country, stocked with friendly, outgoing people and in which every pedal stroke leads towards ever more breathtaking scenery and fascinating experiences.

Facts about Ireland

HISTORY

8000 BC – Ireland's first settlers (hunter-gatherers) arrive at the end of the most recent Ice Age.

300–100 BC – Celtic people reach Ireland, bringing the Iron Age. They control the country for 1000 years and leave a legacy of language and culture that survives today.

432 AD – St Patrick begins converting the Irish to Christianity from his base in Armagh.

9th century – Vikings arrive in Ireland, establishing settlements including Dublin, Wicklow, Waterford and Wexford.

1014 – Irish forces led by Brian Ború defeat Vikings at the Battle of Clontarf.

1175 – Irish kings submit to Henry II under the Treaty of Windsor.

1297 – Irish parliament first meets, in Dublin.

1541 – Irish parliament declares Henry VIII king of Ireland.

1557 – First 'plantation' migrants, from England, displace Irish landholders in counties Laois and Offaly.

1594 – Nine Years' War begins; Irish forces led by Hugh O'Neill of Ulster.

1603 – O'Neill surrenders and signs the Treaty of Mellifont, handing power and authority to the English Crown.

1607 – 'Flight of the Earls'; O'Neill and 90 other Ulster chieftains leave Ireland for Europe.

1610 – Ulster Plantation begins; land confiscated from Irish and given to settlers from Scotland and England.

1641 – Irish and Anglo-Norman Catholics take up arms against Protestant settlers.

1649 – Oliver Cromwell's murderous rampage subdues Irish.

1652 – English Act of Settlement results in more than a quarter of Ireland being handed to Cromwell's supporters.

1690 – James II, deposed Catholic English king, defeated by William of Orange (Protestant king appointed by English parliament to replace him) at the Battle of the Boyne.

1691 – Final surrender of the Irish; Catholic leader Patrick Sarsfield signs the Treaty of Limerick, which includes harsh anti-Catholic laws.

1778 – Catholics hold about 5% of the land in Ireland; Henry Grattan's Patriot Party campaigns for Irish independence.

1782 – Irish parliament wins freedom of legislation from Britain; Crown retains power of veto.

1795 – Protestant Orange Society (later known as Orange Order) founded.

1798 – United Irishmen rising broken by defeat at Vinegar Hill just outside Enniscorthy.

1800 – Act of Union unites Ireland politically with Britain; Irish parliament votes to dissolve itself.

1803 – Failed rebellion led by former United Irishman Robert Emmet.

1823 – Daniel O'Connell, the 'Great Liberator', founds Catholic Association.

1828 – O'Connell elected to parliamentary seat for County Clare; as a Catholic, he is unable to take his seat.

1829 – Act of Catholic Emancipation gives Catholics limited voting rights and the right to be elected as MPs.

1839 – O'Connell campaigns for repeal of the Act of Union and the re-establishment of an Irish parliament.

1840 – Ireland's population numbers around eight million.

1845–51 – The Great Famine; succession of potato crop failures result in mass starvation, emigration and death.

1851 – Ireland's population down to 6.5 million.

1858 – Pro-independence Irish Republican Brotherhood established in Dublin.

1859 – Pro-independence Fenian Brotherhood established in New York.

1867 – Fenian rising; three of the rebels are executed and become known in nationalist circles as the Manchester Martyrs.

1877 – Charles Stewart Parnell becomes leader of the new Home Rule Party, which advocates a limited form of autonomy for Ireland.

1879 – Parnell and Fenian Michael Davitt form the Land League, which agitates for reduced rents and improved working conditions.

1881 – William Gladstone's Land Act creates fair rents and the possibility of tenants owning their land.

1884 – Gaelic Athletic Association (GAA) founded to promote Irish sport and culture.

1885 – Anti-independence Ulster Unionist Party formed.

1890 – Parnell's refusal to resign as leader over a personal crisis splits Home Rule Party.

1892 – Gladstone's Home Rule for Ireland Bill is passed in the House of Commons, but is thrown out by the House of Lords.

1893 – Gaelic League founded to promote Irish culture; pushes for Irish language to be taught in schools.

1907 – Nationalist Sinn Féin party founded.

1912 – Home Rule Act passed under Liberal prime minister Asquith amid strident unionist and conservative British opposition.

1913 – Ulster unionists form the Protestant paramilitary Ulster Volunteer Force (UVF). The republican Irish Volunteers is set up to defend Home Rule.

1914 – Home Rule Act suspended at the outbreak of WWI. Many Irish nationalists support the British war effort in the belief that Home Rule will come after the war.

1916 – Easter Rising by Irish Volunteers and Irish Citizens Army quelled by British forces. Execution of 15 rebels fans support for independence.

1918 – In general election Sinn Féin wins a large majority of Irish seats. Sinn Féin deputies declare Ireland independent and form the first Dáil Éireann (Irish assembly or lower house).

1919 – Dáil convenes in Dublin. Anglo-Irish War begins; Irish Republican Army (IRA) emerges from Irish Volunteers.

1919–21 – Pro-British forces battle IRA 'flying columns' in bloody guerrilla war.

1921 – Anglo-Irish treaty agreed; 26 counties become independent Irish Free State (Éire) while six largely Protestant Ulster counties form Northern Ireland.

1922–23 – Civil war between pro- and anti-treaty forces in Éire; the former prevail.

1927 – Eamon de Valera's Fianna Fáil party wins half the seats in the Dáil.

1932 – Fianna Fáil wins majority of Dáil seats; de Valera becomes *taoiseach* (prime minister).

1937 – De Valera introduces new constitution, which includes claim to sovereignty of Northern counties.

1948 – Fianna Fáil defeated in elections; Free State declared a republic.

1949 – Éire leaves British Commonwealth.

1951 – Ian Paisley establishes the anti-Catholic Free Presbyterian Church in the North.

1955 – Éire becomes a United Nations member.

1964 – Paisley-led protest against flying of Irish tricolour sparks first clashes of modern 'Troubles'.

1965 – Republic Taoiseach Sean Lemass and Northern Ireland Prime Minister Terence O'Neill hold first direct meeting between leaders of South and North since partition.

1967 – Formation of Northern Ireland Civil Rights Association, a broadly based nationalist group.

1968 – First civil rights marches in the North.

1969 – Sectarian rioting in Derry and Belfast; British troops deployed in the North.

1971 – Provisional IRA begins campaign to oust British troops; Northern assembly introduces internment without trial.

1972 – 'Bloody Sunday' in Derry, with civilians shot by British paratroopers. Northern Ireland government and parliament suspended; direct rule from London. UK and Republic of Ireland join European Economic Community.

1973 – Sunningdale agreement forms North/South Council of Ireland.

1974 – Council of Ireland collapses in face of unionist general strike.

1978 – Irish currency (punt) replaces pound sterling in the South.

1980–81 – H-Block hunger strikes in the North; republican prisoners starve themselves to death in an effort to gain the status of political prisoners.

1985 – Anglo-Irish Agreement signed at Hillsborough. Intergovernmental Conference established.

1990 – Mary Robinson elected president of Éire. Northern Ireland secretary Peter Brooke says Britain would accept unification of Ireland by consent of the majority of all Irish, North and South.

1993 – Downing Street Declaration; British government accepts Ireland's right to self- determination.

1994 – Cease-fire declared by the IRA; combined loyalist/unionist paramilitaries follow suit.

1996 – Cease-fire breaks down after Sinn Féin excluded by British government from all-party talks on the North.

1997 – IRA cease-fire resumes; first-ever all-party talks on the North begin in Belfast.

1998 – Good Friday Agreement accepted by all parties. Elections held for Northern Ireland power-sharing government; new Northern Ireland Assembly meets in September.

1999 – First nationalist/unionist coalition government sits.

2001 – Elections in the North favour Sinn Féin and Ian Paisley's Democratic Unionist Party candidates over moderates.

2002 – Northern Ireland Assembly suspended following David Trimble's resignation over the IRA's refusal to disarm.

Island Ireland, South & North

When the distinction between Ireland the island and Ireland the state needs to be made in this book, the state is referred to as the Republic of Ireland, the Republic, the South or Éire. You may also hear Ireland the state referred to as Southern Ireland or the Free State. In this book Northern Ireland is either referred to as such or as the North. You may also hear it dubbed the six counties or Ulster, though the latter is technically incorrect. The province of Ulster actually comprises nine counties, but at the time of partition in 1922 three of these (Cavan, Donegal and Monaghan) went into the Republic of Ireland.

Particularly in the North, it pays to know your faction names – and to understand that the divisions are political as much as religious. Nationalists favour a united Ireland. They're mostly Catholics and the more hardline among them are usually called republicans. Unionists, mostly Protestants, favour continuing ties with Great Britain; those with more extreme views tend to be called loyalists.

History of Cycling

Not surprisingly, Ireland's development as a cycling nation closely parallels Britain's, with interest in and use of bicycles rising from the time the 'ordinary' (penny-farthing) was introduced in the 1870s. In the following decades, technological advances (such as tangential spoking on wheels, the first chain-driven safety bicycle and the subsequent Rover Safety model) appeared on Irish roads. Ireland had no local bicycle manufacturing industry. Bikes were assembled in Ireland, with parts imported from Britain's bicycle-making epicentre, the English Midlands.

Bicycle racing and touring were popular in Ireland in the early 20th century, and the bicycle's worth on often rough Irish roads was ably demonstrated during the Anglo-Irish War (1919–21). In their battle against pro-British forces, IRA guerrillas used bicycles as transport to devastating effect. Their tactics were so successful that military leaders throughout Europe are said to have taken a renewed interest in bikes.

Irish cycle racing has proud and long traditions. The first great Irish road-racing competitor was Harry Reynolds, who became world amateur champion in 1896. Cycle racing declined somewhat for several decades afterwards. Many factors played a role, among them the tumultuous events in Irish politics and the ban (which lasted until the 1940s) on mass-start road races – the 1930s, particularly, are remembered as an era of time-trialling. The next great Irish road racer was Dubliner Shay Elliott, who was second (to Jean Stablinski) in the 1962 world championship. In 1963, Elliott became the first Irishman to wear the Tour de France's famous *maillot jaune* (yellow jersey), which designates the tour's leader.

Irish cycling's greatest moments came during the 1980s and 1990s, the era of Sean Kelly (see the boxed text 'Sean Kelly – High King of Cycling', p124) and Stephen Roche. Legend has it Sean Kelly won his first cycling race near Cork city on a cold St Patrick's Day in 1972. He was Irish junior champion that year and again in 1973. In 1974 he won the Shay Elliott Memorial Classic, a win repeated in 1975, the year he had three stage wins in the Tour of Ireland and one in the Tour of Britain. Kelly turned professional in 1977 and went on to become one of the great champions of the European pro peloton, recording 22 wins in classics (he won Paris–Nice seven times) and multiple stage wins in the big tours.

Dubliner Roche joined the pro peloton in 1981 and celebrated his first season by winning Paris–Nice and the Tour of Corsica, and finishing second in the Grand Prix des

The Wind Beneath Our Wheels

One of the most significant advances in bicycle technology – indeed, in modern wheeled transport – has strong Irish connections. In 1888, the pneumatic rubber tyre was patented by JB Dunlop, a Belfast veterinarian. Born in Scotland in 1840, Dunlop qualified as a vet then worked in Edinburgh for about 10 years before moving to Belfast. He built a successful practice in Ireland but apparently found travel there uncomfortable – what with the rough roads and unforgiving solid wheels on horse-drawn transport. Dunlop began experimenting with ways to make his son's tricycle more comfortable. He'd often used rubber during surgery, and he finally developed a canvas tyre with inflatable rubber inner tube and a rubber tread. The device was patented on 23 July 1888 (this wasn't the first pneumatic tyre patent: Scot RW Thomson patented an air-filled leather tyre in 1845).

Soon Booth's Cycle Agency of Dublin began making a small number of Dunlop's tyres, which were first used in a race (at Queen's College, Belfast) in May 1889. In short order, tyre manufacturing moved to England, and solid-tyred wheels went into a rapid decline. By 1892 few solid-tyred bikes were made, Dunlop was a much wealthier man and the bicycle industry was starting to direct its energy into building inexpensive, practical machines. By 1894, the canny Dunlop had bought patents for two different methods of securing pneumatic tyres to rims (one developed by Scot CK Welch, the other by American WE Bartlett), giving his tyre company great income from licensing fees. In 1896 Dunlop's company was registered in Britain as Byrne Brothers India Rubber Company; in 1900 the name was changed to the enduring Dunlop Rubber Company. Dunlop eventually retired to Dublin, and died there in 1921.

Nations. Several frustrating years of injury and health problems followed, but in 1987 the gods finally smiled upon him. First he won the Giro d'Italia (Tour of Italy), somewhat controversially after getting away from his team leader, Roberto Visentini. Then he beat Pedro Delgado in the Tour de France to become the first Irishman to win the world's best-known cycling race. Roche's 1987 was crowned by victory in the world championship; he became only the second cyclist (the other was the legendary Eddy Merckx) to win the Giro, Tour and world championship in the same year.

In the years since Kelly and Roche retired Ireland's best result on the world cycling stage has been achieved by Sligo man Mark Scanlon, who won the world junior championship in 1998.

One of the brightest stars of contemporary Irish mountain biking is Tarja Owen, from County Wicklow, who became the first Irish female cyclist to represent Ireland at the Olympic Games (in Sydney 2000). Two years later Owen became the first Irish person to be offered an International Olympic Scholarship.

GEOGRAPHY

Ireland is off the northwestern edge of the Eurasian landmass, separated from Britain by the Irish Sea and the St George's and North Channels. The island covers 84,421 sq km (70,282 sq km in the South and 14,139 sq km in the North). It extends 485km north–south and about 300km east–west. The coastline extends for more than 5000km.

The Republic of Ireland has 26 counties and Northern Ireland six. These have traditionally been divided into four provinces: Leinster, Ulster, Connaught and Munster. See Cycling Regions – Index Map (p3) for a province and county breakdown. The six counties of Northern Ireland are often referred to as Ulster, but three of the Republic's counties – Donegal, Cavan and Monaghan – were also in the old province of Ulster.

Most of the higher ground is close to the coast, while the central regions are largely flat. The highest mountains are in the southwest (the tallest mountain in Ireland is Mt Carrauntoohil, 1041m, in County Kerry) and almost the entire western seaboard is a continuous bulwark of cliffs, hills and mountains with few safe anchorages. The only

significant breaches in the chain are the Shannon Estuary and Galway Bay. The flat midlands landscape is mostly rich farmland or raised bogs, huge swathes of which have been harvested. West of the Midlands soils are poorer, fields smaller and stone walls more numerous. On the western seaboard, smallholders make a precarious living by raising sheep, potatoes and some cattle.

The 370km-long Shannon River is Ireland's (and Britain's) longest. It rises in Cavan's Cuilcagh Mountains and flows through the Midlands before emptying into the wide Shannon Estuary west of Limerick town. Lough Neagh in Northern Ireland is the island's largest lake, covering 396 sq km.

GEOLOGY

Mountain-building episodes about 450 and 340 to 280 million years ago laid the foundation of Ireland. Much later volcanic activity (about 60 million years ago) created the Mourne Mountains, in Northern Ireland. The most recent Ice Age was the event with the biggest impact on the modern Irish landscape. For about 90,000 years (until about 10,000 years ago), U-shaped valleys and small, deep-set corrie lakes high on mountainsides were carved out by glaciers. The receding ice sheet left behind many shallow lakes, mainly in central parts. Many of Ireland's mountains and hills have a round, smooth profile, formed by the abrasive effect of moving ice. The ice also deposited soil in its wake, leaving a layer of boulder clay on many parts of the country. There is a large belt of drumlins, small round hills of boulder clay that were dropped and shaped by the passing ice, across the country, from County Cavan to Clew Bay in County Mayo. The result is the characteristic basket-of-eggs topography.

CLIMATE

Ireland has a relatively mild climate for its latitude, with a mean annual temperature of around 10°C. The reason is the moderating effect of the Atlantic Ocean and particularly the Gulf Stream, which brings warm water up to Western Europe from the Caribbean.

The temperature drops below freezing only intermittently during winter, and snow is scarce – perhaps one or two brief flurries every year. The coldest months are January and February, when daily temperatures range

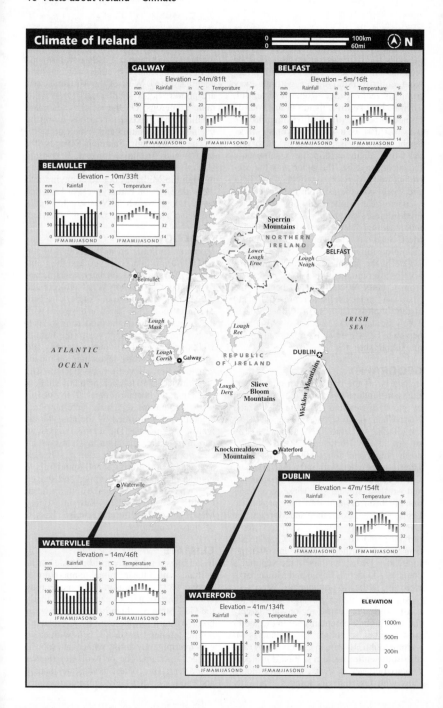

from 4° to 8°C, with 7°C the average. In summer, temperatures during the day are a comfortable 15° to 20°C. During the warmest months, July and August, the average is 16°C. A hot summer's day in Ireland is 22° to 24°C, although it can sometimes reach 30°C. There are about 18 hours of daylight daily during July and August and it's only truly dark after about 11pm. In May and June, Ireland has an average of five to six hours of sunshine a day, while in the southeast during July and August the average is seven hours.

Nationwide, average rainfall is about 1000mm each year, ranging from 750mm in the midlands to over 1300mm in the southwest, where the mountains of southwest Kerry are the wettest part of the country – rain may fall on as many as 270 days a year. The southeast, particularly Counties Wexford and Waterford, is the driest region.

Prevailing winds come from the southwest, bringing rain-bearing clouds from the Atlantic which dump their loads as soon as they meet high ground. Northwesterly changes blow in from Arctic climes and can bring cold and blustery conditions to the north and west.

ECOLOGY & ENVIRONMENT
Ireland's environmental movement was slow to get going by European standards but is now committed and energetic. The conservation (or rehabilitation) of forests and boglands is among key environmental issues. Forests cover only about 8% of Ireland – clearing began (for agriculture) about 6000 years ago. About 17% of the land was once made up of bogland but at the present rate of extraction – for home-fire fuel and garden-enriching peat moss – bogs might soon disappear. Conservation efforts gathered pace late in the 20th century and some areas are now preserved and managed as national nature reserves and national parks.

The rise of the 'Celtic Tiger' – the unprecedented economic growth in the 1990s – has led to a steep increase in private car ownership. Many urban roads are congested and city centres can be smoggy with fumes. Tourist traffic during the peak summer season can create bottlenecks in small towns.

Litter remains a significant problem. Since the Litter Pollution Act became law in 1997, on-the-spot fines and prosecutions for littering have risen more than fivefold.

Some local communities show a greater determination than others to 'clean up'; more than 700 towns and villages take part in the annual National Tidy Towns competition.

Visitors keen to know more about Ireland's environment should contact the Environmental Protection Agency (☎ 053-60600, w www.epa.ie; Johnstown Castle Estate, County Wexford); or Enfo (☎ 01-888 2001, w www.enfo.ie; 17 St Andrew St, Dublin 2; open 10am-5pm Mon-Sat) near the Dublin Tourism Centre. Enfo is the environmental information service of the Department of Environment and Local Government and a public information service.

National Parks & Reserves
Ireland has four national parks – Connemara (Galway), Glenveagh (Donegal), Killarney (Kerry) and Wicklow Mountains (Wicklow). The parks are open year-round (although some attractions within their boundaries may be summer-only). Each has its own information office, but for general information contact Dúchas (see Useful Organisations, p32).

Northern Ireland has no national parks; its national nature reserves (NNRs) are leased or owned by the Environment & Heritage Service. These reserves are defined as areas of importance for their special flora, fauna or geology and include the Giant's Causeway and Glenariff in County Antrim, Marble Arch Forest in County Fermanagh and North Strangford Lough in County Down. For information contact the Environment & Heritage Service (see Useful Organisations, p32).

FLORA & FAUNA
Today, the predominant flora of the Irish landscape is mostly the result of human influence. Only 1% of genuine native oak forest survives. Pine plantations are a major feature of the Irish countryside; species include sitka spruce, lodgepole pine, Douglas fir, Norway spruce and Scots pine. Native plants survive in hedgerows and in wilder parts of the country, and the range of surviving plant species is larger than in many other European countries, where intensive agriculture has a longer history. Hedgerows are a blaze of colour in spring and summer and boglands are home to a unique flora adapted to wet, acidic, nutrient-poor conditions.

The most common native land mammals of any size are foxes and badgers, but they're secretive and rarely seen (except as roadkill). Smaller mammals include rabbits, hares, hedgehogs, red and grey squirrels, shrews and bats. Native red deer are still found in some parts; introduced species include the Japanese sika deer. Rare species such as otter, stoat and pine marten remain in remote areas such as the Burren or Connemara. Sea mammals include grey and common seals, which are found all around the coastline. There are some substantial colonies of grey seals living on uninhabited islands off County Mayo and around the shores of Strangford Lough in Northern Ireland. Dolphins often swim close to land, particularly in the bays and inlets off the west coast.

Ireland is home to a wide range of migrating and locally breeding birds. Brent, barnacle and Greenland white-fronted geese and Bewick's swans are seasonal visitors. April to May and September to October are the main migration periods. The coast is home to a huge variety of sea birds – kittiwakes, razorbills, puffins, Manx shearwaters, storm petrels, cormorants, herons and others. Small Skellig, off Kerry, is the second-largest gannet colony in the world. Other good locations for sea birds are Clear Island in Cork; Hook Head and the Saltee Islands in Wexford; the Burren in Clare; Inishbofin in Galway; Malin Head, Tory Island and the Inishowen Peninsula in Donegal; and Rathlin Island in Antrim. Birds of prey include hen harriers, sparrowhawks, falcons (peregrine, merlin and kestrel) and the odd buzzard.

The main fish species are salmon and varieties of trout (brown, rainbow and sea), species such as mackerel and pollack, off the coast, and pike, bream, perch and roach in lakes and rivers.

Endangered Species

All species native to Ireland's raised bogs are threatened with extinction as their habitat disappears. One of Ireland's rarest native birds is the corncrake, found in some remote and undisturbed areas such as the low-lying flooded grasslands of the Shannon Callows and parts of Donegal. The chough – an unusual crow with bright-red feet and beak – inhabits western coastal areas with extensive sand dunes and Clare Island in Mayo. Other endangered birds are the barn

owl, Canadian brent goose, roseate tern, little tern and red-throated diver. In the Ring of Kerry, the Kerry Bog pony is officially designated a rare breed. The Burren is a stronghold of Ireland's most elusive mammal, the weasel-like pine marten. Other endangered mammals are the whiskered bat, hedgehog, Irish hare, badger and otter.

GOVERNMENT & POLITICS

The Republic of Ireland has a bicameral parliament based on the Westminster system. The Oireachtas (parliament) has a 166-member lower house, the Dáil; members are known as *teachta Dála* (TDs). The government is led by a *taoiseach* (prime minister) and *tánaiste* (deputy prime minister). Elections are held at least every five years.

Members of the Irish upper house, the senate (Seanad), are nominated by the *taoiseach* or elected by university graduates and councillors. The Seanad has limited powers when compared to the British House of Lords.

The constitutional head of state is the president *(an tuachtaran)*, elected by popular vote to a seven-year term. The president has no executive power.

The key political parties are Fianna Fáil, Fine Gael and the Labour Party. Fianna Fáil, founded by Eamon de Valera, has supplied the most Irish governments. Fine Gael and the smaller Labour Party have, on occasion, formed coalition governments. Among the minor parties, Sinn Féin has risen in popularity in the South in recent elections.

The Northern Ireland Assembly was established in the wake of the 1998 Good Friday Agreement, its members voted in under the 1998 Northern Ireland (Elections) Act. The 108-member Assembly's 'cabinet' is the Northern Ireland Executive, which is drawn from all parties. Executive members exercise the power devolved from Westminster in six areas (agriculture, economic development, education, environment, finance and personnel and health and social services), now broken into 11 ministries. The British Secretary of State for Northern Ireland remains responsible for matters such as policing, security policy, prisons, criminal justice, international relations and taxation.

Under the terms of the Good Friday Agreement, the people of Northern Ireland may, through a referendum, choose to unite with the Republic.

POPULATION & PEOPLE

Ireland's total population in 2002 was about 5.6 million – still well below the eight million who inhabited the island before the 1845–51 Great Famine. The Republic's population was about 3.9 million and Northern Ireland's population about 1.7 million.

The most noticeable recent trend in population has been an increase in immigration, through both 'returning' Irish and a growing, number of refugees from Eastern Europe and Africa.

ARTS
Dance

The most important form of dance in Ireland is traditional Irish dancing, performed communally at *ceilidhs* (sessions of traditional music and dancing), often in an impromptu format and always accompanied by an Irish traditional band. Dances include the hornpipe, jig and reel. The west and southwest are strongholds of traditional dance.

Music

Traditional & Folk Most traditional music is performed on the fiddle, the tin whistle, the *bodhrán* (hand-held goatskin drum) and the *uilleann* pipes. Instrumental music fits into five main categories: jigs, reels, hornpipes, polkas and slow airs. There are two main styles of song: *sean nós*, old-style tunes often sung in Gaelic either unaccompanied or with the backing of a *bodhrán*; and more familiar ballads. Traditional music has its strongest following in the Republic, but that's not to say you can't find it in Northern Ireland.

Well-known Irish music groups include the Chieftains, virtuoso instrumentalists playing since the 1960s, and more recently, Lunasa. Groups with more emphasis on vocals include the Clancy Brothers, the Dubliners, the Wolfe Tones and the Fureys. Clannad, Altan, Dervish and Nomos espouse a quieter, more mystical style of singing. The London-Irish band the Pogues, led by Shane Mac-Gowan, added rollicking, rock-roots wildness and contemporary issues to traditional instruments and themes. Contemporary male singer-songwriters include Christy Moore, his brother Luka Bloom, Andy Irvine, Jimmy MacCarthy, Kieran Goss and Paul Brady. Female singer-songwriters include internationally successful Enya (formerly of Clannad), sisters Mary and Frances Black, smoky-voiced Mary Coughlan, innovative accordian player Sharon Shannon, Dolores Keane and Eleanor McEvoy. Giving 'trad' their own contemporary stamp are acts such as Grada, Kila, the Jimmy Cake and John Spillane.

For visitors, the joy of traditional Irish music lies in its sheer accessibility – almost every town and village seems to have a pub renowned for its music where you can show up and find a session in progress, or even join in if you feel so inclined.

Rock & Pop Van Morrison was the first Irishman to make it big in the modern era, and he's still going strong. His best known songs, such as 'Gloria' and 'Brown-eyed Girl', are considered classics. Bands Thin Lizzy and the Boomtown Rats, and performers such as Bob Geldof, Rory Gallagher,

Luka Bloom

Kildare-born singer-songwriter Luka Bloom used to refer to himself as 'a cyclist who sings'. Judging by his six albums and international following, this is perhaps a tad modest. He has always cycled though – getting around town on an old-fashioned Dutch bike, or chilling out in the countryside on his Cannondale hybrid.

A two-week wintertime bike trip through Kerry – 'really cold, but with incredible sunshine' – inspired the title track of his 1992 album *The Acoustic Motorbike*. The song celebrates cycling and the Kerry countryside (complete with the sounds of cows mooing and roosters crowing), and highlights the environmental and social problems caused by Ireland's increasing traffic. Indeed Luka says, if he were to become politically militant, it would be for cyclists' rights: 'Most people can't get their heads around the fact that this is the way I choose to travel.'

Despite the cliched image of old bikes outside old pubs, few Irish people regard cycling as seriously as the foreign visitors who point their handlebars towards the green isle. 'Maybe they know how much it rains!' suggests Luka. But he likes the rain – and, judging by his songs, connects deeply with Ireland's wild places. His favourite cycling destinations? The Burren and Connemara.

So come on, get up on your bike
Pedal on, pedal on, pedal on for miles

Gilbert O'Sullivan, Elvis Costello and Chris de Burgh followed in the 1970s and '80s. Since the early 1980s U2 has been the undisputed, attention-dominating heavyweight of Irish rock, but still bands such as Ash and the Cranberries have broken through. The Corrs combine a touch of the traditional with American pop rhythms and harmonies. Of the so-called 'boy bands', teen idols Westlife attract crowds of screaming female fans. The wonderful, controversial Sinéad O'Connor emerged as a siren-voiced soloist in the late 1980s.

Literature

Ireland's contribution to the literary arts is comprehensive, enduring and impossible to summarise. A fine Irish bookshop is a true delight to the literary traveller. Here are works by the Irish, about them, about their country, about their political and social struggles, sometimes in their own language as well as in English... it's rare to find such a detailed and accessible national record.

The first great work of Irish literature was the Ulaid (Ulster) Cycle, written from oral tradition between the 8th and 12th centuries. The chief story is the *Táin Bó Cúailnge*, about a battle between Queen Maeve of Connaught and Cúchulainn, the principal hero of Irish mythology.

The roll-call of Irish novelists, playwrights and poets includes a healthy representation of acknowledged greats, among them Jonathan Swift, William Congreve, Oliver Goldsmith, Richard Sheridan, Bram Stoker, Oscar Wilde, George Bernard Shaw, WB Yeats, John Millington Synge, Sean O'Casey, James Joyce and Samuel Beckett. Four Irishmen have won the Nobel Prize for Literature: Shaw (in 1925), Yeats (1938) Beckett (1969) and Seamus Heaney (1995).

Among the countless 20th-century male writers who have achieved particular renown are Flann O'Brien (see the boxed text 'The Bicycle, Writ Funny', p70), Brendan Behan, Christy Brown, John Banville, Patrick McCabe and Roddy Doyle.

Female Irish writers with lauded work include Molly Keane (aka MJ Farrell), Iris Murdoch, Jennifer Johnston, Edna O'Brien and Clare Boylan.

The Northern Irish have made an equally strong contribution to the national literary identity, with many of their books in modern times influenced by the long Anglo-Irish struggle. In Brian Moore's *Lies of Silence*, Bernard MacLaverty's *Cal* and Glenn Patterson's *Fat Lad*, Northern Ireland politics act as a backdrop to gritty life in the six counties. Belfast-born Robert McLiam Wilson is highly acclaimed. His first novel was the award-winning *Ripley Bogle*; his *Eureka Street* is set in Belfast.

Southerners have also addressed Irish political history, sometimes through personal experience. *The Informer,* by Liam O'Flaherty, is the classic book about the divided sympathies which plagued Ireland throughout its struggle for independence and the ensuing Civil War (O'Flaherty fought on the republican side). Gerry Conlon was one of the Guildford Four, who were wrongly imprisoned for IRA bombings in Britain in the 1970s. Conlon's true story, *Proved Innocent*, was made into the film *In the Name of the Father.*

The work of Northern playwright and poet Damian Gorman has received considerable praise, particularly *Broken Nails*. Other Irish playwrights worth investigating are Frank McGuinness *(The Carthaginians)*, Martin McDonagh *(The Leenane Trilogy)* and Brian Friel *(Dancing at Lughnasa)*. Young playwrights of renown include Mark O'Rowe *(Howie the Rookie)* and Enda Walsh *(Misterman)*. The literary revival of the late 19th century saw the establishment of Dublin's Abbey Theatre, now Ireland's national theatre. Its role is to present works by former greats such as WB Yeats, JM Synge and Sean O'Casey, as well as to promote modern Irish dramatists.

Nobel winners Yeats and Heaney tower above the ranks of Irish poets, but the works of many others are worth pursuing. Try Patrick Kavanagh *(The Great Hunger* and *Tarry Flynn)*, Irish-language poet Louis de Paor, Tom Paulin *(The Strange Museum)*, Brendan Kennelly, Eavan Boland, Eiléan Ní Chuilleanáin, Paul Muldoon and Derek Mahon.

Painting

Irish painting has a long tradition dating back to the illuminated manuscripts of the early Christian period, most notably the Book of Kells.

The National Gallery in Dublin has an extensive Irish School collection, much of it relating to the Anglo-Irish aristocracy. Early noted portrait painters were Garrett Murphy and James Latham.

In the 18th and 19th centuries, painters worked on landscape and historical themes. Important artists include George Barret, Robert Carver, William Ashford, Roderick O'Connor, James Malton and James Arthur O'Connor.

WB Yeats' younger brother, Jack Butler Yeats, inspired new approaches in the early 20th century, taking Celtic mythology and Irish life as his subjects. Together with Paul Henry and other painters he formed the Society of Dublin Painters in 1920. The influence of European cubism and futurism can be seen in the works of Evie Hone and Mainie Jellett. In the 1950s and 1960s, a school of naive artists appeared on Tory Island, off the coast of Donegal; their most accomplished figure was James Dixon. Much of their work is displayed in the Glebe House and Gallery near Letterkenny. Noted contemporary artists include Michael Cullen, Eithne Jordan, Rita Duffy and Patrick Graham.

Cinema

The modern Irish film industry's biggest break was the 1981 creation of the Irish Film Board, which saw money (and tax incentive packages) directed at a local film industry.

Several Irish films have captured audiences in recent years, among them Neil Jordan's *The Crying Game*, *Michael Collins* and *The Butcher Boy*; Jim Sheridan's *My Left Foot*, *The Field* and *In the Name of the Father*; Noel Pearson's production of Brian Friel's play *Dancing at Lughnasa*; and Pat O'Connor's films of Bernard MacLaverty's *Cal* and Maeve Binchy's *Circle of Friends*.

Irish actors to make a name internationally include Richard Harris, Peter O'Toole, Greer Garson, Maureen O'Hara, Liam Neeson *(Schindler's List)*, Daniel Day-Lewis and Brenda Fricker *(My Left Foot)*, Belfast-born Kenneth Branagh, Aidan Quinn *(Legends of the Fall)*, Stephen Rea *(The Crying Game)*, Fionnula Flanagan *(Some Mother's Son)* and Colm Meaney *(The Commitments)*.

Architecture

Ireland's architectural heritage includes prehistoric graves, ruined monasteries, crumbling castles and cottages and many intact reminders of its long, often dramatic, history. Dúchas (the Irish government heritage service) and An Taisce (National Trust for Ireland) are the best points of contact in the South for travellers interested in exploring Irish architectural heritage. In the North, contact the Environment & Heritage Service or the National Trust (Northern Ireland). See Useful Organisations (p32) for contact details.

SOCIETY & CONDUCT

Ireland today is a nation with a young, expanding population, flourishing arts and a booming economy that has embraced high technology. Social stratification has more to do with personal wealth than birth or background. As is the case in most Western nations, the gap between rich and poor has widened alarmingly in recent decades and, although unemployment has decreased, the number of people living below the poverty line has risen.

With the decline in the power of the Catholic Church there has been a liberalising of sexual mores. Contraceptive pills and condoms are freely available, though in some areas they're still taboo subjects of discussion. In a 1995 referendum, divorce was narrowly accepted. Abortion is still illegal but it's no longer illegal to provide information about it, and women who travel to Britain to terminate their pregnancies do so without fear of legal sanction.

The Republic of Ireland is nominally more than 90% Roman Catholic, but church attendance continues to fall, especially among younger people. Despite its declining power, the Church still wields influence in the South through its control of most primary and secondary schools and hospitals (which are funded by the state); in rural towns and villages, large numbers attend mass every Sunday as part of the weekly social round.

In the North the breakdown is just under 60% Protestant, just over 40% Catholic. Most Irish Protestants are members of the Church of Ireland, an offshoot of the Church of England, and the Presbyterian and Methodist Churches. The primates of both the Roman Catholic Church and the Church of Ireland sit in Armagh, Northern Ireland, the traditional base of St Patrick.

People tend to be friendlier and more courteous towards cyclists on the road the further you are from large cities. In remote areas, it's practically compulsory for road users, whatever their mode of transport, to acknowledge one another with a friendly wave. If you stop to ask for directions, expect a lot more than a 10-second pointing session – the Irish tend to be generous with time and knowledge.

Social Graces
On the whole, Irish people of all political or religious persuasions are friendly and accommodating towards foreigners. However, religion and politics are inextricably mixed, especially in the North, and, whenever these subjects come up, as a visitor it's probably better to listen and learn rather than offer opinions. On most matters that have entered the national debate – among them racism, homosexuality, conservation, contraception, divorce and abortion – older rural people tend to be more conservative than younger urban dwellers. Again, it's better to relax and listen rather than get embroiled in discussion.

LANGUAGE
English is the main language of Ireland, but it's spoken with a distinctive Irish lilt. Irish, a Celtic language, is the first language in parts of western and southern Ireland; these areas are collectively called the Gaeltacht. Officially the Republic is bilingual, and most official documents and road signs are in Irish and English. Even in the Gaeltacht heartland, English is the language of communication with visitors, so you won't need a grasp of even survival-level Irish.

However, it's worth learning to recognise common public signs (see the boxed text 'Irish-Language Signs').

In addition, the Glossary (p271) includes a comprehensive list of Irish terms you're likely to find in public places, on maps and in guidebooks.

Lonely Planet's *Europe phrasebook* devotes a chapter to the Irish language.

Irish-Language Signs

Irish	Pronunciation	English
Fir	*fear*	Men
Mná	*me-naw*	Women
Leithreas	*lehrass*	Toilets
Garda	*garda*	Police
Oifig an	*if-ig on*	
Phoist	*pwist*	Post Office
Telefón	*tay lay foan*	Telephone
An Lár	*an laah*	Town Centre
Stáid	*sroyed*	Street
Bóthar	*bowher*	Road
Baile	*bollyeh*	Town
Cathair	*kawher*	City
An Banc	*an bonk*	Bank
Siopa	*shuppa*	Shop
Óstán	*oh stahn*	Hotel/Hostel
Céad mhíle	*kade meela*	
fáilte	*fawlcha*	Welcome

Facts for the Cyclist

HIGHLIGHTS
Best Coastal Scenery
In the southeast, the coast between Wexford and Youghal (Southeast Coast Cruise ride, p123), includes tranquil tidal inlets, the isolated Hook Peninsula, sea-ravaged cliffs and bathing bays and beaches.

Heading west, the north side of the Beara Peninsula (Ring of Beara ride, p141) features terrific views of the Iveragh Peninsula across Kenmare Bay. The coast around Slea Head, passed on the Dingle Peninsula ride, is spectacular.

In north of the Republic, the entire Donegal coast is a highlight, with some isolated points deserving special mention – Bloody Foreland and Horn Head (Donegal to Derry ride, p199) and the north coast of the Inishowen Peninsula (Inishowen Circuit ride, p211). Northern Ireland's Antrim Coast from Portrush to Ballygalley (Antrim Coast ride, p236) is a revelation, with the steep road between Ballyvoy and Cushenden perhaps the best section.

Best Ascent
Day 2 of the Tipperary & Waterford Highlands ride (p107) heads steadily uphill in the Silvermine Mountains for about 20km, mostly at an easy pace, until the road tops out at a mountain plateau about halfway through the day. The Connor Pass (Dingle Peninsula ride, p153), at 456m, is Ireland's highest pass; in spite of a steady gradient, the 6.5km climb is steep enough to be a slog. By comparison, the 287m Healy Pass (Ring of Beara ride, p141) is a 6km steady climb – it steepens only in the final 500m, and is a complete joy to ride. In Northern Ireland, the 4.6mi (7.4km) climb past Slieveanorra Forest (Glens of Antrim ride, p240) is gradual and gloriously free of noisy traffic.

Best Descent
The 8km swoop from the top of the Knockmealdown Mountains to Lismore (Day 3 of the Tipperary & Waterford Highlands ride, p107) makes a great finale to a tough and memorable day. It's a total adrenaline rush for the initial 5km of the 7.9km descent from Connor Pass (Dingle Peninsula ride, p153), and made all the sweeter by passing other cyclists slogging their way up. The reward for climbing past the Spelga Dam (Mourne Mountains Circuit ride, p249) is a rollicking 8.4mi (13.5km) downhill, all of it on good roads with magnificent views of the mysterious Mournes.

Best Fitness Challenge
Undulating is the general outlook for Irish cycling, worsening to serial climbing and descending in patches. Four major climbs make the 90.5km one-day Comeragh Mountains ride (p115) a memorable slog – it will be etched indelibly into the memory of any cyclist.

In the west and north, flat sections are so rare that one's tempted to stop and picnic alongside them, just to savour the feeling. The 77.8km Day 2 of the Ring of Beara ride (p141) includes two exhausting sections of roller coaster, of which the ups are steep or long enough to break any momentum gained from the downs. They're followed by the 6km climb to Healy Pass – easy in comparison.

The apparently modest 64.1km Day 2 of the Inishowen Circuit ride (p211) serves up 9.5km of steep or moderate climbs in its last third, including a final, cruel 4.8km grind out of Kinnagoe Bay.

Best Guinness & Craic Ride
They say the closer to the brewery the better the brew, so it's hard to go past Dublin, where Guinness has been brewed since 1759. Exploring the city on the Dublin Orientation ride (p71) gives ample opportunity to sample a pint. Clonakilty (Harbour Hopping in Southwest Cork ride, p134) is a great town for music and pubs. On the Clare Circuit ride (p164), Doolin and Milltown Malbay are musical hotbeds (but can also be filled with camera-toting tourists); Ennis is a good bet for pubs and music, as is Kinvara, which isn't as well known. County Donegal (Northern Éire chapter, p193) is strewn with welcoming pubs, and traditional music is a strong part of the heritage; it's not unusual to catch brilliant musicians in a friendly bar in an entirely out-of-the-way place.

Best Irish-Language & Culture Ride

For entire rides, standouts are the Beaches & Bogs ride (p185; especially the Achill Island section) and the Donegal to Derry ride (p199). The latter passes through the heart of the Donegal Gaeltacht, and towns and regions with especially strong cultural traditions, such as Glencolmcille, Gweedore and Gortahork. Inishmór and the mainland in the southernmost Connemara region (Days 1 to 3 of the Connemara & Inishmór ride, p173) are strong Gaeltacht areas, as are the western reaches of the Iveragh Peninsula (Day 3 of the Ring of Kerry ride, p145) and the Dingle Peninsula (Day 2 of the Dingle Peninsula ride, p153).

SUGGESTED ITINERARIES
One Week

From Dublin, do the Into the Wicklow Mountains ride (p96); take transport to Wexford and ride to Dungarvan on the Southeast Coast Cruise ride (p123); and head to Clonmel to tackle the Comeragh Mountains ride (p115).

For a tough but scenic week, do the Ring of Beara (p141) and Ring of Kerry (p145) rides. The Connemara & Inishmór ride (p173) takes seven days but, by leaving out the trip to Inishmór, it's shortened to five or six. The Clare Circuit ride (p164) is especially convenient if you're flying in to Shannon Airport.

The Donegal to Derry ride (p199) nicely fills five days and gives a taste of the North. For a week-long trip in the North, try the Across Ulster ride (p229), followed by the Derry to Portstewart section of the Around Ireland ride (p251) then the Antrim Coast ride (p236); the journey starts and ends in Belfast.

Two Weeks

From Dublin, do the Heart of Ireland Explorer ride (p74) for green scenery and magical sights. Take transport south to Wexford and do the Southeast Coast Cruise ride (p123) as far as Dungarvan, then head north to Clonmel for the Comeragh Mountains ride (p115).

Alternatively, pack in all the rides from the Southwest chapter (p129), or take a more relaxed pace and do three peninsulas – the Ring of Beara (p141), Ring of Kerry (p145) and Dingle Peninsula (p153) rides –

plus some exploring in Killarney National Park and perhaps a Skellig Island trip. Two weeks is ample time to cover the Connemara & Inishmór ride (p173) plus the Beaches & Bogs ride (p185), with a rest day or two included.

In the north, take transport to Sligo and follow the Around Ireland (p251), Donegal to Derry (p199) and Antrim Coast (p236) rides for nine days, ending in Belfast. Spend another three days on either the Inishowen Circuit ride (p211) if you'd like to see more of Donegal, or the Down South ride (p242) for more of the North.

One Month

The best advice is to aim for a particular region or combination of regions, using transport or sections from the Around Ireland ride (p251) to link areas. The grandest tour of all, obviously, would be to complete the 42-day Around Ireland ride; notionally possible in a month, though the average daily distance would rise from 66km to just under 100km.

In the South, it's hard to go past the Wicklow Mountains, southern counties and scenic coastline, with barely a dull spot all the way to Galway. From Dublin, do the Into the Wicklow Mountains ride (p96) then take transport to Arklow, and do the first two days of the Wicklow, Carlow & Wexford ride (p100), as far as New Ross. Nip across to Waterford to tackle the Waterford, Kilkenny & Cashel ride (p118), then continue via a combination of the Around Ireland (p251) and Southeast Coast Cruise (p123) rides to Cork. Continue with all the rides in the Southwest chapter (p129) to fill the month; the free days will be a welcome rest, both from riding and *craic* (fun, good times).

Another highlight-strewn month could be built on rides in the southwest and west. Start in Cork and do the Harbour Hopping in Southwest Cork (p134) and Ring of Beara (p141) rides; pick up Day 2 of the Ring of Kerry ride (p145) in Kenmare and follow it with the Dingle Peninsula ride (p153). From Tralee, ride to Kilkee (Around Ireland ride, p251) and continue with the Clare Circuit ride (p164). From Kinvara (Days 4 and 5 of the Clare Circuit ride), head to Galway (using the Around Ireland ride, p251). Add on the Connemara & Inishmór ride (p173) but branch off at Westport for the Beaches & Bogs ride (p185) before finishing at Galway city.

For the northern region, take transport to Sligo then follow the Around Ireland ride (p251) to Ballyshannon and complete the Kingfisher Country ride (p216). Continue on the Donegal to Derry ride (p199) then complete the Inishowen Circuit ride (p211) and take the train to Belfast. Follow with the

Across Ulster ride (p229), the Around Ireland ride (p251) to Portstewart, and Antrim Coast (p236) and Glens of Antrim (p240) rides to return to Belfast. Finish up with the Down South (p242) and Mourne Mountains Circuit (p249) rides, the Newcastle to Drogheda section of the Around Ireland ride (p251), then cruise back into Dublin following Day 8 of the Heart of Ireland Explorer ride (p85).

Equipment Check List

This list is a general guide to the things you might take on a bike tour. Your list will vary depending on the kind of cycling you want to do, whether you're roughing it in a tent or using hotels, and on the time of year. Don't forget to take on board enough water and food to see you safely between towns.

Bike Clothing
- ☐ cycling gloves
- ☐ cycling shoes and socks
- ☐ cycling tights or leg warmers
- ☐ helmet and visor
- ☐ long-sleeved shirt or cycling jersey
- ☐ padded cycling shorts (knicks)
- ☐ sunglasses
- ☐ thermal undershirt and arm warmers
- ☐ T-shirt or short-sleeved cycling jersey
- ☐ visibility vest
- ☐ waterproof jacket and pants
- ☐ windproof jacket or vest

Off-Bike Clothing
- ☐ change of clothing
- ☐ spare shoes
- ☐ swimming costume
- ☐ sunhat
- ☐ fleece jacket
- ☐ thermal underwear
- ☐ underwear and spare socks
- ☐ warm hat and gloves

Equipment
- ☐ bike lights (rear and front) with spare batteries (see torch)
- ☐ elastic cord
- ☐ camera and spare film
- ☐ cycle computer
- ☐ day-pack
- ☐ handlebar bag (small) and/or map case
- ☐ medical kit* and toiletries
- ☐ sewing/mending kit

- ☐ panniers and waterproof liners
- ☐ pocket knife (with corkscrew)
- ☐ sleeping sheet
- ☐ tool kit, pump and spares*
- ☐ towel (small)
- ☐ torch (flashlight) with spare batteries and globe – some double as (front) bike lights
- ☐ water containers
- ☐ water purification tablets, iodine or filter

Camping
- ☐ cooking, eating and drinking utensils
- ☐ clothesline and dishwashing items
- ☐ portable stove and fuel
- ☐ insulating mat
- ☐ matches or lighter and candle
- ☐ sleeping bag
- ☐ tent
- ☐ toilet paper and trowel

*see the boxed texts 'First-Aid Kit' (p36) and 'Spares & Tool Kit' (p53).

Gosh! Lots of luggage. Where's your bike?

In there... somewhere!

DON HATCHER

WHEN TO RIDE

Without question, it's best to aim for May and early June. In all but a few parts of Ireland, these are statistically the driest months. The weather is warming (although some cooler days can be expected early in May), crowds are building (but are below the July/August peak) and daylight hours, while not as long as in midsummer, are more than enough for long days on the bike. Both midsummer (for the rise in crowds and prices) and mid-winter (miserable weather, short daylight hours and reduced tourist facilities) are less than ideal times to ride.

WHAT TO BRING

Keep weight to a minimum but be wise about it. Given Ireland's climate, it's better to leave out an extra camera lens than a spare dry shirt. See the Your Bicycle chapter (p47) for tips on choosing a bicycle and necessary tools and spares. See the boxed text 'First-Aid Kit' (p36) for suggested first-aid supplies.

Clothing

Take clothes that are light and dry quickly. You'll save weight with any item that can be worn on and off the bike.

On the Bike For maximum comfort it's best to use cycling-specific clothing, waterproofs and footwear. Wear padded Lycra bike shorts (knicks), which prevent chafing, or shy shorts, which look like ordinary shorts and have a lightweight, knick-style inner. Lightweight, breathable cycling tops, made from fabrics such as CoolMax or InterCool, are best. Long sleeves are the best option – wear sleeves down for cool or very sunny days, and rolled up for milder weather. For cool and/or wet days you'll need to carry warm and waterproof clothing: Lycra or thermal (usually polypropylene) tights and breathable, waterproof overpants; plus a warm top and quality raincoat. Waterproofs come in a range of fabrics. Some, such as Activent or Pertex, are compact and lightweight but won't really withstand heavy rain; these are a good choice for longs. Gore-Tex is still the preferred fabric for jackets. Choose bright colours for all your cycling gear, especially the wet-weather top. They're cooler and more visible to motorists.

Fingerless cycling gloves reduce jarring on the hands, stop sunburn and protect the palms in a fall. Full-finger gloves – water resistant – are a sensible addition for cycling in Ireland, even in summer. Helmets aren't compulsory in Ireland but it's always wise to wear one. Sunglasses protect the eyes from UV radiation, insects and from drying out in the wind.

Stiff-soled cycling shoes transfer power more efficiently from pedal stroke to pedal. Soft-soled training shoes lack the same 'drive' and using them can leave you with sore feet. Neoprene booties and thermal socks may be useful if you're touring on the fringes of cool months.

Off the Bike Pack as little additional clothing as you can reasonably get away with. Your preferred accommodation is probably the main consideration. Campers need to place greater emphasis on warm clothing, including thermal underwear, hats and tops. Lightweight synthetic trousers with zip-off legs are useful; wear thermals underneath them for additional warmth on cold nights. Take a separate pair of shoes to wear off the bike (sandals aren't a great option in Ireland).

Bicycle

As rides in this book include only brief excursions onto unsealed trails, a touring bike is sufficient, although many tourers are using mountain bikes nowadays. It's well worth fitting mudguards to whatever bike you use.

Camping Equipment

If you're camping you'll need to take a lightweight, waterproof tent, sleeping mat, sleeping bag, torch (flashlight) or bike light, camping stove (open fires are generally not allowed) and cooking and eating utensils. The cities, especially Dublin and Belfast, are the best places to find outdoor equipment shops if you choose to buy upon arrival. In Dublin, a handful of outdoor shops are concentrated in the Liffey St Upper/Mary St/Capel St area.

Buying & Hiring Locally

The larger bike shops in cities are well stocked with a range of bicycles and accessories, including specialist touring bikes. In small towns the cycle shop may double as a general sporting goods, motorcycle or lawnmower outlet. Most smaller shops do repairs and stock essentials such as standard-sized tyre tubes and puncture kits.

In Dublin, a basic but adequate touring bike (most are straight-bar hybrids) will cost about €500 to €600. Prices rise with quality, but you'd expect to get a fine bike for around €1000. Top-class touring bikes are a lot more expensive. Decent rear panniers should be in the range of €75 to €130. Good helmets are up to €130, but you'll get an adequate one for around €40 to €50. Gore-Tex rain jackets range from €210 to more than €380.

Hiring a bicycle is a good option, provided you're prepared (and have the know-how) to personalise the set-up. There are hire shops (often part of a bicycle retail business) throughout the island, and many accommodation providers rent bikes. The largest network is Raleigh Rent-a-Bike, which has outlets in 20 counties. Its rates are €20 per day and €80 (more for better-quality bikes) per week. A smaller number of outlets participate in Raleigh's 'premier' scheme, that allows you to collect your bike in one outlet and return it to another (for an additional €20). Panniers and other equipment can also be rented. For details of the outlet closest to your point of entry, contact Eurotrek Raleigh Ireland (☎ 01-465 9659, W www.raleigh.ie).

ORGANISED RIDES
Bicycle Tour Companies Within Ireland

There are many companies offering bicycle tours in different parts of Ireland. Most tours are for small groups covering a set route with vehicle support and accommodation in B&Bs, guesthouses or hotels. Some will customise tours for individuals. Bord Fáilte and the NITB provide contacts for some tour operators; their websites are a good place to start looking (see Tourist Offices, p258, for contact details).

Costs vary enormously depending on the location, type and length of tour, and type of accommodation en route. Some companies include bikes as part of the package, but most offer them for hire separately so you have the option of taking your own. There's also an extra charge if you're travelling alone – most of the accommodation is set up for two people sharing. A week-long supported tour could cost anything from €500 to €2000+. Some likely tour companies include:

Celtic Trails (W celtictrails.com) This company concentrates on the west (Clare and Galway) and northwest (Mayo, Sligo and Donegal).

The Emerald Trail (☎ 028-9081 3200, W www .emeraldtrail.com) Based in the North this company's tours take in parts of the northeast, the Fermanagh/Leitrim/Sligo lakelands and Donegal; it also offers a tour in Connemara.

Irish Cycling Safaris (☎ 01-260 0749, W www.cyc lingsafaris.com) Among the larger and longest-surviving tour companies this one has an excellent reputation. It runs supported tours in Donegal, the North, southwest (Kerry), southeast and Connemara.

Irish Cycling Tours (☎ 095-42302, W www.irish cyclingtours.com) This outfit specialises in Kerry and Connemara; it's also long-established.

Bicycle Tour Companies Abroad

The Internet is a great place to begin searching; the Cyber Cyclery site (W cycling.org) contains hundreds of links to touring-company sites, many of which include Ireland in their itineraries. Other resources include your travel agency, classified sections in bicycle or adventure travel magazines and the small ads in newspaper travel pages. Also contact Bord Fáilte or the NITB (see Tourist Offices, p258) for the names of tour operators based in your home country.

MAPS

Two mapping agencies cover the island: Ordnance Survey of Ireland (OSI; ☎ 01-802 5379, W www.osi.ie; Phoenix Park, Dublin 8) in the South; and Ordnance Survey of Northern Ireland (OSNI; ☎ 028-9025 5768, W www.osni.gov.uk; Colby House, Stranmillis Court, Malone Lower, Belfast BT9 5BJ) in the North. A wide variety of sheet maps and atlases produced by OSI, OSNI and many external publishers, such as Michelin, are available.

The OSI/OSNI *Complete Road Atlas of Ireland* (1:210,000) is the best investment for planning; it includes detailed town maps of most major centres. Also very useful and highly reliable apart from the odd isolated inaccuracy is the OSI/OSNI 1:250,000 Holiday map series, four maps conveniently titled *Ireland North*, *Ireland South*, *Ireland East* and *Ireland West*.

For greater detail the OSI 1:50,000 Discovery series is invaluable – accurate and full of additional information, particularly contours (interval 10m) and the locations of ancient sites.

Maps and atlases are widely available in bookshops, with the larger outlets in Dublin and Belfast stocking the best range.

PLACE NAMES

All over Ireland, spellings of towns can vary from signpost to signpost as well as from signpost to map, often veering phonetically rather than formally, eg Bonmahon or Bunmahon. In most cases we try to use the OSI 1:250,000 Holiday map spelling.

DIGITAL RESOURCES

The Internet is a rich resource for travellers to Ireland. At the Lonely Planet website (w www.lonelyplanet.com) you'll find succinct summaries on travelling to Ireland, postcards from other travellers and the Thorn Tree bulletin board, which has a cycling branch where you can ask questions and give advice.

The websites of the large tourist boards, Bord Fáilte and the NITB (see Tourist Offices, p258), are comprehensive and have many links. Other comprehensive general sites include IOL's Interactive Travel Guide to the best of Ireland (w www.iol.ie/~discover) and w theirishguide.com).

For cyclists, the Cyber Cyclery (w cyc ling.org) is a fine place to start; it's a huge resource for information, advice, links and much more. Cycling Ireland (w www.cyc lingireland.org) provides news, information, event calendars and links.

BOOKS

For a general overview of Irish writers and literature see Literature (p20). Most bookshops in Ireland have huge Irish-interest sections with many local and regional guidebooks and maps. Most cities and many towns have more than one good bookshop; big chains include Waterstone's and Eason's.

Lonely Planet

Lonely Planet also publishes *Ireland*, *Dublin*, *Dublin Condensed*, *Walking in Ireland* and *World Food Ireland*. Under its Journeys imprint Lonely Planet also publishes *Home with Alice: A Journey through Gaelic Ireland* and Eric Newby's classic

Round Ireland in Low Gear (see Cycling, below). Lonely Planet's *Dublin City Map* is essential if you're planning an extended stay in Ireland's biggest city.

Cycling

Eric Newby's *Round Ireland in Low Gear* is a light-hearted study of rides in Ireland made by Newby and his wife, Wanda. While Newby's book is focused on the South, Dervla Murphy's *A Place Apart* is set in Northern Ireland and at a much less hopeful period of its history. Time has changed some of what Murphy experienced, but her book remains a wonderful backgrounder.

Many local tourist authorities produce brochures and pamphlets detailing routes and various services. These are usually available in tourist information centres (TICs).

General

North and South, Ireland must be one of world's most-written-about places. Beyond the staggering array of regularly updated general guides there are guidebooks to assist all the various travel tribal groups: literary travellers, historical and architectural travellers, genealogists, golfers, fishers, pub goers, music lovers, horsey types... and more. Many titles are available over the Internet, otherwise wait until you arrive in Dublin and make straight for one of the big bookshops, such as Eason's or Hodges Figgis.

The *Irish Almanac & Yearbook of Facts* is a good reference, with lots of information on many different aspects of Irish life, on both sides of the border. Tony Hawks' *Round Ireland with a Fridge* well captures the mood of an Irish journey – allowing for the fact that few of us elect to hitchhike around the island with a small refrigerator for company.

History & Politics

Concise general histories abound. For a detailed account of Irish history read *The Oxford Companion to Irish History*, edited by SJ Connolly. Thomas Cahill's scholarly and readable *How the Irish Saved Civilization* explores the role of early Irish Christians in Western religion, art and literature; it adds a rich veneer to travels in Ireland.

All the key events in Irish history are covered, usually by multiple titles. Cecil Woodham-Smith's *The Great Hunger* remains the classic study of the Great Famine.

Max Caulfield's *The Easter Rebellion* is an enlightening study of the 1916 Easter Rising. *The Long War*, by Brendan O'Brien, traces the evolution of Sinn Féin and the IRA up to the period before the 1994 IRA cease-fire. Tim Pat Coogan's *Wherever Green is Worn: The Story of the Irish Diaspora* explores the spread of Irish people around the world.

The range of books about Northern Ireland's late-20th-century history is staggering; with the possibility of peace waxing and waning in recent years, many works have gone quickly out of date and there's the additional problem of finding a truly impartial account.

Endgame in Ireland, by Eamonn Mallie & David McKittrick, is a standout for coverage of the peace process from 1981 to late 2001. It was inspired by, and is based on interviews conducted for, the acclaimed BBC/RTE documentary films of the same name.

A serious, far-reaching but readable attempt to get to grips with Ulster's story is *A History of Ulster*, by Jonathan Bardon. Brian Barton's *A Pocket History of Ulster* is a concise introduction to the history of the North.

Among other works, journalist Peter Taylor's trilogy *Provos*, *Loyalists* and *Brits* is a detailed exploration of the three main players in the North's conflict. Tim Pat Coogan's readable *The Troubles: Ireland's Ordeal 1966–1996 & the Search for Peace* sketches the origins of the Troubles and the long history of the attempt to find a solution.

NEWSPAPERS & MAGAZINES

In the South, the *Irish Times* and *Irish Independent* are reliable broadsheet dailies, the former a bastion of liberal opinion and good journalism and the latter somewhat lighter in content, with more features and gossip. The main evening paper is the *Evening Herald*, published in Dublin.

In the North, papers include the tabloid and staunchly Protestant *News Letter* and the pro-nationalist *Irish News*. The pick of the bunch is probably the apolitical evening *Belfast Telegraph*. All the major British newspapers are available, North and South.

Taking Photos Outdoors

For cyclists, photography can be a vexed issue – all that magnificent scenery but such weight and space restrictions on what photographic equipment you can carry. With a little care and planning it is possible to maximise your chance of taking great photos on the ride.

Light and filters In fine weather, the best light is early and late in the day. In strong sunlight and in mountain and coastal areas where the light is intense, a polarising filter will improve colour saturation and reduce haze. On overcast days the soft light can be great for shooting wildflowers and running water and an 81A warming filter can be useful. If you use slide film, a graduated filter will help balance unevenly lit landscapes.

Equipment If you need to travel light carry a zoom in the 28 to 70mm range, and if your sole purpose is landscapes consider carrying just a single wide-angle lens (24mm). A tripod is essential for really good images and there are some excellent lightweight models available. Otherwise a pannier, bike seat or even a pile of rocks can be used to improvise.

Camera care Keep your gear dry – a few zip-lock freezer bags can be used to double wrap camera gear and silica-gel sachets (a drying agent) can be used to suck moisture out of equipment. Sturdy cameras will normally work fine in freezing conditions. Take care when bringing a camera from one temperature extreme to another; if moisture condenses on the camera parts make sure it dries thoroughly before going back into the cold, or mechanisms can freeze up. Standard camera batteries fail very quickly in the cold. Remove them from the camera when it's not in use and keep them under your clothing.

For a thorough grounding in photography on the road, read Lonely Planet's *Travel Photography*, by Richard I'Anson, a full-colour guide for happy-snappers and professional photographers alike.

Gareth McCormack

Coverage of cycle sports and issues in the newspapers is sound but hardly exhaustive. Most of the well-known British and American cycling magazines are available, but there's no Irish equivalent. Much local cycling information is disseminated through Cycling Ireland's website (see Useful Organisations, p32).

WEATHER FORECASTS

Most newspapers, and radio and television news services have detailed weather reports. The Irish weather service, Met Éireann, has a telephone forecast service called Weather-dial which updates forecasts for the four provinces (see Cycling Regions – Index Map, p3, for a province map) three times daily. Dial ☎ 155 0123, plus ☎ 850 for Munster, ☎ 851 for Leinster, ☎ 852 for Connaught, ☎ 853 for Ulster and ☎ 854 for Dublin.

RADIO & TV

The Republic has six national radio networks (four run by the state-owned Radio Telefís Éireann, RTÉ) and a host of regional stations. RTÉ Radio 1 has the best news and current affairs. Popular stations often play classic international rock and pop music. The state-run TV channels in the Republic are RTÉ 1 and 2 and the Irish-language Teilifís na Gaeilge (TG4). TV3 is the commercial station.

Northern Ireland electronic media is derived from British parent companies. Two TV stations, BBC NI and UTV, mix their own programming with input from Britain's BBC and ITV.

PHOTOGRAPHY

Landscapes will dominate the photographic record of an Irish journey so the best results come from a 35mm SLR camera and transparency film. Light can be low, so it's best to use film rated 200 or 400 ISO at the minimum. If you're more experienced and favour unusual or professional films, remember that they're rarely available outside of major centres, so stock up wherever possible. Print film is readily available.

Irish people are usually obliging if you wish to take portraits but always ask before aiming the camera. In the North, it's always best to ask before taking pictures of fortified police stations or army posts. In gen-

---

Touring with Children

Children can travel by bicycle from the time they can support their head and a helmet, at around eight months. There are some small, lightweight, cute helmets around, such as the L'il Bell Shell.

To carry an infant or toddler requires a child seat or trailer. Child seats are more common for everyday riding and are cheaper, easier to move as a unit with the bike and let you touch and talk to your child while moving. Disadvantages, especially over long distances, can include exposure to weather, the tendency of a sleeping child to loll, and losing luggage capacity at the rear. The best makes, such as the Rhode Gear Limo, include extra moulding to protect the child in case of a fall, have footrests and restraints, recline to let the child sleep and fit very securely and conveniently onto a bike rack.

With a capacity of up to 50kg (versus around 18kg for a child seat), trailers can accommodate two bigger children and luggage. They give good, though not always total, protection from sun and rain and let children sleep comfortably. It's also handy to be able to swap the trailer between adults' bikes. Look for a trailer that is lightweight, foldable, brightly coloured with a flag, and that tracks and handles well.

Be sure that the bike to which you attach a child seat or trailer is sturdy and low-geared to withstand – and help you withstand – the extra weight and stresses. Seats and trailers are treated as additional luggage items when flying.

IS THAT DOG STILL FOLLOWING US ?

DON HATCHER

eral, Northerners are relaxed about tourists photographing sectarian murals.

Airport Security
The major airports all have inspection systems that do not damage film or other photographic material carried in hand luggage.

CYCLING WITH CHILDREN
Cycling routes that follow relatively flat traffic-free trails and minor roads are best suited to children. Some of the routes in this book are suitable, and regional and local TICs (listed under the Information heading in rides chapters) can provide more information on local conditions.

Ireland is one of the more child-friendly countries in Europe, with provision often made for children in hotels and restaurants. They're welcome in B&Bs, though you need to check on facilities when you book. Children are generally allowed in pubs (but not to consume alcohol) until 7pm or 8pm, and in smaller towns this restriction is often treated with customary Irish flexibility.

You can often buy a family ticket for admission to attractions, and family passes are available on public transport. Special events occur during the year aimed specifically at children; check in the events guides published by the tourist boards.

For further general information grab a copy of Lonely Planet's *Travel with Children* by Cathy Lanigan.

MOUNTAIN BIKING
Ireland's climate isn't particularly suited to mountain-bike riding (compared to say, Southern California's) and the available terrain isn't vast, but there's still a very passionate (if relatively small) mountain-biking scene. The main cycling bodies (see Useful Organisations, p32) can direct you to mountain-bike clubs but probably the best way to get in touch with local mountain bikers and to learn of the best places to ride is through local bike shops.

On the Internet, w www.mtbireland.com gives a good overview of competitive mountain biking (and cyclo-cross racing) in Ireland. A fine starting point for news, views, links and information on the growing mountain-biking scene in Northern Ireland is w www.mtbrider.com.

Touring with Children

From the age of about four, children can move on to a 'trailer-bike' (effectively a child's bike, minus a front wheel, which hitches to an adult's bike) or to a tandem (initially as 'stoker' – the rider at the back – with 'kiddy cranks', or crank extensions); this lets them help pedal. The tandem can be a long-term solution, keeping you and your child together and letting you compensate if the child tires.

Be careful of children rushing into touring on a solo bike before they can sustain the effort and concentration required. Once they are ready and keen to ride solo, at about age 10 to 12, they will need a good-quality touring bike, properly fitted.

Bike touring with children requires a new attitude as well as new equipment. Be sensitive to their needs – especially when they're too young to communicate them fully. In a seat or trailer, they're not expending energy and need to be dressed accordingly. Keep them dry, at the right temperature and protected from the sun. Keep their energy and interest up. When you stop, a child travelling in a seat or trailer will be ready for action, so always reserve some energy for parenting. This means more stops, including at places for children to play. Older children will have their own interests and should be involved in planning a tour. Before setting off on a major journey, try some day trips to check your set-up and introduce your child to cycling.

Children need to be taken into account in deciding each day's route – traffic and distances need to be moderate and facilities and points of interest adequate. Given the extra weight of children and their daily needs, you may find it easier to opt for day trips from a base. The very fit and adventurous may not need to compromise to ride with children, but those who do will still find it worthwhile.

As with other activities, children bring a new perspective and pleasure to cycle touring. They tend to love it.

Alethea Morison

USEFUL ORGANISATIONS
National Cycling Organisations

Cycling Ireland (☎ 01-855 1522, W www.cycling ireland.org; Kelly Roche House, 619 North Circular Rd, Dublin 1) The peak national cycling body, formerly known as the Irish Cycling Federation, this organisation runs road- and mountain-bike racing events and maintains comprehensive listings of affiliated clubs and leisure-cycling events.

Dublin Cycling Campaign (DCC; W www.con nect.ie/dcc; 12 Millmount Grove, Windy Arbour, Dublin 14) This organisation strictly isn't national, but it is the largest cycle-campaign group and can provide links to other Irish campaign groups.

Northern Ireland Cycling Federation (W www .nicycling.homestead.com) The governing body for cycling in Northern Ireland draws members from clubs around the province and caters for racing, touring, mountain biking and leisure cycling.

Sustrans Northern Ireland (☎ 028-9043 4569, W www.nationalcyclenetwork.org.uk; Marquis Building, 89–91 Adelaide St, Belfast BT2 8FE) This group lobbies for the use of sustainable transport and oversees the creation of National Cycle Network routes in Northern Ireland.

Touring Clubs

The UK-based Cyclists' Touring Club (CTC; W www.ctc.org.uk; Cotterell House, 69 Meadrow, Godalming, Surrey GU7 3HS) has affiliated groups in Dublin and Northern Ireland that organise leisure rides. The Dublin-based CTC Ireland group (W home page.eircom.net/~ctc) has its own website and a full calendar of rides and events.

Other Organisations

Dúchas (☎ 01-647 3000, W www.heritageire land.ie; 6 Ely Place Upper, Dublin 2) The government heritage body operates many parks, monuments and gardens in the South. For €20 a Heritage Card permits free access to these sites for one year. For more information call ☎ 1850 600 601 (within Ireland) or visit the website.

Environment & Heritage Service (EHS; ☎ 028-9025 1477, W www.ehsni.gov.uk; Commonwealth House, 35 Castle St, Belfast) Many country parks and historical monuments in Northern Ireland are maintained and managed by this body.

National Trust Northern Ireland (NT; ☎ 028-9751 0721, W www.nationaltrust.org.uk; Rowallane House, Saintfield, Ballynahinch, Co Down, BT24 7LH) Annual membership (£32.50) entitles you to free entry to its properties.

An Taisce (☎ 01-454 1786, W www.antaisce.org; Tailors Hall, Back Lane, Dublin 8) The National Trust for Ireland is a key player in saving natural and built heritage throughout the South. Annual membership (€35) entitles you to reduced-price entry to heritage properties.

CYCLING ROUTES
Route Descriptions

This guide covers what its authors considered to be the best on-road cycle touring routes in Ireland, including the 42-day Around Ireland ride (p251), mostly drawn from shorter tours in regional chapters. To select the routes, authors researched material from several sources, including existing routes suggested by Sustrans (in Northern Ireland) and local cycling or tourism authorities. In some cases, part or all of a route in this book follows one of these existing routes. The routes described range from day rides to rides of several days in length and, in many cases, can be linked to create longer tours. Transport options – including cycling – for getting to and from each ride are given. Each day's riding finishes at a suggested town, for which we provide information on accommodation options, places to buy food or dine out, and points of interest.

Ride Difficulty

Each ride is graded according to its difficulty in terms of distance, terrain, road surface and navigation. The grade appears both in the Table of Rides (p4) and the introduction to each ride.

Grading is unavoidably subjective and is intended as a guide only. The degree of difficulty of a ride will vary according to the weather, a rider's fitness and the weight carried. Many rides involve easy and hard days, which are balanced when the ride's overall grade is considered.

Easy These are rides of only a few hours' duration, over mostly flat terrain on good road surfaces. Navigation is straightforward, presenting few challenges.

Moderate These rides present a moderate challenge to someone of average fitness. They are usually days of three to five hours long, are likely to include hills, may feature poor road surfaces and may require more detailed navigation.

Hard These rides are suited to fit and experienced cyclists. They may include long daily distances and/or challenging climbs, traverse some rough road surfaces and present navigational challenges.

Times & Distances

A suggested riding time is given for each day's riding; this should be used only as a guide. Riding times are based on average speeds of between 10km/h and 18km/h and do not take into account time spent on side trips, rest or meal stops. Daily riding distances are determined by individual authors and vary from less than 40km to more than 90km.

Cue Sheets & Elevation Charts

Most riding days include an elevation profile; those without aren't necessarily *flat*, but they don't include major climbs. See Cue Sheets (p9) for a description of how to use cues.

ACCOMMODATION

It's generally not hard to find a place to stay in Ireland, although some of the smallest villages may lack options, and some of the most popular may fill up at peak times. Bord Fáilte and the NITB (see Tourist Offices, p258) list B&Bs, hotels, camping grounds and other accommodation options on their websites and in a range of annual publications. In addition, there are many places that aren't 'tourist board approved' but are in no way inferior. Most Bord Fáilte and NITB offices book local accommodation (for a small fee). A reservation service (Gulliver Ireland) can be accessed via the tourist board websites, directly at w www .goireland.com or on ☎ 800 3698 7412. This service requires a nonrefundable 10% deposit, and booking fee (€4 for up to four people), to be charged to a credit card at the time of booking.

Irish accommodation providers are sympathetic to cyclists and rarely turn away tourers. Most can offer secure and/or undercover storage for bikes. The NITB's invaluable *Walkers and Cyclists Accommodation Guide* contains contact details for more than 250 accommodation providers in the North who have particular facilities for cyclists, such as areas for drying clothing and equipment.

Prices quoted in this book are for high-season accommodation (July and August).

Camping

In general, camping grounds and caravan parks aren't as common as in the rest of Europe, but there's certainly a higher concentration of them in popular counties in the South, such as Kerry, Cork and Waterford. In County Donegal they're rare indeed. Some coastal parts of the North are well served, but inland camping grounds are rare. Some hostels also have space for tents and offer the use of the kitchen and shower facilities, which often makes them better value than the main camp sites. At commercial parks, a night's camping typically costs €5 to €7 per person (South) or £6 to £10 per site (North). Facilities vary; come prepared for coin-operated showers.

Farmers will often give permission for free camping in their fields (or, at worst, they might ask for a small fee). Don't camp on private land without first seeking permission.

Hostels

The total number of 'official' and independent hostels in Ireland is staggering – there are hundreds. From May to September and on public holidays hostels, like all accommodation, can be heavily booked. Per night, dorm beds typically cost from €8 to €13 (South) or £7 to £10 (North), depending on the hostel's location, size and facilities. Most hostels also offer accommodation in small dorms, double or twin rooms and private rooms, with prices rising accordingly. Some serve a simple breakfast (toast and jam) as part of the tariff, or for an additional (usually modest) fee.

An Óige (Irish Youth Hostel Association; ☎ 01-830 4555, w www.irelandyha.org) and Hostelling International Northern Ireland (HINI; ☎ 028-9032 4733, w www.hini .org.uk) are the two associations linked with Hostelling International (HI). In theory, HI membership holders (see Visas & Documents, p258) pay lower rates but many hostels don't seem too fussy about this.

The main independent hostel organisations are Independent Hostel Owners (IHO; ☎ 21-437 1583, w www.holidayhound.com/ihi) and Independent Holiday Hostels (IHH; ☎ 01-836 4700, w www.hostels-ireland .com). They account for about 250 hostels between them. Both publish annual guides that are widely available in TICs. In recent years, some independent hostels have been given over to accommodation for refugees and may not have beds available for passing travellers; it pays to call ahead and check.

B&Bs & Guesthouses

It sometimes seems as if every other house in Ireland is a B&B: you'll stumble upon them in the most unusual and remote locations. The best are private homes with welcoming, knowledgeable hosts; breakfasts can be big and healthy or big and greasy – they're rarely small. Expect to pay a minimum of about €20 (South) or £15 (North) per person per night, with prices in the cities and big towns, or for luxurious B&Bs, sometimes rising well above that. B&Bs, like hotels, tend to offer better value for travellers in pairs or small groups; singles are often stung with a supplement. B&Bs are usually small, with two to four rooms. Guesthouses are usually larger establishments, with six or more rooms. Outside big cities most B&Bs accept cash only.

Hotels

Hotels range from the local pub to medieval castles. Rates usually include breakfast. Prices vary enormously; small, family-run hotels won't charge much – if any – more than local B&Bs. Large, multi-star hotels in the cities have prices comparable to those in most European cities. It's often possible to negotiate better deals than the published rates, especially out of season.

FOOD

Since the rise of the Celtic Tiger economy and Ireland's rediscovered self-confidence, few aspects of Irish life have been transformed as completely as cooking and eating. Several factors have combined to produce what is called by some 'new Irish cuisine'. As Lonely Planet's *World Food Ireland* points out, the astounding feature of new Irish cuisine, 'is that there's very little new about it, just a confident return to tradition'. In the best of modern Irish restaurants, decor and settings are uncluttered, food is simple and flavoursome and service is friendly and never obsequious. It's a high-on-pleasure, low-on-indigestion formula.

World Food Ireland is an essential addition if eating out will be your main off-the-bike activity. The big city bookshops sell several independent guides to Irish restaurants, and both Bord Fáilte and the NITB publish eating-out guides.

Healthy eating for cyclists is discussed under Nutrition (p38).

Local Food

Most Irish menus are big on meat and include beef, lamb, pork, chicken and seafood. Regional variations are sometimes hard to pick – Ireland isn't very big, after all. Throughout Ireland, seafood is a reliable and delicious choice. Atlantic oysters (available September to April) and salmon (preferably wild, 'superior' farmed otherwise) are both worth looking out for. County Westmeath is renowned for quality beef. The southwest is probably the best part of the country for organically grown vegetables, cheese, and health foods; it also has some of the best vegetarian restaurants outside Dublin. It's worth sampling bakery goods, especially soda bread and fadge (a potato bread) in the north; Ulster bakery specialities include sweet bannocks and cake-like, fruity barm bracks.

Vegetarians, and to a greater extent vegans, are in for a relatively hard time in Ireland, so highly does meat and dairy food feature on menus. However, there are some fine vegetarian restaurants, mostly in the larger or more popular centres. Many hotels and nonvegie restaurants feature a vegetarian dish on their menus, but it's rarely anything to get excited about. Meaty breakfasts can also make B&Bs a bad deal for vegetarians who, depending on whether they eat eggs, are likely to start the day with nothing but cereal and toast.

Where to Eat

In cities such as Dublin, Belfast and Cork there's a wide range of cuisines and restaurants; outside of the major centres the variety and quality of places to eat is hugely influenced by the number of visitors. Chinese food, often served in a late-closing restaurant, is one cuisine that has found its way into the countryside. It's rare for a town not to have at least one hotel, pub or restaurant, although you'll sometimes find that they don't serve evening meals – for many Irish, lunch is the main meal of the day. This is true of many pubs, where a bowl of soup and some good bread can make a filling, cheap meal. Note that not all pubs serve food, and some serve it only during the tourist season. Fast food is sometimes the only option; it ranges from traditional fish and chips (buy it from the 'chipper', as fish and chip shops are known) to burgers, pizzas, kebabs and tacos.

DRINKS
Nonalcoholic Drinks

The Irish drink lots of tea, and coffee is growing in popularity. It's easy to get a good cappuccino or latte in larger towns; expect to confront the dreaded instant coffee in out-of-the-way places. In towns and cities tap water is always safe to drink. Bottled sports drinks are available in supermarkets, convenience stores and fast-food fridges, including all the usual 'ades'. See Hydration (p38) for advice on healthy drinking for cyclists.

Alcoholic Drinks

The Irish love their beer – either lager or stout. The best known stout is Guinness, brewed, and consumed at its very best, in Dublin; Murphy's and Beamish are popular in Cork. It's mandatory to at least try stout; if you don't like it, there are a wide variety of lager beers available, the best known probably Harp (brewed by Guinness). Lo-

Irish Whiskey

The Irish were pioneers in the development of distilling whiskey (distilled three times and spelled with an 'e' as opposed to the twice-distilled Scotch whisky). Bushmills in County Antrim, established in 1608, is the world's oldest legal distillery. When ordering a whiskey, the Irish use the brand name of an Irish whiskey (Jameson's, Paddy's, Powers, Bushmills etc). A hot whiskey is a folk remedy for illnesses such as a cold caught after damp days in the saddle. But who needs a medical excuse? It's also a fine settler after an evening pub meal.

cally brewed 'imports' such as Budweiser, Foster's or Heineken are commonly available. Expect to pay about €3 for a pint (570mL); half-pints are cheaper, but drinking them will probably result in a minor loss of credibility if you're partaking with locals.

Health & Safety

Keeping healthy on your travels depends on your predeparture preparations, your daily health care and diet while on the road, and how you handle any medical problem that develops. Few touring cyclists experience anything more than a bit of soreness, fatigue and chafing, although there is potential for more serious problems. The sections that follow are not intended to alarm, but they are worth a skim before you go.

Before You Go

HEALTH INSURANCE
Make sure that you have adequate health insurance for your needs. For details, see Travel Insurance (p258).

IMMUNISATIONS
You don't need any vaccinations to visit Ireland. However, it's always wise to keep up-to-date with routine vaccinations such as diphtheria, polio and tetanus.

FIRST AID
It's a good idea at any time to know the appropriate responses in the event of a major accident or illness, and it's especially important if you are intending to ride off-road in a remote area. Consider learning basic first aid through a recognised course, and carrying a first-aid manual and medical kit.

Although detailed first-aid instruction is outside the scope of this guidebook, some basic points are listed in the section on Traumatic Injuries (p44). Undoubtedly the best advice is to avoid an accident in the first place. The Safety on the Ride section (p45) contains tips for safe on-road and offroad riding, as well as information on how to summon help should a major accident or illness occur.

PHYSICAL FITNESS
Most of the rides in this book are designed for someone with a moderate degree of cycling fitness. As a general rule, however, the fitter you are, the more you'll enjoy riding. It pays to spend time preparing yourself physically before you set out, rather than let a sore backside and aching muscles draw

First-Aid Kit
A possible kit could include:

First-Aid Supplies
☐ **bandages & safety pins**
☐ **butterfly closure strips**
☐ **elastic support bandage** for knees, ankles etc
☐ **gauze swabs**
☐ **latex gloves**
☐ **nonadhesive dressings**
☐ **scissors (small pair)**
☐ **sterile alcohol wipes**
☐ **sticking plasters (Band Aids)**
☐ **syringes & needles** – for removing gravel from road-rash wounds
☐ **thermometer** (note that mercury thermometers are prohibited by airlines)
☐ **tweezers**

Medications
☐ **antidiarrhoea**, **antinausea drugs** and **oral rehydration salts**
☐ **antifungal cream** or **powder** – for fungal skin infections and thrush
☐ **antihistamines** – for allergies, eg, hay fever; to ease the itch from insect bites or stings; and to prevent motion sickness
☐ **antiseptic powder** or **solution** (such as povidone-iodine) and **antiseptic wipes** for cuts and grazes
☐ **calamine lotion**, **sting relief spray** or **aloe vera** – to ease irritation from sunburn and insect bites or stings
☐ **cold** and **flu tablets**, **throat lozenges** and **nasal decongestant**
☐ **laxatives**
☐ **nappy rash cream**
☐ **painkillers** (eg, aspirin or paracetamol/cetaminophen in the USA) – for pain and fever

Miscellaneous
☐ **insect repellent**, **sunscreen**, **lip balm** and **eye drops**
☐ **water purification tablets** or **iodine**

Getting Fit for Touring

Ideally, a training programme should be tailored to your objectives, specific needs, fitness level and health. However, if you have no idea how to prepare for your cycling holiday these guidelines will help you get the fitness you need to enjoy it more. Things to think about include:

Foundation You will need general kilometres in your legs before you start to expose them to any intensive cycling. Always start out with easy rides – even a few kilometres to the shops – and give yourself plenty of time to build towards your objective.

Tailoring Once you have the general condition to start preparing for your trip, work out how to tailor your training rides to the type of tour you are planning. Someone preparing for a three-week ride will require a different approach to someone building fitness for a one-day or weekend ride. Some aspects to think about are the ride length (distance and days), terrain, climate and weight to be carried in panniers. If your trip involves carrying 20kg in panniers, incorporate this weight into some training rides, especially some of the longer ones. If you are going to be touring in mountainous areas, choose a hilly training route.

Recovery You usually adapt to a training programme during recovery time, so it's important to do the right things between rides. Recovery can take many forms, but the simple ones are best. These include getting quality sleep, eating an adequate diet to refuel the system, doing recovery rides between hard days (using low gears to avoid pushing yourself), stretching and enjoying a relaxing bath. Other forms include recovery massage, spas and yoga.

If you have no cycling background this programme will help you get fit for your cycling holiday. If you are doing an easy ride (each ride in this book is rated; see Cycling Routes, p32), aim to at least complete Week 4; for moderate rides, complete Week 6; and complete the entire programme if you are doing a hard ride. Experienced cycle tourists could start at Week 3, while those who regularly ride up to four days a week could start at Week 5.

Don't treat this as a punishing training schedule: try cycling to work or to the shops, join a local touring club or get a group of friends together to turn weekend rides into social events.

	Monday	Tuesday	Wednesday	Thursday	Friday	Saturday	Sunday
Week 1	10km*	–	10km*	–	10km*	–	10km*
Week 2	–	15km*	–	15km*	–	20km*	–
Week 3	20km*	–	20km†	25km*	–	25km*	20km†
Week 4	–	30km*	–	35km*	30km†	30km*	–
Week 5	30km*	–	40km†	–	35km*	–	40km†
Week 6	30km*	–	40km†	–	–	60km*	40km†
Week 7	30km*	–	40km†	–	30km†	70km*	30km*
Week 8	–	60km*	30km†	–	40km†	–	90km*

* steady pace (allows you to carry out a conversation without losing your breath) on flat or undulating terrain
† solid pace (allows you to talk in short sentences only) on undulating roads with some longer hills

The training programme shown here is only a guide. Ultimately it is important to listen to your body and slow down if the ride is getting too hard. Take recovery days and cut back distances when you feel this way. Don't panic if you don't complete every ride, every week; the most important thing is to ride regularly and gradually increase the length of your rides as you get fitter.

For those with no exercise background, be sure to see your doctor and get a clearance to begin exercising at these rates. This is especially important for those over 35 years of age with no exercise history and those with a cardiac or respiratory condition of any nature.

Kevin Tabotta

your attention from some of the world's finest cycle touring countryside.

Depending on your existing level of fitness, you should start training a couple of months before your trip. See the boxed text 'Getting Fit for Touring' for a training programme.

As you train, you'll discover the bike adjustments needed to increase your comfort – as well as any mechanical problems.

Staying Healthy

The best way to have a completely lousy holiday (especially if you are relying on self-propulsion) is to become ill. Heed the following simple advice and the only thing you're likely to suffer from is that rewarding tiredness at the end of a full day.

Reduce the chances of contracting an illness by washing your hands frequently, particularly after working on your bike and before handling or eating food.

HYDRATION

You may not notice how much water you're losing as you ride, because it evaporates in the breeze. However, don't underestimate the amount of fluid you need to replace – particularly in warmer weather. The magic figure is supposedly 1L per hour, though many cyclists have trouble consuming this much – remembering to drink enough can be harder than it sounds. Sipping little and often is the key; try to drink a mouthful every 10 minutes or so and don't wait until you get thirsty. Water 'backpacks' can be great for fluid regulation since virtually no physical or mental effort is required to drink. Keep drinking before and after the day's ride to replenish fluid.

Use the colour of your urine as a rough guide to whether you are drinking enough. Small amounts of dark urine suggest you need to increase your fluid intake. Passing reasonable quantities of light yellow urine indicates that you've got the balance about right. Other signs of dehydration include headache and fatigue. For more information on the effects of dehydration, see Dehydration & Heat Exhaustion (p42).

Water

While tap water is always safe to drink in Ireland unless there is a sign to the contrary, the intestinal parasite *Giardia lamblia* has been found in water from lakes, rivers and streams. Giardia is not common but, if you want to be certain, water from these sources should be purified before drinking. For more information see Giardiasis, p43.

The simplest way of purifying water is to boil it thoroughly. Vigorous boiling for five minutes should do the job.

Simple filtering will not remove all dangerous organisms, so if you can't boil water treat it chemically. Chlorine tablets will kill many pathogens, but not giardia. Iodine is very effective in purifying water and is available in tablet and liquid form, but follow the directions carefully and remember that too much iodine can be harmful. Flavoured powder will disguise the taste of treated water and is a good thing to carry if you are spending time away from town water supplies.

Sports Drinks

Commercial sports drinks such as Gatorade and PowerAde are an excellent way to satisfy your hydration needs, electrolyte replacement and energy demands in one. On endurance rides especially, it can be difficult to keep eating solid fuels day in, day out, but sports drinks can supplement these energy demands and allow you to vary your solid-fuel intake a little for variety. The bonus is that those all-important body salts lost through perspiration are restocked. Make sure you drink plenty of water as well; if you have two water bottles on your bike (and you should), it's a good idea to fill one with sports drink and the other with plain water.

If using a powdered sports drink, don't mix it too strongly (follow the instructions) because, in addition to being too sweet, too many carbohydrates can actually impair your body's ability to absorb the water and carbohydrates properly.

NUTRITION

One of the great things about bike touring is that it requires a lot of energy, which means you can eat more. Depending on your activity levels, it's not hard to put away huge servings of food and be hungry a few hours after.

Because you're putting such demands on your body, it's important to eat well – not just lots. As usual, you should eat a balanced diet from a wide variety of foods. This is easy in Ireland, with fresh food widely available (see Food, p34).

The main part of your diet should be carbohydrates rather than proteins or fats. While some protein (for tissue maintenance and repair) and fat (for vitamins, long-term energy and warmth) is essential, carbohydrates provide the most efficient fuel. They are easily digested into simple sugars, which are then used in energy production. Less-refined foods, such as pasta, rice, bread, fruits and vegetables, are all high in carbohydrates.

Eating simple carbohydrates (sugars, such as lollies or sweets) gives you almost immediate energy – great for when you need a top-up (see the boxed text 'Avoiding the Bonk'); however, because they are quickly metabolised, you may get a sugar 'high' then a 'low'. For cycling it is better to base your diet around complex carbohydrates, which take longer to process and provide 'slow-release' energy over a longer period. (But don't miss the opportunity to indulge in scones with jam and cream.)

Cycle Food: A Guide to Satisfying Your Inner Tube, by Lauren Hefferon, is a handy reference for nutrition and health advice with practical recipes.

Day-to-Day Needs

Eat a substantial breakfast – wholegrain cereal or bread is best – and fruit or juice for vitamins. If you like a cooked breakfast, include carbohydrates (such as porridge, toast or potatoes). Try to avoid foods high in fat, which take longer to digest.

Avoiding the Bonk

The bonk, in a cycling context, is not a pleasant experience; it's that light-headed, can't-put-power-to-the-pedals, weak feeling that engulfs you (usually quite quickly) when your body runs out of fuel.

If you experience it the best move is to stop and refuel immediately. It can be quite serious and risky to your health if it's not addressed as soon as symptoms occur. It won't take long before you are ready to get going again (although most likely at a slower pace), but you'll also be more tired the next day so try to avoid it.

The best way to do this is to maintain your fuel intake while riding. Cycling for hours burns considerable body energy, and replacing it is something that needs to be tailored to each individual's tastes. The touring cyclist needs to target foods that have a high carbohydrate source. Foods that contain some fat are not a problem occasionally, as cycling at low intensity (when you're able to ride and talk without losing your breath) will usually trigger the body to draw on fat stores before stored carbohydrates.

Good on-bike cycling foods include:

- bananas (in particular) and other fruits
- bread with jam or honey
- breakfast and muesli bars
- rice-based snacks
- prepackaged high-carbohydrate sports bars (eg, PowerBar)
- sports drinks

During lunch stops (or for breakfast) you can try filling potato-based dishes such as boxty and colcannon, fadge (potato bread), spaghetti, cereal, pancakes and baked beans.

It's important not to get uptight about the food you eat. As a rule of thumb, base all your meals around carbohydrates of some sort, but don't be afraid to also indulge in local culinary delights.

Bread is the easiest food for lunch, topped with ingredients like cheese, peanut butter, salami and fresh salad. Filled rolls make for a satisfying meal (chips or pizza, with their high fat content, will feel like a lump in your stomach if you continue straight away).

Keep topping up your energy during the ride. See the boxed text 'Avoiding the Bonk' (p39) for tips.

Try to eat a high-carbohydrate meal in the evening. If you're eating out, Mexican, vegetarian, Italian or Asian restaurants tend to offer more carbohydrate-based meals.

Rice, pasta and potatoes are good staples if you're self-catering. Team them with fresh vegetables and ingredients such as instant soup, canned beans, fish or bacon. Remember that even though you're limited in terms of what you can carry on a bike, it's possible – with some imagination and preparation – to eat camp meals that are both delicious and nutritious.

AVOIDING CYCLING AILMENTS
Saddle Sores & Blisters
While you're more likely to get a sore bum if you're out of condition, riding long distances does take its toll on your behind. To minimise the impact, always wear clean, preferably padded bike shorts (also known as knicks). Brief, unfitted shorts can chafe, as can underwear (see Clothing, p26). Shower as soon as you stop and put on clean, preferably non-synthetic, clothes. Moisturising or emollient creams or baby nappy rash cream also help guard against chafing – apply liberally around the crotch area before riding. For information on correctly adjusting your bike seat, see the Your Bicycle chapter (p47).

If you do suffer from chafing, wash and dry the area and carefully apply a barrier (moisturising) cream.

You probably won't get blisters unless you do a very long ride with no physical preparation. Wearing gloves and correctly fitted shoes will reduce the likelihood of blisters. If you know you're susceptible to blisters in a particular spot, cover the area with medical adhesive tape before riding.

Knee Pain
Knee pain is common among cyclists who pedal in too high a gear. While it may *seem* faster to turn the pedals slowly in a high gear, it's actually more efficient (and better for your knees) to 'spin' the pedals – that is, use a low enough gear so you can pedal quickly with little resistance. For touring, the ideal cadence (the number of pedal strokes per minute) ranges from 70 to 90. Try to maintain this cadence even when you're climbing.

It's a good idea to stretch before and after riding, and to go easy when you first start each day. This reduces your chances of injury and helps your muscles to work more efficiently.

You can also get sore knees if your saddle is too low, or if your shoe cleats (for use with clipless pedals) are incorrectly positioned. Both are discussed in greater detail in the Your Bicycle chapter (p47).

Numbness & Backache
Pain in the hands, neck and shoulders is a common complaint, particularly on longer riding days. It is generally caused by leaning too much on your hands. Apart from discomfort, you can temporarily damage the nerves and experience numbness or mild paralysis of the hands. This can be prevented by wearing padded gloves, cycling with less weight on your hands and changing your hand position frequently (if you have flat handlebars, fit bar ends to provide more hand positions).

When seated your weight should be fairly evenly distributed through your hands and seat. If you're carrying too much weight on your hands there are two ways of adjusting your bike to rectify this: either by raising the height of your handlebars or, if you are stretched out too much, fitting a smaller stem (talk to your local bike shop). For more guidance, see the Your Bicycle chapter (p47).

Fungal Infections
Warm, sweaty bodies are ideal environments for fungal growth, and physical activity, combined with inadequate washing of your body and/or clothes, can lead to fungal infections. The most common are athlete's foot (tinea) between the toes or fingers, and infections on the scalp, in the groin or on the body (ringworm). You can get ringworm (which is a fungal infection, not a worm) from infected animals or other people.

To prevent fungal infections, wash frequently and dry yourself carefully. Change out of sweaty bike clothes as soon as possible.

If you do get an infection, wash the infected area at least daily with a disinfectant or medicated soap, and rinse and dry well. Apply an antifungal cream or powder like tolnaftate. Expose the infected area to air as much as possible, avoid artificial fibres and wash all towels and underwear in hot water, change them often and dry them in the sun.

Staying Warm
Except on extremely hot days, put on another layer of clothing when you stop cycling – even if it's just for a quick break. Staying warm when cycling is as important as keeping up your water and food intake. Particularly in wet or sweaty clothing, your body cools down quickly after you stop working. Muscle strains occur more easily when your body is chilled and hypothermia can result from prolonged exposure (for prevention and treatment, see Hypothermia). Staying rugged up will help prevent picking up chest infections, colds and the flu.

In Ireland you *can* get caught suddenly in bad weather at any time of year. No matter when you go, always be prepared with warm clothing and a waterproof layer. Protect yourself from the wind on long downhill stretches. Even stuffing a few sheets of newspaper under your shirt cuts the chill considerably.

Medical Problems & Treatment

ENVIRONMENTAL HAZARDS
Whatever the season, cyclists in Ireland should be prepared for difficult conditions. For suggestions on appropriate clothing and equipment, see also What to Bring (p26).

Cold
Cycling in cold weather can be a joy if you're prepared and experienced; if not, it can be both unpleasant and hazardous. The physical exertion of pedalling is a great way to stay warm in low temperatures, but on the coldest days it's essential to dress appropriately, to ward off wind chill and stay dry, and to ensure that you have enough to eat.

Beware of frosty roads on cold mornings. Cycling during a snowfall is quite a novelty and always dangerous. Avoid setting out if snow is forecast. If there's snow overnight, don't continue your tour until roads are cleared and ice-free. If you're caught out in a severe snowstorm, seek shelter at the first opportunity – don't try to push on.

Hypothermia This is a real danger in Ireland because of the changeable weather.

Hypothermia occurs when the body loses heat faster than it can produce it and the core temperature of the body falls. It is surprisingly easy to progress from very cold to dangerously cold due to a combination of wind, wet clothing, fatigue and hunger, even if the air temperature is above freezing.

Symptoms of hypothermia are exhaustion, numb skin (particularly toes and fingers), shivering, slurred speech, irrational or violent behaviour, lethargy, stumbling, dizzy spells, muscle cramps and powerful bursts of energy. Irrationality may take the form of sufferers claiming they are warm and trying to take off their clothes.

To prevent hypothermia, dress in layers (see Clothing, p26). A strong, waterproof outer layer is essential. Protect yourself against wind, particularly for long descents. Eat plenty of high-energy food when it's cold; it's important to keep drinking too.

To treat mild hypothermia, first get victims out of the wind and/or rain, remove wet clothing and replace it with dry, warm clothing. Give them hot liquids – not alcohol – and some high-kilojoule, easily digestible food. Do not rub victims: instead, allow them to slowly warm themselves. This should be enough to treat the early stages of hypothermia; however, medical treatment should still be sought urgently if the hypothermia is severe. Early recognition and treatment of mild hypothermia is the only way to prevent severe hypothermia, which is a critical condition and potentially fatal.

Sun
Even in Ireland, even under cloud cover, it's possible to get sunburnt surprisingly quickly. Take sun protection seriously – unless you want to be fried and increase your chances of heatstroke and skin cancer:

• Cover yourself wherever possible: wear a long-sleeved top with a collar, and a peaked helmet cover – you may want to go the extra step and add a 'legionnaire's flap' to your helmet to protect the back of your neck and ears. Make sure your shirt is sunproof: very thin or loosely woven fabrics still let sun through. Some fabrics are designed to offer high sun protection.

- Use high protection sunscreen (30+ or higher). Choose a water-resistant 'sports' sunscreen and reapply every few hours as you sweat it off. Don't forget to protect your neck, ears, hands, and feet if wearing sandals. Zinc cream is good for sensitive noses, lips and ears.
- Wear good sunglasses; they will also protect you from wind, dust and insects and are essential protection against sticks and flying objects if you're mountain biking.
- Sit in the shade during rest breaks.
- Wear a wide-brimmed hat when off the bike.

Mild sunburn can be treated with calamine lotion, aloe vera or sting-relief spray.

Heat

Extreme heat is rare in Ireland. If heatwave conditions are forecast, consider staying off the bike through the middle part of the day. Generally, if you cycle through the cool of the morning and during the long mid-summer evenings you'll have plenty of time to stay on schedule.

Dehydration & Heat Exhaustion Dehydration is a potentially dangerous and generally preventable condition caused by excessive fluid loss. Sweating and inadequate fluid intake are common causes of dehydration in cyclists, but others include diarrhoea, vomiting and high fever – see Diarrhoea for details on appropriate treatment in these circumstances.

The first symptoms are weakness, thirst and passing small amounts of very concentrated urine. This may progress to drowsiness, dizziness or fainting when standing up and, finally, coma.

It's easy to forget how much fluid you are losing via perspiration while you are cycling, particularly if a strong breeze is drying your skin quickly. Make sure you drink sufficient liquids (see Hydration, p38). Refrain from drinking too many caffeinated drinks such as coffee, tea and some soft drinks (which act as a diuretic, causing your body to lose water through urination) throughout the day; don't use them as a water replacement.

Dehydration and salt deficiency can cause heat exhaustion. Salt deficiency is characterised by fatigue, lethargy, headaches, giddiness and muscle cramps; salt tablets may help, but adding extra salt to your food is probably sufficient.

If one of your party suffers from heat exhaustion, lie the casualty down in a shady spot and encourage them to drink slowly but frequently. If possible, seek medical advice.

Heatstroke This serious and occasionally fatal condition can occur if the body's heat-regulating mechanism breaks down and the body temperature rises to dangerous levels. Continuous periods of exposure to high temperatures and insufficient fluids can leave you vulnerable to heatstroke.

The symptoms are feeling unwell, not sweating very much (or at all) and a high body temperature (39° to 41°C or 102° to 106°F). Where sweating has ceased, the skin becomes flushed and red. Severe, throbbing headaches and lack of coordination will also occur, and the sufferer may be confused or aggressive. Eventually the victim will become delirious or convulse.

Hospitalisation is essential, but in the interim get the casualty out of the sun, remove their clothing, cover them with a wet sheet or towel and then fan continuously. Give them plenty of fluids (cool water) if conscious.

INFECTIOUS DISEASES
Diarrhoea

Simple things like a change of water, food or climate can cause a mild bout of diarrhoea, but a few rushed toilet trips with no other symptoms are not indicative of a major problem. More serious diarrhoea is caused by infectious agents transmitted by faecal contamination of food or water, by using contaminated utensils, or directly from one person's hand to another. Paying particular attention to personal hygiene, drinking purified water and taking care of what you eat are important measures to take to avoid getting diarrhoea while touring.

Dehydration is the main danger with any diarrhoea, particularly in children or the elderly, as it can occur quickly. Under all circumstances, the most important thing is to replace fluids (at least equal to the volume being lost). Urine is the best guide to this – if you have small amounts of dark-coloured urine, you need to drink more. Weak black tea with a little sugar, soda water, or soft drinks allowed to go flat and diluted 50% with clean water are all good. With severe diarrhoea it's better to use a rehydrating solution to replace lost minerals and salts. Commercially available oral rehydration salts should be added to boiled or bottled water. In an emergency, make a solution of six teaspoons of sugar and a half teaspoon of salt in a litre of boiled or bottled water. Keep drinking small amounts often. Stick to a bland diet as you recover.

Gut-paralysing drugs such as diphenoxylate or loperamide can be used to bring relief from the symptoms, although they do not actually cure the problem. Only use these drugs if you do not *have* access to toilets, that is, if you *must* travel. These drugs are not recommended for children under 12 years of age, or if you have a high fever or are severely dehydrated.

Seek medical advice if you pass blood or mucus, are feverish or suffer persistent or severe diarrhoea.

Another cause of persistent diarrhoea in travellers is giardiasis.

Giardiasis

This intestinal disorder is contracted by drinking water contaminated with the Giardia parasite. The symptoms are stomach cramps, nausea, a bloated stomach, watery and foul-smelling diarrhoea, and frequent gas. Giardiasis can appear several weeks after you have been exposed to the parasite. The symptoms may disappear for a few days and then return; this can go on for several weeks. Seek medical advice if you think you have giardiasis but where this is not possible, tinidazole or metronidazole are the recommended drugs. Treatment is a 2g single dose of tinidazole or 250mg of metronidazole three times daily for five to 10 days.

BITES & STINGS
Bees & Wasps

These are usually painful rather than dangerous. However, anyone allergic to these can suffer severe breathing difficulties and will need urgent medical care.

Calamine lotion or a commercial sting-relief spray will ease discomfort, and ice packs will reduce the pain and swelling. Antihistamines can also help.

Midges

Midges – small blood-sucking flies – can be a major problem in the west and northwest from June to September. They're at their worst in the evening, or in still and shady conditions, and can make life miserable for the unprepared.

To avoid being bitten, cover yourself up with light-coloured clothing (a netting veil, available from most outdoor shops is also worth considering) and use repellent containing DEET or DMP (note that prolonged overuse of DEET may be harmful, especially to children). Treat bites with antihistamine.

WOMEN'S HEALTH

Cycle touring is not hazardous to your health, but women's health issues are relevant wherever you go, and can be a bit more tricky to cope with when you are on the road.

If you experience low energy and/or abdominal or back pain during menstruation, it may be best to undertake less strenuous rides or schedule a rest day or two at this time.

Gynaecological Problems

If you have a vaginal discharge that is not normal for you with or without any other symptoms, you probably have an infection.

- If you've had thrush before and think you have it again, it's worth self-treating for this (see the following section).
- If not, get medical advice, as you may need a laboratory test and an appropriate course of treatment.
- It's best not to self-medicate with antibiotics because there are many causes of vaginal discharge, which can only be differentiated with a laboratory test.

Thrush (Vaginal Candidiasis) Symptoms of this common yeast infection are itching and discomfort in the genital area, often in association with thick white vaginal discharge (said to resemble cottage cheese). Many factors, including diet, pregnancy, medications and hot climatic conditions can trigger this infection.

You can help prevent thrush by wearing cotton underwear off the bike and loose-fitting bicycle shorts; maintaining good personal hygiene is particularly important when wearing cycling knicks. It's a good idea to wash regularly, but don't use soap, which can increase the chance of thrush occurring. Washing gently with a solution of 1tsp salt dissolved in 1L warm water can relieve the itching. If you have thrush a single dose of an antifungal pessary (vaginal tablet), such as 500mg of clotrimazole is an effective treatment. Alternatively, you can use an antifungal cream inserted high in the vagina (on a tampon). A vaginal acidifying gel may help prevent recurrences.

If you're stuck in a remote area without medication, you could use natural yoghurt (applied directly to the vulva or on a tampon and inserted in the vagina) to soothe and help restore the normal balance of organisms in the vagina.

Avoid yeasty products such as bread and beer, and eat yoghurt made with acidophilus culture to balance the bacteria in your gut.

TRAUMATIC INJURIES

Although we give guidance on basic first-aid procedures here remember that, unless you're an experienced first aider and confident in what you're doing, it's possible to do more harm than good. Always seek medical help if it is available, but if you are far from any help, follow these guidelines.

Cuts & Other Wounds

Here's what to do if you suffer a fall while riding and end up with road-rash (grazing) and a few minor cuts. If you intend continuing on your way, there's likely to be a high risk of infection, so the wound needs to be cleaned and dressed. Carry a few antiseptic wipes in your first-aid kit to use as an immediate measure, especially if no clean water is available. Small wounds can be cleaned with an antiseptic wipe (only wipe across the wound once with each). Deep or dirty wounds need to be cleaned thoroughly:

- Clean your hands before you start.
- Wear gloves if you are cleaning somebody else's wound.
- Use bottled or boiled water (allowed to cool) or an antiseptic solution like povidone-iodine.
- Use plenty of water – pour it on the wound from a container.
- Embedded dirt and other particles can be removed with tweezers or flushed out using a syringe to squirt water (you can get more pressure if you use a needle as well) – this is especially effective for removing gravel.
- Dry wounds heal best, so avoid using antiseptic creams that keep the wound moist; instead apply antiseptic powder or spray.
- Dry the wound with clean gauze before applying a dressing – alternatively, any clean material will do as long as it's not fluffy (avoid cotton wool), because it will stick.

Any break in the skin makes you vulnerable to tetanus infection – if you didn't have a tetanus injection before you left, have one now.

A dressing will protect the wound from dirt, dust and flies. Alternatively, if the wound is small and you are confident you can keep it clean, leave it uncovered. Change the dressing regularly (once a day to start with), especially if the wound is oozing, and watch for signs of infection.

If you have any swelling around the wound, raising the affected limb can help the swelling settle and the wound to heal.

It's best to seek medical advice for any wound that fails to heal after a week or so.

Major Accident

Crashing or being hit by an inattentive driver in a motor vehicle is always a possibility when cycling. When a major accident does occur what you do is determined to some extent by the circumstances you are in and how readily available medical care is. However, remember that emergency services may be different from what you're used to at home.

And, as anywhere, if you are outside a major town they may be much slower at responding to a call, so you need to be prepared to do at least an initial assessment and to ensure that the casualty comes to no further harm. First of all, check for danger to yourself. If the casualty is on the road ensure oncoming traffic is stopped or diverted around you. A basic plan of action is:

- Keep calm and think through what you need to do and when.
- Get medical help urgently; send someone to phone ☎ 112 or ☎ 999 in the Republic and ☎ 999 in the North.
- Carefully look over the casualty in the position in which you found them (unless this is hazardous for some reason, eg, on a cliff edge).
- Call to the casualty to see if there's any response.
- Check for pulse (at the wrist or on the side of the neck), breathing and major blood loss.
- If necessary (ie, no breathing or no pulse), and you know how, start resuscitation.
- Check the casualty for injuries, moving them as little as possible; ask them where they have pain if they are conscious.
- Don't move the casualty if a spinal injury is possible.
- Take immediate steps to control any obvious bleeding by applying direct pressure to the wound.
- Make the casualty as comfortable as possible and reassure them.
- Keep the casualty warm by insulating them from cold or wet ground (use whatever you have to hand, such as a sleeping bag).

Safety on the Ride

ROAD RULES

Traffic in Ireland, both South and North, travels on the left. Bicycles are classified as road-using vehicles and cyclists are expected to obey all signs and signals, to indicate turns (with hand signals) and so on. Remember that drink-driving laws also apply to cyclists. Unless signs indicate otherwise, it's illegal to cycle on the footpath (pavement).

The rules for roads and traffic in the South are reasonably close in form and content to those in the North. Northern Ireland's Highway Code is widely available at booksellers and newsagents. It closely resembles the British Highway Code, which can be viewed at W www.highwaycode .gov.uk.

Bleeding Wounds

Most cuts will stop bleeding on their own, but if a blood vessel of any size has been cut it may continue bleeding for some time. Wounds to the head, hands and at joint creases tend to be particularly bloody.

To stop bleeding from a wound:

- Wear gloves if you are dealing with a wound on another person.
- Lie the casualty down if possible.
- Raise the injured limb above the level of the casualty's heart.
- Use your fingers or the palm of your hand to apply direct pressure to the wound, preferably over a sterile dressing or clean pad.
- Apply steady pressure for at least five minutes before looking to see if the bleeding has stopped.
- Put a sterile dressing over the original pad (don't move this) and bandage it in place.
- Check the bandage regularly in case bleeding restarts.

Never use a tourniquet to stop bleeding as this may cause gangrene – the only situation in which this may be appropriate is if the limb has been amputated.

BICYCLE EQUIPMENT

Helmets aren't compulsory (South or North) although the authorities point out the obvious: that wearing one may reduce the risk of head injury. If riding at night your bicycle must have a red rear reflector, and front and rear lights. A bell or horn is essential if you're cycling in the cities or on cycle paths shared with pedestrians.

RIDING OFF-ROAD

The Irish mountain-biking scene isn't particularly large but there's some superb riding especially in County Wicklow and in some of the forest parks in Northern Ireland. While this book concentrates on Ireland's wealth of road-touring options the main cycling bodies (see Useful Organisations, p32) can put you in contact with mountain-biking clubs. Etiquette requires mountain bikes to yield to walkers and both to yield to equestrians. But it's more important just to use common courtesy. Bike paths are often shared with pedestrians, so be mindful of them: ring your bell or give a shout before passing, and always pass on the right.

The Mountain-Biking Code of Conduct also recommends that you minimise impact by carrying out all human-made elements that you bring into a wilderness area; stay on paths and take care to avoid soil erosion (muddy trails are more vulnerable to damage); never scare animals; control your speed and wear a helmet at all times.

One of the first rules of mountain-bike riding is never do it alone. It's not uncommon for people to go missing either through injury or after losing their way. It's best, if possible, to go in a small group – four is usually considered the minimum number. This way, if someone in the group has an accident or is taken ill, one person can stay with the casualty and the others can go for help.

Always tell someone where you are going and when you intend to be back – and make sure they know that you're back. Take warm clothing, matches and enough food and water in case of emergency. Carry enough tools so that you can undertake any emergency bicycle repairs (see the Your Bicycle chapter, p47, for advice on a basic tool kit).

Carry a map and take note of your surroundings as you ride (terrain, landmarks etc), so if you do get lost, you're more likely to find yourself again. If you get really lost, stay calm and stop. Try and work out where you are or how to retrace your route. If you can't, or it's getting dark, find a nearby open area, put on warm clothes and find or make a shelter. Light a fire for warmth and assist searchers by making as many obvious signs as you can (such as smoke, brightly coloured items, or symbols out of wood or rocks).

TOURING DANGERS & ANNOYANCES

As far as crime is concerned, Ireland is safer than most countries in Europe but the usual precautions should be observed. In Dublin, drug-related crime is quite common and the city has its fair share of pickpockets and sneak thieves waiting to relieve the unwary of unwatched bags. It's the one place in Ireland where it's best never to leave a bicycle unattended.

In Northern Ireland, violence due to the Troubles is well documented but it's unusual to come across any personally, and the on-again off-again peace process offers promise that violence should diminish.

If you are the victim of crime, the Garda (police in the South) may refer you to the Tourism Victim Support Service (☎ 1800 661 771, W www.victimsupport.ie/tourist.html; Harcourt Square, Harcourt St, Dublin 2).

Ireland's roads are said to be the least congested in Europe but there's been a huge increase in car ownership over the past 10 or 15 years and, predictably, the greatest danger to touring cyclists is the four-wheeled monster. Back-country roads and lanes remain relatively car-free but constant vigilance is required as there's usually little room for passing. Happily, the average Irish driver (outside of urban areas) is a fairly cheerful and easy-going soul.

Irish farm dogs appear to have a particular penchant for cyclists and wandering livestock is a relatively common sight, especially on minor roads in isolated areas (see the boxed texts 'Look Out: Dogs About!', p112, and 'Beware the Baa Brigade', p208).

Emergency Numbers

In case of emergency dial the following numbers:

Northern Ireland	☎ 999
The Republic	☎ 112 or ☎ 999

EMERGENCY PROCEDURES

If you or one of your group has an accident (even a minor one), or falls ill during your travels, you'll need to decide on the best course of action, which isn't always easy. Obviously, you will need to consider your individual circumstances, including where you are and whether you have some means of direct communication with emergency services, such as a mobile phone (cell phone). Some basic guidelines are:

- Use your first-aid knowledge and experience, as well as the information in this guide if necessary, to make an assessment of the situation.
- For groups of several people, leave one person with the casualty, leaving as much equipment, food and water as you can sensibly spare. Have the rest of the group go for help.
- If there are only two of you, the situation is more tricky and you will have to make an individual judgement as to the best course of action.
- If you leave someone, mark their position carefully on the map (take it with you); you should also make sure they can be easily found by marking the position with something conspicuous, such as bright clothing or a large stone cross on the ground. Leave the person with warm clothes, shelter, food, water, matches and a torch (flashlight).
- Try attracting attention by using a whistle or torch, lighting a smoky fire (use damp wood or green leaves) or waving bright clothing; shouting is tiring and not very effective.

The uncertainties associated with emergency rescue in remote wilderness areas should make it clear how important careful planning and safety precautions are, especially if you are travelling in a small group.

YOUR BICYCLE

Fundamental to any cycle tour you plan is the bicycle you choose to ride. In this chapter we look at choosing a bicycle and accessories, setting it up to best accommodate your needs and learning basic maintenance procedures. In short, everything you need to gear up and get going.

CHOOSING & SETTING UP A BICYCLE

The ideal bike for cycle touring is (strangely enough) a touring bike. These bikes look similar to road bikes but generally have relaxed frame geometry for comfort and predictable steering; fittings (eyelets and brazed-on bosses) to mount panniers and mudguards; wider rims and tyres; strong wheels (at least 36 spokes) to carry the extra load; and gearing capable of riding up a wall (triple chainrings and a wide-range freewheel to match). If you want to buy a touring bike, most tend to be custom-built these days, but Cannondale (w www.cannondale.com) and Trek (w www.trekbikes.com) both offer a range of models.

Of course you can tour on any bike you choose, but few will match the advantages of the workhorse touring bike.

Mountain bikes are a slight compromise by comparison, but are very popular for touring. A mountain bike already has the gearing needed for touring and offers a more upright, comfortable position on the bike. And with a change of tyres (to those with semi-slick tread) you'll be able to reduce the rolling resistance and travel at higher speeds with less effort.

Hybrid, or cross, bikes are similar to mountain bikes (and therefore offer similar advantages and disadvantages), although they typically already come equipped with semi-slick tyres.

Racing bikes are less appropriate: their tighter frame geometry is less comfortable on rough roads and long rides. It is also difficult to fit wider tyres, mudguards, racks and panniers to a road bike. Perhaps more significantly, most racing bikes have a distinct lack of low gears.

Tyres Unless you know you'll be on good, sealed roads the whole time, it's probably safest to choose a tyre with some tread. If you have 700c or 27-inch wheels, opt for a tyre that's 28–35mm wide. If touring on a mountain bike, the first thing to do is get rid of the knobby tyres – too much rolling resistance. Instead, fit 1–1½ inch semi-slick tyres or, if riding unpaved roads or off-road occasionally, a combination pattern tyre (slick centre and knobs on the outside).

To protect your tubes, consider buying tyres re-inforced with Kevlar, a tightly woven synthetic fibre very resistant to sharp objects. Although more expensive, Kevlar-belted tyres are worth it.

Pedals Cycling efficiency is vastly improved by using toe clips, and even more so with clipless pedals and cleated shoes. Mountain-bike or touring shoes are best – the cleats are recessed and the soles are flexible enough to comfortably walk in.

 Fold & Go Bikes

Another option is a folding bike. Manufacturers include: Brompton (w www.bromptonbike.com), Bike Friday (w www.bikefriday.com), Birdy (w www.birdybike.com), Slingshot (w www.slingshotbikes .com) and Moulton (w www.alex moulton.co.uk). All make high-quality touring bikes that fold up to allow hassle-free train, plane or bus transfers. The Moulton, Birdie, Brompton and Slingshot come with suspension and the Bike Friday's case doubles as a trailer for your luggage when touring.

Touring Bike

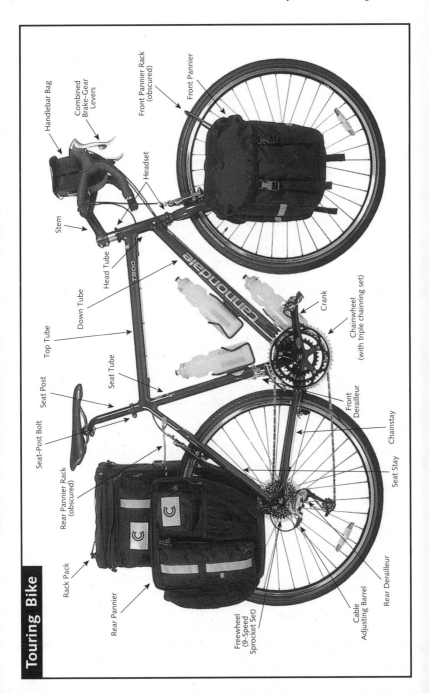

Handlebar Bag

Combined Brake-Gear Levers

Front Pannier Rack (obscured)

Front Pannier

Headset

Stem

Head Tube

Down Tube

Top Tube

Seat Tube

Seat Post

Seat-Post Bolt

Rear Pannier Rack (obscured)

Rack Pack

Rear Pannier

Freewheel (9-Speed Sprocket Set)

Cable Adjusting Barrel

Rear Derailleur

Seat Stay

Chainstay

Front Derailleur

Chainwheel (with triple chainring set)

Crank

Mudguards Adding mudguards to your bike will reduce the amount of muddy water and grit that sprays you when it rains or the roads are wet. Plastic clip-on models are slightly less effective but not as expensive, and they can be less hassle.

Water Bottles & Cages Fit at least two bottle cages to your bike – in isolated areas you may need to carry more water than this. Water 'backpacks', such as a Camelbak, make it easy to keep your fluids up.

Reflectors & Lights If riding at night, add reflectors and lights so you can see, and others can see you. A small headlight can also double as a torch (flashlight). Flashing tail-lights are cheap and effective.

Pannier Racks It's worth buying good pannier racks. The best are aluminium racks made by Blackburn. They're also the most expensive, but come with a lifetime guarantee. Front racks come in low-mounting and mountain bike styles. Low-mounting racks carry the weight lower, which improves the handling of the bike, but if you're touring off-road it is a better idea to carry your gear a bit higher.

Panniers Panniers range from cheap-and-nasty to expensive top-quality waterproof bags. Get panniers that fit securely to your rack and watch that the pockets don't swing into your spokes.

Cycle Computer Directions for rides in this book rely upon accurate distance readings, so you'll need a reliable cycle computer.

Other Accessories A good pump is essential. Make sure it fits your valve type (see p54). Some clip on to your bicycle frame, while others fit 'inside' the frame. Also carry a lock. Although heavy, U- or D-locks are the most secure; cable locks can be more versatile.

Riding Position Set Up

Cycling is meant to be a pleasurable pursuit, but that isn't likely if the bike you're riding isn't the correct size for you and isn't set up for your needs.

In this section we assume your bike shop did a good job of providing you with the correct size bike (if you're borrowing a bike get a bike shop to check it is the correct size for you) and concentrate on setting you up in your ideal position and showing you how to tweak the comfort factor. If you are concerned that your bike frame is too big or small for your needs get a second opinion from another bike shop.

The following techniques for determining correct fit are based on averages and may not work for your body type. If you are an unusual size or shape get your bike shop to create your riding position.

Saddle Height & Position

Saddles are essential to riding position and comfort. If a saddle is poorly adjusted it can be a royal pain in the derriere – and legs, arms and back. In addition to saddle height, it is also possible to alter a saddle's tilt and its fore/aft position – each affects your riding position differently.

Saddle Tilt Saddles are designed to be level to the ground, taking most of the weight off your arms and back. However, since triathletes started dropping the nose of their saddles in the mid-1980s many other cyclists have followed suit without knowing why. For some body types, a slight tilt of the nose might be necessary. Be aware, however, that forward tilt will place extra strain on your arms and back. If it is tilted too far forward, chances are your saddle is too high.

Fore/Aft Position The default setting for fore/aft saddle position will allow you to run a plumb bob from the centre of your forward pedal axle to the protrusion of your knee (that bit of bone just under your knee cap).

Fore/Aft Position: To check it, sit on your bike with the pedals in the three and nine o'clock positions. Check the alignment with a plumb bob (a weight on the end of a piece of string).

Saddle Height The simplest method of roughly determining the correct saddle height is the straight leg method. Sit on your bike wearing your cycling shoes. Line one crank up with the seat-tube and place your heel on the pedal. Adjust the saddle height until your leg is almost straight, but not straining. When you've fixed the height of your saddle pedal the cranks backwards (do it next to a wall so you can balance yourself). If you are rocking from side to side, lower the saddle slightly. Otherwise keep raising the saddle (slightly) until on the verge of rocking.

The most accurate way of determining saddle height is the Hodges Method. Developed by US cycling coach Mark Hodges after studying the position of dozens of racing cyclists, the method is also applicable to touring cyclists.

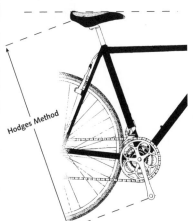

Hodges Method

Standing barefoot with your back against a wall and your feet 15cm apart, get a friend to measure from the floor passing over your knee and ankle joints. Measure each leg (in mm) three times and average the figure. Multiply the average figure by 0.96.

Now add the thickness of your shoe sole and your cleats (if they aren't recessed). This total is the distance you need from the centre of your pedal axle to the top of your saddle. It is the optimum position for your body to pedal efficiently and should not be exceeded; however, people with small feet for their size should lower the saddle height slightly. The inverse applies for people with disproportionately large feet.

If you need to raise your saddle significantly do it over a few weeks so your muscles can adapt gradually. (Never raise your saddle above the maximum extension line marked on your seat post.)

Handlebars & Brake Levers

Racing cyclists lower their handlebars to cheat the wind and get a better aerodynamic position. While this might be tempting on windy days it doesn't make for comfortable touring. Ideally, the bars should be no higher than the saddle (even on mountain bikes) and certainly no lower than 75mm below it.

Pedals

For comfort and the best transference of power, the ball of your foot should be aligned over the centre of the pedal axle (see right).

If using clipless pedals consider the amount of lateral movement available. Our feet have a natural angle that they prefer when we walk, run or cycle. If they are unable to achieve this position the knee joint's alignment will be affected and serious injury may result. Most clipless pedal systems now have some rotational freedom (called 'float') built in to allow for this, but it is still important to adjust the cleats to each foot's natural angle.

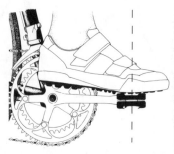

Comfort Considerations

Now that you have your optimum position on the bike, there are several components that you can adjust to increase the comfort factor.

Handlebars come in a variety of types and sizes. People with small hands may find shallow drop bars more comfortable. Handlebars also come in a variety of widths, so if they're too wide or narrow change them.

Pedal Alignment: The ball of your foot should be over the centre of the pedal axle for comfort and the best transfer of power.

With mountain bike handlebars you really only have one hand position, so add a pair of bar-ends. On drop bars the ends should be parallel to the ground. If they're pointed up it probably means you need a longer stem; pointed down probably means you need a shorter stem.

On mountain bikes the **brake levers** should be adjusted to ensure your wrist is straight – it's the position your hand naturally sits in. For drop bars the bottom of the lever should end on the same line as the end section.

Getting the right **saddle** for you is one of the key considerations for enjoyable cycling. Everybody's sit bones are shaped and spaced differently, meaning a saddle that suits your best friend might be agony for you. A good bike shop will allow you to keep changing a new (undamaged) saddle until you get one that's perfect. Women's saddles tend to have a shorter nose and a wider seat, and men's are long and narrow.

Brake Levers: Adjust your drop bars so the end section is parallel to the ground and the brake lever ends on this same line.

If you feel too stretched out or cramped when riding, chances are you need a different length **stem** – the problem isn't solved by moving your saddle forward/aft. Get a bike shop to assess this for you.

 Record Your Position

When you've created your ideal position, mark each part's position (scratch a line with a sharp tool like a scribe or use tape) and record it, so you can recreate it if hiring a bike or when reassembling your bike after travel. The inside back cover of this book has a place to record all this vital data.

MAINTAINING YOUR BICYCLE

If you're new to cycling or haven't previously maintained your bike, this section is for you. It won't teach you how to be a top-notch mechanic, but it will help you maintain your bike in good working order and show you how to fix the most common touring problems.

If you go mountain biking it is crucial you carry spares and a tool kit and know how to maintain your bike, because if anything goes wrong it's likely you'll be miles from anywhere when trouble strikes.

If you want to know more about maintaining your bike there are dozens of books available (*Richard's 21st Century Bicycle Book*, by Richard Ballantine, is a classic; if you want to know absolutely everything get *Barnett's Manual: The Ultimate Technical Bicycle Repair Manual* or *Sutherland's Handbook for Bicycle Mechanics*) or inquire at your bike shop about courses in your area.

Predeparture & Daily Inspections

Before going on tour get your bike serviced by a bike shop or do it yourself. On tour, check over your bike every day or so (see the boxed text 'Pre-Departure & Post-Ride Checks', p57).

Spares & Tool Kit

Touring cyclists need to be self-sufficient and should carry some spares and, at least, a basic tool kit. How many spares/tools you will need depends on the country you are touring in – in countries where bike shops aren't common and the towns are further spread out you may want to add to the following.

Multi-tools (see right) are very handy and a great way to save space and weight, and there are dozens of different ones on the market. Before you buy a multi-tool though, check each of the tools is usable – a chain breaker, for example, needs to have a good handle for leverage otherwise it is useless.

Adjustable spanners are often handy, but the trade-off is that they can easily burr bolts if not used correctly – be careful when using them.

The bare minimum:
- ☐ pump – ensure it has the correct valve fitting for your tyres
- ☐ water bottles (2)
- ☐ spare tubes (2)
- ☐ tyre levers (2)
- ☐ chain lube and a rag
- ☐ puncture repair kit (check the glue is OK)
- ☐ Allen keys to fit your bike
- ☐ small Phillips screwdriver
- ☐ small flat screwdriver
- ☐ spare brake pads
- ☐ spare screws and bolts (for pannier racks, seat post etc) and chain links (2)

For those who know what they're doing:
- ☐ spoke key
- ☐ spare spokes and nipples (8)
- ☐ tools to remove freewheel
- ☐ chain breaker
- ☐ pliers
- ☐ spare chain links (HyperGlide chain rivet if you have a Shimano chain)
- ☐ spare rear brake and rear gear cables

Always handy to take along:
- ☐ roll of electrical/gaffer tape
- ☐ nylon ties (10) – various lengths/sizes
- ☐ hand cleaner (store it in a film canister)

Fixing a Flat

Flats happen. And if you're a believer in Murphy's Law then the likely scenario is that you'll suffer a flat just as you're rushing to the next town to catch a train or beat the setting sun.

Don't worry – this isn't a big drama. If you're prepared and know what you're doing you can be up and on your way in five minutes flat.

Being prepared means carrying a spare tube, a pump and at least two tyre levers. If you're not carrying a spare tube, of course, you can stop and fix the puncture then and there, but it's unlikely you'll catch that train and you could end up doing all this in the dark. There will be days when you have the time to fix a puncture on the side of the road, but not always. Carry at least two spare tubes.

1 Take the wheel off the bike. Remove the valve cap and unscrew the locknut (hex nut at base; see Valve Types) on Presta valves. Deflate the tyre completely, if it isn't already.

2 Make sure the tyre and tube are loose on the rim – moisture and the pressure of the inflated tube often makes the tyre and tube fuse with the rim.

3 If the tyre is really loose you should be able to remove it with your hands. Otherwise you'll need to lift one side of the tyre over the rim with the tyre levers. Pushing the tyre away from the lever as you insert it should ensure you don't pinch the tube and puncture it again.

4 When you have one side of the tyre off, you'll be able to remove the tube. Before inserting the replacement tube, carefully inspect the tyre (inside and out); you're looking for what caused the puncture. If you find anything embedded in the tyre, remove it. Also check that the rim tape is still in

Valve Types

The two most common valve types are Presta (sometimes called French) and Schraeder (American). To inflate a Presta valve, first unscrew the round nut at the top (and do it up again after you're done); depress it to deflate. To deflate Schraeder valves depress the pin (inside the top). Ensure your pump is set up for the valve type on your bike.

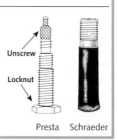

Unscrew

Locknut

Presta   Schraeder

place and no spoke nipples (see pp62–3) protrude through it.

5 Time to put the new tube in. Start by partially pumping up the tube (this helps prevent it twisting or being pinched) and insert the valve in the hole in the rim. Tuck the rest of the tube in under the tyre, making sure you don't twist it. Make sure the valve is straight – most Presta valves come with a locknut to help achieve this.

6 Work the tyre back onto the rim with your fingers. If this isn't possible, and again, according to Murphy's Law, it frequently isn't, you might need to use your tyre levers for the last 20–30cm. If you need to use the levers, make sure you don't pinch the new tube, otherwise it's back to Step 1. All you need to do now is pump up the tyre and put the wheel back on the bike. Don't forget to fix the pucture that night.

Fixing the Puncture

To fix the puncture you'll need a repair kit, which usually comes with glue, patches, sandpaper and, sometimes, chalk. (Always check the glue in your puncture repair kit hasn't dried up before heading off on tour.) The only other thing you'll need is clean hands.

1. The first step is to find the puncture. Inflate the tube and hold it up to your ear. If you can hear the puncture, mark it with the chalk; otherwise immerse it in water and watch for air bubbles. Once you find the puncture, mark it, cover it with your finger and continue looking – just in case there are more.

2. Dry the tube and lightly roughen the area around the hole with the sandpaper. Sand an area larger than the patch.

3. Follow the instructions for the glue you have. Generally you spread an even layer of glue over the area of the tube to be patched and allow it to dry until it is tacky.

4. Patches also come with their own instructions – some will be just a piece of rubber and others will come lined with foil (remove the foil on the underside but don't touch the exposed area). Press the patch firmly onto the area over the hole and hold it for 2–3 minutes. If you want, remove the excess glue from around the patch or dust it with chalk or simply let it dry.

5. Leave the glue to set for 10–20 minutes. Inflate the tube and check the patch has worked.

Chains

Chains are dirty, greasy and all too often the most neglected piece of equipment on a bike. There are about 120 or so links in a chain and each has a simple but precise arrangement of bushes, bearings and plates. Over time all chains stretch, but if dirt gets between the bushes and bearings this 'ageing' will happen prematurely and will likely damage the teeth of your chainrings, sprockets and derailleur guide pulleys.

To prevent this, chains should be cleaned and lubed frequently (see your bike shop for the best products to use).

No matter how well you look after a chain it should be replaced regularly – about every 5000–8000km. Seek the advice of a bike shop to ensure you are buying the correct type for your drivetrain (the moving parts that combine to drive the bicycle: chain, freewheel, derailleurs, chainwheel and bottom bracket).

If you do enough cycling you'll need to replace a chain (or fix a broken chain), so here's how to use that funky-looking tool, the chain breaker.

1 Remove the chain from the chainrings – it'll make the whole process easier. Place the chain in the chain breaker (on the outer slots; it braces the link plates as the rivet is driven out) and line the pin of the chain breaker up with the rivet.

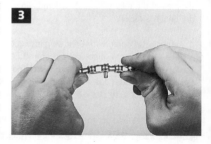

2 Wind the handle until the rivet is clear of the inner link but still held by the outer link plate.

3 Flex the chain to 'break' it. If it won't, you'll need to push the rivet out some more, but not completely – if you push it all the way out, you'll have to remove two links and replace them with two spare links. If you're removing links, you'll need to remove a male and female link (ie, two links).

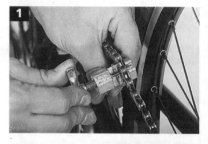

4 Rejoining the chain is the reverse. If you turn the chain around when putting it on you will still have the rivet facing you. Otherwise it will be facing away from you and you'll need to change to the other side of the bike and work through the spokes.

Join the chain up by hand and place it in the breaker. Now drive the rivet in firmly, making sure it is properly lined up with the hole of the outer link plate. Stop when the rivet is almost in place.

5 Move the chain to the spreaders (inner slots) of the chain breaker. Finish by winding the rivet into position carefully (check that the head of the rivet is raised the same distance above the link plate as the rivets beside it). If you've managed to get it in perfectly and the link isn't 'stiff', well done!

Otherwise, move the chain to the spreaders on the chain breaker and gently work the chain laterally until the link is no longer stiff.

If this doesn't work (and with some chain breakers it won't), take the chain out of the tool and place a screwdriver or Allen key between the outer plates of the stiff link and carefully lever the plates both ways. If you're too forceful you'll really break the chain, but if you're subtle it will free the link up and you'll be on your way.

Chain Options

Check your chain; if you have a Shimano HyperGlide chain you'll need a special Hyper-Glide chain rivet to rejoin the chain. This will be supplied with your new chain, but carry a spare.

Another option is to fit a universal link to your chain. This link uses a special clip to join the chain – like the chains of old. You'll still need a chain breaker to fix a broken chain or take out spare links.

Pre-Departure & Post-Ride Checks

Each day before you get on your bike and each evening after you've stopped riding, give your bike a quick once-over. Following these checks will ensure you're properly maintaining your bike and will help identify any problems before they become disasters. Go to the nearest bike shop if you don't know how to fix any problem.

Pre-Departure Check List

☐ brakes – are they stopping you? If not, adjust them.
☐ chain – if it was squeaking yesterday, it needs lube.
☐ panniers – are they all secured and fastened?
☐ cycle computer – reset your trip distance at the start.
☐ gears – are they changing properly? If not, adjust them.
☐ tyres – check your tyre pressure is correct (see the tyre's side wall for the maximum psi); inflate, if necessary.

Post-Ride Check List

☐ pannier racks – check all bolts/screws are tightened; do a visual check of each rack (the welds, in particular) looking for small cracks.
☐ headset – when stationary, apply the front brake and rock the bike gently; if there is any movement or noise, chances are the headset is loose.
☐ wheels – visually check the tyres for sidewall cuts/wear and any embedded objects; check the wheels are still true and no spokes are broken.
☐ wrench test – wrench (pull) on the saddle (if it moves, tighten the seat-post bolt and/or the seat-clamp bolt, underneath); wrench laterally on a crank (if it moves, check the bottom bracket).

Brakes

Adjusting the brakes of your bike is not complicated and even though your bike shop will use several tools to do the job, all you really need is a pair of pliers, a spanner or Allen key, and (sometimes) a friend.

Check three things before you start: the wheels are true (not buckled), the braking surface of the rims is smooth (no dirt, dents or rough patches) and the cables are not frayed.

Begin by checking that the pads strike the rim correctly: flush on the braking surface of the rim (see right and p59) and parallel to the ground.

Calliper Brakes

It's likely that you'll be able to make any minor adjustments to calliper brakes by winding the cable adjusting barrel out. If it doesn't allow enough movement you'll need to adjust the cable anchor bolt:

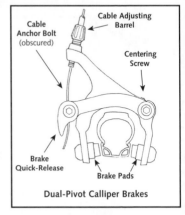

Dual-Pivot Calliper Brakes

1 Undo the cable anchor bolt – not completely, just so the cable is free to move – and turn the cable adjusting barrel all the way in.

2 Get your friend to hold the callipers in the desired position, about 2–3mm away from the rim. Using a pair of pliers, pull the cable through until it is taut.

3 Before you tighten the cable anchor bolt again, check to see if the brake lever is in its normal position (not slack as if somebody was applying it) – sometimes they jam open. Also, ensure the brake quick-release (use it when you're removing your wheel or in an emergency to open the callipers if your wheel is badly buckled) is closed.

4 Tighten the cable anchor bolt again. Make any fine-tuning to the brakes by winding the cable adjusting barrel out.

 Brake Cables

If your brakes are particularly hard to apply, you may need to replace the cables. Moisture can cause the cable and housing (outer casing) to bond or stick. If this happens it's often possible to prolong the life of a cable by removing it from the housing and applying a coating of grease (or chain lube) to it.

If you do need to replace the cable, take your bike to a bike shop and get the staff to fit and/or supply the new cable. Cables come in two sizes – rear (long) and front (short) – various thicknesses and with different types of nipples.

Cantilever Brakes

These days most touring bikes have cantilever rather than calliper brakes. The newest generation of cantilever brakes (V-brakes) are more powerful and better suited to stopping bikes with heavy loads.

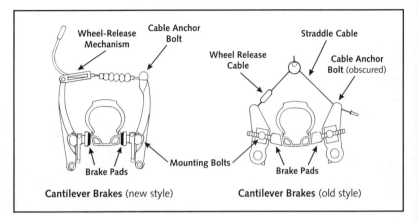

Cantilever Brakes (new style)   **Cantilever Brakes** (old style)

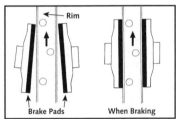

Cantilever Brake Toe-In: This is how the brake pads should strike the rim (from above) with correct toe-in.

On cantilever brakes ensure the leading edge of the brake pad hits the rim first (see left). This is called toe-in; it makes the brakes more efficient and prevents squealing. To adjust the toe-in on cantilever brakes, loosen the brake pad's mounting bolt (using a 10mm spanner and 5mm Allen key). Wiggle the brake pad into position and tighten the bolt again.

If you only need to make a minor adjustment to the distance of the pads from the rim, chances are you will be able to do it by winding the cable adjusting barrel out (located near the brake lever on mountain bikes and hybrids). If this won't do you'll need to adjust the cable anchor bolt:

1 Undo the cable anchor bolt (not completely, just so the cable is free to move) and turn the cable adjusting barrel all the way in. Depending on the style of your brakes, you may need a 10mm spanner (older bikes) or a 5mm Allen key.

2 Hold the cantilevers in the desired position (get assistance from a friend if you need to), positioning the brake pads 2–3mm away from the rim. Using a pair of pliers, pull the cable through until it is taut.

3 Before you tighten the cable anchor bolt again, check to see if the brake lever is in its normal position (not slack as if somebody was applying it) – sometimes they jam open.

4 Tighten the cable anchor bolt again. Make any fine-tuning to the brakes by winding the cable adjusting barrel out.

Gears

If the gears on your bike start playing up – the chain falls off the chainrings, it shifts slowly or not at all – it's bound to cause frustration and could damage your bike. All it takes to prevent this is a couple of simple adjustments: the first, setting the limits of travel for both derailleurs, will keep the chain on your drivetrain, and the second will ensure smooth, quick shifts from your rear derailleur. Each will take just a couple of minutes and the only tool you need is a small Phillips or flat screwdriver.

Front Derailleur

If you can't get the chain to shift onto one chainring or the chain comes off when you're shifting, you need to make some minor adjustments to the limit screws on the front derailleur. Two screws control the limits of the front derailleur's left and right movement, which governs how far the chain can shift. When you shift gears the chain is physically pushed sideways by the plates (outer and inner) of the derailleur cage. The screws are usually side by side (see photo No 1) on the top of the front derailleur. The left-hand screw (as you sit on the bike) adjusts the inside limit and the one on the right adjusts the outside limit.

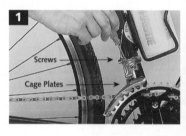

Front Derailleur: Before making any adjustments, remove any build up of grit from the screws (especially underneath) by wiping them with a rag and applying a quick spray (or drop) of chain lube.

After you make each of the following adjustments, pedal the drivetrain with your hand and change gears to ensure you've set the limit correctly. If you're satisfied, test it under strain by going for a short ride.

Outer Limits Change the gears to position the chain on the largest chainring and the smallest rear sprocket. Set the outer cage plate as close to the chain as you can without it touching. Adjust the right-hand limit screw to achieve this.

Inner Limits Position the chain on the smallest chainring and the largest rear sprocket. For chainwheels with three chainrings, position the inner cage plate between 1–2mm from the chain. If you have a chainwheel with two chainrings, position the inner cage plate as close to the chain as you can without it touching.

Rear Derailleur

If the limit screws aren't set correctly on the rear derailleur the consequences can be dire. If the chain slips off the largest sprocket it can jam between the sprocket and the spokes and could then snap the chain, break or damage spokes or even break the frame.

The limit screws are located at the back of the derailleur (see photo No 2). The top screw (marked 'H' on the derailleur) sets the derailleur's limit of travel on the smallest sprocket's (the highest gear) side of the freewheel. The bottom screw ('L') adjusts the derailleur's travel towards the largest sprocket (lowest gear).

Outer Limits Position the chain on the smallest sprocket and largest chainring (see photo No 3). The derailleur's top guide pulley (the one

Guide
Pulleys

closest to the sprockets) should be in line with the smallest sprocket; adjust the top screw ('H') to ensure it is.

Inner Limits Position the chain on the largest rear sprocket and the smallest chainring (see photo No 4). This time the guide pulley needs to be lined up with the largest sprocket; do this by adjusting the bottom screw ('L'). Make sure the chain can't move any further towards the wheel than the largest sprocket.

Cable Adjusting Barrel

If your gears are bouncing up and down your freewheel in a constant click and chatter, you need to adjust the tension of the cable to the rear derailleur. This can be achieved in a variety of ways, depending on your gear system.

The main cable adjusting barrel is on your rear derailleur (see photo No 5). Secondary cable adjusting barrels can also be found near the gear levers (newer Shimano combined brake-gear STI levers) or on the downtube of your frame (older Shimano STI levers and Campagnolo Ergopower gear systems) of some bikes. Intended for racing cyclists, they allow for fine tuning of the gears' operation while on the move.

Raise the rear wheel off the ground – have a friend hold it up by the saddle, hang it from a tree or turn the bike upside down – so you can pedal the drivetrain with your hand.

To reset your derailleur, shift gears to position the chain on the second smallest sprocket and middle chainring (see photo No 6). As you turn the crank with your hand, tighten the cable by winding the rear derailleur's cable adjusting barrel anti-clockwise. Just before the chain starts to make a noise as if to shift onto the third sprocket, stop winding.

Now pedal the drivetrain and change the gears up and down the freewheel. If things still aren't right you may find that you need to tweak the cable tension slightly: turn the cable adjusting barrel anti-clockwise if shifts to larger sprockets are slow, and clockwise if shifts to smaller sprockets hesitate.

Replacing a Spoke

Even the best purpose-made touring wheels occasionally break spokes. When this happens the wheel, which relies on the even pull of each spoke, is likely to become buckled. When it is not buckled, it is considered true.

If you've forgotten to pack spokes or you grabbed the wrong size, you can still get yourself out of a pickle if you have a spoke key. Wheels are very flexible and you can get it roughly true – enough to take you to the next bike shop – even if two or three spokes are broken.

If you break a spoke on the front wheel it is a relatively simple thing to replace the spoke and retrue the wheel. The same applies if a broken spoke is on the non-drive side (opposite side to the rear derailleur) of the rear wheel. The complication comes when you break a spoke on the drive side of the rear wheel (the most common case). In order to replace it you need to remove the freewheel, a relatively simple job in itself but one that requires a few more tools and the know-how.

If you don't have that know-how fear not, because it is possible to retrue the wheel without replacing that spoke *and* without damaging the wheel – see Truing a Wheel (below).

1 Remove the wheel from the bike. It's probably a good idea to remove the tyre and tube as well (though not essential), just to make sure the nipple is seated properly in the rim and not likely to cause a puncture.

2 Remove the broken spoke but leave the nipple in the rim (if it's not damaged; otherwise replace it). Now you need to thread the new spoke. Start by threading it through the vacant hole on the hub flange. Next lace the new spoke through the other spokes. Spokes are offset on the rim; every second one is on the same side and, generally, every fourth is laced through the other spokes the same way.

Spoke Key

3 With the spoke key, tighten the nipple until the spoke is about as taut as the other spokes on this side of the rim. Spoke nipples have four flat sides – to adjust them you'll need the correct size spoke key. Spoke keys come in two types: those made to fit one spoke gauge or several. If you have the latter, trial each size on a nipple until you find the perfect fit.

Truing a Wheel

Truing a wheel is an art form and, like all art forms, it is not something mastered overnight. If you can, practise with an old wheel before leaving home. If that's not possible – and you're on the side of the road as you read this – following these guidelines will get you back in the saddle until you can get to the next bike shop.

1 Start by turning the bike upside-down, so the wheels can turn freely. Check the tension of all the spokes on the wheel: do this by

squeezing each pair of spokes on each side. Tighten those spokes that seem loose and loosen those that seem too tight. Note, though, the spokes on the drive side of the rear wheel (on the same side as the freewheel) are deliberately tighter than the non-drive side.

2 Rotate the wheel a couple of times to get an idea of the job at hand. If the wheel won't rotate, let the brakes off (see pp58–9).

3 Using the chalk from your puncture repair kit, mark all the 'bumps'. Keep the chalk in the same position (brace the chalk against the pannier rack or bike's frame) and let the bumps in the wheel 'hit' the chalk.

4 In order to get the bumps out you'll need a constant point of reference – to gauge if the bumps are being removed. Often, if it is not a severe buckle, you can use a brake pad. Position the brake pad about 2–3mm from the rim (on the side with the biggest buckle).

5 With your spoke key, loosen those spokes on the same side as the bump within the longest chalked area, and tighten those on the opposite side of the rim. The spokes at the start and the finish of the chalked area should only be tightened/loosened by a quarter-turn; apply a half-turn to those in between.

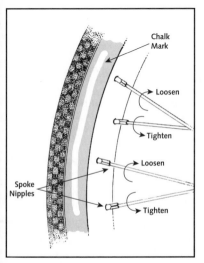

6 Rotate the wheel again; if you're doing it correctly the buckle should not be as great. Continue this process of tightening and loosening spokes until the bump is as near to gone as you can get it – as the bump is removed turn the nipples less (one-eighth of a turn on the ends and a quarter-turn in between). Experienced exponents can remove buckles entirely, but if you can get it almost out (1mm here or there) you've done well.

7 If the wheel has more than one bump, move onto the second-longest chalk mark next. As each bump is removed you might find it affects the previous bump slightly. In this case, remove the previous chalk mark and repeat Steps 4–6. Continue to do this until all the buckles are removed.

Don't forget to readjust the brakes.

If you've trued the wheel without replacing the broken spokes, have them replaced at the next bike shop.

Dublin & the Northeast

HISTORY

The region, which falls within the old province of Leinster, has played the lead role in all stages of Irish history, from the first Stone-Age farmers to modern Nationalist struggles.

Brú na Bóinne in the Boyne Valley, a fertile, sheltered Neolithic settlement was known far and wide around 3000 BC for its passage tomb constructions, which would have required hundreds of people to build.

The Celtic high kings established the Hill of Tara as the main seat of power in Leinster during their heyday (AD 200–400). In the 5th century St Patrick is said to have demonstrated the religious symbolism of the shamrock on either Tara or the Hill of Slane above the Boyne Valley. In August 1843 Tara also saw one of the greatest crowds ever to gather in Ireland. Daniel O'Connell, the 'Liberator' and leader of opposition to union with Great Britain held one of his monster rallies there, attracting over 750,000 people.

During Oliver Cromwell's 1649 campaign of subjugation, he ransacked his way down the eastern seaboard, from Drogheda, the site of a notorious massacre of townsfolk, to Wexford where Cromwell's men once again ran amok among the civilian population.

Forty years later in 1690 William of Orange defeated the English king James II at the Battle of the Boyne and confirmed Protestant rule in Ireland.

Thereafter, the English consolidated their power from Dublin. Since independence, Dublin has been the capital of Éire and the seat of its government.

NATURAL HISTORY

The main geographical features of the Northeast are low-lying bogland, lakeland and rich grazing country. Before mass drainage and extraction, the Bog of Allen stretched 80km from west of Dublin to the River Shannon. It was created by great reservoirs of water, formed by the retreat of the glaciers that became trapped between eskers (low ridges formed by glacial debris), on which humans built fortifications and settlements.

Lakes with unmatched angling conditions are concentrated around Mullingar in Westmeath. The Shannon, the longest river

---

In Brief

Highlights
- The **National Stud** at Kildare
- Magnificent views crossing the **Slieve Bloom Mountains**
- The ancient monastic site of **Clonmacnoise**
- The historically resonant **Boyne Valley** and 5000-year-old **Newgrange passage tombs**

Terrain
Mostly low-lying and predominantly farmland, stretching from Dublin in the east to the Shannon in the west, with extensive bog in the central area and the Slieve Bloom Mountains to the southwest.

Special Events
- **Curragh Racecourse Derby Festival** (June) County Kildare
- **Dublin Theatre Festival** (Oct)
- **Mullingar Bachelor Festival** (July) County Westmeath
- **St Patrick's Day Parade** (weekend nearest 17th Mar) Dublin
- **Samba Festival** (July) Drogheda
- **Punchestown Racecourse National Hunt Festival** (Apr) County Kildare

Cycling Events
- **Drogheda Wheelers Leisure Tour** 10km, 20km, 50km (July) Drogheda
- **RÁS** national stage race (May) various locations
- **Shay Elliott Memorial Road Race** (May) Wicklow Mountains

Food & Drink Specialities
Guinness and seafood in Dublin, **Cashel blue cheese**, **beef** and **steak** in County Westmeath and **bread** in Drogheda.

---

in Ireland (and Britain), is linked to Dublin and the Irish Channel by the Royal and Grand Canals.

Uplands are rare, the main area being the Slieve Bloom Mountains on the border of Offaly and Laois.

CLIMATE

Regional temperatures meet the 10°C national yearly average; the summer high is around 15° to 20°C, and the winter high is about 7°C. Central Ireland is sheltered from the full force of the Atlantic Ocean weather system, with an average rainfall of 750mm, about half of which falls in the southwest.

INFORMATION
Maps & Books

The OSI 1:250,000 Holiday map *Ireland East* covers the entire region.

Information Sources

East Coast & Midlands Tourism Board (☎ 042-933 5484, e dundalktouristoffice@ eircom.net) provides general information.

GATEWAY CITY
Dublin

☎ 01

Little less than a major revival has taken place in Dublin. Once notoriously impoverished, the political and cultural hub of the Celtic Tiger – unprecedented economic growth in the 1990s – boomed, though the economy has since slowed. Nevertheless, the capital of a country that has suffered more than its fair share of woes continues to leap ahead with gusto, not to mention fistfuls of euros.

Against a romantic background of creamy Guinness and Georgian architecture modern commerce is pursued relentlessly, illustrated nicely by the painted frontages of period houses where advertisements for mobile phones vie for attention with the Guinness toucan. The cobbled streets of the old town, Temple Bar, have been transformed into a global drinking village and rents along the banks of the Liffey soar. Yet only a step away is Leinster House, home to the Irish parliament, and the 300-year-old hallowed quads of Trinity College, which also houses the ancient Book of Kells.

The River Liffey marks the centre of Dublin and is lined with old quays and buildings. Its flow bisects the city socially as well as geographically. To the north, the important streets for visitors are O'Connell St and Henry St, the major shopping drags. Further north, away from the river, the cityscape becomes more run down.

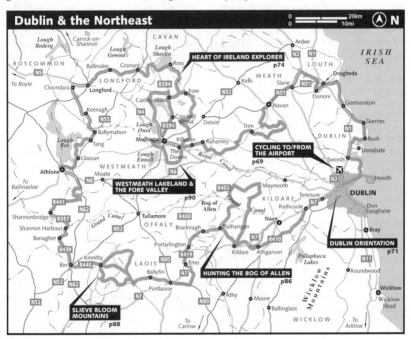

Dublin & the Northeast

Táin Trail

The Táin Trail is a 585km circular cycling route that follows the route immortalised in the Irish saga *Táin Bó Cuailnge* (see Literature, p20), taking in sites of deed and legend. The story is of Queen Maeve and her armies who set off to obtain the finest bull in the land, and their encounters with Cúchulainn, Ireland's heroic warrior. The circuit travels from Maeve's seat at Royal Rathcroghan in County Roscommon through the heart of the country to the Cooley Peninsula on the east coast, and back. The East Coast & Midlands Tourism Board (see Information Sources, p65) publishes a pamphlet with a sketch map and track notes.

South of the river is, by contrast, smart and touristy and the location of most sights, including the outstanding Georgian squares, Temple Bar and pedestrianised Grafton St.

Information All TICs in Dublin are exclusively walk-in and do not provide a phone service. For telephone inquiries contact Tourism Ireland (☎ 476 3400, Ⓦ www.tourismireland.com).

In the city centre, the main TIC is Dublin Tourism (St Andrews Church, Suffolk St, Ⓦ www.visitdublin.com), 300m south of O'Connell Bridge and west of Grafton St. North of the Liffey there's another central office (14 O'Connell St) and there is an information desk at the Bord Fáilte office (☎ 602 4229, Baggot St Bridge) 1.5km north of centre. On arrival by air or sea you'll also find TICs at the airport and on the waterfront at Dun Laoghaire.

There are numerous banks around the city centre with exchange facilities. The Bank of Ireland operates a bureau de change (34 College Green, open 9am-9pm Mon-Sat, 10am-7pm Sun).

Bike shops are friendly and well distributed. Two central bike shops lie on opposite sides of the river. Cyclelogical (☎ 872 4678, 3 Bachelor's Walk, Ⓦ www.cyclelogical-bikes.com), which specialises in racers, is on the north bank near Ha'penny Bridge. Cluttered Square Wheels Cycleworks (☎ 679 0838, Temple Lane South), near the south bank in Temple Bar, is a good place

for advice about cycling holidays, repairs and will store your bike (for a modest charge) while you tour and shop. The large Cycleways (☎ 873 4748, 185-186 Parnell St, Ⓔ cycleway@indigo.ie) 600m north of centre, off the top of O'Connell St, stocks a comprehensive range of panniers. McDonald's Cycles (☎ 475 2586, 38 Wexford St, Ⓔ alecmcd@indigo.ie) is 1km south of the centre, just west of St Stephen's Green.

Maps widely available in Dublin's book shops. The main branch of Eason's in O'Connell St is well stocked, carrying the OSI 1:250,000 Holiday and 1:50,000 Discovery map series. The Dublin Bookshop at 24 Grafton St is another good source.

Things to See & Do The Dublin Orientation ride (p71) passes many of Dublin's main sights.

Guinness is supposed to taste better the closer you are to the source, which means the brew available at the **Guinness Hop Store** (Crane St) must be as good as it gets. This building stored the essential ingredient for the 26-hectare **St James Gate Guinness Brewery** (James's St), which still brews four million pints a day, enough to slake the thirst of half the country.

A poignant reminder of Ireland's struggle for independence from Britain is **Kilmainham Gaol** (☎ 453 5984, Inchicore Rd), west of Heuston Station, in which leaders of many Irish uprisings were imprisoned. The executions of 14 men in its gloomy yard in 1916 have etched the prison deeply into the Irish political consciousness. Tours leave every hour or so from 9.30am to 5pm daily.

Places to Stay In the high summer months Dublin fills to the gills, so reserve accommodation in advance. Apart from the hostels, prices are quite steep in the centre. The cheaper suburban B&Bs are a short ride away.

A call to Gulliver Ireland (☎ 800 3698 7412) which serves the whole country including Dublin, can save ringing round; see Accommodation (p33) for details.

Camping & Budget The closest camping ground is ***Shankill Caravan & Camping Park*** (☎ 282 0011, *N11 Wexford Rd*), 16km south of centre. Tent sites €9 plus €2 per person. Take bus 45 or 84 from Eden Quay (no bikes). *Donabate Caravan Park (☎ 843 6008)*, on the beach road off N1, is 1km north of Donabate village (16km north of Dublin). Tent sites €10.

Dublin centre has plenty of budget beds, many in dorms. An Óige's *Dublin International Youth Hostel (☎ 830 1766, W www.irelandyha.org/anoige/dublin1.html, 61 Mountjoy Square)* has dorm beds costing €18, breakfast included. This big well-equipped hostel is 1.5km north of O'Connell Bridge. The IHH *Isaacs Hostel (☎ 836 3877, W www.isaacs.ie, 2 Frenchmans Lane)* has dorm beds/singles/doubles €12/31/53. A central well-converted warehouse near Busáras (the bus station).

B&Bs & Guesthouses Cycling out to the suburbs will get you B&Bs for not much more than €30 per person. B&Bs are also abundant in the centre. Around 1km north of O'Connell Bridge they cluster around rather rundown Gardiner St. *Stella Maris (☎ 874 0835, 13 Upper Gardiner St)* Doubles/triples €71/107. *Carmel House (☎ 874 1639, 16 Upper Gardiner St)* Singles/doubles from €45/77. *Harvey's Guesthouse (☎ 874 8384, W www.harveysguesthouse.com, 11 Upper Gardiner St)* Doubles from €100; secure bike lock-up.

Morehampton Lodge (☎ 283 7499, 113 Morehampton Rd) Single/doubles from €83/110. This place offers smart accommodation 2km southeast along the N11. *Dún Gealáin (☎ 269 1729, 23 Woodbine Ave)* Singles/doubles €36/58. A neat suburban semi 5km southeast along the N11.

Clontarf, 3km northeast of centre beside the estuary, is rich in B&Bs. *Glenbrook (☎ 833 1117, 34 Howth Rd)* and *Eldar (☎ 833 9091, 19 Copeland Ave)* both have singles from €32.

Dublin's Cycling Scene

Sightseeing by Bike

For good urban cycling head west to the green sea of **Phoenix Park**, one of the world's largest city parks, where you can happily lose yourself for days. Commercial vehicles are banned from the roads, and there are cycle paths on both sides of main Chesterfield Avenue, with light traffic only on the side roads.

It is possible to cycle either of the waterways that start in the city centre. Both the **Royal Canal** on the north side and the **Grand Canal** to the south were built during the 18th century to connect Dublin to the River Shannon in the west, and carried passengers, as well as grain and minerals. The canals fell into disuse after the arrival of the railways in the mid-19th century. Ireland has rediscovered its watery treasures and restoration work has reopened stretches to boats. In theory you can cycle them too, but the towpath is often narrow and broken and would test the patience of a cycling saint. This view is supported by Eric Newby in his book *Round Ireland in Low Gear*, after he rode 129km along the Grand Canal. However, riding a short section can be a pleasant contrast to the city streets encountered on the Dublin Orientation ride (p71).

Events & Racing

Much of the success in expanding Dublin's nascent cycle-path network rests with the Dublin Cycling Campaign (see Useful Organisations, p32). Cycling events in the city include the monthly ad hoc Critical Mass ride, which takes over the roads in the name of sanity (or insanity, depending on your take). There's also the annual illegal bicycle-courier race, in which dispatchers risk their necks in the name of short cuts and second-shaving.

Also based in the capital is Cycling Ireland (see Useful Organisations), which runs the road-racing calendar. In 1998 Dublin was the venue for the opening prologue time trial of the Tour de France. Le Tour en Irelande included a section in Phoenix Park and stages in the Wicklow Mountains and Cork. The annual Tour of Ireland, the RÁS, takes place over eight days, finishing in Dublin.

Mountain Biking

Mountain biking in the Wicklow Mountains to the south has tailed off because of conflict with walkers and the resurgence of road riding. It remains to be seen if mountain-bike routes are developed in the future, as local cyclists wish.

DUBLIN & THE NORTHEAST

Warning – Bike Thieves

⚠️ Dublin has some skilled bicycle thieves. One fable tells of a thief sawing through the seat tube of the bike to release the U-lock, taping up the tube and making good their getaway (though it can't have been *that* good, considering the potential for disaster!). This might be rare, but it's better to leave your bike somewhere secure (see Information, p66) rather than leaving it unlocked even for a second while you explore town. Report any thefts to the Garda (police).

Small guesthouses include **Wynn's Hotel** (☎ 874 5131, e info@wynnshotel.ie, 35 Abbey St Lower) Weekday/weekend doubles €121/140. Very central, between O'Connell St and Custom House. The **Fitzwilliam** (☎ 662 5155, 41 Fitzwilliam St Upper) Singles/doubles €77/128. This place is 1.5km southeast of centre, south of Merrion Sq, and is an original townhouse in the longest street of Georgian terraces in Europe.

Places to Eat North of the Liffey, the **Moore St markets** are a real slice of life, and *the* place for self-caterers. Fruit, vegetables and fresh fish are on offer at this practically tourist-free local market.

At least until you get your bearings, the simplest place to head for a meal and a brew is Temple Bar, the old quarter. This maze of revitalised cobbled streets and alleys between Christ Church and O'Connell Bridge is the heart of the entertainment scene. On summer evenings an international drinking party takes place along East Essex St between the Norseman and Temple Bar pubs.

The **Oliver St John Gogarty** (58 Fleet St) Starters from €8, mains from €16. Trad-modern eatery and bar in Temple Bar with big Irish menu and traditional music. Nearby **Cornucopia** (☎ 677 7583, 19 Wicklow St) Mains from €8 serves big portions of well-priced tasty wholefood and has friendly service.

Dublin's grand canteen institutions are **Beshoff's** (6 Upper O'Connell St • 14 Westmoreland St), with fish and chips from €5, and **Bewley's** (78 Grafton St • 11 Westmoreland St • 13 South Great George's St • 40 Mary St), where hot, substantial, predictable food is served throughout the day in original-decor surroundings.

Mona Lisa (☎ 677 0499, cnr D'Olier & College Sts) Pasta from €13 (nice selection), pizza €9-13. This good-value place has half price from 5pm to 6.30pm every day, as well as €7 lunch deals. It gets busy so book ahead.

Nude (☎ 672 5577, 21 Suffolk St) Smoothies and juices €4, vegan wraps €4. Open seven days, good for a vegie lunch on the run. **O'Neill's Bar** (2 Suffolk St) Soup €3, mains from €9. Decent food and authentic ambience – if you can overlook the tourist hordes (it's opposite the Dublin Tourism office).

Acapulco (☎ 677 1085, 7 South Great Georges St) Nachos €6, quesadilla mains €10, margaritas €6. This isn't great Mexican if you've been to Mexico (or even Texas) but it's popular and lively, south of centre.

Foodie window-shoppers on the north side may enjoy the **Epicurean Food Hall** (Liffey St Lower) not far from Ha'penny Bridge. A dozen separate businesses in one little 'bazaar' include patisserie, sushi, bagels, Mexican and more.

Also on the north side; **Café Kylemore** (cnr O'Connell St & Earl St North) serves fast and efficient continental/cooked breakfast for €4/7. **Bangkok Café** (☎ 878 6618, 106 Parnell St) is one of the city's best Thai restaurants, with popular dishes like kaeng pàa néua (Thai country beef curry) for €10.

Getting There & Away For information about international services see Getting There & Away in the Travel Facts chapter (p263).

Air This is the fastest but most expensive way of travelling between Ireland's major centres. Dublin's international airport (☎ 814 1111, w www.dublin-airport.com) is 10km north of the city. You can leave bicycles at left luggage (☎ 814 4633) for a daily charge of €5. Dublin Bus' Airport Express (Airlink) service No 747/748 links Busáras (the central bus station) and the airport (€5, 35 minutes, every 20 minutes) via Connolly, Tara St and Heuston train stations, and O'Connell St (near the Dublin Bus office). Bikes are carried for free. A taxi into town will cost around €18.

Aer Arann (☎ 814 1058, w www.aer arann.ie) flies between Dublin and Cork

Cycling to/from the Airport

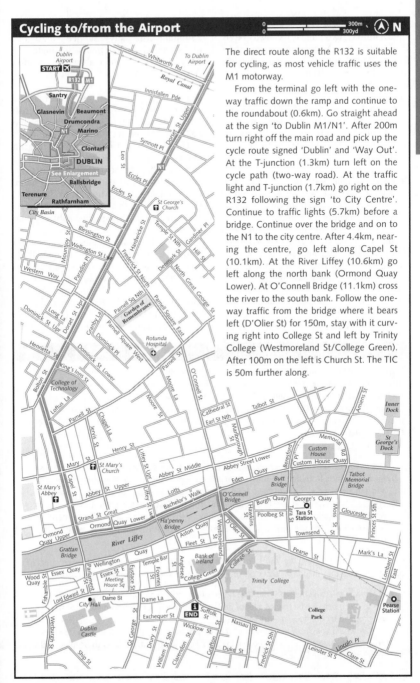

The direct route along the R132 is suitable for cycling, as most vehicle traffic uses the M1 motorway.

From the terminal go left with the one-way traffic down the ramp and continue to the roundabout (0.6km). Go straight ahead at the sign 'to Dublin M1/N1'. After 200m turn right off the main road and pick up the cycle route signed 'Dublin' and 'Way Out'. At the T-junction (1.3km) turn left on the cycle path (two-way road). At the traffic light and T-junction (1.7km) go right on the R132 following the sign 'to City Centre'. Continue to traffic lights (5.7km) before a bridge. Continue over the bridge and on to the N1 to the city centre. After 4.4km, nearing the centre, go left along Capel St (10.1km). At the River Liffey (10.6km) go left along the north bank (Ormond Quay Lower). At O'Connell Bridge (11.1km) cross the river to the south bank. Follow the one-way traffic from the bridge where it bears left (D'Olier St) for 150m, stay with it curving right into College St and left by Trinity College (Westmoreland St/College Green). After 100m on the left is Church St. The TIC is 50m further along.

(€96, 55 minutes, seven Monday to Friday, three Saturday, two Sunday), Galway (€66, 45 minutes, five Monday to Friday, three Saturday and Sunday), Donegal's Carrickfinn (€45 to €70, 50 minutes, once daily) and Sligo (€45 to €70, 45 minutes, twice daily)

British Airways (☎ 0845 773 3377 in the UK, ☎ 1800 626 747 in Ireland, w www .britishairways.com) operates flights between Derry and Dublin (£45, 50 minutes, twice daily).

Bus The Republic's national bus line, Bus Éireann (☎ 836 6111, w www.buseireann.ie) operates services to and from Busáras (Store St), Dublin's central bus station.

Service No 200, run in conjunction with Northern Ireland's Ulsterbus (☎ 028-9066 6630), links Dublin and Belfast's Europa bus centre (€16, two hours 55 minutes, seven Monday to Saturday, six Sunday).

Bus Éireann operates two direct services between Dublin and Cork's Parnell Place (☎ 021-450 8188): No 7 goes via Kilkenny (€19, 6¼ hours, at least two daily) and No

8 is routed through Caher (€19, four hours 25 minutes, six daily). Service No 20 goes to Galway (€12, three hours 40 minutes, 15 daily), arriving at the Galway Bus Station (☎ 091-562 000).

Train The Republic's trains are operated by Iarnród Éireann (☎ 836 6222, w www.irish rail.ie) from Dublin's Connolly (☎ 836 3333) and Heuston (☎ 836 5421) stations.

The cross-border *Enterprise* service, run in conjunction with Northern Ireland Railways (☎ 028-9066 6630) links Dublin Connolly and Belfast Central (€29, two hours five minutes, eight Monday to Saturday, five Sunday). It isn't the fastest of services, but is much less stressful and subject to delays than driving.

Iarnród Éireann operates services from Dublin Heuston to Cork (€45, around three hours, four daily) and to Galway (€33, two hours 55 minutes, four daily).

Car By road the distance from Dublin to Belfast is 167km; the bits and pieces of the M1 are gradually being joined up between

The Bicycle, Writ Funny

Bicycles feature rarely in literature or poetry, coming way down the list after themes such as unrequited love, the pointlessness of war, conspiracy theory and a not-so-clever bear with a fondness for honey. But this is Ireland, land of literary imagination – expect better!

Comic writer Flann O'Brien, pen-name of one Brian O'Nolan, was responsible for numerous musings on the bicycle in a column in the *Irish Times* (written under a second pseudonym, Myles na Gopaleen) that ran for 25 years.

From the 'Cruiskeen Lawn' column (published in the *Irish Times* from 1940 to 1966):

Has it ever occurred to the reader that the bicycle has a personality and a private life? It is the only vehicle I can think of to which man has deigned to concede the attribute of male and female bicycles. Often I have tried to analyse the ineffable otherness of female bicycles...it is not a simple question of anatomy. The simplest way for a man to get a laugh is to go on stage dressed as a woman. A far more extreme and less laughable incongruity is presented by the spectacle of a man riding a lady's bicycle. I always look away in demure, nunlike evasion.

O'Brien's fantastical novel *The Third Policeman* (written in 1939, but published much later) expounds the idea that the longer a person spends on a bike, the more like one they become.

When a man lets things go so far that he is half or more than half a bicycle, you will not see so much because he spends a lot of his time leaning with one elbow on walls or standing propped by one foot against kerbstones.

How would you know a man with a lot of bicycle in his veins? If he walks too slowly or stops in the middle of the road he will fall down in a heap and will have to be lifted and set in motion again by some extraneous party.

Dublin and the border with Northern Ireland so the route is now dual carriageway as far as Drogheda, but can be plagued by frustrating delays. The linking major roads in Northern Ireland are generally better. The road distance between Dublin and Cork is 257km via the N7 and N8; between Dublin and Galway it's 219km via the M4, N4 and N6. The M50 virtually rings Dublin and removes the need to go anywhere near the city on cross-country routes. Late in 2002 it was still incomplete, but the end is somewhere in sight. A toll of €2 is charged between junctions 6 (for the N3 to Navan and Cavan) and 7 (for the N4 to Mullingar).

Dublin Orientation

Duration	2–3 hours
Distance	11.6km
Difficulty	easy
Start/End	Custom House

A pleasant afternoon pedal around Dublin is a grand way to earn a pint of the black stuff. This ride travels clockwise around the centre and shows off Dublin's various faces: handsome, down-at-heel and historic. Two pieces of attractive towpath, along the Grand and Royal Canals, whet the appetite for countryside touring to come.

PLANNING
When to Ride
In the city centre the roads on both banks of the Liffey are truck routes, so although the ride is generally OK as regards traffic, the centre is more savoury on Sundays. Pubs are open even if shops are not.

Maps & Books
The laminated Lonely Planet *Dublin City Map* features greater Dublin in outline and the inner city street-by-street. The OSI *Dublin City Centre street atlas* covers the ride with named streets.

GETTING TO/FROM THE RIDE
Custom House is 400m northeast of the main TIC (see Information, p66), near the bottom of Grafton St. Flow with the traffic through College Green into Westmoreland St, go over O'Connell Bridge and turn right along the north bank.

THE RIDE (see map p72)
The route starts at the imposing **Custom House** on the north bank of the Liffey. The copper-domed landmark was built by Dublin's pre-eminent 18th-century architect, James Gandon, who also designed the Four Courts (seen later).

Heading over the Liffey the first 1km of the route is grotty with traffic and takes close navigation through one-way streets. Merrion Square (1.1km) signals the start of the lovely Georgian cityscape and easier route finding. Around 100m short of the square is the entrance to **College Park** (through the buildings at the southern end of Westland Row). The green sward of **Trinity College** is a good place to spot basking swots. The historic college is also home to one of Dublin's 'must-sees', the **Book of Kells**. One of the oldest books in the world, the brightly illustrated and minutely detailed edition of the four gospels was created by monks around AD 800.

On the western side of Merrion Square is a cluster of buildings at the heart of Irish power and intellect: **Leinster House**, home to the Irish parliament, the domed **Government Buildings** and the trio of **National Gallery**, **National Library** and **National Museum**. The Treasury in the museum houses the national collection of Celtic gold objects, many retrieved from peat bogs.

At the eastern corner of Merrion Square, opposite the handsome old National Maternity Hospital (1.4km), turn right (southwest) up Merrion Square East/Fitzwilliam St into a straight kilometre of Georgian townhouses, the longest street of such terracing in Europe.

At the far end things go green at the **Grand Canal** (2.4km). Go right (westward) along the near bank for 1.7km, either along the towpath or the parallel roads. The old pub 800m along, by Portobello Bridge, is the *Portobello*, which has music on weekends.

Leaving the canal at Robert Emmet Bridge (4.1km), turn north along Clanbrassil St Upper. **St Patrick's Cathedral** (5.3km), on the right in Patrick St, stands on one of Dublin's earliest Christian sites where the saint is said to have baptised converts at a well. Jonathan Swift, tireless campaigner for fair treatment for the Irish and eccentric author of *Gulliver's Travels* was the dean from 1713 to 1745.

Dublin Orientation

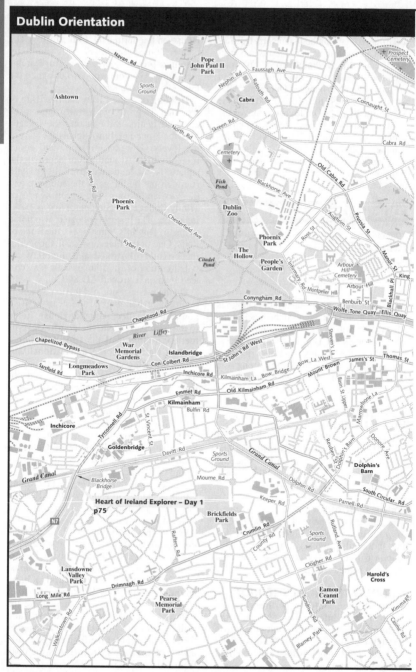

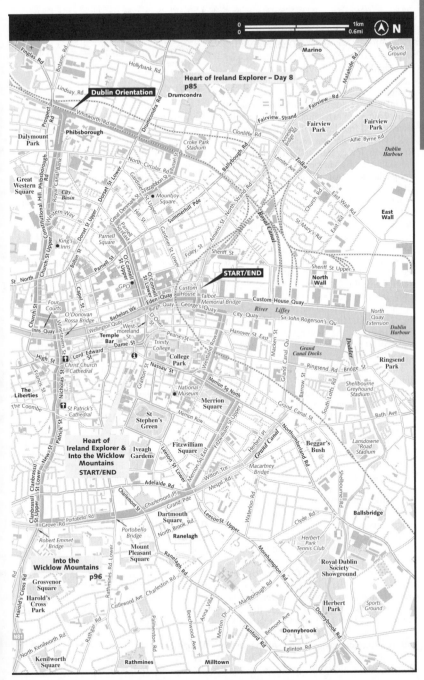

Overlooking the river further on is **Christ Church Cathedral** (Christ Church Place) on the southernmost edge of Dublin's Viking settlement. Like St Patrick's, it fell on hard times in the 18th and 19th centuries and little remains of the original building, although the later structure is still impressive.

On the north side of the Liffey is Gandon's **Four Courts** (6km) which (unsurprisingly) once housed four levels of court. During the 1922 Civil War it was held by anti-treaty Republican forces and shelled to rubble from the south bank by Michael Collins' pro-treaty troops. In the destruction the Public Records Office was also lost, including records of generations of Irish people.

Micro-navigation is needed to find narrow **Broadstone Park** (7.2km), created from a disused arm of the **Royal Canal**; after **King's Inns** (a fine building set in parkland), go right at Western Way and 100m further on the left see the passageway that leads through to Royal Canal Bank, then pick up the park after a few hundred metres on the right.

There are steps at the top of the park where the arm originally branched off the Royal Canal (8.2km). The view eastward down the locks includes the soaring grandstand of **Croke Park** stadium, passed at (9.5km).

The last 200m of the towpath to the stadium may be glass-strewn. A short diversion is to turn right (south) at Dorset St Lower, then take the fourth left (North Circular Road) and third right (Fitzgibbon St) to rejoin the route.

Mountjoy Square (9.9km) is one of north Dublin's part-shiny, part-ramshackle Georgian quadrants. About 500m further on lies **Parnell Square** (10.4km), which features the striking sculpture of the Children of Lir and the Garden of Remembrance which commemorates those who died fighting for Irish independence.

At the head of **O'Connell St** (10.6km), the city-centre bustle hits again. Halfway down on the right is the porticoed landmark of the independence struggle, the **General Post Office** (11km). In the 1916 Easter Rising the proclamation of the republic was read on the steps by Patrick Pearse. The siege that followed reduced the 1818 building to a smoking ruin, and holes in the facade from then, and from fighting in 1922, can still be seen.

At the Liffey (11.2km) go left. Custom House is 400m along the quayside.

Heart of Ireland Explorer

Duration	8 days
Distance	557.3km
Difficulty	easy–moderate
Start/End	Dublin

It's easy to overlook the inland counties in the hurry to get to the better-known west. But after the Ring is rung and the Burren bagged – or maybe on the way there – the Midlands are well worth discovering.

Running clockwise from Dublin, this trip goes through Counties Kildare, Laois and Offaly as far as the mighty River Shannon, and returns via Longford, Westmeath, Meath and County Dublin. The cup runneth over with lovely landscapes, special places and empty roads. A-list sights include the National Stud at Kildare, the Great Telescope at Birr Castle, the ruins of Clonmacnoise on the Shannon and the passage tombs of Newgrange, Knowth and Dowth. Even the B-list includes such gems as Trim Castle, the Hill of Tara and the site of the Battle of the Boyne.

You could use this ride as a scenic route to the Atlantic coast. The first two to three days put you within striking distance of Limerick, Galway and Clare. Longford (Day 4) is a day's ride from Sligo.

NATURAL HISTORY

The once-vast Bog of Allen is now mostly low-lying farmland. To the west, the humpback Slieve Bloom Mountains form the only high land of note. Further north, gleaming fish-rich lakes abound, while the northeastern Midlands, where the River Boyne flows en route to the sea, are undulating.

PLANNING
When to Ride

The ride is great year-round, but several of the headlining sights, particularly Clonmacnoise and Newgrange, can be overwhelmed by visitors in July and August, when accommodation costs also rise. The months of May and September combine decent weather with fewer people.

Maps

The area is covered by the OSI 1:250,000 Holiday map *Ireland East*.

ACCESS TOWN
Dublin
See Dublin (p65).

THE RIDE (see maps pp72 & 76)
Day 1: Dublin to Rathangan
3½–6½ hours, 66.2km

Escape from Dublin to lush, rolling County Kildare, where a visit to the National Stud (57.3km) is a tranquil afternoon break. Today is a good warm-up: the pedalling is mostly easy, with one rise to Kilteel (24.6km) in the morning.

After the city centre the route runs beside the **Grand Canal** for 3.8km. Thereafter an 11.7km section along the busy N7, the main road southwest, is unavoidable. Cyclists can use the broad hard shoulder, but lorry traffic is very heavy – cross the slip roads with great care.

Kildare is the home of the Irish thoroughbred industry. Local residents include three Arab sheikhs, while a dozen stud farms smarten up the landscape. En route lie **Punchestown racecourse** (34.7km), the striking heathland of the **Curragh** (47km), and the **Curragh racecourse** (50.2km). Find details of race days at [w] www.iha.ie/iharace.

The town of Kildare (55.8km) has a bike shop and all facilities. Kildare is also the start/end point of the Hunting the Bog of Allen ride (p86).

There are few places to refuel or restock on the way; Kilteel and Athgarvan have limited facilities.

Side Trip: National Stud
10 minutes, 3km return

Whether you are into horseracing or not – and the Irish are, passionately – the National Stud (☎ 045-521 617, [w] www.irish-national-stud.ie), 1.5km south of Kildare town (follow signs from the centre), is a good mid-afternoon goal. The tour of the stables and paddocks, and the terraced cafeteria are very pleasant. Champion stallions, unaware of their extraordinary value, graze and mate repeatedly for the benefit of the Irish bloodstock industry and the public purse. You are often able to see newborn foals.

Leave time to savour the 20 stages of life represented in the exquisite **Japanese Gardens** at the same site. Meandering along the Honeymoon Path and pausing at the Chair of Old Age, is a good time to pat yourself on the

Heart of Ireland Explorer –
Day 1

Cue		
start		Dublin TIC (Suffolk St)
0km		go N on Church Lane
	⬏	(50m) Dame St
0.8	⬏	Patrick St (N81)
2.3	⬑	Grand Canal towpath/Parnell Rd
6.1	⬏	N7 'the West', Blackhorse Bridge
17.8	⬏	'to Kilteel'
18.2	⬑	'to Beech Pk golf course'
24.6		Kilteel
27.9	⬑	T-junction, Rathmore
	⬏	(50m) 'to Eadestown'
30.0	⬑	R410 'to Punchestown', Eadestown
33.0	⬏	'to Punchestown'
34.7	✳	*Punchestown racecourse*
38.5	⬑	R448
	⬏	(20m) 'to Athgarvan'
45.6	↑	'to Curragh', Athgarvan
47.0	⬑	R413 (no sign)
49.4	⤴	(3rd exit) 'to Rathangan'
	↑	(50m) (2nd exit) 'to Rathangan'
50.2	✳	*The Curragh racecourse*
55.8	↑	R401 'to Rathangan', Kildare
	● ●⬏	*National Stud 3km* ↻
64.1	⬏	'to Rathangan'
66.2		Rathangan post office

back and remember a cyclist is said to have the body of someone up to 10 years younger.

Rathangan
☎ 045

This quiet little town sits on the periphery of the once-vast Bog of Allen, undisturbed by traffic or tourism. Half a dozen traditional bars on the main street fill in the evenings with farmers-cum-turfcutters while their kids drive around in 4WDs. The main street features Victorian houses, many with archways leading to backyards which were originally used for 'parking' horses and carts. The silos beside the Grand Canal are used to store grain destined for the Guinness brewery in Dublin.

Information Rathangan is too small for a TIC or banks yet is karmically blessed with the Bike Shop (☎ 524 326, The Square), run by Leo Conway and open from 'after 11am' to 6pm Monday to Saturday.

Places to Stay & Eat It's best to ring ahead for a bed in Rathangan as there's only one establishment. The *Village Pump* (☎ 524 597, *Main St)* Doubles from €64. This is a B&B

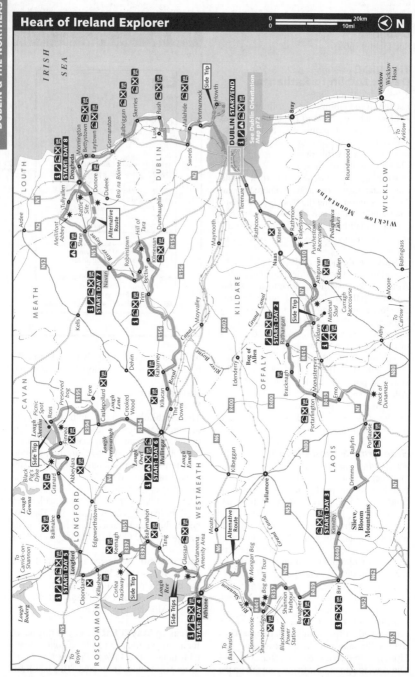

pub with four rooms, run by a local family of peatcutters. Other nearby accommodation options include **Castleview Farm** (☎ 521816, *Lackaghmore*) Singles/doubles from €26/36. A friendly farmhouse; to reach it go 8km south down the R414 Monasterevin road; it's east of Lackagh, north of the N7.

There are no restaurants in Rathangan. The late-night **grocery** *(Main St)* stocks ready-to-cook pizzas, which your B&B host may heat for you. Simple pub grub like cheese toasties (€4) is available in the several Main St **pubs**.

Day 2: Rathangan to Kinnitty
4–7 hours, 73.2km
A pootle through bog and farmland to the ruins of the Rock of Dunamase contrasts with a meaty climb over the Slieve Bloom Mountains to charming Kinnitty.

The striking castle ruins are set on the 200m-high **Rock of Dunamase** (33.4km) atop an esker. It was a strategic site for over 2000 years. The first residents were Iron Age tribes, followed by the Celts and Vikings. The ruins seen today are of an Anglo-Norman castle, constructed over the 11th and 12th centuries, which was destroyed by Cromwell in 1650. Access is on the southeastern side. There are no facilities.

The highlight of the day's pedalling is the 15km scenic traverse of the **Slieve Bloom Mountains**. Rising to over 500m, the iso-lated massif is covered with blanket bog and pine forest. An 8km climb steepens and slackens as the vistas improve. From the road's high point (450m; 63.8km) on the Laois/Offaly county border, the descent drops sharply along the forested valley to Kinnitty. The only shelter comes from the occasional skinny pine, so watch the weather and carry waterproofs and snacks. From Kinnitty it is possible to pick up the Slieve Bloom Mountains ride (p88).

Towns en route where you can restock include pleasant Portarlington and bigger Portlaoise (pronounced Port-leash), which has a shopping mall. Limited supplies are also available at Bracknagh.

When it comes to navigational hazards, pay attention on 8km of little lanes between Emo (25.1km) and the Rock; if in doubt head for the Rock.

Kinnitty
See Kinnitty (p89).

Day 3: Kinnitty to Athlone
4½–8 hours, 80.5km
This is a day of delights for legs and mind on an easy scenic route that takes in Clonmacnoise monastic site on the Shannon.

Take supplies on early at Birr (13.8km), which has all facilities (Banagher and Shannonbridge are smaller, but also have stores).

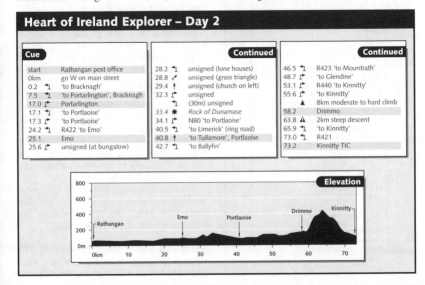

Heart of Ireland Explorer – Day 2

Cue					Continued			Continued
start	Rathangan post office		28.2	unsigned (lone houses)		46.5	R423 'to Mountrath'	
0km	go W on main street		28.8	unsigned (grass triangle)		48.7	'to Glendine'	
0.2	'to Bracknagh'		29.4	unsigned (church on left)		53.1	R440 'to Kinnitty'	
7.5	'to Portarlington', Bracknagh		32.3	unsigned		55.6	'to Kinnitty'	
17.0	Portarlington			(30m) unsigned			8km moderate to hard climb	
17.1	'to Portlaoise'		33.4	Rock of Dunamase		58.2	Drimmo	
17.3	'to Portlaoise'		34.1	N80 'to Portlaoise'		63.8	2km steep descent	
24.2	R422 'to Emo'		40.5	'to Limerick' (ring road)		65.9	'to Kinnitty'	
25.1	Emo		40.8	'to Tullamore', Portlaoise		73.0	R421	
25.6	unsigned (at bungalow)		42.7	'to Ballyfin'		73.2	Kinnitty TIC	

Elevation chart (Rathangan, Emo, Portlaoise, Drimmo, Kinnitty), 0m–800m, 0km–70km.

Birr is also the start of the Tipperary & Waterford Highlands ride (p107). If possible, visit **Birr Castle Demesne** (☎ 0509-20336), the stately pile of the Earls of Rosse, aka the pioneering Parsons, a family of astronomers, engineers and gardeners still in residence. The highlight is the enormous telescope (see the boxed text 'The Great Telescope', p108) in the gardens and grounds. The Historic Science Centre in the stable-block tells of the family's other achievements, including the invention of the steam turbine engine.

From Birr go north and track the mighty River Shannon through shockingly green farmland and swathes of brown peat. At the boating hamlet of Shannon Harbour (31km) the Grand Canal arrives from Dublin to join the river system.

On the road to Shannonbridge come to grips with the bog on the unique **Bog Rail Tour** (38km; €5) run by Bord na Móna (the peat board), a 45-minute trip on part of a 1200km narrow-gauge rail network used to shunt turf. Further on peatland falls beneath the blades of the demonic cutting machines serving the **Blackwater power station** (41.5km).

From Shannonbridge, the scenic road runs along an esker to **Clonmacnoise**, a 'must-see', with the added convenience of a *café* (49km; ☎ 090-967 4195). Overlooking a great curve in the Shannon, Ireland's most important early Christian site comprises a compact walled collection of religious ruins that goes back 1500 turbulent years. The first monastery was built in AD 548, founding a community that lasted 1000 years. But the centuries saw upheaval and bloodshed, as the settlement survived vicious attacks from the Vikings et al rowing up the Shannon. The final bell tolled in 1552 when English troops plundered the last items of value. A museum tells the story and houses carved high crosses. Good replicas stand outside. A TIC (☎ 090-967 4134, open Apr-Sept) is also on site.

On leaving Clonmacnoise, to pick up the scenic Pilgrim's Road that continues along the esker, you have to make a circuitous 1.4km detour round to the eastern edge of the site. **Mongan Bog** nature reserve lies to the right (52.3km). Soon after, at 57.8km, the route takes a scenic 7km meander through more bogland. If you wish to cut this out continue straight ahead on the alternative route and pick up the fast, hairy N62 into Athlone earlier.

Athlone
☎ 090

The largest town on the ride since Dublin, Athlone (Baile Átha Luain) straddles the Shannon, with a foot in the province of Connaught to the west, and the remainder in Leinster to the east. Lying just south of great Lough Ree, the town is a centre for fishing and river cruising.

Information Facilities are easy to find. The castle houses the TIC (☎ 649 4630, open daily June-Sept, closed Sun Apr, May & Oct) – a museum and heritage centre. The entrance is up the ramp beside the bridge. The Bank of Ireland (Northgate St) is just up from Custume Place.

Bike shops are Hardiman's (☎ 647 8669, Irishtown), 500m east of centre and DB Cycles (☎ 649 2280, 30 Connaught St), which lies west of the town centre.

Things to See & Do Athlone occupies a strategic position on an old ford across the Shannon in the geographical heart of the

Heart of Ireland Explorer – Day 3

Cue		
start		Kinnitty TIC
0km		go W on R421
13.7	↱	'to Athlone'
13.9	↑	R439 'to Banagher', Birr
26.1	↱	'to Shannon Harbour', Banagher
28.8	↰	'to Shannon Harbour'
31.0		Shannon Harbour
33.4	↰	R357 'to Shannonbridge'
38.0	✻	Bog Rail Tour
41.7	✻	Blackwater power station
42.7	↱	R444 'to Clonmacnoise', S'bridge
49.1	✻	Clonmacnoise
49.7	↰	unsigned (white bungalow)
52.3	✻	Mongan Bog reserve
55.5	↘	(due east)
57.8	↰	unsigned (sharp, downhill)
▪▪ ↑		alt route: N62 5km
65.5	↘	unsigned
70.2	↰	N62
		alt route rejoins (continue)
75.3	↰	N6 'to Athlone'
76.7	↘	(2nd exit) 'to Athlone'
80.5		Athlone TIC (in castle)

country. Loyal in the 17th century to the Catholic English King James, the **castle**, which dates back to medieval times, withstood siege by the Protestant forces of William of Orange in 1690, but fell the next year to a determined return force of 25,000 troops. The castle has a visitor centre (☎ 649 4630), runs tours and has tearooms.

Boat tours upriver to lovely Lough Ree (1½ hours) leave from the Jolly Mariner Marina (☎ 647 2892) north of the railway bridge, and the Strand (☎ 0902-73383) near the castle. A novel three-hour **Viking ship cruise** (☎ 647 3383) down river to Clonmacnoise also leaves from the Strand. Sailing times depend on bookings; phone to inquire.

Places to Stay & Eat For a night out, head to the little streets of the west bank (near the castle), where boldly painted houses, pubs and restaurants exude a jolly air and the strains of live music.

B&Bs in this area include *Marie's* (☎ 649 2494, 8 High St) Ensuite doubles from €52. *The Bastion* (☎ 649 4954, e bastion@iol.ie, 4 Bastion St) Singles/doubles from €28/49.

Bushfield House (☎ 647 5979, Blyry) Ensuite doubles from €51. Neat and modern this place is 3km northeast of centre, north of the N6 bypass.

Pubs and restaurants are abundant near the castle. *Left Bank Bistro* (☎ 649 4446, Fry Place) Fish- and meat-based menu with mains such as char-grilled halibut with couscous from €20. *Tribeca* (☎ 649 8805, Bastion St) Within the purple and blue exterior, find calamari starters (€6) and pizzas (from €8). The all-day *Mordyke Coffee Dock* (Church St) in the Royal Hoey Hotel serves omelette and chips for €6.

Enjoy live music at *Sean's Bar*, claimed to be the oldest bar in Ireland, behind the castle.

Day 4: Athlone to Longford
3½–6½ hours, 65km

The route continues north on lanes parallel to Lough Ree into County Longford via a curious reed-choked stretch of the Royal Canal. In the middle of nowhere (about mid-afternoon) lies the fascinating ancient Corlea Trackway where a piece of bog road is preserved in a sophisticated building (39.8km, see Side Trip, p80).

Take time to enjoy the Lough. At several points, rather unappealingly named 'Amenity

Heart of Ireland Explorer – Day 4

Cue		
start		Athlone TIC
0km		go E across river
0.3	↘	'to Cavan (N55)'
3.8	⬏	'to Ballymahon, De Porres accomm'
5.2	↑	join N55
	⬏	(50m) 'Lakeside Hotel & Marina'
6.9	✳	Portaneena Amenity Area
8.9	⬏	Glasson
9.4	⬏	'Lough Ree Tour'
12.4	⬑	'to Portlick Bay'
13.9	↘	'to Portlick Bay'
14.3	●●⬏	Portlick Amenity Area 2.4km ↻
15.1	↑	'Lough Ree Tour'
	●●⬏	Portlick Inn, 'to K'more' 2km ↻
17.6	⬏	'Lough Ree Tour'
19.1	⬑	'Lough Ree Tour'
20.7	⬏	'Lough Ree Tour' (T-junction)
22.6	⬏	unsigned (not 'Tour')
26.8	⬏	unsigned (Forgney church, N55)
30.4	⬏	N55 'to Cavan', Ballymahon
31.0	↑	R392
34.2	⬑	R397 'to Keenagh'
39.3	⬏	'to Lanesborough', Keenagh
39.8	⬑	unsigned (nearside Royal Canal)
	●● ↑	Corlea Trackway 4km ↻
41.1	⬏	T-junction
41.7	⬏	over bridge
	⬑	(20m) beside canal
45.1	↑	cross R398
48.3	⬏	N63 'to Lanesborough', Killashee
	⬑	(80m) unsigned (Donlon grocery)
50.0	↙	unsigned (bungalow)
54.3	⬏	Cloondara
55.8	⬑	N5
64.3	⬑	N5, Main St
64.8	⬑	'to Westport'
65.0		Longford TIC

Areas', you can turn off to the water's edge for a breather. **Portaneena** (6.9km) comes early on, **Portlick**, a short side trip, a little later (14.3km). The prettiest lakeside point can be seen as another short side trip, lying below the isolated, very rough and ready Portlick Inn (15.1km), where, if you're lucky, the bar might brew you up a coffee.

The myriad lanes around the lough here can be confusing. The route roughly follows the Tour of Lough Ree (a local cycling tour), so the signposting is usually an aid – but not always. Be warned that the lane below the inn along the lovely shoreline is a dead end, although the OSI Holiday map shows it as a through-road.

Ballymahon (30km) is the main town en route, with both banks and *stores*, while limited supplies are available at Keenagh, Glassan and Killashee.

The afternoon's cycling highlight is 4km along an overgrown section of **Royal Canal** (from 41.km), where reeds and sphagnum moss are recolonising the shallow water. Work is in progress to reopen the canal for boats, meanwhile, enjoy the sight of nature creeping back.

Side Trip: Corlea Trackway
15 minutes, 4km return

The day's historical surprise, **Corlea Trackway** (☎ 043-22386, open Apr-Sept), appears like an oasis in the 'desert' of bog near Keenagh. Access is by guided tour on the hour from 10am to 5pm. An 18m section of oak causeway typical of an extensive network across the bogs in the Iron Age is preserved in humidified conditions. Dated to 148 BC, the trackway is one of 57 structures that have been unturfed in the area. You get plenty of exhibition for your money, not to mention the cyclist's beacon – a tearoom.

To get to the trackway, beyond Keenagh (39.3km), where the route meets the Royal Canal (39.8km), continue straight ahead for 2km rather than turning right.

Longford
☎ 043

Comfortably off the tourist trail, the county town of Longford (An Longfort) is a pleasant all-Irish place with elaborately decorated pubs and shopfronts along Main St, and a centrally located hostel. The town VIP is Albert Reynolds, the long-standing Fianna Fáil MP for Longford-Westmeath and former taoiseach (prime minister) of Ireland (1992–94). He played a significant role in the early-1990s peace talks with British leader John Major.

Information The TIC (☎ 46566, open Mon-Sat Apr-Sept) is at the top of town in the civic building beside the supermarket in Market Square.

The town's two bike shops are Denniston's (☎ 46345, Centenary Square), past Denniston's Fishing, and KM Cycles (☎ 41656, Kelly's Arcade), just east of the Longford Hotel.

Things to See & Do Civic buildings of note are the 1792 **courthouse**, which awaits a long-promised refurbishment, and the great domed renaissance-style **St Mel's cathedral**, built in the 19th century, more recently than it might appear. Italianate **33 Main St**, now a solicitor's practice, dates from 1885 and was once the town gentleman's club.

Pubs with music on Main St include *Patrick Fallons* on Wednesday nights, and *Foley's* for Foster and Allen–style Irish country music. On Main St – left at the top (eastern) end of Ballymahon St – is *An Bodhrán*, where you can inquire about music sessions.

Places to Stay & Eat Near Newtownforbes, 10km northwest of the town along the N4 Carrick-on-Shannon road, is *Longford*

Fionn McCumhaill & the Salmon of Knowledge

Here's a Boyne-based tale from the Fenian Cycle, a collection of ancient Irish legends which tells of the deeds of Fionn McCumhaill (Finn McCool) and his roving warbands, the Fianna.

The wisdom of the sage Finegas was widely regarded, and Fionn McCumhaill, the young man who would become the greatest warrior in Ireland, journeyed to his home on the banks of the Boyne to gain instruction.

When he arrived the master was trying to catch the Salmon of Knowledge, a legendary golden fish with magic powers, which despite Finegas' cunning had eluded him for years. Just as Fionn arrived, Finegas felt a tug on his line, and all of a sudden he found he had landed the great salmon. Thrilled, he set it on the fire to cook, but had to go off for a while. He told Fionn to watch the fish, and warned him to eat none of it.

On his return, Finnegan noticed something different about the lad, and asked if he had disobeyed his instructions. Fionn answered that when he turned the fish, a drop of oil burned his thumb and he sucked it to ease the pain. The old man, realising Fionn had been given the knowledge, told him to eat the rest of the fish. From that day, whenever Fionn wanted to see into the future, he only had to suck his thumb.

Caravan & Camping (☎ 45503, Kilmacannon). Tent sites €8. Open May-Sept.

Riverbeds independent hostel (☎ 41000, e info@riverbeds.com, Gt Water St) Dorm beds from €16. This place has laundry facilities and meals. Turn right off Main St from below the Longford Arms Hotel.

B&Bs here include *Viewmount House* (☎ 42906, e viewmt@iol.ie, Dublin Rd) Doubles from €64. Georgian building 1km southeast from centre down the N4. Further out, on the Day 5 route, is *Cumiskeys Farmhouse* (☎ 24854, e kc@iol.ie) Singles/doubles from €40/32. A handsome place 8km northeast of Longford on the R194 Granard road. *Longford Arms Hotel* (☎ 46296, e longfordarms@itnet.ie, Main St) B&B singles/doubles from €58/102. The grand town hotel is comfortable and central.

Self-caterers can pick up choice meats at *Herterichs* (Ballymahon St), a butcher and meatpacker near Market Square. There's also a *supermarket* on Market Square, where the route ends.

Daytime eating is easy, but dinner is quite hard to track down. *The Coffee Shop* at the Longford Arms Hotel opens until 8pm serving good cafeteria food, such as carvery platters from €8. *Café Torc* (Ballymahon St) from Market Square, is stylish chocoholic heaven. Enjoy hearty savouries (tomato and basil soup costs €3) and the owner's own confections, such as Torc Chocolate and Mokachino, in a café decorated with choc-loving quotes. *Valentine's Bar* (Main St) does great pub grub but only until 6pm Monday to Friday; Saturdays mean soup and sarnies.

Day 5: Longford to Mullingar
4½–8 hours, 80.7km

Leave County Longford for Westmeath through lovely rolling farmland with long views and a loughside lunch stop. Enjoy cruising the countryside – there's nothing in particular to visit.

Restock before you quit town as there are few sizable communities en route. Limited supplies may be found at Ballinalee, Granard, Abbeylara, Finnea and Castlepollard. One possible if remote place for a picnic break is the short side trip to the secluded mooring on Lough Sheelin (41.4km). This lies at the end of a quiet forest track used by anglers. There are no signs to speak of

Heart of Ireland Explorer – Day 5

Cue		
start		Longford TIC
0km		go W on Ballymahon St
	↱	(150m) N5 (N4) 'to Dublin'
0.3	↰	R194 'to Ballinalee'
12.5		Ballinalee
24.6	↰	N55, Granard
25.3	↱	R194 'to Ballyjamesduff'
25.9	↱	R396 'to Abbeylara'
28.5	↰ ✳	'to Finea', Abbeylara
31.7	↱	R194 'to Ballyjamesduff'
32.6	✳	Black Pig's Dyke
33.8	↱	R394 'to Ballyjamesduff'
35.5		Finnea
36.2	↰	'to Mount Nugent'
37.3	↱	'to Mount Nugent (Ross House)'
38.0	✳	preserved bog
41.4	●●↰	Lough Sheelin 3.2km ↻
42.2	↱	Ross
44.3	↰	unsigned (crossroads, 'Yield')
44.8	↰	'to Oldcastle'
47.0	↱	unsigned (opp double poles, no 7)
50.5	↱	unsigned ('Yield')
52.6	↑	unsigned (through buildings)
55.2	↱	R195 'to Castlepollard'
60.1	↰	R394 'to Mullingar', Castlepollard
79.3	↰	'to town centre'
80.6	↰	'to Tullamore', Pearse St
80.7		Mullingar TIC (LHS)

around the tracks; 1.2km after leaving the road turn right. Solo riders, women in particular, might find the place lonely.

No sight demands a visit, but pieces in the jigsaw of ancient Irish history are strewn about. Abbeylara (28.5km) has a picturesque, crumbling 13th-century **Cistercian abbey**. A little further on, the route cuts through **Black Pig's Dyke** (32.6km), part of the country's greatest border barrier. Originally, this thick, high bank stretched for hundreds of kilometres between Donegal Bay and the Irish Sea.

The road between Finnea and Ross passes through a preserved bog (38km) giving an idea of what once covered great expanses of the Midlands.

Navigating the rural lanes between Ross and Castlepollard is a good test of observation! Watch the cues closely. After Castlepollard, traffic on the fast, narrow R394 to Mullingar can be tight. In Mullingar you can pick up the Westmeath Lakeland & the Fore Valley ride (p90).

Mullingar
See Mullingar (p91).

Day 6: Mullingar to Navan
4–7 hours, 72km

Bid farewell to bog and lake and say hello to Meath, a fertile farming county, whose past is rich in historic events that had a powerful influence on modern politics. The day's middling distance may allow time for a lunchtime visit to Trim castle (50.1km) and an afternoon tour of the Hill of Tara (60.2km).

The route picks up the **River Boyne**, following it for the next two and a half days from pastoral scenery inland via the Boyne Valley to Drogheda and on to the Irish Sea.

Trim (50.1km; Baile Átha Troim) is the place to combine lunch with a visit to Ireland's largest **castle** (☎ 046-943 8618, open mid-June–mid-Sept). The great moated Anglo-Norman defence has a 20-sided keep

(main tower) and long curtain walls, with the Boyne on one side.

Beyond Trim lies a 3km climb up the **Hill of Tara** (60.2km), the high grassy seat of Ireland's Celtic rulers during their heyday, AD 200–400. Earlier settlements on the hill date back to 2500 BC, proving that the site, with great views over the plains of Meath, had central importance throughout the long pre-Christian millennia. The visitor centre (☎ 046-902 5903) in the former Protestant church, brings to life the mounds and ditches that are all that remain of structures like a Neolithic passage tomb, and Celtic royal palace and banquet hall.

Returning to the banks of the Boyne, the route passes Bective (65.3km) and the ruins of **Bective Abbey**, founded in 1147, the first Cistercian offspring of Mellifont Abbey in County Louth.

Trim is the main town of the day, with a good choice of *cafés* and *stores*. Some supplies are available at Killucan and Raharney.

Heart of Ireland Explorer – Day 6

Cue		
start		Mullingar TIC
0km		go E on O Plunkett St, Dublin Rd
2.6	↰	'to Dublin'
2.9	↱	N4 'to Dublin'
6.9	↰	R156 'to Killucan', The Downs
14.4		Killucan
17.7		Raharney
17.9	↱	'to Shay Murtagh'
23.8	↰	'to Trim'
27.4	↰	R161 'to Trim'
28.5	↱	'to Longwood'
30.2	↰	'to Longwood'
30.7	✻	River Boyne
31.0	↰	'to Trim'
33.3	↰	unsigned (white house)
34.7	↱	R161 'to Trim'
35.4	↰	unsigned (not 'to Trim')
39.4	↰	R156
39.7	↱	unsigned (blind cnr & farmhouse)
40.2	↑	'to Trim'
43.2	↰	'to Kildalkey' (not Trim)
46.1	↱	'to Trim'
49.4	↱	R154 'to town centre'
50.1	↰ ✻	R154 Dublin Rd, Trim
54.1	↰	'to Kilmessan'
56.8	↱	'to Tara', Kilmessan
56.9	↰	'to Tara'
57.9	↱	'to Tara'
59.6	↰	unsigned (T-junction)
60.2	✻	Hill of Tara
61.2	↰	unsigned (farm wall)
	⚠	1.6km rough steep descent
61.6	↱	'to Navan'
62.3	↰	'to Bective Abbey'
65.3	↱	'to abbey', Bective
65.6	✻	Bective Abbey
66.0	↑	cross R161 'to Athboy'
66.9	↱	'to Navan'
71.5	↱	Brews Hill (T-junction)
72.0	↱	Ludlow St
72.0		(50m) Navan TIC (RHS)

Navan
☎ 046

The bustling county town of Meath, Navan (An Uaimh) has a small number of good places to stay and eat but no irresistible attraction. The town lies at the confluence of the Boyne and Blackwater rivers at head of the Boyne Valley.

The TIC (☎ 907 3426, 21 Ludlow St) is 500m around the corner from Market Square, the hub of Navan. Clarke's Sports (☎ 902 1130), at the back of Navan Indoor Market on Trimgate St, does bike repairs and is a Raleigh Rent-a-Bike dealer. The Allied Irish Bank (cnr Kennedy Rd & Trimgate St) has an ATM.

Live **pub music** is easy to find most evenings of the week. Try *O'Flaherty's* and *Bernard Reilly's* on Trimgate St (off Market Square) or the tiny *Birmingham's Pub* (Ludlow St), which hosts music on Thursdays. Irish music nights are held at the *Lantern Lounge* at the bottom of Watergate St and at *Henry Loughran's* (Trimgate St).

Places to Stay & Eat The nearest hostel is in Slane town (11km northeast of Navan along the undulating N51) and has camping. *Slane Farm Hostel* (☎ 041-988 4985, e paddymacken@eircom.net, Harlinstown House) Dorm beds €16, doubles €40.

Heart of Ireland Explorer – Day 7

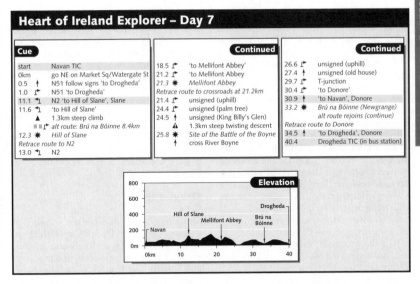

Cue

start	Navan TIC
0km	go NE on Market Sq/Watergate St
0.5 ↑	N51 follow signs 'to Drogheda'
1.0 ⌐	N51 'to Drogheda'
11.1 ⌐	N2 'to Hill of Slane', Slane
11.6 ⌐	'to Hill of Slane'
▲	1.3km steep climb
∎∎⌐	alt route: Brú na Bóinne 8.4km
12.3 ✳	Hill of Slane
Retrace route to N2	
13.0 ⌐	N2

Continued

18.5 ⌐	'to Mellifont Abbey'
21.2 ⌐	'to Mellifont Abbey'
21.3 ✳	Mellifont Abbey
Retrace route to crossroads at 21.2km	
21.4 ⌐	unsigned (uphill)
24.4 ⌐	unsigned (palm tree)
24.5 ↑	unsigned (King Billy's Glen)
25.8 ✳	Site of the Battle of the Boyne
↑	cross River Boyne

Continued

26.6 ⌐	unsigned (uphill)
27.4 ↑	unsigned (old house)
29.7 ⌐	T-junction
30.4 ⌐	'to Donore'
30.9 ↑	'to Navan', Donore
33.2 ✳	Brú na Bóinne (Newgrange)
	alt route rejoins (continue)
Retrace route to Donore	
34.5 ↑	'to Drogheda', Donore
40.4	Drogheda TIC (in bus station)

Elevation

(Elevation profile: Navan ~200m at 0km, rising to Hill of Slane just after 10km, dipping to Mellifont Abbey ~20km, Brú na Bóinne ~30km, Drogheda ~400m near 40km)

Meadow View (☎ 902 3994, ⓔ *meadow view@eircom.net, N51 Slane Rd*) Singles/doubles from €30/44. B&B with fine gardens and luxury fittings just northeast of centre. *Athlumney Manor* (☎ 71388, ⓔ *pboylan@eircom.net, R153 Duleek Rd*) Ensuite singles/doubles from €33/50. Overlooks 16th-century Athlumney castle, 2km southeast of centre.

Navan has plenty of **fast food outlets** and you can get dinner at a couple of restaurants. *Vivaldi's* (☎ 71555, 15 Hudson St) Pasta and other Italian dishes from €8. *Hudson's Bistro* (☎ 29231, Railway St) Mains from €13. Open Tues-Sat. A classy, Egon Ronay–rated restaurant. Visit *Bernard Reilly's* (Trimgate St) and *O'Flaherty's* (Brews Hill) for pub grub.

Day 7: Navan to Drogheda
2–4 hours, 40.4km

After Navan the River Boyne sinks into a deep green dale as historic as it is lovely. The short distance allows time to visit a quartet of significant sights, of which the Newgrange passage tomb at Brú na Bóinne is unmissable. The route is intended as a morning tour of the 120m Hill of Slane, Mellifont Abbey and the site of the Battle of the Boyne, visiting some awe-inspiring tombs in the afternoon.

Generally, navigating is easy: the valley is hard to miss and has a scenic road either side. As sights do not occur in a cycling-friendly line, you can pick and mix them. Be aware though that the only river crossing other than en route (25.8km, at the battle site) is at Slane. This is given on the alternative route that remains in the valley, going direct to Brú na Bóinne and avoiding the climb out of the valley to the Hill of Slane, Mellifont and back to the site of the Battle of the Boyne.

The **Hill of Slane** (12.3km), after a 1.3km climb out of Slane, has magnificent views. This is where St Patrick is said to have plucked the shamrock and used the leaves to illustrate the union of the Father, Son and Holy Ghost. The hill bears evidence of defensive and religious settlements from the 5th to the 16th centuries.

A few kilometres further on, remaining high outside the valley, are the ruins of **Mellifont Abbey** (21.3km; ☎ 041-982 6459, open May-Oct), the country's first and most magnificent Cistercian abbey. The most recognisable building is the *lavabo*, an octagonal wash house for the monks built in the 13th century.

From Mellifont, mind the steep descent down King Billy's Glen (24.5km) and prepare for the story behind the name at the **site of the Battle of the Boyne**. On 12 July 1690 Protestants and Catholics from all over Europe amassed for a fight that would decide the English crown and shape Ireland in the future. The 300-year-old clash on the banks of the Boyne is still invoked today to stoke old conflicts.

There is little to see and plenty to imagine at the battle site (see the boxed text 'Battle of the Boyne'). The local West Ferrard Boyne Development Group (☎ 041-984 1644) runs the humble information cabin beside the river at the bottom of King Billy's Glen (24.5km).

Brú na Bóinne (33.2km) the 'dwelling place of the Boyne' is a stretch of riverside between Slane and Drogheda of extraordinary archaeological importance. Designated a World Heritage site, the valley is dense with remains, many still unexcavated, headlined by three extraordinary passage tombs at Newgrange, Knowth and Dowth. Built before the pyramids, these mound 'buildings' have survived 5000 years virtually unaltered, and still keep out the rain!

The only access to the tombs is via shuttlebus tour from the sophisticated visitor centre (☎ 041-988 0300, open daily), with *café*,

which has been sensitively built into the verdant slopes on the south bank of the Boyne.

The Newgrange tomb is over 75m in diameter, and has a 19m corridor leading to a cruciform burial chamber at its heart. The tour takes you right into the chamber, for the evocative demonstration of a sunbeam penetrating the gloom at dawn on the winter solstice. The Knowth tomb is even larger, with two passages, decorated chambers and 18 'satellite' tombs. The mound at Dowth is under excavation and closed to the public.

En-route supplies can be obtained at Slane and Donore.

Drogheda
☎ 041

Straddling the Boyne within a bulge of County Louth is Drogheda (Droichead Átha). The town has a bloody and political past, due to its strategic position on the river and relative proximity to Dublin. Nowadays, building sites pepper the grubby tidal banks in the centre. Along with the elegant bridge of the new M1 Dublin–Belfast motorway, they are the unmistakable product of the country's recent boom.

Drogheda lies on the old Ulster-Leinster frontier and figures in bloody conflicts of Irish nationhood. By the 15th century it was one of Ireland's four major walled towns and the venue for many sessions of the Irish parliament.

The 17th century saw the darkest chapter in the town's history. In 1649 the forces of Oliver Cromwell massacred 3000 people after the town put up unexpectedly strong resistance to his march north from Dublin. When his men gained control, they were commanded to slaughter all and sundry, as an example to the rest of Ireland.

In 1690 the town was defended by a garrison loyal to the James II and, following defeat by William's army at the Battle of the Boyne, was again forced to surrender to a foreign Protestant force.

Information The TIC (☎ 983 7070) is easy to find in the bus station offices on the main N1 on the south bank of the river. Most of the main banks are on West St. Quay Cycles (☎ 983 4526) is on North Quay, the north bank, east of centre.

Drogheda hosts a highly successful **Samba Festival** (☎ 983 3946) one weekend

---

Battle of the Boyne

Lined up facing each other at a shallow point on the River Boyne 300 years ago, were the 36,000-strong Protestant alliance of Dutchman William of Orange and the 25,000-strong Catholic force headed by his father-in-law, James II, the king of England and Scotland. William, oddly, had the backing of the Pope, who was threatened in Europe by the ambition of the king of France, Charles II, who in turn supported James.

William hid thousands of his men up the steep lane north of the battle site, now called King Billy's Glen. He then sent a decoy force of 10,000 men around to James' western flank (crossing the ford at Newgrange), which fooled James into sending two-thirds of his troops off to defend it. At low tide William's Protestant soldiers jumped out of the glen, forded the river via the islands and in a matter of hours overwhelmed the vulnerable Catholic front line.

William became king of England, and is commemorated in the title of the Loyal Orange Order, the Protestant organisation that works to maintain Northern Irish union with Britain.

every July. The streets bounce to the beat of bands from the Caribbean and USA as well as Drogheda's finest. The pubs, naturally, fill to the brim.

Things to See & Do Drogheda's sights bring to mind its grim history. Cromwell's 1649 rampage saw the tower of **St Peter's Church of Ireland** (William St) burned down, killing 100 people who had sought sanctuary inside. The church was rebuilt in 1748.

In a soaring reliquary in the Catholic **St Peter's Church** (West St) lies the mummified head of the martyr St Oliver Plunkett. The primate of all Ireland, he was hanged by the English in 1681 on spurious charges of treason in a time of feverish anti-Catholic paranoia.

South of the river is the mysterious mound of **Millmount**, which could be another tomb like Newgrange but has not yet been excavated. The surrounding village enclave and 18th-century barracks house craft shops, a museum (☎ 983 3097) and a restaurant. A room at the museum is dedicated to the Cromwellian siege and the Battle of the Boyne.

Places to Stay & Eat In the town centre is *Green Door Hostel* (☎ 983 4422, w *www .greendoorhostel.com, 47 John St)* Dorm beds from €14. This modern hostel on the north bank of the river, 150m from the TIC, has family rooms and serves meals.

Abbeyview (☎ 983 1470, Mill Lane, off Trinity St) Doubles from €46. A central B&B 300m west of centre. *Riverbank House* (☎ 984 1005, Rathmullan Rd)* Doubles from €52. A short distance west of the TIC, along the riverbank (turn off the N1 on the south bank, where it bends and crosses the river).

Westcourt Hotel (☎ 983 0965, West St) Doubles from €106. On the main street in the centre. *Boyne Valley Hotel* (☎ 983 7737, Dublin Rd) Doubles from €140. The best hotel in town, this lies on the main N1 southeast.

Monks Espresso Bar & Café (North Quay) has spicy bean burritos for €7 and is good for lunch. *La Pizzeria* (☎ 983 4208, Peter St) serves huge pizzas, also lasagne and steaks from €12. *Lucky Ned Peppers* (☎ 984 3343, West St) Tex-Mex mains from €12. *Black Bull Bar* (N1 Dublin Rd) Good

pub grub, lasagne, steak and chips until about 10pm. It's 1km southeast of town – look out for the bull on the roof.

Day 8: Drogheda to Dublin
2½–5 hours, 79.3km
The route turns south back to Dublin down a shoreline with sandy beaches and picturesque estuaries via resorts of varying attraction.

Good for a break is colourful Skerries (30.8km), which has a fine harbour and views north to the Mourne Mountains. Likewise affluent Malahide (56.7km), where Dubliners go to promenade on the waterfront, is worth a stop.

The hilly **Howth Peninsula** (66.3km) is a dramatic knob of land on the tip of the northern edge of Dublin Bay which makes

Heart of Ireland Explorer – Day 8

Cue		
start		Drogheda TIC
0km		go E on N1
0.2	↰	'to town centre' (to bridge)
	↱	(20m) 'to Mornington' (riverbank)
6.6	↑	R151, Mornington
9.6		Bettystown
11.9		Laytown
12.2	↰	through car park to riverside
		(40m) cross river on footbridge
12.3	↑	rejoin roadway
13.6	↖	'to Castlehill Centre'
15.5	↘	unsigned (lane veers right)
16.6	↱	unsigned
17.3	↰	N1
17.5	↰	N1 'to Gormanston'
24.1	↰	R127 'to Skerries', Balbriggan
24.7	↰	'to Skerries Mills'
25.0	↱	'to Skerries Mills'
30.6	↰	'to harbour and centre'
30.8	↱	R128 'to Rush', Skerries
37.7	↱	R128 'to Dublin', Rush
41.7	↰	'to Civic Amenity'
45.9	↰	R127
46.4	↰	N1 'to Dublin'
52.3	↰	R106
55.1	↰	R106
56.7		Malahide
62.3	↰	'to Howth'
64.7	↰	R106 'to Howth'
66.3	↱	'to centre'
	↰●●Howth Peninsula 12km ↻	
78.3	↑	cross River Liffey (Custom House)
78.5	↱	George's Quay
78.8	↰	D'Olier St
79.0	↰	College St/Dame St
79.3	↰	Church Lane
79.3		(50m) Dublin TIC

a perfect 12km side trip, with views and moored yachts. It's also great as a day trip from Dublin.

Two sections along the main N1 prove unavoidable: a bearable 3km (from 17.3km) to Balbriggan, and a nail-bitingly tight 5.9km (from 46.4km) before Swords.

The exit from Drogheda along the R150 is easy to miss. Resembling an industrial service road, it starts directly on the south bank of the town bridge spliced between the N1 and the river. Also, leaving Lay-town, where the road turns inland, leave the road left (12.2km), cross to the far corner of the gravel car park, and take the footbridge over the river beneath the railway line. (The OSI Holiday map doesn't mark the river.)

The final 12km into central Dublin is easy. Go with the flow from the turn-off to the Howth Peninsula (66.3km) to the banks of the Liffey (78.3km) beside Custom House.

Hunting the Bog of Allen

Duration	4½–8 hours
Distance	82.9km
Difficulty	easy
Start/End	Kildare

Forty-eight kilometres west of Dublin lies a chunk of what is left of the Bog of Allen, formerly a huge expanse of peatland that stretched as far as the River Shannon.

This ride strikes north from the busy little town of Kildare to search out pieces of this great brown bog, and returns via Peatland World, a low-key but fascinating bogland education centre. Although extensive, the bog is strangely hard to find; 30km are covered before the first sighting.

NATURAL HISTORY

Once one of the largest peatlands in Ireland, the Bog of Allen is a shadow of its former self, the patches that remain either scheduled for extraction, or painstakingly preserved for posterity.

Rich in fauna and flora despite their harshness, bogs have been called the Irish Eden. Plants include bog cotton, cranberry and the bog bean, and insectivorous species such as sundew and bladderwort that supplement their diets with bugs. Insect life includes swooping dragonflies, emerald damselflies

and zig-zagging butterflies. Mammals such as Irish hares and foxes make the bog their home, and the birdlife is renowned, with snipes, meadow pipits and curlews. The skylark provides a lovely ambient bog song.

PLANNING
When to Ride

Spring and summer bring colour back to the greened-over ex-peatlands, with wildflowers. The flat, low-lying land is not particularly exposed until you hit the hectares of extracted bog, where the wind can be fierce.

Maps

OSI 1:50,000 Nos 45 and 59 Discovery maps cover the ride, as does OSI 1:250,000 Holiday map *Ireland East*.

ACCESS TOWN
Kildare
☎ 045

A small town that would be nicer without the N7 thundering through its heart, Kildare (Cill Dara) has plenty of facilities, but little warmth. Nevertheless, it is the site of the perpetual flame of St Brigid, Ireland's most revered saint after St Patrick. Lit in the 5th century, according to legend, the flame burned here until the dissolution of the monasteries in 1537. The restored fire pit lies in the grounds of the 13th-century Protestant St Brigid's Cathedral near the town square.

Building a Bog

The Bog of Allen grew in the lakes formed by retreating glaciers 5000 years ago. Stagnant water became trapped between eskers (low ridges formed by glacial debris) and was supplemented by high rainfall.

There are several stages in the development of a raised bog from an esker lake. First, chalk-like marl is laid down, sealing the lake bed. Dead plants build up on that as a layer of fen peat. The peat eventually fills up the lake entirely, and the fen plants diminish as they lose touch with the mineral-rich groundwater. This clears the way for colonisation by sphagnum moss, which has lengthy roots that draw up moisture from below and can hold water – the main ingredient in a bog – like a sponge. A sphagnum moss bog grows upwards at about 1mm per year, reaching on average 10m deep.

Ireland's Disappearing Bogs

Peat is 100% organic, made up of undecomposed plant matter, and since ancient times has been cut into briquettes, dried and used as fuel. Originally dug by hand, new bog growth could keep pace with human consumption. But machine extraction has accelerated the process beyond a sustainable level. While once about 17% of Ireland was made up of bogland, at the present rate of extraction there could soon be none left.

The idea of bog conservation is a recent development. Previously the habitats were considered at best fuel banks and at worst useless-cum-dangerous ground. No-one valued bogs culturally either; people were happy to let the stereotypical image of the turf cutter with his donkey fade into the past.

The bog-conservation movement is receiving determined scientific help from Holland, which realised too late the significance of its own bogland and is trying to regenerate the remaining sections at considerable expense. While the current aim is to preserve 10% of bogland, some argue that all extraction should cease immediately.

As well as providing fuel bogs preserve ancient remains. Just as with plant matter, human artefacts fail to decompose in the sterile environment created by acidity and lack of oxygen. Remains from 5000 years ago, such as human bodies, wooden trackways, wheels and buckets, have been discovered.

For more information, or to become a Friend of the Bog, contact the Irish Peatland Conservation Council (☎ 01-872 2397, e ipcc@indigo.ie; Capel Chambers, Capel St, Dublin 1).

Kildare is also the capital of the Irish thoroughbred trade, and is twinned with its US equivalent Lexington Fayette in Kentucky.

Information The seasonal TIC (☎ 521 240, Market House, open 10am-5.30pm Mon-Sat May-Sept) is in the central Market Square.

The Bike Shop (☎ 522 309, Claregate St; closed Sun, Mon & Wed afternoon) is on the main road 200m west of centre.

Things to See & Do A visit to the **National Stud & Japanese Garden** is recommended (see Day 1 of the Heart of Ireland Explorer ride (p75).

The solid presence of **St Brigid's Cathedral** looms over Kildare's town square. It has a fine west-facing stained-glass window that depicts the three main saints of Ireland: Patrick, Brigid and Colmcille. The 10th-century round tower is Ireland's second highest at 32.9m.

Places to Stay & Eat *Fremont (☎ 521 604, Tully Rd)* Doubles from €51. B&B 200m south of the square. *Castleview Farm (☎ 521 816, Lackaghmore)* Doubles from €56. A friendly farmhouse 4.5km west of Kildare, signposted 3km off the N7. *Singleton (☎ 521964, 1 Dara Park)* Doubles from €46. A modern house just off Station Rd north of the square. *Curragh Lodge*

(☎ 522144, Dublin St) Doubles from €102. A two-star hotel with ensuite rooms.

Groceries, takeaways and pubs are found on the main square. *Silken Thomas* pub *(☎ 521 695, Dublin Rd)* In a converted cinema, the restaurant serves dishes such as fine Irish oak-smoked salmon (€7) and beef stroganoff (€16). Speedy *Macari's Food Fare* does sit-down kebabs and chip butties from €6.

Getting There & Away Lying 40km west of Dublin, Kildare is very well served by trains. They run between Dublin and Kildare (€11, 30 minutes to one hour, four hourly) on the Dublin to Galway, Waterford, Limerick/Ennis and Cork lines.

A fast and frequent Bus Éireann (☎ 01-836 6111) service runs between Kildare and Dublin (€8, one hour, hourly); another runs to Limerick (€14, 2¾ hours, hourly).

By bicycle access Kildare near the end of Day 1 of the Heart of Ireland Explorer ride (p75).

THE RIDE (see map p88)
From Kildare town ride north past the Hill of Allen to cross the Grand Canal at the picturesque hamlet of Robertstown (16km) and on to **Donadea Forest Park** (29.9km), a good place for a picnic lunch. The park is the woodland grounds of a former estate, complete with an abandoned castle.

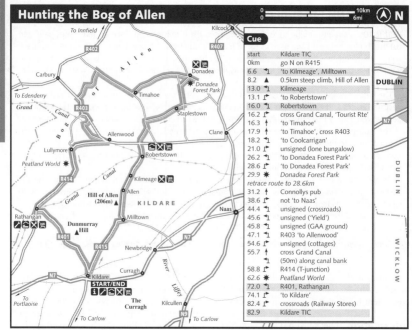

Hunting the Bog of Allen

Cue		
start		Kildare TIC
0km		go N on R415
6.6	↰	'to Kilmeage', Milltown
8.2	▲	0.5km steep climb, Hill of Allen
13.0	↰	Kilmeage
13.1	↱	'to Robertstown'
16.0	↱	Robertstown
16.2	↱	cross Grand Canal, 'Tourist Rte'
16.3	↑	'to Timahoe'
17.9	↑	'to Timahoe', cross R403
18.2	↰	'to Coolcarrigan'
21.0	↱	unsigned (lone bungalow)
26.2	↰	'to Donadea Forest Park'
28.6	↱	'to Donadea Forest Park'
29.9	✳	Donadea Forest Park
retrace route to 28.6km		
31.2	↑	Connollys pub
38.6	↱	not 'to Naas'
44.4	↰	unsigned (crossroads)
45.6	↰	unsigned ('Yield')
45.8	↰	unsigned (GAA ground)
47.1	↰	R403 'to Allenwood'
54.6	↱	unsigned (cottages)
55.7	↑	cross Grand Canal
	↰	(50m) along canal bank
58.8	↱	R414 (T-junction)
62.6	✳	Peatland World
72.0	↰	R401, Rathangan
74.1	↱	'to Kildare'
82.4	↱	crossroads (Railway Stores)
82.9		Kildare TIC

The first sighting of the **bog** (at about 35km) comes between Donadea Forest Park, Timahoe and the turn-off (47.1km) before Carbury. The expanse of brown stretches as far as the eye can see. Another stretch (at about 62km) occurs on the road between Allenwood and Lullymore.

No sizable towns lie en route, although there are *grocery stores* at the petrol station (24km) before the gates of Donadea Forest Park, and in Rathangan. Limited supplies can be bought at Kilmeage and Robertstown.

Navigation takes concentration in places – one *boreen* (lane) can look much the same as another. Late in the ride, a turn-off 2.1km after Rathangan ('to Kildare', 74.1km) is easy to miss. The R401 here is marked on maps as the through-road, but it is necessary to turn right off the through-road, on to what looks like a minor road.

In the last few kilometres, the route passes **Peatland World** (62.6km; ☎ 860 193), a low-key converted farmstead on a mission to educate local children as much as visitors about the ecology and harvesting of the bog, people's dependence on peat for fuel, and bog flora and fauna.

Slieve Bloom Mountains

Duration	3–5½ hours
Distance	55km
Difficulty	hard
Start/End	Kinnitty

This is a spectacular, tough and satisfying ride over isolated Slieve Bloom in the heart of Ireland. For fit cyclists, or those who can afford to take all day, we traverse the hills twice. From the summit of Mt Arderin on a clear day it is said you can see 15 counties.

NATURAL HISTORY

Topping out at 526m on Mt Arderin, the Slieve Bloom Mountains are not alpine, but high enough to sport a harsh upland climate where blanket bog is boss.

The surviving bog on the summit (elsewhere much has been destroyed) was designated a nature reserve in 1985. A rare information board is the only man-made sign of the habitat's status.

Blanket bogs form in areas where the average annual rainfall is over 1200mm and rain falls at least 235 days a year. But how does upland soil, on slopes as steep as 20 degrees, remain waterlogged allowing peat to form? Heavy rainfall washes minerals such as iron down to the lower layers of the soil, where they form an impermeable barrier called an iron pan. Mountain blanket bog, so-called above 152m, grows to an average depth of 1.2m to 3m.

PLANNING
When to Ride
The summer season brings a trickle of visitors to Kinnitty, but the village retains an isolated feeling year-round. Spring and summer bring a cycle of wildflowers in bloom; heather can be seen from late summer into autumn.

Maps & Books
The Slieve Bloom Rural Development Society (☎ 0509-37299) produces its own recreational sketch map of the hills, showing the glens and the Slieve Bloom Way walk. However, if you wish to venture from the road, you need the OSI 1:50,000 No 54 Discovery map.

What to Bring
The uplands are dogged by anti-cycling weather; rain falls two out of every three days. Check the forecast, carry wet-weather gear and hope for a clear day. Carry supplies for the whole ride.

ACCESS TOWN
Kinnitty
☎ 0509
In the northwestern shadow of the Slieve Bloom Mountains lies pretty Kinnitty, an easy place to kick back after the day's climbing. The smart village plays host to visitors to the mountains, and to renowned Kinnitty Castle Hotel, the turreted venue of celebrity weddings nearby.

Information The local development society (☎ 37299, open Tues-Fri & Sun afternoon June-Aug) in the Community Centre at the top of the green, offers tourist information.

Things to See & Do Kinnitty's attractions are the mountains and pubs. The **Slieve Bloom Mountains** are wild and sweeping, yet little visited. The summit area is one of

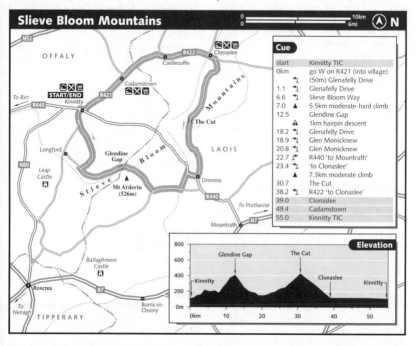

Slieve Bloom Mountains

Cue	
start	Kinnitty TIC
0km	go W on R421 (into village)
	(50m) Glenafelly Drive
1.1	Glenafelly Drive
6.6	Slieve Bloom Way
7.0	5.5km moderate-hard climb
12.5	Glendine Gap
	1km hairpin descent
18.2	Glenafelly Drive
18.9	Glen Monicknew
20.8	Glen Monicknew
22.7	R440 'to Mountrath'
23.4	'to Clonaslee'
	7.3km moderate climb
30.7	The Cut
38.2	R422 'to Clonaslee'
39.0	Clonaslee
49.4	Cadamstown
55.0	Kinnitty TIC

the largest areas of mountain blanket bog in the country. Vales worth exploring on foot or by bike include Glendine, Glenafelly and the road heading north to Cadamstown and Clonaslee.

Although this is good mountain-bike country, no trails or facilities have been established. The 80km **Slieve Bloom Way** is a circular walk; check out its cycling potential at the TIC.

A local curiosity is the **pyramid** that marks the Bernard family vault in the graveyard. The Bernards were formerly lords of Kinnitty Castle; the vault was built after one son visited Egypt.

Leap Castle (pronounced **lep**) was largely ruined during the 1922 civil war. It is reputedly inhabited by a smelly ghost as well as the distinguished (and very much alive) Sean Ryan, who frequently puts on Irish music sessions (inquire at the Community Centre) and may show visitors round, although the castle is not officially open to the public. Leap Castle is 10km south off the R421 to Roscrea.

Places to Stay & Eat You can nearly always find a pillow and fry-up in Kinnitty. Whenever surplus guests at Kinnitty Castle fill the B&Bs, private homes get the call.

Ardmore House (☎ 37009, e *ardmore house@eircom.net)* Doubles from €52. Enjoy a peat fire, traditional furnishings and freshly baked scones for breakfast. *Slieve Bloom Bar* (☎ 37010, e *tjbyrne@iol.ie)* Doubles from €52. This pub has comfy modern rooms, and live music at weekends. *Kinnitty Castle* (☎ 37318, w *www.kinnitty castle.com)*, 1.5km northeast on R421, has doubles from €240. Luxury in a restored neo-Gothic fantasy.

Self-caterers will find only a small village store with basic supplies. If dining out try *Glendine Bistro* (☎ 37973) Set dinner €26. A high-class restaurant with a cosmopolitan atmosphere, serving dishes such as Atlantic mussels and honey-roast duck. B&B (singles/doubles from €45/64) is available upstairs. Otherwise toasties in the *pub* are your grub.

Getting There & Away The nearest Bus Éireann services run to Birr (p108), a reasonable 14km ride to the west. The nearest train station is Tullamore, which lies 26km

northeast, on the Dublin–Galway and Dublin–Westport/Ballina lines. Services to/from Dublin (€13, 1¼ hours, eight Monday to Saturday, five on Sunday). By bike access Kinnitty on Day 2 of the Heart of Ireland Explorer ride (p77).

THE RIDE

Cross the mountains twice on this short and strenuous circuit that showcases plunging glens and lonesome pines. The two high passes are the Glendine Gap (410m; 12.5km), heading southwest, and the Cut (430m; 30.7km), returning northeast. The hairpin plummet off Glendine Gap is tricky, especially if you ogle the best view in the region down Glendine East on the way.

Clonaslee (39km) back down at sea level, is the first place to get *refreshments*. Further on, Cadamstown (49.4km) is another nice place for a break. A romantic disused mill and ruins of St Luna's abbey lie next to the road on the Silver River (which enters little ravines).

Westmeath Lakeland & the Fore Valley

Duration	4½–8½ hours
Distance	83.8km
Difficulty	easy
Start/End	Mullingar

Take a pleasant day trip around the green and easy lakeland north of Mullingar. The ride wends around the boggy nose of Lough Derravaragh and touches the tips of Loughs Lene and Ennell. The pivot point is the picturesque little valley and village of Fore, the site of the mythical Seven Wonders of Fore and synonymous pub.

This lakeland region is highly regarded in the world of angling. Myriad lakes pepper the area.

PLANNING
When to Ride
This low-lying landscape can be cycled year-round, depending on daily conditions.

Maps & Books
The Westmeath Tourism Council (☎ 044-48571; Presentation House, Harbour St, Mullingar) produces a leaflet for the Fore

Trail, on which this ride is based, with a sketch map and tourist information. The OSI 1:250,000 Holiday map *Ireland East* covers the ride.

ACCESS TOWN
Mullingar
☎ 044

With a great choice of traditional drinking holes and good restaurants, lively Mullingar (An Muileann gCearr) is famous for its beef. Most establishments are on the main street, which changes name four times, from the west: Dominick St, Oliver Plunkett St, Pearse St and Austin Friars St.

Information Mullingar TIC (☎ 48650, Oliver Plunkett St) is at the traffic-light junction with Mount St. There's a number of banks on the main street. The Bike Shop (☎ 40487, Mount St) is south of the TIC traffic lights on the junction with the N52 Tullamore Rd. Kenny's Cycles (☎ 41671, Austin Friars St) is down an alley beside the Druid's Chair bar.

Things to See & Do Mullingar reels in the visitors with excellent fishing on Loughs Ennell, Owel and Derravaragh and countless other smaller lakes nearby.

About 5km south of town on the shores of Lough Ennell is **Belvedere House, Gardens & Park** (☎ 49060, N52 Tullamore Rd, open daily). This magnificent, restored, 18th-century stately home stands in 160 acres of grounds. A visitor centre tells the

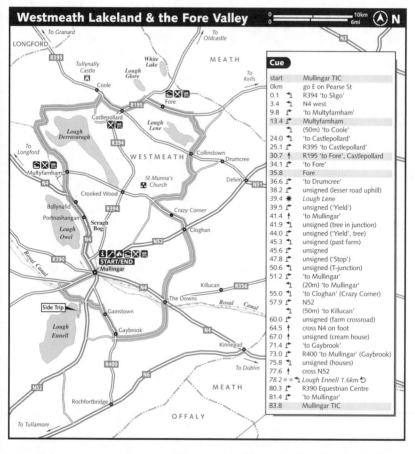

Westmeath Lakeland & the Fore Valley

0 —— 10km
0 —— 6mi

Cue	
start	Mullingar TIC
0km	go E on Pearse St
0.1 ↰	R394 'to Sligo'
3.4 ↰	N4 west
9.8 ↱	'to Multyfarnham'
13.4 ↱	Multyfarnham
↰	(50m) 'to Coole'
24.0 ↰	'to Castlepollard'
25.1 ↱	R395 'to Castlepollard'
30.7 ↑	R195 'to Fore', Castlepollard
34.1 ↱	'to Fore'
35.8	Fore
36.6 ↱	'to Drumcree'
38.2 ↱	unsigned (lesser road uphill)
39.4 ✳	*Lough Lene*
39.5 ↱	unsigned ('Yield')
41.4 ↑	'to Mullingar'
41.9 ↰	unsigned (tree in junction)
44.0 ↰	unsigned ('Yield', tree)
45.3 ↰	unsigned (past farm)
45.6 ↱	unsigned
47.8 ↱	unsigned ('Stop')
50.6 ↰	unsigned (T-junction)
51.2 ↱	'to Mullingar'
↰	(20m) 'to Mullingar'
55.0 ↰	'to Cloghan' (Crazy Corner)
57.9 ↱	N52
↰	(50m) 'to Killucan'
60.0 ↱	unsigned (farm crossroad)
64.5 ↑	cross N4 on foot
67.0 ↑	unsigned (cream house)
71.4 ↱	'to Gaybrook'
73.0 ↱	R400 'to Mullingar' (Gaybrook)
75.8 ↰	unsigned (houses)
77.6 ↑	cross N52
78.2 ●●↰	*Lough Ennell 1.6km* ↻
80.3 ↱	R390 Equestrian Centre
81.4 ↱	'to Mullingar'
83.8	Mullingar TIC

To Granard
LONGFORD
R395
Tullynally Castle
Coole
White Lake
Lough Glore
MEATH
To Oldcastle
N3
To Kells
Fore
R195
Lough Lene
Castlepollard
Lough Derravaragh
R394
WESTMEATH
Collinstown
Drumcree
To Longford
Multyfarnham
N4
Crooked Wood
St Munna's Church
Delvin
N51
Ballynafid
R394
Crazy Corner
Portnashangan
Scragh Bog
Cloghan
Lough Owel
N4
N52
Royal Canal
R390
START/END
Mullingar
Killucan
R356
The Downs
Royal Canal
Side Trip
Gainstown
Lough Ennell
Gaybrook
N4
Kinnegad
R400
To Dublin
N6
N52
MEATH
Rochfortbridge
OFFALY
To Tullamore

estate's story, including the earl's 31-year imprisonment of his wife, and, don't panic, there is a *café*.

The town is famous for beefcake as well as beef. The annual **Mullingar Guinness Bachelor Festival** (☎ 48571) takes place every July when bachelors from all around the world undertake tasks that test their manliness and personality, such as completing an army obstacle course and performing a party piece on stage. Spectators meanwhile supportively drink copious amounts to their health.

Traditional pubs with music sessions include *Danny Byrnes* (Pearse St), *Hughes Corner House* (cnr Castle & Pearse Sts) on Wednesdays and *Temple Bar* (Mount St), round the corner from the TIC, on Sunday afternoons.

Places to Stay & Eat The nearest camping ground is *Lough Ennell Caravan & Camping* (☎ 48101, N55 Tullamore Rd). Tent sites €13. This place lies close to the lake 8km south of town.

B&Bs include *Woodside* (☎ 41636, Dublin Rd) Singles/doubles €34/51. A family home 1km east of centre along the main street towards Dublin. *Southfield Court* (☎ 84666, Lynn Rd) Singles/doubles €35/52. A big bungalow 2km south down the N52 Tullamore Rd.

The *Greville Arms Hotel* (☎ 48563, Pearse St) Singles/doubles/triples €64/115/132. The welcoming three-star town hotel, slap-bang in the centre, has a comfortable carvery and bar. Guest James Joyce immortalised the place in his writings and is in turn immortalised in wax on the stairs.

Mullingar boasts several good restaurants. *Oscar's* (☎ 44909, 21 Oliver Plunkett St)*, featuring a menu that varies from 300g steak (€19) to ricotta tortellini (€5). *Le Lys*

(☎ 84844, 28 Oliver Plunkett St) This French restaurant has a chef's menu featuring burgundy snails in garlic sauce (€10) and good vegetarian choice (vegetable strudel in wild mushroom sauce costs €11).

Sunday beef roast (€8) at the Greville Arms *Coffee Shop* (open 9am-7pm) is an institution. Also on offer are quiche and salad (€7) and Baileys cheesecake (€3).

Getting There & Away Bus Éireann runs frequent services from Mullingar to Dublin (€10, 1½ hours, four daily), on its Dublin–Longford/Sligo route. The pick-up point in Mullingar is Castle St. Lying on the Dublin–Sligo line Mullingar is also well served by trains to Dublin (€13, 1¼ hours, four daily). On your bike access Mullingar on Day 5 of the Heart of Ireland Explorer ride (p81).

THE RIDE (see map p91)
Follow the cues carefully for a gentle, if not-so-short day out; don't be confused by several nameless junctions drowned in greenery.

Turf cutting may be in progress in the bogland around Lough Derravaragh (around 16km) and there are long views of **Lough Lene** (39.4km) and Lough Ennell (on a short side trip down to the shore at 78.2km).

The picturesque **Fore** (35.8km) and its nearby Christian ruins fall about halfway. The remains of St Fechin's Church, the Anchorite Cell and Benedictine Priory give the day historical spice, while the village has a pub named after the legend of the Seven Wonders of Fore. These include water that flows uphill and the tree that won't burn, and all arise from the religious beliefs of the old settlers.

Some supplies are available en route at Fore, Castlepollard and Multyfarnham.

Southeast

HISTORY

Strategically, the southeast was, and is, the natural gateway from Britain and Europe. The first landing of the Anglo-Normans in 1169 was at Bannow Bay, prompting 800 years of English involvement in Ireland.

During his bloody 1649 tour Oliver Cromwell sacked Wexford and killed 1500 civilians, including all the town's Franciscan friars.

Several towns have memorials to leaders of abortive rebellions against the English. The 1798 rising led by Father John Murphy was sparked by torture of anyone suspected of belonging to the United Irishmen, a group which demanded home rule by any means. Murphy's men had a number of minor victories until defeat at Vinegar Hill near Enniscorthy. Fifty years later, sparked by the Great Famine and minor revolutions in Europe, the Young Ireland movement rose up in the region, but was quelled.

NATURAL HISTORY

Southeastern Ireland is fertile and undulating, dominated by agriculture, with much smaller areas of bogland than the Midlands, and quite a number of middling mountain ranges. Until the advent of modern farming, it was the only region in Ireland where grain could be grown.

CLIMATE

The southeastern counties are the sunniest and driest part of what is a damp little island, with an average of seven hours' sunshine a day during July and August, an hour more than elsewhere. The region also enjoys the warmest sea temperatures in the country.

INFORMATION
Maps

OSI 1:250,000 Holiday map *Ireland East* covers most of the area, the *Ireland West* and *Ireland South* maps feature in the western perimeters.

Information Sources

The South East Regional Tourism Authority (☎ 051-875 823, ⓦ ireland-southeast .travel.ie; The Granary, 41 Merchants Quay, Waterford) is responsible for tourism in the area.

GATEWAY CITIES
Dublin

See Dublin (p65).

Waterford
☎ 051

The principal city in southeast Ireland, Waterford (Port Lairge) is a busy commercial centre and port with a small number of visitor attractions. As for the last 1000 years, the 1km-long quayside on the River Suir provides the focal point of the settlement. The south bank is lined with sleek public places and pubs. Behind it lies the old town, which was once completely walled, and nowadays seethes with shoppers during the day and drinkers in the evenings. The hand-blown Waterford crystal made here is one of Ireland's most famous exports and attracts tourists in droves.

Information The busy TIC (☎ 875 823, W ireland-southeast.travel.ie; The Granary, 41 Merchants Quay, open 9am-7pm Mon-Sat year-round & 11am-5pm Sun July-Aug) is in a converted warehouse. There are several

banks along the Quay. Ulsterbank has an ATM and a bureau de change.

Altitude Cycle & Outdoor shop (☎ 870 356, e altitude@indigo.ie, 22 Ballybricken), located behind and above the main town centre, also hires out bikes.

Things to See & Do Waterford's main attraction is the **Museum of Waterford Treasures** (☎ 304 500, Merchants Quay, adult/student €6/4), in the same building as the TIC. Audio guides are available for a tour of gold, bronze and crystal treasures, and some fascinating history.

Waterford was so critical in the defence and control of the southeast coast and waterways that **city walls** were constructed around 1000 and extended by English King

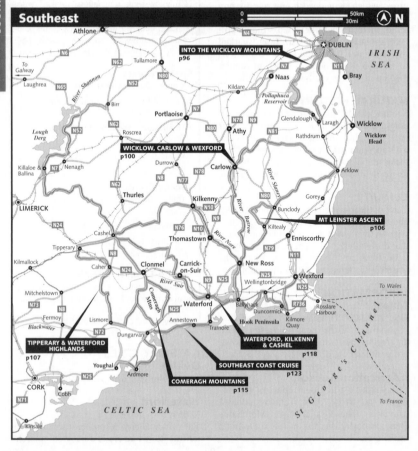

John from 1200. Remnants can be seen near the Theatre Royal at the southeastern end of the quayside. The best of the several remaining towers is **Reginald's Tower** (☎ 304 220, The Mall, adult/student €2/1), at the southeastern corner of the riverfront. Built by the Normans 800 years ago with walls three to four metres thick, these towers were the city's key fortification.

Waterford's fine neighbouring riverways can be enjoyed on a **Classic Galley Cruise**, which serves lunch (noon, €18), tea (3pm, €11) or dinner (7pm, €32) from Easter to September. Book at the TIC and catch the boat at Meagher Quay nearby.

Waterford's **Light Opera Festival** contends with Wexford's serious opera festival, putting on productions such as *Jesus Christ Superstar*. The 12-day festival takes place every September. Contact the Theatre Royal box office (☎ 874 402).

From the 3034-piece Harrods fountain to the not-so-humble hand-cut whiskey tumbler (from €30), **Waterford Crystal** has made the town a household name around the world. At the factory are organised tours (☎ 373 311, adult/student €6/4) of the workshops and the showroom, where the sound of beeping tills mingles with that of tinkling chandeliers. The factory employs 1600 workers; the highly skilled glass blowers, cutters and engravers take eight to 10 years to learn their trade. It lies on the main N25 Cork road, 2km southwest of the town centre.

Places to Stay Despite its size Waterford is not good for budget accommodation. The nearest camping grounds are at Tramore (p126) seaside resort, 10km to the south. An Óige **Arthurstown Hostel** (☎ 389 411) Dorm beds €8. It's 10km east at Arthurstown via the Passage East ferry.

For B&Bs try **Beechwood Guesthouse** (☎ 876 677, 7 Cathedral Square) Doubles €42. Cheap and facing the cathedral at the eastern end of town centre in a pedestrian area. **O'Connell House** (☎ 874 175, 3 O'Connell St) Singles/doubles €32/57. A Georgian town house in the street parallel to the quayside behind the TIC. **Sion Hill House** (☎ 851 558, e sionhill@eircom.net, Ferrybank) Singles/doubles from €39/62. A spacious Georgian house 300m east of the city bridge on the N25.

Dooleys Hotel (☎ 873 531, Merchants Quay) Singles/doubles €102/140. A comfortable, friendly place with a fine restaurant and Sunday lunch carvery.

Places to Eat Off Broad St pedestrian square is the funky, ethical **Cafe Bia** (Arundel Lane) Dairy-free No Moo smoothie is €3; breakfasts include steamy paninis. **Bewley's** (Barronstrand Lane) Good standard fare; located between the pedestrian area and the quayside. **California Cafe** (8 The Mall) Gourmet coffee and imaginative light meals at around €6, in a trendy little place near Reginald's Tower.

Dinnertime, head to the pub/hotel complexes. The **Reginald** (☎ 855 087, The Mall) Pork and walnut parcels for €17, also vegetarian dishes till 10.30pm and a complete early-bird dinner from 3pm to 7.30pm for €16; near Reginald's Tower. **Dooleys Hotel** (Merchants Quay) Lunchtime carvery (€8) in the bar every day (12.30pm to 2.30pm) and à la carte thereafter in the restaurant.

Haricots (☎ 841 299, O'Connell St) A good wholefood restaurant up behind the TIC. Hummus pancake and salad €9, blackcurrant layer cake €3. **Chicago Pie Pizzaria** (☎ 878 211, 10 O'Connell St) Good value tasty pizzas from €6.

Getting There & Away Following the demise of Euroceltic Airways in 2003 there were no passenger flights operating to Waterford Airport (☎ 875 589) at the time of writing. Phone to inquire if services have resumed.

Bus The Bus Éireann station (☎ 879 000) is on the far side of the river from town to the quay near the TIC. Buses run to Dublin (€13, 2¾ hours, hourly, two on Sunday), Rosslare Harbour (€18, 55 minutes, four daily, three on Sunday), Limerick (€21, 1½ hours, four daily, three on Sunday) and Cork (€20, 1¼ hours, hourly).

RapidExpress Coaches (☎ 872 149) has a stop in Parnell St (200m inland from Reginald's Tower) with services to Carlow (€9, 1¼ hours, more than 10 daily), Dublin (€13, three hours, ten daily) and Dublin Airport (€17, four hours, nine daily).

Train From Plunkett Station (☎ 873 401, 24-hour talking timetable ☎ 01-805 4233) on the northern side of the river there are direct services to Dublin (€22, 2½ hours, four daily; bikes are not allowed on the 4.30pm service from Dublin), Kilkenny (€7, 45 minutes, four daily), Kildare (€21, two hours, four daily) and Rosslare Harbour (€11, 1½ hours, twice daily Monday to Saturday).

Rosslare Harbour
☎ 053

Rosslare Harbour (Ros Láir) is one of Ireland's four passenger ports, serving the southeast corner of the country with ferries between Wales (for Britain) and France. There is a youth hostel, and B&Bs, widely scattered around the area, offer passengers an early breakfast if required.

Rosslare Strand to the north has a long sandy windsurfing beach, and the harbour lies on the Wexford coastal path. Otherwise this is a no-frills ferry port.

Information The TIC (☎ 33232, open daily Apr-Sept) lies at Kilrane, 3km along the main N25. There is a Bank of Ireland with an ATM and bureau de change on St Martin's Rd, which runs off the N25.

Places to Stay & Eat An Óige *Rosslare Harbour Hostel (☎ 33399, e rosslareyh@ oceanfree.net)* Dorm beds €12. Uphill from the harbour near the supermarket, it has several smaller rooms. It opens early and late for ferry passengers.

Many B&Bs overlook the harbour and line the N25 out of the port. *Elmwood (☎ 33321)* Singles/doubles €33/50. Open May-Sept. Close to ferry near the town church. *Marianella (☎ 33139, Kilrane)* Singles/doubles €30/50. Easy to find on the N25 1km out of harbour with restaurants nearby. *Hotel Rosslare (☎ 33110, atop the cliff)* Singles/doubles €63/100. More upmarket with views across St George's Channel.

On the N25 is *MacFadden's Bar & Restaurant (☎ 33590, Kilrane)* Mains €10-13. This place, about 2.4km from the harbour terminal, serves meals between noon and 9.15pm.

Getting There & Away Rosslare Harbour is well serviced by trains and buses. For details of international ferry services to the UK and France see Getting There & Away in the Travel Facts chapter (p258).

Bus Bus Éireann (in Waterford ☎ 051-879 000) runs buses to Dublin (€13, 3¼ hours, nine to 12 daily), Wexford (€4, 20 minutes, 16 daily, fewer on Sunday), Waterford (€12, 1¼ hours, three to five daily), Cork (€18, 3¾ hours, two to four daily) and Galway via Limerick (€22, 6¾ hours, twice daily).

Train Services from Rosslare Europort station at the end of the harbour run to Dublin (€15, 3½ hours, three to four daily) via Wexford (€3, 30 minutes, three to four daily). There are also trains to Waterford (€8, 1½ hours, two per day Monday to Saturday), Limerick (€16, four hours, one per day Monday to Saturday) and Cork (€16, five hours, one per day Monday to Saturday).

Bicycle Rosslare Harbour lies a little way off Day 1 of the Southeast Coast Cruise ride (p125). The most direct route to Wexford is to follow the N25. To pick up the ride at its nearest point westward (towards Kilmore Quay and Waterford) set off also on the N25 and after 4km (at Tagoat) go left on the R736. After approximately 9km go left signed for Kilmore Quay (the town is about 21km from Rosslare Harbour and good for a first stop). You can pick up the ride at a second point, cutting out Kilmore Quay, if you continue on the R736 for another 9km to near Duncormick (at 30.7km go left 'to Carrick on Bannow').

Into the Wicklow Mountains

Duration	2 days
Distance	115.7km
Difficulty	moderate–hard
Start/End	Dublin

The Wicklow Mountains, slap-bang on Dublin's doorstep, are full of geographical variety – waterfalls, lakes, mountains of all shapes and sizes, forests and open moorland.

On this weekend ride each day has an up-and-over profile that showcases the main east–west passes, the Sally Gap and the Wicklow Gap. The overnight stop is Laragh, the pleasant village nearest the ancient monastic site of Glendalough. (From Laragh the Around Ireland ride, p251, continues to Arklow for the night.)

Book of Kells, Trinity College

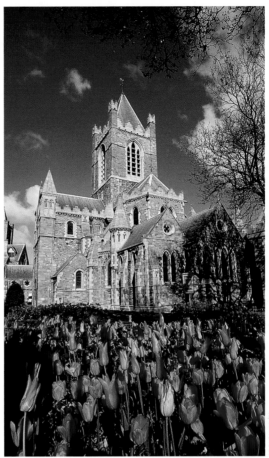
Christ Church Cathedral, Dublin

Don't tell this bike what to do!

Ha'penny Bridge, Dublin

Phoenix Park, Dublin

U2 it ain't, but here's rock'n'roll rural-style; rock on up to the Rock of Cashel in County Tipperary...

...and roll on down the verdant slopes of County Wexford.

Each day also has an aquatic highlight. Below the Sally Gap is the lovely Glenmacnass valley and waterfall. Beyond the Wicklow Gap lie the picturesque shores of Pollaphuca reservoir, the storehouse for Dublin's potable water.

HISTORY

From the suburbs to Laragh the ride follows the old Military Road, constructed by the British in the 19th century to reach the Wicklow rebels. A feat of engineering, the road traverses open bog and barren mountainscapes for 50km, continuing from Laragh southwest over Cullentragh Mountain down into Glenmalure and on to Aghavannagh.

NATURAL HISTORY

During the last Ice Age glaciers filled the upper reaches of the range, the most obvious impact being the carving of deep, steep-sided valleys, notably Glendalough (Gleann dá Loch; 'valley of the two lakes') on Day 1.

Much of the higher ground is covered with blanket bog. The steeper and drier ground supports a cover of ling and bell heather, and bilberry. The most varied plant and animal life is found in the valleys. Sessile oaks and their natural companions, birch, rowan, holly, hazel and ash, have staged a recovery from near extinction following 17th-century decimation felling for building materials and charcoal.

With luck you may see deer, hybrids of the red and Sika species, which are now plentiful. Red squirrels live in the conifers beside the Upper Lake at Glendalough and on a quiet day you may see foxes and hares, and smell, if not see, feral goats. The moors are home to red grouse, skylarks and meadow pipits. More elusive kestrels, merlins and peregrine falcons may also be spotted.

PLANNING
When to Ride

Any time of year is good, although as a mountain ride with exposed sections check the weather forecast before leaving, and expect the temperature to drop and the winds to strengthen as you climb. The tops are utterly without shelter.

In July and August the mountains are busy with visitors, especially coach parties to the main attraction, Glendalough.

Maps

OSI 1:50,000 Discovery map Nos 50, 56 and 62 cover the ride, also the OSI 1:250,000 Holiday map *Ireland East*.

What to Bring

Carry all supplies for Day 1; after the suburbs (there's shopping at Rathfarnham) there are no villages until Laragh, which has a *store*, but no bank or bike shop.

ACCESS TOWN
Dublin

See Dublin (p65).

THE RIDE (see maps p72 & p98)
Day 1: Dublin to Laragh

2½–5 hours, 47.4km

This memorable day has a big early climb, a remote traverse of high ground and descent via a waterfall (not literally) to Laragh and the side trip to Glendalough, the monastic site in the heart of the mountains. This sub-50km ride may allow a few hours there.

Escaping the city's clutches involves hard pedalling up the skirts of the mountains. As the gradient steepens the buildings give way to woodland, the air freshens and a sense of freedom returns. The 15.5km ascent starts at the turn-off for the Sally Gap on the R115 (8.7km) and finishes just below the summit of Powerscourt Mountain (24.2km) near the top of the Wicklow Mountains.

The big climb done, the next 9km is a spectacular cruise along the desolate Military Road surrounded by blanket bog and bare summits. Glacial valleys fall away sharply to the east at Glencree and from the Sally Gap crossroads (27.7km) to Loughs Tay and Dan.

On the swooping descent to Laragh the road drops into the wooded head of the valley of **Glenmacnass** beside the spectacular cascade (40.7km). This is a good place for a more sheltered breather after the high moorland plateau.

When navigating the suburbs, follow directions carefully. The route takes the most direct way to the Sally Gap and Glendalough, although this is not well signposted until after Rathfarnham at about 5km.

Warning: the climb out of Dublin may be interrupted by youths racing cars up and down the hillside. Hug the gutter whenever a roaring engine becomes audible.

Side Trip: Glendalough
20 minutes, 4km return

To reach Glendalough follow signs from Laragh village green (along R756). Sprinkled around the shores of the Upper and Lower Lakes in the lovely glacial Vale of Glendalough, the monastic 'city' founded by St Kevin in the 6th century shows monks could pick a site. In early Christian times it catered for thousands of students and teachers, and during the Dark Ages helped earn Ireland its reputation as a country of saints and scholars.

The visitor centre (☎ 0404-45325, adult/student €3/2) shows an informative film, *Ireland of the Monasteries*, about the community. The small and evocative buildings are reached on a well-trodden path, the **Lower Lake cluster** lies a few hundred metres from the visitor centre. The **Upper Lake** is 2km up the valley, in a situation worth the walk. The Lower Lake has the more interesting buildings, including a graveyard, the 10th-century 33m-high **round tower**, the **Cathedral of St Peter and St Paul** and the **Priest's House**. A guided tour is recommended.

Laragh
☎ 0404

Pretty Laragh (Láithreach) nestles between the mountains at the point where the Glenmacnass, Glendasan and Avonmore rivers converge on their way to the sea.

Laragh has plenty of places to get a nibble, including a fine pub, and plenty of beds. In July and August book ahead; the

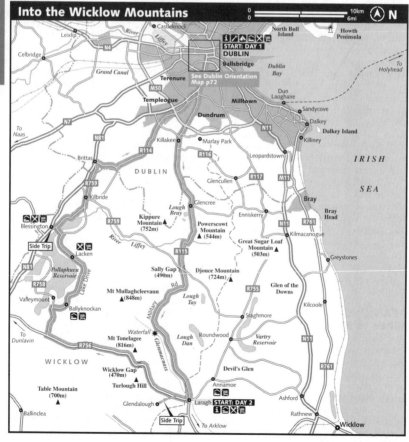

Into the Wicklow Mountains – Day 1

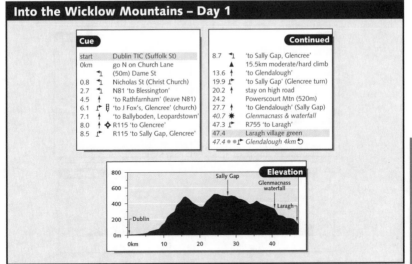

Cue			Continued
start	Dublin TIC (Suffolk St)	8.7 ↰	'to Sally Gap, Glencree'
0km	go N on Church Lane	▲	15.5km moderate/hard climb
↱	(50m) Dame St	13.6 ↑	'to Glendalough'
0.8 ↰	Nicholas St (Christ Church)	19.9 ↰	'to Sally Gap' (Glencree turn)
2.7 ↰	N81 'to Blessington'	20.2 ↑	stay on high road
4.5 ↑	'to Rathfarnham' (leave N81)	24.2	Powerscourt Mtn (520m)
6.1 ↱ 🅿	'to J Fox's, Glencree' (church)	27.7 ↑	'to Glendalough' (Sally Gap)
7.1 ↑	'to Ballyboden, Leopardstown'	40.7 ✳	Glenmacnass & waterfall
8.0 ↑ ◆	R115 'to Glencree'	47.3 ↰	R755 'to Laragh'
8.5 ↰	R115 'to Sally Gap, Glencree'	47.4	Laragh village green
		47.4 ● ● ↰	Glendalough 4km ↩

Elevation — Dublin, Sally Gap, Glenmacnass waterfall, Laragh (elevation profile, 0km to 40+, 0m to 800m)

---

place is a honey pot for visitors. The Glendalough TIC (☎ 455 808, open Tues-Sun June-Sept) is in Laragh.

Places to Stay & Eat An Óige *Glendaloch* (☎ 45342, e glendaloughyh@ireland.com, The Lodge, Glendalough) Dorm beds €16. On the road to the Upper Lake of Glendalough 2km west of Laragh. *Glendalough River House* (☎ 45577, e glendaloughriver house@hotmail.com, Derrybawn) Singles/ doubles €51/72. A 200-year-old house, 1km west of Laragh on the walking route to Glendalough. *Glendale* (☎ 45410, e merrigan@ eircom.ie, Glendalough) Singles/doubles €36/50. About 1.5km east of Laragh on R755 Annamoe road. *Carmel's* (☎ 45297, e carmelsbandb@eircom.net, Annamoe) Ensuite doubles €50. About 3km east along R755 Annamoe road from Laragh.

Weather permitting *Ann's Coffee Shop* serves lunches and teas on the green outside her house. *May's Tearooms* does toasties, scones and teas for around €4. *Lynhams Inn*, a welcoming old pub on the green, serves food until 8.30pm, with a dinner menu of €25 (eg, Laragh-style black pudding with red-wine sauce and roast stuffed leg of Wicklow lamb). *Wicklow Heather Restaurant* (Glendalough Rd) An unpretentious family-run place that does Irish stew €12, also baguettes and toasties.

Day 2: Laragh to Dublin
4–7 hours, 68.3km
The return leg to Dublin climbs the mountains early via the Wicklow Gap, then floats downward to the real highlight of the day, a shimmy around the shores of the Pollaphuca reservoir (also spelt Poulaphouca, and known as Blessington Lakes).

The **Wicklow Gap** (7.8km) is at 470m, where boggy moorland and craggy slope rule. Neither the climb nor the descent is particularly steep, although they are exposed. The gap lay on the second stage of the 1998 Tour de France en Irelande. The descent follows a reshaped valley that is part of Dublin's hydroelectric power scheme.

Created in 1940 when the rising waters drowned 76 farmhouses and cottages, the **Pollaphuca reservoir** is the holding tank for Dublin's drinking water. The route around the shores has fine, long views. In the 1820s Ballyknockan (25km) became home to quarrymen and stonecutters who hewed granite for the building of Dublin. The hamlet's **buildings** display skilful carvings and architectural features.

Halfway along, the town of Blessington on the far side of the reservoir (2km return) is suitable for a lunchtime stop with a small number of *pubs* and *eateries*.

Late in the day watch out for an easy-to-miss turn. At 50.1km, without a signpost, the

SOUTHEAST

Into the Wicklow Mountains – Day 2

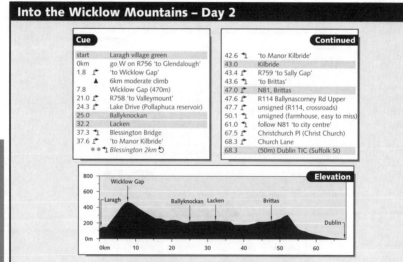

Cue	
start	Laragh village green
0km	go W on R756 'to Glendalough'
1.8 ↱	'to Wicklow Gap'
▲	6km moderate climb
7.8	Wicklow Gap (470m)
21.0 ↱	R758 'to Valleymount'
24.3 ↱	Lake Drive (Pollaphuca reservoir)
25.0	Ballyknockan
32.2	Lacken
37.3 ↰	Blessington Bridge
37.6 ↱	'to Manor Kilbride'
● ● ↰	*Blessington 2km* ↺

	Continued
42.6 ↰	'to Manor Kilbride'
43.0	Kilbride
43.4 ↱	R759 'to Sally Gap'
43.6 ↰	'to Brittas'
47.0 ↱	N81, Brittas
47.6 ↱	R114 Ballynascorney Rd Upper
47.7 ↱	unsigned (R114, crossroads)
50.1 ↰	unsigned (farmhouse, easy to miss)
61.0 ↰	follow N81 'to city centre'
67.5 ↱	Christchurch Pl (Christ Church)
68.3 ↱	Church Lane
68.3	(50m) Dublin TIC (Suffolk St)

Elevation

R114 (just a lane) turns left at right angles off the lane you have been travelling on, to a lesser lane. The junction is tiny, the only feature being a stone farmhouse on the corner. Don't miss it if you don't want to cross the mountains a second time.

Wicklow, Carlow & Wexford

Duration	3 days
Distance	216.3km
Difficulty	easy–moderate
Start/End	Arklow

Dramatic mountain backdrops, fine towns and the lovely River Barrow mark this tour of choice landscapes in Counties Wicklow, Carlow and Wexford.

From Arklow, the route runs to the foot of Lugnaquila, the tallest peak in the Wicklows, then exits the high land cross-country to Carlow, a party town on the Barrow where the half-castle tells a blinding tale. The trip next day down the river is a highlight of the region. Glassy waters lead between high verdant land via the prettiest towns and villages. At New Ross, don't miss the famine ship, SS *Dunbrody*. The final side of the triangle leads along the eastern skirts of the Blackstairs Mountains back to Arklow.

PLANNING
When to Ride

Rarely, the road to Aghavannagh on Day 1 might be blocked by bad weather, but only in the depths of winter. Otherwise, this is a year-round ride with the universal proviso that accommodation is harder to get, and costs more, in July and August.

Maps

The ride is covered by the OSI 1:250,000 Holiday map *Ireland East*.

What to Bring

Carry all provisions for the 30km between Aughrim and Baltinglass (43.3km), the first feasible stopping point after the mountains on Day 1. Rathdangan also has a small store.

ACCESS TOWN
Arklow
☎ 0402

Arklow (An tInbhear Mór) is a small and busy town on the mouth of the Avoca river. All facilities are easy to find, including a night out on the town at any of the plentiful pubs and good restaurants.

Information The TIC (☎ 32484, Main St, open Mon-Sat May-Sept, Mon-Fri Oct-Apr) is operated by the community rather than the tourist board from October to April.

The town bike shop is Blacks Cycle Centre (☎ 31898, Wexford Rd).

Things to See & Do From its start as a minor fishing village, Arklow became one of the country's busiest ports and a centre of boat-building. Sir Francis Chichester's *Gypsy Moth IV* (now on show at Greenwich in London) and the Irish training vessel *Asgard II* were built here. In 1841 there were 80 schooners working from the harbour. A walk along the **quayside** is pleasant although it bears few marks of the town's maritime history.

During the 1798 rising, 20,000 Irishmen led by Father John Murphy tried to storm the town. They were defeated, however, by the better equipped and trained British Army.

Murphy and 700 rebels died in the battle. A **monument** in front of St Mary & St Peter's church commemorates them.

Places to Stay & Eat On the road out to Dublin, 300m from the centre, is *Avonmore House Hostel* (☎ 32825/33855, e avonmorehouse@eircom.net, Ferrybank) Dorm beds €13, doubles €26.

Vale View (☎ 32622, e pat.crotty@ifi.ie, Coolgreaney Rd) Doubles from €52. This edwardian house with rooftop sun lounge, lies 200m off the roundabout on R772 Main St. *Valentia* (☎ 39200, e valentiahouse@esatclear.ie, Coolgreaney Rd) Singles/doubles from €33/54. Comfortable family home. *Inver Dea* (☎ 33987, Ferrybank) Singles/doubles from €33/50. About 500m from

SOUTHEAST

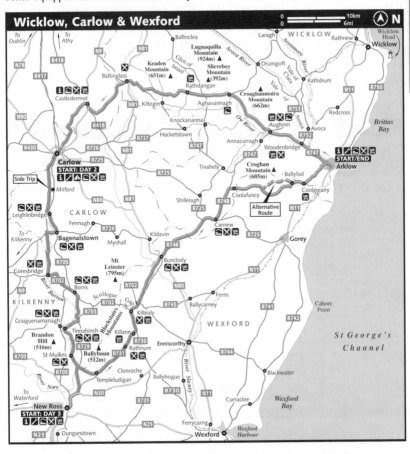

centre on the Dublin road. ***Royal Hotel*** (☎ *32524, Main St*) Singles/doubles from €45/78. Central with a comfy bar.

Head to Main St for dinner by 8pm; seafood is big on the menu. ***Oscars*** (☎ *32683, 31 Main St)* Grills and seafood. Also BBQs Monday to Thursday on a garden terrace with retractable roof. Jazz sessions from 6.30pm to 8.30pm on Sunday. ***Lazy Lobster Restaurant*** at Birthistles pub *(☎ 32253, Main St)* Red snapper daily for €9. ***Garden View Restaurant*** upstairs at Murphy's pub (☎ *32781, 49 Main St)* An early-bird menu 6pm to 7.30pm for €19. Lunch is served in the pub: salmon, duck or a sizzling vegetarian platter (€14).

Getting There & Away Bus Éireann runs services from Arklow to Dublin (€9, 1½ hours, 10 daily), Wexford (€11, 1¾ hours, 10 daily), New Ross (€11, 1½ hours, four daily) and Waterford (€14, two hours, four daily). Trains go to Dublin (€11, 1¾ hours, five daily) and Wexford (€11, 1¼ hours, five daily).

To access Arklow by bike see the Around Ireland ride (p251); it is also 30km south-

east of Laragh, the overnight stop on the Into the Wicklow Mountains ride (p96).

THE RIDE (see map p101)
Day 1: Arklow to Carlow
3½–6½ hours, 67.5km
Scenic valleys, the Wicklow's highest peak, a round tower and arrival at the River Barrow sum up the first day of the ride.

From Arklow head inland along the wooded valleys of the Avoca and Aughrim rivers to Aughrim town (13.6km). This is the mouth of the glen that leads to Aghavannagh and is overlooked by Lugnaquilla Mountain (924m), the highest in the Wicklows. The route stays low despite the surrounds until a 1.6km climb over a shallow, exposed saddle (25.8km) at the head of the valley. The An Óige ***Ballinclea youth hostel*** (☎ *045-404 657)* also lies at the head of the valley.

At Castledermot (54.7km) any atmosphere of the **religious ruins** is spoiled by appalling lorry traffic. The ruins are of a 13th-century Franciscan friary, two 10th-century high crosses, a 20m-high round tower topped with a medieval battlement and a 12th-century Romanesque church doorway.

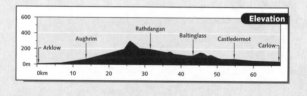

Wicklow, Carlow & Wexford – Day 1

Cue				Continued
start	Arklow TIC	44.0 ↑		unsigned (not 'to Ballitor')
0km	go W on Main St (uphill)	47.5 ⬏		'to Castledermot'
0.2 ⬏	R747 'to Avoca'	54.7 ⬏		R418
6.6 ⬑	'to Aughrim', Woodenbridge	⬏ ✳		(30m) N9, Castledermot
13.4 ⬏	R753 'to Rathdrum'	55.4 ⬑		R418 'to Athy'
13.6 ⬑	'to Aghavannah', Aughrim	⬑		(20m) unsigned (minor road)
14.4 ⬏	'to Aghavannah'	58.4 ↑		unsigned (not left, wall)
22.9 ↑	unsigned (low road)	59.1 ⬑		unsigned (gate)
24.2 ↑	'to Rathdangan' (nr Aghavannah)	61.1 ⬑		unsigned (T-junction, bridge)
▲	1.6km moderate climb	62.4 ⬏		'to Carlow'
31.5	Rathdangan	65.6 ↑		cross N80, Dublin St
37.9 ⬑	'to Baltinglass'	66.8 ↑		'to town centre'
40.2 ⬏	R747 'to Baltinglass'	67.2 ⬑		Tullow St (Irish Nationwide)
43.3	Baltinglass	67.5 ⬑		College St
43.5 ↑	cross river 'to Ballitor'	67.5		(20m) Carlow TIC (LHS)

Elevation

600 / 400 / 200 / 0m — Arklow — Aughrim — Rathdangan — Baltinglass — Castledermot — Carlow

0km   10   20   30   40   50   60

Carlow

☎ 059

Carlow (Ceatharlach) has plenty of buzz for a regional Irish town. Loads of shops, innumerable pubs, live music and a tasty spread of cookhouses make it ideal for a weekend on the tiles. Tourists have little else to attract them, other than the remarkable Browne's Hill Dolmen on the outskirts – one of Ireland's postcard stalwarts.

The town sits astride the River Barrow, one of Ireland's loveliest waterways, which empties into Waterford harbour. A towpath runs along the west bank.

The shops and pubs are broadly arranged around Dublin St, which runs north–south, and Tullow St, which runs east off the southern end. The N9 Dublin–Waterford road bypasses east of the centre.

Information The TIC (☎ 913 1554, open Mon-Fri, Sat July-Aug) is neatly hidden in College St, just south of the cathedral off Tullow St. It shares premises with the library, which fronts Tullow St, but has its own side entrance.

A well-stocked bike shop, Coleman Cycles (☎ 913 1273), is on the main north–south Dublin St.

Things to See & Do Strolling around Carlow in good weather can be pleasant. Wander along the **River Barrow** west of centre past the rowing clubhouse and south towards **Graiguecullen Bridge**, one of the oldest and lowest on the Barrow.

Set back from the gushing weir and lock are the remains of once mighty **Carlow Castle**. Built in the 12th century, the great keep stood intact for 700 years, and even survived a 17th-century Cromwellian assault. Things took a turn for the worse in the 19th century when a local doctor decided to convert the castle into an asylum. That, he reckoned, required enlarging the arrow-slit windows with dynamite. The explosions destabilized most of the structure and practically three-quarters of the keep had to be demolished. All that remains are a single wall and two corner towers. Welcome contemporary enhancements include a walkway and bower.

Northeast of town, next to the train station, is **Carlow Microbrewery** (☎ 913 4356, admission €4), a seedling of the American craft breweries, where traditional Celtic

nectar is made using local ingredients and methods. Beer tasting and a beer garden cater for visitors' needs, and Guinness should watch out in case the award-winning O'Hara's Celtic stout catches on.

The area around Tullow St was the site of fierce fighting in the 1798 rising between United Irish rebels and the English. The bloodiest fight of the rebellion saw 640 Irish killed, and their bodies thrown into a mass grave. A Celtic high cross marks what is known as the **Croppie Grave**, after the men's short haircuts, a signal of their allegiance to the independence movement. Find the grave in Barrow St, on the west bank north of Graiguecullen Bridge.

The monster capstone of **Browne's Hill Dolmen** portal tomb, or *cromlech*, is the largest of its kind in Europe and weighs over 100 tonnes. Various theories exist as to how Neolithic people lifted the stone into place, slanting it over four smaller portal stones. The site would have been created sometime between 1500 and 3000 BC for funerary rites and ceremonies. It sits without pomp in a field and can be seen from the road 3km east of town, along the R726 Hacketstown road (from the outer end of Tullow St, turn to face north along the N9 and immediately go right).

Among others, catch **Irish music sessions** at the *Carlovian*, and live music Saturdays at *McHughs*. *The Foundry Club* *(Tullow St)* has live bands 11pm to 2.30am most nights.

Places to Stay & Eat IHH *Otterholt Riverside Lodge* (☎ 913 0404, Kilkeeny Rd N9) Dorm beds/doubles €13/17. A grubby, tatty hostel (with camping) on the banks of the Barrow.

Red Setter House (☎ 914 1848, 14 Dublin St) Doubles €52. Dead central B&B. *Barrow Lodge* (☎ 914 1173, e georgepender@eir com.net, The Quay) Singles/doubles €33/56. Central B&B by the river near the rowing club. *Carlow Guesthouse* (☎ 913 6033, e carlowguesthouse@eircom.net) Singles/doubles €39/64. A B&B 1km north of the centre on N9; one of a cluster. *Barrowville Town House* (☎ 914 3324, w www.bar rowvillehouse.com) Singles/doubles €45/70. An elegant Georgian guesthouse leaving little to be desired by way of comfort, 1km south of town on the busy N9.

SOUTHEAST

Óstan Din Rí (☎ *914 3311, Tullow St*) Singles from €51. Modern lodgings in the heart of Carlow's nightclub land, designed so that people can fall upstairs into their rooms from the nightclub below. *Seven Oaks* (☎ *913 1308, Athy Rd*) Doubles from €50. North of Dublin St, this more traditional hotel also has a leisure centre.

Pubs with good restaurants are easy to find, as are coffee shops and fast-food joints all along Dublin and Tullow Sts. *Bon Appetit* (*133 Tullow St*) has a full Irish breakfast for €5. *Supermac's* (bottom of Dublin St) serves decent all-Irish burgers and chips. *The Beams* (☎ *913 1824, 59 Dublin St*) is a recommended old coaching inn.

The *Carlovian Restaurant* (☎ *913 0911, Tullow St*) Serves a wide menu until 9pm: guinea fowl (€17), polenta moussaka (€11). *McHugh's Court House Hotel* (☎ *913 3243, Dublin St*) The Jury House Restaurant is open Saturday and Sunday until 10pm, serving the same menu in the bar Monday to Friday: stir-fry chicken (€10), fajitas (€13) and lamb cutlets (€14).

Day 2: Carlow to New Ross

3½–6 hours, 61km

The River Barrow flows smoothly south to its estuary at New Ross through reedy banks, weirs and wharves, and a clutch of picturesque towns. The best sight comes last: the riverside ruins of St Mullins.

Don't pass over the side trip to **Milford Mills** (7.2km) where the 18th-century water management is awesome. The mill generated the power that made Carlow the first inland town with electric street lighting. **Leighlinbridge** (12.5km) has an ancient bridge, ruined castle and marina and in summer positively swings (with hanging baskets).

St Mullins (47.4km) proves the pick of the day. High on the river bank on the edge of the village this place of antiquity and tranquillity was once abundant in little churches and high crosses. The ruins date to the 10th century and are faced by modern-day graves. The village green is in fact the bailey (the wooden-staked encampment) of the motte (earthen mound with a fort on top) built in the 12th century by Anglo-Normans. There are toilets and a *café* on the way out of the village, but little else by way of facilities.

Between Carlow and Borris (31.4km), the route runs at river level. Thereafter the valley deepens between the Blackstairs Mountains and Brandon Hill (516m) and the road rises and falls about 60m or so half a dozen times.

Watch out for one quite dangerous descent approaching New Ross on the R729 at 50.7km. The twisting, narrow road is used by heavy lorries and is slippery in the wet.

New Ross
☎ 051

An estuary town where the Barrow broadens towards the sea, New Ross (Ross Mhic Thriúin) is full of wharves and lorries and has a cheerful main street where refreshments are easy to find.

In May 2001 the town jumped squarely aboard the tourist trail with the opening of the SS *Dunbrody* famine ship moored at the quayside in the middle of town. The ship is a full-size replica of a three-masted barque that just 150 years ago carried hundreds of Irish people away from starvation to the New World.

Information The TIC (☎ 425 239, open 9am-6pm daily) and SS *Dunbrody* Visitor

Wicklow, Carlow & Wexford – Day 2

Cue		
start		Carlow TIC
0km		go S on College St
	⤵	(20m) Tullow St
0.2	↑	Castle St (cross Dublin St)
0.3	⤵	Kennedy St (to bridge)
0.6	⤴	Leighlin St ('to golf club')
7.2	⤴●	*Milford mill 1km* ↻
11.5	⤵	N9 'Barrow Drive'
	⤴	(30m) 'to Leighlinbridge'
12.3	⤴	cross bridge
12.5	⤵	R705 'to B'town', Leighlinbridge
16.6	⤵	Flame Fireplaces, Bagenalstown
16.8	⤵	R724 'to Kilkenny'
18.5	⤴	'to Goresbridge', R Oak (not N9)
25.0	⤴	R702, Goresbridge (Kelly's bar)
31.4		Borris
32.6	↑	R729 'to Graiguenamanagh'
37.4	⤵	R703 'to Graiguenamanagh'
41.0	⤴	'to St Mullins', T'hinch/G'managh
45.3	⤵	'to St Mullins'
47.4	⤴	'to St Molings Mill', St Mullins
50.2	⤵	R729 'to New Ross'
50.7	⚠	500m twisting descent with traffic
51.4	⤤	unsigned (RH bend)
57.0	⤵	N30, 'to New Ross'
60.5	⤵	Bridge St (New Ross)
60.6	↑	South Quay (N25)
61.0		New Ross TIC (SS Dunbrody)

Centre share premises on the quayside next to the ship.

Fred James Cycles (☎ 421 328, Priory St) is a well-stocked bike shop. There's also Paddy Meyler (☎ 640 626, 6 New Bridge St).

SS Dunbrody A guided tour (☎ 425 239, admission €6) on and below the decks of the SS *Dunbrody* is an eye-opener; a close-up of the cramped conditions endured by millions of Irish people trying to escape disease and starvation. A film show is included in the frequent tours, and a database held below decks contains records of more than two million passengers who emigrated to the USA between 1820 and 1920.

Although their transports were known as 'coffin ships', 97% of passengers survived the 45-day crossing. Among them were the Kennedys, a local family that went on to great things stateside. The project is an American creation involving funding from the JFK Trust.

Places to Stay & Eat The IHH *Mac-Murrough Farm Hostel (☎ 421 383, w www.macmurrough.com)* Dorm beds €12, doubles €26. Family rooms and laundry. There is farm produce in season at this well-run hostel 3.5km northeast of town.

Venroode (☎ 421 446, e michelstom@ hotmail.com, Southknock) Singles/doubles €33/50. This hotel, off William St Lower, overlooks the river. *Riversdale House (☎ 422 515, e riversdalehse@eircom.net, William St Lower)* Singles/doubles with en-suite €37/52. A modern house 500m from the centre. *Brandon House Hotel (☎ 421 703)* Singles/doubles from €77/116. The best address in town, it is located off the N25, to the south.

Boosted partly by the *Dunbrody*'s appeal, eating out in New Ross is a good experience. *River View Cafe (South St)* does Irish breakfast for €6. The best selection of coffee in town is found at *Café Nutshell (South St)*, which doubles as a health-food shop. *Bewleys (South St)*, Ireland's famous tearoom chain, has a decent quiche lunch for €4.

Opposite the ship, the restaurant at *John V's pub (☎ 425 188, South Quay)* serves a broad menu until 9pm including Atlantic scallops (€20) and vegetarian tomato mornay

SOUTHEAST

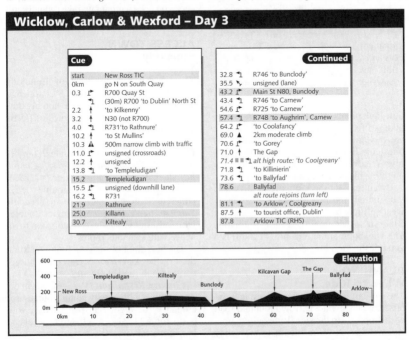

Wicklow, Carlow & Wexford – Day 3

Cue			Continued		
start		New Ross TIC	32.8 ↰		R746 'to Bunclody'
0km		go N on South Quay	35.5 ↘		unsigned (lane)
0.3	↱	R700 Quay St	43.2 ↱		Main St N80, Bunclody
	↰	(30m) R700 'to Dublin' North St	43.4 ↰		R746 'to Carnew'
2.2	↑	'to Kilkenny'	54.6 ↱		R725 'to Carnew'
3.2	↑	N30 (not R700)	57.4 ↰		R748 'to Aughrim', Carnew
4.0	↰	R731 'to Rathnure'	64.2 ↱		'to Coolafancy'
10.2	↑	'to St Mullins'	69.0 ▲		2km moderate climb
10.3	◮	500m narrow climb with traffic	70.6 ↱		'to Gorey'
11.0	↱	unsigned (crossroads)	71.0 ↑		The Gap
12.2	↑	unsigned	71.4 ▮▮ ↰		*alt high route: 'to Coolgreany'*
13.8	↰	'to Templeludigan'	71.8 ↰		'to Killinierin'
15.2		Templeludigan	73.6 ↰		'to Ballyfad'
15.5	↱	unsigned (downhill lane)	78.6		Ballyfad
16.2	↰	R731			*alt route rejoins (turn left)*
21.9		Rathnure	81.1 ↰		'to Arklow', Coolgreany
25.0		Killann	87.5 ↑		'to tourist office, Dublin'
30.7		Kiltealy	87.8		Arklow TIC (RHS)

Elevation

(€9). Nearby on South Quay the kitchen at *Katie Pat's* (☎ *422 404*) is also open until 9pm, with another menu for all tastes, including items such as seafood platter (€8). *Il Primo* (☎ *425 262, South St*) is a smart and popular Italian joint with pizzas from €7.

Day 3: New Ross to Arklow
5–8½ hours, 87.8km

The final day of the ride swivels back northwest along the eastern skirts of the Blackstairs ridge and makes a moderate crossing of the Croghan outcrop down to Arklow. The views are good considering the effort is light. Navigating and finding a bevvy are easy too.

The lovely Barrow valley north of New Ross gets the juices flowing before a steady haul up to Templeludigan (15.2km). The great radio mast of 795m-high Mt Leinster keeps you company on lanes as far as Bunclody (43.2km), a pleasant place for lunch, and the start/end of the Mt Leinster Ascent ride. Thereafter lanes undulate to Croghan Mountain for a civilised 2km traverse of the Gap (71km). An alternative high route has better views to the coast, and is detailed in the cues, but falls late in the day.

Mt Leinster Ascent

Duration	2–3 hours
Distance	42.4km
Difficulty	hard
Start/End	Bunclody

Few high points in Ireland are accessible by bike, so for *seriously* serious cyclists who are travelling on mountain bikes the conquest of 795m Mt Leinster on the Carlow–Wexford border is a mission they might be insane enough to accept.

By cutting out the last extreme 2.4km to the summit, the rest of us can also enjoy what still makes a lovely cruise around the Blackstairs Mountains' gentle gradients. The viewpoint at the turn-off (11.5km) is a good destination in itself.

PLANNING
When to Ride

The summit of Mt Leinster is bare and exposed, reached via a narrow mountain road with drop-offs to the side. Ride only in fine, still weather. A warm breeze in the valley

Warning: Tough Riding

⚠ The full-length climb and descent of Mt Leinster is extremely steep and very tough. The ride should be tackled only by strong, competent cyclists in calm weather, on a mountain bike.

will be a cold gale at the top. If the weather deteriorates on approach, quit. If riding alone, tell someone your plans.

Maps

The OSI 1:250,000 Holiday map *Ireland East* covers the ride.

What to Bring

Carry full weatherproof gear, including a bivvy bag or tent and survival blanket. Also bring all water and food; there are no services until Kiltealy (29.9km).

Those attempting the summit may like to leave their full panniers behind at their accommodation, while still carrying the items recommended above. Remember summiteers, you need a mountain bike (which can't be hired locally).

ACCESS TOWN
Bunclody
☎ 054

The tree-lined main street of Bunclody (Bun Clóidí) lends the town a continental air. Though small, it serves the holiday traffic for Mt Leinster, with a choice of B&Bs and a good restaurant.

Places to Stay & Eat En route 200m before town is *Weston House* (☎ *76435, Church Rd*) Doubles €52. *Moss Cottage* (☎ *77828,* e| *bgilsenan@eircom.net*) Doubles €52. Off Irish St, 300m south of town. *Meadow Side* (☎ *76226, Ryland St*) Singles/doubles with ensuite €36/64. A Georgian town house with spacious rooms.

The best dinners are to be found on Main St. Try the *American Style Diner* burger bar, and pub food at *Deanes*.

Chantry Restaurant (☎ *77482, Main St*) Top choice with meaty main courses for around €10, vegetarian penne pasta with pesto for €11, also a self-serve, weekend lunchtime carvery.

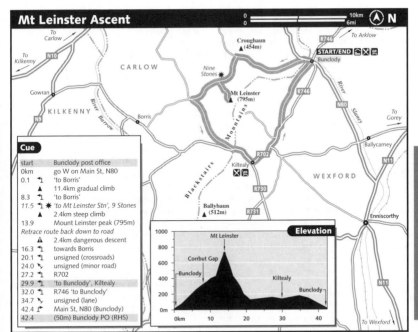

Mt Leinster Ascent

Cue	
start	Bunclody post office
0km	go W on Main St, N80
0.1 ↰	'to Borris'
▲	11.4km gradual climb
8.3 ↰	'to Borris'
11.5 ↰ ✳	'to Mt Leinster Stn', 9 Stones
▲	2.4km steep climb
13.9	Mount Leinster peak (795m)
Retrace route back down to road	
⚠	2.4km dangerous descent
16.3 ↰	towards Borris
20.1 ↰	unsigned (crossroads)
24.0 ↳	unsigned (minor road)
27.2 ↰	R702
29.9 ↰	'to Bunclody', Kiltealy
32.0 ↰	R746 'to Bunclody'
34.7 ↳	unsigned (lane)
42.4 ↰	Main St, N80 (Bunclody)
42.4	(50m) Bunclody PO (RHS)

Getting There & Away Bunclody lies on Day 3 of the Wicklow, Carlow & Wexford ride. It has no train station or national bus service.

THE RIDE

Why tackle the awesome climb to the great radio mast on top of 795m Mt Leinster? For wannabe rally-car drivers, because it's there. For a minority of extremely fit cyclists, because they can't resist a challenge and love an extraordinary view.

The road from Bunclody rises steadily in 11km to around 400m elevation on a road used by driving locals and day-trippers. The turn-off for the peak (11.5km, altitude 430m) doubles as a beauty spot with a great view of six counties of Leinster and the location of the stone circle, the **Nine Stones of Leinster**.

The last rough stage to the peak radio station is another story. The desperately steep track gains 365m in 2.4km, an *average* gradient of 1:6.5 steepening to 1:5. The mountain track is officially private, but locals drive it when the gates are open (and drive round the gates when they're shut) and the

peak is never closed to walkers. It's steep, exposed and rough with drops to the side.

The danger lies in the descent. Take it easy, especially on loose corners. Don't look at the fabulous views when you should be sizing up a rut.

Tipperary & Waterford Highlands

Duration	4 days
Distance	304.6km
Difficulty	easy–moderate
Start	Birr
End	Cashel

A family of compact mountain ranges jumps out of the plains across the southern counties of Ireland, particularly in this corner of Tipperary and Waterford. Between them the Silvermines, the Slieve Felims, the Galtys, Knockmealdowns, Comeraghs and Monavullaghs feature no summit above 1000m, yet each rises dramatically from the green farmland, with a character and colour all of its own.

The ride resembles the shape of a wiggly eye hook. The three mountain days pivot around the heritage town of Cashel. The connecting opening day comes down from Birr via the shores of Lough Derg.

Despite the title, the ride is suitable for riders of middling fitness. The route may ascend and descend four ranges like a lumbering rollercoaster, but the greater percentage of riding is at farmland level, or follows the contours.

PLANNING
When to Ride
Traversing four mountain ranges requires good weather day by day even in summer. Check the weather forecast and carry wet-weather gear and food supplies. The pesky rhododendron on the high slopes of the Knockmealdowns are indisputably glorious from May to June.

Maps
The ride is mostly covered by the OSI 1:250,000 Holiday map *Ireland East*, but near Birr (in the northwest of the ride)

The Great Telescope

You may be forgiven for rubbing your eyes at the sight of the enormous wooden barrel and the high, stone supports of the Great Telescope on the castle lawns at Birr. No doubt William Parsons, the third Earl of Rosse, blinked a little in 1845 when the project bore fruit and he pinpointed the first spiral galaxy through his monstrous creation.

Built in 1840 using just the workers on the estate, and containing a giant mirror (speculum) of polished metal, the telescope appears crude by today's standards. But for 77 years this instrument, open to the elements, was the largest in the world. Astronomers came to Birr Castle from all over the globe to boldly peer into the final frontier. Only in 1917 did a 100-inch reflector constructed in California surpass 'the leviathan of Parsonstown'.

Rosse's discovery of the spiral structure of the nebula Messier 51 near the tail of the Great Bear was a breakthrough he recorded along with other nebulae, including spirals, in a catalogue in 1850. Today, the document is one of astronomy's historic artefacts.

---

nudges into the *Ireland West* and *Ireland South* maps.

What to Bring
Mountain roads mean exposure. Carry wet-weather gear and some food supplies at all times.

ACCESS TOWN
Birr
☎ 0509
The Georgian town of Birr has a gentrified air courtesy of Birr Castle Demesne, the home of the pioneering Parsons family from the 17th century to this day.

The town was laid out by the original Parsons, Sir Laurence (who named it Parsonstown) during the Plantation in 1620 when the English colonised the country by systematically taking over lands from the resident Irish.

Granted the title of Earls of Rosse, the family later won more wholesome renown for important discoveries in the field of astronomy and photography at the castle.

Information The TIC (☎ 20110, 14 Main St, open May-Sept) is on the street that runs down south from Emmet Square.

Bike shop WM Smyth (☎ 20203, Connaught St), is on the street off Main St behind Emmet Square.

Birr Castle Demesne A visit to the Parsons family seat (☎ 20336, w www.birrcastleireland.com/new, adults/students €7/5) is recommended – allow half a day if possible. The entrance lies 500m west of Emmet Square on the Banagher road.

The most fascinating feature is the Great Telescope (see the boxed text) on the lawns a few hundred metres from the castle. Demonstrations of the recently restored telescope take place throughout the day and on request. To see the original speculum (mirror), however, you must travel to the Science Museum in London.

The Parsons were a multi-talented family and their story, together with that of other inventors, is told in the Irish Historic Science Centre, in the Galleries of Discovery in the converted castle stable-block.

While the earl stargazed, his wife, Mary, the third Countess of Rosse, pushed the limits of photography. On show are her early

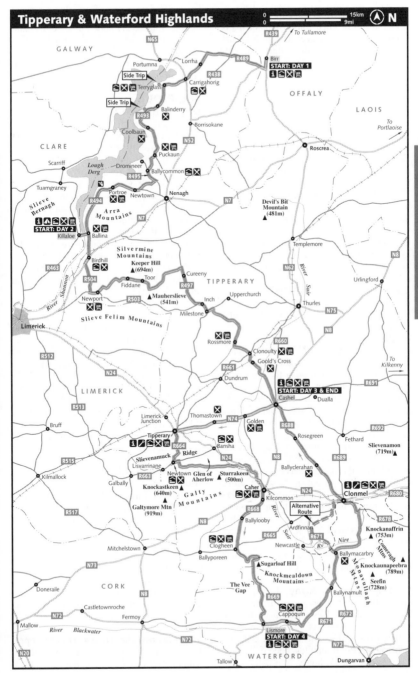

photographs, cameras and darkroom dating from the 1850s. Their sons also made major contributions to science. The fourth earl, Laurence, invented a device that accurately calculated the surface temperature of the moon a century before man landed. His brother Charles invented the high-speed steam turbine, which powered his steamship *Turbinia* with its record-breaking top speed of 35 knots.

The 50-hectare park and separate formal gardens are maintained by the current seventh Earl of Rosse and his wife. They feature the 200-year-old tallest box hedges in the world, a 90-year-old wisteria and a suspension bridge that dates from 1820. Meanwhile no less than 50 of the estate's trees are listed in the book *Champion Trees of the British Isles*.

Places to Stay & Eat Blessed with award-winning restaurants, trad pubs, and cosy accommodation, Birr is a fine place to refresh.

Ring Farmhouse (☎ 20976, e ring farm@gofree.indigo.ie) Singles/doubles from €32/52. This is a comfortable family-run dairy farm B&B, 2km southeast of Birr off the Roscrea road.

Dooly's Hotel (☎ 20032, Emmet Square) Two-bed room per person €45. There's always something going on at the cosy town coach hotel built in 1747. To eat here, choose between the *Emmet Room* restaurant, the self-service all-day *Coach House* bistro (lamb chops €8, open until 10pm) and the cosy *bar*.

Spinners Town House (☎ 21673, Castle St) Singles/doubles from €45/64, in a medieval room €58/90. This is a converted 19th-century woollen store near the castle with a lovely private courtyard garden. *Spinners Bistro* (open to 10pm daily in summer, Wed-Sun in winter) This high-quality restaurant has dishes such as salmon cakes with chive mayonnaise.

Kong Lam (Market Square) serves Kung Po and Szechuan Chinese dishes.

Getting There & Away Buses, which stop in the main square, aren't frequent, so check the times. Bus Éireann (☎ 01-836 6111) goes to Dublin (€17, 2¼ hours, once daily), Cork (€13, four hours, once daily), Athlone (€10, 50 minutes, once daily) and Limerick (€13, 1½ hours, four daily).

Kearn's Coaches (☎ 22244) runs services to Dublin (€7, 2½ hours, twice daily) and Galway (€7, 1¾ hours, once daily Friday to Monday).

To access Birr by bike see Day 3 of the Heart of Ireland Explorer ride (p77).

THE RIDE (see map p109)
Day 1: Birr to Killaloe
4–7 hours, 71.9km

Lough life is the theme of the day, although the ride, partially following the Lough Derg cycleway, runs mostly inshore. During the holidays cruiser owners whoosh past in 4WDs to their watery escapes and children pad around the towns in wellingtons. The day ends at the picturesque twin towns of Killaloe and Ballina astride Lough Derg's mouth on the Shannon.

There are several chances to leave the route and explore peaceful inlets and harbours along the way, on diversions both signposted (Terryglass, 26.2km and Mota quay, 33.9km) and spontaneous.

Towards the end of the day, the road rises steadily to skirt the Arra Mountains, where there is a fabulous view of the lough from the lookout (62.4km), in good weather.

A good place for elevenses is the comfortable *Derg Bar* at Terryglass Harbour (26.2km), which also serves food. No sizable towns lie en route, but pubs and stores are well spaced for a cycle tourist. Navigation is mostly straightforward, but there are fiddly lanes between Puckaun (45km) and Portroe (58.7km) where the directions need close attention.

Killaloe & Ballina
☎ 061

The splendid medieval 13-span bridge between Killaloe and Ballina is one of the principal crossings of the River Shannon. The twin towns occupy a lovely setting at the point where Lough Derg narrows back to river at a gateway through high land formed by the Slieve Bernagh Hills to the west and the Arras to the east. From this point the river is navigable as far north as County Sligo. In summertime the weekend sailors are out in force.

Information The TIC (☎ 376 866, open 10am-6pm daily May-Sept), is part of the Killaloe Heritage Centre on the west end of

Tipperary & Waterford Highlands – Day 1

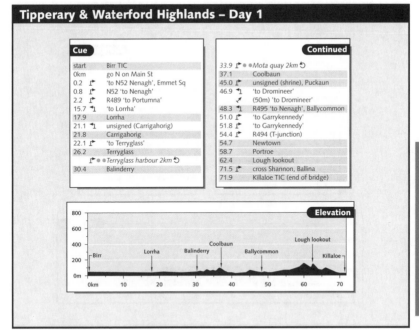

Cue	
start	Birr TIC
0km	go N on Main St
0.2	'to N52 Nenagh', Emmet Sq
0.8	N52 'to Nenagh'
2.2	R489 'to Portumna'
15.7	'to Lorrha'
17.9	Lorrha
21.1	unsigned (Carrigahorig)
21.8	Carrigahorig
22.1	'to Terryglass'
26.2	Terryglass
	Terryglass harbour 2km
30.4	Balinderry

Continued	
33.9	Mota quay 2km
37.1	Coolbaun
45.0	unsigned (shrine), Puckaun
46.9	'to Dromineer'
	(50m) 'to Dromineer'
48.3	R495 'to Nenagh', Ballycommon
51.0	'to Garrykennedy'
51.8	'to Garrykennedy'
54.4	R494 (T-junction)
54.7	Newtown
58.7	Portroe
62.4	Lough lookout
71.5	cross Shannon, Ballina
71.9	Killaloe TIC (end of bridge)

Elevation

SOUTHEAST

the bridge by the canal. The nearest bike shop is in Nenagh, 17km northeast.

Things to See & Do The lovely setting makes the twin towns a perfect place to linger in good weather. A **cruise** on Lough Derg is another way to relax and enjoy the views. The *Derg Princess* leaves daily at 2.30pm from the TIC (tickets available there) and returns beneath the bridge up the canal. The *Spirit of Killaloe* leaves from the quayside at Ballina.

The town's annual **Iniscealtra Festival of Arts** (☎ 927 290) takes place late May/early June with performances of poetry and traditional music.

Places to Stay & Eat At a scenic site on the shores of the lough 5km north of Killaloe along the Scarriff road, is *Lough Derg Holiday Park* (☎ 376 329). Tent sites €11.

Kincora House (☎ 376 149, Church St, Ballina) Dorm beds €32. *Carramore Lodge* (☎ 376 704, Roolagh) Beds €26, singles with ensuite €35. Family home overlooking the Shannon, around 500m from Ballina centre.

Lantern House (☎ 923 034) Beds €30. This guesthouse, 10km north along the Scarriff Road, overlooks the Shannon and has its own restaurant.

Crotty's Courtyard has outdoor tables in Killaloe. *Cherry Tree* (☎ 375 688; Lakeside, Ballina) has a varied modern menu.

The *Anchor Inn* near the bridge runs sessions with traditional music and dancing and serves pub grub.

Day 2: Killaloe to Cashel

4–7 hours, 77.1km

Enjoy long vistas on a high passage over the Silvermine Mountains, then a resounding finale at the snaggle-toothed Rock of Cashel.

About half the ride (20km to 60km) is up and over high ground. Climb steadily along a remote valley below Keeper Hill (694m), cross a long saddle past the bosomy outline of Mauherslieve (Mother Mountain, 541m) and drop gradually back down again. In bad weather the top road (27km to 36km) is absolutely exposed with no shelter other than infrequent farms. Find out the forecast and carry all supplies between Newport (14.5km) and Rossmore (60.6km).

Tipperary & Waterford Highlands – Day 2

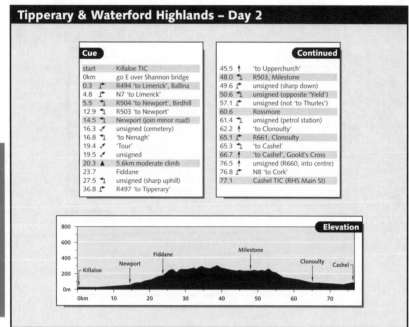

Cue	
start	Killaloe TIC
0km	go E over Shannon bridge
0.3	R494 'to Limerick', Ballina
4.8	N7 'to Limerick'
5.5	R504 'to Newport', Birdhill
12.9	R503 'to Newport'
14.5	Newport (join minor road)
16.3	unsigned (cemetery)
16.8	'to Nenagh'
19.4	'Tour'
19.5	unsigned
20.3	5.6km moderate climb
23.7	Fiddane
27.5	unsigned (sharp uphill)
36.8	R497 'to Tipperary'

Continued	
45.5	'to Upperchurch'
48.0	R503, Milestone
49.6	unsigned (sharp down)
50.6	unsigned (opposite 'Yield')
57.1	unsigned (not 'to Thurles')
60.6	Rossmore
61.4	unsigned (petrol station)
62.2	'to Clonoulty'
65.1	R661, Clonoulty
65.3	'to Cashel'
66.7	'to Cashel', Goold's Cross
76.5	unsigned (R660, into centre)
76.8	N8 'to Cork'
77.1	Cashel TIC (RHS Main St)

Elevation

Killaloe — Newport — Fiddane — Milestone — Clonoulty — Cashel
(elevation profile from 0km to 77km, 0m to 800m)

Approaching the high farms, you may encounter dogs unused to visitors (see the boxed text 'Look Out: Dogs About', (p196).

Cashel
See Cashel (p114).

Day 3: Cashel to Lismore
4½–8½ hours, 84.9km
Mountain bagging is the name of today's game. Line after line of highlands rear their heads on a tough and memorable ride with great views and two major climbs. In between, much of the route is flat, so riders can catch their breath between efforts.

After Tipperary (18.6km), the first ascent climbs the sharp ridge of **Slievenamuck** which has a stunning view from the southern escarpment over the Glen of Aherlow to the Galty Mountains (thankfully inaccessible by bike). After Caher (48.9km) come the **Knockmealdown Mountains** (72.4km), which the ride traverses steadily (300m over 8km) on a great hairpin road known as the **Vee**. Good descents reward both climbs, especially the scenic 8km down southern side of the Knockmealdowns to Lismore.

Weather permitting, you can picnic at points with outstanding views at the Slievenamuck ridge overlooking the Glen of Aherlow (25.6km), and in two places on the Knockmealdowns (67.2km, 70.6km). The latter halt has long views over the Tipperary plain to the north. In late spring the purple blooms of rhododendron enliven the slopes. But the non-native plant is a colourful blot on the landscape, as it threatens to defy containment and engulf native fauna.

Treat the ride as a day in the mountains, carry wet weather gear and supplies, and check the forecast. There is no shelter on the Knockmealdowns between Clogheen and Lismore.

Tipperary (18.6km) has all facilities, including a bike shop (Carl's, Main St), but the town is run down. Any renown is more due to the song *It's a Long Way to Tipperary* (composed by an Englishman who chose the word for its sound) than character or history.

Lismore
☎ 058
In the 7th and 8th centuries Lismore (Lios Mor) was a centre of great monastic learning,

the seat of a flourishing university established by St Cartach. After the 10th century, despite several sackings at the hands of the Vikings, the town hung on as a religious capital until the 17th century, when the remains of eight churches could still be seen.

Latter-day Lismore developed from an estate town around the vast Lismore Castle, which occupies an attractive riverside position next to the bridge coming into the town.

The TIC (☎ 54975, Chapel St, open daily Apr-Oct, closed Sun morning) is in the Heritage Centre in the old courthouse.

Things to See & Do Built in 1633, **St Carthage's Cathedral** sits in peaceful gardens. Noteworthy tombs inside include a MacGrath family crypt dating from 1557.

The **Heritage Centre** (admission €4) shows a film every half-hour on local history and attractions. The seven-acre **gardens at Lismore Castle** (☎ 54424, admission €4, open April-Sept), home to the Duke of Devonshire, feature contemporary sculpture as well as lovely views. The interior of the castle is not open to the public.

Places to Stay & Eat On the eastern side of town, with a drying room that will be useful after rain crossing the mountains, is **Beechcroft** (☎ 54273, Deerpark Rd) En-suite singles/doubles €32/50.

Pinetree House (☎ 53282) Doubles €50. To the southwest of centre. **Northgrove** (☎ 54325, e johnhoward1@eircom.net, Tourtane) Singles/doubles €30/48. Big new house on the outskirts.

Lismore Hotel (☎ 54304, Main St) Doubles €90. Dead centre, opposite the Heritage Centre, Lismore's hotel also serves mains, typically steak or chicken, from €13. Hear live 'easy-listening' Irish music in the evening on Saturday and Sunday.

Dining out is limited. **Eamon's Place** (Main St) is a cosy pub with a beer garden that provides steaks, salads and fish.

Day 4: Lismore to Cashel
4–7 hours, 70.7km

The third day in the mountains dramatically crosses the Comeraghs, then returns via Clonmel to Cashel.

Cruise on quiet lanes around the eastern skirts of the Knockmealdowns. Then, at

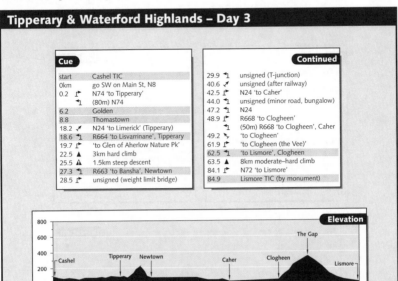

Tipperary & Waterford Highlands – Day 3

Cue

start	Cashel TIC	
0km	go SW on Main St, N8	
0.2	N74 'to Tipperary'	
	(80m) N74	
6.2	Golden	
8.8	Thomastown	
18.2	N24 'to Limerick' (Tipperary)	
18.6	R664 'to Lisvarrinane', Tipperary	
19.7	'to Glen of Aherlow Nature Pk'	
22.5	3km hard climb	
25.5	1.5km steep descent	
27.3	R663 'to Bansha', Newtown	
28.5	unsigned (weight limit bridge)	

Continued

29.9	unsigned (T-junction)	
40.6	unsigned (after railway)	
42.5	N24 'to Caher'	
44.0	unsigned (minor road, bungalow)	
47.2	N24	
48.9	R668 'to Clogheen'	
	(50m) R668 'to Clogheen', Caher	
49.2	'to Clogheen'	
61.9	'to Clogheen (the Vee)'	
62.5	'to Lismore', Clogheen	
63.5	8km moderate–hard climb	
84.1	N72 'to Lismore'	
84.9	Lismore TIC (by monument)	

Elevation

Ballymacarbry (27.2km), recharge your batteries at the ***Nire View Bar*** for the climb ahead. Patron Pat Melody is a fount of knowledge on the local highlands and runs pony-trekking from the location.

The ascent up the Nire Valley and over the northern saddle of the Comeraghs is steady. This mountain traverse is definitely the scenic route to Clonmel (the alternative R671 continues 15km along the valley bottom with less pizzazz and effort). Views north are easy to miss on the 13.7km descent – a lookout (35km) offers a second chance for appreciation. The gradient slackens as you lose height, bringing you into Clonmel (the start/end of the Comeragh Mountains ride) over the River Suir at the foot of the massif.

Be fully prepared for mountain weather on high. Study the forecast and carry all supplies between Cappoquin and Clonmel. The kilometres in the lanes soon after Cappoquin are the trickiest to navigate.

Cashel
☎ 062

A small, pleasant town, Cashel's (Caiseal) draw since the 5th century has been the Rock of Cashel north of the main street. Hot status on the tourist trail means plentiful meals and beds but the places fill up in high summer. The Rock itself becomes very crowded and tours can be delayed, so it's best to visit early or late in the day.

Information The TIC (☎ 61333, Main St, open 9.30am-6pm Mon-Sat Apr-Sept) is in the town hall. To help get your bearings a model of 1640s Cashel is on show in the small **heritage centre** in the neighbouring rooms. The Allied Irish Bank (AIB) and Bank of Ireland on Main St have ATMs. Paddywell's (☎ 63106) in Friar Street, is considering doing bike hire and repairs.

The Rock of Cashel A limestone outcrop bristling with defensive and religious buildings, the Rock (☎ 61437, admission €5) is one of Ireland's most spectacular medieval sites. For over 1000 years it was the base of the kings and churchmen who ruled the region, and for some 400 years rivalled the Hill of Tara as the centre of Irish power.

The Rock's finest structure is **Cormac's Chapel** on the south side of the cathedral.

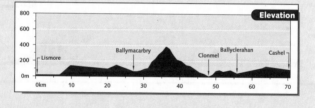

Tipperary & Waterford Highlands – Day 4

Cue	
start	Lismore TIC
0km	go N on N72 'to Cappoquin'
6.7 ↑	R669, Cappoquin
7.7 ↱	Glenshelane River Walk
8.9 ↰	'to Newcastle'
9.4 ↗	unsigned (thatched house)
↑	(50m) unsigned (whitewashed farm)
15.8 ↑	unsigned (crossroads)
20.1 ↱	Ballynamult (beyond bridge)
20.3 ↰	R671 'to Clonmel'
22.5 ↰	R671 'to Clonmel'
27.2 ↱	Nire Drive, Ballymacarbry
▲	9km moderate climb
▰ ▰ ↑	*alt route: R671 to Clonmel 15km*
32.3 ↰	Comeragh Drive

	Continued
34.1 ↰	Nire Drive
37.2 ⚠	3km steep descent
40.5 ↰	R678 'to Clonmel'
47.7 ↑	over River Suir (cross R680)
48.0 ↰	'to town centre', Clonmel
	alt route rejoins (turn left)
↱	(40m) Dillon St (flower r'about)
48.3 ↰	The Crescent
48.7 ↑	Queen St (not 'all routes')
48.8 ↱	R688 'to Cashel'
55.8	Ballyclerahan
63.8	Rosegreen
70.6 ↰	N8 'to Cork' (Cashel)
70.7	Cashel TIC (RHS)

Elevation

800
600
400 — Ballymacarbry — Clonmel — Ballyclerahan — Cashel
200 — Lismore
0m

0km   10   20   30   40   50   60   70

Built from 1127 and still completely intact, it is small and stone-roofed with unusual square towers either side. Compared with other churches of the era, the chapel is sophisticated in design and shows influence from Britain and the Continent. The dark interior has a fine archway to the east chancel. Inside the main door on the left is the sarcophagus, said to house King Cormac, dating from 1125 to 1150.

The Hall of the Vicars Choral is the restored entrance house, where a 17-minute film runs every half-hour detailing the Rock's history. Exhibits downstairs features very rare silverware and Bronze Age–axes, also a badly-worn 12th-century cross. Tradition held that the kings of Cashel and Munster were inaugurated at its base – a replica stands outside in situ.

The 13th-century Gothic **cathedral** overshadows the other ruins with its huge square tower and turrets. Scattered throughout are monuments and panels. At the western end is the **Archbishop's Residence**, a four-storey, 15th-century castle. The **Round Tower** dates from the 11th or 12th century and stands 28m tall with the door 3.5m above the ground, perhaps for defensive reasons.

Places to Stay & Eat There is no camping ground in or close to town; the nearest is 16km away: *Ballinacourty House Camping & Caravanning* (☎ 56000) Tent sites per person/tent €2/11. It's southwest in the lovely Glen of Aherlow near Newtown.

O'Brien's Holiday Lodge (☎ 61003, St Patrick's Rock, Dundrum Rd, e obriens holidayhostel@eircom.net) Dorm beds €13. This old coach house northwest of town has top views of the Rock with family rooms and laundry. *Cashel Holiday Hostel* (☎ 62330, 6 John St) Dorm beds €12, doubles €32. In a quiet turning off Main St.

Abbey House (☎ 61104, e teachnamain streach@eircom.net, 1 Dominic St) Beds/singles €26/39. A modern bungalow 150m from the Rock. *Rockville House* (☎ 61760, Dominic St) Doubles €50. *Ashmore House* (☎ 61286, w www.ashmorehouse.com) Doubles €60. Georgian family home in peaceful street, with dinner for €18. *Baileys* (☎ 61937, Main St) Doubles €64. A fine Georgian townhouse on busy main road with Rock views and restaurant. *Grove* (☎ 62382) Singles/doubles €30/52. An accommodating

family house 1km south of town on the R668 Clonmel road.

Cashel Palace Hotel (☎ 62707, Main St) Rooms from €89. Luxurious rooms in a 1730 Queen Anne hotel with its own footpath to the Rock, a cellar bar and restaurant serving fresh salmon and trout.

A well-known local delicacy available in the *supermarkets* is Cashel blue cheese. Opposite the TIC *Bakehouse (Main St)* serves light meals and good coffee till 9pm, also bread baked in the basement.

Ryan's Daughter (Ladyswell St) East of the TIC; home cooking till 9pm. *Hannigan's Bar & Restaurant (Ladyswell St)* Home-cooked meals till 9.30pm Monday to Saturday, and 9pm Sunday. A traditional pub that caters for vegetarians. *Pasta Milano (Ladyswell St)* Mains €10. Open till midnight Sat & Sun. Serves tasty Italian fare.

Getting There & Away Cashel is on the Bus Éireann lines between Dublin (€16, three hours, six daily), Cork (€13, 1¼ hours, seven daily) and Athlone (€13, 50 minutes, once daily).

For cyclists Cashel acts as a hub. This ride visits twice. The town is also the halt (from Kilkenny) on Day 2 of the Waterford, Kilkenny and Cashel ride (p122).

Comeragh Mountains

Duration	5–9 hours
Distance	90.5km
Difficulty	hard
Start/End	Clonmel

This is a long and tough mountain ride for fit cyclists who want an Irish challenge.

Four climbs mark a complete circuit of the Comeragh Mountains and sister range the Monavullaghs. The views are long and dramatic, particularly of the eastern face of the Comeragh ridge in the morning, and the Mahon Falls if you have the energy to appreciate them. And if you're lucky the sun will warm your front going out, and your back coming home, 90km later.

NATURAL HISTORY
The Comeragh Mountains and Monavullagh Mountains are a small range of rolling uplands with several summits above 700m.

The eastern side boasts fine high corries (cirques or hollows) cradling small tarns (alpine lakes) and feeding scenic waterfalls.

Wild flowers are scarce because sheep graze the entire upland area, but meadow pipits and skylarks sweeten the bleating and baa-ing.

PLANNING
When to Ride
Ride when the weather is calm and warm, which can happen in September rather than the summer months.

Maps
This ride is covered on OSI 1:250,000 Holiday map *Ireland East*, and OSI 1:50,000 Discovery map Nos 74 and 75.

The Nire Valley Heritage map (from Clonmel TIC or Melody's Nire View bar at Ballymacarbry) is a sketch map of the area at the northern end of the circuit showing ancient sites like cooking places (*fulachta fiadh*) and Ogham stones (stones inscribed with an early form of Irish writing).

What to Bring
Food and water are in short supply throughout this ride, as there are only two watering holes, at Rathgormuck and Ballymacarbry. A little store with ad-hoc opening hours is found at the hamlet of Mahon before the steep climb to Mahon Falls.

This ride is exposed and extended, which means wet-weather gear, repair kit and tools should be carried.

ACCESS TOWN
Clonmel
☎ 052
Sitting at the foot of the mountains, Clonmel (Cluain Meala) is Tipperary's largest and most cosmopolitan town and a good base for exploring the Comeragh, Knockmealdown and Galty ranges.

The main street runs east–west, starting off as Parnell St, becoming Mitchel St and O'Connell St, then passing through West Gate, to become Irishtown and Abbey Rd.

Information The friendly TIC (☎ 22960, 8 Sarsfield St, open 9.30am-6pm Mon-Sat July-Aug, 9.30am-5pm Mon-Fri Sept-June) is just south off the eastern end of the main street opposite the Clonmel Arms Hotel.

TNT Cycles (☎ 25322) lies just outside Westgate, at that end of the main street. Worldwide Cycles (☎ 21146) lies 200m north of the Main Guard, the renovated courthouse at the eastern end of the main street; or try Frank Ryan Cycles (☎ 23363, 34 Upper Gladstone St).

Places to Stay & Eat Two camping grounds are a distance out of town. *Apple Camping & Caravanning Park* (☎ 41459) Tent sites per person €6. Open May-Sept. It's 9km west of Clonmel along the busy but flat N24. *Power's the Pot Caravan & Camping Park* (☎ 23085) Tent sites per person €6. This adventurously sited camping ground is high up the slopes of the Comeraghs, 9km southeast of town along the R678.

Benuala (☎ 22158) Doubles €46. Comfortable family house 1km west of centre along Marlfield Rd, turn left off Abbey Rd. *Lisarda* (☎ 22593/22294, Old Spa Rd) Singles/doubles with ensuite €33/58. Modern bungalow walking distance to centre. *Amberville* (☎ 21470, e amberville@eir com.net, Glenconnor Rd, off Western Rd) Singles/doubles €33/50. Modern bungalow northwest of centre. *Clonmel Arms Hotel* (☎ 211 233, Sarsfield St) Doubles €116. The fine town hotel is just off Main St opposite the TIC.

On the far side of the Comeraghs from Clonmel, above Ballymacarbry just off the route is B&B *Cnoc-na-Ri* (☎ 36239) Doubles €52. It's 5km above Ballymacarbry in the Nire Valley, just beyond the Metal Bridge. Modern comfy isolated bungalow in the hills.

Getting There & Away Bus Éireann (call the Limerick office for information ☎ 061-313 333) services travel from Clonmel to Dublin (€11, 3½ hours) and Cork (€17, 1¾ hours) three times daily and twice on Sundays; and from Clonmel to Limerick (€13, 1½ hours), Waterford (€14, one hour) and Tipperary (€9, 50 minutes) seven times daily and six on Sundays.

Rapid Express Coaches (☎ 29292) runs between Dublin (Gresham Hotel) and Clonmel (€8, three hours, at least two daily).

Clonmel is on the train line between Waterford (€11, 50 minutes, once a day) and Limerick Junction (€13, 1½ hours). Connections head via Waterford to Dublin, and via Limerick Junction to Cork.

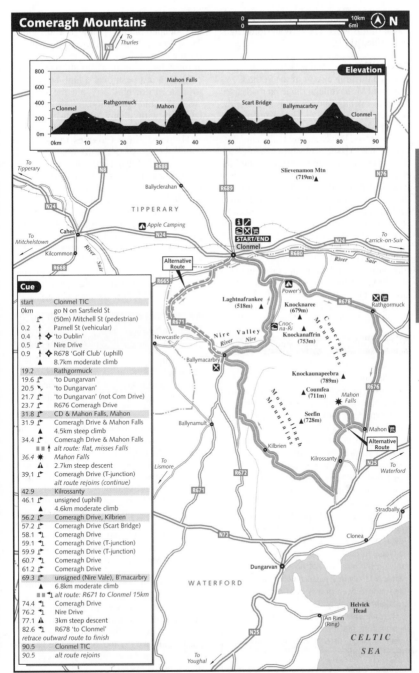

Comeragh Mountains

Elevation

Clonmel	Rathgormuck	Mahon	Mahon Falls

Scart Bridge — Ballymacarbry — Clonmel

Cue

start	Clonmel TIC
0km	go N on Sarsfield St
	(50m) Mitchell St (pedestrian)
0.2	Parnell St (vehicular)
0.4	◆ 'to Dublin'
0.5	Nire Drive
0.9	◆ R678 'Golf Club' (uphill)
▲	8.7km moderate climb
19.2	Rathgormuck
19.6	'to Dungarvan'
20.5	'to Dungarvan'
21.7	'to Dungarvan' (not Com Drive)
23.7	R676 Comeragh Drive
31.8	CD & Mahon Falls, Mahon
31.9	Comeragh Drive & Mahon Falls
▲	4.5km steep climb
34.4	Comeragh Drive & Mahon Falls
▪▪▪	*alt route: flat, misses Falls*
36.4 ✳	Mahon Falls
⚠	2.7km steep descent
39.1	Comeragh Drive (T-junction)
	alt route rejoins (continue)
42.9	Kilrossanty
46.1	unsigned (uphill)
▲	4.6km moderate climb
56.2	Comeragh Drive, Kilbrien
57.2	Comeragh Drive (Scart Bridge)
58.1	Comeragh Drive
59.1	Comeragh Drive (T-junction)
59.9	Comeragh Drive (T-junction)
60.7	Comeragh Drive
61.2	Comeragh Drive
69.3	unsigned (Nire Vale), B'macarbry
▲	6.8km moderate climb
▪▪▪	*alt route: R671 to Clonmel 15km*
74.4	Comeragh Drive
76.2	Nire Drive
77.1 ⚠	3km steep descent
82.6	R678 'to Clonmel'
	retrace outward route to finish
90.5	Clonmel TIC
90.5	*alt route rejoins*

If you're cycling Clonmel connects with Day 4 of the Tipperary & Waterford Highlands ride (p113).

THE RIDE (see map p117)

Here's a thrilling circuit of the 700m Comeragh and Monavullagh range on roads used by local cycling hero Sean Kelly (see the boxed text 'Sean Kelly – High King of Cycling', p124).

Few riders, however, tackle the complete tour of the massif, a blistering 90km-hack with four major climbs and descents, including a very steep pitch to the Mahon Falls just below the ridgeline. Not for the faint-legged, this is a long day with over 1100m of height gain and loss with precious few places to shelter and refresh. You need a degree of fitness to enjoy it: tourers well into their trip will treasure the memories.

The initial moderate 8.7km ascent from Clonmel is a good warm-up. From the saddle (290m) at the top you are in the mountains proper.

The second climb of the day is the hardest. From the hamlet of Mahon (31.8km)

the road climbs 300m in 4.5km in steeper and steeper pitches to the **Mahon Falls**. These tumble spectacularly off the edge of the high corrie. From the mountain car park at the falls (36.4km, 414m altitude, no facilities), a last push over a high bank leads to a steep downhill. (Avoid the last and steepest 2km of the climb, missing the falls but still with plenty of high-level eye-candy, on an alternative route at 34.4km).

The third climb traverses the southern end of the massif (50.7km), on an exposed moorland plod that gains 200m in 4.6km.

The western slopes of the massif are gentler and greener. The final crossing climbs the **Nire Valley** over a northern saddle, a steady gain of 320m in 6.8km (duplicating Day 4 of the Tipperary & Waterford Highlands ride, p113). You can avoid this late climb by taking the R671 from Ballymacarbry around the mountains back to Clonmel.

Navigation is relatively simple, but where the lane junctions are closely spaced and unsigned follow the cues closely.

The Magic Road of Mahon

In a land of myths and legends, here's a cyclist's dream you can test out yourself.

On the route high against the mountains about a kilometre before the Mahon Falls, lies a stretch known locally as the magic road. At this point (about 35.4km, about 50m beyond a cattle grid), with the slopes to the north and the sea in the distance to the south, occurs a phenomenon well known to the folk in the area that affects cars and should affect bicycles if you could stop and stay upright in reverse long enough.

It is said, at the right point, that a mysterious force pulls the vehicle up the hill on its own. So powerfully, it is said, that cars can be difficult to control. The author tried to test this on the bike but got no reaction. Meanwhile a family in a passing Volvo swore they had indeed been drawn from a stop up the road against gravity.

If true, what a godsend for struggling riders nearing the top of a difficult climb and grateful for any help they can get from this or the spirit world.

Waterford, Kilkenny & Cashel

Duration	3 days
Distance	209.3km
Difficulty	easy–moderate
Start/End	Waterford

Using skeins of the finest scenery this ride weaves historic towns into a charming tapestry of the southern counties.

From Waterford, catch the Passage East ferry across the harbour, visit the JFK homestead and picture-perfect Inistioge on the Nore and bed down in Kilkenny, the country's best-preserved medieval town. Continue over the gentle Slieveardagh hills to the Rock of Cashel and return to Waterford via intriguing Fethard and the small lanes of Slievenamon through the hometown of one of Ireland's cycling heroes (see the boxed text 'Sean Kelly – High King of Cycling', p124) back to Waterford.

There are no mountain climbs, although the gradient up from the ferry is steep, the ups and downs of the Nore valley need a push on the pedals, and the elongated ascent of the Slieveardagh needs patience more than it needs brawn.

PLANNING
When to Ride
Kilkenny and Cashel are hotspots on the tourist trail, and during July and August, accommodation prices rise and availability falls. At this time queues are known to form at the Rock of Cashel; visit early or late in the day.

Maps
The OSI 1:250,000 Holiday map *Ireland East* covers all ground.

ACCESS TOWN
Waterford
See Waterford (p93).

THE RIDE
Day 1: Waterford to Kilkenny
4–7 hours, 73km
The ride heads off along scenic valleys through picturesque towns to the medieval city of Kilkenny. The road rollercoasts between meadows and high outlooks along Rivers Barrow and Nore, the most scenic stretch being between New Ross and Inistioge. The day's cultural highlight is Jerpoint

Abbey (see Side Trip, p120), once one of Ireland's finest religious monuments.

The ferry (cyclists €3) at Passage East (11.5km) carries cars and pedestrians over the River Barrow between the cliffs of Counties Waterford and Wexford. At Ballyhack and Passage East this ride overlaps with the Southeast Coast Cruise ride (p123).

A little further on lies **Dunbrody Abbey** (17km; ☎ 061-388 603, admission €2), a 12th-century Cistercian establishment, with a visitor centre and *café*.

The Kennedy clan has roots in this area and the family is commemorated at the **Kennedy Homestead** (☎ 051-388 264, admission €4) at the hamlet of Dunganstown (24.6km). The house was the birthplace of John F Kennedy's great-grandfather and an exhibition tells the tale of the emigrant Kennedys and those who stayed behind.

In New Ross (31.4km) the **SS Dunbrody Famine Ship**, moored in the town centre on the quayside, is worth a visit (see New Ross, p104).

The exquisite little town of **Inistioge** (Inish-**teeg**; 47.6km) on the Nore is a bit of a film star, appearing in *Widow's Peak*

SOUTHEAST

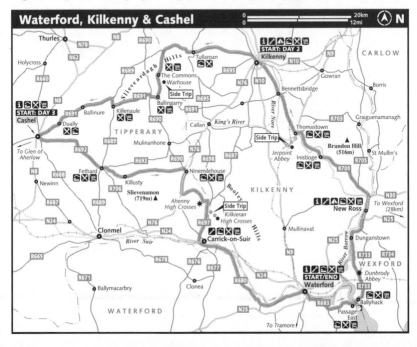

(1994) and *Circle of Friends* (1994). The medieval 10-span stone bridge is edged by a manicured sward of green, and visitors are lavished with hotels and *teahouses*.

The lovely road between Inistioge and Thomastown is marred by fast traffic, and route finding is tricky in the lanes between Dunbrody Abbey (following the turn-off to Great Island at 17.8km) and New Ross; follow the cues closely. Around the Kennedy Homestead the lanes along the Barrow's reedy banks are charming. The sharpest climb of the day is straight up from the ferry above Ballyhack. Several short climbs lie along the Nore valley to Inistioge.

Side Trip: Jerpoint Abbey
15 minutes, 4km return

Lying 1.5km southwest of Thomastown (55.4km), directly on the N9, are the spectacular ruins of Cistercian **Jerpoint Abbey** (☎ 056-772 4623, adult/student €3/2). The Romanesque details of the church date from the 12th century and the superb sculptured cloisters from the 15th century. The exhibition in the visitor centre explains the abbey's rise and fall.

Kilkenny
☎ 056

Kilkenny (Cill Chainnigh) is a smart little town and a tourist magnet. Over the centuries the largely medieval layout and fine historic buildings somehow escaped destruction at the hands of invaders. By dint of the town's international air and affluence art and crafts flourish, with cultural festivals and a number of art-show venues.

Kilkenny's castle was built in the 13th century by the Earl of Pembroke, the son-in-law of the Norman conqueror Strongbow. In the same period the town was intermittently capital of Ireland, and the venue for an Anglo-Norman parliament, which passed apartheid-like laws to prevent assimilation with the Irish. The laws failed to work; the indigenous way of life has proved attractive to occupiers and visitors alike for centuries.

In the 1640s Cromwell besieged Kilkenny for five days, destroying much of the castle and ending the town's influence in national affairs.

Information The busy TIC (☎ 775 1500, Rose Inn St) is in the heart of things on the

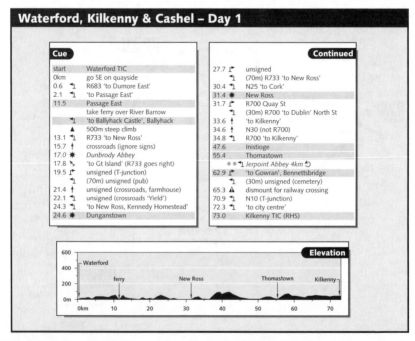

Waterford, Kilkenny & Cashel – Day 1

Cue				Continued
start	Waterford TIC	27.7 ↱	unsigned
0km	go SE on quayside	↰	(70m) R733 'to New Ross'
0.6 ↰	R683 'to Dumore East'	30.4 ↰	N25 'to Cork'
2.1 ↰	'to Passage East'	31.4 ✳	New Ross
11.5	Passage East	31.7 ↱	R700 Quay St
	take ferry over River Barrow	↰	(30m) R700 'to Dublin' North St
↰	'to Ballyhack Castle', Ballyhack	33.6 ↑	'to Kilkenny'
▲	500m steep climb	34.6 ↑	N30 (not R700)
13.1 ↰	R733 'to New Ross'	34.8 ↰	R700 'to Kilkenny'
15.7 ↑	crossroads (ignore signs)	47.6	Inistioge
17.0 ✳	Dunbrody Abbey	55.4	Thomastown
17.8 ↘	'to Gt Island' (R733 goes right)	● ●↰	Jerpoint Abbey 4km ↻
19.5 ↱	unsigned (T-junction)	62.9 ↱	'to Gowran', Bennettsbridge
↰	(70m) unsigned (pub)	↰	(30m) unsigned (cemetery)
21.4 ↑	unsigned (crossroads, farmhouse)	65.3 ▲	dismount for railway crossing
22.1 ↰	unsigned (crossroads 'Yield')	70.9 ↰	N10 (T-junction)
24.3 ↰	'to New Ross, Kennedy Homestead'	72.3 ↰	'to city centre'
24.6 ✳	Dunganstown	73.0	Kilkenny TIC (RHS)

Elevation chart: Waterford, ferry, New Ross, Thomastown, Kilkenny — axis 0km to 70, elevation 0m to 600.

main road 100m west from old John Bridge. There is an AIB (3 High St) with an ATM. You can also change money in the TIC.

Wall's Cycle Shop (☎ 772 1236, Maudlin St) lies on the east side of town (go east over John Bridge and take the first right) and is a Raleigh Rent-a-Bike dealer.

The August Kilkenny Arts Festival (☎ 775 2175) presents music, poetry and street plays. The Rhythm & Roots Festival (☎ 775 2520) takes place around May.

Things to See & Do Strolling around Kilkenny can be pleasant. A nice 1.5km **walk** starts from the square below the castle, crosses the old John Bridge, runs along the eastern riverbank to the modern Greens Bridge and returns via St Canice's Cathedral and the old main street (High St/Parliament St/Irishtown).

An hour-long **guided walk** run by Tynans Tours (☎ 776 5929) tells the town's medieval story in full. It sets off from the TIC six times daily (four on Sunday) and costs adult/student €5/4.

Grandiose **Kilkenny Castle** (☎ 772 1450, adult/student €5/2, open daily Apr-Sept) is the remodelled 12th-century ancestral pile of the region's ruling Butler family. Added to the three surviving 1190s towers are the splendid Victorian library, drawing room, bedrooms and beautiful **Long Gallery**. The former kitchen is now the café. Admission is by 50-minute guided tour only. Access to the lovely 20-hectare castle **parkland** is free.

St Canice's Cathedral (☎ 776 4971) at the northern end of town was constructed in the 13th century on what was likely a much older Christian site. The round tower (admission €2), which you can climb for a fine view, dates from the 9th century. Around the cathedral are a graveyard and 18th-century bishop's palace, and there are also medieval carvings, brass work and stained glass.

Places to Stay & Eat Campers should head to *Tree Grove Caravanning & Camping* (☎ 777 0302, [e] *treecc@iol.ie, Danville House*) Tent sites €11. Small camping ground near the river 1.5km south on R700 New Ross road.

Kilkenny Tourist Hostel (☎ 776 3541, [e] *kilkennyhostel@eircom.net, 35 Parliament St*) Dorm beds/doubles €13/17. Central with family rooms and laundry facilities.

The Kilkenny Cats

They sound like a Canadian hockey team, but the fable of the Kilkenny cats battling to destruction probably originates at the time of Cromwell's occupation in 1650.

The story goes that bored soldiers garrisoned in Kilkenny invented a bizarre form of entertainment to while away the hours. They tied a pair of cats together by the tails and threw them across a line, whereupon the enraged animals lashed out at the only foe they could get their claws on, their unfortunate fellow prisoner.

On hearing about the sport, the commander of the garrison outlawed it. So the soldiers continued in secret until one night an officer on patrol heard caterwauling and went to investigate. Sensing his footsteps a soldier cut off the cats at the tails, allowing them to escape but leaving the bloody appendages dangling on the line. At the sight, the officer could only conclude that the cats had eaten each other. Hence the poem:

There once were two cats in Kilkenny;
Each thought there was one cat too many.
So they fought and they fit,
They scratched and they bit,
'Til excepting their nails
And the tips of their tails,
Instead of two cats there weren't any.

Banville's (☎ 777 0182, [e] *mbanville@ eircom.net, 49 Walkin St*) Singles/doubles €33/50. Comfortable rooms 500m west of centre. *Anna Villa* (☎ 776 2680, *4 College Rd*) Singles/doubles from €33/55. Town house 500m southwest of centre. *Glendhu* (☎ 772 2481, *Waterford Rd*) Singles/doubles €39/52. Modern bungalow 1km southwest of centre along N10 close to several other B&Bs.

Zuni (☎ 772 3999, *26 Patrick St*) B&B singles/doubles from €63/90, good weekend deals available also including dinner. Trendy new town house hotel with good restaurant 50m from the TIC.

Berkeley House Hotel (☎ 776 4848, *5 Lower Patrick St*) Singles/doubles from €51/70. A three-star Georgian guesthouse 100m up from the TIC.

SOUTHEAST

Crotty's Coffee House (St Kieran's St)
Sit at outside tables for lunch and cappuccino in good weather. Decent fast-food joint *Abrakebabra (Rose Inn St)* is on the west bank near John Bridge.

Fléva Brasserie (☎ 777 0021, 84 High St) Mains around €20. Creative Irish cuisine such as monkfish with squid ink pasta, at the *tholsel* (city hall) end of the main shopping street. *Lautree's Brasserie (☎ 776 2720, Kieran St)* does pizza and pasta mains, and dishes like marinated chicken in lemongrass sauce for €16. *Rinuccini (☎ 776 1575, The Parade)* serves Irish and Italian dishes for around €10.

Day 2: Kilkenny to Cashel
3–5½ hours, 57.1km
Take the scenic high road over the rolling Slieveardagh Hills to the Rock of Cashel. The ride climbs the 300m hump, runs along the top and descends to Ballingarry. From there, it undulates on a quiet road into Cashel.

On a good day the views are gorgeous from the top (22.4km), northwest and west across the vale. Turning anticlockwise from north see the notched Devilsbit Mountain, the Silvermines, Slievefelim, the Galtys, the Knockmealdowns, Slievenamon and behind that to the south, the Comeraghs.

A major point of interest, the **Warhouse** (☎ 087-908 9972, open 2.30pm-5.30pm Wed-Sun Apr-Sept, 2pm-4pm Sat-Sun Oct-Mar) is reached via a side trip at 25.9km involving a steep climb of 1km. This isolated hilltop cottage was a focal point of the Young Irelander rising in 1848, when rebels under Protestant nobleman William Smith O'Brien besieged police there. An exhibition tells the story.

The climb up the Slieveardagh is substantial but very steady. There are short steeper sections nearing the secondary summit (8km) before Tullaroan and the main summit at Monablanchameen. The hilltop is exposed, so on grim days consider staying in Kilkenny and drinking coffee instead. There are no reliable services for 16km between Tullaroan and Ballingarry.

Navigating the lanes over the hills requires attention, but once past Ballingarry, route-finding is a breeze.

Cashel
See Cashel (p114).

Day 3: Cashel to Waterford
4½–8 hours, 79.2km
Here's an easy day of idyllic lanes and tranquil historic sites. The return to Waterford wends its way to medieval Fethard, around bulky Slievenamon and past ancient high crosses to Carrick-on-Suir, home of cycle-racing legend Sean Kelly.

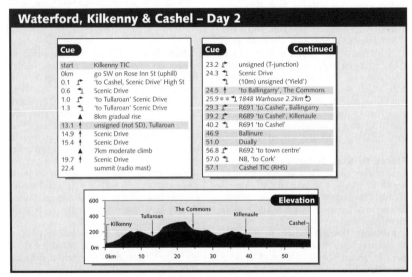

Waterford, Kilkenny & Cashel – Day 2

Cue		
start	Kilkenny TIC	
0km	go SW on Rose Inn St (uphill)	
0.1	⬏	'to Cashel, Scenic Drive' High St
0.6	⬑	Scenic Drive
1.0	⬏	'to Tullaroan' Scenic Drive
1.3	⬑	'to Tullaroan' Scenic Drive
▲	8km gradual rise	
13.1	↑	unsigned (not SD), Tullaroan
14.9	↑	Scenic Drive
15.4	↑	Scenic Drive
▲	7km moderate climb	
19.7	↑	Scenic Drive
22.4	summit (radio mast)	

Cue		Continued
23.2	⬏	unsigned (T-junction)
24.3	⬑	Scenic Drive
	⬑	(10m) unsigned ('Yield')
24.5	↑	'to Ballingarry', The Commons
25.9 ● ●	⬑	*1848 Warhouse 2.2km* ↻
29.3	⬏	R691 'to Cashel', Ballingarry
39.2	⬏	R689 'to Cashel', Killenaule
40.2	⬑	R691 'to Cashel'
46.9	Ballinure	
51.0	Dually	
56.8	⬏	R692 'to town centre'
57.0	⬑	N8, 'to Cork'
57.1	Cashel TIC (RHS)	

Elevation

Elevation profile (metres, 0m–600m vertical; 0km–50+ horizontal) showing: Kilkenny, Tullaroan, The Commons, Killenaule, Cashel.

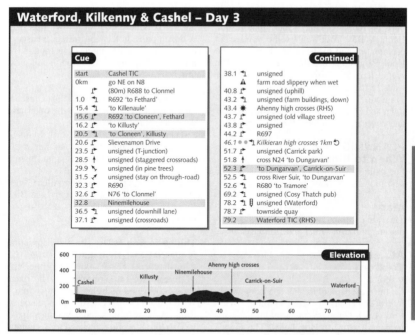

Waterford, Kilkenny & Cashel – Day 3

Cue				Continued	
start	Cashel TIC		38.1	↰	unsigned
0km	go NE on N8			⚠	farm road slippery when wet
	↱	(80m) R688 to Clonmel	40.8	↲	unsigned (uphill)
1.0	↰	R692 'to Fethard'	43.2	↰	unsigned (farm buildings, down)
15.4	↰	'to Killenaule'	43.4	✴	Ahenny high crosses (RHS)
15.6	↲	R692 'to Cloneen', Fethard	43.7	↲	unsigned (old village street)
16.2	↲	'to Killusty'	43.8	↲	unsigned
20.5	↰	'to Cloneen', Killusty	44.2	↲	R697
20.6	↲	Slievenamon Drive	46.1	● ● ↰	*Kilkieran high crosses 1km* ↻
23.5	↲	unsigned (T-junction)	51.7	↲	unsigned (Carrick park)
28.5	↑	unsigned (staggered crossroads)	51.8	↑	cross N24 'to Dungarvan'
29.9	↘	unsigned (in pine trees)	52.3	↲	'to Dungarvan', Carrick-on-Suir
31.5	↙	unsigned (stay on through-road)	52.5	↰	cross River Suir, 'to Dungarvan'
32.3	↲	R690	52.6	↰	R680 'to Tramore'
32.6	↲	N76 'to Clonmel'	69.2	↰	unsigned (Cosy Thatch pub)
32.8		Ninemilehouse	78.2	↰ 🏠	unsigned (Waterford)
36.5	↰	unsigned (downhill lane)	78.7	↲	townside quay
37.1	↲	unsigned (crossroads)	79.2		Waterford TIC (RHS)

Tiny lanes are rough in places around the mountain between Fethard (15.6km) and Ninemilehouse (32.8km), and between the N76 turn-off (36.5km) and Ahenny high crosses (43.4km). Wet lanes are downright slippery where you pass farms – be warned! For navigating purposes, the ride follows mostly the better-worn through-route.

First halt is riverside Fethard where little fuss is made of remnants of a major **Anglo-Norman settlement**. These include 17th-century fortified tower houses, a good length of the 15th-century town wall, a 14th-century Augustinian friary, also Holy Trinity Church and medieval churchyard wall.

Visit 8th-century **high crosses** in grave-yards at Ahenny (43.4km) and on a short side trip at Kilkieran (46.1km). The Ahenny crosses are covered in interlacing designs and topped with mitre capstones. These are said to cure headaches if placed on the sufferer's head. The Kilkieran site has three intact crosses, of which the needle-like Long Shaft Cross is unique in Ireland.

Carrick-on-Suir (52.3km), a fine town with *cafés* and *pubs*, is home to cycling champion Sean Kelly (see the boxed text

'Sean Kelly – High King of Cycling', p124). Foley's bike shop (☎ 051-640 318, Bridge St) is on the street leading to a seven-arched, **15th-century bridge**. For centuries this was the first crossing up the Suir from its mouth at Waterford Harbour.

The R680 from Carrick to Waterford carries occasional fast traffic. You leave this at 69.2km on a detour which may avoid the hellish N25, but does rise and fall several times before eventually dropping to end on the Waterford quayside.

Southeast Coast Cruise

Duration	2 days
Distance	160.5km
Difficulty	moderate
Start	Wexford
End	Youghal

Showcasing seascapes and coastal settlements this ride is rugged and charming in equal measure. Trees grow bent in the wind, and waves wash cliffs and dunes along a picturesque coastline.

SOUTHEAST

Soon after Wexford comes the little fishing port of Kilmore Quay, then picturesque Bannow Bay, followed by the windswept promontory and medieval lighthouse of the Hook Peninsula (reached on a site trip). The scenic ferry trip across Waterford Harbour leads to the sandy swathes of holiday town Tramore. The best stretch between Annestown and Dungarvan is riddled with beaches and coves against a mountain backdrop.

PLANNING
When to Ride
For calmer, warmer weather and seas, the best months are May to September.

Maps
The ride overlaps two OSI 1:250,000 Holiday maps *Ireland East* and *Ireland South*.

ACCESS TOWN
Wexford
☎ 053
On the west bank of the River Slaney where it broadens into Wexford Harbour, Wexford (Loch Garman) has a 600m quayside peppered with drinking holes. The town's cheerful streets exude well being. The shops are family owned and well stocked, and dining out is rather good for a town this size. A dozen pubs, hotels and restaurants serve hearty, occasionally interesting food. Live music sessions are easy to find to suit most tastes.

Information The TIC (☎ 23111, Crescent Quay) is on a curving blip in the otherwise dead-straight waterfront.

There are two banks on North Main St near Common Quay St, and another at the corner of Common Quay St and Custom House Quay; all have ATMs.

Satisfy cycling needs at Dave Allen Cycles (☎ 22516, 84 Main St South) and the Bike Shop (☎ 22514, 9 Selskar St) at the northern end of the high street.

Things to See & Do The main attraction is the **National Heritage Park** (☎ 20722, adults/students €7/6), 4km along the N25 Waterford road at Ferrycarrig. The place cans 1000 years of Ireland's history into a series of outdoor reconstructions, such as Stone Age–dwellings and a Viking ship.

Wexford is world renowned for its annual **Opera Festival** in October. Rare works are

Sean Kelly – High King of Cycling

In or around Carrick-on-Suir you may glimpse a chap who throughout much of the 1980s dominated international cycle racing.

When Sean Kelly retired in 1994, his home town named a square after him (near the southern end of the old bridge). Today, while busy with TV race commentating and charity rides, he is still a common sight in Carrick, although he's more likely to be wearing wellies than flashing past in a blur of rubber and metal.

Every year after the end of race season, Kelly returned to Carrick and the family farm; he now runs his own. Kelly was never one for show and townsfolk see the hard man of professional cycling as just another one of the locals.

Kelly began cycling aged about 13. He joined the Carrick Wheelers and worked his way up the amateur ranks, racing at every opportunity, and riding every Sunday on the roads of Waterford and Tipperary. The region provided a fine training ground, especially the climbs of the Comeragh Mountains and the Vee on the Knockmealdowns.

From that humble background, Kelly became a professional rider on the Continent, earning a reputation as a tough contender who could withstand gruelling conditions. Between 1980 and 1990, he persistently triumphed in the great one-day classics; Paris–Nice (seven times), the Paris–Roubaix, Milan–San Remo, Liége–Bastogne–Liége and the Tour of Lombardy. He never won the Tour de France but took the green points jersey four times and won the inaugural World Cup league in 1989. Kelly led the world rankings for a staggering total of five years to 1990.

A man of few words, he was once asked how he kept on training in the rain. 'You don't know how wet and cold it is until you're in it,' was the stoic reply. Now there's inspiration for a cycle tourist on the damp Emerald Isle!

performed to enthusiastic audiences, and booking at the Theatre Royal box office (☎ 22144, e boxoffice@wexfordopera.com) three months in advance is essential.

Places to Stay There's a good selection of accommodation options. *Ferrybank Camping and Caravan Park* (☎ 44378, *Ferrybank*) Tent sites €11. About 1km northeast across the bridge over the Slaney River. *Kirwan House* (☎ 21208, *3 Mary St*) Dorm beds/twins €12/16. A comfortable hostel 200m behind the TIC, across the main street.

B&Bs are plentiful and may serve early breakfast for Rosslare ferry passengers. *Auburn House* (☎ 23605, e *mary@obriens auburnhouse.com, 2 Auburn Terrace, on Redmond Rd*) Singles/doubles €39/64. One of a clutch of three B&Bs with a river view beyond Redmond Square at the north end of town. *Blue Door* (☎ 21047, e *bluedoor@ indigo.ie, 18 Lower George St*) Singles/doubles €39/64. A Georgian town house to the north of centre near the traditional music pubs. *Villa Maria* (☎ 45143, *Ivy Lane, Coolcots*) Singles/doubles €32/50. Around 1km north of town.

White's Hotel (☎ 22311, e *info@whites hotel.iol.ie, George's St*) B&B singles/doubles €81/120. A trad-modern hotel that combines coaching inn and leisure centre.

Places to Eat Wexford's abundant good restaurants allow a little menu-shopping.

Robertino's (☎ 23334, *19 South Main St*) Pasta and pizza from €9. The Wexford river salmon costs €17. *La Riva* (☎ 24330, *Crescent Quay*) Mains around €20. Serves modern dishes with Mediterranean vegetables and goat cheese, and duck leg in white wine. *Harpers Restaurant* (☎ 22311, *George's St*) Carvery and à la carte meals available. The gammon plate is €8 while the salmon is €17. The entrance is on North Main St.

Waterfront pubs serving chow include *Wren's Nest* (☎ 22369, *Custom House Quay*) All home-made food.

Cappuccino's (*Main St*) Bagels and panini from €6. *Yellow River* (*Common Quay St*) Eat-in or takeaway post-pub noodles from €5, open until midnight most nights and 3am Sundays.

Getting There & Away Frequent Bus Éireann (☎ 23939) services pass through Wexford, travelling between Dublin (€11, 2¾ hours, approximately hourly, fewer on Sundays) and Rosslare Harbour (€4, 25 minutes, approximately hourly). There are also buses from Waterford (€10, one hour, five daily, four on Sundays).

Wexford lies on the north–south train line between Dublin Connolly (€12, three hours, three daily) and Rosslare Europort (€3, 28 minutes, three daily) line. Dial the 24-hour timetable on ☎ 01-805 4288. O'Hanrahan Station (☎ 22522) is at the northern end of town on Redmond Place.

By bike Wexford is on the Around Ireland ride (p251), reached after a 67km stage from Arklow.

THE RIDE (see map p126)
Day 1: Wexford to Tramore
4½–8 hours, 83.5km
This long and very memorable day follows a wind-buffeted shoreline of dunes, estuaries, cliffs and coves. In good weather the Ring of Hook alternative route is a treat if you can manage the extra distance.

First stop is **Kilmore Quay** (21.9km), an isolated fishing port with several nice *watering holes* and a Blue Flag (EU listed as clean and safe) marina. Around Wellington-bridge (41.9km), the route follows the shores of lovely **Bannow Bay**. On the far western flank follow tiny lanes down to a 3km stretch of deserted waterside (49km), and the little town of Saltmills (51.5km). Soon after, you reach the turn-off for the Ring of Hook alternative route (55km).

Inland from the peninsula, the ferry (cyclists €3) between Passage East and Ballyhack (66.1km) links Counties Wexford and Waterford between the river cliffs of Waterford Harbour. The ferry runs all day and takes 10 minutes. Here the route briefly overlaps with Day 1 of the Waterford, Kilkenny & Cashel ride (p119).

There are two sticky navigation points: first in the tiny lanes after Wellingtonbridge that lead towards Bannow Bay and; second, after the ferry crossing, where you have to spot the left turn (73km) off the R683 to Tramore on to a back road.

Traffic-wise, there's a 2km stretch on the narrow, straight R733 after Wellingtonbridge that prompts hellish fast driving. Put on your sprinting legs, and complete it as quickly as you can.

Alternative Route: Ring of Hook
1½ hours, 25.1km

The remote, windswept **Hook Peninsula** thrusts into the ocean to form the east side of Waterford Harbour. At its tip sits an impressive 13th-century **lighthouse** (☎ 051-397 055) that, amazingly, is still in commission after 700 years, following a few enhancements such as electrification. With such open landscape and the call of warmth and refreshments at the lighthouse, the 25.1km detour is recommended. A guided tour of the lighthouse costs adult/student €5/4.

However, adding the Ring of Hook to the ride increases the day's distance to over 100km. The good news is, if you decide to break the journey, *watering holes* and B&Bs are plentiful (although they fill up July to August) in the holiday towns of Fethard (1.5km from start of alternative route), Duncannon (61.3km) and Arthurstown (64.8km). Arthurstown also has an An Óige *youth hostel (☎ 051-389 411)* and Fethard has a *camping ground (☎ 051-397 123)*.

Tramore
☎ 051

Perched on cliffs overlooking a vast Blue Flag beach, Tramore (Trá Mhór) is number one on the family holiday scene and packs out in July and August, when amusements and chip stalls cram the promenade. The town is neat and busy and returns to normality out of season. The 3km-long beach is backed by dunes and becomes a great expanse of sand at low tide.

Information The TIC (☎ 381 250, Lower Branch Rd) opposite the bus station has highly seasonal opening periods, which vary throughout June, July and August depending on demand. Pedal Power Cycles (☎ 381 252, Market St) takes care of cycling needs.

Things to See & Do Oceanic Manoeuvres (☎ 390 944, 3 Riverstown) and Tramore Bay Surf Club (☎ 391 297) at end of the promenade provide **surfing** equipment and tuition, while the main attraction is **Splashworld** (☎ 390 176), an outsize swimming pool near the promenade.

About 3km west near Westown, signposted 'scenic view', are the bathing coves of **Guillamene** (once men-only) and **Newtown**. Walkways add atmosphere to neighbouring pools where people are said to swim every day of the year.

Places to Stay & Eat Good facilities near the bathing coves west of town on the R675 to Dungarvan are provided by *Newtown Cove Camping & Caravan Park (☎ 381 979)* Tent sites per person €12.

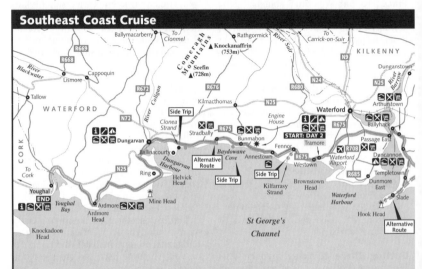

Southeast Coast Cruise

Woodview (☎ *390 376, 9 Tivoli Terrace*) Doubles €52. Central, with TV in rooms. *Church Villa* (☎ *381 547, Church Road*) Doubles €46. Cheap, rather shabby lodging 500m up Gallwey's Hill (at the end of the promenade). A cluster of smart B&Bs is located just off Church Road. *Venezia House* (☎ *381 412,* ⓔ *veneziahouse@ireland.com*) Doubles €52. Smart bungalow. Near the bathing coves is *Radharc na Mara* (☎ *381 606, Westown*) Singles/doubles €26/42. Modern bungalow 2km southwest of town.

Majestic Hotel (☎ *381 761, Turkey Rd*) Singles/doubles €61/77. Three-star lodgings with nightly live music in the holiday season.

Dinner in Tramore means mostly grills and seafood for families coming off the beach. *Waterfront* (☎ *381 149, Gallwey's Hill*) Mains from €13. Overlooks the beach. *Apicius* (☎ *390 955, Turkey St*) Pizza from €8, pasta from €9. Italian joint with varied mains from around €13.

Day 2: Tramore to Youghal
4–8 hours, 77km

The best seaside day in the region follows a cliff-lined shore with a multitude of beaches and coves. Remote surrounds awaken the soul, a cuppa is never far away and the views are uplifting. Given sunny weather, this day could happily stretch to two or more.

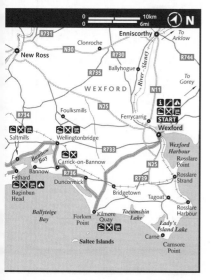

Southeast Coast Cruise – Day 1

Cue	
start	Wexford TIC
0km	go SE on Crescent Quay
2.2 ↱	'to Bridgetown'
14.6 ↰	'to Kilmore Quay'
21.9	Kilmore Quay
retrace outward route 3.2km	
25.1 ↰	'to Wellingtonbridge'
27.8 ↰	'to Wellingtonbridge'
30.7 ↰	'to Carrick-on-Bannow'
37.1	Carrick-on-Bannow
38.2 ↱	'to Wellingtonbridge'
41.9 ↰	R733 'to Arthurstown', W'bridge
44.5 ↰	unsigned, take right fork
46.2 ↱	unsigned (crossroads & stone)
46.9 ⚠	slippery descent
48.2 ↰	unsigned (bungalow crossroad)
50.9 ↰	unsigned (T-junction)
51.5	Saltmills
54.6 ↰	'Ring of Hook'
55.0 ↱	unsigned (minor road)
▪▪▪ ↑	*alt route: Ring of Hook 25.1km*
58.1 ↱	'to Campile' (T-junction)
	alt route rejoins (continue)
58.3 ↰	'to Duncannon'
60.5 ↰	'to Duncannon'
61.3 ↱	'to Arthurstown', Duncannon
63.7 ↰	R733 'to Arthurstown' (T-Junction)
64.8	Arthurstown
66.1	Ballyhack
	take ferry over River Barrow
↱	'to Waterford', Passage East
72.2 ↱	R683 'to Waterford'
73.0 ↰	unsigned (opposite Orpen's pub)
73.8 ↰	'to Dunmore East'
↱	(50m) unsigned (fencing)
78.3 ↰	'to Tramore' (T-junction)
81.9 ↰	R675 'to Tramore'
83.5	Tramore TIC (bus station)

SOUTHEAST

The highlight is the early stretch between Annestown (9.9km) and Bunmahon (17.3km) where the road clings to the **clifftop** with long views around the coast. The area between Tramore and Stradbally (24.5km) is known as the Copper Coast, with several structures left behind from the 19th-century mining industry. From the ruined **engine house** (15km) before Bunmahon, shafts run 7km underground.

However, beaches and coves are the day's main attraction. Kilfarrasy Strand is an early side trip at 5.1km. Annestown and Bunmahon are quaint clusters of civilisation where rivers break through to the sea. Numerous coves are signposted en route including Ballydowane (side trip at 20.3km) and Ballyvooney (alternative route at 22.4km).

Clonea Strand (side trip at 33.4km) is a popular holiday beaches, complete with *chip and tea stands* and a beachside hotel.

After Dungarvan (37.4km) the road crosses the Drum Hills and falls to remote **Ballyquinn Strand** (59km) and the popular beach town of Ardmore (64km).

Youghal
☎ 024

A charming old port at the mouth of the River Blackwater, Youghal (Eochaill, pronounced y-all) has a long river quay which doubles as the main road to Cork, yet remains strangely unspoiled by the juggernauts. The main street runs parallel to the quayside with painted shops, and cafés and restaurants where seafood is a speciality.

The river forms the border between Counties Cork and Waterford.

Information The TIC (☎ 20170, Market Square) is on the quayside. The town **walking trail** starts from the TIC, and an interesting 1½-hour **guided walk** (€3) of the walls and old buildings leaves at 11am daily, June to August.

For bicycle supplies, Hennessy's Sport & Leisure (☎ 90884, 45 South Main St) sells minor parts and may do overnight repairs.

Things to See & Do The 8km-long **Blue Flag beach** concludes at the town end with a funfair and amusements.

The **old walls** of the medieval town of Youghal originally reached to the water's edge along Main St. But the Blackwater silted up and jumped course, and the town broadened with it. The inshore portion of the wall still exists and can be seen from the grounds of **St Mary's Collegiate Church**, built in 1220 and one of the oldest churches in Ireland still used for worship.

Places to Stay & Eat At the Cork end of town is *Avonmore House* (☎ 92617, e avonmoreyoughal@eircom.net, South Abbey) Singles/doubles from €33/50. A fine Georgian house located where the one-way traffic system starts. *Roseville* (☎ 92571, e rosevillebandb@eircom.net, New Catherine St) Singles/doubles from €32/50. Welcoming big house at the inland end of town. *Devon View* (☎ 92298, Pearse Square) Singles/ doubles from €32/50. Georgian house with

antique furniture, also at the Cork end of the one-way traffic circuit.

Walter Raleigh Hotel (☎ 92011, O'Brien's Place) Singles/doubles from €45/78. Bar meals start at €9, with restaurant mains, such as grills, seafood and roasts from €13, served until 8.30pm.

Tides Restaurant & Accommodation (☎ 93127, Upper Strand) Singles/doubles €58/90. Rooms with all the trimmings, also a specialist seafood restaurant serving dinner until 10pm daily; the house dish is a symphony of seafood with salmon, cod, oysters, mussels and prawns for €33. For plain fish and chips there's the *Roma Grill (North Main St)* near the post office.

Getting There & Away Bus Éireann vehicles ply through Youghal on the way to Rosslare Harbour (€16, two hours, four daily, two on Sundays), Waterford (€12, 1½ hours, hourly), Cork (€13, 50 minutes, hourly) and Killarney (€18, 2¾ hours, hourly, fewer on Sundays).

By bike Youghal is the Day 5 stop on the Around Ireland ride (p251), reached after a 77km stage from Tramore.

Southeast Coast Cruise – Day 2

Cue	
start	Tramore TIC
0km	go SW on Turkey St/Gallweys Hill
1.6 ⌐	'to Fennor'
5.1 ● ● ⌐	*Kilfarrasy strand 6km* ⤵
9.9	Annestown
15.0 ✳	*Engine house*
17.3	Bunmahon
17.8 ⌐	'to Stradbally' (thatched cottage)
20.3 ● ● ⌐	*Ballydowane cove 0.5km* ⤵
22.4 ■ ■ ⌐	*alt route: Ballyvooney cove 3km*
23.2 ⌐	'to Stradbally' (T-junction)
24.5 ⌐	'to Dungarvan' Stradbally
	alt route rejoins (turn left)
27.8 ⌐	R675 (T-junction)
33.4 ⌐● ●	*Clonea Strand 3km* ⤵
37.4	Dungarvan
37.6 ⌐	'all routes' (ACC bank)
38.7 ⌐	N25 'to Cork'
41.1 ⌐	R674 'to Helvick, Ardmore'
45.0 ⌐	'to Ardmore' (uphill, not Ring)
	3km moderate climb
57.0 ⌐	R673 'to Ardmore'
64.0 ⌐	'to Youghal', Ardmore
69.0 ⌐	N25 'to Youghal'
76.1 ⌐ ●	N25 'to Cork'
77.0	Youghal TIC (quayside)

County Wicklow's enchanting Glendalough (Into the Wicklow Mountains ride)

Sculptural decoration, Kilkenny Castle

Cloister carving, Jerpoint Abbey, County Kilkenny

Stop off for a feed...

...before heading to the Beara Peninsula (Ring of Beara ride).

County Kerry's twisting, hilly roads challenge and reward cyclists

Moss-covered yew woods, Killarney National Park

Southwest

You don't get to be one of the most visited regions in Ireland without some aces up your sleeve. The Southwest has several: magnificent mountains, lakes and coast; spring and early summer weather as good as anywhere in the country; a rich concentration of ancient monuments, including some fascinating and extraordinarily preserved clues to the region's cultural past; and some gourmet (and not-so-gourmet) culinary hotspots.

Throw in another few high-scoring trump cards – a good range of accommodation, a bike-friendly ethos (cycling is the region's third-most popular tourist activity), interesting villages and lively pubs – and it's no surprise that the Southwest wins one third of all international cyclists visiting Ireland.

With so many drawing cards, the tourists come thick and fast. But the Southwest wins by playing its joker: quieter roads early in the season, when the weather is best. Come in May or early June and you'll get the best Ireland has to offer – it's on the cards.

HISTORY
Though not restricted to Ireland's southwest, Stone Age forts, standing stones, Ogham stones and stone circles are very common in the region. Likewise, early Christian monuments abound, shining examples of which include the monastery 12km offshore on Skellig Michael and Dingle Peninsula's Gallarus Oratory. Indeed, an extraordinary number of ecclesiastical sites exist on Dingle.

Kinsale was the site of a battle that marked a significant turning point in Irish history. In 1601, the English defeated Ulster chiefs O'Neill and O'Donnell, who had marched the length of Ireland (in winter) to join their Spanish allies. The defeat is said to have been the beginning of the end of Gaelic Ireland. In what is now called the 'Flight of the Earls', the defeated Ulster chiefs later left Ireland, which opened the way for the Ulster Plantation settlement of subjects loyal to the Crown.

Cobh, on Cork harbour, was the departure point for millions of emigrants during the 18th and 19th centuries, including convicts, and later orphan girls, bound for Australia; and victims of the 1845–51 Great Famine bound mostly for the USA and Britain.

In Brief

Highlights
- **Beara Peninsula** for quiet roads and awesome, rugged beauty
- **Killarney National Park** and the stunning **Gap of Dunloe**
- The magic of the fantasy-like **Skellig Islands**
- Dingle's Stone Age and early Christian **monuments**

Terrain
Undulating along the south coast, more pronounced on the west-coast peninsulas; steep sections and long climbs on the Beara, Iveragh and Dingle Peninsulas.

Special Events
- **Cork International Choral & Folk Dance Festival** (Apr/May) Cork
- **Mussel Fair** (street entertainment and food events; May) Bantry
- **Summer Splash Festival** (concerts and regatta; July) Waterville
- **Rose of Tralee Festival** (events and music culminating in a beauty contest; Aug) Tralee

Food & Drink Specialities
Fish and **seafood**, organically grown **vegetables**, **cheeses**, and **health foods**.

Daniel O'Connell (1775–1847), the 'Great Liberator' who fought for Catholic voting rights, lived at Caherdaniel, although his parliamentary seat was in County Clare. Another hero, Michael Collins (1889–1922; see the boxed text 'Michael Collins… The Big Fella', p137), who led the resistance against the British during the War of Independence (1919–21), was born near Clonakilty and killed close by.

NATURAL HISTORY
The terrain in southwest Cork undulates around river valleys and a series of sheltered inlets. A range of red-sandstone uplands cuts across northern Cork and into Kerry, the

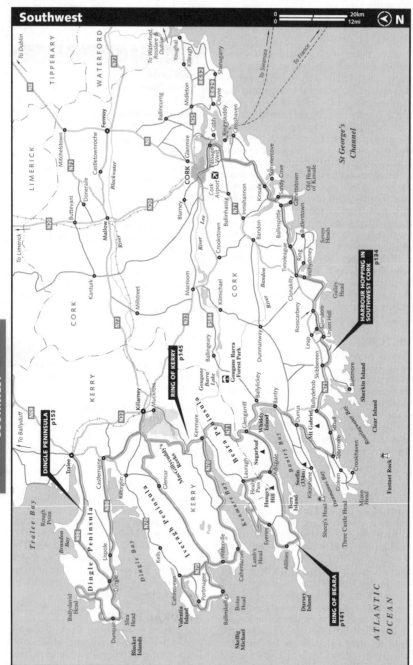

Southwest

| 0 | 20km |
| 0 | 12mi |

N

To Dublin

TIPPERARY

WATERFORD

To Waterford, Rosslare & Dublin

Youghal

Killeagh

N8

N72

To Swansea

To France

St George's Channel

Fermoy

Ballincurrig

Midleton

R632

Cloyne

R629

Shanagarry

Mitchelstown

Castletownroche

Blackwater

N8

Glanmire

Cobb

Ringaskiddy

Crosshaven

LIMERICK

N20

Doneraile

N25

CORK

Passage West

Summercove

N20

Buttevant

Mallow

Blarney

Cork Airport

Innishannon

Kinsale

Garrettstown

Old Head of Kinsale

Sandy Cove

To Limerick

River Lee

Ballinhassig

N71

To Ballyduff

Kanturk

Crookstown

Bandon

Ballinspittle

Seven Heads

N59

Millstreet

River Lee

Crookstown

River Bandon

Butlerstown

Ring

Timoleague

N20

Macroom

N22

Kilmichael

CORK

Clonakilty

Inchydoney

HARBOUR HOPPING IN SOUTHWEST CORK p134

CORK

N72

Ballingeary

Gougane Barra Forest Park

Dunmanway

Roscarbery

Galley Head

Killarney

KERRY

Muckross

N22

RING OF KERRY p145

Gougane Barra Lake

Ballylickey

Bantry

Glandore

Union Hall

Leap

N71

Skibbereen

Baltimore

Sherkin Island

Kenmare

Glengarriff

Ballyvourney

Whiddy Island

Durrus

Ballydehob

Schull

Clear Island

DINGLE PENINSULA p153

Tralee

Castlemaine

Killorglin

Glencar

MacGillycuddy's Reeks

Iveragh Peninsula

KERRY

Beara Peninsula

N71

Sugarloaf

Bantry Bay

Mt Gabriel

Toormore

Crookhaven

Goleen

Fastnet Rock

Tralee Bay

Rough Point

Kenmare River

N70

Lauragh

Healy Pass

Adrigole

Hungry Hill

Seefin (334m)

Dunmanus Bay

Sheep's Head

Mizen Head

Roaringwater Bay

Brandon Bay

Dingle Peninsula

N86

Lispole

Dingle Bay

Glenbeigh

Kells

Waterville

Bere Island

Kilcrohane

Three Castle Head

Ballydavid Head

Dunquin

Slea Head

Blasket Islands

Cathciveen

Portmagee

Valentia Island

Ballinskelligs

Bolus Head

Skellig Michael

Caherdaniel

Lamb's Head

Eyeries

Allihies

Dursey Island

RING OF BEARA p141

ATLANTIC OCEAN

N85

N86

N6

N70

N22

N71

more mountainous county, in which lies Ireland's highest peak, Carrauntoohil (1041m).

The handful of finger-like peninsulas that make up west Cork and Kerry reach into the Atlantic, their mountainous spines rugged and picturesque. Almost one-third of Ireland's coastline belongs to Cork and Kerry.

A climate warmed by the Gulf Stream fosters the growth of relatively lush vegetation. Introduced plants such as richly coloured rhododendrons and fuchsias are especially conspicuous; a colourful display of summer meadow flowers lines the roadsides. The Glengarriff woods in Cork, plus Kerry's Killarney National Park and Derrynane National Historic Park protect remnants of oak forest.

The coast of, and particularly the islands off, West Cork and Kerry are good birdwatching areas. Species include guillemot, kittiwake, puffin, gannet, shag and razorbill. Seals, dolphins and, occasionally, whales are also seen. An aquaculture industry has developed in the long, sheltered waters of Roaringwater and Bantry Bays, from which shellfish gathering was a traditional activity.

Native mammals include the red deer, foxes, badgers and pine martens. They're not easy to spot, but Killarney National Park would be a good place to try, if you're keen. On a more practical matter, watch out for unrestrained small yappy dogs that like to chase and snap at cyclists (see the boxed text 'Look Out: Dogs About!', p196).

CLIMATE

With Ireland's weather blowing in from the Atlantic on the prevailing southwesterly wind, the mountains of west Cork and Kerry bear the brunt of it. That said, the saving graces of southerly latitude and proximity to the Gulf Stream ensure the region receives a good share of warm sunny weather as well. Indeed, it's not unheard of for rain to fall over much of the country while west Cork bathes in sunshine.

The driest, sunniest period is from April to June, after which average rainfall increases steadily month-by-month. Heavy rain and strong winds are more likely in August and September.

Temperatures are warmest from June to September. The average minimum and maximum temperatures in April are 5°C and 13°C, in June and September 10°C and 17°C, and in August 12°C and 18°C.

For a daily regional weather forecast, phone ☎ 1550-123 694.

INFORMATION
Maps & Books

The OSI 1:250,000 Holiday map *Ireland South* covers the region. Useful references from Cork Kerry Tourism include the *Beara Way Cycle Route* map and the booklet *Ireland South West: Cycling Routes in Cork & Kerry*, which offers a detailed overview of signed and proposed cycling routes throughout the region.

Tim Severin's *The Brendan Voyage* is an account of his replication of St Brendan's 6th-century voyage from the Dingle Peninsula to America (see the boxed text 'St Brendan's Voyage', p158). Inhabitants of Great Blasket Island near Dingle became famous for the wealth of literature they produced. Classics include Maurice O'Sullivan's *Twenty Years A-Growing*, Peig Sayers' *Peig* and Tomás O'Crohán's *The Islandman*.

Information Sources

Cork Kerry Tourism (☎ 021-427 3251, w www.corkkerry.ie) maintains a regional network of Bord Fáilte TICs that cover almost all places in this chapter. (Note that Tralee falls into the Shannon Region and may not stock Cork Kerry publications.)

Cork Kerry Tourism produces the *Ireland South West Counties: Cork & Kerry* brochure, a useful guide to visitor services, tours and attractions.

Place Names

Place names are almost exclusively in Irish in Gaeltacht areas such as the western reaches of the Iveragh and Dingle Peninsulas, and to a lesser extent in other areas.

GATEWAY CITY
Cork
☎ 021

The Republic's second-largest city (population 180,000) began in the 6th century when St Finbarr, the city's patron saint, founded a monastery on the bank of the River Lee.

Central Cork is a small island between two channels of the green river. A dense cluster of narrow streets bounded and dissected by wide boulevards, it's Cork's most engaging area. Along with the city centre, Shandon, which rises steeply from the north bank, it is

SOUTHWEST

one of the oldest areas. Apart from a couple of attractions, Shandon is rather drab.

As a university town, Cork is a much-cycled city; however, cyclists should be prepared to negotiate hills to the north and south, considerable traffic and a network of one-way streets.

Information The TIC (☎ 427 3251, W www .corkkerry.ie, open 9.30am-5.30pm Mon-Fri, 9.30am-4pm Sat, open later plus Sun July & Aug) is at the southern end of Grand Parade. Look for the *Cork City at a Glance* visitor map free from local businesses.

The major banks (with ATMs and bureaus de change) are all along St Patrick St. Bureau de Change facilities also operate at the post office (cnr Oliver Plunkett and Pembroke Sts) and the TIC.

Rothar Cycles (☎ 431 3133, W www.rct .foundmark.com, 55 Barrack St) is a Raleigh Rent-a-Bike agent; weekly rental costs €51. Rothar (Irish for bike; pronounced Roh-her) also offers a buy-back scheme and repairs. Robbie has the lowdown on single-track spots around Cork and Kerry. Kilgrews Cycle Centre (☎/fax 427 6255, 6 Kyle St) has a better range of new bikes and offers a buy-back scheme and repair service.

Waterstone's Bookshop (☎ 427 6522, 69 Patrick St) is useful. Try Great Outdoors (☎ 427 6382; Daunt Square, Grand Parade) for outdoor equipment.

A left-luggage service (☎ 455 7150) operates at the bus station, on the corner of Parnell Place and Merchant's Quay.

Things to See & Do Visitors talk enthusiastically about **Cork City Gaol** (☎ 430 5022, at Sunday's Well on Convent Ave), west of the city, especially the moving individual sound tour.

The stepped tower of the 18th-century **St Anne's Church** dominates Shandon. The church bells are said to be unique and the salmon-shaped weathervane was apparently chosen because the monks reserved for themselves the right to fish salmon in the river. Nearby is the old Butter Exchange through which once passed all of Ireland's butter for export – it's now the **Butter Museum** (☎ 430 0600, O'Connell Square).

South of the river, the imposing, Protestant **St Finbarr's Cathedral** (Bishop St) was designed by William Burges and completed in 1879. It has been the site of a cathedral since the 6th century.

It's worth a day (or half-day) trip to some of Cork's best attractions, which are outside the city itself. **Cobh** (pronounced Cove) is the picturesque town on Great Island in Cork Harbour, for many years the port of Cork. Lovely to wander around, Cobh has an impressive **Heritage Centre** (☎ 481 3591, admission €6). It includes multimedia displays on the mass emigrations, the era of the great liners and the tragedies of the *Titanic* and *Lusitania*. Cobh is 16.4km from Cork. To get there, follow Day 1 of the Harbour Hopping in Southwest Cork ride (p134) to the Glenbrook ferry ramp (12.7km). The five-minute crossing costs €1/2 one way/ return. From the ferry, go right on the R624 'to Cobh'. A train service runs to Cobh (via Fota), but does not carry bikes.

On the north side of Great Island is **Fota Wildlife Park** (☎ 481 2678, admission €7, arboretum and gardens free), a 28-hectare open-range zoo with more than 90 exotic species. To cycle from Cobh (7.4km), retrace the outward route but, instead of taking the ferry, continue on the R624. Return to Cork via the busy (but shouldered) N25 (14km) or cycle back to the ferry.

The **Blarney Stone** at the top of the 15th-century Blarney Castle (☎ 438 5252) is the county's best known attraction, where visitors feel compelled to kiss the stone and receive the gift of the gab. Blarney is 8km northwest of Cork. From the TIC, take Grand Parade, Washington St, North Main St and, after crossing the river, go left on Blarney St.

Places to Stay The closest camping is 10.5km away at *Blarney Caravan & Camping Park* (☎ 438 5167, R617) Tent sites per person €6, including showers. The four-star site is 2.5km north of Blarney Village (signposted).

An Óige *International Youth Hostel* (☎ 454 3289, 1-2 Redclyffe, Western Rd) Dorm beds €13-16, twins €37. Kitchen facilities are limited in this clean Victorian house, 1.5km west of town; ask if your bike can go in the shed. *Sheila's Budget Accommodation* (☎ 450 5562, e sheilas@iol.ie, 4 Belgrave Place) Dorm beds €12-14, doubles €32-35. Despite box-like dorms, Sheila's facilities are good; it's off Wellington Rd (and up a steep hill from town).

Cheaper B&Bs lie along Lower Glanmire Rd, near the train station; the other main B&B area is Western Rd, near the university. *Tara House (☎ 450 0294, 52 Lower Glanmire Rd)* Singles €32, standard/ensuite doubles €46/51. Friendly lodgings near the train station. *Deans Hall Summer Village (☎ 431 2623, w www.deanshall.com, Crosses Green)* Singles/doubles €32/58 with continental breakfast, self-catering apartments for four/six people from €96/121. Central student residences with laundry and cooking facilities; available mid-June to September. *Garnish House (☎ 427 5111, w www.garnish.ie, Western Rd)* Ensuite singles €45-58, doubles €77-96. Welcoming, with an excellent breakfast menu and laundry facilities. *Westbourne House (☎ 427 6153, Western Rd)* Ensuite doubles €56. This pleasant house is nonsmoking throughout.

Imperial Hotel (☎ 427 4040, e imperial@iol.ie, South Mall) Room only €88/101 weekdays/weekends (higher during special events). Attractively refurbished, central, three-star hotel; continental/full Irish breakfast costs €7/11. *Isaacs Hotel (☎ 450 0011, 48 MacCurtain St)* Singles/doubles €74/102 B&B. Once a storage warehouse for the British army, three-star Isaacs has only outdoor bike storage. MacCurtain St is noisy; ask for a rear room. *Isaacs Hostel (☎ 450 8388)* is also part of the complex. Dorm beds €11-18.

Places to Eat For groceries, don't miss the *English Market (Grand Parade to Princes St)*. The olive stall alone is worth a visit; also excellent bread, fresh fish, vegetables and local cheeses. *Tesco (Paul St Shopping Centre)* Open 8.30am-8pm (noon-6pm Sunday).

Hillbilly's Fried Chicken (cnr Grand Parade & Oliver Plunkett St) Boxes €5-6. Open late.

Quay Coop Vegetarian Restaurant (Sullivan's Quay) Mains €6-7. Open Mon-Sat. Cafeteria-style, attractive dining area; an easy place to eat alone. Wholefoods store downstairs. Across river from TIC.

Kethner's (9 Paul St) Mains €8-18. Cosy place, opposite Tesco, offering a standard menu at better value than many. *Scoozi (3 & 4 Winthrop Ave)* Mains €8-11. Another good place for budgeters; Italian-style.

Cafe Mexicana (Careys Lane) Mains €11-18. Tucked away, it's popular, with tasty food. *Pico's Bistro (4 Bridge St)* Mains €10-15. Excellent, flavoursome food, fresh and organic ingredients; intimate atmosphere.

Getting There & Away You can get to Cork by air, land or sea.

Air Cork Airport, 10.7km south of the city, receives direct flights from European destinations including London, Manchester, Paris and Amsterdam – and, of course, from Dublin.

Bus Éireann (☎ 450 6066) operates an airport-city service (€4/5 one-way/return, 25 minutes, 15 daily); bikes must be boxed. A taxi fare between the airport and the city centre costs around €10.

The cycle to the city begins with a long descent: from the airport exit road, go left onto the N27; right 'to Grange' at 3.1km (towards the bottom); stay right until 6.2km; go left then continue straight, ignoring 'to city centre' signs. At 10km, turn hard right into Douglas St (the signing is confusing here: it looks like Abbey St), left into Dunbar St and left again into George's Quay. Follow the 'to city centre' signs over the river.

Bus The Bus Éireann Travel Centre (☎ 450 6066) is on Parnell Place, on the corner of Merchant's Quay, 1km east of the city centre. Services to/from Cork include: Youghal (€8, 50 minutes, 13 daily), Dublin (€18, 4½ hours, six daily) and Ennis (€14, three hours, 12 daily), continuing on to Galway. Bikes, carried subject to space, cost €9 on any journey.

Train Iarnród Éireann (☎ 1850 366 222) runs services between Cork and Ennis (€18, 3¼ hours, two daily, change at Limerick and Limerick Junction), Dublin (€45, 3½ hours, four to seven daily), and Cobh (€3, 30 minutes, regular services). Bikes are not permitted on Cobh services.

The train station (☎ 450 6766, recorded timetable information ☎ 450 4544) on Lower Glanmire Rd is 2.8km northeast of the TIC.

To ride from the station, go right (east) on Lower Glanmire Rd, right at the traffic lights and right again along the wharves. At 1.7km, go left over the bridge, then immediately right (at the bus station) on Merchant's Quay; at 2.1km, left on St Patrick's St and continue to the TIC.

Boat Regular ferries link Cork with the UK and France. The ferry terminal, at Ringaskiddy, is about 20km southeast of the city. From the terminal, go west on the N28; turn right after 2.2km, and hard right onto the R610 almost 1km later. From here, follow (in reverse) Day 1 of the Harbour Hopping in Southwest Cork ride (note that Anglesea St and South Mall are one-way).

Swansea Cork Ferries (☎ 427 1166, ⓦ www.swansea-cork.ie) runs four to six services each week between Swansea (Wales, UK) and Cork. Brittany Ferries (☎ 427 4090, ⓦ www.brittany-ferries.com) runs weekly services between Cork and Roscoff (France).

Harbour Hopping in Southwest Cork

Duration	4 days
Distance	220km
Difficulty	moderate
Start	Cork
End	Kenmare

Tracing the dozen or so bays and harbours along the coast of County Cork, this ride begins in Ireland's second-biggest city, visits its most southwesterly point, and ends in Kerry just short of its highest mountain.

Waterside villages, roadside wildflowers, extensive gardens and a general laid-back ambience make the kilometres roll easily by. And there's no shortage of fuel around these parts: Kinsale is Ireland's undisputed gourmet capital; Schull has some excellent, unpretentious eateries; and Cork city's wide choice includes the wonderful English Market. This is among the best regions for health foods and locally grown organic vegetables.

PLANNING
When to Ride
Late spring and early summer are best for weather and quieter roads; however, some services may not open until mid-June.

Maps
The OSI 1:250,000 Holiday map *Ireland South* covers the route.

ACCESS TOWN
Cork
See Cork (p131).

THE RIDE
Day 1: Cork to Clonakilty
4½–7 hours, 81.6km
A longish first day mingles inland meandering with coastal dalliance. Traversing Cork's undulating countryside, the route features Cork and Kinsale Harbours, the

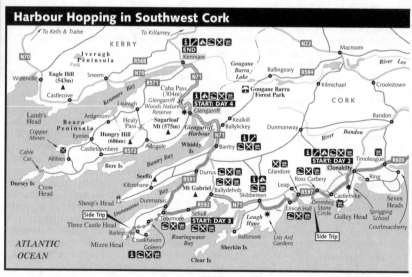

Harbour Hopping in Southwest Cork

lovely beaches of Courtmacsherry Bay, and a handful of quiet villages. Traffic can be busy through Cork city and surrounds (easing after the ferry to Cobh, 12.7km) and, again, nearing Carrigaline (21.2km) and Kinsale (40.5km).

The journey could be broken at Kinsale, a pretty harbour village, also dubbed Ireland's gourmet capital. Its medieval centre makes for a pleasant (and mouth-watering) wander; a guided **historic stroll** (☎ 021-477 2873) leaves the TIC daily. Many restaurants and B&Bs are pricey (lunchtime generally less so), and booking is advised. *Pisces Bistro (☎ 021-477 7933, cnr Main & Market Sts)* offers a €17 early bird evening menu; otherwise, evening mains cost a reasonable €12-18. *Castlepark Marina Hostel (☎ 021-477 4959)*, across the bridge, has €13 dorm beds. Contact the TIC (☎ 021-772 234, Pier Rd) for B&Bs.

Old Head of Kinsale is a promontory 13km south of Kinsale town. Unfortunately, it's no longer possible to visit the lighthouse at the end of the promontory: the land is now closed to all but members of the Old Head Golf Links. However, a side trip (51.3km) to the castle at the narrow neck affords great views of the coast and countryside on the return downhill run.

The shallow inlet to Courtmacsherry Bay attracts a variety of water birds, some of

which migrate from Arctic regions. At its head is the village of Timoleague (71.9km), and the impressive remains of its 14th-century **Franciscan friary**.

Clonakilty
☎ 023

With plenty of live music, arts and crafts plus the beach nearby, Clonakilty is a lively small town. Most shops and restaurants are on the long main street known, in different sections, as The Strand, Wolfe Tone St, Ashe St and Pearse St. Restored and old buildings (including several from the linen industry, Clonakilty's mainstay for centuries) give the place character. Read about them in the free brochure, *Clonakilty: Beach Centre of West Cork*, available from local businesses. Clonakilty's most famous son, the Irish patriot Michael Collins, was born 7km west of the town in 1889.

Information Visit the TIC (☎ 33226, 25 Ashe St, open 9.30am-5.30pm Mon-Sat Mar-Oct, until 7pm daily July-Aug). Bank of Ireland (with bureau de change) and Allied Irish Bank (AIB) are on Pearse St; Trustee Savings Bank (TSB) is on Rossa St; all have ATMs.

MTM Cycles (☎ 33584, 33 Ashe St, open 8.30am-7.30pm Mon-Sat, 9.30am-12.30pm Sun) can help with cycling needs.

Things to See & Do Clonakilty's **Model Village** (☎ 33224, Inchydoney Rd) features local icons in miniature and a working model of the West Cork Railway circa 1940.

Michael Collins' first home is now the **Michael Collins Memorial Centre**, 7km west of Clonakilty, signposted off the N71.

Inchydoney Beach has beautiful white sands, but be careful of the dangerous riptide. It's a 10km return ride along the tidal flats – watch for water birds.

You'll find **live music** at many of the pubs; best bets for trad are *De Barra's Folk Club* or *An Teach Beag* behind O'Donovan's (see Places to Stay); if you're over Irish, try *The Venue*.

Places to Stay Camping and B&B are available at *Desert House (☎ 33331, Ring Rd)* Tent sites per person €6, B&B farmhouse singles/doubles €28/44 (€31/50 with ensuite). Overlooking Clonakilty Bay, 380m from the roundabout (signed).

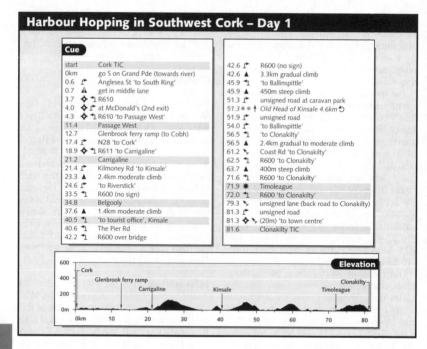

Harbour Hopping in Southwest Cork – Day 1

Cue

start	Cork TIC		42.6	↱	R600 (no sign)
0km	go S on Grand Pde (towards river)		42.6	▲	3.3km gradual climb
0.6	↰ Anglesea St 'to South Ring'		45.9	↰	'to Ballinspittle'
0.7	▲ get in middle lane		45.9	▲	450m steep climb
3.7	◆ ↰ R610		51.3	↱	unsigned road at caravan park
4.0	◆ ↱ at McDonald's (2nd exit)		51.3 ● ● ↑		Old Head of Kinsale 4.6km ↻
4.3	◆ ↰ R610 'to Passage West'		51.9	↱	unsigned road
11.4	Passage West		54.0	↱	'to Ballinspittle'
12.7	Glenbrook ferry ramp (to Cobh)		56.5	↰	'to Clonakilty'
17.4	↱ N28 'to Cork'		56.5	▲	2.4km gradual to moderate climb
18.9	◆ ↰ R611 'to Carrigaline'		61.2	↘	Coast Rd 'to Clonakilty'
21.2	Carrigaline		62.5	↰	R600 'to Clonakilty'
21.4	↱ Kilmoney Rd 'to Kinsale'		63.7	▲	400m steep climb
23.3	▲ 2.4km moderate climb		71.6	↰	R600 'to Clonakilty'
24.6	↱ 'to Riverstick'		71.9	✳	Timoleague
33.5	↰ R600 (no sign)		72.0	↰	R600 'to Clonakilty'
34.8	Belgooly		79.3	↘	unsigned lane (back road to Clonakilty)
37.6	▲ 1.4km moderate climb		81.3	↱	unsigned road
40.5	↰ 'to tourist office', Kinsale		81.3	◆ ↘	(20m) 'to town centre'
40.6	↰ The Pier Rd		81.6		Clonakilty TIC
42.2	↰ R600 over bridge				

Elevation

(Elevation profile showing: Cork, Glenbrook ferry ramp, Carrigaline, Kinsale, Timoleague, Clonakilty; vertical axis 0m–600m; horizontal axis 0km–80km)

Old Brewery Hostel (☎ *33525, Emmet Square*) Dorm beds €11. Nonsmoking hostel; comfy beds and a good kitchen.

Pauline's B&B (☎ *33157, 5 Strand Rd*) Singles/doubles €21/42. Easy-going family home. ***Wytchwood B&B*** (☎ *33525, Emmet Square*) Ensuite singles/doubles €32/58. A lovely place: spacious, pleasing decor; non-smoking throughout.

O'Donovan's Hotel (☎ *33250, Pearse St*) Ensuite singles/doubles €63/89. Comfortable family-run hotel; many rooms have bath and shower. Book ahead.

Places to Eat Groceries are available from ***Walshes Foodmarket*** (*Pearse St*). ***Old Market House Food Store*** (*Connolly St*) West Cork produce. ***Rossa Grill*** (*8 Rossa St*) Fast food €2-7.

Fionnualas Little Italian Restaurant (*30 Ashe St*) Pasta and pizza €9-17. Cosy, licensed place with good vegetarian options. ***Cafe Asia: Fusion Food Bar*** (*The Venue, O'Donovan's Hotel*) Mains €11-18. Relaxed café-cum-music club; has a fair crack at contemporary Asian food (music after 9pm). ***Shama Pakistani Indian Restaurant*** (*12 Ashe St*) Mains (including rice) €7-14. Good vegetarian selection. ***An Súgán*** (☎ *33498, The Strand*) Mains €11-22. Known for seafood, the menu is identical in both the atmospheric bar and the restaurant.

Day 2: Clonakilty to Schull
3–6 hours, 59.6km

The undulating route to Schull features ancient monuments and stories of more recent history. A pattern emerges of a series of descents into (and climbs out of) townships; the biggest hill, after Ross Carbery, is steep at times.

Meadow flowers enliven the roadside, along with occasional statues of the Virgin Mary; Glandore Harbour and The Narrows offer more scenic treats. Towards Schull, Roaringwater Bay and the looming spectre of Mt Gabriel whet the appetite for the rugged west coast peninsulas.

The delightful descent into tiny Castlefreke is punctuated by stones explaining points of historical interest. The **sprigging school** (9km) is worth a quick visit: the old schoolhouse now houses a small museum of local history. Watch for the unsigned turn

Michael Collins... The Big Fella

Michael Collins was born on 16 October 1889 and reared in West Cork. As a young man he left Ireland to work as a civil servant in London. At the age of 26 he returned to take part in the 1916 Easter Rising and became committed to the continued armed struggle against the British. During the War of Independence (1919–21), he earned a reputation as a ruthless organiser of guerilla warfare.

Collins inspired tremendous respect among the Irish and fear among the British, who offered a large reward for his capture. He became a living legend, not least for the ease with which he evaded arrest, seldom bothering to disguise himself and riding freely around Dublin on his bicycle.

Eamon de Valera sent Collins to Downing St, London, to negotiate a truce. Collins resisted the order, but to no avail. In going to London, he was forced to give up his most important weapon – his anonymity. Reluctantly, Collins signed a treaty which partitioned Ireland, leaving the six counties of the North under British rule. He considered the partition a stepping stone to a completely independent Ireland and believed it was the best deal that could be secured at the time, while prophetically declaring, 'I may have signed my death warrant tonight'.

The treaty split the Irish people and a brutal civil war followed its acceptance, with de Valera heading the anti-treaty faction. Collins was killed on 22 August 1922 in an ambush near Macroom in Cork.

Much of Neil Jordan's film *Michael Collins* (1996) was shot in West Cork. Despite some inevitable 'Hollywoodising' of the story, it remains a worthwhile, accessible introduction to the 'Big Fella', played by Liam Neeson.

into Castlefreke Wood (9.5km), through stone gate posts.

A side trip (19.6km) near the top of the climb from Ross Carbery leads to the impressive **Drombeg stone circle**, 17 stones probably arranged around 100 BC. In a nearby cooking trough, hot stones can boil around 320L of water in 18 minutes. You'll need to walk the last 150m to the site.

Views across the harbour make immaculate Glandore (22km) a nice lunch stop; *Glandore Inn* serves bar food and sandwiches. With more choice, including a *grocery store*, Union Hall (24.8km), across the water, is more down-to-earth.

The Liss Ard foundation's expansive **gardens** (34.7km) offer a nice resting spot – although the gardens themselves are some way from the entrance.

Skibbereen (35.9km) was hard-hit by the Great Famine: almost 10,000 people were buried in local mass graves. Spend half an hour at the **Heritage Centre** (☎ 028-40900) for an insight into the famine's impact; a separate natural history display features an interesting video on the ecology of nearby Loch Hyne.

Schull
☎ 028

Delightful little Schull sits on a harbour of Roaringwater Bay below Mt Gabriel. The community is sprinkled with artists and European expatriates and, except during summer (particularly early August, when the yachties come in), it's a pretty relaxed place.

Information No TIC exists but the *Visitors Guide to Schull* booklet (free from village businesses) is very useful. An AIB bank (with ATM) is at the top end of Main St. For emergency bike repairs, try McCarthy's Garage (Main St).

Things to See & Do Schull is home to the Republic's only **planetarium** (☎ 28552, Community College, Colla Rd). Phone ahead for Star Show times. Local **walks** are suggested in the *Visitors Guide to Schull* (see Information); or take a day ride to **Mizen Head** (see the Day 3 Side Trip, p139); it's 50.4km return from Schull.

West Cork Coastal Cruises (☎ 39153, e westcorkcruises@eircom.net) runs **boat trips** between Schull, Cape Clear and Baltimore, and to Fastnet Rock lighthouse, from mid-June to August.

Places to Stay It's wise to book ahead, especially in July and August. IHH *Schull Backpackers Lodge* (☎ 28681, w www.schull backpackers.com, Colla Rd) Tent sites (limited) per person €7; dorm beds €12. Pretty farm location 400m south of town.

SOUTHWEST

Harbour Hopping in Southwest Cork – Day 2

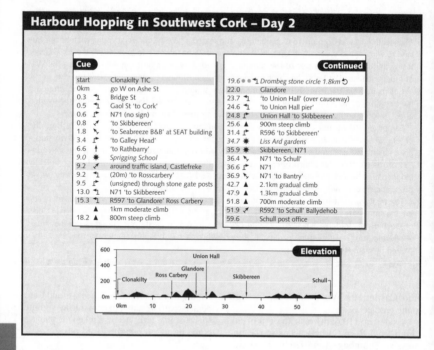

Cue			Continued
start	Clonakilty TIC	19.6 ● ● 1	Drombeg stone circle 1.8km ⮌
0km	go W on Ashe St	22.0	Glandore
0.3 1	Bridge St	23.7 1	'to Union Hall' (over causeway)
0.5 1	Gaol St 'to Cork'	24.6 1	'to Union Hall pier'
0.6 1	N71 (no sign)	24.8 1	Union Hall 'to Skibbereen'
0.8 ↗	'to Skibbereen'	25.6 ▲	900m steep climb
1.8 ↘	'to Seabreeze B&B' at SEAT building	31.4 1	R596 'to Skibbereen'
3.4 1	'to Galley Head'	34.7 ✳	Liss Ard gardens
6.6 ↑	'to Rathbarry'	35.9 ✳	Skibbereen, N71
9.0 ✳	Sprigging School	36.4 ↘	N71 'to Schull'
9.2 ↗	around traffic island, Castlefreke	36.6 1	N71
9.2 1	(20m) 'to Rosscarbery'	36.9 ↘	N71 'to Bantry'
9.5 1	(unsigned) through stone gate posts	42.7 ▲	2.1km gradual climb
13.0 1	N71 'to Skibbereen'	47.9 ▲	1.3km gradual climb
15.3 1	R597 'to Glandore' Ross Carbery	51.8 ▲	700m moderate climb
	▲ 1km moderate climb	51.9 ↗	R592 'to Schull' Ballydehob
18.2 ▲	800m steep climb	59.6	Schull post office

Adele's B&B (☎ 28459, *Main St*) Singles/doubles €26/51. Smallish rooms above the coffee shop (see Places to Eat) ooze character; good-sized continental breakfast. *Glencairn B&B* (☎ 28007, *Ardmanagh Dr*) Singles/doubles €26/51 (€58 with ensuite). Smallish but pleasant family home; welcomes singles, bikes outside.

Grove House (☎ 28067, w *www.cork-guide.ie/schull/grove/welcome.html, Colla Rd*) Singles/doubles €84/102. An elegant former 18th-century hotel, it's smoke-free.

Places to Eat Good eating options decrease after 6pm, especially outside the summer months. But any lack of quantity is balanced by some fine foodies, include two cheese makers.

Centra Supermarket (*Main St*) Open late daily. *The Courtyard* (*Main St*) The best place for supplies: its well-stocked bakery and delicatessen includes local cheeses (closed Sunday).

The Mermaid's Takeaway (*Main St*) Burgers €2-6, plus fish and chips.

Adele's Coffee Shop (*Main St*) Mains €7-9. Closes 6pm. Excellent Mediterranean-style meals (try bean stew with garlic bread), good coffee, bread and baked treats; non-smoking downstairs. *The Courtyard Bar & Restaurant* (behind The Courtyard store) Bar meals €7-13 (until 5.30pm; closed Sunday); restaurant mains €11-18 (6pm-9pm Tues-Sat). A friendly place with Mediterranean and Irish cuisine (including vegetarian pasta). *The Waterside Inn* (☎ 28203, *Main St*) Bar meals €7-11; restaurant mains €18-24. Best option for pub grub (phone ahead for vegetarian).

Day 3: Schull to Glengarriff
3–5 hours, 51.4km

Mostly undulating, the ride to Glengarriff is not hard; longer climbs are generally gradual. The day is extended considerably by including the side trip to Mizen Head, Ireland's most southwesterly tip. This is well worth the effort; it could also be done as a day trip from Schull, without panniers. Traffic becomes heavier back on the N71 from just before Bantry to Glengarriff, but the wide shoulder makes it easily bearable.

The Mizen Peninsula's rocky spine, green fields and roadside flowers make for pleasant riding to Toormore (8.6km), the turn-off point for Mizen Head light station.

Durrus (24.4km) is the village at the entrance to the Sheep's Head Peninsula – another popular cycling area – said to be even quieter and more laid-back than the Mizen.

Bantry (34.4km) has a lovely, wide harbour, filled with mussel farms. A sizable town, it's not particularly engaging, although it has the last serious bike store – Kramers (☎ 027-50278), on Glengarriff Rd (with early closing Wednesday) – until Kenmare. Its other major attraction is **Bantry House & Gardens** (☎ 027-50047), the former home of the Earl of Bantry. However, its future is in question.

After some undulation around Bantry Bay, a gradual climb (42.6km) yields views of the Sheep's Head and Beara Peninsulas, before a descent into Glengarriff.

Side Trip: Mizen Head
2–3 hours, 33.5km
To assist ships through the dangerous Atlantic waters, a signal station was completed at Mizen Head in 1910. The station was automated in 1993 and an exhibition, Mizen Vision, was established in the old keepers quarters. The light station, at the end of the head, is a 10-minute walk from the Mizen Head visitor centre and *café* (☎ 028-35115). It costs €5 to walk down, and it's

worth paying: apart from the Mizen Vision exhibition, the scenery is far more dramatic beyond the gate. Look out for dolphins, seals and sea birds; whales are frequently seen off Mizen Head during July and August. Allow an hour (including walking time) to visit the exhibition.

A few hills lie between the turn-off and Mizen Head, including a 4.6km climb (to around 100m) from the inlet near Barleycove beach. The return trip offers spectacular views of the peninsula and Fastnet Island. The village of Goleen, 6.3km from the turn-off, has a small TIC, a *store* and *places to eat*.

Glengarriff
See Glengarriff (p141).

Day 4: Glengarriff to Kenmare
1½–2¾ hours, 27.4km
Though it's on the N71 all the way, traffic is reasonably light. Climbing starts through the leafy Glengarriff Woods Nature Reserve 1.3km from town, and continues steadily for almost 8km to the Caha Pass, emerging onto characteristic open rocky hills. It's not steep; towards the top, it (deceptively) looks almost flat. Views are expansive: as the road snakes around to the south, Glengarriff appears far below and, later, the Iveragh Peninsula mountains become visible to the north. A 200m tunnel, blasted through the

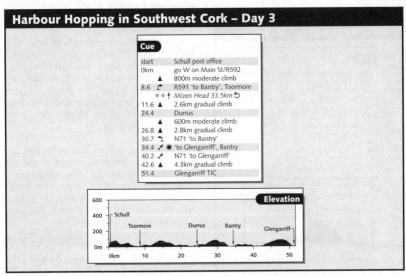

Harbour Hopping in Southwest Cork – Day 3

Cue	
start	Schull post office
0km	go W on Main St/R592
▲	800m moderate climb
8.6 ⌐	R591 'to Bantry', Toormore
● ● ✝	*Mizen Head 33.5km* ↰
11.6 ▲	2.6km gradual climb
24.4	Durrus
▲	600m moderate climb
26.8 ▲	2.8km gradual climb
30.7 ⌐	N71 'to Bantry'
34.4 ↗ ✳	'to Glengarriff', Bantry
40.2 ↗	N71 'to Glengarriff'
42.6 ▲	4.3km gradual climb
51.4	Glengarriff TIC

Elevation

Schull — Toormore — Durrus — Bantry — Glengarriff

(600 / 400 / 200 / 0m — 0km / 10 / 20 / 30 / 40 / 50)

hill, is the highest point (304m), after which it's more or less downhill all the way to Kenmare. It's worth stopping for delicious cream tea at the welcoming *O'Connors Store*, Bonane post office (16.3km).

Kenmare
☎ 064

Despite the tourist influx, lively little Kenmare retains its soul. A planned, X-shaped town with a central market square, it sits at the point where the Finnihy, Roughty and Sheen Rivers flow into the Kenmare River. A lace industry providing jobs for women was established here in the 1860s and became a national centre of excellence.

Information Visit the TIC (☎ 41233, The Square, open 9am-5pm Mon-Sat, 10am-5pm Sun July-Aug). Also try **w** www.nei din.net and **w** www.kenmare.com for local information. The bureau de change on Main St charges no commission on non-Euro currencies. Bank of Ireland and AIB banks (both with ATM) are on The Square.

Kenmare Cycle Centre (☎ 41031, cnr Henry & Shelbourne Sts) is a Raleigh dealer. It's behind Finegans, a tacky souvenir shop.

Kenmare Bookshop (☎ 41578, cnr Shelbourne & Main Sts) stocks local maps and guides. Noel & Holland Books (☎ 42464, Bridge St) sells second-hand books.

Harbour Hopping in Southwest Cork – Day 4

Cue	
start	Glengarriff TIC
0km	go W on N71
0.3 ↗	N71 'to Killarney'
1.3 ✳	Glengarriff Woods Nature Reserve
▲	7.9km moderate climb
9.2	Caha Pass
▲	200m tunnel
10.1 ▲	40m tunnels
10.4 ▲	80m tunnel
16.3	O'Connors Store
27.3 ↰	N71 'to Killarney'
27.4	Kenmare TIC

Things to See & Do Inside the TIC, **Kenmare Heritage Centre** succinctly covers local history, including Bronze Age stone circles, local Gaelic clans, the Cromwellian era, the founding of Kenmare town, the Great Famine and nationalism. Upstairs, the **Lace Centre** displays handiwork from Kenmare's lace industry.

The TIC's free *Kenmare Heritage Trail* brochure details **historical sites** of interest, including the largest stone circle in Ireland's southwest. Some other **walks** are detailed in *The Kenmare Way: A Pocket Guide for Walkers & Cyclists* (available from Kenmare Bookshop).

Places to Stay The closest camping is 4.5km west. *The Ring of Kerry Caravan & Camping Park (☎ 41648, Reen)* Tent sites for one/two €6/8. Good facilities, 800m off the N70.

IHH *Fáilte Hostel (☎ 42333, cnr Shelbourne & Henry Sts)* Dorm beds €11. Central and pleasant, bikes not under cover.

*Hawthorn House (☎ 41035, **e** haw thorn@eircom.net, Shelbourne St)* Ensuite singles €26-32, doubles €51-64. Central and hospitable with good breakfast options; book ahead. *Rockcrest House (☎ 41248, **e** dowdy@eircom.net, Gortamullen)* Ensuite singles/doubles €32/54. Good views, laundry and drying available; book ahead. *Limestone Lodge (☎ 42541)* Singles/doubles €32/56. Worth trying if others are full; it's across the footbridge.

Henry St has several pubs with B&B. *The Wander Inn (☎ 42700)* Ensuite singles/ doubles €45/64. Small, pleasantly furnished rooms (ask for a quiet one). *O'Donnabhain's (☎ 42106, **w** www.odonnabhain-kenmare .com)* Ensuite singles/doubles €64/77. Spacious, more luxurious rooms, some non-smoking. Book ahead.

Places to Eat Self-caterers have choice in Kenmare. The Wednesday open-air *market (The Square)* has wonderful olive and cheese stalls. *Super Valu (Main St)* Kenmare's better supermarket. *The Pantry (☎ 42233, Henry St)* Open Mon-Sat. Organic produce, wholefoods.

Jam Bakery, Deli & Cafe (Henry St) Daytime light meals €3-6; also bread, delicious cakes and pastries. *Cafe Mocha (The Square)* Best bet for coffee.

Hanks (Main St) Good takeaway variety. *The New Delight (18 Henry St)* Hot meals €8. Vegetarian café (closes 8pm May to August, earlier other times).

Foleys (16 Henry St) Bar meals €10-13; restaurant mains €10-18, three-course set menu (all night) €25. Restaurant menu includes vegetarian, pasta and risotto dishes. *The Wander Inn* (see Places to Stay) Pub grub €9-17; early bird menu (6pm-8pm) €17. Nought for vegetarians; lamp-lit pub.

Giuliano's Pizzeria/Trattoria (Main St) Pasta €10-18; 10-inch pizzas. Open Mon-Sat. Good tasty Italian food, but tourist prices. *Lime Tree Restaurant & Art Gallery (☎ 41225, Shelbourne St)* Meat and seafood mains €16-23. It's great; treat yourself!

Getting There & Away Follow the Ring of Kerry ride, Day 1 of which ends at Kenmare (p140).

Bus Éireann (☎ 021-450 8188) runs via Kenmare mid/late June to mid-September. Kenmare to Cork (€17, four hours, one daily) is on the Tralee–Cork service which also runs via Glengarriff and Killarney. Buses stop in Kenmare outside Brennans Pub on Main St. Services from Cork to Glengarriff and Killarney run year-round.

The 34km ride to Killarney on the N71 takes in the spectacular Ladies View and Killarney National Park. After the 9.6km climb to Molls Gap, it's *mostly* downhill all the way to Killarney.

Ring of Beara

Duration	2 days
Distance	130.3km
Difficulty	hard
Start/End	Glengarriff

With far less traffic than the peninsulas to the north, Beara's awesome rugged landscape and colourfully painted villages make it a special place to ride. In the heart of the touristy southwest, it's surprisingly low-key, overshadowed by the famous Ring of Kerry on the neighbouring Iveragh Peninsula (see the Ring of Kerry ride, p145).

It's in Beara's villages that you might find an entire community filling the low-ceilinged pub after a funeral, or the shopkeeper's daughter explaining the legend of a local landmark. Tour buses are rare, and the Irish as much as visitors come here to relax.

NATURAL HISTORY

The dramatic, mountainous core of the Beara Peninsula is a rocky sandstone, glacier-carved spine. Such an imposing, barren landscape might seem inhospitable, were it not for the lushness of the valleys below. Colourful fuchsias and rhododendrons are everywhere. The 300-hectare oak woodland, Glengarriff Woods Nature Reserve, at the peninsula's eastern end, features Atlantic species including St Patrick's cabbage, kidney leaved saxifrage and the strawberry tree. The mild climate also encourages the growth of mosses and ferns. Similar forest once covered a far greater area, but was extensively cut during the 17th century to produce charcoal for iron smelting. The *Glengarriff Woods Nature Reserve* brochure (from Glengarriff's private TIC) explains more.

PLANNING
When to Ride

Beara is probably most enjoyable outside of July and August. Weatherwise, May and June are best.

Maps

Cork Kerry Tourism's *Beara Way Cycle Route* map is available from Kenmare and Glengarriff TICs. Its route varies slightly from that presented here. The website ⓦ www.bearatourism.com/visitor/cycle.html also publishes the map.

Otherwise, the OSI 1:250,000 Holiday map *Ireland South* covers the route.

ACCESS TOWN
Glengarriff
☎ 027

On a sheltered inlet of Bantry Bay, Glengarriff is bounded by the oak and pine Glengarriff woods. A popular retreat for the wealthy English during the second half of the 19th century, its lush setting is attractive, and marred only slightly by touristy sweater shops. The sea is obscured from the main village by gardens, more pleasant than their name – Blue Pool Amenity Area – implies.

Information There is a small Bord Fáilte TIC (☎ 63084, N71, open 9.30am-5.30pm mid-June–Sept, closed Wed & Sun). Bantry

TIC (☎ 50229) covers the Beara region at other times. There is a good private TIC (☎ 63201, open daily May-Sept) next to the Garinish Island ferry. Bureau de change facilities operate from the post office, the Bord Fáilte TIC and The Spinning Wheel, all on the N71.

Jem Creations (☎ 63113, Castletownbere Rd) is a Raleigh Rent-a-Bike agent and may be able to help with emergency repairs.

Things to See & Do The area around Glengarriff is great for **walking** or **cycling**. Good routes (and natural history information) through the Glengarriff woods are detailed in the *Glengarriff Woods Nature Reserve* brochure (available at the private TIC).

On the 15-hectare **Garinish Island** (Illnacullin) is an Italianate garden created in the early 20th century by English architect Harold Peto. The mild climate enables a varied collection of exotic plants to flourish. Blue Pool Ferries (☎ 63333) makes the 12-minute sailing from the centre of the village. Allow two hours to explore.

Places to Stay & Eat A camping ground lies 2.5km west of the village. *Dowlings Caravan and Camping Park* (☎ 63154, Castletownbere Rd) Tent sites for one/two €6/11. Good facilities, including launderette; a bar opens nightly in the high season.

IHH *Murphy's Village Hostel* (☎ 63555, N71) Dorm beds €11. Friendly, family-run hostel next to the private TIC; a *café* operates during summer.

Rockwood House (☎ 63097, Castletownbere Rd) Singles/doubles €32/49. Cheerful and accommodating; may also help with laundry. *Conimar Guest House* (☎ 63405, Castletownbere Rd) Singles/doubles €30/51. Good facilities for cyclists; next to Jem Creations. *The Cottage Bar & Restaurant* (☎ 63226, N71) Ensuite singles/doubles €26/44. Adequate but small, plain units behind the pub. Book ahead. Bar meals (including vegetarian) €9-19.

Eccles Hotel (☎ 63003, N71) Singles/doubles €70/140. A grand, older-style hotel overlooking the harbour at the eastern end of town. Bar meals €7-16, bistro mains €10-19; both include vegetarian options.

For groceries try *Spar supermarket* (cnr N71 & Castletownbere Rd). *Johnny Barry's* (N71) Bar and restaurant meals €6-16, including seafood and vegetarian. Probably the best food option. *Rainbow Restaurant* (N71) Mains €9-17, including vegetarian. An obvious choice, but uninspiring, with somewhat pushy service.

Getting There & Away Bus Éireann (☎ 021-450 818) runs services between Cork and Glengarriff (€14, 2½ hours, two

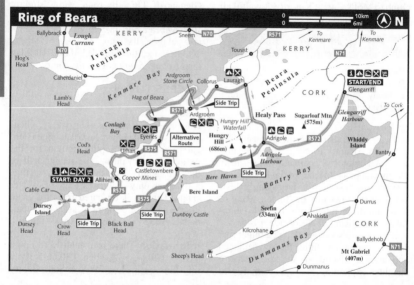

Ring of Beara

to three daily) and, from mid-June to mid-September, between Glengarriff and Killarney via Kenmare (€11, 1½ hours, one to two daily). Buses stop outside, and opposite, the post office.

THE RIDE
Day 1: Glengarriff to Allihies
3–5 hours, 52.5km

The peninsula's craggy spine dominates early on: the views unfold during the first of the ride's three long climbs, beginning less than 3km from Glengarriff. Over the hill undulating terrain continues for most of the day, with little sign of habitation before the scattered 'village' of Adrigole. Hungry Hill (685m), the peninsula's highest peak, looms behind Adrigole Harbour. From here flows Ireland's highest **waterfall**, the Hungry Hill Waterfall. To see it, take the side trip (at 19.5km) from Adrigole. It's about 4km return, climbing to get there.

Castletownbere (33.5km), Beara's main town and Ireland's largest whitefish port, is a good lunch stop, with several stores, pubs and restaurants. At *Murphy's Restaurant* near the harbour, mains including burgers and vegetarian dishes cost €5-10. Friday to Sunday, the *creperie van* in the square serves sweet and savoury pancakes for €2-4. Opposite *Harrington's Foodhall*, the surprisingly grand **Sacred Heart Cathedral** is wedged among buildings up the steps. From Castletownbere, it's possible to take a ferry to Bere Island. You can cycle the island, but accommodation is very limited.

Dunboy Castle (side trip at 36.1km; admission €1) makes another nice picnic spot. The ruined 19th-century mansion belonged to the Puxley family who made a fortune mining copper at Allihies. Past the mansion are the remains of a 14th-century castle that was the fortress of the O'Sullivans Bere.

Waterside lushness is left behind in a long climb (at 37.6km) that ends among giant boulders; the steady gradient and unfolding views make for easy climbing.

A final hill (46.1km) affords views of coastal cliffs and **Dursey Island**, a haven for wild birds and whales. Visit the island on a side trip (at 48.4km); it's a place to walk or watch wildlife rather than cycle, although there's a tough 8km ride to the cable car (€4 return) that transports locals, livestock and tourists (in that order) across to the island.

After the pass, picture-postcard views of Allihies are delightful, as is the swoop down to it. The day ends with an unexpected tough little climb into the village itself.

Allihies
☎ 027

Tiny, colourful Allihies is nestled against a dramatic, rocky backdrop. The poor surface

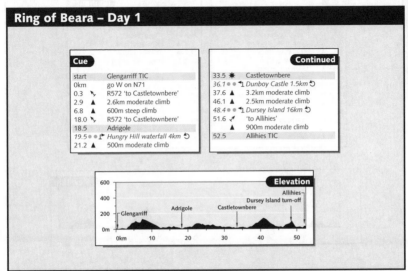

Ring of Beara – Day 1

Cue	
start	Glengarriff TIC
0km	go W on N71
0.3 ⬈	R572 'to Castletownbere'
2.9 ▲	2.6km moderate climb
6.8 ▲	600m steep climb
18.0 ⬈	R572 'to Castletownbere'
18.5	Adrigole
19.5 ● ● ⬉	*Hungry Hill waterfall 4km* ↺
21.2 ▲	500m moderate climb

Continued	
33.5 ✳	Castletownbere
36.1 ● ● ⬉	*Dunboy Castle 1.5km* ↺
37.6 ▲	3.2km moderate climb
46.1 ▲	2.5km moderate climb
48.4 ● ● ⬉	*Dursey Island 16km* ↺
51.6 ⬈	'to Allihies'
▲	900m moderate climb
52.5	Allihies TIC

Elevation graph: Glengarriff, Adrigole, Castletownbere, Dursey Island turn-off, Allihies; vertical axis 0m to 600m; horizontal axis 0km to 50+km.

of the street, the smell of silage and the close community give it an air of old-worldliness. Of the dozen or so buildings in the village, four are pubs. Allihies was a copper mining area from 1810 to 1962. Men, women and children were employed in poor conditions and for low wages by the landed Puxley family who became very wealthy. Though you'd never know, the attractive strand below the village was made with sand from the mines.

A small volunteers-staffed information kiosk may be operating near the church during July and August. Both the post office and the supermarket operate bureau de change facilities.

Walking just about anywhere is pleasant; signs point the way to the old **copper mining** area just north of the village. If you're more energetic, ride back up the hill and take the side trip to **Dursey Island** (see Day 1) to watch wildlife. Otherwise, listen to **music** at any of the village pubs.

Places to Stay & Eat By the beach is *Anthony's Campsite (☎ 73002, The Strand)* Tent sites €8. Facilities are basic (showers €1); call at the yellow house opposite.

The Village Hostel (☎ 73107) Dorm beds €13. Excellent facilities; clean and smoke-free throughout.

Seaview Guest House (☎ 73004) Ensuite singles/doubles €32/54. Comfortably furnished, airy rooms with views; laundry and drying available. *Veronica's B&B (☎ 73072)* Singles/doubles €18/36. Older-style, smaller rooms, but good value. Full Irish breakfast available for nonresidents €6; plus tea, coffee and sandwiches.

There are few eating options: the *supermarket* opens to 9pm daily. *Lighthouse Bar (☎ 73000)* Pub grub €5-9. *O'Neill's Bar & Restaurant (☎ 73008)* Mains €10-17. The à la carte menu features the usual meat, fish, chicken and a couple of vegetarian options.

Day 2: Allihies to Glengarriff
4¼–7¾ hours, 77.8km
A tough ride through some spectacular coastal and mountain scenery, this stage begins with a punishing roller coaster of short steep climbs. A mercifully flat stretch offers respite before the long, steady climb up to Healy Pass and a few shorter hills on the way back to Glengarriff.

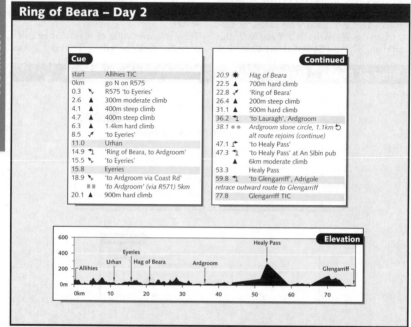

Ring of Beara – Day 2

Cue

start	Allihies TIC
0km	go N on R575
0.3 ↘	R575 'to Eyeries'
2.6 ▲	300m moderate climb
4.1 ▲	400m steep climb
4.7 ▲	400m steep climb
6.3 ▲	1.4km hard climb
8.5 ↙	'to Eyeries'
11.0	Urhan
14.9 ↰	'Ring of Beara, to Ardgroom'
15.5 ↘	'to Eyeries'
15.8	Eyeries
18.9 ↘	'to Ardgroom via Coast Rd'
▮▮	'to Ardgroom' (via R571) 5km
20.1 ▲	900m hard climb

Continued

20.9 ✳	Hag of Beara
22.5 ▲	700m hard climb
22.8 ↗	'Ring of Beara'
26.4 ▲	200m steep climb
31.1 ▲	500m hard climb
36.2 ↰	'to Lauragh', Ardgroom
38.1 ●●	Ardgroom stone circle, 1.1km ↺
	alt route rejoins (continue)
47.1 ↰	'to Healy Pass'
47.3 ↰	'to Healy Pass' at An Sibín pub
▲	6km moderate climb
53.3	Healy Pass
59.8 ↰	'to Glengarriff', Adrigole
	retrace outward route to Glengarriff
77.8	Glengarriff TIC

Elevation

600
400
Eyeries
Healy Pass
200
Allihies   Urhan   Hag of Beara   Ardgroom   Glengarriff
0m
0km   10   20   30   40   50   60   70

SOUTHWEST

The most strenuous riding is through the striking, rocky scenery of the northern Beara Peninsula. The folds of rock are clearly evident; at times it feels like being on an island of pure rock. Atop the first steep climb, the Kerry mountains lie dramatically across the water. A short respite comes between Urhan (11km) and Eyeries (15.8km), after which some steep ascents and swooping descents lie before Ardgroom.

If you're feeling weary, you can avoid the strenuous 15km stretch between Eyeries and Ardgroom (albeit sacrificing views to the Ring of Kerry): take the direct R571 to Ardgroom instead of the coastal route at 18.9km.

It's a half-minute walk to the **Hag of Beara** (20.9km), a stone, covered with offerings of coins, shells and pebbles, said to be the petrified remains of a Celtic harvest goddess.

From Ardgroom, the road feels silky-smooth and flat, in comparison with the earlier section. A 1.1km partly unsealed side trip (plus five-minute walk) at 38.1km leads to the **Ardgroom stone circle** (a €2 donation is requested at an honesty box).

The climb to the **Healy Pass** (287m) is a highlight of the ride. The gradient of the steady climb is moderate, steepening only in the final 500m. It's said to be one of the most spectacular passes in Ireland and the views are indeed amazing: surrounding Glanmore Lake, the rugged hills of Beara's interior unfold as you ascend; Kenmare Bay and the mountains of the Iveragh Peninsula become visible in the distance. On the southern side, great walls of folded rock dominate the treeless landscape; as the road snakes down, it yields to wide open hillsides and eventually shrubs and small fields again.

From Adrigole (59.8km), the route retraces Day 1 back to Glengarriff.

Ring of Kerry

Duration	4 days
Distance	221.9km
Difficulty	moderate–hard
Start/End	Killarney

Ah, the famous Ring of Kerry. Beginning in beautiful Killarney, it heads through Ireland's highest mountains and down to the sea, the countryside growing hillocky and more rugged as it travels west. Rocks, like

a bad case of warts, pepper the landscape, and with level ground at a premium, even the tiniest flat spots are used to grow potatoes or hay. The coastal views around Derrynane are magnificent.

It's a beautiful place, all right. Trouble is, everyone wants to 'do the Ring', and most of them are in cars or tour buses – which is not such a beautiful thing if you happen to be cycling. That's why this route isn't quite the traditional 'Ring'. For a start, it travels clockwise; tour buses do the opposite (and several convoys whooshing past are easier to bear if they're on the other side of the white line). Day 3 takes the less-travelled 'Skellig Ring'; and Day 4, instead of tracing the Iveragh Peninsula's northern edge, heads through the middle – 'the way of Oisín' (see the boxed text, p146). Since the Day 1 route is partly closed to traffic, Day 2 is really the only section where you'll battle the buses.

NATURAL HISTORY

Killarney National Park, created in 1932, was Ireland's first national park. The park, immediately southwest of the town, covers an area of 102 sq km. In 1981 it was designated a Unesco Biosphere Reserve.

Ireland's only remaining wild herd of native red deer lives among the remote areas of blanket bog on the park's red sandstone uplands. On the lower slopes are 1200 hectares of old-growth oak woodland, the likes of which once covered much of Ireland. The woods support wildlife including the woodmouse, fox, badger, red and sika deer, red squirrel and pine marten, along with the chaffinch, robin, goldcrest, blue tit and wren. The yew woodland on the lowland limestone of Muckross Peninsula is thought to be one of only three pure yew woods in Europe.

Dominating the national park are the three lakes: Lough Leane (Lower Lake or 'Lake of Learning'), Muckross Lake and Upper Lake, which support brown trout, salmon, arctic char and Killarney shad.

Bird species recorded within the park number 141. Common summer species include the swallow, swift and cuckoo. Rarer are the Greenland white-fronted goose, peregrine falcon and osprey.

Other noteworthy species include the northern emerald dragonfly, found nowhere else in Ireland, the strawberry tree and the insectivorous greater butterwort. Exotic species include the rhododendron, sika deer and American mink

Derrynane National Historic Park near Caherdaniel is another area of oak woodland, while the offshore Skellig Islands (see the boxed text, p151) are home to billions of sea birds. Most obvious are puffins on Skellig Michael and gannets on Small Skellig; other species include storm petrel, kittiwake, fulmar, guillemot and razorbill.

PLANNING
When to Ride
Try to avoid July and August (especially bank holidays) when the area is thick with tourists (otherwise book accommodation well ahead). Early June is ideal; May weather is often good, though some services may be limited.

Maps
The OSI 1:250,000 Holiday map *Ireland South* covers the route. The 1:100,000 map *Ring of Kerry Cycle Route* is available from TICs. Its route varies considerably from that presented here.

What to Bring
Carry sturdy shoes if you plan to visit the Skellig Islands.

ACCESS TOWN
Killarney
☎ 064

Yes, it's touristy, it's ritzy, it's busy in summer. Killarney is, nevertheless, an attractive town beside the lakes, mountains and woods of beautiful Killarney National Park – it's worth spending a day or two exploring its environs.

Information Killarney TIC (☎ 31633, Beech Rd, open daily) can help with tourist information. All the major banks on New St have ATMs and bureaus de change. Another option is American Express (☎ 35722, East Avenue). The post office is on New St.

O'Sullivan's Cycles (☎ 31282, Bishop's Lane), off New St, is a Raleigh Rent-a-Bike agent, with a good range of new and rental bikes, outdoor gear and a repair workshop. Weekly rental costs €45, including panniers. It opens daily till late.

The Way of Oisín

The centuries-old Irish legends remain alive and well. That many of them relate to or explain actual geographical sites further enlivens these stories (typically, of noble deeds, heroic adventures, romance and tragedy) for the romantics among us. Occasional cryptic signs (like 'The Children of Lir mythical site') point to places that are part of a story.

The legend of Oisín (pronounced o-**sheen**) and the land of Tír na nÓg (Land of Eternal Youth) relates to the Ballaghisheen (literally 'Way of Oisín') Pass. Here's how the story goes:

Oisín and his father Fionn MacCumhaill (Finn McCool) were hunting near Lough Leane in Killarney when a white cloud approached them, from which appeared Niamh Cinn Óir (Niamh of the Golden Hair), riding a white stallion. She told them her father was the king of Tír na nÓg and invited Oisín to come with her.

Enveloped in cloud, Niamh and Oisín disappeared over the western horizon. Despite Oisín's promise to return, the saddened Fionn knew that he would never see his son again.

Deliriously happy with Niamh in the paradise of Tír na nÓg, Oisín was only troubled by his promise to his father: no-one had ever returned from Tír na nÓg before. He begged Niamh to let him go back once more. Niamh agreed, reluctantly, warning him to stay on the horse until he was back in Tír na nÓg.

Oisín was surprised to find people in Ireland much smaller than he had remembered. He was dismayed to find his father's fortress a moss-covered ruin. Dumbfounded, he realised that three centuries had passed since he'd left.

Riding sorrowfully through Gleann na Smól near Dublin, he came across some men struggling to move a large rock. Amazed at how small and weak they were, he leaned down to help them, easily moving the rock. In doing so the saddle slipped and he fell off the horse. In an instant, he became a shrivelled old man and crumbled into dust.

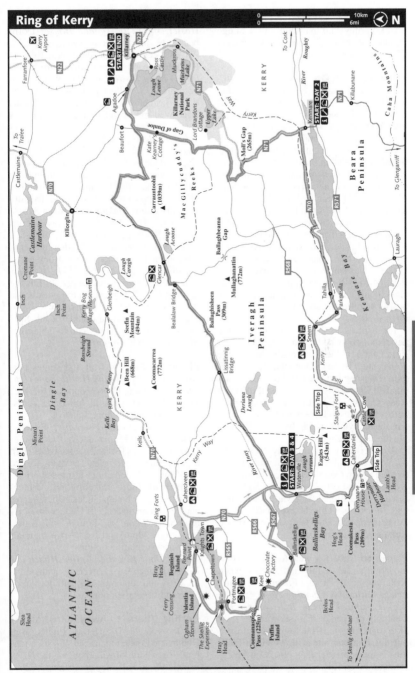

Trailways Outdoor Centre (☎ 39929, [e] trailwayskillarney@hotmail.com, 11 College St) also does rental (€39 per week, panniers €7) and repairs.

Things to See & Do Dominating the northern entrance of town, **St Mary's Cathedral** was designed by Augustus Pugin and built between 1846 and 1855. The **Museum of Irish Transport** (☎ 34677, East Avenue Rd) features vintage cars and bicycles.

It's well worth exploring **Killarney National Park**. Walking and cycling trails are generally well signed; maps from the TIC include the *Killarney Area Guide*, the *Simple Pocket Maps for Walkers & Cyclists in Killarney* and the OSI 1:25,000 National Park Series map *Killarney National Park*.

The core of Killarney National Park is the Muckross Estate, 5km south of Killarney, on the N71. Now managed by Dúchas, the stately Victorian **Muckross House & Gardens** (☎ 31440) shows upper- and servant-class living, and traditional handicrafts. The nearby **traditional farms** represent farming circa 1930.

It's a pleasant 2.4km ride through the park (start opposite St Mary's Cathedral) to **Ross Castle** (☎ 35851). Probably built in the 15th century by an O'Donoghue Ross chieftain, it was the last place in Munster to succumb to Cromwell's forces. A **boat trip** from Ross Castle takes you (and your bike) across the lakes to Lord Brandon's Cottage, from where you can ride back to Killarney via the Gap of Dunloe.

A deservedly popular **day trip** is the 57.5km circuit through the Gap of Dunloe to Moll's Gap (follow Day 1 of the Ring of Kerry ride, p149), returning to Killarney through the national park via Ladies View and Muckross. This is especially worth doing if you began the Ring of Kerry ride at Kenmare.

Places to Stay It's wise to book accommodation ahead in July and August, when Killarney really hops. *Fleming's White Bridge Caravan & Camping Park (☎ 31590, [e] fwbcamping@tinet.ie, Ballycasheen Rd)* Camping per person €6 (showers €1). At 3km east of town, it's not quite the closest, but this four-star site with excellent facilities is much prettier than others on Muckross and Fossa Rds.

An Óige *Killarney International Youth Hostel (☎ 31240, Agadoe House)* Dorm beds €13, private rooms per person €18. An 18th-century mansion 5.5km west of Killarney, in tiny Agadoe. *Neptune's Killarney Town Hostel (☎ 35255, [w] www.neptuneshostel.com, Bishops Lane)* Dorm beds €11-13, singles/doubles from €25/34. This large well-run hostel is near O'Sullivan's Cycles.

Leen's B&B (☎ 32819, [e] siobhanleen@eircom.net, 22 Marion Terrace) Ensuite singles/doubles €32/51. Central with good-sized rooms; excellent value. *Sunnybank (☎ 34109, Fairhill)* Ensuite singles/doubles €35/56. Opposite the bus station, friendly with airy rooms. *Oaklawn House (☎ 32616, Muckross Dr)* Ensuite singles/doubles €39/69. Spacious and beautifully furnished house with a well-tended garden; owner is a former national park ranger. Book early.

Fairview House (☎ 34164, [w] www.fairviewkillarney.com, College St) Ensuite doubles €77. The most central guesthouse in Killarney. *Glena House (☎ 32704, Muckross Rd)* Ensuite doubles €89. Spacious, nonsmoking rooms; comfortable common areas; drying rooms.

Places to Eat For fruit and vegies plus wholefoods, try *Horans Healthfoods (Innisfallen Shopping Centre)* opposite the TIC. *Tesco (New St)* opens till 7pm (later Thursday and Friday, till 6pm Sunday).

Stonechat (Fleming's Lane) Evening mains €10-13 (cheaper lunches). Good vegetarian food plus fish and chicken. Off High St. *The Caragh (106 New St)* Mains €5-15. Old-fashioned food at old-fashioned prices.

Taste of India (St Anthony's Place) Mains €8-13. Menu includes balti, tandoori and vegetarian dishes. Off College St. *Mustang Sally (Main St)* Mains €8-17. Music bar (after 9.30pm) and Tex-Mex restaurant; pasta and vegetarian options.

Blue Door Bistro & Coffee House (57 High St) Lunch €4-11, evening mains €14-23. Cosy and contemporary, with local produce and vegetarian options.

Getting There & Away Kerry Airport (☎ 066-976 4644) receives flights from Dublin and London Stanstead. It's at Farranfore, 16km north of Killarney (via the N22). A taxi to/from Killarney costs around €19.

Bus Éireann (☎ 30011, Park Rd; left luggage ☎ 37509, 7.30am-7pm daily) operates a Kerry Airport bus service (€4, 20 minutes, regular services). Other services to/from Killarney include Cork (€12, 1¾ hours, several daily), Shannon Airport (€14, four hours, three to 13 daily), Rosslare Harbour (€21, 6½ hours, one to four daily) and Dublin (€20, 6¼ hours, five daily).

Iarnród Éireann (☎ 1850 366 222) runs services between Killarney and Tralee (€7, 45 minutes, four daily), which connect with trains to Limerick and Dublin. For services between Killarney and Cork, you must change at Mallow (€18, 2½ hours, two to three daily). Killarney train station (☎ 1850 366 222) is off East Avenue Rd, opposite the Great Southern Hotel. Phone ☎ 1890 200 493 for 24-hour timetable information.

THE RIDE (see map p147)
Day 1: Killarney to Kenmare
2¼–4 hours, 42.2km

With some of Kerry's best mountain scenery and two gaps to climb through, this is a rewarding, if strenuous ride.

The Gap of Dunloe separates Ireland's highest mountains, MacGillycuddy's Reeks, from Purple Mountain. The Gap road starts at *Kate Kearney's Cottage* (☎ 064-44146), a touristy little complex, which serves bar food. It was originally a coaching inn,

where Kate bewitched customers with her beauty (or was it the illegal poteen – potato-based firewater – that she served?).

The Gap road is supposedly closed to motor traffic, but don't expect solitude: in summer it's packed with pony traps, walkers and cyclists – and the odd naughty car (hardly surprising with scenery this good). The climb is not a steady one: chunks of altitude are gained in short, steep bursts and, though it's all paved, expect to encounter some loose gravel and rough surfaces, especially on the steeper sections.

The glorious Black Valley lies to the other side. Look back from the valley and it seems that a wall of mountains surrounds you.

A turn-off at 21.7km leads to Lord Brandon's Cottage and the Upper Lake, from where boats sail to/from Killarney (see Things to See & Do in Killarney).

The climb to Moll's Gap is shorter (2.4km) but also has some steep pinches. A *café* capitalises on the views at the top; from here, it's all downhill to Kenmare.

Kenmare
See Kenmare (p140).

Day 2: Kenmare to Waterville
3¼–6 hours, 60.3km

The route passes through some of the more spectacular scenery on the 'Ring', though

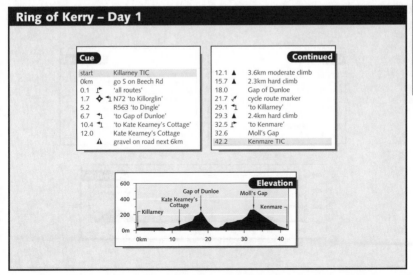

Ring of Kerry – Day 1

Cue				Continued
start	Killarney TIC	12.1 ▲	3.6km moderate climb	
0km	go S on Beech Rd	15.7 ▲	2.3km hard climb	
0.1 ↱	'all routes'	18.0	Gap of Dunloe	
1.7 ✦ ↰	N72 'to Killorglin'	21.7 ↗	cycle route marker	
5.2	R563 'to Dingle'	29.1 ↰	'to Killarney'	
6.7 ↰	'to Gap of Dunloe'	29.3 ▲	2.4km hard climb	
10.4 ↰	'to Kate Kearney's Cottage'	32.5 ↱	'to Kenmare'	
12.0	Kate Kearney's Cottage	32.6	Moll's Gap	
▲	gravel on road next 6km	42.2	Kenmare TIC	

Elevation

SOUTHWEST

most of it not until late in the day. The road undulates more past Sneem, although climbing is generally gradual. The most significant hill is the 5km climb to Coomakesta Pass (52.7km) – it's beautifully graded. Traffic is reasonably heavy, and the road surface patched and bumpy at times. Tour buses, which travel anticlockwise from Killarney, reach this section around 2pm to 5pm.

Travelling past fields and forest, the coast is barely visible for 14km, after which you're right by it, briefly. The mountains appear around Sneem (26km), a town seemingly geared for the tour bus crowd. However, as the largest settlement before Waterville, it's the best lunch option. The *Riverside Cafe & Coffee Shop*, across the bridge, does soup and sandwiches; otherwise, picnic on the north square or the river, or try the *pubs*.

In tiny Castle Cove, plaques commemorate local sons, including Joseph White, All-Ireland Cycling Champion from 1952 to 1954. Soon after, a side trip (at 40.8km) leads to 2000-year-old **Staigue Fort**, one of Ireland's finest dry-stone buildings, which sits 120m above sea level.

Caherdaniel (46.7km) has the closest *camping* to Waterville. From here there is a side trip to **Derrynane House** (☎ 066-947 5113), home of 'the Great Liberator' Daniel O'Connell, set in the oak woods of Derrynane National Historic Park. The €3 entry

fee includes an informative audiovisual presentation. Wander the gardens for free or walk to the lovely beach nearby (beware of strong currents). *Annies Cafe*, by the house, is locally recommended for daytime meals and cakes.

Climbing from Caherdaniel, the views over Derrynane National Historic Park, the harbour and islands are magnificent. At Coomakesta Pass, a coach parking bay by the Madonna statue allows bus-bound tourists to feel the fresh air and take in the views through their camera lenses.

Waterville
☎ 066

Built along the wide front of Ballinskelligs Bay, Waterville itself is fairly plain, especially compared with the scenery that surrounds it. In 1866, the transatlantic telegraph cable connected Europe and America through cable stations at Waterville, and at nearby Valentia Island and Ballinskelligs. Today, the town is largely dependent on tourism. Accommodation is heavily booked during the Summer Splash festival (generally the second weekend in July), even more so during the August bank holiday weekend.

Information The TIC (☎ 947 4646, open June-Sept) is on the foreshore. Contact the Killarney TIC (☎ 064-31633) at other times.

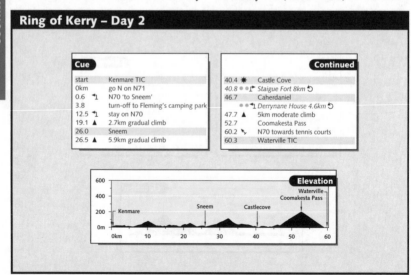

Ring of Kerry – Day 2

SOUTHWEST

Cue	
start	Kenmare TIC
0km	go N on N71
0.6 ↰	N70 'to Sneem'
3.8	turn-off to Fleming's camping park
12.5 ↰	stay on N70
19.1 ▲	2.7km gradual climb
26.0	Sneem
26.5 ▲	5.9km gradual climb

Continued	
40.4 ✳	Castle Cove
40.8 ● ● ↳	*Staigue Fort 8km* ↻
46.7	Caherdaniel
● ● ↳	*Derrynane House 4.6km* ↻
47.7 ▲	5km moderate climb
52.7	Coomakesta Pass
60.2 ↘	N70 towards tennis courts
60.3	Waterville TIC

Skellig Islands

The Skellig Islands jut out of the Atlantic Ocean, 12km from the mainland. A trip to these rocky other-worlds is an experience for which the description 'unforgettable' is truly apt. Both islands have a fantasy-like magic to them. The larger, puffin-populated Skellig Michael was, incredibly, the site of a monastic settlement between the 6th and 12th centuries. Despite Viking raids in the 8th and 9th centuries the monastery remains largely intact. Climb – as the monks must have – 150m above sea level, to the beehive oratories and cells. A sense of peace pervades the site, the enclosing wall offering some protection from the wind.

The craggy, castle-like Small Skellig is a bird sanctuary, home to 20,000 pairs of gannets; seals are often seen on the rocks at the base.

Boat trips leave from Ballinskelligs, the closest port to the islands (14.6km from Waterville); from Portmagee; and from Derrynane, near Caherdaniel. Ballinskelligs operators include Joe Roddy (☎ 066-947 4268), Sean Feehan (☎ 066-947 9182) and JB Walsh (☎ 066-947 9147). Sean O'Shea (☎ 066-947 5129) sails from Derrynane. Ask whether the boat operator will pick you up from Waterville (or ask your B&B or hostel about transport to the boat). Visitors to the island are limited and you must book at least by the night before to guarantee a place on the boat. Expect to pay €32 (some boats cost more in the high season) for the trip, which involves two hours on Skellig Michael and at least an hour each way on the boat. The crossing can be rough (you'll probably get wet), and won't be made at all in bad weather. The islands have no toilets or shelter; bring warm and waterproof clothes, stout shoes, food and water.

If you can't get to the islands, **The Skellig Experience** (☎ 066-947 6306), on Valentia Island (see Day 3 of the Ring of Kerry ride, p152) has exhibitions, and a 16-minute audiovisual show, about the monks' life on Skellig Michael. Other displays focus on wildlife, and the lighthouse on Skellig Michael.

The website W www.waterville-insight.com also supplies local information.

Banks on Main St include the Bank of Ireland (open 10.15am-12.30pm Tues year-round, Fri June-Sept) and AIB (open 10am-12.30pm Mon year-round, Thurs June-Sept). Neither has an ATM. The TIC, post office (opposite the TIC) and several businesses have bureau de change facilities.

Quinlan Cycles (☎ 947 4307, open 9am-7pm) is attached to a house at the southern end of Main St.

Things to See & Do Behind the TIC, the Skellig Reflections **Photography Exhibition** opens 10am to 2pm weekdays.

The best thing to do in Waterville is to take a trip to the Skellig Islands (see the boxed text).

Places to Stay & Eat The closest camping to Waterville is 1.5km east of Caherdaniel at *Wave Crest Caravan Park* (☎ 947 5188, N70) Tent sites per person €6, showers €1. Coastal camping site with laundry facilities, a store and shelter. *Mannix Point Camping & Caravan Park* (☎ 947 2806)

Tent sites per person €7, showers €1; 1.5km west of Caherciveen.

Peter's Place Hostel (*Main St*) Dorm beds €11. Easy-going; no telephone or bookings.

The Old Cable House B&B (☎ 947 4233, W www.old-cable-house.com) Standard/ensuite doubles €49/64; singles supplement €7. Airy rooms have folksy elegance; warm welcome for cyclists. Downstairs is *Browns Restaurant* Early bird two-course special €16-20 5pm to 7pm; otherwise, mains €13-16. Small, pleasant restaurant, generally open nightly in summer. *Clifford's B&B* (☎ 947 4283, Main St) Singles €32, doubles €44-51. Spacious rooms, plus laundry and drying facilities.

Silver Sands Guesthouse (☎ 947 4161, Main St) Singles/doubles €20/39 (with ensuite €32/51). Brightly painted rooms; laundry/drying service.

O'Dwyers The Villa (☎ 947 4248, Main St) Ensuite singles/doubles €32/64. Small-ish, comfortable hotel rooms are away from the pub noise; unsheltered (secure) bike storage. Bar mains €7-19 (no vegetarian). More a local pub than a tourist haunt.

SOUTHWEST

Centra supermarket The best grocery store, a few doors along from the post office.

Beachcove Cafe Pizzas €5-6, other fast food plus soup and sandwiches. Licensed; next to the post office. **An Corcán** Mains €7-17 including vegetarian. Good value but ordinary; licensed. **Shéilin Seafood Restaurant** (☎ 947 4231) Early bird special €18 from 6pm to 7.30pm; otherwise, mains €14-22 (Ballinskelligs Bay lobster €26/lb). Cosy, licensed restaurant near the supermarket. **Lobster Bar** (Main St) Mains €7-19, including vegetarian. Popular pub.

Day 3: The Skellig Ring & Valentia Island

3–5¾ hours, 58km

Leave your panniers behind for the 'Skellig Ring', a signed circuit at the peninsula's western end, which starts and ends in Waterville. It's separate from, and much less travelled than, the main 'Ring of Kerry' (tour buses are prohibited); remote and sleepy, it's literally 'land's end'.

The terrain is mainly undulating with three main climbs. The second, to Coomanaspig Pass, is very steep and often walked. Rough patches mar the descent. Sections of the road on Valentia (sometimes spelt Valencia) Island are also rough and potholed.

Leaving the N70, the route heads southwest to the tiny settlement of Ballinskelligs (Baile an Sceilg; boats to the Skellig Islands leave nearby) and climbs through patchwork fields to the western edge of the peninsula and the Atlantic. The **pub** at Ballinskelligs is the last place for food until Portmagee.

Stone walls cut through the fields to the cliffs above the ocean. On misty days sheep and white cottages are bright spots among the green and grey. Ruined houses hint at the hardship here during the Great Famine: many were forced to leave.

It's an unlikely landscape in which to find a **chocolate factory**, but don't miss Skelligs Mixed Truffles (20.7km; ☎ 066-947 9119). Tastings of the enormous variety of truffles are free, and bags are packed small enough to please your pocket and your pannier.

Over the Coomanaspig Pass (225m) is Portmagee (29.8km) and the bridge to Valentia Island. Just across the bridge is **The Skellig Experience** (see the boxed text 'Skellig Islands', p151).

Ring of Kerry – Day 3

Cue			Continued	
start	Waterville TIC		25.5	Coomanaspic Pass
0km	go NW 'to Golf Links'		⚠	steep descent, rough patches
1.6 ↱	Ring of Kerry bike sign		29.8 ↱	'to Valencia Island', Portmagee
2.7 ↘	N70 Ring of Kerry bike sign		30.1 ↗	'to Valencia Island' over bridge
3.6 ↘	'to Skellig Ring'		30.6 ✳	The Skellig Experience
4.9 ▲	500m moderate climb		30.9 ↰	'Valentia Ring'
5.4 ↰	R567 'Skellig Ring'		32.5 ↗	'Valentia Ring'
10.5 ↑	ignore Ring of Kerry bike sign		33.9 ▲	1.4km moderate climb
11.2 ↰	R566		35.2 ✳	Ogham stones (RHS)
14.6 ↱	'Skellig Ring', Baile an Sceilge		37.9 ↰	'Valentia Ring'
▲	2.6km moderate climb		38.0 ↱	'Valentia Ring'
15.0 ↘	'Skellig Ring'		40.7 ↘	'Valentia Ring', Knights Town
15.2 ↗	'Skellig Ring'		41.2	ferry landing
17.7 ▲	400m steep climb		catch ferry to mainland	
21.0 ✳	chocolate factory		43.8 ↱	N70
21.8 ↰	'to Portmagee', Keel		55.3 ↗	N70 'to Waterville'
23.1 ▲	1km moderate climb		58.0	Waterville TIC
24.1 ▲	1.4km very steep climb			

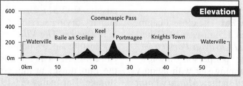

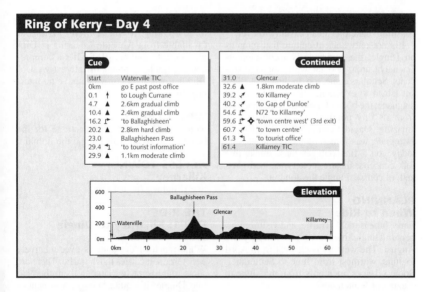

Ring of Kerry – Day 4

Cue			Continued	
start	Waterville TIC	31.0	Glencar	
0km	go E past post office	32.6 ▲	1.8km moderate climb	
0.1 ↑	to Lough Currane	39.2 ↗	'to Killarney'	
4.7 ▲	2.6km gradual climb	40.2 ↗	'to Gap of Dunloe'	
10.4 ▲	2.4km gradual climb	54.6 ↱	N72 'to Killarney'	
16.2 ↱	'to Ballaghisheen'	59.6 ↱ ✧	'town centre west' (3rd exit)	
20.2 ▲	2.8km hard climb	60.7 ↗	'to town centre'	
23.0	Ballaghisheen Pass	61.3 ↰	'to tourist office'	
29.4 ↰	'to tourist information'	61.4	Killarney TIC	
29.9 ▲	1.1km moderate climb			

On Valentia Island, look out for **archaeological monuments**, including Ogham stones, close to the road. The ferry (€3, five minutes) from Knights Town, once the only access to Valentia Island, was stopped when the Portmagee bridge was built, only to be reinstated at the locals' insistence.

Day 4: Waterville to Killarney
3–6 hours, 61.4km

In contrast to the well-trodden 'Ring', the interior of the Iveragh Peninsula is peacefully quiet. Only after Glencar does traffic become noticeable (and the roads more potholed). Though it's surrounded by mountains, the route mostly follows the valleys. However, it's also known locally as 'the road over the pass'; Ballaghisheen Pass (23km) is a tough climb: almost 3km of moderately steep gradient incorporates a couple of very steep sections. Just before the top, you can see down the valley to the sea. At the pass, MacGillycuddy's Reeks, among which is Carrauntoohil, Ireland's highest peak, lie ahead.

The day's first 20km, along the valley of the River Inny, is fairly easy riding, through farmland, bogs and pine forest, and overlooking Lough Currane and Deriana Lough.

A long gradual descent to Glencar (which, they say, translates to 'Valley of the Friendly People') follows the initial swoop down from Ballaghisheen Pass. *The Climbers Inn*

(☎ *066-976 0101, Glencar*), at 31km, is one of the few services on the route. It has a basic store, picnic tables and bar food all day. It also has hostel and B&B accommodation plus free camping (no facilities).

A picturesque climb (at 32.6km) by a rushing stream ends just past Lough Acoose, after which a long, slow descent around MacGillycuddy's Reeks continues almost to Killarney.

Dingle Peninsula

Duration	3 days
Distance	176.6km
Difficulty	moderate–hard
Start	Killarney
End	Tralee

Compared with the rugged, rocky peninsulas to the south, Dingle appears more rounded and somehow softer, although it's here that you'll climb Ireland's highest pass.

The highlight is exploration of the tranquil region west of Dingle town on Day 2. Here is the greatest concentration of ancient sites in Kerry (if not in the whole of Ireland), and the superb Blasket Centre at Dunquin, which features less ancient, but equally fascinating, life on the recently abandoned Blasket Islands. Cultural attractions aside, its gentle gradients, sweeping vistas and dramatic coastline make this area heavenly to cycle.

It's not only ancient culture that remains on Dingle: the peninsula is a conspicuous Gaeltacht area, popular with language students. Scholars came, too, to the Great Blasket Island to experience traditional life and language; the body of literature that emanated from its tiny population last century was amazing. David Lean's 1970 film, *Ryan's Daughter*, was filmed on the peninsula, and today you'll find pub sessions, smoke-free folk concerts, theatre, pottery, stained glass and, of course, Fungie the dolphin.

PLANNING
When to Ride
Early June is ideal. Traffic, and visitor numbers in Dingle town, are heavier in July and August. The weather is clearest from April to June, warmest from June to September. Some services open only from mid-June to August or September.

Maps & Books
The OSI 1:250,000 Holiday map *Ireland South* covers the route. For Day 2, it's well worth purchasing Maurice Sheehy's *Motorists Guide to the Dingle Peninsula* (available from An Cafe Liteártha in Dingle, see Information, p155). It's a comprehensive guide to points of interest west of Dingle town, many of which have no interpretation at the site.

What to Bring
You'll need a swimming costume for the beach or to swim with Fungie the dolphin.

ACCESS TOWN
Killarney
See Killarney (p146).

THE RIDE
Day 1: Killarney to Dingle
3½–6½ hours, 65.8km
While much of the route is over relatively easy terrain, it carries much traffic. There are some rough stretches, among them the N86 into Dingle: it's quite bumpy. A strenuous 9.3km section (at 47.4km), virtually traffic-free, avoids the busy but flat N86 (hillophobes and truckophiles could continue on the main road here).

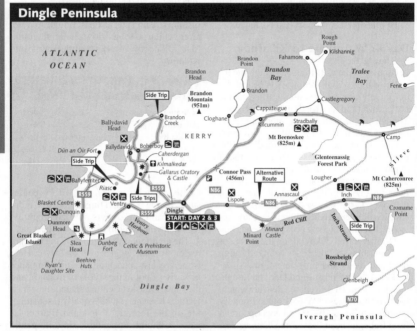

As MacGillycuddy's Reeks fade behind you, the Slieve Mish mountains, to the north, loom ever closer. The countryside is noticeably greener on Dingle than on the rugged and rocky peninsulas further south. In June, expect to encounter hay-carting tractors.

From Castlemaine, the road undulates gently between the mountains and Dingle Bay. If you're a vegetarian, don't miss *The Phoenix* (☎ 066-976 6284) farmhouse organic vegetarian café at 28km; lunch mains are €5-8. Extensive gardens and greenhouses supply some of the produce. Camping, hostel and B&B accommodation is also available; it's a hippie kind of place, with creative, Indian-influenced furnishings.

Otherwise, the short side trip to Inch Strand is a perfect lunch option. The wide sand spit stretches into Dingle Bay, looking across to the Ring of Kerry. Along with picnic tables, there's a small *store*, a *café*, plus a *pub* across the road.

Heading back inland, watch for the narrow lane at 47.4km – the turn is unsigned except for a walking marker. The climb affords wonderful views right along the peninsula's patchwork valley.

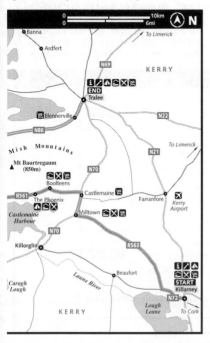

Minard Castle (51.7km) by tiny Storm Beach was built in 1560 but destroyed in 1649 by Cromwellian forces. The rounded boulders on the beach were once part of the sandstone cliffs.

Another strenuous climb lies between the beach and the main road. Watch for the left turn (54.7km) on the downhill: it also is signed only with a walking marker.

Dingle
☎ 066

Signposted as 'An Daingean', the town's proper name, Daingean Ui Chuis, is said to mean 'Hussey's fortress', which is thought to refer to the settlement of a 13th-century Flemish family. Though it becomes very busy with visitors during the summer, especially on weekends, Dingle has a healthy local community, rich in fisherfolk, artists and musicians – and is famous for longtime resident, Fungie the dolphin.

Information The TIC (☎ 915 1188, open 9.15am-5pm Mon-Sat, until 6pm June-Sept, 10am-5pm Sun) is at the Quay and operates a bureau de change. Bank of Ireland and AIB banks on Main St have ATMs and bureau de change facilities, as does the post office, also on Main St.

Paddy's Bike Shop (☎ 915 2311, Dykegate Lane) does repairs and rentals. Mountain Man (☎ 915 2400, Strand St) supplies camping and outdoor equipment. An Cafe Liteártha (Dykegate St) is an excellent bookshop with a café behind.

Things to See & Do St James's Church (Lower Main St) hosts **folk concerts** on Monday and Thursday (7.30pm); it's wise to buy advance tickets from Murphy's Icecream (see Places to Eat).

Visit Díseart (☎ 915 2476), next to St Mary's Church, for extraordinary **stained-glass windows** made in 1924 by renowned Irish artist, Harry Clarke.

Regular boat trips to see **Fungie**, Dingle's playful wild dolphin, include an 8am trip to swim with him. Book trips with Dingle Boatmen's Association (☎ 915 2626) at the Quay. **Boat trips** with Dingle Marine Eco Tours (☎ 086-285 8802), next door, incorporate archaeology, geology, history and wildlife. Alternatively, see the marine life indoors at **Dingle Oceanworld** (☎ 915 2111, Strand St).

SOUTHWEST

Places to Stay Camping is available at the two best hostels, both outside the town centre. *Rainbow Hostel (☎ 915 1044)* Camping €7, dorm beds €12. Excellent farmhouse-style hostel; great kitchen but smallish dorms. Western end of town, 600m north of the roundabout. *Ballintaggart House (☎ 915 1454, N86)* Camping €6, dorm beds €12-14. Large, friendly hostel in an 18th-century hunting lodge; 2.2km east of town.

D'Coileáin B&B (☎ 915 1937, Holyground) Ensuite singles/doubles €36/51. Central; friendly hosts, airy rooms and a garden: a lovely place to stay. *Kirrary B&B (☎ 915 1606, Avondale)* Singles €28-32, standard/ensuite doubles €51/56. Shares garden with D'Coileáin; nonsmoking, with bright, comfortable rooms; rents out bikes. *Tower View B&B (☎ 915 2990, High Rd)* Ensuite singles/doubles €36/59. Comfortably furnished spacious rooms; 100m east of the western roundabout.

Benners Hotel (☎ 915 1638, Main St) Singles/doubles €81/115. A Best Western hotel; large rooms with folk-style furniture.

Places to Eat It's worth booking for dinner during summer in Dingle. *Super Valu (Holyground)* Open late in summer. *An Grianán Wholefood Shop (Dykegate St)* Health foods, plus gourmet deli. *O Curnain Bakery (Dick Mack's Yard, Green St)*.

Murphy's Icecream (cnr Strand St & Holyground) Nonsmoking; yummy desserts, home-made ice cream, and coffee. *Next Door (cnr Holyground & Bridge St)* Take-away next to Greany's.

Greany's (☎ 915 0924, Holyground) Evening mains €7-18. Locally recommended: good food and good value. Breakfast from 9am (cereals and fruit; full Irish €7). *Paudie's Bar (☎ 915 1231, Strand St)* Bar meals €8-13 including vegetarian. Good-value, bustling pub, with atmosphere – and tourists. *The Loft (☎ 915 2431, Dick Mack's Yard)* Mains €10-17. Flavoursome Mediterranean- and Mexican-style dishes; tucked away off Green St.

Global Village (☎ 915 2325, Main St) Mains €13-19. Modern place with dishes from around the world (vegetarian options). *Fentons Restaurant (☎ 915 2172, Green St)* Early bird three-course special €23 (6pm-7.30pm); otherwise, mains €16-22 (including vegetarian). Highly regarded modern cuisine; a meal to linger over.

Day 2: Slea Head Circuit
3–6 hours, 63.3km

There's so much on this ride that you'll need a full day, despite the mostly gentle terrain. Unless you despise history and archaeology, it's worth spending two days in this lovely area. Hostel and B&B accommodation is

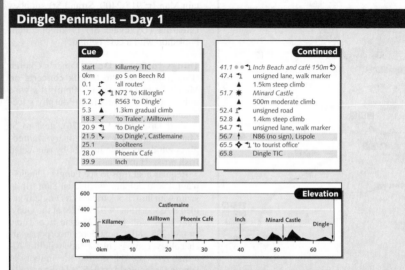

Dingle Peninsula – Day 1

Cue	
start	Killarney TIC
0km	go S on Beech Rd
0.1	↱ 'all routes'
1.7	✧ ↰ N72 'to Killorglin'
5.2	↱ R563 'to Dingle'
5.3	▲ 1.3km gradual climb
18.3	↙ 'to Tralee', Milltown
20.9	↰ 'to Dingle'
21.5	↘ 'to Dingle', Castlemaine
25.1	Boolteens
28.0	Phoenix Café
39.9	Inch

	Continued
41.1	● ● ↰ Inch Beach and café 150m ↩
47.4	↰ unsigned lane, walk marker
	▲ 1.5km steep climb
51.7	✳ Minard Castle
	▲ 500m moderate climb
52.4	↱ unsigned road
52.8	▲ 1.4km steep climb
54.7	↰ unsigned lane, walk marker
56.7	↑ N86 (no sign), Lispole
65.5	✧ ↰ 'to tourist office'
65.8	Dingle TIC

Elevation

Killarney — Milltown — Castlemaine — Phoenix Café — Inch — Minard Castle — Dingle

(600, 400, 200, 0m; 0km, 10, 20, 30, 40, 50, 60)

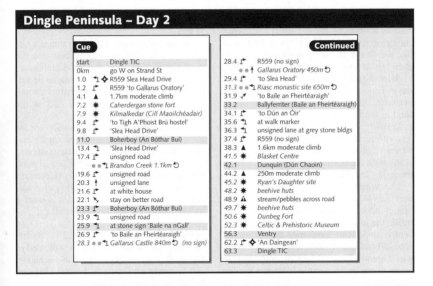

Dingle Peninsula – Day 2

Cue			Continued	
start	Dingle TIC	28.4 ⌐	R559 (no sign)
0km	go W on Strand St	● ● ✝	*Gallarus Oratory 450m* ↻
1.0	⬏ ✦ R559 Slea Head Drive	29.4 ⌐	'to Slea Head'
1.2	⌐ R559 'to Gallarus Oratory'	31.3 ● ● ⬏	*Riasc monastic site 650m* ↻
4.1	▲ 1.7km moderate climb	31.9 ↙	'to Baile an Fheirtéaraigh'
7.2	✳ *Caherdergan stone fort*	33.2	Ballyferriter (Baile an Fheirtéaraigh)
7.9	✳ *Kilmalkedar (Cill Maoilchéadair)*	34.1 ⌐	'to Dún an Óir'
9.4	⌐ 'to Tigh A'Phoist Brú hostel'	35.6 ⬏	at walk marker
9.8	⌐ 'Slea Head Drive'	36.3 ⬏	unsigned lane at grey stone bldgs
11.0	Boherboy (An Bóthar Buí)	37.4 ⌐	R559 (no sign)
13.4	⬏ 'Slea Head Drive'	38.3 ▲	1.6km moderate climb
17.4	⌐ unsigned road	41.5 ✳	*Blasket Centre*
● ● ⬏	*Brandon Creek 1.1km* ↻	42.1	Dunquin (Dún Chaoin)
19.6	⌐ unsigned road	44.2 ▲	250m moderate climb
20.3	↑ unsigned lane	45.2 ✳	*Ryan's Daughter site*
21.6	⌐ at white house	48.2 ✳	*beehive huts*
22.1	↘ stay on better road	48.9 ⚠	stream/pebbles across road
23.3	⌐ Boherboy (An Bóthar Buí)	49.7 ✳	*beehive huts*
23.9	⬏ unsigned road	50.6 ✳	*Dunbeg Fort*
25.9	⬏ at stone sign 'Baile na nGall'	52.3 ✳	*Celtic & Prehistoric Museum*
26.9	⌐ 'to Baile an Fheirtéaraigh'	56.3	Ventry
28.3 ● ● ⬏	*Gallarus Castle 840m* ↻ *(no sign)*	62.2 ⌐ ✦	'An Daingean'
		63.3	Dingle TIC

available at Ballyferriter (Baile an Fheirtéaraigh; 33.2km) and Dunquin (Dún Chaoin; 42.1km); and camping near the Gallarus Oratory (28.4km).

The route is described anticlockwise, since the main traffic flow is clockwise (as is signposting). Traffic is heaviest between Dingle, Dunquin and the Gallarus Oratory; fewer tourists travel out to Brandon Creek. Consider travelling clockwise if you want to be sure to see the Blasket Centre.

The *Motorists Guide to the Dingle Peninsula* (see Maps & Books, p154) covers the area comprehensively; following is a selection of interesting sites.

Caherdergan (7.2km) is a ring fort with beehive huts; **Kilmalkedar** (Cill Maoilchéadair; 7.9km), a 12th-century church on the site of St Maolchéadair's 7th-century monastery; and **Brandon Creek** (side trip at 17.4km), the place from which St Brendan allegedly set sail (see the boxed text 'St Brendan's Voyage', p158).

An unsigned lane (28.3km) leads to the 16th-century **Gallarus Castle**. More famous is the incredibly preserved **Gallarus Oratory** (side trip at 28.4km), unaltered since its construction in the 7th or 8th century. The €3 entry fee includes a 15-minute video (which also shows scenery you may have missed in bad weather). Remains of the 5th- or 6th-century **Riasc Monastic Settlement**

(side trip at 31.3km) offer an inkling of community life.

The scattered village of Dunquin looks across to the celebrated Blasket Islands, which were inhabited until 1953. Leave at least 1½ hours to visit the **Blasket Centre** (41.5km; ☎ 915 6444), which offers a fascinating insight into life (and literature) on Great Blasket Island; last admission 6.15pm in the high season. **Blasket Island ferries** depart regularly for the Islands from Dunquin Pier (☎ 915 6422).

Around Slea Head is some of the ride's more spectacular scenery. The **beach** that featured in *Ryan's Daughter* is at 45.2km. **Beehive huts** and other ruins pepper the hillside east of Slea Head; inside the cliff-edge **Dunbeg Promontory Fort** (50.6km) are the remains of a house and underground passage. Entrepreneurial land owners charge €2 to visit any of these sights.

The impressive private collection at the **Celtic & Prehistoric Museum** (52.3km; ☎ 915 9941) includes a woolly mammoth skull.

Day 3: Dingle to Tralee
2½–4¾ hours, 47.5km

The Connor Pass (456m), Ireland's highest pass, is the highlight of this ride (or the heartbreak, depending on how you view it). The 6.5km steady slog culminates in terrific views north and south, weather permitting. And as if reaching the top wasn't heavenly enough in itself, a harpist plays at the pass in fine weather. For more punishment, walk up even higher from the car park at the saddle.

After the pass, it's pretty much plain sailing to Tralee. The road undulates only gently between the mountains and the golden-sand beaches of Brandon and Tralee Bays.

Traffic increases considerably after the turn-off to Castlegregory (24.3km), more so on rejoining the N86 (32.2km). This, along with the patched road surface, makes the going less pleasant for the final leg.

The **windmill** (☎ 712 1064) at Blennerville (44km) is the largest working mill in Ireland or Britain. Along with displays inside the mill is an exhibition in the visitor centre about the thousands of emigrants who left Ireland in 'coffin ships' from what was County Kerry's largest embarkation point. Close by, the **Jeanie Johnston Visitor Shipyard** (☎ 712 9999) has built a replica of an emigrant ship that made at least 16 voyages between Tralee and the new world. Although she eventually sank, she never lost a passenger. The replica sailed to the USA in 2003.

St Brendan's Voyage

It hardly looks like the place to begin a momentous voyage, but Brandon Creek was where St Brendan allegedly set sail, in AD 535, bound for Tír na nÓg (Land of Eternal Youth). His mission? To convert the inhabitants to Christianity.

According to legend, he spent 40 days fasting and praying on nearby Brandon Mountain before embarking, with his band of monks, in a *curragh* (traditional rowing boat). Brendan recorded the journey in his manuscript *Navigatio Sancti Brendani Hobatis*. It appears, from his descriptions, that the land he found (after seven years) was North America.

Adventurer Tim Severin retraced St Brendan's voyage in a similar vessel in 1977, showing that it could indeed have been done hundreds of years before Columbus, and that the lands St Brendan described visiting on his journey were probably the Hebrides, the Faroes, Iceland and Greenland. His book *The Brendan Voyage* is his account.

Tralee
☎ 066

With a population of 20,000, Tralee is a sizable town handily positioned between the west Kerry peninsulas and the Shannon region to the north. Attractive gardens lie immediately south of the town centre; beyond, in the distance, is the eastern end of the Slieve Mish mountain range.

Tralee is famous internationally for its Rose of Tralee festival, a big bash at the end of August, which culminates in the contest to crown 'the Rose' – an overseas girl with Irish blood (plus beauty and talent). Accommodation is heavily booked and pricier during the festival. Otherwise, Tralee is more a locals' town than a glitzy tourist affair.

Information Tralee TIC (☎ 712 1288), beside the Ashe Memorial Hall, is at the end of Denny St. It has a café and bureau de change.

The banks on Castle St have ATMs and bureau de change facilities.

Tralee Gas Supplies (☎ 712 2018, Strand St) is a Raleigh Rent-a-Bike agent and does repairs. Rental costs €45 per week, all-inclusive; special rates can be negotiated for long-term rental. Call of The Wild (☎ 712 3820, Ivy Terrace) is a well-stocked outdoor and camping centre.

Things to See & Do Siamsa Tíre, the **National Folk Theatre** (☎ 712 3055), off Ivy Terrace, has productions based on Celtic culture most nights from April to September. It's highly regarded; book ahead to guarantee seats.

Also well regarded is the **Kerry the Kingdom** museum (☎ 712 7777) in Ashe Memorial Hall. Its three exhibitions use audiovisual and interactive media to give a concise history of Ireland with the emphasis on County Kerry.

Places to Stay Excellent camping is just south of the town centre: *Woodlands Park* (☎ 712 1235, e wdlands@eircom.net, Dan Spring Rd) Cyclists per person €7, showers €1. Facilities include an indoor room, games room, laundry and left luggage.

Tralee has an odd bag of hostels. Those in the centre are semi-hotel style: expensive, with mediocre facilities. *Collis Sandes House* (☎/fax 712 8648, Oakpark) Camping €6, dorm beds €12. Former convent with large, multibed dorms; bikes are not sheltered. It's 2.5km north of town, off the N69. *Westward Court* (☎ *718 0081, Mary St)* Beds in 4-bed dorms €16. Comfy, but small ensuite rooms; the tiny kitchen isn't adequate.

Leeside B&B (☎ *712 6475,* [e] *dowlings bandb@hotmail.com; N69, Oakpark)* Ensuite singles/doubles €26/51. Smallish, but bright, comfy rooms. *Alverna* (☎ *712 6970; 26 Liosdara, Oakpark)* Singles/doubles €30/44, ensuite doubles €49. Smallish rooms, quiet street and handy to train and bus. *Bricruiú* (☎ *712 6347, 20 Old Gold Links Rd)* Ensuite doubles €49. Homely like Grandma's, smallish rooms.

Imperial Hotel (☎ *712 7755, 25 Denny St)* Ensuite singles/doubles €51/89. A central, older-style hotel. A curry house should be operating from the restaurant by now.

Places to Eat Self-caterers should head to the grocery precinct on Abbey Court, off The Square. Try *Tesco (Abbey Court)*. *Seancara Wholefood Grocer (Abbey Court)* Bakery and health foods plus takeaway bargains (vegie chilli and rice €4). *The Rolling Pin Homebakery (Russell St)* Probably Tralee's best bakery (café adjoining).

New Yorkers & Liberty Pizza Co (Bridge St) Pizzas €7-11, plus burgers, chicken, fish and chips; open late. *La Scala (The Square)* Mains €6-14. Cheap and cheerful Italian, good pasta selection; open late. *Val's Bistro* (☎ *712 1559, 4 Bridge St)* Mains €9-19. Decent modern cuisine (including pastas); trendy, yet cosy, atmosphere. Upstairs from Val O'Shea's Bar; bookings are advised. *Finnegans Cellar Restaurant* (☎ *718 1400, 17 Denny St)* Mains €12-22. Best bet for good food; traditional-style, limited vegetarian options.

Getting There & Away Kerry Airport (☎ *976 4644)* receives flights from Dublin and London Stanstead. It's at Farranfore, 19km southeast of Tralee (via the N22). Bus Éireann's Tralee-Cork-Rosslare service stops at Farranfore on request; Tralee-Farranfore costs €4 (20 minutes). A taxi to/from Tralee costs around €30.

Dingle Peninsula – Day 3

Cue	
start	Dingle TIC
0km	go E on Strand St
0.0 ↗	(70m) 'The Tracks'
0.3 ↑ ◆	'to Connor Pass'
0.6 ↰	Main St
0.6 ↱	(10m) 'to Connor Pass'
0.9 ↗	'to Connor Pass'
▲	6.5km hard climb
7.4	Connor Pass
20.7	Strandbally
44.0 ✳	Blennerville
44.4 ↗	N86 'to Tralee'
46.3 ↰◆	'to centre' Prince's Quay
47.0 ↗	Russell St
47.1 ↖	The Mall
47.2 ↱	Denny St
47.5 ↖	'to tourist office'
47.6	Tralee TIC

Iarnród Éireann (☎ 1850 366 222) runs services between Tralee's Casement Station (☎ 712 3522) and Limerick (€20, 2½ hours, four daily), Dublin (€46, four to five hours, three to four daily), Killarney (€7, 45 minutes, four daily) and Cork (€18, 2½ hours, three to four daily).

The Bus Éireann Travel Centre (☎ 712 3566) is at Casement Station, on the corner of Oakpark (N69) and John Joe Sheehy Rds. Services to/from Tralee include Shannon Airport (3¼ hours, five to eight daily), Tarbert (€8, 45 minutes, one per week), Cork (€13, 2½ hours, 10 to 14 daily) via Killarney (€6, 40 minutes, 10 to 14 daily), and Rosslare Harbour (seven hours, one to four daily).

The 38.1km ride to Killarney climbs over the eastern shoulder of the Slieve Mish mountains (much easier than the Connor Pass!) to Castlemaine, from where it retraces the Day 1 route. From the TIC, go west on Ivy Terrace, left into Princes St, and continue, ignoring signs to Killarney. Turn left 'to Castlemaine' around 3km and right (unsigned) onto the N70 at 4.4km. Traffic is moderately light throughout.

West

Think of the west of Ireland and you'll likely conjure up images of misty mountains and lonely bogs – the territory of fairies and leprechauns. That wild romantic west is certainly there to be found – but the magic extends much further. Other charms include hearing the Irish language (widely spoken in Connemara and Mayo), dozens of golden-sand beaches, the majestic Cliffs of Moher, the bizarre and compelling Burren, Ireland's only fjord, the most ancient farm in the world and other special places undiscovered by the tourist masses.

The west, devastated by the Great Famine, is less populated than the rest of Ireland; yet abundant evidence of earlier habitation exists in Stone Age–monuments, early Christian monasteries, and the deserted villages of 19th-century tenant farmers. Today you'll find settlements ranging from cosmopolitan Galway city to remote one-pub hamlets – and some villages so enchanting they became movie sets.

But the most magical thing of all is that the best scenery is on the quietest roads – with few noisy cars around to break the spell.

HISTORY

Ireland's west has always been beautiful, but its ruggedness and relative infertility have made it not always desirable – 'beauty is no good if you can't eat it' was the wry observation of hungry farmers.

Some who did choose to live in isolated pockets of the harsh region were monks, around the 6th century.

In the 12th century the Anglo-Normans pushed the cattle-herding Celtic chieftains west from their fertile land. Richard de Burgh captured a fort from the O'Flahertys in 1234 and began building Galway city. The O'Flahertys remained defiant, however, and the city's western gate was once inscribed with: 'From the fury of the O'Flahertys, good Lord deliver us'.

The legendary Granuaile (Grace O'Malley; 1530–1603), daughter of a Connaught chief, married into the O'Flaherty family. She became a powerful and ruthless pirate queen who controlled the coast of Connemara and southern Mayo (see the boxed text 'Grace O'Malley', p182).

In Brief

Highlights
- The fascinating limestone expanse of **the Burren**
- Majestic **Dún Aengus** and other fascinating archaeological features on **Inishmór**
- Magical mountains and wild bogs in **Connemara**
- Uncrowded **Blue Flag beaches** in north-west Mayo

Terrain
Undulates gently to moderately; longer hills through the Burren and the Connemara mountains; hilly coastal sections on Achill Island and in northern Mayo.

Special Events
- **Willie Clancy Irish Music Festival** (July) Milltown Malbay
- **Galway Arts Festival** (July/Aug) Galway
- **Scoil Acla** (traditional arts and music summer-school festival; July/Aug) Keel, Achill Island
- **Féile Iorras** (folk arts festival; July) Belmullet

Cycling Events
- Sheeffry Challenge (Aug) Westport

Food & Drink Specialities
Wholesome fare such as **beef**, **Irish stew** and freshly caught **seafood**.

In 1649, Oliver Cromwell arrived and during his subsequent rampage – in which many native Irish were killed or sent into slavery – he gave the survivors a choice of 'Hell or Connaught' (the province comprising Galway, Mayo, Sligo, Roscommon and Leitrim), banishing them from the more valuable Midlands.

After the Battle of the Boyne in 1690, the victorious William of Orange confiscated good land from Catholic Anglo-Normans but rewarded those who converted to the established church with poorer land in Connemara.

By the time of the Great Famine of 1845–51, the population of landlords and tenant farmers far exceeded that of the region today.

County Mayo and the Connemara region were, along with Counties Kerry and Clare, particularly devastated during the Famine. Deserted villages and memorials to famine victims of this time are evident, particularly around southern Mayo.

NATURAL HISTORY
Taking in Counties Clare, Galway and Mayo, this region stretches north from the River Shannon to the Burren; across Galway Bay to Galway's Connemara region; then around County Mayo's Clew Bay to golden beaches, Achill Island and the cliff-lined north coast.

The Aran Islands in Galway Bay share the geological characteristics of the Burren, the natural history of which is detailed further under Natural History (p165) for the Clare Circuit ride.

The southern Connemara region and much of northwest Mayo are characterised by extensive areas of blanket bog. Northern Connemara is a stunning, glacier-carved quartzite mountainous region (often called Joyce Country), which includes the Twelve Bens (or Pins) and the Maumturk Mountains. The Mweelrea Mountains and Croagh Patrick, the holy mountain, lie north of Killary Harbour, in southwest Mayo.

Blanket bog or peat (an accumulation of decayed plant material) is thought to have spread across the poorly drained lowlands after Neolithic farmers (around 3000 BC) felled the oak and hazel forests that had previously covered the area. Prominent bogland flora includes purple moor grass, heath, heathers, sphagnum moss, insectivorous butterworts, sundews and bog cotton. Local animals include birds such as meadow pipits, skylarks, plovers, kestrels and ravens; hares, foxes and red deer.

CLIMATE
Like the mountains in County Kerry, Connemara is one of Ireland's wettest regions. The Aran Islands can be drier than the mainland, however, with moisture in the sea air not condensing until it reaches the Connemara mountains. Mist, fog and steady drizzle occur often in the West – although these 'soft' days are most likely between October and April. April to June is the driest period; the average August rainfall tends to be significantly higher, as the warm,

The Great Famine

> Okay, I want to talk about Ireland
> Specifically, I want to talk about the 'famine'
> About the fact that there never really was one
> Sinead O'Connor, 'Famine'

The Great Famine of 1845–51 was one of the great tragedies of Irish history. The disaster was all the greater because, while a million people died and another million fled on overcrowded 'coffin ships', Ireland continued to export food.

The penal laws enacted in 1695 prohibited Catholics from, among other things, entering government and buying land. By the 19th century Ireland's population was four million. Around 5000 landlords owned 90% of the land, renting it out to Irish tenant farmers.

By 1841, the population had rocketed to eight million. Most were practically subsistence farmers, dependent on potatoes for food and to pay their rent. Many lived in wretched, crowded conditions: large families (and their animals) typically shared single-roomed, virtually windowless cottages (landlords charged higher rent for windows).

Rapid population growth meant more pressure on the land and, between 1845 and 1851, blight destroyed most of the potato crop. Catastrophe was inevitable: without their staple food, people starved; without the means to pay rent, they were evicted. Even those who grew grain had to choose between eating and being evicted or staying and starving. Those who could scrape together the passage (or whose landlords paid it) left for the New World on overcrowded and unregulated 'coffin ships' on which disease ran rife and, typically, a third of the passengers died.

By 1851, Ireland's population was around six and a half million.

West

0 — 40km
0 — 24mi

N

BEACHES & BOGS p185

CONNEMARA & INISHMÓR p173

CLARE CIRCUIT p164

ATLANTIC OCEAN

ATLANTIC OCEAN

MAYO

SLIGO

GALWAY

CLARE

KERRY

Erris Head
Broad Haven Bay
Doonamo Point
Belderrig
Pollatomish
Downpatrick Head
Lackan Bay
Kilcumin
Sligo Bay
Sugo
N15
Belmullet
Mullet Paninsula
Lake Carrowmore
Killala
Killala Bay
Ballysadare
Colloney
N59
Slieve Gamph (Ox Mountains)
Blacksod Bay
Bangor
Crossmolina
Ballina
N17
Blacksod Point
Nephin Beg (628m)
Lough Conn
N26
Swinford
Doogort
Ballycroy
N59
Mt Nephin (806m)
N26
N58
N5
Knock Airport
Achill Head
Keel
Achill Island
Nephin Beg Range
Straide
Mulranny
Newport
Castlebar
N17
Knock
Ballyhaunis
Castlerea
Clare Island
Clew Bay
Westport
Murrisk
Balla
Roonagh Quay
Louisburgh
Ballintubber
Claremorris
N60
Inishturk
Killadoon
Croagh Patrick (765m)
MAYO
Tourmakeady
Lough Carra
N17
Inishbofin
Killary Harbour
R335
Ballinrobe
Cleggan
Leenane
Lough Mask
Cong
Tuam
Letterfrack
Connemara National Park
N59
Maam
Lough Corrib
GALWAY
Mount Bellew
Clifden
Recess
Maam Cross
Oughterard
N17
Ballyconneely
N59
Cashel
GALWAY
Scriob
N59
Roundstone
Carna
Casla
Galway
Athenry
N6
Rossaveal
R336
Spiddal
N18
Aran Islands
Black Head
New Quay
N66
Lough Rea
Inishmór
Kilrónan
Kinvara
Coole Park
Inishmaan
Ballyreen
The Burren
Gort
Inisheer
Doolin
Lisdoonvarna
Kilfenora
Carron
R460
Cliff of Moher
Kilnaboy
Corofin
N18
Feakle
Scarriff
Hug's Head
Lahinch
Spanish Point
Miltown Malbay
N85
Ennis
Quin
Kilmurry
Mutton Island
Quilty
R474
CLARE
N68
Shannon Airport
N18
Cratloe
Donegal Point
N67
Doonbeg
Knockalough
R473
Shannon
Kilkee
N67
Kilrush
Labasheeda
River Shannon
Limerick
Carrigaholt
Loop Head
Kilbaha
Shannon Estuary
Tarbert
Shanagolden
N69
N21
Rathkeale
KERRY

moist westerly airflow brings heavier rain and sometimes thunder.

The Gulf Stream contributes to mild conditions on the west coast. The average temperature climbs steadily from April to July and August, the warmest months. In County Clare, the average inland minimum and maximum temperatures in April are 5° and 13°C, respectively; by June, they are 10° and 18°C (the maximum is likely to be a touch lower on the coast). The pattern is similar in County Mayo, where inland averages for April are 3° and 12°C; for June, 8° and 17°C.

Prevailing winds are from the southwest and west (although east and northeasterlies are not unknown) and calm days tend to be the exception rather than the rule.

INFORMATION
Maps
The OSI 1:250,000 Holiday map *Ireland West* covers the region.

Information Sources
Shannon region and Ireland West maintain networks of TICs within Counties Clare, Galway and Mayo. The main offices for the region are in Ennis, Galway (p174) and Westport (p185).

The Connemara Walking Centre (☎ 1850 266 636, w www.walkingireland.com), in Clifden has information about walking (not just in Connemara).

Place Names
In strong Gaeltacht (Irish-speaking) areas such as Inishmór and Achill Island, place names on signs are almost exclusively in Irish. You will also see this in other areas, if to a lesser extent.

GATEWAY CITY
Ennis
☎ 065
Though it's one of Ireland's larger regional towns, and the capital of County Clare, Ennis has a population of only around 18,000. Its attractive centre, with narrow, paved streets and the remains of a 13th-century friary, testify to a medieval past. During the 17th and 18th centuries, Ennis was a busy market town, and it continues to buzz – notably, with traditional music in its atmospheric pubs. A monument to Daniel O'Connell commemorates the man's victory in the 1828

Clare election; it's a popular congregating place for the local youth.

Information Ennis TIC (☎ 682 8366, w www.shannon-dev.ie/tourism) is in the new complex between O'Connell Square, the Temple Gate Hotel and Ennis Friary. It operates a bureau de change.

Bank of Ireland, Ulster and National Banks are on O'Connell Square; the Allied Irish Bank (AIB) is on Abbey St. All have bureaus de change; the National has no ATM.

Tierneys Cycles, Fishing and Hobbies (☎ 682 9433, w www.ennisrentabike.com, 17 Abbey St) is a Raleigh Rent-a-Bike agent, has new bikes and does repairs. Book ahead for rental, which costs €51 per week, including helmets, repair kit and locks; panniers cost €7 extra.

Things to See & Do Inside the TIC, 'The Riches of Clare' exhibition, with displays on traditional farm life, fishing, religion, archaeology and modern Clare, is a good introduction to the county.

The 13th-century **Ennis Friary** (☎ 682 9100, Abbey St) was founded by king of Thomond, Donnchadh Cairbreach O'Brien, and in the 15th century was one of Ireland's great centres of learning.

Ennis: A Walking Trail, a free brochure from the TIC, guides a walking tour of the town's **historic buildings and monuments**.

You'll find **traditional music** in several Ennis pubs; *Cruises Pub* (☎ 684 1800, Abbey St) has nightly sessions. The *Traditional Irish Music Pubs: Shannon Region* brochure (free from the TIC) lists pubs in the Shannon region.

Places to Stay The closest camping to Ennis is around 15km north in Corofin. *Corofin Village Caravan & Camping Park* (☎ 683 7683, e corohost@iol.ie, Main St) Tent sites per person €7.

Abbey Tourist Hostel (☎ 682 2620, Harmony Row) Dorm beds €13. The only hostel accommodation in town, it could be a better place with more inspired management.

There's plenty of B&B accommodation, but it's worth booking in high season. *Cloneen* (☎ 682 9681, Clon Rd) Standard singles/doubles €32/46, ensuite doubles €49. With comfortable and pleasant older-style rooms, this nonsmoking house has a garden for guests. *Grey Gables* (☎ 682 4487, e *marykeane.ennis@eircom.net, Station Rd)* Singles/doubles €26/45, with ensuite €32/51. Friendly and very central; ensuite rooms are newer, bright and spacious. *Railway View* (☎ 682 1646, Tulla Rd) Ensuite singles/doubles €32/51. Country-style, spacious rooms, nonsmoking, quiet location 1km north of centre.

Temple Gate Hotel (☎ 682 3300, w *www .templegatehotel.com, The Square)* Ensuite singles/doubles from €86/127. Opposite the TIC the former Sisters of Mercy convent has been converted into a gracious three-star hotel.

Places to Eat The main supermarket is inside an arcade *Dunnes Stores (O'Connell St). The Bakers Oven (Salthouse Lane)*, off Parnell St. Abbey St has takeaways: try *Enzo's Fast Foods (Abbey St)* Chicken boxes €4.

Sicilian (☎ 684 3873, Cabey's Court, Parnell St) Mains €6-23, three-course set menu €21. Good list of pastas and pizzas, bright, contemporary café, reservations advised Fri-Sat. *Punjab Balti & Tandoori Restaurant* (☎ 684 4655, 59 Parnell St) Mains €8-16 plus rice. Good vegetarian selection. *Brogans Bar & Restaurant* (☎ 682 9859, 24 O'Connell St) Bar menu €7-13, restaurant mains €10-20. Locally recommended for decent pub grub.

Cruises Pub & Restaurant (☎ 682 8963, Abbey St) Bar meals €6-11, restaurant mains €11-20. Atmospheric pub c. 1658 has traditional music, good wine list and award-winning food.

The Cloister Restaurant (☎ 682 9521, Abbey St) Mains €12-19. Lovely dining area was once the old abbey's kitchen area. It has a shortish menu, mostly meat-based.

Getting There & Away Just as accessible from Shannon Airport as the larger Limerick, Ennis is a more attractive base, not least for its proximity to the coast.

Air Shannon Airport (☎ 061-712 155, w www.shannonairport.com, is a major gateway to Ireland, receiving flights from the UK, Europe and, particularly, the USA. The airport's TIC (☎ 061-471 664) can book accommodation.

Bus Éireann runs buses between Ennis and the airport, which is 24.3km south (€5,

45 minutes, regular services); buses to Limerick cost the same. Taxis to either Ennis or Limerick cost around €24.

To cycle from the airport, follow the exit drive, go left at the roundabout (3.9km) on the R472, following signs to Newmarket-on-Fergus. At 7.9km, veer left 'to Ballygireen'; at 9km, go right at the 'Cahergal Farm B&B' sign; then, at 15.2km, turn left onto the N18, following it into Ennis. Though the N18 is busy, it's not too unpleasant – the ride's earlier section is relatively quiet.

Bus Ennis bus station (☎ 682 4177) is by the train station, southeast of the TIC on Station Rd. Bus Éireann services to/from Ennis include Cork (€14, three hours, 12 daily), Galway (€10, 1¼ hours, 13 daily) and Limerick (€7, regular services). Change at Limerick for services between Ennis and: Dublin (€14, five hours, four to six daily), Killarney (€15, 3½ hours, five daily) and Waterford (€16, five hours, four to five daily).

Train Ennis train station (☎ 684 0444) is on Station Rd, southeast of the TIC. Iarnród Éireann (☎ 1850 366 888) runs services between Ennis and Limerick (€7, one hour, two daily except Sunday), Dublin (€27, 3¼ hours, one to two daily; you may need to change at Limerick or Limerick Junction or both) and Cork (€18, 3¼ hours, two daily; change at Limerick and Limerick Junction).

Clare Circuit

Duration	6 days
Distance	348km
Difficulty	moderate
Start/End	Ennis

Clare, a county with only one land border, offers considerable variety for cyclists. This ride (of which only one day is landlocked) rolls through the fertile lowlands flanking the Shannon estuary to towns with Blue Flag beaches (EU listed as clean and safe) and dramatic cliffs facing the Atlantic; then on, through music hotbeds, Milltown Malbay and Doolin, to the intriguing, elephant-grey Burren. Ask the Irish about their favourite places and chances are the Burren will be among them. Lingering for a deeper exploration of its flora, archaeology and interesting sites, the ride finishes with a sojourn into Yeats' country, and a visit to the impressive 12th-century Kilmacduagh monastic site, before sauntering home through County Clare's gentle patchwork countryside.

HISTORY

As with most of the country, County Clare offers plenty of historical interest. Evidence from farmers 6000 years ago abounds in the Burren, and well-preserved Christian sites exist at Ennis and at Kilmacduagh near Gort.

Champion of the Anglo-Irish literary revival, William Butler Yeats, lived at Thoor Ballylee, a secluded Norman tower near Gort. His friend and patron, Lady Gregory, lived nearby at Coole. They met at Doorus House (now a youth hostel), northwest of Kinvara, in 1898; their conversations led to the founding of Dublin's Abbey Theatre.

Clare has also seen some significant political figures. Kerry man Daniel O'Connell (1775–1847), stood for and easily won a County Clare seat in the 1828 election. Catholics were still prohibited by law from holding a seat and O'Connell's victory provoked the British Parliament to pass the 1829 Act of Catholic Emancipation.

In 1917, Eamon de Valera was elected Sinn Féin MP for East Clare, becoming Sinn Féin president from 1917 to 1926. He went on, as leader of the Fianna Fáil, to govern the new Irish state from 1932 to 1948.

NATURAL HISTORY

Away from the lowlands by the River Shannon, the land is generally rocky and poor for farming. Many farmers were unable to support themselves during the Great Famine and emigrated during the 1850s.

In terms of natural history, it is the Burren in the county's north, that holds most fascination. Called Boireann, meaning 'rocky country', in Irish, it is the most extensive limestone region, or karst, in Ireland or Britain. Though it was once lightly wooded and soil-covered, thousands of years ago farmers began clearing the woodlands and using the slopes for grazing.

Despite appearances, the Burren is not barren, cracks in the limestone support more than two thirds of Ireland's plant species (including subarctic, alpine, Mediterranean and woodland species!). It's one of the most floristically diverse regions in Europe.

The Burren is a stronghold of the elusive pine marten; hares, foxes, pygmy shrews and stoats are also inhabitants. Otters and seals live along the shores around Bealaclugga, New Quay and Finavarra Point. More than 28 of Ireland's 33 species of butterfly are found here, as are 84 species of bird.

PLANNING

Days 2 and 5 are self-contained circuits, which could be left out if time is limited.

When to Ride

June is perhaps the ideal month. May and June are best for wildflowers in the Burren, while some accommodation opens only from June through August. Since County Clare is less touristy than its southern neighbour, traffic and visitor numbers are less of an issue.

Maps & Books

The OSI 1:250,000 Holiday map *Ireland West* adequately covers the region. Tim Robinson's *Burren Map & Guide* shows that area, especially points of interest, in far greater detail.

The Book of the Burren, by Richard Broad, Jeff O'Connell and Anne Korff, is a comprehensive, illustrated reference to the Burren's archaeology, geology, natural history, flora, and its ancient, medieval and recent history.

ACCESS TOWN
Ennis
See Ennis (p163).

THE RIDE (see map p166)
Day 1: Ennis to Kilkee
3¾–7 hours, 70.5km

Tracing the path of the River Shannon almost all the way to the coast, this day heads through pleasant rolling countryside, the green pastures bound by hedges and stone walls. Early glimpses of the Shannon estuary later become wide vistas of a mighty river and shipping route. Sections by the water's edge are exposed to the prevailing southwesterly wind, which can make for a longish day. Traffic, for the most part, is not intrusive, but it thickens a little after joining the N67 at Killimer (48.9km).

Gentle undulations become more continuous and rolling, particularly between Labasheeda (35.1km) and Kilrush (57.4km). After climbing out of Kilrush, it's blessedly flat for 5km and, indeed, climbs slightly during the remaining stretch to Kilkee.

You'll find *stores*, *pubs* and picnic tables at Killadysert (22.8km), picnic tables at Labasheeda's small quay, and more *eateries* at Killimer and Kilrush.

Car ferries cross the River Shannon between Tarbert and Killimer, the point at which the Around Ireland ride (p251) joins this ride.

Kilkee
☎ 065

Very much a seaside town, Kilkee's centre is replete with amusements for kids, fast-food joints and accommodation. Built around the horseshoe-shaped, Blue Flag beach, the town became a popular resort in Victorian times among Limerick folk who could afford to 'take the sea air'. July and August are busy and accommodation is more expensive, particularly at weekends so try to stay midweek. Some services operate only June to August.

Information The TIC (☎ 905 6112, O'Connell St, open daily late-May–Aug, other times contact Ennis TIC) exchanges currency. The Bank of Ireland (with ATM) and AIB banks on O'Curry St also exchange currency.

The closest bike shop is Gleesons (☎ 905 1127, Henry St) in Kilrush.

Things to See & Do The spectacular **cliffs** southwest of Kilkee feature on Day 2 but, if you haven't time for the whole ride, head to the cliffs by starting the ride in reverse.

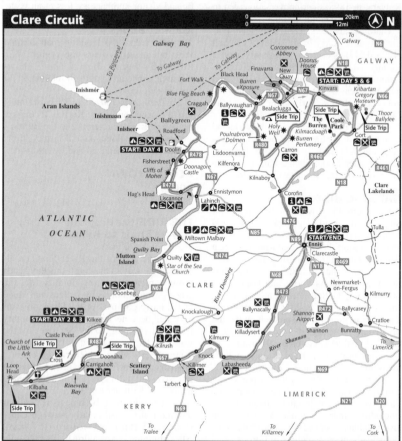

Kilkee is a well-known **diving** location. Contact Kilkee Dive Centre (☎ 905 6707), East End, near the pier.

At Carrigaholt, 12.3km southwest (see Day 2), you can take a **dolphin-watching cruise** on the River Shannon. Dolphinwatch Carrigaholt (☎ 905 8156) runs two-hour trips (€14) three times daily (weather permitting); phone ahead.

Places to Stay Book accommodation well ahead during July and August, especially on weekends.

Camping in Kilkee is available only from June to August. *Cunningham's Holiday Park* (☎ 905 6430, e cunninghams@eircom .net) Tent sites per person €6. Central site (off Marine Parade), laundry facilities and games room. *Green Acres Caravan & Camping Park* (☎ 905 7011) Tent sites per person €6. A two-star site, it's 6km south of town on the R487, and opens Easter to October.

Kilrush offers the closest hostel accommodation. *Katie O'Connors Holiday Hostel* (☎ 905 1133, e katieoconnors@eircom.net, 49-50 Frances St, Kilrush) Dorm beds €11.

Nolans B&B (☎ 906 0100, Kilrush Rd) Ensuite singles/doubles €32/51. Almost 1km east, Nolans is excellent with spacious, light rooms and drying facilities. *Kitty's Easy Rest B&B* (☎ 905 6640, Circular Rd) Singles/doubles €32/46. Away from the seafront (but central), Kitty's is friendly and better value than most; singles more welcome for two-night stays. *Murphy's B&B* (☎ 905 6026, 1 Marine Parade) Doubles €51. Central, with beach views from the breakfast room.

Stella Maris Hotel (☎ 905 6455, e stella marishotel@eircom.net, cnr O'Connell & Erin Sts) Ensuite singles/doubles €39/77. Good-value B&B with comfortable, older-style rooms. *Halpin's Hotel* (☎ 905 6032, Erin St) Ensuite singles €58-64, doubles €89-108. Prices vary according to which rooms have sea views or baths – book well ahead.

Places to Eat Supermarkets include *Mace Central Stores* (O'Curry St). Other options include *Savoy Take-away* (O'Curry St) Burgers €2-3, chicken lunchboxes €5. Locally recommended as the best takeaway. *The Pantry* (O'Curry St) Mains €8-9. Cafeteria-style, run by an inspired home-economics teacher; open late-May to August,

Clare Circuit – Day 1

Cue

start		Ennis TIC
0km		go W on Arthurs Row (walk)
0.1	↰	O'Connell St
0.4	↰ ⑂	N18 'to Limerick'
2.5	⌐	R473 'to Killadysert'
10.8	▲	800m gradual climb
14.8	▲	800m moderate climb
16.0		Ballynacally
16.5	▲	1.8km moderate climb
22.8	↘	R473, Killadysert
23.3	▲	800m moderate climb
26.5	▲	700m moderate climb
30.4	▲	500m moderate climb
35.0	▲	400m moderate climb
35.1	⌐	Labasheeda
36.7	↘	'to Kilrush'
41.3		Kilmurry
42.4	↰	R486 'to Killimer'
45.2		Knock
46.5	▲	1.5km moderate climb
48.9		Killimer
49.2	▲	1.7km moderate climb
57.2	↰	'to Kilkee'
57.4	⌐	'to Kilkee', Kilrush
57.7	▲	800m moderate climb
70.5		Kilkee TIC

8.30am-7.30pm. Good food at good value, plus an excellent bakery at the back.

Stella Maris Hotel (see Places to Stay) Restaurant mains €13-22, bar specials €9-18. Probably the nicest place for a pub meal. Modern *Myles Creek* (☎ 905 6771, O'Curry St) is best value (most mains under €11). *Scott's Bar* (☎ 905 6061, O'Curry St) is cosy. *Yeung's Chinese Restaurant* (☎ 905 6866, O'Curry St) Chinese dishes €10-12, western-style steaks €13. Menu includes little for vegetarians (ask and they'll make it).

It's advisable to book restaurants, especially at weekends. *The Old Bistro* (☎ 905 6898, O'Curry St) Mains €13-20. Good food, lots of potatoes and friendly service but a little pricey. *The Strand Restaurant* (☎ 905 6177, Strand Line) Mains €14-19. The place for a nice meal: mostly meat and seafood mains that are a notch up from the usual fare.

Day 2: Loop Head Day Circuit
3–5 hours, 54.9km

Despite its dramatic cliff scenery, the often-overlooked Loop Head peninsula remains quiet and unhurried. This day ride to Loop Head passes through the small villages of

WEST

the peninsula's southern side, returning via the northern cliffs. The landscape undulates gently, with a couple of hills, including a longish climb up to the lighthouse. Traffic, mostly very light, increases a little around the cliffs area.

Charming views over gentle patchwork fields are tempered by the (somewhat less charming) aromas of silage and slurry (farmyard manure used as fertiliser).

Along with its attractive beach and the remains of 15th-century **McMahon castle**, the major attraction at Carrigaholt (12.3km) is dolphin watching trips (see Things to See & Do in Kilkee, p166).

The wall built around Rinevella Bay (15.5km), along with the stones washed loose onto the road, are testament to the joint power of high tides and fierce winds. The peninsula is indeed subject to the elements and there's little shelter from a strong southwesterly (a perfect excuse to rest inside a *pub* at tiny Kilbaha). Closed to the public, the **lighthouse** (reached via a side trip at 28.2km) on the barren point is at the end of the road. The first of the magnificent cliffs is visible on the descent.

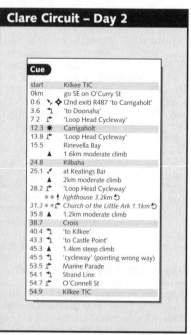

Clare Circuit – Day 2

Cue	
start	Kilkee TIC
0km	go SE on O'Curry St
0.6 ↘ ◆	(2nd exit) R487 'to Carrigaholt'
3.6 ↱	'to Doonaha'
7.2 ↱	'Loop Head Cycleway'
12.3 ✳	Carrigaholt
13.8 ↱	'Loop Head Cycleway'
15.5	Rinevella Bay
▲	1.6km moderate climb
24.8	Kilbaha
25.1 ↙	at Keatings Bar
▲	2km moderate climb
28.2 ↱	'Loop Head Cycleway'
● ● ↑	lighthouse 3.2km ↻
31.3 ● ● ↱	Church of the Little Ark 1.1km ↻
35.8 ▲	1.2km moderate climb
38.7	Cross
40.4 ↱	'to Kilkee'
43.3 ↱	'to Castle Point'
45.3 ▲	1.4km steep climb
45.5 ↱	'cycleway' (pointing wrong way)
53.5 ↱	Marine Parade
54.1 ↱	Strand Line
54.7 ↱	O'Connell St
54.9	Kilkee TIC

A short side trip at 31.3km leads to the **Church of the Little Ark**, where you can see the Little Ark itself – a small wooden altar used by Catholics during the 1850s, when Catholicism was outlawed. The altar was wheeled below the high-tide mark, where it was outside the jurisdiction of the Protestant landlord, for the priest to celebrate mass. More descriptions of the repressive penal times are inside the church.

A decent climb (45.3km) leads to the most spectacular **coastal scenery**, which includes cliffs, arches, stacks and rocks sculpted by wind and waves. The waves are dramatic on a windy day.

Day 3: Kilkee to Doolin
3½–6 hours, 62.6km

Start the day with a climb out of Kilkee, after which the patchwork fields of Clare are spread before you. A spin by the seaside is the last of a long flat stretch. The road rolls a little more from Milltown Malbay, through the Blue-Flag beach towns of Lahinch (sometimes spelled Lehinch) and Liscannor, before climbing to the magnificent Cliffs of Moher. Though it's largely on the N67, traffic is reasonably light.

The early 16th–century **Doonbeg Castle** (11.1km) was owned by the O'Briens of Thomond. In 1598, Tadhg McMahon garrisoned the castle, surrendering a year later to the Earl of Thomond who promptly had the garrison hanged in couples face to face.

The **seaweed** liberally strewn about the seashore near Quilty was traditionally an important fertiliser on coastal farms. Quilty remains a centre for seaweed products, which are also used in toothpaste, beer, agar and cosmetics.

The **Church of our Lady Star of the Sea** (27.8km) was built in 1909 but looks older because of its round tower. A poem inside – indeed, the church itself – commemorates the epic rescue by local fishermen of the crew of a French sailing boat wrecked in Quilty Bay in 1907.

Milltown Malbay (33.9km) hosts the major annual **Willie Clancy Irish Music Festival**. If you happen to be there in early July, you'll find plenty of revelry, with streets and pubs filled with musos, listeners and atmosphere. In any case, with a *bakery*, *pubs* and *stores*, the town is a good lunch option.

Late afternoon is an ideal time to view the **Cliffs of Moher** when, if you're lucky, the sun will be shining on the cliff face. The final descent into Doolin culminates in a short very steep section (at 61.4km), past the (privately owned) Doonagore Castle.

Doolin
☎ 065

A rather spread-out little town, Doolin is set around the pretty Aille River, back about 1.6km from the coast. With two 'centres' (Roadford is the upper, northern end of town and Fisherstreet, the lower, southern end) the town is known as the heart of Irish traditional music, and, according to local propaganda, many famous musicians cut their teeth in the local pubs. Its far-reaching reputation for excellent music ensures many camera-toting tourists. It's an attractive and popular chill-out spot on the backpacker circuit, with plenty of B&Bs and some good restaurants, but little in the way of other services.

Information The closest TIC is the Cliffs of Moher Visitor Centre (☎ 708 1171) 6.4km south, which books accommodation and exchanges currency. *Paddy's Doolin Hostel* (☎ 707 4006) in Fisherstreet is the village's basic information point: it has some tourist brochures and operates a bureau de change. A mobile Ulster Bank (near O'Connors Pub, Fisherstreet; Thurs 11am-11.45am) visits Doolin. It offers currency exchange and €60 maximum withdrawal on Visa or Access (no ATM).

Doolin Ferries (☎ 707 4155) sail from the pier (1.5km west of Fisherstreet) to Inishmór between April and September (one-way/return €16/33, daily). The Aran Islands can also be reached from County Galway (see Day 1 of the Connemara & Inishmór ride, p177).

Things to See & Do Historical sites and points of interest, plus local walks, are detailed in the *Doolin Guide Map* from Paddy's Village Hostel.

All of Doolin's three pubs have nightly **music sessions** during the summer. *O'Connors* in Fisherstreet is best known; *McGanns* and *MacDermott's* (MacDiarmada's) in Roadford are also well frequented. Ask around for what's on.

Clare Circuit – Day 3

Cue

start		Kilkee TIC
0km		go N towards beach
0.1	↱	'to Milltown Malbay'
0.4	↗	'to Doonbeg'
0.6	▲	500m moderate climb
1.8	▲	1.4km moderate climb
6.2		Bealaha
11.1	✳	Doonbeg
13.9	↘	'to Lahinch'
16.6	↗	'to Lahinch'
	▲	1.6km gradual climb
20.9	⬎	'Coast Road'
23.8	↱	stay on sealed road
27.8	✳	*Star of the Sea Church*
28.2	↘	N67 'West Clare Cycleway'
28.4		Quilty
31.2	↑	'to Milltown Malbay'
33.9	↘	N67 'to Lahinch', Milltown Malbay
34.1	⬎	N67 'to Lahinch; W Clare Cycleway'
43.9	↘	'West Clare Cycleway'
45.5	↘	N67, 'to Liscannor', Lahinch
45.7	↗	N67
45.8	↘	R478 'to Liscannor'
50.4		Liscannor
50.6	▲	400m moderate climb
52.7	↗	R478 'to Cliffs of Moher'
53.2	▲	600m steep climb
54.1	↘	'to Cliffs of Moher'
	▲	500m steep climb
54.9	▲	1.9km moderate climb
56.1	✳	*Cliffs of Moher*
60.8	⬎	'Shannon Cycleway'
61.4	⚠	very steep descent
61.5	↘	unsigned lane (downhill)
62.6		Paddy's Doolin Hostel

Places to Stay Accommodation fills up quickly in July and August, book to be sure of a bed. *O'Connors Riverside Camping* (☎ 707 4314) Tent sites per person €6. Central, by Aille River, with indoor eating area.

Aille River Hostel (☎ 707 4260, e *aille river@esatclear.ie*) Tent sites per person €6, dorm beds €11. Opposite the camping ground, friendly Aille River has free laundry and a lovely, cosy atmosphere, although the kitchen can be crowded. *Rainbow Hostel* (☎ 707 4415, Roadford) Dorm beds €11. The archaeologist owner offers guests free guided walks at this small hostel.

Rainbow's End B&B (☎ 707 4900, Roadford) Singles €32-39, doubles €49-51. Spacious, new rooms, free guided walks and a laundry service. *Doolin Cottage B&B*

WEST

(☎ 707 4762) Standard/ensuite doubles €36/41. Centrally located, next to Aille River Hostel, this friendly place is exceptional value. **Churchfield B&B** (☎ 707 4209, [e] churchfield@eircom.net, Roadford) Ensuite singles/doubles €39/51. One of Doolin's original B&Bs offers a friendly welcome, breakfast includes homemade jams. **Horseshoe House** (☎ 707 4006, [e] horseshoe@eircom.net, Fisherstreet) Doubles €60. Nonsmoking, comfortable, efficiently run, lovely lounge/dining area.

Doolin Activity Lodge (☎ 707 4888, [w] www.doolinlodge.com) Self-catering singles/doubles €26/51, B&B €32/64. Central, towards Fisherstreet. Self-contained apartments (linen and towels included). This nonsmoking complex has excellent facilities including a drying room.

Places to Eat The best eating in Doolin is in Roadford; all places cater for vegetarians. **Doolin Deli** (Fisherstreet) is a small grocery store, often serving hot takeaway food, open 9am-7pm.

McGanns (☎ 707 4133, Roadford) Pub mains €8-16. Busy and atmospheric, good pub grub includes big bowls of scrummy apple crumble (€4). **MacDermott's** (☎ 707 4328) Mains €8-13. The menu is in English, French and German.

You'll need to book restaurants during July and August. **Doolin Café** (☎ 707 4795, Roadford) Mains €13-18, early-bird three-course meal (6pm-7pm) €18. Highly regarded locally; traditional food in a contemporary style; closed Thurs Sept-May. **Lazy Lobster Seafood Restaurant** (☎ 707 4852, Roadford) Mains €11-17. Intimate, with country views from the nonsmoking conservatory, it also serves poultry and steak (closed Mon).

Day 4: Doolin to Kinvara

3–5½ hours, 56.8km

Cut between the relentlessly grey, yet captivating, limestone expanse of the Burren and the sparkling blue of Galway Bay, the coast road to Kinvara makes a wonderful ride. The moderate amount of traffic increases somewhat on the N67 after Ballyvaughan but is generally not worrisome.

Although the bleached rock rises steeply from the coast, there's little real climbing in this ride; it undulates, but not exhaustingly.

Clare Circuit – Day 4

Cue		
start		Paddy's Doolin Hostel
0km		go N (to Roadford)
1.0	▲	900m moderate climb
2.7	▲	2.2km gradual climb
4.9	↘	'Coast Rd, Burren Cycleway'
8.0	▲	1.9km gradual climb
14.1		Craggah
16.3	✳	Blue Flag beach
20.5		Black Head
	✳	fort walk
29.2		Tea & Garden Rooms
29.7	↰	'to Galway', Ballyvaughan
30.8	✳	Burren eXposure
36.8	↘	'to Kinvara', Bealaclugga
37.1	▲	400m moderate climb
39.9	↘	'to Finavarra'
41.2	▲	400m moderate climb
41.8	↰	'to Martello Tower', Finavarra
42.5	↱	unsigned lane
45.9	↰	unsigned road
46.5		New Quay
48.5	↘	N67 (unsigned)
56.7	↱	'to post office'
56.8		Kinvara post office

The longest uphill stretch is the gradual climb out of Doolin for 3.9km. The coast road is exposed but the usual southwesterly wind should push you along. A northerly will slow things considerably.

On a nice day, it's worth spending time among the limestone rocks and platforms – the early section before Craggah (14.1km) is particularly good for wandering. The **Blue Flag beach** at 16.3km is nice for a swim. It's also possible to walk from Black Head (20.5km) up a steep spur to a **fort**, from which the views are excellent. There's no track – the fort is around 700m southsouthwest of Black Head.

Ballyvaughan (29.7km; sometimes Ballyvaghan) has a range of eating options, including the **Tea and Garden Rooms** (☎ 707 7157) west of the town centre, where the generous slices of cake bring to mind great aunts serving tea in the parlour.

The Burren eXposure (30.8km; ☎ 707 7277) is a 30-minute audiovisual display, an interesting introduction to the history, geology and flora of the Burren. It's also the TIC for the Burren region (but doesn't book accommodation).

A detour off the main N67 (at 39.9km) is substantial enough that few cars bother with it. You may have Galway Bay to yourself on this little, occasionally patchy road, which takes in the tiny, untouristed villages of Finvarra and, at 46.5km, New Quay – home to the well-regarded *Linane's Lobster Bar*.

Kinvara
☎ 091

On the main route between Galway and the Burren, Kinvara sees some through traffic during the day, but is more down-to-earth and far less touristy than Ballyvaughan, 22km west. A sweet little place on Kinvarra Bay, it has a friendly population and you'll usually find live music or set dancing inside the pubs at night.

Information The nearest TIC is the Burren eXposure (☎ 707 7277) near Ballyvaughan. It has money-changing facilities; for accommodation bookings contact Galway TIC (☎ 537 700).

In Kinvara, the post office and the Merriman Hotel both change money. For emergency bike repairs, go to McMahons petrol station up the hill on Main St.

Things to See & Do For a description of historic sites and buildings, natural features and local wildlife buy *Kinvara: A Ramblers Map & Guide*, available from the post office.

Locals who are out to listen to music may frown if you talk through it. Ask around for what's on, but generally **Winkles** has step dancing on Friday and bands on weekends while **Plaid Shawl** and **Keoghs** have music on Thursday.

If you fancy sailing a **hooker** (traditional Galway vessel; ☎ 087-231 1779), trips leave from the pier. Call ahead to arrange one.

Places to Stay Just west of town is the privately owned **Burren Vision Camping Site**. Tent sites per person €6 (includes showers). Pleasant enough, but fairly basic.

Johnstons Hostel (☎ 637 164, Main St) Tent sites per person €6, dorm beds €11. Open July-Aug. In previous incarnations a hotel, drapery, dance hall and cinema, this excellent hostel's future was uncertain at the time of writing.

An Óige *Doorus House (☎ 637 512, Doorus)* Dorm beds €12. Peaceful location 6.4km northwest of Kinvara (3.2km off the Ballyvaughan Rd, signed), meals available by arrangement. It was in this house that Lady Gregory and WB Yeats met and the idea for Dublin's Abbey Theatre germinated.

Fallon's B&B (☎ 638 088, Main St) Singles €32, doubles €51-64. Nonsmoking,

---

Lots in a Name

If you're confused that the place where you thought you were sounds rather different from the name on your map, don't worry. Most Irish towns have at least two different names – one in Irish and one in English – with further possible spelling variations.

The names of many towns and villages were anglicised in the 1830s during the British Ordnance Survey of Ireland (see the boxed text 'Mapping Ireland', p225). The difficulties faced by the army in anglicising place names are highlighted in Brian Friel's play *Translations*. Set in a hedge school in Baile Beag (literally 'small village'), Donegal, in 1833, the play uses the interaction of the Baile Beag community with the British soldiers to explore the issues of language, culture and colonialism (not to mention love…).

In the play, it quickly becomes clear that mapping Ireland in English is far more complex than simply 'translating' place names. Some names tell a story, the meaning or complexity of which is easily lost in a simple anglicised version. For example, Kilmacduagh is just a name but, in Irish, Cill Mhic Dhuach literally means, 'the church of St MacDuach' – it's where St Colman Mac Duach founded a monastery in the 7th century. But how do you translate such complexity into one English word?

A degree of political unrest becomes increasingly apparent as characters express concern that standardising place names into 'the King's English' will erode their culture. A further complication is the blossoming love between a soldier and a village girl who communicate without knowing a word of each other's language.

The tension is unresolved at the play's end, but there is no mistaking the inevitable and irrevocable impact of the Ordnance Survey on the culture of Baile Beag and, by implication, that of Ireland.

renovated house with private guest patio (behind Spar supermarket).

Cois Cuain *(☎ 637 119, The Quay)* Singles/doubles €36/56. Central, small and homely, book ahead. ***The Meadow B&B*** *(☎ 637 245)* Doubles €46-49. Nonsmoking, fresh rooms 500m east of the post office on the Day 5 route.

Merriman Hotel *(☎ 638 222)* Ensuite singles/doubles €70/108. Claims Ireland's largest thatched roof, but inside it's your standard three-star hotel.

Places to Eat The bigger supermarket is *Londis (Main St)*.

Café on the Quay *(The Quay)* Hot dishes €7-9. Breakfast (from 9am); spaghetti bolognese, curries and other light meals.

Rosaleen's Restaurant *(☎ 637 503, The Square)* Mains €10-18. Café-style, good vegetarian selection plus traditional meat and Mexican-influenced dishes. ***Keoghs*** *(☎ 637 145, The Square)* Pub grub €10-19, limited vegetarian options. ***The Pier Head*** *(☎ 638 188, The Quay)* Mains €11-22. Modern (as compared with Keogh's traditional) pub dining; mostly meat, fish and poultry dishes.

Day 5: East Burren Day Circuit

2¾–5 hours, 52.2km

Penetrating into the heart of the Burren, with fabulous views across and beyond the lunar landscape, this circuit features the famous Poulnabrone Dolmen; Irelands' oldest perfumery; a limestone cave, once the den of bears; and an imposing 12th-century abbey.

Traffic is negligible for the ride's first half. It increases on the road to Poulnabrone, and is heaviest between Ballyvaughan and Kinvara (other than the quiet section past the abbey). The two major hills are longish, though steady.

The first part of the ride climbs steadily, emerging from the hedges onto a lonely wide plateau. Keep an eye out for St Fachtnan's **Holy Well** (Tobar na Fiachtnan; 14.9km), scantily signed on the descent. A simple square cairn with a cross marks the tiny well, which has coins at the bottom. Watch, too, for wildflowers growing between the rocks.

The Burren's rich and diverse flora inspired the sense-delighting **Burren Perfumery** (15.7km; ☎ 065-708 9102). A 12-minute audiovisual, more aesthetic than informative, features beautiful photography of Burren flora. By the distillery (watch the action on weekends) is a large herb garden.

Though it's about 50m from the road, you can hardly miss the much-photographed **Poulnabrone Dolmen** (28km) – just look for the parked cars. The stone table, set among giant knucklebones of weathered limestone pavement, is thought to be a 5000-year-old tomb. Despite literature which asks people

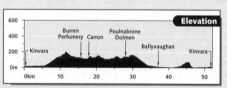

Clare Circuit – Day 5

Cue			Continued			Continued
start	Kinvara post office	16.8 ↗	unsigned road	34.1 ●●↰	Aillwee Cave 1.9km ↻
0km	go N to main road	17.5 ▲	700m moderate climb	35.5 ↱	N67 'to Ballyvaughan'
0.0 ↰	(10m) 'to Ballyvaughan'	17.9 ↰	'to Corofin', Carron	37.1 ↱	'to Kinvara', Ballyvaughan
0.9 ↰	'to B&Bs' opposite old mill	23.2 ↱	'to Ballyvaugan'	41.2 ↱	'to Corofin', Bealaclugga
1.7 ↘	unsigned road	23.6 ▲	2.1km gradual climb	41.5 ●●↰	Corcomroe Abbey 2.8km ↻
5.3 ▲	3.3km gradual climb	26.8 ▲	700m moderate climb	42.1 ↰	'to Kinvarra'
7.6 ▲	3.9km moderate climb	28.0 ✳	Poulnabrone Dolmen	43.5 ▲	2km moderate climb
8.2 ↘	'to Burren Perfumery'	28.9 ↗	'to Ballyvaughan'	46.3 ↱	'to Kinvara'
14.9 ✳	Holy Well (RHS)	▲	1.1km moderate climb	52.2	Kinvara post office
15.7 ✳	Burren Perfumery	30.3 ✳	megalithic tombs		

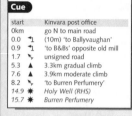

Elevation chart showing Kinvara, Burren Perfumery, Carron, Poulnabrone Dolmen, Ballyvaughan, Kinvara along route from 0km to 50km, with elevation from 0m to 600m.

not to alter the landscape, a collection of 'monuments' mimicking the dolmen now forms a backdrop to the real thing. Nearby, two more **megalithic tombs** (30.3km) can be viewed only from the road (access to the property is prohibited).

Pause on the glorious descent into Ballyvaughan to visit **Aillwee Cave** (side trip at 34.1km; ☎ 065-707 7036). Regular tours (€7) of the cave, which penetrates 600m into the mountain, take 35 minutes. Inside the grounds is a good *café*; cheese and other treats are made on site.

Another side trip (at 41.5km) leads to 12th-century **Corcomroe Abbey**. Though roofless, the dignified building retains grandeur, and, with soft light falling through the narrow arch windows, a sense of peace.

Day 6: Kinvara to Ennis

2¾–5 hours, 51km

It's an easy end to the ride, gently undulating through classic Clare countryside. However, with plenty of interest along the way, it may take all day! Apart from a 3.6km stretch into Gort and another (4.3km) into Ennis, traffic is fairly light.

The **Kiltartan Gregory Museum** (10.6km; ☎ 632 346) celebrates the author and playwright, Lady Gregory, and the Irish literary revival. Photographs, manuscripts, maps and memorabilia are displayed in the old National School building.

A side trip at 10.8km leads to **Thoor Ballylee** (☎ 631 436, open daily June-Aug, closed Sun other times), the Norman tower in which WB Yeats wrote.

Yeats' patron and friend, Lady Gregory lived at **Coole Parke** (side trip at 12.1km), which is now a leafy nature reserve. Though the house no longer exists, the visitor centre (€3) has a one-hour audiovisual show on Coole's literary connection, and natural history displays. It's free to visit the grounds (the walled garden makes an ideal picnic place), and a detailed guide to the park's walking trails can be purchased.

Less genteel than the more visited towns of the Burren, Gort (14.4km), has decent *pub grub*, and good cakes or light meals at *Christophers Coffee Shop (Market Square)*.

A 34m-high round tower beckons a visit to Kilmacduagh (20km). The remains of the **monastery** founded by St Colman Mac Duach early in the 7th century are impressive.

Clare Circuit – Day 6

Cue

start	Kinvara post office	
0km	go SE 'to Gort'	
▲	300m moderate climb	
7.9	'to Gort'	
10.6	at museum	
✳	Kiltartan Gregory Museum	
10.8	N18 'to Gort'	
●●⤵	Thoor Ballylee (Yeats' tower) 9.6km ⟳	
12.1 ●●	Coole Park 3.2km ⟳	
13.5 ▲	shoulder disappears	
14.4	R460 'to Oranmore', Gort	
14.9	'to Kinvara, Kilmacduagh'	
17.7	stay on R460 'to Hazelwood B&B'	
17.8	stay on R460	
20.0	R460 'to Ennis'	
●●⤵	Kilmacduagh 800m ⟳	
20.5	'to Corofin' (not to Ennis)	
25.8 ▲	1.8km gradual climb	
35.8	'to Corofin'	
▲	800m moderate climb	
36.6 ⤴✳	R476 'to Ennis', Corofin	
46.7 ⤴	N85 'to Ennis'	
50.2 ↑ ◆	'to town centre'	
50.6	Abbey St	
50.9	O'Connell Sqare	
↑	(20m) Arthur's Row (walk)	
51.0	Ennis TIC	

Undulation is a tad more pronounced along the Corofin Rd. At Corofin (36.6km) is the **Clare Heritage Centre** (☎ 065-683 7955), which incorporates a Genealogical Centre. Though it's an exhibits-in-glass-cases museum, the descriptions of 19th-century Clare are interesting and informative. With *eateries* and a *store*, Corofin is also the last refuelling opportunity before Ennis.

Connemara & Inishmór

Duration	7 days
Distance	349.2km
Difficulty	moderate
Start/End	Galway city

From engaging Galway, the ride visits Inishmór, the largest of the Aran Islands, before traversing wild lonely bogs towards the magical mountains and loughs of Connemara.

Inishmór is an enigmatic bag of ancient-historical and natural goodies. The prize gobstopper is Dún Aengus, a fascinating fort with its southern side a sheer 70m drop to the ocean.

WEST

The romance of Connemara is in its mist-covered mountains, its long dark loughs, the golden seaweed that adorns its convoluted harbours, and the fluffy bog cotton and hazel grasses that soften rocky bogs. Add to this charming villages like Leenane or Cong, and it's the sort of place you might see in the movies – perhaps you already have.

Defying its horizon, the ride contains little serious climbing; the few steep sections are relatively short. Coupled with fabulous scenery and mostly quiet roads, it's little wonder that Connemara is one of the country's most popular cycling areas. You're bound to come across other two-wheeled travellers – in some places, perhaps more often than motorists.

PLANNING
When to Ride
May and June are ideal – being the sunniest months, they're subject to less tourist traffic, although, with a choice of roads, peak-season traffic isn't as busy as in places like County Kerry. July and August are warmer, but rain is more likely. This is also festival time – book accommodation well ahead.

Maps & Books
The OSI 1:250,000 Holiday map *Ireland West* covers the region, although it shows only the major road on Inishmór. More detailed are the ferry companies' free maps. However, for exploring the island's more remote sites, it's advisable to use something with a larger scale, such as the OSI 1:25,000 map *Oileáin Árann*, or Tim Robinson's 1:28,160 map *Oileáin Árann* (Aran Islands), to which an accompanying guide is also available.

What to Bring
Bring walking gear, if you plan to walk in Connemara National Park or climb Croagh Patrick, and a bike lock.

ACCESS TOWN
Galway
☎ 091
One of Ireland's liveliest and most engaging cities, Galway is a delight, with its narrow streets, old stone and wooden shopfronts, good restaurants and bustling pubs. The city streets, which are always full of people, are brightened by musicians.

Galway is a university town, and attracts a bohemian crowd of musicians, artists, intellectuals and young people. Its summer arts festival is hugely popular and the place goes wild during Galway Race Week in the last week of July.

From its origins as a small fishing village, Galway became a walled merchant town during the Middle Ages. Governed first by the Anglo-Normans under Richard de Burgh, who captured territory from the O'Flahertys in 1232, the city came under the rule of an oligarchy of 14 (mostly English or Norman) merchant families or 'tribes' after a royal charter was granted, hence the name 'City of the Tribes'. Its Irish name Gaillimh is thought to have come from *'na Gall'*, the ancient word for foreigners.

Information Galway TIC (☎ 537 700, w www.irelandwest.ie; Fairgreen, Forster St, open Mon-Sat, longer hours and daily July-Aug) is the place for tourist information.

National Bank, Bank of Ireland and Trustee Savings Bank (TSB) on Eyre Square have ATMs and bureaus de change, as does the AIB branch (cnr Shop & Abbeygate Sts). You can also change money at the TIC and at the post office (Eglington St).

Mountain Trail Bike Shop (☎ 569 888, Corn Store Arcade, Middle St) rents out bikes for €64 per week (including panniers and accessories). It's not in the Raleigh Rent-a-Bike scheme, but has agents in the west where you can leave bikes if you're not returning to Galway. The shop operates a buy-back scheme and sells ex-rental bikes for around €130. It's advisable to book ahead for rental and inquire early for second-hand bikes, which sell quickly. The shop also sells panniers, does repairs, runs on- and off-road tours, and gives excellent advice on local mountain-bike trails.

Kearney's Cycles (☎ 563 356, e mkearney@indigo.ie; Terryland Retail Park, Headford Rd) is a Raleigh Rent-a-Bike agent (€51 per week; extra for panniers and helmet) and does repairs.

Things to See & Do Galway is a charming and compact city to wander around. You can walk along the River Corrib from the **Spanish Arch** at the southern end of town to the Salmon Weir Bridge near the imposing **St Nicholas' Roman Catholic**

Cathedral, a stylistically mixed structure, which the critics love to hate.

The protestant **Collegiate Church of St Nicholas of Myra**, on Shop St, is Ireland's largest medieval parish church still in use. The Lynch family – the most powerful of the 14 ruling Galway 'tribes' – are buried here. James Lynch, mayor of Galway in 1493 found his own son guilty of murder and, when none of the townsfolk would act as executioner, the justice-upholding mayor did it himself, and then retired into seclusion. The nearby **Lynch's Castle** (now a branch of the AIB) holds a memorial to his 'stern and unbending justice'.

A Galway walking tour is detailed in Junior Chamber's pocket-sized *Galway Tourist Guide* (free from the TIC). Literary walking tours of Galway (☎ 589 544) take one hour.

Places to Stay Book accommodation well ahead during the Arts Festival and Race Week.

Galway city's closest camping is 5.4km west of the centre. *Salthill Caravan Park* (☎ 523 972, W www.galway.net, Salthill Rd) Tent sites per person €7. It's a flat, grassy site on Galway Bay.

Kinlay House (☎ 565 244, e kinlay.gal way@usitworld.com, Merchants Rd) Dorm beds €14-18, standard/ensuite doubles €21/ 23. Large and central, dedicated bike lock-up and cheap laundry make this Galway's best hostel option. *Sleepzone* (☎ 566 999, W www.sleepzone.ie, Bóthar na mBán) Dorm beds €14-18, singles/doubles/twins €26/ 40/44. Galway's newest large purpose-built hostel, just north of the central area.

Cill Cuana (☎ 585 979, 16 Grattan Park) Ensuite singles/doubles €34/51. Nonsmoking, pleasantly homely, eight minutes walk to town; welcomes cyclists. *Consilio* (☎ 586 450, 4 Whitestrand Ave) Ensuite singles €32-36, doubles €51. Nonsmoking B&B on a quietish street towards Salthill, 10 minutes' walk from the centre. *Rossa B&B* (☎ 562 803, 21 St Brendans Ave) Singles/doubles €32/45. Central and nonsmoking, with smallish homely rooms. *Inishmore Guesthouse* (☎ 582 639, e inishmorehouse@eir com.net; 109 Fr Griffin Rd, Lower Salthill) Singles/doubles €58/77. Country-style rooms and cosy guest lounge; German spoken.

Most of Galway's hotels don't cater well for bike storage. *Foster Court Hotel* (☎ 564 111, W www.fostercourthotel.com) Singles/ doubles €108/121. Smart, spacious three-star hotel stores bikes in the basement.

Places to Eat For food choice and quality, Galway is one of the best places around. It's wise to book during July and August.

You'll find *supermarkets* in Eyre Square Centre. *Healthwise Wholefoods* (☎ 568 761, 4 Lower Abbeygate St) sells health foods. *Griffins Bakery* (cnr High & Mainguard Sts) is popular. Gourmets should visit *Sheridan's Cheesemongers* (☎ 564 829, 14-15 Churchyard St).

Mocha Beans (☎ 565 919, 2 Lower Cross St) Galway's best coffee plus pastries, breakfast and lunch. *Food for Thought* (☎ 565 854, Lower Abbeygate St) Breakfast €2-6, lunch from €4. Cafeteria-style wholesome meals from 7.30am (closed Sun).

McDonagh's (☎ 565 001, Quay St) Eat in/takeaway fish and chips €6, adjoining restaurant mains €9-22. A Galway institution – it's recommended; the menu makes a good read, and the illustrated guide to fish is in nine languages.

Couch Potatas (☎ 561 664, Upper Abbeygate St) Mains €7-11. Substantial meals with baked potatoes of many flavours (even pizza potato). *Scoosi* (☎ 568 010; Fishmarket) Pizza and pasta mains €7-11. Overlooks the river and has some outdoor tables.

The River God Café (☎ 565 811, 2 Quay St) Mains €11-14. Excellent fusion food with a French influence; creative assortment of flavoursome veg, meat and seafood dishes. *Spikes* (☎ 556 770, 2 High St) Mains €6-14. Fresh, tasty contemporary food (including veg and pasta). Their motto is 'Get stuffed at Spikes'.

Getting There & Away See the Tralee to Galway section of the Around Ireland ride (p251) for how to cycle the 32km from Kinvara on the Clare Circuit ride (p164) to Galway.

The Bus Éireann Travel Centre (☎ 562 000) and the train station (☎ 561 444) are on Station Rd just off Eyre Square.

Carnmore Airport (☎ 091-755 569) is 10km east of Galway city, near the N18. See Air (p268) for more information on flights to Galway.

Bus Éireann (☎ 562 000) services to/from Galway include Westport (€12, two hours,

Connemara & Inishmór

four daily), Shannon Airport (€12, three hours, 10 daily; change in Ennis), Dublin (€12, four hours, 13 daily) and Belfast (€24, 6½ hours, three daily).

Iarnród Éireann (☎ 1850 366 888, after-hours timetable information ☎ 01-805 4222) runs services between Galway and Dublin (€21, €30 Sun & Fri; three hours, five daily).

THE RIDE (see map p176)
Day 1: Galway to Kilronan
2–3½ hours, 39.2km

Today's ride culminates in a 40-minute ferry ride to one of the Aran islands, Inishmór. It's advisable to book your ticket a day ahead during high summer. Island Ferries (☎ 568 903, after hours ☎ 572 273) has three offices, including one at the TIC in Galway, and another at the ferry terminal. It's the longer established operator, with more space for bikes on board (one-way/return €16/20, bikes €3/6; three daily). Boats may be cancelled in very bad weather. Island Ferries also sails to the smaller islands Inishmaan (Inis Meain) and Inisheer (Inis Oirr). ó

You can sail direct from Galway city to the islands with O'Brien Shipping (☎ 567 676), also in the TIC (one-way/return €16/20, bikes free; two hours, daily to Inishmór, less frequently to other islands). You can also reach the Aran Islands from Doolin (p169).

The ride from Galway city to the ferry at Rossaveal is straightforward, lightly undulating with a couple of minor climbs. The road is mostly in good condition and wide, although traffic is moderately heavy.

Although it remains fairly built up until the attractive village of Spiddal (19.5km), the route is quite scenic, with good views across Galway Bay to the Burren. After Spiddal, the country opens out to the wild rocky Connemara countryside and, in the distance, the magnificent Twelve Bens.

The last 5.7km leaves the R336, the main road to the ferry, in favour of a quieter route past a popular Travellers (itinerant people; also known as Tinkers) halting site, and thatched cottages.

Kilronan
☎ 099

Inishmór (Big Island), or Árainn, is the largest of the three Aran islands: it's 14.5km long and a maximum of 4km wide. It's also the most visited of the three, be-

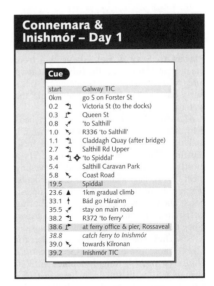

Connemara & Inishmór – Day 1

Cue		
start		Galway TIC
0km		go S on Forster St
0.2	↰	Victoria St (to the docks)
0.3	↱	Queen St
0.8	↙	'to Salthill'
1.0	↘	R336 'to Salthill'
1.1	↰	Claddagh Quay (after bridge)
2.7	↰	Salthill Rd Upper
3.4	↰ ✧	'to Spiddal'
5.4		Salthill Caravan Park
5.8	↘	Coast Road
19.5		Spiddal
23.6	▲	1km gradual climb
33.1	↑	Bád go Há:rainn
35.5	↙	stay on main road
38.2	↰	R372 'to ferry'
38.6	↱	at ferry office & pier, Rossaveal
38.8		*catch ferry to Inishmór*
39.0	↘	towards Kilronan
39.2		Inishmór TIC

coming very busy – particularly with day trippers – in July and August. Although a number of tour minibuses roam the island, the roaring trade is in the rental of bicycles, the main mode of transport here.

A loose cluster of buildings near the pier, Kilronan (Cill Rónáin) is the main entry/exit point on the island. In summer, the central intersection, with its few gift shops, pubs and eateries, is strewn with parked bicycles and clogged with wobbling day cyclists. The place quietens considerably after the last ferry departure.

Information The TIC (☎ 61263) is 300m west of the pier.

Bank of Ireland (open Wed year-round & 10am-3pm Thurs July-Sept; closed for lunch) is on the main road, about 650m northwest of the pier. The post office, about 550m northwest of the pier, changes money and, next to it is a bureau de change (open Fri-Tues).

Aran Bike Hire (☎ 61132) by the pier rents decent bikes for €8 per day and will help out with repairs if possible.

Ionad Árann Aran's Heritage Centre, Ionad Árann (☎ 61355) provides an excellent overview of the island, with informative displays about its geology, natural and archaeological sites of interest, and traditional life. Robert O'Flaherty's 1934 film, *Man of Aran*,

WEST

an unusual documentary on island life, is screened here several times daily.

Places to Stay & Eat About 2km from the pier, in Mainistir, is the *Inishmór Camp Site (☎ 61185)* Tent sites per person €4. It's fairly basic (no showers) but overlooks the water on the coast road.

Mainistir House (☎ 61169) Dorm beds €11. The best value you'll find anywhere; includes a breakfast of porridge and fresh muffins. The nonsmoking hostel offers a mostly vegetarian two-course buffet evening meal (€11), also available to nonresidents. It's highly recommended, but fills up, so book ahead. Otherwise, the self-catering kitchen is somewhat spartan. It's about 2km along the main road; bikes are stored outside.

Few B&Bs on the island have shelter for bikes. Those listed here do. *St Brendan's House (☎ 61149)* Singles/doubles €23/46 ensuite €51 with full Irish breakfast (€3 less for continental breakfast). Built in 1910, and a B&B since 1923, this place is not slick and new, but has lovely character. *Nóirín Uí Ghoill (☎ 61297, e noirinuighoill@hot mail.com, Cill Éinne)* Ensuite doubles €51. On the Killeany (Cill Éinne) Bay, 1.5km from the village, the rooms are new and spacious. It's right near the *Tigh Fitz* pub *(☎ 61213)*, which serves food until 7pm. *An Crugán (☎ 61150, w www.ancrugan.com)* Ensuite singles/doubles €39/51. Plain but comfortable rooms, about 1km from the pier (signposted off the main road).

Spar supermarket opens 9am-8pm (10am-6pm Sun). Most places in Kilronan (including the pubs) serve food only until early evening. *Lios Aengus (☎ 61030)* next to Spar serves light meat meals (€7), soup and sandwiches (€3-6), 10am-7pm. *The Auld Pier (☎ 61228)* does overpriced eat-in fast food until around 8pm.

Pier House (☎ 61417, e pierh@iol.ie) Ensuite singles/doubles €69/102. Three-star guesthouse; very pleasant with great views and more atmosphere than the average three-star hotel. Adjoining is the *Pier House Restaurant* Delicious-sounding gourmet pizzas (with good veg options) €16 (Tues only); à la carte mains €19-20 (vegetarian on request, around €14, Wed-Sun). Specialising in seafood, local and organic produce, this place even uses local seaweed in some dishes.

Aran Fisherman Restaurant & Bar (☎ 61104) Evening mains €16-23. One of the few places open after 8pm, the fairly standard menu is pricey for what you get.

Day 2: Inishmór Day Circuit
1½–2½ hours, 30km

The best way to cycle Inishmór is to understand the basic orientation of the island, take note of the things you particularly want to visit and follow your nose. We haven't provided cues – Inishmór is not large, or difficult to navigate; and you can easily cycle it in a day, stopping to visit sites of interest on the way. It's also an excellent place for walking. Indeed, most of the attractions are accessible only on foot.

Three roughly parallel roads run between Kilronan (Cill Rónáin) and Kilmurvy (Cill Mhuirbhigh). The island's busiest stretch is the middle main road. Look for seals on the lower (northern) coast road (from Kilronan, turn-off opposite Joe Watty's pub). Well worth exploring is the quiet southern (high) road. From Kilmurvy it's a steep climb east through an extraordinary landscape of tiny walled fields. So rocky are the fields that the hundreds of walls look like rock deposits built as much to expose ground as to fence the fields. From high up, the views are terrific, although the road peters out into a hard-packed rocky track. Two tracks to the left drop steeply to the main (middle) road, so road bikers may prefer to retrace their steps to Kilmurvy.

The roads leading west from Kilmurvy, and, southeast of Kilronan, around Killeany Bay are also relatively quiet.

Sites to visit include Stone-Age forts, early Christian buildings and intriguing natural formations. **Dún Aengus** (Dún Aonghasa), perched on the sheer southern cliff south of Kilmurvy, is one of the most amazing archaeological sites in the country. Be *very* careful when approaching the cliffs: there are no guard rails; tourists have been blown off and fallen to their death.

The circular **Dún Eochla**, halfway between Kilronan and Kilmurvy, on the highest point, has the best view of the Aran Islands, Connemara and the Burren.

Off the southern (high) road, south of Gort na gCapall, is **Serpent Hole** (Poll na bPéist), which is a natural rectangular pool connected to the ocean by an underwater passage.

WEST

If you're up for a swim, try the Blue Flag **beach** at Kilmurvy.

Day 3: Kilronan to Clifden
3–5½ hours, 56.4km

Heading into the wild expanse of Connemara, this ride is not hard (unless a strong westerly is blowing). It undulates most of the way across the lonely bogs and around scalloped harbours, their rocks strewn with golden seaweed. The only climb to really get you puffing (at 24.5km) bucks and swerves for 1.5km before easing into a steadier gradient.

After leaving the ferry traffic the roads are quiet – on the bog roads you'll probably see more bikes than cars. For the most part surfaces are good (the bog roads occasionally have rough patches).

The few services en route include a *Spar* supermarket (1.7km) and Cashel's (36.8km), *store* and *Willie Boulger's Fireside Bar*, which sells soup and sandwiches.

The desolate beauty of the bogs is the highlight of the ride: this is Ireland's 'wild west'. The appeal is subtle and heightened by travelling slowly enough to appreciate the colours of the grasses in different lights – emeralds, hazels and straw – and to notice the pink and yellow wildflowers, and the fluffy white bog cotton in the turf diggings. Small and irregular wind-whipped loughs lie among rocky hillocks, spotted sheep wander over the road, and on the northern horizon loom the Twelve Bens.

Clifden
☎ 095

At the head of narrow Clifden Bay, Connemara's 'capital' is one of the youngest towns in Ireland. It was founded around 1812 by landlord John D'Arcy, whose vision was to kick-start the poverty-stricken region by creating a commercial centre and then exploit the area's resources of wool, fish and marble. The D'Arcy family was ruined by the Great Famine and their estate along the Sky Rd is now in ruins.

Clifden is also a centre for Connemara ponies. The annual Connemara Pony Show is held in August.

Information Clifden TIC (☎ 21163, w www .irelandwest.travel.ie, Galway Rd) is opposite St Joseph's Church. It operates a bureau de change, as do the AIB (Market Square)

Connemara & Inishmór – Day 3

Cue	
start	Kilronan pier
catch ferry to Rossaveal	
0km	go south along Rossaveal pier
0.2 ↰	R372 (retrace route), Rossaveal
1.7	Spar supermarket
2.5 ↰	'to Casla'
4.2 ↱	R336 'to Scriob', Casla
15.6 ↰	R340 'to An Gort Mor'
23.4 ↑	minor road (leave R340 Coast Rd)
24.5 ▲	2.3km moderate climb
33.0 ↱	'to Cashel'
33.6 ↰	R342 'to Cashel'
36.8	Cashel
41.4 ↘	'to Roundstone', across bridge
43.1 ↑	bog road 'to Clifden'
52.7 ↱	R341 'to Clifden'
55.9 ↰	'to town centre'
56.1 ↱ ◆	Main St
56.4	Clifden TIC

and the Bank of Ireland (Seaview); both have ATMs.

Manions Cycles (☎ 21160, Bridge St) can help with cycling needs. The Outdoor Shop (☎ 22838, Market St) sells camping gear.

Things to See & Do The local countryside is worth exploring further, either on foot or by bike. Richard at the Brookside Hostel is full of suggestions for local routes. The well-known **Sky Rd** around the narrow peninsula east of town passes the ruined Clifden Castle where the D'Arcy family lived. The 16km circuit involves some hard climbing and terrific views. **Roundstone**, 20.9km southeast, is another good destination: a pretty harbour town, where works a *bodhrán* (hand-held goatskin drum) maker.

The Connemara Walking Centre (☎ 1850 266 636, w www.walkingireland.com, Market St) sells walking guidebooks and runs specialist walking tours, eg, with an archaeology or natural history theme.

Places to Stay The closest camping, 2.3km north, is: *Shanaheever Campsite* (☎ 22150) Tent sites per person €6, including showers. Reasonably basic, it's quiet and offers covered facilities. The signed turn-off is 1.8km along the Day 3 route.

Brookside Hostel (☎ 21812, e *brook sidehostel@eircom.net, Hulk St)* Dorm beds

Are Ye Lost?

The Irish have something of a reputation for storytelling – or, more particularly, for leading gullible souls up the garden path. Bear this in mind when inquiring about the distance to somewhere. The locals obligingly help with directions. Stop to look at your map and a passing farmer will inevitably ask, 'Are ye lost?' Ask them how far to the next town/ pub/turn-off and they'll usually reply, 'Oh, it's about a mile'. After two, three, or maybe four miles, you'll probably reach the location in question. Be warned!

€11-12. Bike-friendly, the owner has excellent local knowledge.

Ben View House (☎ 21256, *Bridge St*) Singles €24-25, ensuite doubles €50-58. With a 1950s Cyclists Touring Club plaque, welcoming and accommodating Ben View has been a B&B since 1926. ***Kingstown House*** (☎ 21470, *Bridge St*) Ensuite doubles €51. Next door to the bike shop, with inside storage. ***Dún Rí Guesthouse*** (☎ 21625, e dunri@anu.ie, *Hulk St*) Ensuite singles/ doubles €45/64. Comfortable rooms furnished with antique-style dressers.

Places to Eat Self-caterers should head to ***Super Valu*** (*Market St*) or, for speciality and organic foods, ***Connemara Hamper*** (*Market St*).

Walsh's Coffeeshop & Bakery (*Market St*) Continental/full Irish breakfast €4-6. ***Connemara Diner & Takeaway*** (*Seaview*) €2-5. Burgers, chicken, fish and chips.

EJ Kings (☎ 21330, *Market Square*) Bar meals €7-11; restaurant mains €11-19, including vegetarian. Live music after 9pm in the lively bar; the upstairs restaurant serves food till late. ***Crannmer Italian Restaurant*** (☎ 21174, *Church Hill*) Pizza and pasta €8-18. Large servings in a small place, hidden away up the hill from Main St. ***Cullen's Bistro & Coffee Shop*** (*Market St*) Mains €7-13. Café-style (burgers to salmon) with retro lighting and colourful tablecloths.

O'Grady's Seafood Restaurant (☎ 21450, *Market St*) Mains €14-17. Reputed to be one of the best restaurants in western County Galway.

Day 4: Clifden to Leenane
2–4 hours, 39.7km

Leaving the bogs, this ride takes in some magnificent Connemara landscapes. The day begins with some moderate climbing and continues to roll throughout, ending with a descent along Killary Harbour. The N59 carries a moderate – not unpleasant – amount of traffic; the coast road is quieter, especially during the week.

After climbing out of Clifden, the wonderfully warty Twelve Bens dominate the horizon. Letterfrack (14.3km) lies on the Ballynakill Harbour at the edge of **Connemara National Park** (visitor centre ☎ 41054, admission €3). Visit the park on a side trip at 14km, the entrance is at the western edge of the village. The visitor centre contains an exhibition on the history and natural history of Connemara over the last 10,000 years. There's an excellent 15-minute audiovisual show and a *café*. Three short nature trails are nearby. Guided nature walks (two to three hours) happen in July and August. Letterfrack makes a good base for serious walking: visitors recommend the ***Old Monastery Hostel*** (☎ 41132), which also has tent sites. The village also has B&Bs, and a couple of *pubs* make it a good lunch stop.

Beautifully positioned **Kylemore Abbey** (☎ 41146) is an easy 4.2km side trip east of Letterfrack. The spectacular neo-Gothic abbey, built on the estate of a wealthy surgeon from Manchester, is a big tourist drawcard. Between Letterfrack and the abbey is the estate's **Victorian Walled Garden**. It costs €6 to visit the garden and €5 for the abbey (combined ticket €9). Allow an hour for each.

The coast road west of Tully Cross looks out to the Atlantic and the mouth of Killary Harbour. Side roads head down to a couple of white-sand beaches. ***Connemara Campsite*** (☎ 43865) is by one of them (23.6km).

Heading back towards the mountains, the road skirts Loughs Muck and Fee. Names aside, these dark, brooding loughs are stunning in their peacefulness, which is characterised by the sound of water gently lapping, sheep bleating and the occasional buzz of a fishing line. Just when it seems things couldn't get any more beautiful, the road descends along the Killary Harbour fjord into Leenane.

Leenane

☎ 095

Sometimes spelled Leenaun, and pronounced Lee-nan, Lee-naan and, sometimes, Lee-nawn, this tiny village is gloriously located at the foot of the mountains and the head of Killary Harbour. *The Field* was filmed in and around the village in 1989, a fact not forgotten by one local pub.

The best bet for information is the **Leenane Cultural Centre** (☎ 42323, open 9am-6pm daily Easter-Oct). It's not a TIC, but the friendly operators have good local knowledge. The post office, which has a bureau de change and small *store,* is inside *Hamiltons Bar* (☎ 42266).

Things to See & Do Inside the **Leenane Cultural Centre** is an exhibition of the wool industry, which thrived a century ago, including spinning and weaving demonstrations. Forget the touristy 12-minute video.

Surrounding Leenane are some excellent walks, including one to **Aasleagh Falls**, north of town.

The Killary Adventure Company offers guided **adventure activities**, from walking and mountain biking through kayaking, windsurfing and archery. The company operates out of the Killary Centre, 5.5km west of town (see Places to Stay & Eat).

Places to Stay & Eat The closest official camping is 16.2km west at *Connemara Campsite* (see Day 4). There's little flat, dry land around Leenane, but you could try asking landowners for permission to camp in their fields.

Killary Centre (☎ 43411, ⓦ www.killary.com, Kylemore Rd) 5.5km up the hill, operates two accommodation centres. The newly built Killary Centre, K2 with dorm beds for €16-23 and doubles for €56, offers budget accommodation (includes breakfast). There's no kitchen, pre-ordered three-course meals cost €18. At Killary Lodge, 1km away, B&B singles/doubles cost €50/100 (including three-course dinner €74/148).

The Convent Guesthouse (☎ 42240, Westport Rd) Ensuite singles/doubles €26/51. With stained glass windows and pews in the dining area, large sitting rooms and harbour views, this place is a treat; book early. *Sancta Maria* (☎ 42250, Maam Rd) Singles/doubles €22/44. This old-fashioned, homely B&B

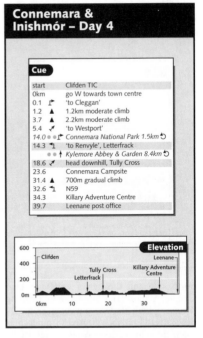

Connemara & Inishmór – Day 4

Cue

start	Clifden TIC
0km	go W towards town centre
0.1 ↱	'to Cleggan'
1.2 ▲	1.2km moderate climb
3.7 ▲	2.2km moderate climb
5.4 ↙	'to Westport'
14.0 ●●↱	Connemara National Park 1.5km ↻
14.3 ↰	'to Renvyle', Letterfrack
●●↑	Kylemore Abbey & Garden 8.4km ↻
18.6 ↙	head downhill, Tully Cross
23.6	Connemara Campsite
31.4 ▲	700m gradual climb
32.6 ↰	N59
34.3	Killary Adventure Centre
39.7	Leenane post office

Elevation

was one of the first in town. *Leenane Lodge* (☎ 42377, Westport Rd) Singles/doubles €32/51. Open June–mid-Sept. Characterful, if not typical, B&B, run by a talkative American; has a self-catering kitchen.

Leenane Hotel (☎ 42249, ⓔ leenanehotel@eircom.net, Kylemore Rd) Singles/doubles €61/122. This 200-year-old inn retains an olde worlde character. Book well in advance. In the restaurant, mains cost €14-15 (vegetarian available, around €11).

The Village Grill Eat-in fast food €2-14, sandwiches and fry ups until 10pm.

The Blackberry Café (☎ 42240) Meals €7-18. Don't be put off by Richard Clayderman on replay – the food here is good: excellent Irish stew (€12), plenty of fish, but little for vegetarians. Closes 8pm.

Portfinn Lodge Restaurant (☎ 42265) Mains €14-21. Specialising in seafood, it's pricey, but locally recommended.

Day 5: Leenane to Westport

2½–5 hours, 51.8km

The magnificent scenery continues especially for the first half of this ride, which undulates gently along Killary Harbour's

WEST

Connemara & Inishmór – Day 5

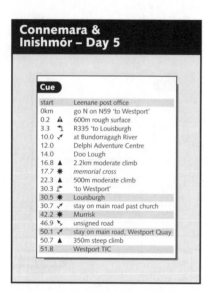

Cue	
start	Leenane post office
0km	go N on N59 'to Westport'
0.2 ⚠	600m rough surface
3.3 ⮱	R335 'to Louisburgh'
10.0 ⤴	at Bundorragagh River
12.0	Delphi Adventure Centre
14.0	Doo Lough
16.8 ▲	2.2km moderate climb
17.7 ✳	memorial cross
22.3 ▲	500m moderate climb
30.3 ⮱	'to Westport'
30.5 ✳	Louisburgh
30.7 ⤴	stay on main road past church
42.2 ✳	Murrisk
46.9 ⤵	unsigned road
50.1 ⤴	stay on main road, Westport Quay
50.7 ▲	350m steep climb
51.8	Westport TIC

north side and through a valley to Doo Lough. A short pass climbs onto a rolling plateau which flattens out as it gradually descends to Louisburgh. Apart from a short steep climb in Westport itself, the rest of the route is relatively flat, heading around Clew Bay past the famous pilgrimage mountain, Croagh Patrick, to Westport.

Traffic is relatively light and moves slowly through the mountains; it's heavier and faster from Louisburgh. The road surface is rough in patches around Killary Harbour.

At the pass above Doo Lough is a **memorial** to the world's hungry poor. During the Great Famine, 600 men, women and children walked 17.7km (11mi) from Louisburgh to Delphi Lodge in the hope that the landlord would offer them food. They were refused and around 400 perished on the return journey.

Other than a *café* at Delphi Adventure Centre (12km; an outdoor activity and accommodation centre), there is no food until Louisburgh (30.5km), which has *shops*, *pubs* and *eateries*. Here, too, is the **Granuaile Interpretive Centre** (☎ 098-66341), which celebrates the life and times of Granuaile (aka Grace O'Malley), a 16th-century pirate queen. An interesting 25-minute documentary tells her story. See also the boxed text.

Tiny Murrisk (42.2km) is inundated on the last Sunday of every July when pilgrims come to climb **Croagh Patrick**, the mountain at whose feet it lies, and on which St Patrick is said to have stood when he expelled the snakes from Ireland in AD 441. The Croagh Patrick Information Centre (☎ 098-64114) incorporates a photographic exhibition and a *café*. It takes around three hours (return) to climb 'The Reek' (as it's known). Across the road is the striking **National Famine Memorial**; and just off the road is the ruined **Murrisk Abbey**, founded in 1457.

Westport

See Westport (p185).

Grace O'Malley

Grace O'Malley (1530–1603), also called Granuaile, the daughter of a Connaught chief, established her own fleet and commanded her own army. From her Clare Island base she controlled the Clew Bay area and attacked the ships of those who had submitted to the English. In 1566 she married Richard Burke, a neighbouring clan chief (her first husband, Donal O'Flaherty, had died years earlier), and her power grew to such an extent that the merchants of Galway pleaded with the English governor to do something about her.

In 1574 her castle (Carrigahowley Castle, now called Rockfleet Castle, near Newport) was besieged, but she turned the siege into a rout of the English and sent them packing. In 1577 she was held in prison but mysteriously managed to get herself released on a promise of good behaviour. Over the next few years she craftily entered a number of alliances, both with and against the English.

In 1593 she travelled to London and was granted a pardon after meeting Elizabeth I, who offered to make her a countess. Grace declined, for she already considered herself the Queen of Connaught.

Back in Ireland she appeared to be working for the English, but it seems likely that she was still fiercely independent. In the final recorded reference to her, in the English State Papers of 1601, an English captain tells of meeting one of her pirate ships, captained by one of her sons, on its way to plunder a merchant ship.

Day 6: Westport to Cong

3½–6 hours, 60.2km

Heading back inland, Day 6 features the great island-studded Lough Mask, a brief flirtation with the mountains, and a touch of the Twilight Zone.

Skirting around the Partry Mountains on the R330, the route turns southwest and follows Lough Mask to the Connemara foothills. Undulating gently to moderately for most of the way, the ride's only serious climb is a relatively steep one (at 38.8km) from Lough Mask over to the valley of Lough Nafooey, before switching back east towards Cong. Traffic, moderate leaving Westport, gradually lessens; it's barely noticeable after leaving the R330.

Is it for real? The village of Killavally (12.2km), surrounded by bogs, is little more than *McEvilly's Pub*, an undertaker and a 'Caution: Dangerous Junction' sign.

There are plenty of more comfortable stopping places along Lough Mask, including several picnic tables. Tourmakeady (26.2km) has a *store*; just past the village a side trip leads to a picnic area by a waterfall.

Towards the lough's western end the mood changes as the steep, glacier-carved spurs of **Maumtrasna** (673m), layered like the folds of a theatre curtain, sing their siren song.

More exquisite, mist-shrouded mountains drop to another water-filled valley over the pass. Stop at delightful Finny (44.3km) for the wonderful 'turf' (chocolate) cake or tea and scones at the *Happy Kettle*.

Cong
☎ 094

Another small movie village, Cong was the setting for John Ford's 1951 film, *The Quiet Man*, starring John Wayne and Maureen O'Hara. Many of the local B&Bs, pubs and restaurants are named after the film or its characters, yet it generally manages to retain charm rather than tackiness.

Cong TIC (☎ 954 6542, Abbey St) operates a bureau de change, as does the post office(Main St).

O'Connor's Esso service station (☎ 954 6008) is a Raleigh Rent-a-Bike agent and can do bike repairs.

Things to See & Do A community of scholars and metalworkers thrived at Cong during the early Christian period. The 12th-century Augustinian **Cong Abbey** was founded by the last high kings of Ireland, Turlough, Rory and Cathal O'Connor, on the site of an earlier monastery.

The **Quiet Man Heritage Cottage** (☎ 954 6089, Abbey St) replicates the 'White O'Mornin' cottage in the film and claims to be typical of cottages of the 1920s. Also contained within it is the **Cong Archaeological**

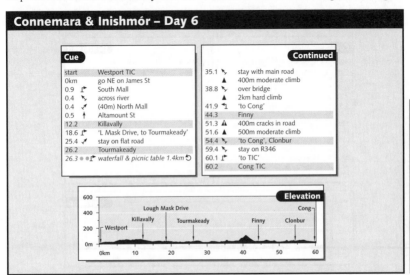

Connemara & Inishmór – Day 6

Cue			Continued	
start	Westport TIC	35.1 ↘	stay with main road
0km	go NE on James St	▲	400m moderate climb
0.9 ↱	South Mall	38.8 ↘	over bridge
0.4 ↘	across river	▲	2km hard climb
0.4 ↗	(40m) North Mall	41.9 ↰	'to Cong'
0.5 ↑	Altamount St	44.3	Finny
12.2	Killavally	51.3 ⚠	400m cracks in road
18.6 ↱	'L Mask Drive, to Tourmakeady'	51.6 ▲	500m moderate climb
25.4 ↗	stay on flat road	54.4 ↘	'to Cong', Clonbur
26.2	Tourmakeady	59.4 ↘	stay on R346
26.3 ● ● ↱	waterfall & picnic table 1.4km ↻	60.1 ↱	'to TIC'
		60.2	Cong TIC

Elevation chart: Westport, Killavally, Lough Mask Drive, Tourmakeady, Finny, Clonbur, Cong — 0m to 600m over 0km to 60km.

WEST

and Historical Exhibition, which explores almost 9000 years of Cong's history.

South of town, **Ashford Castle** (☎ 954 6003) was once the home of the Guinness family and is now an exclusive hotel (Pierce Brosnan of James Bond 007 fame was married here in 2001), which charges €6 just to look at the outside.

Places to Stay & Eat About 1.6km east is An Óige-affiliated **Cong Hostel** and **Cong Caravan & Camping Park** (☎ 954 6089, Quay Rd, Lisloughrey) Tent sites per person €6 (showers €1), dorm beds from €10. Facilities include an excellent kitchen and theatrette, which screens *The Quiet Man* every night.

Cong Travel Inn (☎ 954 6310, Circular Rd) Ensuite twins/doubles €32. Clean, central motel-like hostel.

Nymphsfield House (☎ 954 6320, Gortroe) Ensuite singles/doubles €32/49. Signed 1.2km from village this place has spacious rooms and is friendly and accommodating (dubbed the 'singles club' for willingness to take singles).

At Drumshiel, an undulating 1½ to 2km ride northwest of Cong, is a raft of B&Bs (signposted), the closest of which is **Dolmen House** (☎ 954 6466) Ensuite singles/doubles €35/51. Spacious, plush pink rooms and mountain views.

Danaghers Hotel (☎ 954 6028, Abbey St) Ensuite singles/doubles €45/89. Fine older-style hotel. Rooms above the bar can be noisy, ask for a quieter one. Pub grub €9-16 (no veg); probably the cheapest meal in town. Soak up the bar atmosphere or watch the world go by from outside tables.

O'Connor's *Spar* supermarket *(cnr Main St & Circular Rd)* is next to the Esso station.

Micilín's Restaurant (☎ 954 6655, Main St) Mains €13-18. Micilín was *The Quiet Man's* matchmaker – and it looks a suitably romantic establishment, serving fish, poultry, steak and vegetarian dishes.

Echoes Restaurant (☎ 954 6059, Main St) Mains €14-25. The place for a well-cooked meal: classic dishes using local produce.

Day 7: Cong to Galway
4–7 hours, 71.9km

The massive Lough Corrib is never far from this ride: Cong sits a handful of good stones' throws from its shore. The route skirts its northwestern edge and the lough comes into view again much later on. Galway city is built around its exit to the sea.

After a short steep climb at 15.4km, the Maumturks lie ahead. Savour the view: at Maam (21.4km) the route turns its back and, with a longish climb out of the valley, farewells the mountains. From Maam Cross (29km), it's pretty much plain sailing on

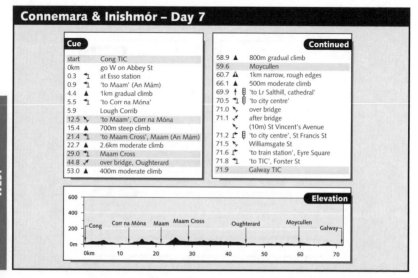

Connemara & Inishmór – Day 7

Cue		
start		Cong TIC
0km	⬐	go W on Abbey St
0.3	⬐	at Esso station
0.9	⬐	'to Maam' (An Mám)
4.4	▲	1km gradual climb
5.5	⬐	'to Corr na Móna'
5.9		Lough Corrib
12.5	⬎	'to Maam', Corr na Móna
15.4	▲	700m steep climb
21.4	⬐	'to Maam Cross', Maam (An Mám)
22.7	▲	2.6km moderate climb
29.0	⬐	Maam Cross
44.8	↗	over bridge, Oughterard
53.0	▲	400m moderate climb

		Continued
58.9	▲	800m gradual climb
59.6		Moycullen
60.7	⚠	1km narrow, rough edges
66.1	▲	500m moderate climb
69.9	↑ 🏠	'to Lr Salthill, cathedral'
70.5	⬐ 🏠	'to city centre'
71.0	⬎	over bridge
71.1	↗	after bridge
	⬎	(10m) St Vincent's Avenue
71.2	⬑ 🏠	'to city centre', St Francis St
71.5	⬎	Williamsgate St
71.6	⬑	'to train station', Eyre Square
71.8	⬐	'to TIC', Forster St
71.9		Galway TIC

Elevation

Cong — Corr na Móna — Maam — Maam Cross — Oughterard — Moycullen — Galway

WEST

the N59 all the way back to Galway. Traffic here increases and is faster, although mostly not too intrusive. The terrain undulates gently with a couple of short climbs.

Few services exist until later in the ride: Corr na Móna (12.5km) has a *store* and a *pub*, as does Maam (21.4km); at Maam Cross (29km) is a touristy *hotel/gift-shop/restaurant* complex. Sizeable Oughterard (44.8km), the so-called 'gateway to Connemara', has *shops*, *pubs*, *restaurants* plus hostel and B&B accommodation.

Beaches & Bogs

Duration	4 days
Distance	303.9km
Difficulty	moderate–hard
Start/End	Westport

Northwest Mayo is one of Europe's least inhabited areas. Its wild open spaces and numerous Blue Flag beaches attract those in the know (Irish holiday-makers), but it's certainly off the beaten tourist trail.

This ride explores traditional villages and the wonderful coastline of Achill Island, which alone claims five Blue Flag beaches. It heads north through bleak blanket bog to the very Irish villages of Belmullet and Killala and takes in the oldest farm in the world.

PLANNING

Budget accommodation is limited north of Achill Island. Camping is permitted, but facilities are not provided. No hostels exist between Pollatomish (early on Day 3) and the end of the ride.

It's possible to make the ride easier by turning it into five shorter days. On Day 1, finish at Achill Sound (42.7km), instead of Keel. On the second day, ride the Achill Island sections unloaded: ie to Keel, plus the side trip to Keem Bay, returning to Achill Sound via the Atlantic Drive section of Day 2 (53.4km plus side trip). On the third day, ride to Belmullet (62.8km). On the fourth day, take the shorter option via the R314 to Killala (see Day 3). Follow the Day 4 ride description on the fifth day.

When to Ride

May to July is best. Average monthly rainfall is lowest between April and July, and

Warning

⚠ Unspoilt beaches are one of the treasures of Mayo. However (apart from Blue Flag beaches, which are considered safe), some of the best-looking beaches are the most treacherous, with dangerous currents. Always check locally before swimming.

increases markedly in August. The reasonably light tourist traffic increases in July and August, particularly on Achill Island.

Maps

The OSI 1:250,000 Holiday map *Ireland West* covers the region. It's worth buying the *Achill Island Map Guide* (available from Westport and Achill Tourism TICs) for the interesting and informative descriptions.

What to Bring

Budget travellers should carry camping equipment.

ACCESS TOWN
Westport
☎ 098

Built around the River Carrowbeg and Clew Bay, Westport has two parts, divided by a hill: Westport Quay and Westport town proper. It is a planned town; the river runs down the middle of The Mall. The focal point of the centre is the Octagon Monument, erected in 1845. St Patrick now graces its podium, replacing an earlier statue (decapitated during the Civil War) of a local banker.

The last Sunday in July, Reek Sunday, is when pilgrims flock to climb Croagh Patrick, 10km to the southwest. Be sure to book accommodation well ahead on this weekend, as Westport will be inundated.

Information The TIC (☎ 25711, ⓦ www .visitmayo.com, James St) has extended hours in July and August.

The AIB (Shop St) has an ATM and bureau de change, as do the Bank of Ireland and Ulster Bank on The Mall. James St has an AIB ATM.

Sean Salmon runs Fuel & Cycle (☎ 25471, James St), a Raleigh Rent-a-Bike and repair business, from an unlikely looking premises in a yard (next to the barber shop).

Things to See & Do If you're into stately houses, **Westport House** (☎ 25430) is County Mayo's only one – though it's pricey and rather commercial (entry to the grounds is free). It's 3.2km from the centre, off Westport Quay Rd.

Clew Bay Heritage Centre (☎ 26852), in Westport Quay, has a collection of local artefacts and documents.

You can hear **music** in several Westport pubs. *Matt Molloy's (Bridge St)*, owned by Matt Molloy of the Chieftains, is crowded and noisy. Others to try include *Hobans (The Octagon)*, *Hennighans (Bridge St)* and *Clew Bay Hotel (James St)*.

For walking around Westport, the TIC sells *Westport Walks*, which details one- to three-hour walks.

Places to Stay Westport has two camping options. *Parkland Caravan & Camping Park* (☎ 27766, w www.westporthouse.ie) Tent sites €17. Pricey, it's on the Westport House estate, 3.2km from the town centre. An Óige *Club Atlantic Holiday Hostel* (☎ 26644, Altamount St) Tent sites per person €6, dorm beds €10. Near the train station; good facilities, though the atmosphere is a touch school-camp. The *Old Mill Hostel* (☎ 27045, James St) Dorm beds €11 (linen €2). Relaxed and located behind the TIC.

Altamount House (☎ 25226, Altamount St) Singles/ensuite doubles €25/54. One of Westport's older B&Bs, comfortable and bike-friendly.

Anna Lodge (☎ 28219, Distillery Court) Ensuite singles/doubles €36/49. Bright

new nonsmoking townhouse in a quiet court. *St Anthony's B&B* (☎ 28887, e *sk@ achh.iol.ie, Distillery Rd*) Doubles €64. Comfortably elegant, nonsmoking, with a large garden and good breakfast.

The *Olde Railway Hotel* (☎ 25166, w *www.anu.ie/railwayhotel, The Mall*) En-suite singles/doubles €83/115. This 220-year-old hotel, loaded with character, has smoke-free rooms furnished in period style.

Places to Eat Reservations are advised during July and August.

Super Valu supermarket *(Shop St)* is near the Octagon. *Country Fresh Greengrocer (Shop St)* is opposite. *Curry's Cottage Home Bakery (James St)*, has a tempting range (closed Mon except mid-Jun–mid-Sept).

Westport's most popular and tasty eateries are Italian-style. *Antica Roma* (☎ 28778, *Bridge St*) Mains €4-16. With pizzas (all under €9), burgers and grills, this place isn't bad value. *Sol Rio Restaurant* (☎ 28944, *Bridge St*) Mains €7-17. A cosy upstairs joint with pizzas and pastas all under €11. *La Bella Vita* (☎ 29771, *High St*) Mains €9-19. A little pricier, pasta here is delicious and service good (just as well, with a 10% service charge).

The Lantern (☎ 29912, *Bridge St*) Mains €7-15 plus rice. Chinese and Thai food. *O'Malleys Bar & Restaurant* (☎ 27307, *Bridge St*) Mains €12-20. Mixed cuisines, including Mexican, Italian and Asian; popular but a little pricey.

Getting There & Away Buses stop on Mill St near the Garda station. For timetable information, contact the TIC (☎ 25711) or the train station (☎ 25253). Services to/from Westport include: Dublin (€15, five hours, one to four daily); Galway (€12, two hours, four daily); and Sligo (€13, 2¼-2¾ hours, one to four daily).

The train station is on Ballinrobe Rd, near the Club Atlantic hostel. Trains travel between Westport and Dublin (€21, 4¼ hours, one to three daily).

THE RIDE
Day 1: Westport to Keel
3½–6 hours, 64.3 km
The scenery, Blue Flag beaches and old villages of Achill Island, which are all in the second half, are the highlights of this ride.

Beaches & Bogs – Day 1

Cue		
start		Westport TIC
0km		go NE on James St
0.3	▲	400m steep climb
1.6	▲	500m moderate climb
11.7	↘	N59 over bridge, Newport
12.1	↘	N59 'to Achill Sound'
28.3		Mulranny
29.3	↑	stay on N59
29.4	↘	R319 'to Achill Sound'
42.7		Achill Sound
47.3		Cashel
50.2	↰	'to Valley'
54.5	↱	'to Blue Flag beaches', Valley
56.0	▲	1.1km moderate climb
56.7	▲	200m rough surface
57.5		Doogort
57.9		Doogort Strand
58.1	✓	unsigned road
58.4	▲	900m moderate climb
58.6	✳	Achill Mission & St Thomas Church
59.8	▲	400m moderate climb
62.2	↱	unsigned road
	● ●↰	deserted village 900m ↰
64.1	↰	into village
64.3	● ● ↑	Keem Bay 16km ↰
64.3		O'Malleys store, Keel

But first comes a section on the N59, which is busy enough to detract from the enjoyment, particularly after Newport, where the road is straighter and the traffic faster. Off the N59, traffic is halved. It's practically nonexistent after the turn-off to Valley at 54.5km.

Beginning with a hilly section out of Westport, the road rises and dips all the way, more markedly between Newport and the Achill turn-off. It's rarely steep, however, except for one or two short sections on Achill.

From the turn-off to Achill Sound (29.4km) the change in scenery is dramatic: from unremarkable rolling pastures, the landscape suddenly becomes rocky, mountainous and sea-bound.

Achill Sound (42.7km) is an alternative stopover (see Planning, p185); accommodation includes *Wild Haven Hostel* (☎ 45392), *Breegeann House B&B* (☎ 45592) and *Achill Island Hotel* (☎ 45138).

At Cashel (47.3km) are the TICs of both Bord Fáilte and Achill Tourism (see Keel, p188, for details), but there is little else in the way of services.

Near the second Blue Flag beach on Achill's north side, and in the shadow of Mt

Slievemore, is Doogort (57.5km), a delightful, traditional whitewashed village. Though there are few services, *Seal Caves Caravan & Camping Park* (☎ *098-43262*) makes a quieter alternative to the huge park at Keel.

Nearby is the **Achill Mission** site, established by the Church of Ireland in the early 1830s, and St Thomas Church (58.6km). This was the first mission established among the native Irish, using the Irish language, and it prospered – to the consternation of the local Catholic clergy, who soon set about establishing their own schools.

A side trip at 62.2km leads to the **Slievemore deserted village**. Why and when the village was abandoned remains unclear; although the Great Famine is a likely contributor. It's incredible, looking at the tiny ruined cottages, to think that each one probably housed 10 children plus a cow! Today it's a peaceful place – although some sense the villagers' ghosts in the stillness...

Side Trip: Keem Bay
1–2 hours, 16km return

Talk to anyone who knows Achill and they're sure to say: 'You *must* go down to Keem Bay!' It's spectacular, but it comes at a price: there's a big climb in and out. From Keel, the smaller climb into neighbouring Dooagh serves as a warm up and from here you'll see the challenge ahead. Climbing along a cliff side, the tiny Blue Flag beach is visible below. From the beach itself, you might see the Minaun Cliffs back at Keel. It's a tough cycle, but worth the effort.

Keel
☎ 098

The island's main settlement sits by Trawmore, its longest beach (a Blue Flag beach, also called Keel). Keel is largely a one-street town; the newer 'suburb', Newtown, is at the western end. The neighbouring village of Dooagh is a further kilometre west. From late July, the villages host Scoil Acla (literally, Achill School) a two-week festival/summer school of traditional music and culture. Keel (and Achill, generally) is popular with Irish holiday-makers. The busiest period is July to August, especially during Scoil Acla.

Information Two TICs are at the Cashel Esso station, 17km east of Keel. There's the Bord Fáilte TIC (☎ 45384, open Jul-Aug) and

on the north side, Achill Tourism's TIC (☎ 47353, W www.achilltourism.com, open June-Aug), has free copies of *A Visitor's Guide to Achill* and *Achill Tourist Directory*.

Apart from an ATM (at Sweeny's Restaurant & Souvenir shop) in Achill Sound, Achill has no permanent banks. An AIB mobile bank (outside O'Malleys supermarket, open 10.45am-12.30pm Mon & Wed) visits Keel. Ulster Bank (Minaun Bar, open 11am-noon Tues) also visits.

Things to See & Do It's all about **outdoor activities** on Achill. These include walking (climb Mt Slievemore from behind the deserted village; ask Achill Tourism about other walks), rock climbing, windsurfing and diving – contact Achill Island Scuba (☎ 087-234 9884) at Keel's Purteen Harbour.

Places to Stay By Trawmore Strand is *Keel Sandybanks Caravan & Camping Park* (☎ *43211*). Tent sites €9 (showers €1). Large four-star site overlooking the Minaun Cliffs.

Rich View Hostel (☎ *43462, Newtown, Keel*) Dorm beds/doubles €9/26. Small, friendly and easy-going; book ahead mid-July to August.

Fuchsia Lodge (☎ *43350*, e *fuchsia lodge@eircom.net, Newtown, Keel*) Ensuite singles/doubles €32/51. Bright rooms, down-to-earth.

Achill Isle House (☎ *43355*, e *achill isle@eircom.net*) Singles/doubles €32/44. Welcomes singles even in the high season.

Joyce's Marian Villa Guest House (☎ *43134*) Ensuite singles €39-51, doubles €64-102 (some with sea views). Warm welcome; tastefully furnished rooms; enclosed veranda and cosy lounge; beach nearby.

Places to Eat The best eating depends on the year's summer staff: ask locals for recommendations.

O'Malleys *Spar* supermarket (☎ *43125*) incorporates the post office and bike hire (no repairs). The *Fish Shop* (☎ *43310, Newtown*) has freshly caught (not cooked) fish; locals recommend it. *Max Fast Food* (☎ *43268, The Annexe Inn*) is another option; open July, August and bank-holiday weekends.

The *Beehive* (☎ *43134*) Lunches €3-7. Cafeteria-style with great cakes and coffee. Good craft shop in the front.

Chalet Seafood Restaurant (☎ *43157*) Mains €9-18. Three-course early-bird menu €14. Fish and seafood plus a good variety of middle-of-the-road dishes, including vegetarian; smoking and nonsmoking areas. *Calvey's Restaurant* (☎ *43158*) Mains €12-19, including vegetarian. Decent wine list; local lamb and beef.

Day 2: Keel to Belmullet
5–8½ hours, 94.6km

From the spectacular mountain and coastal scenery of Achill's Atlantic Drive to the lonely bogs of sparsely populated northern Mayo, this ride is a long one – although once on the northbound N59, it's mostly flat.

Not so the Atlantic Drive, which rides between the dramatic Atlantic coast and bizarrely shaped mountains and rock outcrops. The road zigzags to a high point above Ashleam Bay (19.1km), becoming more sedate by the sheltered waters past the southern tip. In bad weather, or if the distance is daunting, the Atlantic Drive section could be left out – although, as the islanders say, you haven't really seen Achill until you've experienced Atlantic Drive.

Traffic is busiest on Achill during summer weekends. The N59 north of Achill is far quieter than the section further east. The main traffic concern is fast local vehicles on the R313 between Bangor and Belmullet.

Stop for a peek inside the 15th-century **Kildavnet Castle** (24.3km), a fortified tower used (and possibly built) by Grace O'Malley (see the boxed text, p182).

Among the Celtic crosses at **Kildavnet cemetery** (24.6km) are two commemorating victims of tragedies. In 1894, 32 young islanders drowned on their way to go 'tatie hokin' (potato harvesting) in Scotland. Another 10 died in Scotland in the 1937 Kirkintillock fire disaster.

Around Ballycroy (59.1km) is one of Europe's largest peatland expanses and the 1000 sq km Ballycroy National Park. Few services break the open stretch of blanket bog until Bangor (75.8km), which has places to stay and eat.

An alternative route at 77.4km leads to Pollatomish and Kilcommon Lodge (see Places to Stay & Eat for Belmullet (p190).

Belmullet
☎ 097

The main town on the remote, Irish-speaking Mullet Peninsula, Belmullet (Béal an Mhuirthead) is a very Irish town. With a population of around 1000, it has a strong local community. Few tourists make it a destination, although musicians the world over come to participate in the annual Féile Iorras (Erris International Folk Arts Festival), held in the last week of July.

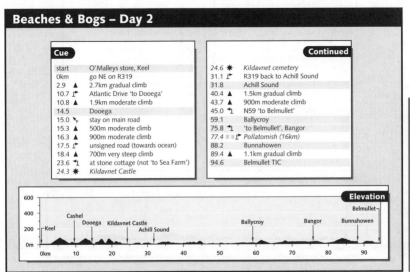

Information The locally run TIC (☎ 81500, W www.mayoerris.com, Barrack St) is opposite the Anchor Pub.

The Bank of Ireland and Ulster Banks on the main roundabout (The Square) have bureaus de change and ATMs.

Walshes Garage (☎ 82260, Chapel St) repairs bikes.

Things to See & Do Come in late July for **Féile Iorras** (W www.feileiorras.org).

For local walks, pick up a free copy of *A Series of Circular Walks in the Beautiful Barony of Erris or Siúlóidí Iorrais* (Erris Walks) from the TIC.

Places to Stay & Eat No official camping ground exists; ask local farmers for permission to camp on their land. *Camping* is also permitted at the (rather exposed) picnic spot by Trawmore Bay: go west on Main St, turn left at the water and continue for 1km.

The closest hostel is 21km northeast, at Pollatomish (see Day 3); it can be accessed on Day 2 by turning off (at 77.4km) after Bangor. *Kilcommon Lodge* (☎ 84621, W www.kilcommonlodge.net, Pollatomish)

Tent sites per person €4 (by prior arrangement), dorm beds/doubles €10/22. An excellent hostel; beautiful garden and terrific views; good local knowledge. Breakfast (€4-5) and four-course evening meal (€9) available. Book ahead July to August.

Drom Caoin (☎ 81195) Ensuite singles/doubles €34/51. Nonsmoking; excellent breakfast with views of Achill Island.

Highdrift B&B (☎ 81260, e anne .reilly@ireland.com, R313) Ensuite singles €31-34, doubles €51. Friendly; overlooks the water on the entrance to town.

Western Strands Hotel (☎ 81096, e westernstrandshotel@eircom.net, Main St) Ensuite singles/doubles €32/51. Family-run, great value, clean and friendly; book ahead. The best place for an evening feed: three-course meal €20; mains mostly €11-12; little for vegetarians.

Self-caterers should visit *Londis Supermarket (The Square)*. Other options are *Snoopy's Restaurant & Takeaway (☎ 81272, The Square)* Pizzas €4-8; also burgers and chicken boxes. *Square Meal (☎ 20984, The Square)* Traditional mains €7. Closes 6pm (4pm Sunday).

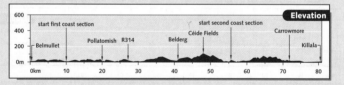

Beaches & Bogs – Day 3

Cue		Continued	
start	Belmullet TIC	57.2 ▲	sand on road 20m
0km	go SE on Barrack St	58.5 ↰	unsigned road
4.0 ↘	'to Céide Fields'	60.3 ●●↰	Downpatrick Head 4km ↺
10.0 ↰	Coast Rd 'to Inver'	60.8 ▲	1km moderate climb
■■↑	alt route: R314 (9km)	64.1 ▲	800m steep climb
15.5 ▲	400m moderate climb	65.8 ▲	water on road, bump
20.1	Pollatomish	65.9 ▲	500m steep climb
20.6 ▲	400m moderate climb	66.4 ↗	unsigned road (not 'to Lacken Pier')
21.0	Kilcommon Lodge	69.7 ✻	sculpture of soldier
27.2 ↰	R314 (unsigned)	71.8	Carrowmore
	alt route rejoins (continue)	74.8 ↰	R314 (unsigned)
40.7 ▲	2.6km gradual climb		alt route rejoins (continue)
41.0	Belderg	76.0 ↶	across bridge
44.8 ▲	600m moderate climb	76.1 ↰	by river
46.8 ▲	1.1km moderate climb	80.3 ↶	up hill
47.7 ✻	Céide Fields	80.4 ↰	'to Ballina'
50.0 ▲	500m gradual climb	80.9	Killala TIC
55.6 ↰	'Western Way'		
■■↑	alt route: R314 (8.8km)		

Elevation chart: start first coast section, start second coast section. Belmullet, Pollatomish, R314, Belderg, Céide Fields, Carrowmore, Killala. Elevation 0m–600m, distance 0km–80km.

Day 3: Belmullet to Killala

4½–8 hours, 80.9km

Owing to two coastal diversions, this day is longish and reasonably strenuous, undulating for much of the way (steeply at times). It can be made shorter and less hilly by taking the more direct R314 all the way to Killala. Traffic, not overly heavy on the R314, is very light on the coast roads.

On a fine day, the wonderful coastal views around Broad Haven include the Mullet Peninsula's northern end, and eroded cliffs and sandy beaches near the entrance to Sruwaddacon Bay.

The excellent *Kilcommon Lodge* hostel (see Places to Stay & Eat in Belmullet) is in the tiny, spread-out village of Pollatomish, the name of which translates to 'the valley of tranquillity'. Indeed, it's the perfect place for a tranquil rest day to relax and regain energy. The village also has two *pubs* and a *store*.

The **Céide Fields** (47.7km; ☎ 096-43325) are around 1000 hectares of 5000-year-old stone remains, buried beneath blanket bog. They were discovered in the 1930s by a local teacher digging turf. The buried system of stone walls, believed to be built by Neolithic farmers, is the earliest known farmstead in the world. A 40-minute guided tour explores the site; inside the visitor centre are exhibits and an audiovisual display, which describe its architecture, botany and geology. Use the disabled entrance so you can lock bikes by the visitor centre.

The road via Downpatrick Head is the one to avoid if you want to shorten the ride: it's quite strenuous and, though attractive and peaceful, the scenery is not as spectacular as the earlier coast. It begins on a narrow country lane, which has bumps but charm as well.

A side trip at 60.3km leads to **Downpatrick Head**, where a fenced-off blowhole occasionally shoots up plumes of water.

In 1798, General Humbert and 1000 troops from France landed in Killala Bay, with the plan that the Irish peasants would rise in rebellion and help Napoleon in his war against the British. Despite early success, Humbert was defeated within weeks. A **sculpture** of a French revolutionary soldier (69.7km) marks the place where the first French soldier died on Irish soil.

Killala

☎ 096

Its skyline dominated by a 25m-high round tower and the Church of Ireland cathedral, Killala (sometimes Kilala) is believed to have originated as a 5th-century monastery, whose first bishop was appointed by St Patrick himself. The village's irregular town plan adds to its medieval ambience.

The community-operated TIC (☎ 32166, e kkc@eircom.net, Ballina Rd, open Mon-Fri June-Sept), 500m from the town centre, is in the Community Council offices.

The village has no bank, but the post office on Market St has a bureau de change.

Both the **round tower** and **cathedral** are worth a look, and it's a pleasant walk along the harbour. The tiny, Blue Flag **Ross Beach** is 4km north of town (signposted).

Places to Stay & Eat Killala has no official camping ground; unofficially, it's possible to camp on public land by Ross Beach (which has clean toilet facilities). It's signposted 'Ross Strand' 1km from Killala on the Ballycastle road. After 2.9km, veer left over a small rise to the beach. Around 11km south is *Belleek Caravan & Camping Park* (☎ 71533) Tent sites per person €5 (showers €1). It's signed off the R314 near Ballina.

Avondale House (☎ 32229, e bilbow@eircom.net, Quay Rd) Singles/doubles €25/42 (with ensuite €28/46). Central, well-kept and excellent value; evening meals available by arrangement. *Gardenhill Farmhouse* (☎ 32331, Crossmolina Rd) Ensuite singles/doubles €25/49. Nonsmoking rooms 1km from the village on the Day 4 route.

Golden Acres (☎ 32183) B&B ensuite singles/doubles €32/64. The welcome is as cosy as the bar in this well regarded, family-run pub. Good evening meals (veg available) cost €8-11.

If your accommodation is full, two B&Bs are 3.5km away near Ross Beach: *Chez Nous* (☎ 32056) and *Beach View House* (☎ 32023). Both offer ensuite singles/doubles for €28/46 and evening meals by arrangement.

Wards supermarket *(cnr Market & Church Sts)* has a basic range. *Byrnes Fish Shop* (☎ 32717, the pier) sells locally caught fresh fish weekdays 8.45am–4pm.

The *Anchor Bar* (☎ 32050, Georges St) Mains (including vegetarian) €7-16. A cosy

WEST

Beaches & Bogs – Day 4

Cue

start	Killala Post Office
0km	go S on Market St
0.2 ↘	'to Crossmolina'
11.0 ↘	unsigned road
15.6 ↗	into village
15.8 ↱	past Bank of Ireland, Crossmolina
15.9 ↙	'to Castlebar'
19.8 ↙	'to Newport'
22.1 ▲	500m moderate climb
25.2 ▲	300m moderate climb
26.3 ▲	1.2km moderate climb
27.8 ✳	standing stone LHS
30.3 ⚠	steep descent before intersection
30.8 ↱	R312 (Nephin Drive) 'to Castlebar'
42.2 ✳	Bealtra Lough parking area

Continued

42.8 ↱	unsigned lane, at old Garda station
43.5 ↗	unsigned lane
45.7 ▲	300m steep climb
46.4 ▲	400m moderate climb
50.0 ↰	R311 (unsigned)
50.5 ↱	unsigned lane
51.6 ↑	stay on low road after crossroads
53.5 ↰	N59 (no sign)
61.1 ▲	500m moderate climb
62.6 ▲	400m moderate climb
63.5 ↰	'to town centre'
63.6 ↱	Bridge St
63.9 ↱	Shop St
64.0 ↱	James St at The Octagon
64.1	Westport TIC

Elevation

Killala — Crossmolina — Beltra Lough parking area — N59 to Westport — Westport

600 / 400 / 200 / 0m
0km · 10 · 20 · 30 · 40 · 50 · 60

bar, locally recommended for food. For take-aways, try **Country Kitchen** *(Georges St)*.

Day 4: Killala to Westport
3½–6 hours, 64.1km

From medieval Killala to the planned streets of Westport, this ride heads through delightful Mayo countryside, via the Nephin Beg Mountains and Beltra Lough.

Rather than backtracking to the TIC, today's ride starts at the post office in central Killala. Traffic is very light until the final 10.6km into Westport on the N59, which retraces the Day 1 outward route. The only services are in the attractive village of Crossmolina (15.8km), which has **stores**, **pubs** and places to eat.

Virtually flat until Crossmolina, the road then undulates mildly, before climbing through the peaceful valley, which is over-shadowed by the steep, shaley slopes of Mt Nephin (806m). Watch for the **standing stone** at 27.8km.

Turning onto the R312, the route chases the lively Boghadoon and Crumpaun Rivers to Beltra Lough. A signed parking area by the water's edge (42.2km) makes a great **picnic spot**.

Watch for the sharp right onto a country lane (42.8km) south of the lough – it's easy to miss. The lane's traffic-free, its surface is good, and the views are great, but, in true country-lane fashion, evenly graded it isn't – you'll be rock'n'rollin' for around 5km.

WEST

EOIN CLARKE

The magnificent, sweeping Cliffs of Moher (Clare Circuit ride)

RICHARD MILLS

Connemara's wild coastline (Connemara & Inishmór ride)

GARETH McCORMACK

The ancient limestone landscape of the Burren (Clare Circuit ride)

Missing presumed enjoying the *craic* in Galway city: one cyclist

Seafood, soda bread and a pint of the best at day's end – go on, you deserve it!

Pub music in Ireland's west – the lifeblood of a thriving traditional culture

Northern Éire

This chapter notionally covers the entire region that borders Northern Ireland, but its rides are concentrated in Counties Donegal, Leitrim and Cavan (a few days' riding in Sligo and Louth appear in the Around Ireland chapter). Donegal has arguably the north's greatest variety of scenery, attractions, towns and activities. Donegal also contains Ireland's largest Gaeltacht area (Irish-speaking region) and is a stronghold of traditional culture. Although less visited, Leitrim is a comely and welcoming region of lakes and mountains, which is popular with walkers and anglers.

The weather hereabouts is perhaps the most changeable in Ireland, and the roads can be skull-rattlingly terrible. And yet it's one of the most compelling regions to visit. If you're attracted to rough and out-of-the-way roads, wild skies, peat fires and solitude, this is the place to ride.

HISTORY
Given its lower profile on the Irish tourist trail, the region has a surprising wealth of historical sites. Ancient monuments in many areas date back to Stone Age–times. Reminders of more recent history are abundant, some formally preserved by local or national organisations, others tantalisingly unmarked and decaying in nondescript stonewalled fields. Fewer tourists in these parts means that you'll sometimes be able to enjoy historical sites with little or no company.

Donegal, Cavan and Monaghan were three of the nine counties in the old Irish province of Ulster (since 1922, the other six have made up Northern Ireland, which in modern times is often called Ulster). Neighbouring Leitrim was the northernmost county of Connaught province. Key moments in the region's past several centuries tend to focus around the Ulster Plantation and its implications. In late Elizabethan times, the Gaelic O'Neills and O'Donnells of Ulster led the Nine Years War (1594–1603) against the English but were ultimately defeated. In 1607, scores of Ulster chieftains fled Ireland (from Rathmullan, Donegal) for Europe – an event known as the Flight of the Earls – which effectively signalled the end of Gaelic Ireland. In 1608 the last Gaelic lord,

In Brief

Highlights
- The Donegal **Gaeltacht** and Irish culture
- Beautiful **Gleanveagh National Park**
- The rugged isolation of **Bloody Foreland**, **Horn Head** and **Fanad Head Peninsula**
- The history, beauty and solitude of the **Inishowen Peninsula**

Terrain
Few sections of genuine flatlands – even low-lying lands tend towards drumlins and low ridges; stunning coastline, some soaring cliffs; upland bogs, especially surrounding steep ranges, and prominent peaks.

Special Events
- **Earagail Arts Festival** (July) throughout Donegal
- **Mary from Dungloe Festival** (traditional music and arts; July/August) Dungloe
- **Ballyshannon Folk & Traditional Music Festival** (August)

Cycling Events
- **BorderTrek Cycle for Peace** (June) North/South ride through Counties Fermanagh, Tyrone, Donegal, Sligo, Roscommon, Leitrim and Cavan

Food and Drink Specialities
Bakery goods, especially **soda bread** and **fadge** (potato bread) are a feature; **seafood** is an always-reliable choice on Donegal menus.

Sir Cahir O'Doherty, rebelled and sacked Derry but was killed in Donegal. In 1610, the Ulster Plantation began in Armagh, Cavan, Derry, Donegal, Fermanagh and Tyrone. A later uprising by Owen Roe O'Neill, of Cavan, was ultimately quashed in 1649 by Oliver Cromwell's forces.

NATURAL HISTORY
Donegal's geology attracts rock fans from around the globe. Highlights include the plunging, 600m Slieve League cliffs, which contain many of the rock types that feature

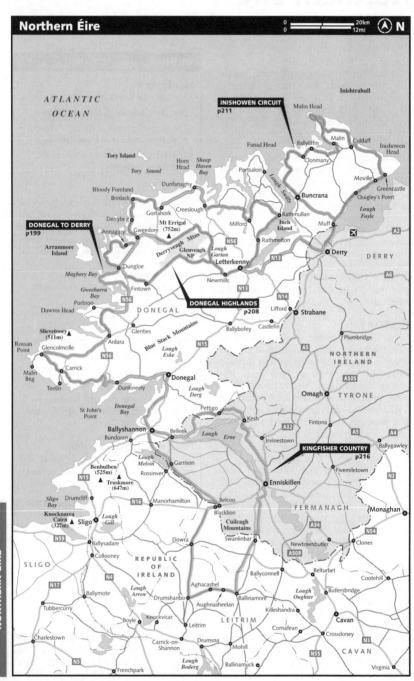

Northern Éire

in the region's geological make-up (such as schists, quartzites, slates, conglomerates and mineral ores). Widespread glaciation during the most recent ice age put the finishing touches on such features as the Derryveagh and Glendowan Mountains and spectacular Glenveagh.

As is the case for much of Ireland, northern Éire's ecology has been greatly altered by human intervention, and the most common sight outside towns and cities is rolling green fields or heath-covered bogs, many of the latter showing signs of turf cutting. One of the region's few pockets of surviving native woodland is found in Glenveagh National Park, where red deer may be encountered during spring and autumn. Other wildlife includes foxes, hares, rabbits and badgers, which are most often seen as roadkill. Birdlife is varied and especially rich along isolated coastline and offshore islands.

CLIMATE

The weather will have the greatest sway on your experience in, and memories of, northern Éire – perhaps more so in Donegal than in any other part of Ireland. As the region's westernmost fringe, Donegal and western Leitrim are exposed to the unpredictability of the Atlantic Ocean. Expect changeable conditions ranging from diabolical (including squally rain, showers and strong winds) to sublime. In general, the weather becomes warmer, drier and more reliable the further east you go. Central north parts – eastern Leitrim, Cavan and Monaghan – seem to shoulder the bulk of the region's bland, grey days. Met Éireann's Weatherdial line for Ulster (☎ 1550 123 853) updates forecasts for the region three times daily; calls cost €0.75 per minute.

INFORMATION
Maps

All rides in this chapter are covered by the OSNI 1:250,000 Holiday map *Ireland North*. The relevant OSI 1:50,000 Discovery map will enhance your experience in some areas, such as the Inishowen Peninsula. About 12 Discovery maps cover the region.

Books

Packie Manus Byrne's *Recollections of a Donegal Man* (1989) provides an interesting social history of Donegal. Leon Uris'

Warning: Be Prepared

⚠ Donegal's notoriously changeable and extreme weather makes good-quality warm and wet-weather clothing essential. Consider carrying overshoes (or waterproof socks), particularly if you're cycling on the cooler fringes of summer.

popular novel *Trinity* is set in Inishowen (and Northern Ireland) and provides entertaining reconstructions of life and key events in pre-partition Ulster.

Information Sources

The North West Regional Tourism Authority has offices in Sligo and Letterkenny (p197); see those cities for contact details. Each office has a wide range of guides, maps and pamphlets, although few are specific to cycling. They'll assist with accommodation reservations.

Place Names

Most road and other signs throughout the region are bilingual; in Donegal's Gaeltacht area you'll encounter signs only in Irish. The recommended *Ireland North* Holiday map includes many town names in both Gaelic and English.

Other Information

It's extremely useful to seek on-the-spot route and road-condition advice from local sources – cycle-shop staff and hostel owners are invariably well informed. Road signs can be as mystifying here as anywhere else in Ireland (see the boxed text 'Sign Sense and Nonsense', p215), and reviewing a route with a local before setting out will often pay dividends.

GATEWAY CITIES
Sligo
☎ 071

Almost swamped in associations with the writer William Butler Yeats, Sligo (Sligeach) is a lively and friendly place, with good transport links and some nice places to eat and drink. Split by the River Garavogue, Sligo is in a splendid setting with Sligo Bay to the west and, north, the looming bulk of erosion-scarred, 525m-high Benbulben.

Information The North West Regional Tourism Authority office doubles as the Sligo TIC (☎ 916 1201, W www.ireland -northwest.travel.ie, Temple St, open Mon-Fri year-round, Sat May-Sept, Sun Jun-Aug). The major banks, most with ATMs and bureaus de change, are on Lower Knox and Stephen Sts. Flanagans Cycles (☎ 914 4477, Market Yard) is the local Raleigh Rent-a-Bike agent; owner Seamus Flanagan is a dab hand at running repairs and has extensive knowledge of local cycling routes.

Things to See & Do A stroll around town yields much of interest. Yeats seekers should visit the **Sligo County Museum and Niland Gallery** (☎ 914 3728, Heritage Centre, Stephen St). Established in 1955, the museum features a fine collection of Yeats material, including his Nobel Prize. The gallery includes artwork by Jack B Yeats, the poet's brother, and several noted 20th-century Irish artists. Just west of the museum on Stephen St, there's a **sculpture of Yeats** inscribed from hat to shoe with his poetry. About 7km north of Sligo town on the N15, **Yeats' grave** forms the key attraction in Drumcliff churchyard. The simple slab headstone carries the famous epitaph from Yeats' poem 'Under Ben Bulben': 'Cast a cold eye / On life, on death / Horseman, pass by!'

The oldest parts of the Dúchas-managed **Sligo Abbey** (☎ 914 6406, Abbey St) date from the 15th century; the abbey was first established in the mid-13th century, and destroyed in 1641.

A short ride southwest of town and worth an extra day's stay are **Carrowmore Megalithic Cemetery** (☎ 916 1534) and **Knocknarea Cairn**. Carrowmore is one of Europe's largest Stone Age–cemeteries; about half of the stones have been removed from its more than 60 stone circles and dolmens, but they're still a compelling sight. About 4km west, Knocknarea – said to be the grave of Queen Maeve of Connaught – rises to 327m. There are fine views from the cairn's summit, a 1.5km uphill walk from the car park. Both sites are well signposted from Sligo; leave town to the west, on Church Hill.

Places to Stay About 1.6km west of town centre is *Gateway Caravan & Camping Park* (☎ 914 5618, N16) Tent sites €7. For a beachside camp try *Greenlands Caravan & Camping Park* (☎ 917 7113, Rosses Point) Tent sites €9. About 8km northwest of Sligo via the R291.

Yeats Hostel (☎ 914 6876, 12 Lord Edward St) Dorm beds €11. Closest to town centre, opposite train station. *Edenhill Holiday Hostel* (☎ 914 3204, Pearse Rd) Dorm

Look Out: Dogs About!

Road stories about dogs, both amusing and harrowing, have featured prominently in the recollections of the authors. From Dingle to Donegal and Drogheda to Dungarvan, our scribes slowed, swerved or pedalled for dear life to avoid pooches ranging in temper from charming to alarming.

At least things are better than before the Dog Act of the late 1980s, when a dog was allegedly entitled to one free bite. Now the mutt is prosecuted on the first nip. The problem is, no-one told the dogs, especially those whose main pastime is to career out of farmyards at the first squeak of approaching wheels.

In theory, the act tackled the problem head on by making owners liable for their pooches' behaviour on and off their land. Owners must have a licence for all dogs and keep them on a leash when outside their own property.

In practice, dogs seem blissfully unaware of their responsibilities in law. They consider the roadway outside their farm as part of their protectorate and anyone who strays on to it must be prepared to account for themselves. If you do have trouble, report the incident to the local Garda station – a dog warden is obliged to investigate and the owner may be fined.

Some locally garnered tips, varying in usefulness, on combatting the canine menace include: wearing hobnailed boots for a good kick; carrying dog treats; carrying a switch (branch with twigs at the top) to swipe at the nose; and carrying a copy of the act to read aloud at the crucial moment.

Richard's Bicycle Book even explains how, when under dangerous attack – to kill a dog by thrusting a pump down its throat – but we recommend you avoid canicide, unless you seriously believe your life is at risk!

beds/doubles €10/28; on town outskirts to the south.

There's a wide choice of B&Bs in and near town. *Renate House (☎ 916 2014, Upper John St)* Singles/doubles €33/44. Close to bus and train stations. *An Crusicin Lan (☎ 916 2857, Connolly St)* Singles/doubles €37/49. With 11 rooms, it's bigger; a short walk to town centre. *Lissadell (☎ 916 1937, Mail Coach Rd)* Singles/doubles €39/56. On the town outskirts to the south. For a room with rural views, try *Glen View (☎ 914 3770, Enniskillen Rd, Drum East)* Singles/doubles €26/49. About 6km northeast of Sligo on Day 26 of the Around Ireland ride (p251).

Clarence Hotel (☎ 914 2211, Wine St) Doubles €120. Small and central, nice bar. *Hotel Silver Swan (☎ 914 3231, Hyde Bridge)* Singles/doubles €61/89. Central and pleasant, alongside the river. *Sligo Park Hotel (☎ 916 0291, Pearse Rd)* Doubles €134. Surrounded by gardens, swimming pools and tennis courts.

Places to Eat There are some good choices for a place this size. For self-caterers, there's a big *Tesco* off Wine St and a late-closing *Spar* supermarket on Lord Edward St. Grab bread at *O'Hehirs Bakery* in Wine St.

For breakfast, try *The Tea House (34 O'Connell St)* Irish breakfast €6, big bacon and eggs €6. *Hy-Breasil Espresso Bar (Bridge St)* is good for morning coffee, snacks and cakes.

Garavogue Bar & Restaurant (☎ 914 0100, rear 15-16 Stephen St) Bar snacks €4-7, mains from €9. Nice pasta choices such as penne with goat's cheese, tomato and olives. *Bistro Bianconi (☎ 914 1744, 44 O'Connell St)* Mains €13-18, gourmet pizzas €6-8. Probably best vegetarian mains in town. *Fiddlers Creek Restaurant & Bar (☎ 914 1866, Rockwood Pde)* Starters €5-7, mains €11-19. Mexican-ish flavours; good vegetarian fajitas €11. *Hotel Silver Swan* has starters from €4 to €9 and mains from €11 to €19. The dining room overlooks the river.

Getting There & Away Being a busy commercial centre, Sligo is well serviced by domestic airline routes, and train and bus links to/from Dublin.

Air Sligo Airport (☎ 916 8280) is at Strandhill, about 8km west of town via the R292.

Aer Arann (☎ 1890 426 726) operates two daily flights to/from Dublin.

Bus Regular Bus Éireann services reach Sligo from Dublin (€14, four hours), Galway (2½ hours) and Derry (2½ hours); the bus terminal (☎ 916 0066) is on Lord Edward St, near the train station. Feda O'Donnell Coaches (☎ 074-954 8114) runs between northern Donegal and Galway; Sligo is the midpoint of the journey (€8 to either Galway or Letterkenny, at least two daily).

Train Iarnród Éireann (timetable information ☎ 01-836 6222) trains run between Sligo and Dublin (€19, three hours, up to four daily).

Bicycle Sligo is 217km northwest of Dublin via the most direct route. Enniskillen, the Day 2 start on the Kingfisher Country ride (p216), is 68km east in Northern Ireland. Sligo is reached on Day 25 of the Around Ireland ride (p251).

Letterkenny
☎ 074

Anyone in Letterkenny (Leitir Ceanainn) will tell you that this is 'the fastest-growing town in Europe' – it's one of several Irish towns and cities in the running for this title. Cyclists can't help but notice one classic indicator: the crowded roads, especially the evening peak-hour traffic jams. Generally, Letterkenny is an easy-going place with a lively pub scene and good bus links to major centres. It's Donegal's largest town and the perfect gateway to the county's central and northwestern parts.

Information The North West Regional Tourism Authority office (☎ 912 1160, Derry Rd, open Mon-Fri year-round, Sat June-Sept, Sun July-Aug) is 1.3km east of the bus terminal and station roundabout. Staff will assist with accommodation reservations. The major banks with ATMs are on Upper Main St (two near Market Square) and Ramelton Rd. Gallagher's Bikes (☎ 912 2510, Pearse Rd) is open Monday to Saturday.

Things to See & Do Letterkenny has grown since the partition of Ireland separated it from Derry, the principal city in this part of Ireland. The skyline is dominated by the soaring spire of 100-year-old **St Eunan's Cathedral**, on Sentry Hill Rd, which features some fine carved ceilings and stained-glass windows. Opposite the cathedral, the yard surrounding **Conwal Parish Church** includes graves dating from the 17th century. The **Donegal County Museum** (☎ 912 4613, High St) is housed in part of the Letterkenny Workhouse, built in 1846. The collection includes Iron Age–artefacts.

It's worth checking what's on at the acclaimed **An Grianán Theatre** (☎ 912 0777, Port Rd), which has a varied program of drama, dance and music. Letterkenny's fairly lively nightlife revolves around its many pubs and a few late-closing clubs, notably the **Golden Grill** and the **Pulse**, both on Ramelton Rd.

Places to Stay There's no camping ground in or near town. *Port Hostel (☎ 912 5315, Port Rd)* Dorm beds/doubles €10/24. Quiet and tucked away yet a short walk from shops, main attractions and eateries. Turn off Ramelton Rd at An Grianán Theatre.

Among B&Bs, try *Covehill House (☎ 912 1038, Port Rd)* Singles/doubles from €23/46. Good value with plenty of space and well located near Port Hostel. Try pleasant *Ardeen (☎ 912 1819, Glencar Rd)* Singles/doubles €32/49. It's about 750m from Main St. There are several B&Bs on Kilmacrennan Rd, on the northern outskirts, some with fine views. *Swilly View (☎ 912 1137)* Singles/doubles from €32/46. *Willow House (☎ 912 1871)* Singles/doubles from €32/43.

Gallaghers Hotel (☎ 912 2066, 110 Upper Main St) Singles/doubles €39/64. Central, has a bit of character. *Quality Court Hotel (☎ 912 2977, 29-45 Lower Main St)* Doubles €180. New and central, close to some good restaurants. Other hotels are further out. *Castle Grove House (☎ 915 1118, Ramelton Rd)* Doubles €190. About 5km from town centre.

Places to Eat Self-caterers are well served by big *Dunnes Stores (Old Town Rd)* and *Tesco (Port Rd, at the bus station)* supermarkets and several late-closing convenience stores.

Café Rico (Oliver Plunkett Rd) Big breakfasts €6. *Bake House (Upper Main St)* Sandwiches and rolls €2-3, decent coffee €2. It's also the place to stock up on bread and cakes.

Pat's Pizza (Upper Main St) Wide range of pizzas €4-11, kebabs and burgers €2. Open until late and the food is reliable and tasty. The *Brewery Bar & Restaurant (☎ 912 7330, Market Square)* Bar food €8-9. Filling but predictable. Some good restaurant mains for around €13. *The Metropolitan Bar & Restaurant (☎ 912 0800, 106 Lower Main St)* Bar food €9. Fine dishes, such as ragout of monkfish and butterbeans. The *Yellow Pepper (☎ 912 4133, Lower Main St)* Mains €12-17. Popular restaurant/bistro with tasty seafood, pasta and vegetarian dishes. The *Lemon Tree (☎ 912 5788, 39 Lower Main St)* Mains €12-19. Nice seafood; fresh sea trout €13.

Getting There & Away This bustling town is well linked by road to many towns, and bus services are frequent and good value

Air Letterkenny is roughly equidistant from both Derry Airport (☎ 028-7181 0784), and Donegal Airport (☎ 954 8284), about 55km west, near Annagary. Aer Arann (☎ 1890 426 726) operates a daily flight to/from Dublin.

Bus Regular Bus Éireann (☎ 912 1309) services reach Letterkenny from Dublin (€13, four hours), Sligo, Derry and points farther afield; the bus terminal is at the station roundabout. John McGinley (☎ 913 5201) buses run to Dublin (3¾ hours, daily) and Belfast International Airport (four times weekly, daily July to August). Feda O'Donnell Coaches' (☎ 954 8114) Galway service stops at Letterkenny (€13, at least two daily), also at the station roundabout. McGeehan Coaches (☎ 954 6150) runs a service between Letterkenny and Glencolmcille (2¼ hours, Monday to Saturday).

Train Derry's (see p227) Waterside train station is about 38km to the west.

Bicycle Letterkenny is about 235km northwest of Dublin and 150km west of Belfast; Derry is an easy 35km to 40km to the east. Letterkenny is reached on Day 4 of the Donegal to Derry ride (p199). It's also the start/end point of the Donegal Highlands ride (p208).

Donegal to Derry

Duration	5 days
Distance	338.2km
Difficulty	moderate
Start	Ballyshannon
End	Derry

This grand tour of the Donegal coastline reveals the variety, extent and splendour of Ireland's northernmost county. The ride passes isolated mountains, loughs, boglands and the stunning coast, and traverses key parts of the Gaeltacht. Expect friendly locals, welcoming pubs, traditional music... and Ireland's least predictable weather. The Donegal Highlands ride (p208) can be picked up at Dungloe or Letterkenny to add some upland Donegal exploration.

PLANNING
When to Ride
Late spring to early autumn (particularly late May to June) is best. Donegal is geared to tourists more in summer, so much so that you may have difficulty finding accommodation – or even a meal – from October to April. Driving rain and lashing wind can occur at any time, but are certainly more bearable in the 'warm' season.

Maps & Books
The ride is covered by the OSNI 1:250,000 Holiday map *Ireland North*. Most TICs have free town maps and sell OSI 1:50,000 Discovery maps covering the local area. It's worthwhile having a basic Irish-language guide with you, such as *Irish for Beginners*, by A Wilkes & J Shackell.

ACCESS TOWN
Ballyshannon
☎ 072

Nestled on steep hills beside the fast-flowing River Erne, Ballyshannon (Béal Átha Seanaidh) is far less hectic than nearby Bundoran, a popular seaside resort, and a good base from which to ride farther north into Donegal, or east to the Fermanagh lakes in Northern Ireland.

Information There's no TIC; an information board on the town diamond, up Castle St, will help you get your bearings. Both Bank of Ireland (Main St) and Allied Irish Bank (AIB; Castle St) have branches with ATMs and bureaus de change.

In summer many pubs have live music and there's a music festival during the first week in August. The **Donegal Parian China Visitor Centre** (☎ 51826), about 1.5km south of town on the N15, displays and sells delicate Donegal Parian China; there's little for under €13 and it's too precious to bounce around in a pannier! There are Blue Flag beaches (listed by the EU as clean, safe beaches, and usually patrolled and water-monitored) about 6km north (at Rossnowlagh) and south (at Bundoran). The poet **William Allingham's grave** is in a churchyard west of Main St (the way is signposted). Allingham (1824–89) wrote the 'The Fairies', which begins, 'Up the airy mountain / Down the rushy glen', declaring strong associations with southwestern Donegal, where Allingham worked for the customs and excise service.

Places to Stay & Eat On the shores of Assaroe Lake, about 1km east of town, is *Lakeside Centre Caravan and Camping Park* (☎ 52822, Belleek Rd) Tent sites €12. *Duffy's Hostel* (☎ 51535, Donegal Rd) Dorm beds/twins €10/23; open Mar–mid-Oct. A bit grubby, but friendly.

B&Bs include *Randwick* (☎ 52545, Bundoran Rd) Singles/doubles €30/49. One of several B&Bs on the N15 approaching from the south, about 1km from centre. Also 1km south is *Bri-Ter-An* (☎ 51490, Bundoran Rd) Singles/doubles €32/49. *Rockville House* (☎ 51106, Belleek Rd) Singles/doubles €35/51. About 500m east of town.

Assaroe Hotel (☎ 51115, Main St) Singles/doubles €26/46, more on weekends and bank holidays. Close to ride start point at town diamond. *Dorrian's Imperial Hotel* (☎ 51010, Main St) Singles/doubles €51/102. Best hotel in town; a lot of tour-group guests.

There's a *Mace* supermarket (Saimer Court Shopping Centre, Main St) and a late-closing *Spar* convenience store (top of Castle St). There's an *Abrakebabra* fast-food outlet (Castle St).

The coffee shop above *Grimes Bakery* (Main St) has breakfasts €3-8 (sausage sandwiches to jumbo fry-ups) and lunches from €5 (baked spuds and salad). On the south side of the river *Maggie's Bar* (Bundoran Rd) also serves breakfast. *Cafe Saimer*

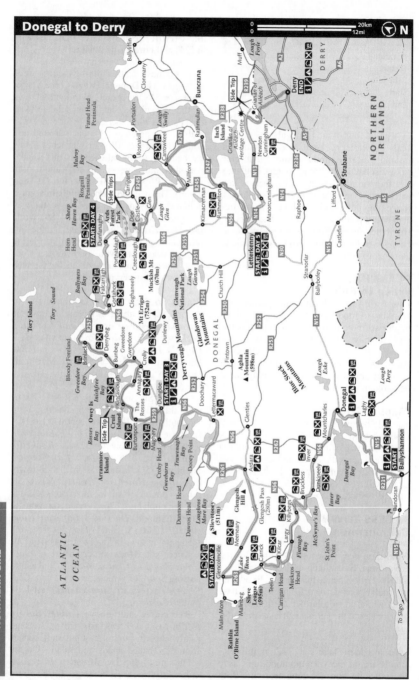

(Saimer Court Shopping Centre) has decent coffee. **Shamrock Chinese** *(Bundoran Rd)*. Starters €4-6, mains €6-9. Meals are filling but predictable.

Try **Embers Restaurant** (☎ *52297, Market St)* above Devine's Bar, or **Dorrian's Imperial Hotel** for more interesting food.

Getting There & Away Bus Éireann runs regular services to Ballyshannon from Dublin (€15, 3¾ hours), Galway (3½ hours) and Derry (1¾ hours). The bus station is just north of the river on the N15. Feda O'Donnell Coaches (☎ 075-48356) runs between Ballyshannon and Galway (€13, at least two daily).

Ballyshannon is reached on Day 26 of the Around Ireland ride (p251) after an easy day ride from Sligo, which has regular train services from Dublin. Ballyshannon is the start/end point of the Kingfisher Country ride (p216).

THE RIDE
Day 1: Ballyshannon to Glencolmcille
5–8½ hours, 84.6km

This is a relatively gruelling but immensely satisfying day. Some nifty navigating keeps you clear of busy roads for about 40km and there are wonderful coast and mountain views throughout. Even unfavourable weather seems more alluring in this part of Ireland – the cold winds off the Atlantic can't diminish the pleasure of a day spent skirting Donegal Bay.

During the early stages of the ride, the Blue Stack Mountains loom to the north. There are several unmarked roads in quiet country between Ballyshannon and Laghy (20km) so careful navigating is needed. Consider breaking the journey overnight in Donegal (Dún na nGall; 25.6km), which has fine **pubs** and **restaurants**. At the least, visit both **Donegal Castle** (☎ 074-972 2405), originally built by the O'Donnell clan in the 1400s, and **Donegal Priory ruins**. The Franciscan priory, founded in 1474, was destroyed in 1601; from it are commanding views of the bay.

The ride runs through Mountcharles (Moin Séarlas; 31.7km) but a bypass may be open by the time you read this; taking it will cut a few hundred metres off the day and avoid the steep climb up Mountcharles Main St. From Bruckless (An Bhroclais;

46.3km), back roads provide the first relief from traffic for about 26km. After clearing Killybegs (Na Ceala Beaga, 55.1km), Ireland's most important fishing port, the ride has noticeably fewer cars.

Beyond Killybegs the ride is very up and down, but climbs pass almost unnoticed given the remarkable views of steep green hills, stonewalled fields and Donegal Bay – particularly striking near Muckros Head (about 65km). Further along, soaring, 595m Slieve League dominates. Both Kilcar (Cill Charthaigh; 68.9km) and Carrick (An Charraig; 74.9km) have **stores** to buy supplies – probably a good idea before the 4.4km uphill that leads past pretty Lake Inna, scarred bogs, and ragged sheep to Glencolmcille.

Glencolmcille
☎ 074

There's a magic about this windswept Gaeltacht outpost (which also appears on maps as Glencolumbcille or Glencolumbkille), spread

NORTHERN ÉIRE

Donegal to Derry – Day 1

Cue	
Start	Ballyshannnon Town Diamond
0km	go SW on Market St
0.0 ⌐	(40m) Main St
0.4 ↑	Bishop St
1.6 ⌐	unsigned road
1.8 ⌐	unsigned road
▲	800m moderate climb
5.8 ⌐	R231 'to Rossnowlagh'
9.5 ⌐	unsigned road
10.6 ⌐	unsigned road
14.9 ⌐	'to Ballintra'
16.6 ⌐	'to Laghy'
17.0 ↘	'to Laghy'
19.4 ⌐	N15 'to Donegal'
20.0	Laghy
21.9 ⌐	R267 'to Donegal Town'
25.6 ↘ ✳	Donegal Town Diamond, Donegal
25.7 ↘	Bridge St (N56)
29.4 ▲	1.7km moderate climb
30.9 ⌐	'to Mountcharles'
31.4 ▲	1.3km steep climb
31.7	Mountcharles
32.3 ⌐	N56
37.8	Inver

	Continued
41.6 ▲	1.9km moderate climb
43.7	Dunkineely
46.3 ⌐	unsigned road, Bruckless
46.4 ⌐	unsigned road
49.5 ✓	unsigned road
53.1 ⌐	R263
55.1	Killybegs
▲	1km moderate climb
57.6 ▲	1.4km steep climb
59.8 ▲	1.6km moderate–steep climb
62.3 ⌐	Coast Road 'Scenic route to Kilcar'
62.7 ▲	1.4km steep climb
66.0 ▲	700m steep climb
68.9 ⌐	R263 'to Gleann Cholm Cille', Kilcar
69.1 ▲	1km steep climb
72.6 ▲	600m steep climb
73.2 ⌐	'to An Charraig'
74.8 ⌐	R263
▲	1.5km moderate climb
74.9	Carrick
76.6 ▲	4.4km moderate climb
84.5 ⌐	'to TIC'
84.6	Glencolmcille TIC

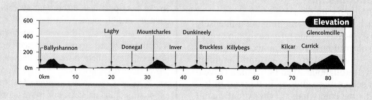

out in a glen that meets the Atlantic at a wild-looking beach, Silver Strand. The Glencolmcille (Gleann Cholm Cille) region provides an alluring mix of isolation, great natural attractions, archaeological finds and traditional culture.

The seasonal information centre (☎ 973 0116, Carrick St, open daily Easter-Sept) is in the Lace House. There's a post office but no banks (many businesses take credit cards).

Things to See & Do Archaeological sites in the area date to 3000 BC; the best of them are remains of **megalithic tombs** near Malin More, about 4km west of town. Glencolmcille is better known for its associations with early Christians (its name is derived from St Colmcille, or Columba) and various **standing stones** that remain from the period. These stones – probably once objects of pagan worship, to which Christian carvings were later added – are the focus of the Turas Colmcille, a 5.6km pilgrimage that takes place each year on 9 June, St Colmcille's feast day.

Irish was the main language here up to the early 20th century, and Glencolmcille remains a centre of learning for Gaelic language and traditional crafts. **Oideas Gael** (☎ 973 0248, e oidsgael@iol.ie) offers courses in Irish language, crafts and music. The wonderful **Folk Village Museum** (☎ 973 0017) features re-created thatched cottages and the old National School building.

Consider taking an extra day here to visit **Slieve League**. It's about 15km from Glencolmcille, via Teelin, to the clifftop car park at Carrigan Head, where there are stunning views of Slieve League's dizzying, sheer 300m cliffs.

Places to Stay & Eat It's hard to go past the friendly ***Dooey Hostel*** *(☎ 973 0130)* Tent sites per person €6, dorm beds/doubles €9/20. Great facilities and outlook; follow the signs from Glenhead Tavern.

There are many B&Bs dotted about town. Quite close to the village shops is ***Corner House*** *(☎ 973 0021)* Singles/doubles €33/49. ***Brackendale*** *(☎ 973 0038)* B&B per person €21-23. ***Millstone*** *(☎ 30295)* Singles/doubles €30/46.

Glencolmcille Hotel *(☎ 973 0003)* Rooms €108-128; 40 comfortable rooms, a few kilometres west at Malin More.

It's best not to be too fussy about food in Glencolmcille. The general store on Carrick St is open until late seven days. You'll find nice cakes and scones at the ***Folk Village Tea House***. ***Lace House Restaurant*** *(☎ 973 0444)* Starters €2-5, filling mains, including steaks and Atlantic salmon up to €12. The fare's a little more interesting at ***An Chistin*** *(☎ 973 0213)* and prices are comparable.

Day 2: Glencolmcille to Dungloe
4–7 hours, 72.1km

Another energetic but satisfying day and one that includes very little flat terrain (thankfully, towards the end). There's some time spent on the N56, the main thoroughfare in the area, but the traffic is heavy only on summer weekends.

The start of the day seems all uphill, with two long climbs past pastures and bogs on the way to Glengesh Pass (280m; 17.7km). Views north from the pass are spectacular, over Ardara (Árd an Rátha) and towards Aghla Mountain. Take care on the descent, which features switchbacks and a host of hill-hugging sheep.

Ardara has strong associations with weaving and has a number of shops specialising in Donegal tweed and knitwear. At the **Ardara Heritage Centre** *(☎ 954 1704)* there are working looms and displays showing the manufacture of Donegal tweed and the history of tweed production in the region.

After some time on the N56, there's a left turn (51.2km) and the real fun starts. Following is about 14km on minor roads that eventually lead to Crohy Head. Particularly from

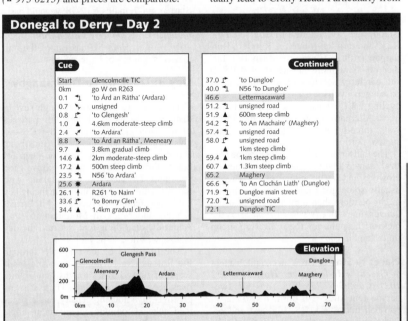

Donegal to Derry – Day 2

Cue			Continued	
Start	Glencolmcille TIC	37.0	'to Dungloe'	
0km	go W on R263	40.0	N56 'to Dungloe'	
0.1	'to Árd an Rátha' (Ardara)	46.6	Lettermacaward	
0.7	unsigned	51.2	unsigned road	
0.8	'to Glengesh'	51.9 ▲	600m steep climb	
1.0 ▲	4.6km moderate-steep climb	54.2	'to An Machaire' (Maghery)	
2.4	'to Ardara'	57.4	unsigned road	
8.8	'to Árd an Rátha', Meeneary	58.0	unsigned road	
9.7 ▲	3.8km gradual climb	▲	1km steep climb	
14.6 ▲	2km moderate-steep climb	59.4 ▲	1km steep climb	
17.2 ▲	500m steep climb	60.7 ▲	1.3km steep climb	
23.5	N56 'to Ardara'	65.2	Maghery	
25.6 ✳	Ardara	66.6	'to An Clochán Liath' (Dungloe)	
26.1 ↑	R261 'to Nairn'	71.9	Dungloe main street	
33.6	'to Bonny Glen'	72.0	unsigned road	
34.4 ▲	1.4km gradual climb	72.1	Dungloe TIC	

Elevation

Glencolmcille — Glengesh Pass — Meeneary — Ardara — Lettermacaward — Marghery — Dungloe

600 / 400 / 200 / 0m — 0km 10 20 30 40 50 60 70

58km to 65km, the going is steep, narrow and painfully slow. But nothing could detract from what you've passed. At first it's the strange stoniness of the land that arrests your attention, but as the ride swings further west, the view opens out to Trawenagh and Gweebarra Bays, and finally out to the Atlantic. On a clear day, you can see south to Slievetooey. Ruined cottages, crumbling stone walls and roaming sheep add to the vista.

Dungloe

☎ 074

Another friendly Donegal town with easygoing locals and good pubs, Dungloe (An Clochán Liath) offers a lovely outlook over Dungloe Bay to Arranmore Island (Arainn Mhór). At the right time – *not* midsummer weekends – Dungloe is not too crowded and not too touristed. It's a good base from which to explore Arranmore and the rolling, lake-strewn region to the north, the Rosses.

Dungloe TIC (☎ 952 1297, off Lower Main St, open Mon-Sat June-Sept, Sun Aug). Three banks have offices on Main St, two have ATMs. Dungloe Garden & Bike (☎ 22382, Carnmore Rd) does repairs.

Things to See & Do To get to **Arranmore Island**, ride 6.6km north of Dungloe on the R259 and turn left (on to the R260) to Burtonport (Ailt an Chórrain), about 1km farther on. Arranmore Ferries (☎ 952 0532) run car-ferry services to the island (foot passengers/cyclists €9 return, daily). The cycling isn't extensive, but it's gloriously quiet. Alternatively, do the Arranmore Way walk: three linked tracks that cover a substantial portion of the island.

The midsummer **Mary from Dungloe Festival** (named after the old song) is a popular, crowded and hectic annual event. There's usually some good music, but the crowds might be more than a cyclist can bear. At quieter times, *Beedy's Bar (Main St)* is the pick of the pubs for the *craic* (fun, good times) and music.

Places to Stay & Eat You can pitch a tent at *Greene's Independent Hostel (☎ 952 1021, Carnmore Rd)*. Tent sites €7, two-person tent sites €9, dorm beds/beds in two-bed dorms €11/13. It's neat and orderly, and close to the town centre. *Crohy Head Hostel (☎ 952 1950)* Dorm beds €9.

This An Óige hostel is 8km southwest in a grand position overlooking the ocean.

Most B&Bs are outside the centre. *Sea View (☎ 952 1353, Mill Rd)* Singles/doubles €33/49. Nice views of Dungloe Bay, about 600m north of the town centre. About 1km east of town is *Lake View (☎ 952 1897, Carnmore Rd)* Singles/doubles €32/51. Easy walk/ride into town. *Morawell (☎ 952 1037, Quay Rd)* Singles/doubles €23/46. About 1.5km southwest of the centre, on the road to Maghery.

There are two bar-guesthouses on Main St: *Atlantic House (☎ 952 1061)* and *Midway (☎ 952 1251)*; both have doubles at €51. *Óstán na Rossan Hotel (☎ 952 2444, Mill Rd)* Doubles €115-130. Has 48 rooms and a swimming pool.

The *Mace* supermarket *(Main St)* is open until 10.30pm daily. The *Coffee Dock (Main St)* Cooked breakfasts €5, toasted sandwiches €2-3. *Fran's Bia Blasta* takeaway *(Main St)* Fry-ups, chicken and chips €5. *Three in One* takeaway *(Lower Main St)* has affordable Indian food, kebabs and fry-ups.

Best for dinner is probably *Riverside Bistro (☎ 952 1062, Lower Main St)* Starters €4-7, mains €12-18, veg and pasta dishes €8-9. Nice seafood, also sandwiches for lunch €3-6. *Doherty's Restaurant (☎ 952 1654, Lower Main St)* has run-of-the-mill pizzas (small €4-5, large €5-8).

Day 3: Dungloe to Dunfanaghy

4–7 hours, 70.1km

This gem of a day passes through several distinct landscapes and three key parishes of the Donegal Gaeltacht – the Rosses, Gweedore and Cloghaneely. It's mostly up and down but lacks the long or steep (or both) climbs of Days 1 and 2, so isn't too strenuous. The views are breathtaking, with the ride's meandering course enhancing key landscape features, especially Mt Errigal (752m) and Muckish Mountain (670m). About the only thing that can ruin the day is poor weather, so be prepared.

The first third of the ride rolls through the Rosses (Na Rosa), an arresting landscape of tucked-away loughs and granite rises between marshy flats. There's a surprisingly high housing density, and a genuine Gaeltacht community feel: small shops, village post offices and people practising Gaelic sports.

NORTHERN ÉIRE

At 11.9km there's a right turn to quiet **Cruit Island** (An Chruit); the side trip to road's end at the island's north – from where there are fine views out to sea and of Owey Island – will add 10km to the day. Continuing, the ride passes through the villages of Kinscalough (Cionn Caslach; 13.5km) and Annagary (Anagaireen) en route to Crolly (Croithsli), home of famous porcelain Crolly dolls.

Once on the R257 (26.3km) the ride passes through the heart of Gweedore (Gaoth Dobhair), the spread-out and jumbled towns of Bunbeg (Bun Beag; about 31km) and Derrybeg (Doirí Beaga; about 33km). Around Brinlack (Bun na Leaca; 39.5km), stone fences catch the eye – many are of an unusual, tapering, one-rock-width design. Going north, the sense of isolation grows as the ride passes Bloody Foreland (named for sunset hues on the rocks). Views north to Tory Island (Oileán Thóraigh) are a feature. Further along, pretty Ballyness Bay and steep-sided Mt Errigal fix the gaze.

The ride returns to the N56 (54.3km) for the last stretch into Dunfanaghy. The towns of Gortahork (Gort an Choirce; 54.8km)

and Falcarragh (An Fal Carrach; 58.8km) both have strong Irish-speaking communities. Afternoon views are dominated by the sea and Horn Head to the north, and Muckish Mountain to the south.

Dunfanaghy
☎ 074

Compact and tidy, Dunfanaghy (Dún Fionnachaidh) is situated on the shore of Sheep Haven Bay, with the green hills of Horn Head stretching to the north. This is a pretty town with stone houses lining its wide, main street.

The post office is at the top of Main St; it has a bureau de change. There's an AIB (no ATM) next to Arnold's Hotel.

Things to See & Do Just south of town on the N56, the **Workhouse heritage centre** (☎ 913 6540, open daily Apr-Sept) provides a window into Famine-era life and local history. It's housed in the restored Dunfanaghy Workhouse, which opened just before the Famine in 1845, and includes craft and coffee shops.

The turn to Horn Head is at the southern end of Main St. There's about 12km to 14km

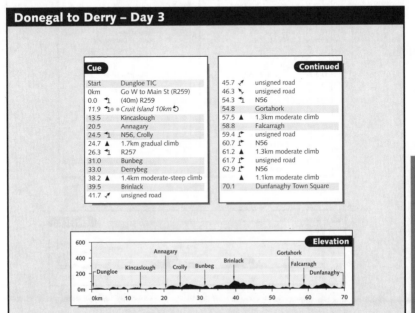

Donegal to Derry – Day 3

Cue	
Start	Dungloe TIC
0km	Go W to Main St (R259)
0.0	(40m) R259
11.9	*Cruit Island 10km*
13.5	Kincaslough
20.5	Annagary
24.5	N56, Crolly
24.7	1.7km gradual climb
26.3	R257
31.0	Bunbeg
33.0	Derrybeg
38.2	1.4km moderate-steep climb
39.5	Brinlack
41.7	unsigned road

	Continued
45.7	unsigned road
46.3	unsigned road
54.3	N56
54.8	Gortahork
57.5	1.3km moderate climb
58.8	Falcarragh
59.4	unsigned road
60.7	N56
61.2	1.3km moderate climb
61.7	unsigned road
62.9	N56
	1.1km moderate climb
70.1	Dunfanaghy Town Square

Elevation chart showing the route from Dungloe (0km) through Kincaslough, Annagary, Crolly, Bunbeg, Brinlack, Gortahork, Falcarragh to Dunfanaghy (70km), with elevation from 0m to 600m.

of road here, but the best views and most spectacular coastal features require some walking.

Places to Stay & Eat In a lovely setting 3.5km south of town on the N56 is *Corcreggan Mill (☎ 913 6409)* Tent sites per person €6. Dorm beds/loft doubles in the kiln house €10/26. Dorm beds/doubles in converted train carriages €13/30.

The Willows (☎ 913 6446, Main St) Singles/doubles €26/46. B&B closest to town centre, comfortable rooms and big breakfasts. *Carrigan House (☎ 913 6276)* and *The Whins (☎ 913 6481)* B&B singles/doubles at both €36/54. Both on the N56, less than 1km west of the town centre and overlooking Sheep Haven Bay.

Carrig Rua Hotel (☎ 913 6133) Rooms €140. *Arnold's Hotel (☎ 913 6208)* Singles €80-110, doubles €100-160. These two hotels at the north end of Main St are lovely but not cheap.

The *Village Shop* is open until 11pm daily. Open summer only, *An Chistín (Main St)* serves food fried and fast. Fish and chips €4, burgers €2. *Patsy Dan's* and *Michael's Bar* are both good for a pint and the *craic*; the latter serves bar food. *Muck 'n' Muffins (Village Square)* is a pottery and coffee shop; fine for a hot beverage.

Arnold's Hotel bistro has starters €3-6 and mains €9-18. There's a fair range of pasta €9-13. The *Carrig Rua Hotel* bistro has starters €3-6 and mains €8-14; the baked local salmon is good value at €10.

Donegal to Derry – Day 4

Cue	
Start	Dunfanaghy Town Square
0km	Go E on N56
2.7	Portnablaghy
6.3	↰● ●Ards Forest Park 6km ↺
8.3	▲ 1.9km gradual climb
10.2	Creeslough
10.3	↰ unsigned road
10.6	↘ 'to Doe Castle'
13.1	↱ unsigned road
	↑ ● ●Doe Castle 0.6km ↺
14.0	↰ R245
15.3	↱ 'to Gleann' (Glen)
	▲ 1.2km moderate climb
17.7	▲ 1.8km moderate–steep climb
18.0	↰ Glen
	↱ (10m) 'to Milford'
	▲ 2.5km moderate climb
25.9	↗ 'to Millford'
28.1	↱ R245 'to Millford'
30.5	▲ 0.9km moderate climb
32.2	↰ 'to Kerrykeel' (Carrowkeel)
33.8	↰ R246 'to Kerrykeel'
34.5	↱ unsigned road

Continued	
34.5	▲ 2.1km moderate climb
38.4	↱ R247 'to Glenvar', Carrowkeel
38.7	▲ 2.9km steep climb
39.4	↱ unsigned road
49.2	↱ R247
59.7	↰ R245 'to Letterkenny'
59.8	Rathmelton
59.9	↱ R245 'to Letterkenny'
	▲ 1.0km moderate–steep climb
60.9	↰ unsigned road
61.0	↱ unsigned road
61.8	▲ 1.3km gradual climb
63.1	↱ 'to Letterkenny'
64.2	↰ unsigned road
65.5	↱ unsigned road
67.8	↰ unsigned road
68.1	▲ 1.1km moderate–steep climb
69.2	↱ unsigned road
70.3	▲ 1.1km moderate climb
72.5	↱ Gortlee Rd
73.6	↱ Ramelton Rd
74.0	Letterkenny Station Roundabout

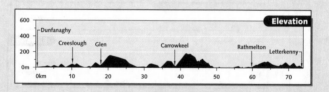

This hotel's *Sheephaven Room* serves à la carte restaurant mains €14-19. *Danny Collin's Restaurant (Main St)* has food of similar quality and price in a less formal setting than the hotels.

Day 4: Dunfanaghy to Letterkenny

4–7 hours, 74km

Rolling terrain – including some rearing climbs, and, towards the end, some zigzagging navigation – to stay off the busy R245 takes its toll. This feels like a very long day. En route there's another picture book's worth of wonderful views, a handful of lovely small towns and some interesting stops.

The day begins easily enough, passing through Portnablaghy. At 6.3km there's a side trip off the rolling N56 to **Ards Forest Park**, where there are nice walks to isolated beaches. Past Creeslough (An Craoslach; 10.2km) the route (and a short side trip at 13.1km) leads to **Doe Castle**. Built in the early 1500s by the MacSweeney family, allies of the O'Donnells, the castle is in a splendid setting overlooking the southern waters of Sheep Haven Bay.

There are wide views to the west, towards Mt Errigal, Muckish Mountain and the Derryveagh Mountains, before the neat village of Glen (An Gleann; 18km), which marks the start of the day's serious climbing and descending. After the climb out of Glen, views east towards Fanad Peninsula open up and there's a rare (for Ireland) long, winding downhill cruise for about 9km. The ride just bypasses Millford (Baile na nGalloglach), as it's only 500m to the town centre. Supplies are available there if necessary. Back roads into and out of Carrowkeel (An Cheathrú Chaol; 38.4km) provide the day's best views and most demanding riding. Be especially careful on the eye-widening descents from about 42km to 47km.

The ride returns to a busier road (the R247) just south of Rathmullan (Ráth Maoláin) and the mostly flat ride into attractive Rathmelton (Ráth Mealtain; 59.8km) hugs the western shore of Lough Swilly. A few cruel little climbs remain between Rathmelton and Letterkenny's outskirts, but a roaring descent brings the ride into town.

Letterkenny

See Letterkenny (p197).

Day 5: Letterkenny to Derry

2–4 hours, 37.4km

This short ride follows mostly busy roads to keep it as brief as possible. It focuses on attractive views of lower Lough Swilly and a visit to the evocative **Grianán of Ailéach**, a restored stone hill-fort 10.8km west of Derry.

The N13 between Letterkenny and the **Grianán Ailigh Heritage Centre** (24.9km; ☎ 936 8512) can be busy but there's a wide sealed verge for most of the way. Displays at the heritage centre give a broad background to the Grianán; there's also a decent *café*.

A steep climb away, the Grianán (side trip at 27.2km) crowns windswept Grianán Hill and offers views over Loughs Swilly and Foyle, the Inishowen Peninsula and Derry. The Grianán is thought to have been established about 2000 years ago; it was destroyed 800 years ago and rebuilt in the 1870s.

The final kilometres (or miles – the border is crossed just past the 32km mark) lead into Derry through the solidly Nationalist Creggan and Bogside areas.

Derry

See Derry (p227).

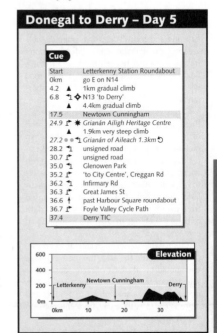

Donegal to Derry – Day 5

Cue		
Start	Letterkenny Station Roundabout	
0km	go E on N14	
4.2	▲	1km gradual climb
6.8	↰✛	N13 'to Derry'
	▲	4.4km gradual climb
17.5		Newtown Cunningham
24.9	↱✸	*Grianán Ailigh Heritage Centre*
	▲	1.9km very steep climb
27.2	●●↰	*Grianán of Aileach 1.3km ↺*
28.2	↰	unsigned road
30.7	↱	unsigned road
35.0	↰	Glenowen Park
35.2	↱	'to City Centre', Creggan Rd
36.2	↰	Infirmary Rd
36.3	↱	Great James St
36.6	↑	past Harbour Square roundabout
36.7	↱	Foyle Valley Cycle Path
37.4		Derry TIC

Elevation

Letterkenny Newtown Cunningham Derry

600
400
200
0m

0km 10 20 30

NORTHERN ÉIRE

Donegal Highlands

Duration	2 days
Distance	121.3km
Difficulty	moderate–hard
Start/End	Letterkenny

The Derryveagh and Glendowan Mountains and Glenveagh National Park feature in this circuit of Donegal's isolated and rugged northern ranges. Highlights include stark Mt Errigal, the county's highest peak, and the extraordinary, steep-sided glen surrounding Lough Beagh.

HISTORY

The Derryveagh-Glendowan area has felt human influence for millennia: the region's extensive boglands formed in the wake of tree-clearing in Neolithic times. Historically, the spectre of John George Adair casts the biggest shadow. At an earlier stage in his life Adair stood for parliament on a tenants' rights platform, but by 1859 he was a major landowner and his holdings included present-day Glenveagh National Park. When his

Beware the Baa Brigade

Isolation and tourist-deterring, unpredictable weather place Donegal's highlands among Ireland's quietest regions to cycle. Often, a rider cresting a climb on a Donegal back road will see nothing but misty rain, boggy moorlands...and a host of sodden sheep.

Often roaming at will in remote areas, these woolly creatures seem especially fond of roads on cold and wet days. Rather than moving calmly to the roadside when a bike or car approaches, they have a tendency to run ahead of moving vehicles. Young lambs, likely to be on the hoof by mid-spring, are particularly dim-witted; if they become separated from their mothers, they'll dart into the path of bikes or vehicles to cross the road and join ewe-know-who.

It's advisable to ride with care at all times – the more remote the area, the more cautious you should be. It's best *never* to descend at speed from high passes in poor weather. A mature sheep is a solid object to T-bone, and more likely to walk away from the collision than a cyclist.

relationship with tenants deteriorated over several issues, including game-shooting rights, Adair had nearly 250 evicted. After Adair's death in 1885, his wife Cornelia reintroduced red deer and improved the estate. American owner Henry McIlhenny kept it running through the mid-20th century, and it was eventually acquired by the state and opened as Glenveagh National Park in 1984.

NATURAL HISTORY

Granite is the main underlying rock type in the region, brought to the surface by millions of years of weathering. In places, later volcanic flows left basalt in granite fissures, where it has subsequently weathered faster than the surrounding granite. Distinctive Mt Errigal is something of an oddity in this geology: it's composed of quartzite. Glacial erosion during the most recent ice age played the biggest role in shaping the land here – its most notable legacies are the Glenveagh valley and the Poisoned Glen.

A great part of the terrain passed during the ride is peat bogland. The large pine plantations on slopes below Aghla More (584m), Aghla Beg (564m) and Crocknalaragagh (471m) are in sight from the northernmost section of Day 2. The remnant woodland on Lough Beagh's southeastern shore is one of few areas of native woodland remaining in Ireland. The park's herd of several hundred red deer is descended from animals introduced in the late 19th century by Cornelia Adair. Despite their relatively large numbers the deer aren't readily seen; encounters with foxes and hares are much more common. Scores of bird species are found in the park and surrounding highlands.

PLANNING
When to Ride

Late spring to early autumn is best, weather permitting. This ride is specifically intended as an adjunct to the Donegal to Derry ride (p199) if the weather is fair. Start at either Dungloe or Letterkenny if a favourable forecast is issued for the following days.

Maps

The ride is covered by the OSNI 1:250,000 Holiday map *Ireland North*. OSI 1:50,000 Discovery map No 6 covers Glenveagh National Park and is useful if you're planning to do some walking in the park.

What to Bring
Weather in these uplands is among the most changeable in Donegal, if not all Ireland. Driving rain, poor visibility and chilly winds can happen without warning. Dress appropriately; see the boxed text 'Warning: Be Prepared', (p195).

ACCESS TOWN
Letterkenny
See Letterkenny (p197).

THE RIDE
Day 1: Letterkenny to Dungloe
3–5½ hours, 54.3km

A slow climb on the northern flank of **Glenveagh National Park**, glorious views down the glen (weather permitting) and a long pedal through remote central Donegal are features of this rewarding day. In unfavourable conditions, it can seem an awfully long 50-odd kilometres to Dungloe, but the countryside has its attractions.

Ironically, given this ride's name, a longish flat stretch leads away from Letterkenny. At 7km, it's worth a stop at **Newmill Corn & Flax Mill** (open June-Sept), a complex of neat, stone industrial buildings, the oldest of which is more than 300 years old. The site includes one of Ireland's largest working waterwheels, powered by the River Swilly. In its heyday, the mill processed flax, oats and barley.

Beyond Glendowan (Gleann Domhain; about 20km), which is a locality rather than a township, there's a real sense of isolation for about 25km. The route first climbs beside the River Bullaba through bleakly beautiful wild moorlands and heath-covered hills to a lookout at the southern end of Glenveagh. Throughout the climb, the 45km-long Glenveagh National Park deer fence (erected in the 19th century) is off to the right. Beyond the lookout, the ride descends into a widening valley flanked by the Glendowan and Derryveagh Mountains; 683m Slieve Snaght is a forbidding presence to the west, although you can often see nothing of the peak except its mist-shrouded lower reaches. This section can be particularly spectacular in poor weather, with mist swirling, rain cascading off the steep granite hills and sheep sheltering as best they can.

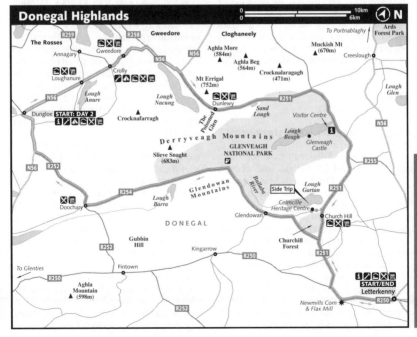

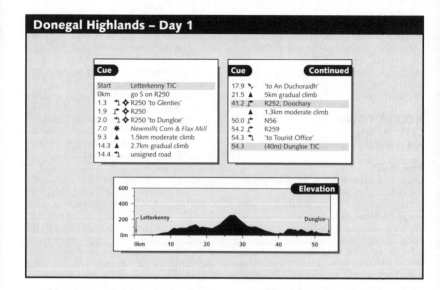

Donegal Highlands – Day 1

Cue	
Start	Letterkenny TIC
0km	go S on R250
1.3	R250 'to Glenties'
1.9	R250
2.0	R250 'to Dungloe'
7.0	*Newmills Corn & Flax Mill*
9.3	1.5km moderate climb
14.3	2.7km gradual climb
14.4	unsigned road

Cue	Continued
17.9	'to An Duchoraidh'
21.5	5km gradual climb
41.2	R252, Doochary
	1.3km moderate climb
50.0	N56
54.2	R259
54.3	'to Tourist Office'
54.3	(40m) Dungloe TIC

Elevation

The ride skirts Lough Barra (about 32km) through rolling farmland that harbours a number of ruined 19th-century cottages. Beyond Doochary (An Dúchoraidh; 41.2km), a popular fishing destination, the route passes through an arresting landscape of granite rises and tiny loughs; the undulating terrain here can be very cruel if a cold wind is blowing down from the northwest. Traffic on the roads between Doochary and Dungloe tends to be fast moving – beware.

Dungloe

See Dungloe (p204).

Day 2: Dungloe to Letterkenny

4–6½ hours, 67km

A rolling start is followed by a superb, arcing journey past Mt Errigal, and through the heart of the Derryveagh Mountains. A visit to Glenveagh National Park is arguably the highlight.

Throughout the first part of the day, 752m Mt Errigal is a beckoning presence, seen at first in the distance behind another quartzite peak, Crocknafarragh. The up-and-down journey on the N56 through the Rosses includes some pretty sights – Lough Anure (about 8km) especially – but it's mostly a transit section, the object being to reach Gweedore and the turn onto the R251 (19.6km) as quickly as possible. Viewed

from the start of the R251, the hulking, pyramidal mass of Mt Errigal dominates views, while the wild-looking, rounded peaks of Slieve Snaght and other high Derryveagh peaks take time to draw attention.

Tiny Dunlewy (Dún Lúiche; 22.5km) is the gateway to walks in this part of the mountains (particularly to Mt Errigal and the Poisoned Glen). The 8km trek up Mt Errigal is Donegal's most popular mountain walk and, if the weather gods smile and deliver a brilliantly clear day, it ought to be considered compulsory. It's best to take an extra day to complete the ride if you do so. There are a couple of *youth hostels* as well as *B&Bs* in Dunlewy.

After a gradual climb past Mt Errigal's southern flank, the ride rises to a high point near Sand Lough then rolls down virtually all the way to the way to Glenveagh National Park (Pairc Naísúnta Gleann Bheatha) entrance at 38.9km. At 140 sq km, Glenveagh is the second largest of Ireland's five national parks and visitors could spend more than an hour exploring it. The park visitor centre (☎ 074-913 7090), which provides background to John Adair and the park's natural systems, and its *restaurant* are a short distance off the main road. It's about 3km further up the valley to **Glenveagh Castle** and its acclaimed gardens. The park is open year-round, but the visitor

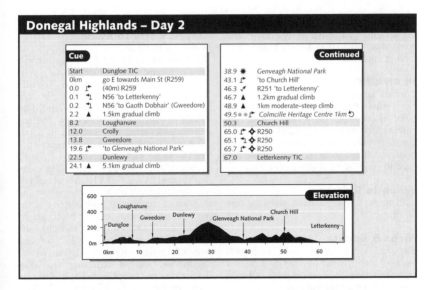

Donegal Highlands – Day 2

Cue	
Start	Dungloe TIC
0km	go E towards Main St (R259)
0.0	↱ (40m) R259
0.1	↰ N56 'to Letterkenny'
0.2	↰ N56 'to Gaoth Dobhair' (Gweedore)
2.2	▲ 1.5km gradual climb
8.2	Loughanure
12.0	Crolly
13.8	Gweedore
19.6	↱ 'to Glenveagh National Park'
22.5	Dunlewy
24.1	▲ 5.1km gradual climb

Continued	
38.9	✳ Genveagh National Park
43.1	↱ 'to Church Hill'
46.3	↙ R251 'to Letterkenny'
46.7	▲ 1.2km gradual climb
48.9	▲ 1km moderate–steep climb
49.5	●●↱ Colmcille Heritage Centre 1km ↻
50.3	Church Hill
65.0	↱ ◆ R250
65.1	↰ ◆ R250
65.7	↱ ◆ R250
67.0	Letterkenny TIC

Elevation

centre and Glenveagh Castle are closed from November to March.

A side trip (49.5km) leads to the **Colmcille Heritage Centre** (☎ 074-913 7306) on pretty Lough Gartan. The centre has multimedia displays to tell St Colmcille's story, and the overall effect is more informative and entertaining than you might expect. The centre is surrounded by extensive grounds that include lakeside *tea rooms.*

Inishowen Circuit

Duration	3 days
Distance	168.5km
Difficulty	moderate–hard
Start/End	Derry

There's an other-worldly quality to the Inishowen (Inis Eoghain) Peninsula, the largest of Donegal's peninsulas and the least visited by tourists. This route mostly follows the mapped and signposted scenic driving route, the Inishowen 100 (Inis Eoghain 100), which takes in the best of the natural sights.

HISTORY

Inishowen was one of the last parts of Ireland to submit to the English and its Nationalist associations continued to modern times. For seven centuries the peninsula was ruled by the O'Doherty family, which had close alliances with the O'Donnells of West Donegal and the O'Neills of Tyrone. In 1608 Sir Cahir O'Doherty of Inishowen, the last of the Gaelic lords and a 'stayer' after the previous year's Flight of the Earls (see History, p193), rebelled. He almost wiped out Derry, then little more than a trading settlement, but was killed in Donegal. In 1798, United Irishmen rebellion leader Theobald Wolf Tone was captured from a French fleet defeated off the Inishowen coast. He subsequently beat the hangman by committing suicide, and the United Irishmen were broken. Their several attempts at rebellion led to the 1801 Act of Union. In 1921, Donegal and its strong Catholic majority remained in the Republic when counties to the east were gathered into Northern Ireland. Thus did Inishowen remain part of the South, even though its northernmost reaches are further north than the North.

NATURAL HISTORY

Most of Inishowen is a declared European Special Area of Conservation and is host to a range of indigenous wildlife and migratory birds. Like much of Ireland, the landscape has been greatly altered by human activity. Inishowen's most alluring attraction is its compactness. Boggy moorlands, plunging sea cliffs, attractive sandy beaches and some steep uplands make it a kind of Ireland in miniature.

PLANNING

Tourists are less catered for here than in other parts of Ireland. To keep riding distances manageable, Days 1 and 2 of the ride end in quiet towns with limited options for accommodation and eating out. It pays to book ahead and to be flexible – you may need to stay a short distance off-route.

When to Ride

Late spring to early autumn gives the best weather.

Maps & Books

The ride is covered by OSNI 1:250,000 Holiday map *Ireland North*. OSI 1:50,000 Discovery map No 3 covers most of Inishowen and is a useful addition.

ACCESS TOWN
Derry

See Derry (p227).

THE RIDE
Day 1: Derry to Malin

4–6½ hours, 68.8km

As is normal for Donegal, the weather will be the biggest factor in determining your enjoyment of this demanding day. The ride twice climbs from sea level to elevated passes – both around 250m – and cold winds or rain can make for slow and uncomfortable going over either high point. However, nothing except dense fog can detract from the views en route.

Start the day on the Foyle Valley cycle path opposite the Derry TIC. About eight of the first 10km out of Derry are spent on the A2, which can be especially busy on weekends. The back roads between Muff (Magh; 10km) and Buncrana (Bun Cranncha; just off-ride at about 26km) provide relief, and views from the road between Eskaheen and Scalp Mountains are outstanding, especially back to the east over Lough Foyle. The ride picks up the Inis Eoghain 100 at 26.3km, just north of Buncrana.

At 35.9km, a 2km side trip leads to **Fort Dunree Military Museum** (☎ 074-936 1817) at windswept Dunree Head, overlooking

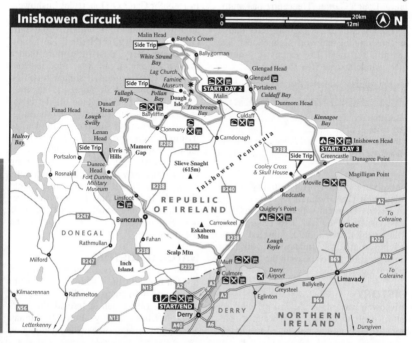

Lough Swilly. Displays include pieces of military equipment and focus on the fort's history. Wolf Tone and his French cohorts planned to reach Derry by way of Lough Swilly, and Dunree was one of the forts built to keep the invaders at bay.

The ride crosses the rugged Urris Hills at the Mamore Gap (An Mam Mór; 41.6km), after a painful push to the top. The views here are outstanding, west over Lough Swilly and towards Fanad Head, and north towards Dunaff Head.

At 58.2km, the turn for the side trip to **Doagh Island Famine Village** (☎ 074-937 6493) is signposted and it's an easy ride. Buildings at this outdoor museum represent Inishowen life over the past 150 or so years, emphasising the period of the Great Famine.

Malin
☎ 074

Neatly arranged around a central village green Malin (Málainn) is well positioned to allow even distances on the ride's longest days. It's a quiet place with limited accommodation and food options, so it's best to book ahead.

The Malin post office and general store face the village green and provide limited tourist information. Arranged around the green are friendly *McGonagle's Bar*, a grocery store/off-licence and the Malin Hotel.

Places to Stay & Eat There are two hostels, *Sandrock* (☎ 937 0289) and *Malin Head Hostel* (☎ 937 0309), near Malin Head, both about 13km into the Day 2 route. Both have dorm beds for around €12.

The *Malin Hotel* (☎ 937 0606) B&B singles/doubles €51/89. Comfortable rooms. *Ashdale Farmhouse* (☎ 937 4017) B&B doubles €49. About 4km south of Malin and close to Carndonagh. There are more B&Bs in Culdaff, about 7km east of Malin, and Ballyliffin, 13km west. If you're cycling in a small group, there are a couple of self-catering cottages near Malin that may be good value, although they're generally let on a weekly basis. Call John and Vivien Holt (☎ 937 0612) to inquire.

The *Malin Hotel* has bar meals €5-13, restaurant starters €3-7 and restaurant mains €11-14. Predictable fare. Veg meals available in both bar and restaurant.

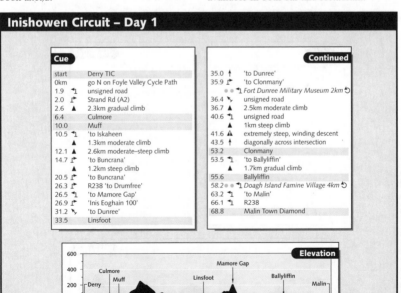

Inishowen Circuit – Day 1

Cue	
start	Derry TIC
0km	go N on Foyle Valley Cycle Path
1.9 ↱	unsigned road
2.0 ↰	Strand Rd (A2)
2.6 ▲	2.3km gradual climb
6.4	Culmore
10.0	Muff
10.5 ↱	'to Iskaheen'
▲	1.3km moderate climb
12.1 ▲	2.6km moderate–steep climb
14.7 ↰	'to Buncrana'
▲	1.2km steep climb
20.5 ↰	'to Buncrana'
26.3 ↰	R238 'to Drumfree'
26.5 ↱	'to Mamore Gap'
26.9 ↰	'Inis Eoghain 100'
31.2 ↘	'to Dunree'
33.5	Linsfoot

	Continued
35.0 ↑	'to Dunree'
35.9 ↱	'to Clonmany'
● ● ↱	Fort Dunree Military Museum 2km ↻
36.4 ↘	unsigned road
36.7 ▲	2.5km moderate climb
40.6 ↱	unsigned road
▲	1km steep climb
41.6 ▲▲	extremely steep, winding descent
43.5 ↑	diagonally across intersection
53.2	Clonmany
53.5 ↱	'to Ballyliffin'
▲	1.7km gradual climb
55.6	Ballyliffin
58.2 ● ● ↱	Doagh Island Famine Village 4km ↻
63.2 ↱	'to Malin'
66.1 ↱	R238
68.8	Malin Town Diamond

NORTHERN ÉIRE

Day 2: Malin to Greencastle
4–6½ hours, 64.1km

This is a solid day with very little flat terrain. The climbs start before the first 10km and the longest and hardest of them are in the ride's second half. Scenery throughout is outstanding and, even though the ride passes through several towns or settlements, there's a feeling of wilderness and isolation about the day. Expect to arrive in Greencastle exhilarated but ready for a rest.

Early in the day the ride passes **Lag Church** (5.6km), the oldest church still in use on the peninsula, set in dunes a few hundred metres from the beach at Black Strand. The best view of the church in its broader setting, with Doagh Isle to the south, is from a lookout on Soldiers Hill, at 8.5km. The best wide-angle view of Malin Head (Cionn Mhálanna), with lovely White Strand Bay in the foreground, is at 11km, as the ride passes White Hill.

It's a steepish climb up to **Banba's Crown** (Fiorcheann Éirann; side trip at 18.7km) but essential viewing. Here, a tower built in 1805 by the British looms above Ireland's northernmost point; it's almost better being here in stormy weather, when the sea seems particularly gloomy and dangerous. In clear weather, there are excellent views of Inishtrahull (Inis Trá Tholl) and the Garvan Isles.

Quiet back roads and one major up-and-down section lead eventually to Culdaff (Cúil Dabhcha; 40.5km) and the Blue Flag beach on Culdaff Bay (about 42km). Have a dip if it's a warm day; the day's remaining 20km are up and down and extremely tiring. A plaque (54.7km) commemorating the 1588 wreck of Spanish Armada vessel *La Trinidad Valencera* in Kinnagoe Bay is the perfect place to rest before the final 4.8km climb. Only about 40 of the 360 aboard *Valencera* died in the wreck; the others headed south once ashore, and about 200 of them were slaughtered outside Derry. Thankfully a far gentler reward is in store for southbound cyclists. From the top of the climb views extend east across Magilligan Point and beyond; the Mussenden Temple near Downhill is visible on clear days. Lough Foyle spreads out to the south and the rolling green hills of County Derry beckon.

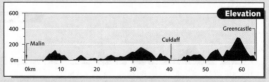

Inishowen Circuit – Day 2

Cue			Continued	
start	Malin Town Diamond	35.9 ↰	'to Culdaff'	
0km	Go W on R242	36.0	Glengad	
5.6 ✳	Lag Church	36.5 ▲	1.1km steep climb	
5.9 ↰	'Inis Eoghain 100'	40.5 ↰	'to Moville', Culdaff	
▲	800m moderate climb	↘	(40m) 'Inis Eoghain 100'	
6.8 ↰	'Inis Eoghain 100'	43.3 ▲	800m moderate–steep climb	
7.2 ▲	1.3km steep climb	44.5 ↰	'to Carrowmena'	
13.7 ↰	'to Malin Head'	48.0 ↰	'to Tremone Bay'	
13.8 ↘	'to Malin Head'	50.1 ▲	2.8km moderate–steep climb	
14.0 ▲	1.6km moderate–steep climb	50.3 ↰	'Inis Eoghain 100'	
14.8 ↱	'to Malin Head'	51.2 ↘	'Inis Eoghain 100'	
18.7 ●●↰	Banba's Crown 1.6km ↺	53.9 ↰	'to Kinnagoe Bay'	
21.7 ↰	'Inis Eoghain 100'	54.7 ↱	'to Moville'	
23.3 ↱	'Inis Eoghain 100'	▲	4.8km steep climb	
25.2 ↰	'to Glengad'	56.5 ↗	'Inis Eoghain 100'	
27.8 ↰	'Inis Eoghain 100'	62.3 ↰	'to Greencastle'	
▲	2km gradual climb	63.3 ↱	'to Maritime Museum'	
30.5 ▲	1.7km moderate climb	64.1	Greencastle Post Office	

Elevation

(elevation profile: 0m–600m scale; markers for Malin, Culdaff, Greencastle; distance axis 0km to 60+)

Greencastle
☎ 074

Directly opposite Magilligan Point, Greencastle (An Cáisleán Nua) is every bit the maritime village. From its busy little harbour, fishing vessels leave to ply the waters of Lough Foyle and the sea beyond.

Some information boards in the park just north of the harbour will help with bearings.

Things to See & Do In an old coastguard station right opposite the harbour is **Inishowen Maritime Museum** (☎ 938 1363). It contains a good collection of memorabilia and photographs, themed displays on the Spanish Armada and emigration (nearby Moville was once a busy emigration port), and a fine collection of boats. There's also a planetarium.

A **coastal walkway** extends south to Moville and north to **Northburgh Castle**, from which Greencastle gets its name. The 14th-century castle was built by Norman Richard de Burgo as a garrison for troops used in subduing the O'Doherty and O'Donnell clans. There's not much of it left today; you'll get the best idea of its scale if you view it from the lough side. Next door, **Greencastle Fort** began life as a Martello tower (defensive structure) in 1801; it and a matching tower at Magilligan were intended to guard the lough entrance. It was extended into a fort by 1812, but these days it's a guesthouse and pub/restaurant.

The *Ferryport Bar* *(Main St)* has live music from time to time.

Places to Stay & Eat Campers should head to *Greencastle Camping and Caravan Park* (☎ 938 1410). For B&B, try *Tardrum Country House* (☎ 938 1051) Singles/doubles €39/72. Dinner €26. *Brooklyn Cottage* (☎ 938 1087) Singles/doubles €28/49. Great sea views, about 500m from town centre.

Castle Inn (☎ 938 1426) Singles/doubles €39/64. Comfortable; many rooms have sea views. Bar-food starters €3-7, mains €7-13. Castle Inn *Conservatory Restaurant* has à la carte starters €3-7 and mains €12-18. Will take requests for vegetarian food if booked in advance. *Greencastle Fort* (☎ 938 1279) Doubles €89; nice beer garden overlooking the sea, bar and à la carte food available.

There's a *Spar* supermarket opposite the harbour. *Kealys Seafood Bar* (☎ 938 1010, *Main St*) serves fresh local seafood dinners Thursday to Sunday. There's a *café* in the Maritime Museum.

Day 3: Greencastle to Derry
2–3½ hours, 35.6km

This easy transit day – a relief after a couple of days among the Inishowen hills – tracks straight down to Derry mainly on the R241 and R238. If it's tackled midweek, traffic won't be a problem (although there'll certainly be more south of Quigley's Point). There are just three easy climbs en route; views over Lough Foyle are peaceful and virtually uninterrupted.

On the outskirts of Moville (Bun an Phobail, 4.4km), take the second right after crossing the River Bredagh bridge for the

NORTHERN ÉIRE

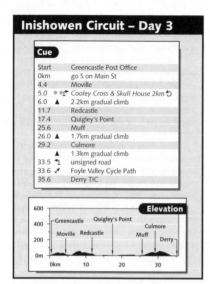

Inishowen Circuit – Day 3

Cue

Start	Greencastle Post Office
0km	go S on Main St
4.4	Moville
5.0	● ⬅ Cooley Cross & Skull House 2km ↻
6.0 ▲	2.2km gradual climb
11.7	Redcastle
17.4	Quigley's Point
25.6	Muff
26.0 ▲	1.7km gradual climb
29.2	Culmore
▲	1.3km gradual climb
33.5 ↱	unsigned road
33.6 ↗	Foyle Valley Cycle Path
35.6	Derry TIC

side trip (5km) to the **Cooley Cross & Skull House**. Keep veering right; you'll see the 3m-high cross after 1km. The nearby stone Skull House still contains some bones; it's thought to have its origins in the 6th century and may have had another use before it became a mortuary.

Kingfisher Country

Duration	3 days
Distance	201.5km (125.2mi)
Difficulty	moderate
Start/End	Ballyshannon

This border-hopping ride is based around the 370km (230mi) Kingfisher Cycle Trail, Ireland's first signposted long-distance National Cycle Network ride. Both this ride and the Kingfisher Cycle Trail wind through the lakelands of Counties Leitrim, Cavan and Fermanagh. Roughly half the ride's total distance is spent in Northern Ireland. Cycling through beautiful scenery on quiet back roads is the main attraction.

HISTORY
This region resisted invaders until the dawn of the 17th century. Enniskillen became a major Plantation centre but the Planters (Protestant immigrants) were never in the majority, and the region retained Nationalist associations into modern times. The current elected MP for Fermanagh and South Tyrone is Michelle Gildernew, the first female Sinn Féin MP since Countess Markievcz in 1918.

The Kingfisher Cycle Trail was developed throughout the late 1990s. It follows a meandering figure-of-eight course that, in its entirety, would be best covered in five to six days.

NATURAL HISTORY
About one third of Country Fermanagh is covered by water – Lough Erne is by far the biggest body. The territory encompasses lakes, rivers and streams, drumlins and some surprisingly steep uplands. The lakes attract many species of waterbird and, in places, are fringed by areas of broadleaf woodland.

PLANNING
The Fermanagh lakes are particularly noted for fishing and boating, and you may consider staying longer in the region to take advantage of these pursuits. Fermanagh TIC (see Enniskillen, p218) provides information on cruise-boat hire and on fishing seasons and licences.

When to Ride
Late spring to early autumn is best because of the milder weather and longer daylight hours.

Maps
The ride is covered by OSNI 1:250,000 Holiday map *Ireland North*. The NCN 1:100,000 *Kingfisher Cycle Trail* map provides much extra detail and should be regarded as an essential addition. It's available from bigger bookshops in the region as well as Fermanagh TIC in Enniskillen.

What to Bring
Although the ride flits seamlessly between Éire and the North (in many places the 'border' isn't even marked) don't forget that currencies change – euros are used in the South and pounds sterling in the North.

ACCESS TOWN
Ballyshannon
See Ballyshannon (p199).

THE RIDE
Day 1: Ballyshannon to Enniskillen
4–7½ hours, 74.4km (46.2mi)

To avoid the busy A47, some meandering in the first half turns this into a fairly tiring day, but splendid cycling on quiet roads and wonderful views are ample compensation.

After a flat, easy first section along Lake Assaroe, the ride crosses into Northern Ireland and quickly enters the neat town of Belleek (Béal Leice; 8.2km; 5.1mi) home of the renowned **Belleek Pottery works** (☎ 028-6865 8501). There are regular weekday tours of the works, which has been producing fine glazed porcelain since 1857. The visitor centre includes a *restaurant* and museum.

Out of Belleek, at 13.7km (8.5mi), consider continuing on the A47 (rather than taking the ride's left turn, which passes Lough Scolban, for the side trip to **Castle Caldwell Forest Park** (☎ 028-6863 1253). The castle, built in the early 17th century, is a ruin, albeit in an evocative setting, while the park includes a Royal Society for the Protection of Birds reserve (with bird hides) and some pleasant walks through woodland and along the Lower Lough Erne shore. After visiting the park, rather than backtracking to 13.7km (8.5mi), continue on the A47 for about another 1.6km (1mi), turn left and pick up the Day 1 ride at the 17.8km (11.1mi) mark.

Between 20km and 30km there's some climbing on gloriously isolated roads. The ride passes Lough Avehy and there are wide

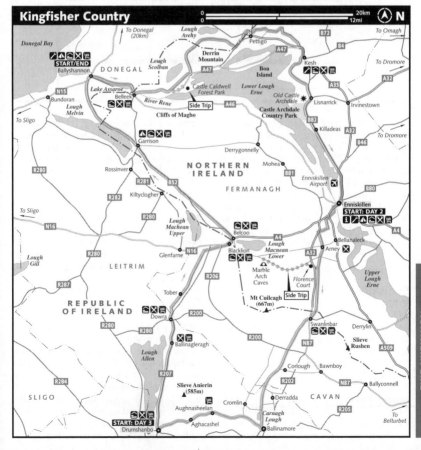

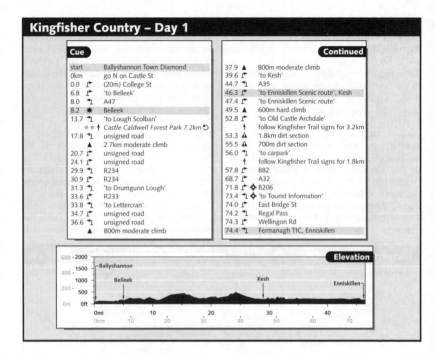

Kingfisher Country – Day 1

Cue		
start		Ballyshannon Town Diamond
0km		go N on Castle St
0.0	↱	(20m) College St
6.8	↱	'to Belleek'
8.0	↰	A47
8.2	✳	Belleek
13.7	↰	'to Lough Scolban'
	● ● ↑	Castle Caldwell Forest Park 7.2km ↺
17.8	↰	unsigned road
	▲	2.7km moderate climb
20.7	↱	unsigned road
24.1	↱	unsigned road
29.9	↰	R234
30.9	↱	R234
31.3	↰	'to Drumgunn Lough'
33.6	↱	R233
33.8	↰	'to Lettercran'
34.7	↱	unsigned road
36.6	↰	unsigned road
	▲	800m moderate climb

		Continued
37.9	▲	800m moderate climb
39.6	↱	'to Kesh'
44.7	↰	A35
46.3	↱	'to Enniskillen Scenic route', Kesh
47.4	↱	'to Enniskillen Scenic route'
49.5	▲	600m hard climb
52.8	↱	'to Old Castle Archdale'
	↑	follow Kingfisher Trail signs for 3.2km
53.3	▲	1.8km dirt section
55.5	▲	700m dirt section
56.0	↰	'to carpark'
	↑	follow Kingfisher Trail signs for 1.8km
57.8	↱	B82
68.7	↱	A32
71.8	↱ ◆	B206
73.4	↰ ◆	'to Tourist Information'
74.0	↱	East Bridge St
74.2	↰	Regal Pass
74.3	↱	Wellington Rd
74.4	↰	Fermanagh TIC, Enniskillen

Elevation

views over southern Donegal, across the undulating, lake-strewn Pullans district to the craggy Blue Stack Mountains.

At 52.8km (32.8mi) the ride passes **Old Castle Archdale**, a fortified farmhouse built in the early 17th century, during the Plantation of Ulster. The building was twice destroyed, in 1641 and again in 1689, during the Williamite Wars; the ruins mark the beginning of the ride's visit to Castle Archdale Country Park, following NCN route 91. Beyond the park, the ride joins the B82 and riders can expect some fast-moving traffic.

Enniskillen
☎ 028

Athwart the watery narrows between Upper and Lower Lough Erne, Enniskillen (Inis Ceithleann) has an easy-going air that's more reminiscent of towns in the South. It's the main centre in the popular Fermanagh Lakelands and has excellent services for visitors.

Information Fermanagh TIC (☎ 6632 3110, e tic@fermanagh.gov.uk, Wellington Rd, open Mon-Fri year-round, Sat & Sun Easter-Sept) is the gateway information

centre for the lakes region. It takes accommodation bookings and has a bureau de change. Banks (all have ATMs) are on High/Townhall Sts and the town diamond. Patrick McNulty & Sons cycle shop (☎ 6632 2423, 24-26 Belmore St) is close to the town centre and good for repairs.

Things to See & Do Walk up the 108 steps inside **Cole's Monument**, a soaring column in Forthill Park, for an overview of town; it's open in afternoons during the warmer months. **Enniskillen Castle** (☎ 6632 5000, off Wellington Rd) includes the Fermanagh Heritage Centre (exhibits cover Fermanagh human and natural history) and the Museum of the Royal Inniskilling Fusiliers (full of weapons and other regimental paraphernalia).

Just southeast of Enniskillen on the A4, **Castle Coole** (☎ 6632 2690) is reputedly Ireland's finest neoclassical house. Completed in 1798 and once the family seat of the Earls of Belmore, the house includes faithfully restored interiors and furnishings. The extensive landscaped grounds feature walks through parks and woodlands.

Places to Stay & Eat Catch the ferry (9am-midnight) from behind the Lakeland Forum, about 250m from the TIC, to **Lakeland Canoe Centre** (☎ *6632 4250, Castle Island*) Tent sites per person £4, dorm beds with/without breakfast £11/9.

HINI **Castle Archdale Hostel** (☎ *6862 8118*) is 17.7km (11mi) north of Enniskillen in Castle Archdale Country Park. Dorm beds £9.

B&Bs include **Will-O-Brook** (☎ *6632 5825, Tempo Rd*) Singles/doubles £18/30. A 19th-century terrace house, opposite Round 'o' Park, 800m west of centre. The **Point** (☎ *6632 3595, Tempo Rd*) Singles/doubles £20/36. Dinner £12. Good value, 2.5km (1.5mi) northwest of centre. **Drumcoo House** (☎ *6632 6672, 32 Cherryville, Cornagrade Rd*) Singles/doubles £24/42. Near the hospital, 1.6km (1mi) north of centre. **Mountview** (☎ *6632 3147, 61 Irvinestown Rd*) Singles/doubles £33/44; dinner £13. Lovely house, also 1.6km (1mi) north of centre.

Belmore Court Motel (☎ *6632 6633, Tempo Rd*) Doubles with kitchenette £45-48. OK value for two people; a short ride from the town centre. **Fort Lodge Hotel** (☎ *6632 3275, 72 Forthill St*) Singles/doubles £45/70. Comfortable and friendly. **Killyhevlin Hotel** (☎ *6632 3481, Dublin Rd*) Singles/doubles £73/105. Four-star hotel; lovely lakeside setting.

For self-caterers, there's a big **Dunnes Stores** supermarket (Forthill St).

Golden Arrow (*Townhall St*) does a big breakfast £4. **Café Cellini** (*East Bridge St*) Tasty filled paninis £4. It has lovely bread. **Crowe's Nest Bistro** (☎ *6632 5252, High St*) Burgers £3, salads £5-6. **Scoffs** (☎ *6634 2622, 17 Belmore St*) Starters £3-4, mains £11-13, good pasta selection £5. **Oscar's** (☎ *6632 737, 29 Belmore St*) Starters £3-5, veg mains £8-10, pastas £8-11. Probably the best in town for food and atmosphere. **Franco's Restaurant** (☎ *6632 4424, Queen Elizabeth Rd*) Starters £4-7, mains £10-19, pastas £7-10, pizzas $7-8. Extensive menu.

Day 2: Enniskillen to Drumshanbo

3½–6 hours, 57.9km (36mi)

This might be the best day's cycling in this part of Ireland. Dipping in and out of the NCN Kingfisher Cycle Trail, the ride is almost entirely on quiet back roads and features rolling farmlands, tree-lined lanes and isolated villages. High country east (Slieve Rushen) and west (Mt Cuilcach) of the ride provides lofty green counterpoints on clear days. The suggested side trips are well worthwhile, but the cycling itself is enough.

At 14km turn right for the side trip to Florence Court, or go all the way to Marble Arch Caves (see Side Trip, p220).

Kingfisher Country – Day 2

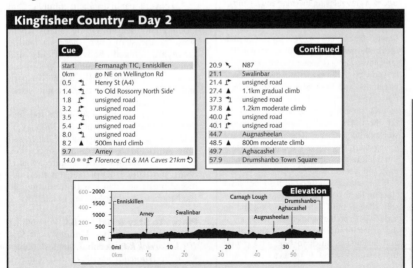

Cue			Continued	
start	Fermanagh TIC, Enniskillen		20.9 ↘	N87
0km	go NE on Wellington Rd		21.1	Swalinbar
0.5 ↱	Henry St (A4)		21.4 ↰	unsigned road
1.4 ↰	'to Old Rossorry North Side'		27.4 ▲	1.1km gradual climb
1.8 ↱	unsigned road		37.3 ↰	unsigned road
3.2 ↱	unsigned road		37.8 ▲	1.2km moderate climb
3.5 ↰	unsigned road		40.0 ↱	unsigned road
5.4 ↱	unsigned road		40.1 ↱	unsigned road
8.0 ↰	unsigned road		44.7	Augnasheelan
8.2 ▲	500m hard climb		48.5 ▲	800m moderate climb
9.7	Arney		49.7	Aghacashel
14.0 ●●↱	Florence Crt & MA Caves 21km ↻		57.9	Drumshanbo Town Square

Elevation

Beyond Swalinbar (An Muileann Iarainn; 21.1km; 13.1mi) the countryside is quiet, mostly fields, cottages, livestock and wide views from a narrow lane. Watch for the fine stone St Patrick's Church in Corlough (Corlach), just off the ride at 30.3km (18.8mi). At 40.1km (24.9mi), near Ballinamore (Béal an Átha Mór), the ride passes a portion of the Shannon-Erne Waterway. This 382km-long system of canals and loughs winds across Counties Leitrim, Cavan and Fermanagh from Leitrim town, on the upper reaches of the River Shannon, to Upper Lough Erne.

Side Trip: Florence Court & Marble Arch Caves
1–2 hours, 21km return
At 14km (8.7mi) a right turn (with NCN signpost) heads to Florence Court, 3.5km (5.6mi) from the turn off, and Marble Arch Caves, 7km (4.4mi) further west. Florence Court (☎ 6634 8249) is an 18th-century Palladian mansion built by the earls of Enniskillen. It's not as grand inside as Castle Coole, but very impressive in its setting, surrounded by broad and peaceful grounds. The

---

Sticky Business

As you cycle country lanes, be prepared to encounter road resurfacing crews – usually comprising a tar-spraying truck, a couple of trucks, a gravel-laying machine and a gang of affable, tool-wielding workers.

The job is a messy affair, and can sometimes delay a rider's progress for several minutes as the machinery is all but impassable. The tar-sprayer lumbers along, jetting an oozing layer on top of the existing roadway, roadside vegetation and the weeds that sprout from the centre of the road. The laying machine follows, spreading fine gravel on top of the tar; the trucks shuttle gravel from a nearby stockpile to the layer. There are rarely any rolling machines to pack the new surface – this is left to passing vehicles over the coming days and weeks.

Riding a freshly resurfaced road requires a steering technique similar to that needed for soft, shallow sand – straight tracking and no sudden jerks on the handlebars. The legacy of the experience is an irregular residue of tar and fine gravel stuck to tyres and frames that's extremely hard to remove.

1780s walled garden is a feature, and views of Mt Cuilcach are outstanding. Marble Arch Caves (☎ 6634 8855) are very popular although they're perhaps a tad too developed. The 1¼-hour guided tour (bookings recommended) includes a short underground boat trip and reveals the cave system's water features, passages and chambers. Phone ahead during inclement weather; the caves are sometimes closed after heavy rain.

Drumshanbo
☎ 071
Primarily a fishing centre, Drumshanbo (Droim Seanbhó) sits at the southern tip of Lough Allen; nearby are Lustia, Drumkeelan and Acres Lakes and Lough Scur. Drumshanbo has a dozen pubs (for a town population of about 600), which does nothing to harm its friendly and cheerful ambience.

Information Drumshanbo post office is on the Market Square, in McKenna's Stationers; it includes a bureau de change. There are Bank of Ireland and National Irish Bank branches, without ATMs, on High St and the Market Square. For cycling needs head to Moran's Cycles (☎ 964 1043, Convent Ave, closed Wed & Sun).

Things to See & Do Audiovisual displays at **Sliabh an Iarainn Visitor Centre** (☎ 964 1522) cover local history and culture (585m Sliabh an Iarainn, or Slieve Anierin, is a mountain northeast of Drumshanbo). About 800m northeast of town, there's a **famine graveyard** tucked between fields and houses. There's not much to see in the stonewall-enclosed yard – a grassy space and some spreading ash trees – but its starkness lends it a certain poignancy.

Drumshanbo's annual **An Tóstal folk festival**, founded by local man Joe Mooney, is held in June, and features music, dance and song. An Tóstal has been running since 1953. If you're as serious about culture as good *craic*, most townspeople reckon the traditional music and dance is better during the Joe Mooney Summer School, in late July.

Places to Stay & Eat It's B&B or nothing in quiet Drumshanbo. *Mooney's* (☎ 964 1013, Carrick Rd) is central; singles/doubles €20/39. *Woodside* (☎ 964 1106, Carrick Rd) Singles/doubles €32/36. This place is a short walk from town. **Paddy Mac's** pub (☎ *964 1128, High St*) does town-centre B&B. About 1km (600 yards) west of town centre is **Fraoch Ban** (☎ *964 1260, Corlough*) Singles/doubles €34/49.

Eating choices are limited and seasonal. There's a late-closing **Spar** supermarket on Market Square. **Enda's Takeaway** (*High St*) does standard fried takeaway food. **Krefeld I** pub (☎ *964 1563, Church St*) has soup, bread, lasagne and salad, all for €5. Cheap, filling meals. Both **The Millrace** (☎ *964 1481, Church St*) and **Henry's Haven** pubs have restaurants open in summer. **Allendale Restaurant & B&B** (☎ *964 1125, Convent Ave*) offers meals and accommodation.

Day 3: Drumshanbo to Ballyshannon

4½–7 hours, 69.2km (43mi)

This fine day in the Leitrim and Fermanagh lakelands requires plenty of energy – especially if there's wet or windy weather. The ride spends a lot of time within sight of Loughs Allen, Macnean Upper and Melvin, and provides wider views of nearby prominent peaks, including Slieve Anierin, Carrignahasta (542m) and Thur Mountain. There are at least seven moderate climbs on the route, plus a number of longer, easier ascents and sundry steep pinches. Exposed sections – especially high points west of Blacklion – can be very trying on a windy day.

The two towns of Blacklion (An Blaic; 34.4km; 21.4mi), in the northwestern tip of County Cavan, and Belcoo (Béal Cú; 35km; 21.7mi), in Fermanagh, illustrate the random path of Irish partition better than most places. The North/South border follows the waterway that connects Lough Macnean Upper and Lower; only a bridge and the narrow flatlands surrounding the river separate the two towns. Imagine children needing to stockpile both euro and sterling coins in order to take advantage of the best 'local' price on sweets!

Superb views of Lough Macnean Upper and a series of climbs punctuate the route to Garrison (An Garastún; 55.3km; 34.3mi). Beyond, the ride runs along Lough Melvin, a popular fishing venue, and some great views are to the southwest, towards soaring Truskmore (647m), on the fringe of County Sligo. Just one gentle ascent breaks pedalling rhythm on the way to Ballyshannon.

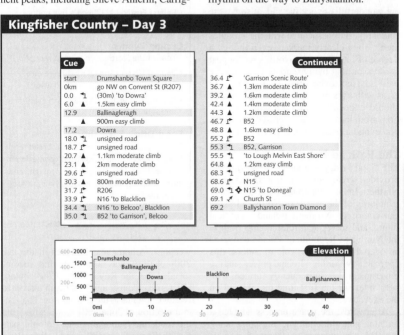

Kingfisher Country – Day 3

Cue		Continued	
start	Drumshanbo Town Square	36.4 ↱	'Garrison Scenic Route'
0km	go NW on Convent St (R207)	36.7 ▲	1.3km moderate climb
0.0 ↰	(30m) 'to Dowra'	39.2 ▲	1.6km moderate climb
6.0 ▲	1.5km easy climb	42.4 ▲	1.4km moderate climb
12.9	Ballinagleragh	44.3 ▲	1.2km moderate climb
▲	900m easy climb	46.7 ↱	B52
17.2	Dowra	48.8 ▲	1.6km easy climb
18.0 ↰	unsigned road	55.2 ↱	B52
18.7 ↱	unsigned road	55.3 ↰	B52, Garrison
20.7 ▲	1.1km moderate climb	55.5 ↰	'to Lough Melvin East Shore'
23.1 ▲	2km moderate climb	64.8 ▲	1.2km easy climb
29.6 ↱	unsigned road	68.3 ↰	unsigned road
30.3 ▲	800m moderate climb	68.6 ↱	N15
31.7 ↱	R206	69.0 ↰ ◆	N15 'to Donegal'
33.9 ↱	N16 'to Blacklion	69.1 ↗	Church St
34.4 ↰	N16 'to Belcoo', Blacklion	69.2	Ballyshannon Town Diamond
35.0 ↰	B52 'to Garrison', Belcoo		

Elevation

Drumshanbo, Ballinagleragh, Dowra, Blacklion, Ballyshannon

0mi 10 20 30 40
0km 20 40 60

NORTHERN ÉIRE

Northern Ireland

It can't be very long before Northern Ireland's allure as a cycling destination, indeed for any mode of tourism, becomes more widely known. Here are fine, fascinating cities; welcoming and often beautiful towns and villages; some spectacular scenery and a backdrop of fascinating history and impassioned politics.

For cyclists, there are three fully mapped National Cycle Network (NCN) routes (more are planned) and an increasing number of urban bike paths and signed on-road routes. Minor roads are quiet and often have better sealed surfaces than equivalent roads in the South. Best is the realisation that the North's tough reputation is unwarranted, at least for foreign visitors. The Northern Irish (Nationalist or Unionist, Catholic or Protestant) are almost universally friendly and helpful.

HISTORY
The North's many historical sites cover evidence of human occupation and endeavour from Stone Age times to the present. Many are wonderfully evocative and, at some, the absence of crowds is a revelation. Understandably, sites associated with the Troubles aren't often clearly marked, even though a degree of interest in the North's recent past is a reason that many tourists visit. You're well advised to be sensitive if you go to areas with a history of sectarian tension, and should expect some no-nonsense suggestions from locals if your interest or questions go beyond a reasonable, objective level.

The Path to Peace
The Good Friday Agreement of April 1998 provided great hope for lasting peace in Northern Ireland. Its central tenet is that only a majority of the people of Northern Ireland can determine Northern Ireland's political future, and subsequent referendums both in the North and Republic of Ireland delivered an overwhelming 'yes' vote to endorse this approach. A Northern Ireland power-sharing government was subsequently formed, with both sides for the first time represented on the executive.

Afterwards, the peace process adopted a lurching gait, the main sticking point being the IRA's reluctance to decommission its

In Brief

Highlights
- The feisty cities of **Belfast** and **Derry**
- Historic **Armagh**
- The beautiful **Antrim Coast** and **glens**, including the **Giant's Causeway**
- The mysterious **Mourne Mountains**

Terrain
Predominantly rolling country with uplands generally closer to the coasts (the rounded Sperrin Mountains, in the northwest interior, are the exception); spectacular coastlines to the north, northeast and southeast; flatlands rare, usually river valleys.

Special Events
- **Belfast Music Festival** (Mar)
- **Orangemen's Day** (High point of the Protestant marching season; 12 July)
- **Hallowe'en Carnival** (Oct) Derry
- **Belfast Festival at Queen's** (Big annual arts festival; Nov)

Cycling Events
- **Tour of the North** (Annual road race; Apr)
- **Tour of Ulster** (Annual road stage race; May)
- **Festival of Cycling** (Displays and events throughout the North; June)

Food/Drink Specialities
Bakery goods, especially **soda bread** and **fadge** (potato bread); **seafood**; **prime lamb** and **beef**; **apples** and **cider** in Armagh; and **dulse** (edible seaweed), especially on the Ards Peninsula.

weapons. Among major moves in the late 20th century was a review that recommended that the Royal Ulster Constabulary (RUC) change its name and begin a drive to recruit Catholics to the police force. The general election of June 2001 saw a shift from the moderate Nationalist and Unionist parties, theSocial Democratic and Labour Party

(SDLP) and Ulster Unionist Party (UUP), towards the more extreme views of Sinn Fein and Ian Paisley's Democratic Unionist Party (DUP). The summer of 2001 brought unsettling developments, including a flare-up of sectarian violence in Belfast's Ardoyne area. The power-sharing executive teetered as Chief Minister David Trimble, a moderate Unionist, threatened to resign on several occasions if the IRA did not move forward with decommissioning.

In October 2001, the IRA began destroying weapons. By year's end Trimble remained in charge of the power-sharing Northern Ireland government and the peace process, although battered, appeared to be progressing. A demonstration of the process's adaptation to change came when

Calling Northern Ireland

If calling Northern Ireland from within the North, you only have to dial the eight-digit number supplied in this chapter.

If calling Northern Ireland from outside the province, you have to use the area code of ☎ 028, followed by the eight-digit number.

However, if calling Northern Ireland from the Republic, there is a cheaper option; you can use the special area code of ☎ 048, followed by the eight-digit number.

Britain's Northern Ireland secretary John Reid gave paramilitary groups an extra five years to get rid of weapons.

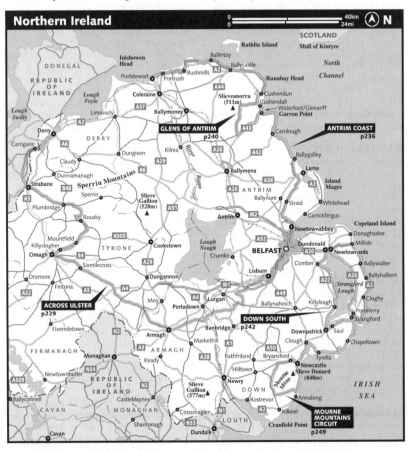

In April 2002, the IRA announced that it had put more weapons out of use. In an extraordinary July – the height of the Loyalist marching season – the IRA was praised by a senior Belfast police officer for quelling the threat of serious violence during Loyalist parades. Later in July, the IRA apologised to the families of 'noncombatants' killed during the Troubles. Overall, the peace process continued to wobble, its biggest problem being the difficulty that Loyalists and Nationalists had trusting each other. Sectarian riots continued through the year and more British military forces withdrew. In October, the power-sharing government was suspended.

In March 2003, British Prime Minister Tony Blair and Irish Taoiseach Bertie Ahern announced that the Assembly elections would take place in late May. After talks aimed at restarting the stalled peace process, the two put forward a document which detailed five key areas of discussion: demilitarisation; policing and justice issues; human rights and equality issues; the return of fugitive terrorists; and the creation of a body to oversee 'acts of completion' (such as the winding up of paramilitaries). Hopes that the peace process would get back on track were high, but many sticking points remained.

NATURAL HISTORY

There's a surprising variety of terrain to enliven cycling, and the North's compactness lends a pleasing sense of scale and achievement to human-powered travel. Upland waypoints such as the Mourne and Sperrin Mountains may, in clear weather, be visible for several hours, if not days, before a route reaches or passes them. Generally there are only small pockets of both flat terrain – the largest of these surrounds the River Bann – and genuine uplands. Much of the remainder is rolling drumlin country (which makes for tiring riding) dominated by green fields and hedgerows.

Expect wildlife and birdlife similar to that encountered in Northern Éire. Colonies of grey seals add great interest to rides around Strangford Lough, in County Down, while the coasts and offshore islands offer the greatest diversity of birds.

CLIMATE

Weather systems moving across from the Atlantic have the greatest influence on the North's weather. The Donegal high country extracts some of the moisture from rain-bearing clouds, but does little to alter the intensity of raking winds, especially cold air coming from the northwest. A midsummer day can be surprisingly warm and, particularly near the coast, free of the haze that tends to hang over the countryside. Weathercheck's telephone weather reports for the North (☎ 09001 333 111 104) cost £0.60 per minute. Met Éireann's Northern Ireland line (☎ 0891 505 327) is marginally cheaper.

INFORMATION
Maps

All rides in this chapter are covered by OSNI's 1:250,000 Holiday map *Ireland North*. About 18 OSI 1:50,000 Discovery maps cover the region.

Information Sources

The Belfast Welcome Centre (☎ 9024 6609, ⓔ belfastwelcomecentre@nitic.net, 47 Donegall Place, open Mon-Sat year-round & Sun afternoons June-Sept), is the main contact point for intending visitors to Northern Ireland. It can supply information on accommodation – including the invaluable booklet *Walkers & Cyclists Accommodation Guide to Northern Ireland* – cycling routes, maps and attractions. Sustrans Northern Ireland (☎ 028-9043 4569, ⓦ www.nationalcyclenetwork.org.uk) lobbies for the use of sustainable transport and oversees the creation of NCN touring and urban routes.

GATEWAY CITIES
Belfast

Northern Ireland's capital is spread at the base of Belfast Lough with steep hills to the west. It's an unexpectedly attractive setting and while parts of Belfast (Beal Feirste) are grim, grey and post-industrial, by and large it's fairly easy on the eye, constantly improving and endlessly fascinating. Recent events have shown that it may take years, possibly generations, for some Belfast people to get past the Troubles, but the overwhelming feeling one gets when visiting the city is of a desire for peace and normality.

Information The Belfast Welcome Centre (see Information Sources) has the largest selection of general information about the city; it also takes accommodation reservations and

Wild, mountainous and off the tourist trail, Donegal's Inishowen Peninsula is unforgettable

WB Yeats, Sligo's favourite son

Political mural in Bogside, Derry

Erosion-scarred Benbulben, a County Sligo landmark

RICHARD CUMMINS

Giant's Causeway (Antrim Coast ride)

IAN CONNELLAN

Hilly riding near Spelga Dam

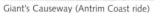

OLD BUSHMILLS WHISKEY

Famous over 300 Years.

RICHARD CUMMINS

A famous local drop, Bushmills

DOUG McKINLAY

A slap-up meal in Belfast

GARETH McCORMACK

Newcastle is framed by the celebrated Mourne Mountains

Mapping Ireland

The Ordnance Survey of Ireland (1824–46) was the first ever large-scale mapping of an entire country. A House of Commons committee recommended the survey to promote uniform land valuations for taxation purposes.

The flatlands east of Lough Foyle were chosen as the site for the critically important base line, which would determine the scale of the triangulation. To measure the line as accurately as possible, the surveyors developed an iron-and-brass compensation bar, about 10ft (3m) long, that was unaffected by temperature changes. It took most of two summers (1827–8) to complete the base-line measurement, which was 41,640.8873ft (about 8mi; 13km). When OSNI surveyors remeasured the base in 1960 using electronic equipment they recorded a difference of about 1 inch (25mm).

Three widely spaced base towers mark the base-line site today. Two of them, at Ballymulholland and Mineary, are on private land. The south base tower is at the edge of a playing field near the Drummond Hotel in Ballykelly, about 13.7mi (22km) from Derry.

has a bureau de change. There are bureaus de change in both the GPO (cnr Royal Ave & Castle Place) in the city centre, and Shaftesbury Square post office, just south and closest to the bulk of our accommodation and restaurant suggestions. ATMs and grocery and convenience stores are common around the city centre and throughout suburban Belfast. Life Cycles (☎ 9043 9959; 35 Smithfield Markets, Winetavern St) is the bike shop nearest the centre.

Things to See & Do With Belfast City Council's free *Historic Belfast* walking guide you can explore the city centre at leisure – it's a fine way to get your bearings. The city's centrepiece, **Belfast City Hall** (☎ 9027 0456, Donegall Square) was completed in 1906. Various statues and memorials dot its extensive grounds and the interior features an Italian marble dome and grand staircase. Facing City Hall, the **Linen Hall Library** (☎ 9032 1707, Donegall Square North) is a must-visit site for anyone interested in Irish politics and culture. Nearby on Great Victoria St, stop for the obligatory

pint (if you can wade through the tourists at the bar) at the ornate **Crown Liquor Saloon** (☎ 9024 9476) and visit or take in a performance at the **Grand Opera House** (☎ 9024 1919). The Opera House first opened in the late 19th century, survived a couple of terrorist bombs in the 1990s and today presents a lively and varied programme of music, theatre, ballet and opera year-round.

The district with the city's toughest factional reputation, West Belfast, is an easy stroll from the city centre. A journey along its arteries, Nationalist Falls Rd and Loyalist Shankill Rd, is an essential Belfast experience; many people choose to take a Black Taxi tour. If you walk or cycle you'll get a closer look at such things as political murals and the Peace Line; it's rewarding being closer to the street atmosphere.

Just south of the city centre, the **Ulster Museum** (☎ 9038 3000) fronts Stranmillis Rd in the **Botanic Gardens**. A small section of the museum's 'Made in Belfast' exhibition is devoted to cycling; it includes a battered old bike once owned by JB Dunlop, the Belfast-based, Scottish-born doctor who in 1888 made the first practical pneumatic tyre, see the boxed text 'The Wind Beneath our Wheels, (p14). Most Botanic Gardens visitors take in the striking 1852 **Palm House**, but the grounds are pretty enough – some of the earliest plantings here date from 1827.

About 3mi (5km) north near Newtownabbey, **Cave Hill Country Park** (☎ 9077 6925) combines prehistoric sites, superb grounds, fine views, a zoo and a castle – it would rate highly among Belfast's most versatile attractions. If you visit in clear weather, consider walking the trail up to Cave Hill's 1207ft (368m) summit. Views extend east over Belfast Lough and south as far as the Mourne Mountains. Belfast's beautiful, peaceful parklands are perhaps its biggest surprise. The first stretch of the Across Ulster ride (p229) follows the **River Lagan Towpath** through Lagan Valley Regional Park and Belvoir Park Forest, and a nicer stretch of traffic-free riding is hard to imagine. Even if you're not planning to do the Across Ulster ride, take a morning to do the return ride to Lisburn on the Lagan towpath.

About 7mi (11km) east of central Belfast, near Holywood, the **Ulster Folk & Transport Museum** (☎ 9042 8428) deserves a full day's attention. Here you'll find cottages, churches and businesses of various types – re-created into a folk village. Farm animals and human extras add an authentic feel, and various traditional crafts and activities are demonstrated (during summer). The transport collection is surprisingly arresting; it includes some bicycles, although the exhibition on the Belfast-built *Titanic* seems to draw most attention.

Places to Stay There's literally one tent site about 5mi (8km) north of Belfast at *Jordanstown Lough Shore Park (☎ 9034 0000, Shore Rd, Newtownabbey)* Tent site £7. There's a maximum stay of two nights. The next-closest camping ground is about 19mi (30km) east near Millisle, at *Ballywhiskin Caravan Park (☎ 9186 2262, 216 Ballywalter Rd)* Tent sites £8.

There's accommodation spread around Belfast, but we've opted for a selection that includes several choices in the Shaftesbury Square/Queen's University area, the so-called Golden Mile, which also has many places to eat. A couple of B&B choices are slightly further out, but all are part of the NITB's Cyclists Welcome scheme. *Belfast International Youth Hostel (☎ 9032 4733, 22 Donegall Rd)* Dorm beds/twins/singles £8/12/16. Affiliated with HINI; big and busy, just off Shaftesbury Square, near Sandy Row; breakfast £3. *Ark Hostel (☎ 9032 9626, 18 University St)* Dorms/twins/singles £9/16/20. Further south, smaller and quieter.

For B&B, try *Tara Lodge (☎ 9059 0900, ⓔ info@taralodge.com, 36 Cromwell Rd)*. Weekday singles/doubles £60/68, weekend £43/60.

About 2mi (3km) south of the city centre, try *Ravenhill House (☎ 9020 7444, ⓔ info@ ravenhillguesthouse.com, 690 Ravenhill Rd)*. Singles/doubles £40/60. Lovely restored Victorian house. Nearby is *Roseleigh House (☎ 9064 4414, ⓔ roseleigh house@ukonline.co.uk, 19 Rosetta Park)* Singles/doubles £38/55.

There are plenty of hotel beds around town and most are more affordable on weekends. *Benedicts (☎ 9059 1999, 7-21 Bradbury Place)* Weekday singles/doubles £60/70, weekend £45/55. Lively location, right near Shaftesbury Square.

Madison's Hotel (☎ 9033 0040, 59-63 Botanic Ave) Weekday singles/doubles £70/ 80, weekend £50/65.

Places to Eat The bulk of our suggestions are clustered in the Golden Mile, but there's plenty to munch on in the city. Around the centre, try the historic pub *Morning Star (17-19 Pottinger's Entry)* Bar snacks from £3, mains to £14. *Cafe Society (3 Donegall Square East)* Bistro mains £4-6, restaurant mains £10-21. Bistro and upstairs restaurant. *Clements (37-39 Rosemary St)* is nice and relaxing for coffee (cappuccinos £2).

In the Golden Mile, for rice, noodles and pasta try *Cayenne (7 Lesley House, Shaftesbury Square)* Mains £9-14. Innovative food and cool atmosphere. *Benedicts* (see Places to Stay) has £6 bar snacks – some a little more inventive than the usual. There's tasty Mexican food at *La Salsa (23 University Rd)* Mains £10-13. *Cafe Vincents (78-80 Botanic Ave)* Mains £9-12. Interesting fare, but limited vegetarian options. For better vegie choices try *Laziz (cnr Botanic Ave & University St)* Mains £9-15. *Gigolo's (☎ 9024 6900, 23 Donegall Pass)* has filling pasta mains for £8 to £11, while pasta mains at *Madison's Hotel* (see Places to Stay) are £7 to £9. *Imperial City (96 Botanic Ave)* Mains from £8. Chinese, good for noodles. *The Other Place (79 Botanic Ave)* is good for coffee and has a student atmosphere. There's also a branch of *Clements (Botanic Ave)*. Grab rolls and pastry treats at *John's Breads and Cakes (Botanic Ave)*.

Getting There & Away For information about international services see Getting There & Away in the Travel Facts chapter (p263). For an overview of all transport services in Northern Ireland have a look at ⓦ www.translink.co.uk.

Air Belfast's International and City airports receive direct flights from throughout Britain and some European cities. Ireland's small size and good rail and bus network make domestic flights all but unnecessary. If you've been touring in the southwest, you may find the Aer Lingus flight from Shannon to Belfast International worthwhile.

Belfast International (☎ 9448 4848) is about 18mi (30km) northwest of city centre via the A26 and A52; the ride includes some solid climbing. It's easier to catch a bus to the Europa Bus Centre (£5, bikes £3), or ride the 5.6mi (9km) north to Antrim, and jump on a Belfast train (£3, bikes £1).

Belfast City Airport (☎ 9045 7745) is about 3.7mi (6km) northeast of the centre. It's an easy ride in via Station, Holywood and Newtownards Rds.

Bus Ulsterbus (☎ 9066 6630) runs services to Belfast from all major, and most minor, towns in Northern Ireland and (in conjunction with Bus Éireann) an express service to Dublin Airport and Dublin (£11/€14, three hours, six to seven daily). Most services arrive at/depart from the Europa Bus Centre on Glengall St. For fare and timetable information for services within Northern Ireland phone ☎ 9033 3000.

Train Belfast has Northern Ireland Railways (NIR; ☎ 9033 3000) links north to Derry/Londonderry via Ballymena and Coleraine, northeast to Larne, east to Bangor and south to Dublin via Newry. Services to all major towns are frequent Monday to Saturday and reduced on Sunday. The Belfast to Dublin Enterprise (£20/€27, two hours, eight per day Monday to Saturday, five on Sunday) is an express service.

Bicycle Belfast is due north of Dublin, 104mi (167km) via main roads, or 255.6mi (411.6km) following (in reverse) the Around Ireland route. Belfast is the starting point for the Across Ulster (p229) and Down South (p242) rides and the finishing point for the Antrim Coast ride (p236).

Derry/Londonderry

This small city (population 95,370) split by the River Foyle is growing in popularity for visitors, and with good reason. Arranged within and around historic city walls, Derry (Doire) is a vibrant and welcoming place. There are fine museums, music, pubs and food, and there's good cycle access via quiet roads and bike paths and a regular train service. Here and there is evidence of Derry's role in the Troubles – political murals in the Nationalist Bogside and Loyalist Waterside the most obvious. But most noticeable is the relaxed friendliness of Derry people – it's a place that's easy to like.

Civil rights marches in Derry in 1968 were a turning point in the rise of the Troubles. Fierce rioting in 1969 – the 'Battle of the Bogside' – led to the first street deployment of British troops, who were welcomed at first. In January 1972, British paratroopers shot and killed 13 Catholic marchers on Bloody Sunday; fresh hearings into the incident begun in 1998 were continuing at the time of writing.

Information The Derry Visitor Centre (☎ 7126 7284, e info@derryvisitor.com, 44 Foyle St, open Mon-Fri year-round, Sat mid-Mar–Oct & Sun July-Sept) has an accommodation booking service, bureau de change and a fine range of maps, guides and giveaway information. There are banks with ATMs at the Waterloo Place end of Strand Rd and in Shipquay St. Bees Cycles (☎ 7137 2155, 4 Waterloo St) is closest to the city centre, just outside the Butcher Gate. Go to Clooney Cycles (☎ 7131 3470, 28 Bonds St) if you're on the Waterside.

Things to See & Do A walking tour of this compact city is essential both for getting your bearings and for interest; tours leave the Visitor Centre Monday to Friday, twice daily in mid-summer and once daily the rest of the year. Grab the free *Derry/Londonderry Visitor Attractions* map and it's easy to get around on your own. A circuit of the **city walls** is free and easy. Interpretive signs along the way give snippets of Derry history, and several other attractions are visible from the various bastions and gates. Of these, the **Tower Museum** (☎ 7137 2411, Union Hall Place, open year-round, closed Sun & Mon Sept-June) represents the fastest way to learn about the city if you're short of time. Exhibits trace Derry's development from prehistoric times and reveal much of life and politics here from the time of St Colmcille onwards. Just over the walls from the museum, the 1890 neo-Gothic **Guildhall** (☎ 7137 7335, open Mon-Fri) was once a symbol of discrimination against Catholics; the IRA bombed it twice in 1972. Its most famous recent incarnation is as the site of the Bloody Sunday Inquiry hearings, which have drawn large crowds and become something of an attraction in their own right. There are some fine stained-glass windows in the building.

Just inside the southernmost corner of the walls is **St Columb's Cathedral** (☎ 7126 7313), completed in 1633 and a survivor of the 1688 siege. It's an austere and intriguing church, and its **Chapter House Museum** contains some interesting exhibits. From the Royal Bastion on the walls, there's a great view to the west of **Free Derry Corner** and the Bogside; to get there, slip out of the city at Butcher's Gate and go left down Fahan St. Around the intersection of Fahan and Rossville streets and Lecky Rd, you'll see the famous 'You Are Now Entering Free Derry' monument (painted on the old end-wall of a row of houses). Nearby are several striking murals, a monument to the H-block prisoners who died on hunger strike in the early 1980s and, tucked off Rossville St a short distance north, a monument to those killed in the Bloody Sunday incident.

Walk or ride across the 1933 **Craigavon Bridge** to the Waterside to get a taste of Protestant Londonderry; the views of hardline Loyalists are summed up in a series of murals around Bonds St. Just up the hill on Glendermott Rd, visit the **Workhouse Museum** (☎ 7131 8328) to see displays that reveal Derry's role in protecting Atlantic convoys during WWII. Upstairs are displays on the Great Famine.

South of the Craigavon Bridge on the city side, the **Foyle Valley Cycle Route** extends for 4mi (6.5km) along the riverfront, following the trackbed of the disused Great Northern Railway. It's a pleasant, flat ride and an extra mile or so on undulating roads past its end will get you to the town of Carrigans in the Republic.

Places to Stay There's no camping close to Derry – the nearest site is at Benone, west of Portstewart. HINI *Derry City Youth Hostel* (☎ 7128 4100, 4-6 Magazine St) Dorm beds/doubles £8/30. Inside the city walls near Butcher's Gate. *Derry City Independent Hostel* (☎ 7137 79898, 4 Asylum Rd) Dorm beds £7, private rooms per person £10. Smaller, almost a mile north of the centre; price includes breakfast and Internet use.

For central B&B, it's hard to resist the beautifully restored Victorian *Saddler's House* (☎ 7126 9691, 36 Great James St) Standard singles/doubles £20/40, with ensuite £25/45. Friendly and knowledgeable owners. *Merchant's House* (☎ 7126 9691, 16 Queen St,) Singles/doubles from £20/40. The same owners, warmth, style and big breakfasts as at Saddler's. South of the walled city is *Happy Days* (☎ 7128 7128, 245 Lone Moor Rd) Singles/doubles £25/40.

Cycling specialists and the Derry Raleigh Rent-a-Bike operators. There are a number of B&Bs north of the centre, some of them cheaper. Try *Country House* (☎ 7135 2932, 153 Culmore Rd) Singles/doubles £15/30. Or *Aarona* (☎ 7135 8684, 20 Thornhill Park, Culmore Rd) Singles/doubles £18/34.

Trinity Hotel (☎ 7127 1271, 22-24 Strand Rd) Singles/doubles £60/80. Closest to city centre and includes bistro. *Quality Hotel Da Vinci's* (☎ 7127 9111, 15 Culmore Rd) Doubles £55. Good value, about 2mi north of the centre.

Places to Eat Both centrally located *Claudes* (Shipquay St) and *The Sandwich Co.* (The Diamond) are good spots for sandwiches (£2 to £3) and coffee. There's a big *Tesco* supermarket in the Quayside shopping centre, facing Strand Rd. *The Bakers Oven* (Ferryquay St) and *Doherty's* (Foyle St) are fine for bread and cakes.

There's plenty of pubs and pub food. *Henry Joy McCrackens* (☎ 7136 0177, 10A Magazine St) is pleasant and friendly. *JD Wetherspoon Freehouse* (The Diamond) Mains under £5. Go to the *Gweedore Bar* or *Dungloe Bar*, both on Waterloo St, for a mixture of trad and modern music.

For pasta, try *Piemonte* (☎ 7136 4036, 2 Clarendon St) Mains from £7. Further east on Clarendon St, popular *Danano* (☎ 7126 6646) also does pizza and pasta. For rice and noodles try *Mandarin Palace* (☎ 7137 3656, Lower Clarendon St) Starters £3-4, mains £6-11. Popular, river views and atmosphere.

O'Brien's American Bar & Restaurant (☎ 7136 1527, 59 Strand Rd) Starters from under £3, mains £6-8. Good value for filling food. Closer to the centre, *Fitzroy's Cafe/Restaurant* (☎ 7126 6211, 2-4 Bridge St) Coffee from £1.50, mains £7-12. Busy and with decent food, but somewhat cold and chrome in atmosphere. *Indigo* (☎ 7127 1011, 27 Shipquay St) Mains mostly above £8. Inside city walls, pleasant and smart.

Getting There & Away Derry offers a variety of transport options.

Air City of Derry Airport (☎ 7181 0784) is just off the A2 about 8mi (13km) northeast of the centre, near Eglinton; it's an easy ride in to Derry. There are regular flights to/from London Stansted, Glasgow, Manchester and

Dublin. For more information about air travel to Northern Ireland see the Getting There & Away section of the Travel Facts chapter (p263).

Bus The main bus terminal is on Foyle St south of the Guildhall. From Derry, Ulsterbus (fare and timetable information ☎ 9033 3000) runs the Maiden City Flyer to Belfast (£8, 1¾ hours, 19 daily Monday to Friday, 14 on Saturday, six on Sunday) and direct or connecting services to most major towns in the North. Bus Éireann (☎ 01-836 6111) services reach Derry from nearby towns in Donegal and further afield, including Dublin (€14, 4¼ hours, five daily).

Train From Derry's Waterside Station (☎ 7134 2228, timetable information ☎ 9033 3000), trains run regularly to Belfast via Coleraine and Ballymena (£8, two hours, nine daily Monday to Friday, seven on Saturday, five on Sunday).

Bicycle Derry is northwest of Belfast, 73mi (117km) via most direct route, or 139.1mi (224.1km) following the Across Ulster ride (p229). Derry is the final stop on the Donegal to Derry ride (p199) and the start/finish point for the Inishowen Circuit ride (p211).

Across Ulster

Duration	3 days
Distance	139.1mi (224.1km)
Difficulty	moderate
Start	Belfast
End	Derry

Drawing inspiration (and some directions) from the NCN Belfast to Ballyshannon and Ballyshannon to Ballycastle routes, this ride winds through the towns, villages and rolling green hills of counties Down, Armagh, and Tyrone. It takes in a fair amount of territory that's off the tourist trail and provides a window to life in rural Northern Ireland.

HISTORY

There's a wealth of historical sites and several fine museums in the region, which together make it highly advisable to plan longer stays in both Armagh and Omagh.

Key prehistoric sites include the Navan Fort (see Things to See & Do in Armagh, p230), which is Northern Ireland's most important archaeological site. In County Tyrone especially, there are many historical sites dedicated to the Ulster roots of Americans, including former presidents Ulysses S Grant and Woodrow Wilson. Reminders of recent history are subtle, but constant; small communities tend to be either strongly Catholic or Protestant, and it's quite engrossing piecing together settlement patterns as the route unfolds.

NATURAL HISTORY

Like much of Ulster, Armagh and Tyrone are dominated by farmlands, but pockets of woodland and several forest parks provide some respite. The best known of these is Gortin Glen Forest Park, north of Omagh.

Marching Season

On 12 July, members of the Loyal Orange Order across Northern Ireland march to commemorate the 1690 victory of Protestant King William III of Orange over Catholic King James II. In the days leading up to the 'twalfth', the ambient mood in the North alters. It's a fascinating, if somewhat disquieting, time – underlaid by the Western world's rawest grass-roots politics.

In staunchly Loyalist towns the marches are colourful and noisy affairs (huge Lambeg drums 'blatter' the day's distinctive rhythm), and usually pass off without trouble. Union Jacks, Red Hands of Ulster and other flags (many of the various Protestant paramilitaries) flutter from flagpoles and streetlamps; enthusiastic crowds line marching routes. In many Nationalist areas the marches tend to be avoided or ignored. In some, usually those where a marching route intersects a Nationalist neighbourhood, there might be resistance to the marchers, and violence sometimes erupts.

It's often suggested that tourists avoid Northern Ireland for the days either side of 12 July, but it's a shame to miss a fascinating aspect of Ulster culture. If you're apprehensive, consider discussing your proposed route with staff at a TIC. They can steer you towards towns with trouble-free marches, and away from places where things might get hectic.

The most significant uplands passed on the route are the Sperrin Mountains, a rounded, bog-covered range of schist and quartzite.

PLANNING
When to Ride
Late May and June are probably best. It can get quite warm in mid-summer when hazy skies tend to reduce the outlook.

Maps
The ride is covered by the OSNI 1:250,000 Holiday map *Ireland North*. The NCN 1:100,000 *Belfast–Ballyshannon* and *Bally-shannon–Ballycastle* maps provide much extra detail for Days 1 and 3.

What to Bring
Insect repellent keeps midges at bay.

ACCESS TOWN
Belfast
See Belfast (p224).

THE RIDE
Day 1: Belfast to Armagh
4½–8 hours, 50.8mi (81.8km)
After a dream start on the River Lagan tow-path, this day turns into something of a mini-epic with a full bag of challenges – undulating terrain, some sections in traffic and tricky navigation.

From the Lagan Lookout in Belfast, there's little to do for about 13.1mi (21km) except follow the NCN signs to Lisburn (Lios na gCearrbhach). The towpath (starting at 3.3mi; 5.3km) is a flat, shady delight, passing through lovely Lagan Valley Regional Park and Belvoir Park Forest. In Lisburn (13.2mi; 21.2km), the **Irish Linen Centre and Lisburn Museum** (☎ 9266 3377) has displays explaining the linen production process and local history. It's worth a look given the importance of linen in Ulster history.

Just outside Lisburn, a collapsed bridge pushes the route off the Lagan towpath, and briefly off the marked NCN trail (14.5mi; 23.3km) and through a housing estate to the A3. The route rejoins NCN markers at 17.4mi (28km) and in the next few miles passes the walls of the infamous Long Kesh (Maze) prison – where the 1981 Republican hunger strikers died – and then crosses Down Royal Racecourse (detours will be in place on race days, which aren't frequent).

Throughout the day's second half the route is relentlessly up and down. The most noticeable feature of the landscape is the lush and orderly appearance of farmlands – this neatness is a feature of most Ulster farmland, and a contrast to the generally more relaxed feel of farms in the South. It's worth a cycle around the heritage town of **Richhill** (45.7mi; 73.6km). The town name is an abbreviation of Richardson's Hill – the name bestowed on it in the 17th century by Major Edward Richardson, High Sheriff and an MP for County Armagh. Many of the small town's fine buildings date from the 18th century, thanks in part to Richhill's prosperous linen market. There's also a bike shop.

Armagh
Armagh (Ard Mhacha) is thought to be one of Ireland's oldest settlements; it has evolved and survived through the coming of Christianity, Viking raids, clan wars and, in recent years, some of the excesses of the Troubles. Tradition has Armagh as the centre of St Patrick's Christian mission; certainly there has been a church on the hilltop west of the city centre since the mid-5th century. Church of Ireland primate, Richard Robinson (appointed 1765), and architects Thomas Cooley and Francis Johnston are largely responsible for Armagh's distinctive, mostly Georgian, appearance. This is a fine, compact city with attractions that merit more than an overnight stay.

Information The Armagh TIC (☎ 3752 1800, e armagh@nitic.net, 40 English St, open daily) is housed in the 1851 Belfast Banking Co building and is part of the Saint Patrick's Trian complex. Banks, with ATMs, are on Thomas St, English St and Market Square. For cycling needs head to Brown's Bikes (☎ 3752 2782, 21a Scotch St).

Things to See & Do There's a lot on offer in Armagh. If you're short of time, **Saint Patrick's Trian heritage centre** (☎ 3752 1801, English St) will provide the best overview of Armagh's long history and its associations with Irish Christianity. 'The least of all the faithful' – the display on St Patrick – is particularly interesting. The Church of Ireland **St Patrick's Cathedral** (☎ 3752 3142, Cathedral Close) reinforces the city's Christian connections. St Patrick

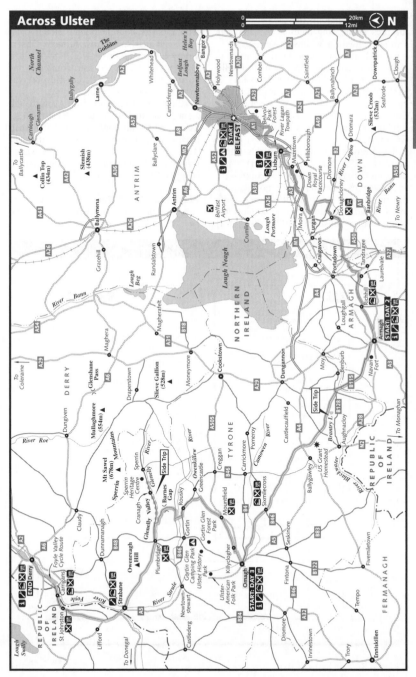

Across Ulster

0 — 20km
0 — 12mi

N

was the congregation's first abbot (444–67); the present building dates from 1268, but various battles (or whims) have seen it remodelled several times through the centuries. Just across the road, **Armagh Public Library** (☎ 3752 3142, open Mon-Fri) is Richard Robinson's greatest legacy to the city. Its hub is Robinson's personal collection of 17th- and 18th-century books; bibliophiles should set aside an entire day to wallow here.

The Roman Catholic **St Patrick's Cathedral** (☎ 3752 2802, Cathedral Rd) is the more imposing of Armagh's cathedrals – its soaring spires are visible from most parts of the city. It was mostly built between 1840 and 1873 and contains striking mosaics. **Armagh County Museum** (☎ 3752 3070, The Mall East) is a fine regional depository filled with artefacts, household items clothing and stuffed animal specimens. **Armagh Observatory & Planetarium** (☎ 3752 3689, College Hill) will interest the astronomically inclined, although the 200-year-old observatory isn't open to the public.

About 2mi (3km) west of Armagh, the ancient **Navan Fort** (Emain Macha) and its associated **Navan Centre** (☎ 3752 5550) can occupy several hours. The hilltop settlement dates back to about 5500 BC. The Navan Centre has displays that explain the archaeology and mythology of the site.

Places to Stay & Eat There's nowhere to camp in the city; *Gosford Forest Park (☎ 3755 1277, 54 Gosford Forest Park),*

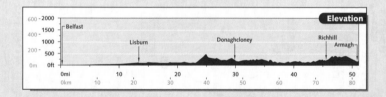

about 7mi (11.3km) southeast near Markethill, has two-person tent sites for £10. *Armagh City Youth Hostel (☎ 3751 1800, 39 Abbey St)* Dorms/twin rooms per person £11/12. Well appointed, pleasant and handy to attractions.

There are three Cyclists Welcome scheme B&Bs. *Fairylands Country House (☎ 3751 0315, [e] info@fairylands.net, 25 Navan Fort Rd)* Singles/doubles £25/40. About 1mi (1.6km) west of city centre. *Hillview Lodge (☎ 3752 2000, 33 Newtownhamilton Rd)* Doubles from £50. About 1mi (1.6km) south of city centre. *Ni Eoghain Lodge (☎ 3752 5633, 32 Ennislare Rd)* Singles/doubles £21/36. Quiet setting about 2.5mi (4km) south of city centre.

De Averell Guest House (☎ 3751 1213, 47 Upper English St) Singles/doubles £30/54. Central and comfortable, dinner £15. *Charlemont Arms Hotel (☎ 3752 2028, 57-65 English St)* Singles/doubles/twins £35/60/62. Central, also has restaurant (see following).

There are several late-closing convenience stores and a big *Sainsbury's* supermarket between English St and The Mall West.

Hester's Place (12 Upper English St) does breakfasts (£2 scrambled eggs and toast) and filling lunches (pasta bake and chips £3). *The Basement Cafe (Market St)* has cappuccinos and £3 club sandwiches. *Cafe Papa (15 Thomas St)* has £1 cappuccinos and lattes, nice cakes and sandwiches. There's a fair range of takeaways, but not too many sit-down places for dinner. Try the *Charlemont Arms Hotel* restaurant (starters £3 to £5, mains £7 to £13) or the *Market Place Restaurant (Market St)* in the Armagh Theatre and Arts Centre. *Elichi Indian Takeaway (29 Lower English St)* Starters £2-4, mains £6-7. Open to midnight daily. Acceptable Indian, also pizzas (£4 to £8) and burgers. *Welcome Chinese Hot Food Bar (14 Lower English St)* has some vegetable dishes (all £4, served with boiled rice).

Day 2: Armagh to Omagh
3½–6 hours, 36.6mi (59km)

This is something of an unexpected gem: a wonderful day in rural Tyrone that delivers pleasant – and fairly easy – cycling and fine views. Climbs, when they occur, tend to be gradual (or moderate at worst).

The 8.5mi (13.7km) spent on the B115 out of Armagh is the day's busiest stretch for traffic. After a few twists and a gradual climb the route leads past a turn (10.8mi; 17.4km) to tucked-away **Brantry Lough**; it's a fine place for a morning side trip – serene enough to make you wish you'd brought your fishing gear. After some more turns and climbs the route passes the **U.S. Grant Homestead** (16.8mi; 27km). The Civil War general and 18th US President never lived here – he was born in Ohio in 1822 – but his maternal ancestors, the Simpsons, did. The site provides some insight into 18th-century life for an Ulster plantation settler.

But it's really the cycling that stars on this day, and arguably the best section begins after the route crosses the busy A4 (19mi; 30.6km). The road winds uphill through hedge-lined pastures before flattening and crossing wide boggy country.

Another great section comes after the route passes through the arresting village of Sixmilecross. For several miles the route follows part of the Marshall Country Trail, a 51mi (82.1km) driving tour that loops from Sixmilecross to Carrickmore, Omagh and Seskinore. The trail honours poet, writer and broadcaster WF Marshall (1888–1959), who was born in Sixmilecross and whose passion for the district inspired much of his work. Marshall wrote the lines: 'Oh High are the hills of Tyrone / But the one I know best has a charm of his own / Green Hill of O'Neill that my boyhood has known / My heart is with you in the heart of Tyrone'. Cycle this route on a clear day and you'll be closer to understanding what Marshall found so moving.

Omagh

Plumb at the confluence of the Camowen and Drumragh Rivers (thereafter the River Strule), Omagh (An Omaigh) is a lively and welcoming town with excellent services. It's the closest major town to some very worthy attractions, all of them within easy cycling distance. Omagh's place in many people's imaginations was sealed by the 1998 Omagh bombing, when 28 were killed and scores injured (one mortally) in the single worst atrocity of the Troubles; a memorial garden on Drumragh Ave commemorates the victims.

Information Omagh TIC (☎ 8224 7831, [e] omagh@nitic.net, 1 Market St, open

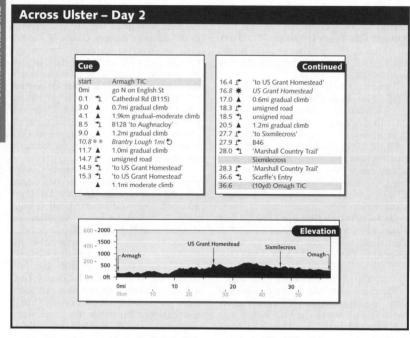

Mon-Sat Apr-Sept, weekdays only rest of the year) has an extensive range of information about the local area and County Tyrone and can assist with accommodation. Several banks have branches (all with ATMs) on High St or Market St. Allen's of Omagh (☎ 8225 1991, Market Arcade) bike shop is off Market St.

Things to See & Do North of Omagh, the **Ulster-American Folk Park** (☎ 8224 3292), 5mi (8km) via the A5 and nearby **Ulster History Park** (☎ 8164 8188), 6mi (10km) via the B48, could easily absorb a day.

The better of the two is probably the Folk Park, an open-air museum dedicated to emigration from Ulster to North America in the 18th and 19th centuries. Its exhibits include typical cottages and businesses, such as a forge, from the period. Costumed guides demonstrate various crafts and flesh out the story. Life-size exhibits at the History Park show the different kinds of settlements that have appeared in Ireland from the Stone Age to Plantation times.

Just east of the History Park, **Gortin Glen Forest Park** includes a 5mi (8km) road through the forest that's peaceful during quiet times and a bit mad with traffic on summer weekends.

A quieter route to the History Park and Gortin Glen Forest is part of the NCN's Belfast–Ballyshannon and Ballyshannon –Ballycastle routes. It's signposted out of Omagh; pick it up on the B48 just north of Drumragh Ave.

Places to Stay & Eat The nearest camping ground is 7mi (11.3km) north of Omagh at *Gortin Glen Caravan and Camping Park* (☎ 8164 8108, Lisnaharney Rd) Tent sites £5-9, depending on tent size. *Omagh Hostel* (☎ 8224 1973, 9a Waterworks Rd) Dorm beds £7. Pleasant rural situation, about 2.5mi (4km) northeast of town.

There's not a great number of B&Bs for a town this size. *Ardmore* (☎ 8224 3381, 12 Tamlaght Rd) Singles/doubles £17/34. Close to town centre; friendly and welcoming. *Four Winds* (☎ 8224 3554, 63 Dromore Rd) Singles/doubles £18/36, ensuite doubles £40. Slightly further out; pleasant house. *Clanabogan Country House* (☎ 8224 1171, 85 Clanabogan Rd) Singles/doubles £25/50.

About 3mi (4.8km) from town centre; lovely house and setting.

Silverbirch Hotel *(☎ 8224 2520, 5 Gortin Rd)* Singles £42-45, doubles £72-84. Two-star, on northern outskirts. If you're feeling indulgent give yourself a treat at ***Hawthorn House*** *(☎ 8225 2005, 72 Old Mountfield Rd)* Singles/doubles £40/60. Lovely place with award-winning restaurant (starters £4 to £7, mains £12 to £17).

There's a big ***Dunnes Stores*** supermarket near the library.

The Pink Elephant *(19 High St)* does £4 carvery lunches. ***Balti Palace*** *(8 Campsie Rd)* Starters £3-4, meat mains £6-7. Fair choice of vegetable dishes (starters £4, mains £5). ***Carlton Licensed Restaurant*** *(29-31 High St)* Starters £3-5, pasta £9-11, seafood mains £9-11. Open seven nights. Big and cheerful. Downstairs is the cheaper ***Carlton Pizzaria.*** Pasta £4, pizzas £6-7. ***La Gondola*** *(80 Market St)* Starters £2-7, meat mains £9-12, pasta £4-7. Authentic Italian – try the fresh tagliatelle. ***The Coach Inn*** *(1 Railway Terrace)* Starters £3-4, meat mains £8-9, vegetable curry £6, big steaks £12-14. Big serves and friendly staff in this pub/restaurant, a short walk from town centre. ***Riverfront Coffee House*** *(38 Market St)* is nice for hot beverages. ***Bakewell's Patisserie*** *(18 Campsie Rd)* Open 8am Mon-Sat.

Day 3: Omagh to Derry
4½–8 hours, 51.7mi (83.3km)

A meandering course to allow a visit to the Sperrin Mountains makes this a long day

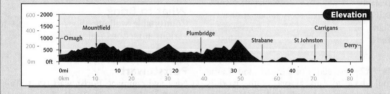

Across Ulster: Day 3

Cue				Continued
start	Omagh TIC	24.2		Plumbridge
0mi	go NW on Market St	24.7 ▲		0.6mi steep climb
0.4 ↘	A505	26.1 ▲		0.6mi moderate cimb
0.9 ↰	Knocknamoe Rd 'to Killyclogher'	27.8 ▲		0.4mi steep climb
1.5 ▲	0.7mi moderate climb	29.0 ▲		1.4mi moderate–steep climb
3.6 ▲	1.1mi gradual climb	34.2 ↱		B72 (unsigned)
5.2 ↰	unsigned road	34.7		Strabane
5.9 ↰	unsigned road	34.8 ↰		'to Lifford'
6.3	Mountfield	37.3 ▲		0.7mi gradual climb
▲	0.6mi moderate climb	40.6 ↑		at 'Yield' sign
6.6 ↑	at 'Yield' signs	42.6 ↱		R236 'to St Johnston'
8.7 ↑	at 'Yield' signs	42.9 ↰		'to St Johnston'
10.5 ↰	unsigned road	43.5 ↱		unsigned road
▲	0.9mi moderate climb	43.6 ↰		'to Newton C'ham', St Johnston
11.4 ↰	B46	44.1 ↱		unsigned road
14.0	Rousky	44.2 ↰		R236 'to Derry'
15.0 ↱	'to Barnes Gap'	45.5		Carrigans
16.0 ↱	'to Barnes Gap'	46.1 ↱		unsigned road 'NCN 92'
▲	2.7mi moderate climb	47.0 ↱		Foyle Valley Cycle Route
19.4 ↰	'to Plumbridge'	51.7		Derry TIC
21.7 ↰	'to Plumbridge'			

Elevation chart: Omagh, Mountfield, Plumbridge, Strabane, St Johnston, Carrigans, Derry with a few solid climbs. If the weather's kind it isn't too demanding; strong winds from the north can render the miles beyond of Strabane rather tiresome. Views throughout are outstanding.

It's a steady and manageable climb to Barnes Gap (18.7mi; 30.1km) and the reason for the effort is immediately apparent. A cool, pine-tree-lined descent follows, into the heart of the beautiful Glenelly Valley with (weather permitting) views of the gently rounded Sperrin Mountain peaks. A side trip will take you to the **Sperrin Heritage Centre** (☎ 8164 8142), near Cranagh (An Crannog), where displays reveal the Sperrin's natural and human background. Take a right turn at 19.4mi (31.2km), then first left and follow to a right onto the B47 to reach the centre.

The route between Plumbridge (Droichead an Phlum; 24.2mi; 39km) and Strabane (An Srath Ban; 34.7mi; 55.9km) is the day's toughest section. It's a tough climb to the radio masts on the ridge southwest of Owenreagh Hill (great views from here in good weather) but the reward is a descent of nearly 4mi (6.5km), all the way to Strabane.

From Strabane, the route mostly follows NCN Route 92 (Ballyshannon–Ballycastle) except for a short stretch on the N14 near Lifford in order to knock a few miles off the total. The day's final 4.7mi (7.6km) is spent on the new Foyle Valley Cycle Route, which follows the track-bed of the former Great Northern Railway – a flat and scenic introduction to the fascinating city of Derry.

Derry

See Derry (p227).

Antrim Coast

Duration	2 days
Distance	92mi (148.2km)
Difficulty	moderate–hard
Start	Portstewart
End	Belfast

The A2 between Portstewart and Larne would have to rank as one of the world's great scenic coastal roads. Its key attractions – particularly the Giant's Causeway – are among Northern Ireland's most popular tourist sites, but they're just part of the story.

Coastal Antrim includes beautiful beaches, welcoming towns and villages, cool woodland tracts and sparkling North Channel waters. Lock into a few days of good weather and this route will be the highlight of a Northern Ireland visit.

HISTORY

Surprisingly, this was one of the last regions in the North where the Irish language was spoken. The Antrim Glens, despite their proximity to Belfast (and some Scottish islands), were isolated until the coast road was hacked and blasted from seaside cliffs in the 1830s.

NATURAL HISTORY

Much of the Antrim Coast's natural beauty is built on a foundation of basalt. Lava flows about 60 million years ago are responsible for the remarkable formations at the Giant's Causeway. Basalts that form the Antrim Plateau were laid down in the same era; they've since been eroded to form the famous Nine Glens of Antrim.

PLANNING
When to Ride

Weekdays in late spring or early autumn are probably best. This is Northern Ireland's most popular region for tourists and roads, attractions and accommodation can be unbearably busy on mid-summer weekends and during holidays.

Maps

The ride is covered by the OSNI 1:250,000 Holiday map *Ireland North*. The NCN 1:100,000 *Ballyshannon–Ballycastle* map provides some useful detail for Day 1. Those planning more detailed investigations of the Glens would benefit from the OSI Discovery map Nos 4, 5 and 9.

What to Bring

Comfortable walking shoes – for visits to various attractions – are advisable.

ACCESS TOWN
Portstewart

Neat and compact, Portstewart (Port Stiobhaird) is, like nearby Portrush, a popular coastal retreat for Northerners. It tends to attract fewer families and children than Portrush though.

Information Portstewart TIC (☎ 7083 2712, The Crescent, open Mon-Sat July-Aug) is in the library, which is part of the town-hall complex. There are three banks on The Promenade, all with ATMs and bureaus de change. The nearest bike shop is Thompson Cycles (☎ 7082 9606, 77b Main St, Portrush).

Things to See & Do Just west of town via Strand Rd, **Portstewart Strand** is a 1.5mi (2.5km) long stretch of firm, fairly clean sand. It's great fun to ride along the strand provided you pick a quiet afternoon – remarkably, cars are allowed right on the beach, a National Trust (NT) site. Much-photographed **Mussenden Temple** sits atop a cliff southwest of Portstewart, near Castle-rock; it's about 11mi (11.7km) to ride, and there's a fine view from the curious, circular temple on clear days towards Magilligan Point and Inishowen.

Places to Stay & Eat About 1.5mi (2.5km) east of town on the A2 is *Juniper Hill Caravan Park (☎ 7083 2023, 70 Ballyreagh Rd)* 2-person tent sites from £10. *Carrick Dhu Caravan Park (☎ 7082 3712, 12 Ballyreagh Rd)* 2-person tent sites from £10, a bit closer to Portrush on the A2. *Rick's Causeway Coast Hostel (☎ 7083 3789, 4 Victoria Terrace)* Dorm beds £7. Friendly and close to town centre.

Cul-Erg House (☎ 7083 6610, 9 Hillside) Singles £18-25, doubles £40-50. Easy walk to town. *Chez-Nous (☎ 7083 2608, 1*

Victoria Terrace) B&B doubles £32. Small and handy to town. ***Craigmore House*** *(☎ 7083 2120, 26 The Promenade)* Singles/ doubles £19/38. Facing the ocean on the main street.

O'Malley's Edgewater Hotel *(☎ 7083 3314, 88 Strand Rd)* Singles/doubles £60/96. Nice rooms and lovely views, dinner available (£20).

You'll find a late-closing ***convenience store*** on The Promenade (and ***supermarkets*** in Portrush and Coleraine).

Heathrhon Diner *(29 The Promenade)* does £3 big breakfasts. ***1st Floor Coffee Shop*** *(16 The Promenade)* Filled baps £3, coffees from £1. Best coffee and best views. Also on The Prom, ***O'Hara's Bar*** has pastas (£6 to £10), and ***Montagu Arms*** has decent mains at £7 to £12. ***Smyths Restaurant*** *(2 Lever Rd)* Starters £3-5, mains £10-14. Fresh food and inventive dishes make this probably the best place in town for dinner. ***Ashiana Tandoori Restaurant*** *(12 The Diamond)* Starters £3-4, mains £6-7. Good selection of vegetable dishes (£45 to £5). ***Griddle Bakery*** *(Strand Rd)* Open Mon-Sat.

Getting There & Away There are several Ulsterbus (☎ 7032 5400 in Coleraine) services daily (fewer on Sunday) between Portstewart and Belfast (£8, two hours) or Derry (£7, 1¼ hours). Buses stop on The Promenade.

There are several NI railways (☎ 7032 5400 in Coleraine) services daily (fewer on Sunday) between Coleraine, about 5mi (8km) from Portstewart, and Belfast (£6) or Derry (£5).

The NCN's Ballyshannon–Ballycastle bike route follows a scenic and meandering 65.5mi (105.5km) course from Derry to Portstewart via Claudy and Limavady. The more direct route from Derry, via the A2 and B201, is about 34mi (55km).

THE RIDE (see map p237)
Day 1: Portstewart to Cushendall
4–7 hours, 43.7mi (70.4km)

Don't let the distance deceive you. A morning of frequent stops to take in interesting sites and an afternoon that includes some extreme climbs and descents will leave you knackered. Given clear weather, this day will *definitely* be the highlight of a Northern Ireland cycling odyssey.

The Port to Port path leads the 3.3mi (5.3km) along the coast to Portrush (Port Rois; 4.4mi; 7.1km) and the ensuing spin around town reveals its wealth of amusement arcades and ice-cream parlours.

Dunluce Castle is reached via a short side trip at 8.1mi (13km). The windswept ruin, perched atop a cliff with commanding views along the coast and to sea, was once the patch of the MacDonnell clan, but they vacated in the mid-17th century. The collapse into the sea of some service rooms, complete with servants and dinner, in 1639, may have hastened their departure.

At 11.4mi (18.4km), another short (well-signposted) side trip leads to the **Bushmills Distillery** (☎ 2073 1521), the world's oldest legal distillery – the first legal drop was produced here in 1608. The tour is interesting and the whiskey-tasting afterwards amusing; it's worth a visit even if you're not a fan of the famous product.

Take as much time as you can spare for the side trip to the **Giant's Causeway** (13.4mi; 21.6km; visitor centre ☎ 2073 1855), Ireland's first World Heritage Site. The Causeway's 37,000-or-so black basalt columns are mostly hexagonal; a few pentagons and other polygons make up the balance. The site's extreme tourist-media exposure can't dent its appeal. The basalt formations were formed by lava eruption about 60 million years ago; Irish legend attributes them to giant Fionn McCumhaill (Finn McCool). He built the causeway to the Scottish island of Staffa (where similar formations are found), home of a giantess he fancied. You'll see the best of the site by walking the North Antrim Cliff Path to Hamilton's Seat, then returning to the visitor centre via the lower path, which passes formations such as Chimney Tops and the Organ before reaching the Causeway itself.

The route beyond the Giant's Causeway passes a magnificent stretch of coastline that includes the 16th-century ruin of **Dunseverick Castle** (16.3mi; 26.2km) and, just beyond, the shining sands of White Park Bay. Just past the pretty village of Ballintoy (Baile an Tuaighe) lies the turnoff (at 20.9mi; 33.6km) for the **Carrick-a-Rede Rope Bridge** side trip. The bridge is another famous North-coast landmark. The narrow, swaying, 20m-long bridge, about 25m above the sea, is erected each spring by workers from the salmon fishery on Carrick-a-Rede Island; it's

Antrim Coast – Day 1

Cue	
start	Portstewart TIC
0mi	go N on The Promenade
1.1 ↘	onto Port to Port Path
3.6 ↰	The Strand
3.8 ↰	Ramore St/Ramore Ave
4.3 ↰	Main St
4.4	Portrush
4.5 ↘	Causeway St/A2
5.4 ▲	2.8km gradual climb
6.5 ↱	B62 'to Ballymoney'
7.0 ↰	Ballymagarry Rd
8.1 ↱	Ballytober Rd
● ● ↱	*Dunluce Castle 500yd* ↻
↰	(40yd) Ballyclogh Rd
▲	0.5mi steep climb
9.7 ↰	Craigaboney Rd
10.8 ↰	B17
11.2 ↱	A2
11.4 ↰	A2, Bushmills
● ● ↱	*Bushmills Distillery 800yd* ↻
11.5 ▲	1.1mi gradual climb
12.5 ↰	B146 'to Giant's Causeway'
13.3 ▲	1.4mi gradual climb
13.4 ● ● ↰	*Giant's Causeway 1.2mi* ↻

	Continued
16.3 ✻	*Dunseverick Castle*
16.6	Dunseverick
▲	2.4mi gradual climb
20.5	Ballintoy
▲	1.4mi steep climb
20.9 ● ● ↰	*Carrick-a-Rede rope bridge 0.8mi* ↻
22.6 ▲	0.7mi moderate climb
25.1 ↰	B15 'to Ballycastle Seafront'
26.6 ↰ ◆	A2 'to Cushendun via coastal route'
	Ballycastle
26.9 ↰	A2 'to Cushendun via coastal route'
27.0 ▲	1.4mi gradual climb
28.9 ↰	'to Cushendun via scenic route'
▲	4.2mi moderate/gradual climb
30.4 ↰	'to Cushendun'
34.4 ▲	0.8mi steep climb
36.1 ▲	0.5mi steep climb
39.7 ↰	B92 'to Cushendun'
40.2	Cushendun
40.9	Knocknacarry
42.1 ↰	A2 'to Cushendall'
42.2 ▲	1.0mi gradual climb
43.7	Cushendall TIC

Elevation

600 - 2000
400 - 1500 Portstewart
1000 Ballintoy Cushendall
200 - 500 Portrush Bushmills Dunseverick Ballycastle Cushendun
0m 0ft

0mi 10 20 30 40
0km 10 20 30 40 50 60 70

free to cross and there are fine coast views from the island. For more spectacular views, stop at the clifftop lookout at 21.9mi (35.4km). It's well worth a break in charming Ballycastle (Baile an Chaistil; 26.6mi; 42.8km), departure point for ferries to nearby Rathlin Island.

The route's final section, from the left turn on the outskirts of Ballyvoy (28.9mi; 46.5km), yields its most arresting scenery and toughest cycling. From 33.1mi (53.3km), the scenic road hugs the steep coast, passing Torr and Runabay Heads and offering spectacular views towards the Mull of Kintyre (just 13mi/21km from Torr Head) and other Scottish islands. At least one uphill section (beginning at 34.4mi; 55.4km) is unrideable (it's almost unpushable!) and the descents

require extreme caution. The NT-owned village of Cushendun (Bun Abhann Duinne; 40.2mi; 64.7km) is a welcome sight; its distinctive whitewashed buildings all date from the early 20th century.

Cushendall

See Cushendall (p241).

Day 2: Cushendall to Belfast

4½–8 hours, 48.3mi (77.8km)

This is a day in three distinct parts. The first 20.2mi (32.5km), entirely flat and rarely more than a stone's throw from the sea, follows the spectacular A2 coast road to Ballygalley. The next 21mi (33.8km) winds through hilly farming country inland of Larne and Carrickfergus, thus avoiding parts of the

Antrim Coast – Day 2

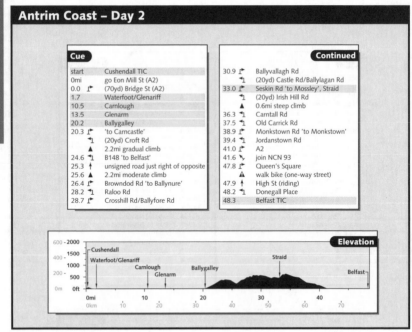

Cue	
start	Cushendall TIC
0mi	go Eon Mill St (A2)
0.0	(70yd) Bridge St (A2)
1.7	Waterfoot/Glenariff
10.5	Carnlough
13.5	Glenarm
20.2	Ballygalley
20.3	'to Carncastle'
	(20yd) Croft Rd
	2.2mi gradual climb
24.6	B148 'to Belfast'
25.3	unsigned road just right of opposite
25.6	2.2mi moderate climb
26.4	Browndod Rd 'to Ballynure'
28.2	Raloo Rd
28.7	Crosshill Rd/Ballyfore Rd

	Continued
30.9	Ballyvallagh Rd
	(20yd) Castle Rd/Ballylagan Rd
33.0	Seskin Rd 'to Mossley', Straid
	(20yd) Irish Hill Rd
	0.6mi steep climb
36.3	Carntall Rd
37.5	Old Carrick Rd
38.9	Monkstown Rd 'to Monkstown'
39.4	Jordanstown Rd
41.0	A2
41.6	join NCN 93
47.8	Queen's Square
	walk bike (one-way street)
47.9	High St (riding)
48.2	Donegall Place
48.3	Belfast TIC

Elevation

A2 that have heavy traffic. The final section, almost all flat and traffic-free, follows NCN route 93 into Belfast.

The A2 south of Cushendall passes three of the Antrim Glens – Glenariff, Glencloy and Glenarm – and the neat towns at their heads. Pretty Carnlough (Carnlach, 10.5mi; 16.9km) has a tiny stonewalled harbour and distinctive stone bridge which once carried limestone-laden trains to the harbour; the creeper-covered *Londonderry Arms* is a nice place for a break. Glenarm (Gleann Arma; 13.5mi; 21.7km) has a wide main street lined with colour-washed buildings; its centrepiece is the old estate gateway.

After the turn inland at Ballygalley, there's a certain amount of climbing and descending, but the route mostly follows ridges, and offers fine views, until descending to the northern reaches of Belfast at solidly Unionist Monkstown (about 39.4mi; 63.4km). A large portion of the final section into Belfast hugs Belfast Lough and the NCN route signs make navigation a breeze in the Belfast Docks area. Only in the day's last few hundred metres, from the Lagan Lookout, will you need to tangle with traffic.

Belfast
See Belfast (p224).

Glens of Antrim

Duration	3–5 hours
Distance	25.3mi (40.7km)
Difficulty	moderate
Start/End	Cushendall

A pleasant day designed to show off some of Antrim's famous glens enables you to also explore some of the high country that surrounds them and visit peaceful Glenariff Forest Park.

NATURAL HISTORY
Underlying the basalt Antrim Plateau is a layer of 200-million-year-old sandstone and red marls. These are covered with two ancient seabeds, one of 150-million-year-old clay and 100-million-year-old limestone. Within the upper layer of 60-million-year-old black basalt are bands of iron ore, which was mined in the Glenariff area in the 1870s and '80s.

PLANNING
When to Ride
Weekdays in late spring or early autumn are best.

Maps
The ride is covered by OSNI's 1:250,000 Holiday map *Ireland North*. OSI 1:50,000 Discovery map No 9 enhances walks in Glenariff Forest Park.

What to Bring
Warm and waterproof clothing is essential, even if the weather forecast is favourable. The route rises to 400m above sea level and can be very cool in exposed sections.

ACCESS TOWN
Cushendall
At the head of Glenballyemon, charming Cushendall (Bun Abhann Dalla) has a welcoming village-community atmosphere, good facilities for visitors and several fine pubs.

Information The Cushendall TIC (☎ 2177 1180, 24 Mill St, open Mon-Sat July-Sept, 10am-1pm Tues-Sat Oct-Dec & Feb-June, closed Jan) is in the Glens of Antrim Historical Society office. There's a Northern Bank office (Shore St) with ATM.

Things to See & Do Cushendall's landmark red sandstone **Curfew Tower**, at the town-centre intersection of Mill and Bridge Sts, was built in 1817 by village landlord Francis Turnly as 'a place of confinement for idlers and rioters'. Turnly had made his fortune with the East India Company and used it to buy the estate that included Cushendall. The ruins of **Layde Old Church** (Layde Rd), about 1km north of town on the coast road to Cushendun, are worth visiting; a scenic clifftop coastal walk to the site begins at the coast road opposite the HINI hostel. The church, believed to have been founded by Franciscans and in ruins for most of the 17th century, was restored and used as a Protestant church until the late 18th century.

Places to Stay & Eat Just 0.6mi east of town on the A2 is *Cushendall Caravan & Camping Park (☎ 2177 1699, 62 Coast Rd)* 2-person tent sites £6-10.

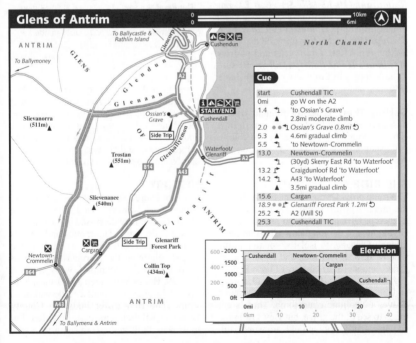

Beware the Irish Mile

Here and there in County Down you'll see old granite milestones, usually half-hidden on roadsides, that give distances in Irish miles, an arcane measure that translates to 1.27 (ordinary) miles, or just over 2km·

All B&Bs listed are in the Cyclists Welcome scheme. *Ashlea* (☎ *2177 1651*, e *martha@ashleareach.totalserve.co.uk, 2 Tromra Rd)* Singles/doubles £19/34. *The Burn* (☎ *2177 1733*, e *theburn63@hotmail.com, 63 Ballyeamon Rd)* Standard singles/doubles £18/34, with ensuite £19/36. *Garron View* (☎ *2177 1018*, e *josiegarronview@yahoo.co .uk, 14 Cloughs Rd)* Singles/doubles £18/32.

The Glens Hotel (☎ *2177 1223, 6 Coast Rd)* Doubles £50, dinner £10. East of town centre.

The *Spar Market (Bridge St)* closes late seven days. *Arthur's Tea & Coffee Warehouse (Shore St)* Coffees £1.50, sandwiches from £2, soup and bread £2. Best for hot beverages and snacks. *Harry's Licensed Restaurant (10-12 Mill St)* Soup £2, bar snacks £3-7, mains from £4.95. À la carte dinner from 6pm. *Homemade Pizza & Fish & Chips (Bridge St)* Fry-ups, cod and chips £4, burgers £1.50. Grab bread and pastries at *Gillian's Home Bakery (Mill St)*. Be sure to have a pint in fascinating *Johnny Joe's (Mill St)* bar.

Getting There & Away Regular Ulsterbus services reach Cushendall from Belfast (£6, two hours) and Derry (£11, two hours).

Cushendall is the Day 1 stop on the Antrim Coast ride (p236).

THE RIDE (see map p241)
The route provides an introduction to five of the nine Antrim Glens: Glenballyemon, Glencorp, Glenaan, Glendun and Glenariff. Highlights are the long slow climb, initially through Glenaan, to isolated country in the shadow of 551m Trostan and 540m Slievenanee, and a visit to Glenariff Forest Park.

Just 2mi (3.2km) from Cushendall, a steep and bumpy side trip leads up to **Ossian's Grave**, a Neolithic court tomb. There's not much to see of the grave, but views from the site, in a gently sloping field, are wonderful.

A stone cairn nearby was erected as a memorial to John Hewitt, 'the poet of the Glens'.

As the climb continues the sense of solitude grows; if you ride midweek before July you'll likely see only a couple of vehicles between the turnoff to Ossian's Grave and Newtown-Crommelin. The road meanders upwards between stands of pine in Slieveanorra Forest, with wind whistling through pine needles and the bubbling waters of the upper Glendun River the only sounds.

There's another longish, gradual climb on the A43 before the start of the thrilling downhill to the entrance of **Glenariff Forest Park** (18.9mi; 30.4km). It's well worth a side trip into the 1185-hectare park which contains beautiful shady woodland that supports foxes, red squirrels and badgers and a variety of birdlife. There are impressive views of wide Glenariff – the so-called Queen of the Glens – and several relatively easy walks. The Glenariff River gorge contains a number of waterfalls, the largest of which (accessible to walkers) is Ess-na-larach falls.

Down South

Duration	3 days
Distance	127.1mi (204.6km)
Difficulty	easy–moderate
Start	Belfast
End	Newcastle

These three days in County Down reveal historic ruins, nature reserves, stunning natural attractions (such as Strangford Lough and the Mourne Mountains) and friendly towns and villages. For most of its course, the route is rarely out of sight of water, and its sternest climbs are short and of moderate intensity.

HISTORY

Ruins of churches, monasteries, mottes and baileys and tower houses are a feature of the region (several are discussed in the ride narratives following). The mottes and baileys (early Norman fortifications) date from the period following the Norman conquest of County Down by John de Courcy in 1177. In 1429, Henry VI offered a £10 subsidy to every leige man who built a castle within 10 years. The first tower house in County Down, at Kilclief, appeared soon after, but most were built in the 16th century.

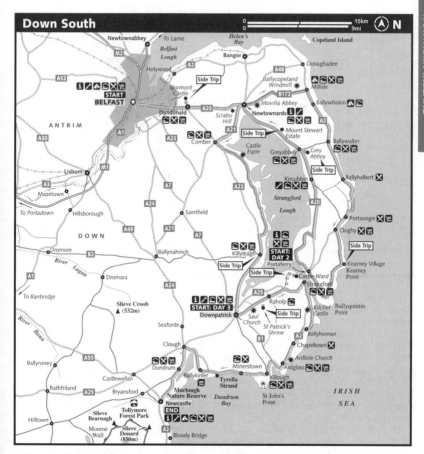

NATURAL HISTORY

Strangford Lough is among Europe's most important wildlife sites; its residents and visitors include seals and otters and a variety of migratory birds. The NT has a wildlife scheme that covers the lough's foreshore and 50-odd islands. Grass and heathlands at the NT's Murlough National Nature Reserve, north of Newcastle, provide nesting sites for birds such as skylarks, meadow pipits and ringed plovers. The Trust also owns Slieve Donard in the Mourne Mountains, Northern Ireland's highest peak.

PLANNING
When to Ride

Weekdays in late spring or early autumn are best.

Maps

The ride is covered by the OSNI 1:250,000 Holiday map *Ireland North*. OSI 1:50,000 Discovery map No 29 is a useful addition and gives greater detail for rides and walks in the Mourne Mountains.

ACCESS TOWN
Belfast

See Belfast (p224).

THE RIDE
Day 1: Belfast to Portaferry

4–7 hours, 43.8mi (70.5km)

The journey from bustling Belfast to quiet Portaferry serves up pleasant countryside, outstanding coast views, several points of interest and easy cycling.

Down South – Day 1

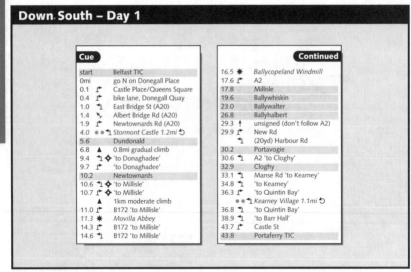

Cue		
start	Belfast TIC	
0mi	go N on Donegall Place	
0.1	Castle Place/Queens Square	
0.4	bike lane, Donegall Quay	
1.0	East Bridge St (A20)	
1.4	Albert Bridge Rd (A20)	
1.9	Newtownards Rd (A20)	
4.0	● ● *Stormont Castle 1.2mi* ⟳	
5.6	Dundonald	
6.8	▲ 0.8mi gradual climb	
9.4	◆ 'to Donaghadee'	
9.7	'to Donaghadee'	
10.2	Newtownards	
10.6	◆ 'to Millisle'	
10.7	◆ 'to Millisle'	
	▲ 1km moderate climb	
11.0	B172 'to Millisle'	
11.3	*Movilla Abbey*	
14.3	B172 'to Millisle'	
14.6	B172 'to Millisle'	

	Continued	
16.5	*Ballycopeland Windmill*	
17.6	A2	
17.8	Millisle	
19.6	Ballywhiskin	
23.0	Ballywalter	
26.8	Ballyhalbert	
29.3	unsigned (don't follow A2)	
29.9	New Rd	
	(20yd) Harbour Rd	
30.2	Portavogie	
30.6	A2 'to Cloghy'	
32.9	Cloghy	
33.1	Manse Rd 'to Kearney'	
34.8	'to Kearney'	
36.3	'to Quintin Bay'	
	● ● *Kearney Village 1.1mi* ⟳	
36.8	'to Quintin Bay'	
38.9	'to Barr Hall'	
43.7	Castle St	
43.8	Portaferry TIC	

On Belfast's eastern outskirts, **Stormont Castle** (☎ 9076 0556) houses the Northern Ireland Assembly. A short side trip (from 4mi; 6.4km) leads up the grand avenue to Stormont's somewhat stolid front, where a statue of stern-faced Edward Carson, who led the campaign that resulted in Ireland's 1921 partition, adds to the exterior's cheerless feeling. The beautiful grounds and gardens include a poignant reconciliation statue, west of the castle.

Just outside Newtownards (Baile Nua na hArda; 10.2mi; 16.4km), the **Movilla Abbey** site (11.3mi; 18.2km) contains the vine-covered ruins of a 13th-century church. It's thought that the monastery here was founded in the 6th century by St Finian; it survived Viking attacks in the 9th and 10th centuries.

Further east, **Ballycopeland Windmill** (16.5mi; 26.6km) juts from a high point on the rolling fields. This is Northern Ireland's only working windmill (there are dozens of windmill ruins in County Down alone); the miller's house and the kiln house have also been faithfully restored.

Some delightful coastal riding (including views to the Isle of Man) eventually leads to picturesque **Kearney village** (side trip from 36.3mi; 58.4km). The whitewashed, slate-roofed cottages in this 18th-century fishing village have been carefully preserved by the National Trust; visitors are welcome to wander about the privately owned houses, which are not open to the public.

Portaferry

Portaferry (Port an Phiere) is a neat complex of streets, dominated by the ruin of a 16th-century tower house. A regular car-ferry service crosses The Narrows to Strangford, traversing the fierce tidal currents that wash in and out of Strangford Lough.

Information Portaferry TIC (☎ 4272 9882, e tourism@ards-council.gov.au, Castle St, open daily Easter-Sept) can help with tourist information. There's a Northern Bank (cnr High St & The Square) with an ATM.

Things to See & Do Next to the TIC, **Portaferry Castle** (Castle St) was built by the Norman Savage family. It's a tower house, with one projecting tower to the south. Next door, **Exploris Aquarium** (☎ 4272 8062) is Northern Ireland's only aquarium and seal sanctuary. Displays reveal the rich and varied marine life sustained by Strangford Lough. About 1.5mi (2.5km) east of town off the A2 are the evocative **Derry Churches** ruins, the remains of two small churches believe to date from the 10th and 12th centuries.

Places to Stay & Eat HINI-affiliated *Barholm* (☎ 4272 9598, 11 The Strand)

Dorm beds £12. Opposite the ferry landing, comfortable and friendly.

For B&B, try *Adair's* (☎ 4272 8412, 22 The Square) Singles/doubles £16/33. Central and reasonable. *Peep O Day* (☎ 4272 9675, 20C Cloughey Rd) Singles/doubles £25/44. Signposted off A2, 1mi (1.6km) east of town centre. *Lough Cowey Lodge* (☎ 4272 8263, 9 Lough Cowey Rd) Singles/doubles £25/40. Off the A20, 2mi (3.2km) north of town.

The Narrows (☎ 4272 8148, 8 Shore Rd) B&B singles/doubles £58/86, with dinner £74/118, starters £3-10, mains £9-15. Three-star, overlooking the water; restaurant meals. *Portaferry Hotel* (☎ 4272 8231, 10 The Strand) B&B singles/doubles £58/95, starters £3-8, mains £10-16. Three-star, overlooking the water; restaurant meals available. Good seafood can be had in both restaurants.

The *Costcutter* (Steel Dickson Ave) supermarket closes late seven nights; there's also a *Spar Market* (High St).

The Ferry Grill (High St) Burgers £2-3, mixed grill £5. *The Cornstore Restaurant & Bistro* (The Shambles) Starters £3-5, pasta £5-6, meat mains £6-12. Pleasant central location, best value for a sit-down meal. *Yukon Palace* (High St) Open to 11pm Wed-Mon. Chinese restaurant. Buy bread at *The Rock Bakery* (The Square).

Day 2: Portaferry to Downpatrick

4–7½ hours, 45.9mi (73.9km)

Lovely scenery around Strangford Lough and a wealth of interesting sites are the stars of this quite tiring day. The cycling required to enjoy the views and sites isn't quite as good; more than half of the day is spent on moderately busy A roads. If you don't fancy the idea of traffic, catch the ferry to Strangford and pick up the Day 3 route at the 8.3mi (13.4km) mark.

A short side trip at 14.3mi (23km) leads to the **Grey Abbey** site, the ruins of a late-12th-century Cistercian monastery. A substantial part of the cruciform chapel – used for parish worship until 1778 – and some walls of the refectory, or frater, are still standing. The ruins are surrounded by lovely lawns and overlooked by the charming gardens of 18th-century Rosemount House.

Not far past the town of Greyabbey (An Mhainistir Liath), the NT-owned **Mount Stewart** estate (16.1mi; 25.9km; ☎ 4278 8387) includes a grand 18th-century house that was home to the marquess of Londonderry. Among many notable features are the 1785 banqueting hall and magnificent 98-acre (40-hectare) grounds, packed with rare and unusual plant species and offering unbeatable views over Strangford Lough.

Down South – Day 2

Cue		Continued	
start	Portaferry TIC	29.3 ↙	Quarry Rd 'to Killinchy'
0mi	go W on Castle St	26.9 ↰	Tullynakill Rd 'to Killinchy'
0.1 ↱	The Strand	31.7 ↘	Killinakin Rd 'to Killinchy'
3.5 ↰	unsigned road	31.9 ▲	0.8mi moderate climb
5.8 ↰	A20	32.8 ↱	'to Killinchy'
10.6	Kircubbin	32.9 ↰	Ballymorran Rd
14.2	Greyabbey	34.0 ↰	Quarterland Rd
14.3 ↰	A20 'to Newtownards'	35.1 ↰	unsigned road ('Ulster Way')
● ● ↑	Grey Abbey 800yd ↻	35.8 ↘	Ringdufferin Rd
16.1 ● ● ↱	Mount Stewart 0.6mi ↻	37.4 ↰	A22
21.5	Newtownards	39.6	Killyleagh
21.5 ↰	A21 'to Comber'	● ● ↱	Killyleagh Castle 600yd ↻
25.5	Comber	45.7 ↱	Market St (A25)
25.6 ↰	A22 'to Castle Espie'	45.8 ↱	'to TIC'
26.1 ↰	Ballydrain Rd	45.9	Downpatrick TIC
28.4 ✻	Castle Espie		

Just past Newtownards the route passes east of Scrabo Hill and the 1857 Scrabo Tower, a 41m memorial to the 3rd marquess of Londonderry. The flat ground hereabouts is dominated by vegetable growing; traffic moves fast on the A22 and it's a relief to turn onto quiet roads just past Comber (An Comar; 25.5mi; 41.1km).

At 28.4mi (45.7km), **Castle Espie** (☎ 9187 4146), a Wildfowl & Wetlands Trust reserve, harbours Ireland's largest collection of ducks, geese and swans. There are peaceful walks through the reserve and, for the ornithologically inclined, three bird hides. The centre's *café* is a fine place for tea and scones.

The succeeding miles roll over typical drumlin country and provide wonderful views of Strangford Lough and some of its larger islands. It's worth a short side trip in Killyleagh (Cill O Laoch; 39.6mi; 63.8km) to see the imposing, privately owned **Killyleagh Castle**, begun in the 12th century by John de Courcy. Take care on the A22 over the final miles into Downpatrick; traffic can be heavy.

Downpatrick

Associations with St Patrick, Georgian architecture and some fine attractions make Downpatrick (Dun Padraig) a worthy destination in itself.

Birthplace of Irish Christianity?

Just outside Downpatrick at Saul (Sabhal), small, neat St Patrick's Memorial Church marks the supposed site of Ireland's first Christian congregation, established in 432. After landing at Strangford Lough, about 2.5mi (4km) from Saul, St Patrick is thought to have converted the local chieftain, Dichu, who granted Patrick his *sabhal* (barn) as a place of worship. Later, St Patrick built a church on the site, which was eventually replaced by an abbey. A cycle of destruction and rebuilding was played out over several centuries; the oldest part of the present-day site is a portion of a church wall that's thought to date from the early 12th century. The present-day church, a simple building with a 60ft (18m) round tower and a rather austere interior, was erected in 1932 to commemorate the 1500th anniversary of St Patrick's arrival.

Information Downpatrick TIC (☎ 4461 2233, e downpatrick@nitic.net, open Mon-Sat year-round, daily July-Aug) is just northwest of Market St in the Saint Patrick Centre. Several banks, all with ATMs, are on Market St. Spares and repairs are available at Down Discount Cycles (☎ 4461 4990, 45 Church St).

Things to See & Do The **Saint Patrick Centre** (☎ 4461 9000, admission £5), or 'ego Patricius', employs video and audio displays in its interpretation of Patrick's life. The displays are a bit gimmicky in parts, but that doesn't detract from a good story that's well told, and casts a great deal of light on the saint's life and influence. It's worth the admission charge just to see the final video presentation – a beautifully filmed, multi-screen perspective of key St Patrick sites throughout Ireland.

Dominating the Hill of Down in the town centre, **Down Cathedral** as it stands today was mostly built in the 18th and 19th centuries, but the site has ecclesiastical connections extending back 1600 years. The interior includes private box-pews (the last of their kind in Ireland) and a fine old organ; outside there's a decaying, 1000-year-old high cross and a rough granite slab inscribed with the word 'Patric' – St Patrick's 'grave'. It's unlikely the saint was buried in this exact spot, but he may rest in the vicinity; legend has it that the remains of Saints Brigid and Colmcille were also brought here in the late 12th century. The slab was installed about 100 years ago, in part to cover the hole dug by earlier, relic-seeking pilgrims.

East of the cathedral on English St is Downpatrick's finest Georgian quarter, which includes the courthouse, Southwell School (founded 1733) and **Down County Museum** (☎ 4461 5218). Housed in a rambling 18th-century jail, the museum's exhibits mainly cover local history; outside, a track leads to the **Mound of Down**, the remains of a Norman motte and bailey.

Places to Stay & Eat About 4.3mi (7km) north of town, off the A22 (closer to Killyleagh), is *Delamont Country Park* (☎ 4482 1833) Tent sites per person £5.

Hillside (☎ 4461 3134, 62 Scotch St) B&B singles/doubles £17/34. Pleasant and centrally located restored Georgian terrace.

NORTHERN IRELAND

Arolsen (☎ 4461 2656, 47 Roughal Park) Singles/doubles £20/36. Close to town centre and comfortable; dinner available (£10). *Dunleath House (☎ 4461 3221, 33 St Patrick's Drive)* Singles/doubles £24/40. Modern home, five minutes to town centre.

Denvir's Hotel (☎ 4461 2012, 14-16 English St) Singles/doubles £30/50, starters £3-5, mains £6-9, steaks £12-15. Central, lovely old coaching inn; restaurant also available. *Abbey Lodge Hotel (☎ 4461 4511, 38 Belfast Rd)* Doubles £60, dinner £13. About 1mi (1.6km) north on the A7.

There's a big *Safeway* supermarket south of the town centre on Market St.

Cafe Plazza (18 The Grove) Soup £2, filled paninis around £3. Light and pleasant, opposite the TIC. *Forum (10 Scotch St)* Starters £2-4, most mains under £5. Fairly typical of the several Chinese takeaways in town. *Samsia Tandoori (20 St Patrick's Ave)* Starters £2-3, mains £4-7. Indian takeaway, good range of vegetable side dishes (£3). *Bits & Pizzas (Church St)* does pizzas (£2 to £7) and burgers. *Oakley Fayre Farmhouse Bakery (Market St)* includes a coffee shop.

Day 3: Downpatrick to Newcastle

3½–6 hours, 37.4mi (60.2km)
A few moments in traffic aside, this is a wonderful day of easy riding and ocean views.

The Lecale Peninsula is quiet and its people relaxed and free of sectarianism. As one local put it: 'Around here, the Protestants play Gaelic (football) and the Catholics play cricket'.

Just 2mi (3.2km) outside Downpatrick, **Saul Church** (see the boxed text 'Birthplace of Irish Christianity?') is a symbol of the roots of Irish Christianity. At 3.2mi (5.2km), Slieve Patrick is topped by St Patrick's Shrine, a 10m (32.8ft) statue of the saint that's a short side trip about half a mile from the road; stations of the cross mark the way to the shrine.

A side trip at 6.8mi (10.9km) leads to **Castle Ward** (☎ 4488 1204), a 750-acre (300-hectare) walled estate overlooking sleek Strangford Lough. Its centrepiece is Castleward House, the intriguing 1760 mansion built by Lord and Lady Bangor. His Lordship favoured the neoclassical design that appears on the front facade; her Ladyship went in for Gothic style, which graces the building's rear facade. Within the grounds are walking paths and the Strangford Lough Wildlife Centre.

The route passes several well-preserved castles south of Strangford. **Kilclief Castle** (10.9mi; 17.5km) marks the entrance to Strangford Lough. It was the first tower house in County Down, built in the first half of the 15th century, and was used by

Down South – Day 3

Cue			Continued	
start	Downpatrick TIC	10.9 ✳	*Kilclief Castle*	
0km	go S to Market St	11.0 ↰	Shore Rd 'to Ballyhornan'	
0.1 ↰	Market St	13.3	Ballyhornan	
0.2 ↰	Irish St (A22)	13.9 ↰	A2 'to Ardglass'	
↱	(20yd) Scotch St	15.4	Chapeltown	
▲	0.9mi moderate climb	16.7 ✳	*Ardtole Church*	
0.3 ↰	Saul St	17.4 ✳	Ardglass	
0.7 ↗	Saul Rd	20.3	Killough	
2.0 ✳	*Saul Church*	23.8	Minerstown	
2.2 ↱	unsigned road	26.6 ↰	'to Ballykinler' (leave A2)	
3.2 ● ●↱	*St Patrick's Shrine 0.8mi* ↻	27.4 ↱	Commons Rd, Ballykinler	
3.8	Raholp	29.2 ↰	A2 'to Clough'	
4.5 ↱	A25	29.9 ▲	0.8mi gradual climb	
6.8 ● ●↰	*Castle Ward 2.5mi* ↻	30.7 ↰	A2 'to Newcastle'	
8.2	Strangford	33.1	Dundrum	
8.3 ↱	A2 'to Ardglass'	37.4	Newcastle TIC	

John Sely, the Bishop of Down from 1429 to 1443.

At 16.7mi (26.9km) you'll see the ruins of **Ardtole Church** off to the left. The church was once dedicated to St Nicholas, patron saint of sailors, and was used by fishermen; there are fine views from its hilltop position. Nearby Ardglass (Ard Ghlais; 17.4mi; 28km) is dotted with castles and fortified homes (only **Jordan's Castle**, near the harbour on Low Rd, is open to the public). The village of Killough (20.3mi; 32.7km) is also a pleasant surprise; its wide, shady, tree-lined main street was planned by Lord Bangor of Castle Ward.

Once you're past Killough, the Mourne Mountains are visible from all but a very few stages and form a beckoning counterpoint to the easy riding and wonderful views of wide Dundrum Bay. If it's a warm day consider taking a dip at Tyrella Beach (25.2mi; 40.6km); after it, there's just one short climb en route to Newcastle.

Newcastle

Main gateway to the Mourne Mountains, Newcastle (An Caislean Nua) is a lively and attractive town with plenty of accommodation and an outlook to die for: 848m Slieve Donard, the North's highest peak, rises abruptly to the south of town. The Shimna River flows out to sea through the centre of town, and there's a 3mi (5km) beach arcing northeast.

Information Newcastle TIC (☎ 4372 2222, 10-14 Central Promenade, open daily year-round) has tourist information. Northern and Ulster Banks both have branches, with ATMs, on Main St. Wiki Wiki Wheels (☎ 4372 3973, 10b Donard St, open daily Easter–Christmas) is the Raleigh Rent-a-Bike agent.

Things to See & Do Pick up a *Newcastle Heritage Trail* map from the TIC before taking a spin around town. There are some interesting 19th-century churches and buildings, and a truly awful modern church: **Our Lady of the Assumption** (Downs Rd). The big attractions in the centre are pubs, ice-cream parlours and rather tacky amusement centres. Better to drop into the **Mourne Countryside Centre** (☎ 3472 4059, 91 Central Promenade) and collect some

The Mourne Wall

The Mourne Wall is surely one of Northern Ireland's more intriguing sights. Stretching for 21.7mi (35km) over 15 Mourne Mountain summits, the 90cm wide stone wall, up to 2.4m high, marks the boundary of the Silent Valley and Ben Crom reservoir catchments. And that's pretty much *all* the wall does. It was built between 1910 and 1922, partly to provide employment. Cyclists will get closest to it on the Mourne Mountains Circuit ride, just past the entrance to Silent Valley.

information on the Mourne Mountains environment, walks and cycle routes.

Plan at least one extra day in Newcastle to walk to **Slieve Donard's summit**. It's a 7.5mi (12km) circuit from town if you walk along the A2 south to Bloody Bridge (5.6mi; 9km if you catch the bus to Bloody Bridge). The walk includes time next to the Mourne Wall (see the boxed text), spectacular views (given clear weather) and, near its end, Donard Park, where the Glen River tumbles over some sparkling waterfalls.

Places to Stay & Eat About 1.9mi (3.4km) northwest of town, off the B180, is *Tollymore Forest Park* (☎ 4372 2428) 2-person tent sites £7. *Newcastle Youth Hostel* (☎ 4372 2133, 30 Downs Rd) Dorm beds £9. Quiet, convenient central location, good facilities.

There are stacks of B&Bs in and near town. *Homeleigh* (☎ 4372 2305, 7 Slievemoyne Park) Singles/doubles £16/30. Good value close to town centre. *Ashmount* (☎ 4372 5074, 19 Bryansford Rd) Singles/doubles £28/45. Away from the busy main drag. *Castle Corrigs House* (☎ 4372 6986, 41 Castewellan Rd) Singles/doubles £20/32. Just north of town centre on the A50; quiet and good value. *Harbour House Inn* (☎ 4372 3445, 4-8 South Promenade) Singles/doubles £30/50. Great location on the harbour, just south of town centre.

Burrendale Hotel & Country Club (☎ 4372 2599, 51 Castewellan Rd) Singles/doubles £80/130, dinner £24. Next to Castle Corrigs House, facilities include swimming pool, gym etc. *Slieve Donard Hotel* (☎ 4372 3681, Downs Rd) Singles/doubles £90/140, dinner from £22. The place to stay if you're feeling prosperous – grand well located.

There's a big *Tesco (Castewellan Rd)* supermarket just north of the centre; it's open seven days.

Shimna Diner (2 Main St) does an all-day big breakfast for around £4. *Jennifer's Kitchen (Savoy Lane)* has filled baked spuds from £3 and big open sandwiches (£4 to £5). Main St dives such as *Pizza Palazzo* and *Bob's Pizzeria and A1 Burgers* do cheap burgers, pizza and chips. *Sea Palace* Chinese restaurant *(135 Main St)* Starters £3-5, mains £6-7. Open until late daily. Some half-decent noodle dishes. *The Percy French Grill Bar & Restaurant (☎ 4372 3175, Railway St)* Starters £2-4, mains £7-14. Tasty food, nice location overlooking the beach. *Mario's Restaurant (☎ 4372 2912, 65 South Promenade)* Starters £4-6, meat mains £13-15. Best place in town for pasta (starters £3 to £4, mains £9 to £10). *The Cookie Jar (Main St)* Open Mon-Sat. Best for bread and pastries.

Getting There & Away There's an hourly Ulsterbus (☎ 4372 2296) service between Belfast and Newcastle (£5, 1¼ hours).

Newcastle is about 37mi (60km) south of Belfast riding the most direct route (via the A24, B175 and A50), through Ballynahinch and Castlewellan.

Mourne Mountains Circuit

Duration	3–5 hours
Distance	27.5mi (44.3km)
Difficulty	moderate–hard
Start/End	Newcastle

Circling the Mourne's highest peaks, this route goes through the heart of the mountains on the B27 and passes well-known features such as Silent Valley, Spelga Dam and Tollymore Forest Park.

NATURAL HISTORY
The granite Mournes were formed about 50 million years ago. Only thin topsoil has formed on the granite surface, which accounts for the Mournes' predominant plant cover of heather and grasses. The main animal types found here are birds, lizards and insects.

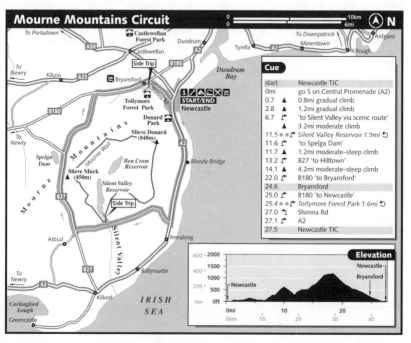

Mourne Mountains Circuit

Cue	
start	Newcastle TIC
0mi	go S on Central Promenade (A2)
0.7 ▲	0.8mi gradual climb
2.8 ▲	1.2mi gradual climb
6.7 ↱	'to Silent Valley via scenic route'
▲	3.2mi moderate climb
11.5 ●●↱	*Silent Valley Reservoir 1.9mi* ↺
11.6 ↱	'to Spelga Dam'
11.7 ▲	1.2mi moderate–steep climb
13.2 ↱	B27 'to Hilltown'
14.1 ▲	4.2mi moderate–steep climb
22.0 ↱	B180 'to Bryansford'
24.6	Bryansford
25.0 ↱	B180 'to Newcastle'
25.4 ●●↱	*Tollymore Forest Park 1.6mi* ↺
27.0 ↰	Shimna Rd
27.1 ↱	A2
27.5	Newcastle TIC

PLANNING
When to Ride
Weekdays in late spring or early autumn are best.

Maps
OSNI's 1:250,000 Holiday map *Ireland North* covers the ride. If you're planning an extended visit to Newcastle and the Mourne Mountains, it's worth obtaining *Mourne & Slieve Croob Cycle Routes*, a pack of excellent map/information sheets that detail seven rides in the area. OSI 1:50,000 Discovery map No 29 is a useful addition.

What to Bring
Warm and waterproof clothing is essential, even if weather reports are favourable. Comfortable walking shoes (for walks in the Mournes) are advisable.

ACCESS TOWN
Newcastle
See Newcastle (p248).

THE RIDE (see map p249)
3–5 hours, 27.5mi (44.3km)
Quiet mountain landscapes, longish and pleasant climbs and an 8.4mi (13.5km) descent feature on this short hop. The A2 south of Newcastle can be busy on weekends.

During the last period of glaciation (up to about 10,000 years ago), the **Silent Valley** (side trip at 11.5mi; 18.5km) was deepened and widened by erosion. The valley's central feature is the Silent Valley Reservoir, a key part of Belfast's water supply. Its earth-and-rock wall was built from 1923 to 1933; the smaller Ben Crom Reservoir, about 3mi (4.8km) further up the valley, was completed in 1957. There are easy walks around the peaceful site, which includes an information centre (☎ 9074 6581) and *restaurant*. Oddly, bikes must be left at the entrance gatehouse (there's a rack in the gatekeeper's sight), apparently a measure to keep cyclists off the walking paths. From the gatehouse it's an easy walk of just under a mile to the dam wall.

The climb into the heart of the Mournes tops out around the 17mi (28km) mark, from where there are spectacular views across the Spelga Dam and west towards County Down farmlands. Just past the Spelga, the day's big yahoo – the 8mi (13km) downhill – begins.

At 25.4mi (40.9km), **Tollymore Forest Park** (☎ 4372 2428) includes some pleasant walks along the Shimna River and lots of glorious green space for picnics. Wildlife in the park includes a variety of birds, badgers, foxes, red squirrels and fallow deer.

Around Ireland

Fancy a couple of months cycling in Ireland? This grand circuit of the Emerald Isle travels clockwise, mostly close to the coast, taking in most major cities, sites and attractions in both the Republic of Ireland and the North. This is your chance for the total Irish experience: from sophisticated Euro cities to bustling market towns to quiet, peat smoke–swathed villages. En route you'll encounter enough Irish hospitality, pubs with traditional music, and weather changes for a lifetime of touring stories.

HISTORY

While some earlier books have suggested complete circuits of Ireland, this isn't a widely recognised long-distance tour such as the USA coast-to-coast ride or Britain's Land's End to John o'Groats. However, what it lacks in fame it more than makes up for with friendly towns, grand sights and varied terrain.

CLIMATE

There's quite a contrast between the relatively sunny and dry southeast, the milder and wetter southwest and west, and the changeable and cooler north and northwest. For an overview of Irish weather, see Climate (p15).

INFORMATION
Maps

The ride is covered by the four OSI/OSNI 1:250,000 Holiday maps (*Ireland North*, *Ireland South*, *Ireland East* and *Ireland West*). A single small-scale map, such as the OSI 1:450,000 *Ireland Touring Map*, is fine for most days but lacks detail for some out-of-the-way minor roads. OSI/OSNI 1:50,000 Discovery maps show great detail; around 55 sheets are required to cover the entire route.

Information Sources

See Tourist Offices (p258) and Information Sources in the introductory sections of each regional chapter.

GATEWAY CITY
Dublin

See Dublin (p65).

PLANNING
When to Ride

Late April to early June is ideal. Throughout Ireland the driest months are April and May, and this warming period of spring is also a quieter time on roads and in towns and villages.

Around Ireland

Duration	42 days
Distance	2798.6km
Difficulty	hard
Start/End	Dublin

THE RIDE (see map p252)
Dublin to Youghal

4 days, 305.4km

From the capital head over the mountains to the southeastern corner of the country then turn westward to Youghal on the Waterford/Cork border. The stage starts with a spectacular traverse of the Wicklows, down past Glendalough monastic site to Arklow on the coast. The shoreline between there and Wexford is unremarkable, but once round the corner two days of lovely seascapes and fascinating places are a treat.

From Dublin follow Day 1 of the Into the Wicklow Mountains ride (p97) continuing from Laragh via Rathdrum and the Vale of Avoca (**Avoca village** is the setting for the BBC's *Ballykissangel*) to Arklow (p100). The following day to Wexford follows the coast road virtually all the way. Go left for Clogga Strand 3km south of Arklow and carry on in the same direction through Courtown Harbour, Kilmuckridge, Blackwater and Curracloe, going left on the R741 at about 63km for the bridge over Wexford Harbour into Wexford (p124). Signposted possible side trips to the shore include Clogga Bay (5.7km), Kilmichael Strand (9.2km), Roney Point (28.8km) and Cahore Point (32.1km).

After Wexford enjoy two days exploring the fine Atlantic shoreline on the Southeast Coast Cruise ride (p123) to Youghal. See some of best scenery in the region en route from picturesque Kilmore Quay to Bannow Bay and the Hook Peninsula. The Ring of

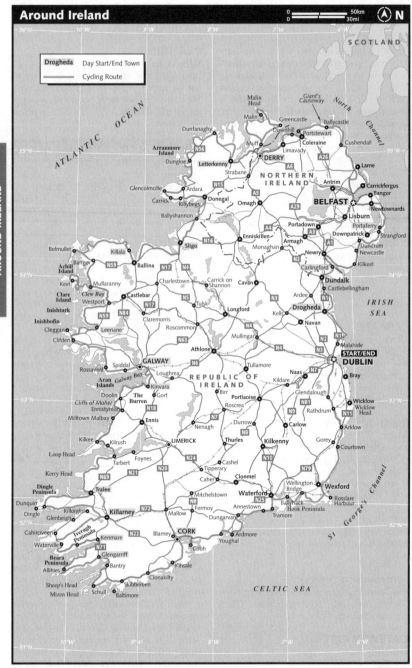

Around Ireland

	0	50km
	0	30mi

N

Drogheda Day Start/End Town

Cycling Route

Around Ireland Quick Guide

day	from/to	distance (km)	ride	page
1	Dublin to Arklow	77.9	Into the Wicklow Mountains	97
2	Arklow to Wexford	67.0	Around Ireland	251
3	Wexford to Tramore	83.5	Southeast Coast Cruise	125
4	Tramore to Youghal	77.0	Southeast Coast Cruise	127
5	Youghal to Cork	54.4	Around Ireland	254
6	Cork to Clonakilty	81.6	Harbour Hopping in Southwest Cork	134
7	Clonakilty to Schull	59.6	Harbour Hopping in Southwest Cork	136
8	Schull to Glengarriff	51.4	Harbour Hopping in Southwest Cork	138
9	Glengarriff to Allihies	52.5	Ring of Beara	143
10	Allihies to Kenmare	73.3	Ring of Beara	144
11	Kenmare to Waterville	60.3	Ring of Kerry	149
12	Waterville to Killarney	61.4	Ring of Kerry	153
13	Killarney to Dingle	65.8	Dingle Peninsula	154
14	Dingle to Tralee	47.6	Dingle Peninsula	157
15	Tralee to Kilkee	94.2	Around Ireland/Clare Circuit	254/165
16	Kilkee to Doolin	62.5	Clare Circuit	168
17	Doolin to Kinvara	56.9	Clare Circuit	170
18	Kinvara to Galway	31.9	Around Ireland	254
19	Galway to Clifden	95.6	Connemara & Inishmór	177
20	Clifden to Leenane	39.8	Connemara & Inishmór	180
21	Leenane to Westport	51.8	Connemara & Inishmór	181
22	Westport to Keel	64.3	Beaches & Bogs	187
23	Keel to Belmullet	94.6	Beaches & Bogs	189
24	Belmullet to Killala	80.9	Beaches & Bogs	191
25	Killala to Sligo	84.5	Around Ireland	255
26	Sligo to Ballyshannon	71.1	Around Ireland	255
27	Ballyshannon to Glencolmcille	84.6	Donegal to Derry	201
28	Glencolmcille to Dungloe	72.1	Donegal to Derry	203
29	Dungloe to Dunfanaghy	70.1	Donegal to Derry	204
30	Dunfanaghy to Letterkenny	74.0	Donegal to Derry	207
31	Letterkenny to Derry	37.4	Donegal to Derry	207
32	Derry to Malin	68.8	Inishowen Circuit	212
33	Malin to Greencastle	64.1	Inishowen Circuit	214
34	Greencastle to Derry	35.6	Inishowen Circuit	215
35	Derry to Portstewart	62.0	Around Ireland	256
36	Portstewart to Cushendall	70.4	Antrim Coast	238
37	Cushendall to Belfast	77.8	Antrim Coast	239
38	Belfast to Portaferry	70.5	Down South	243
39	Portaferry to Newcastle	46.7	Down South	245
40	Newcastle to Carlingford	72.5	Around Ireland	256
41	Carlingford to Drogheda	71.3	Around Ireland	257
42	Drogheda to Dublin	79.3	Heart of Ireland Explorer	85

AROUND IRELAND

Hook alternative route (p126) should not be missed; it's quite remarkable. (You might consider breaking your day at Fethard, Duncannon or Arthurstown to accommodate the extra 25.1km.) Cross Waterford Harbour via the car ferry at Passage East, and head back to the sea at sunny Tramore with its 3km beach. On the last day go bay-watching on a beautiful stretch of undulating cliff road between Annestown and Dungarvan. Resist the siren call of a dozen beaches and coves if you can.

Youghal to Glengarriff

4 days, 247km

Heading through County Cork, the route features the picturesque waters of the south coast, including Cork, Kinsale and Glandore Harbours and Courtmacsherry, Clonakilty, Roaringwater and Bantry Bays. The countryside is mostly undulating, with little long or arduous climbing, and, except around Cork city, little traffic.

Begin on the N25 from Youghal and take the R633 after 4km, turning within 2km onto minor roads that run parallel to (and south of) the N25. Cross the N25 entering and leaving Midleton, and join it again for the final 14km into Cork city (p131). This last section is busy, but the wide shoulder makes for easy cycling. Where there's a choice, stay on the high road. It's worth detouring south (at around 40km – just before hitting the highway) to the pretty harbour town of **Cobh** (see Things to See & Do in Cork, p132). From Cork to Glengarriff, the route follows Days 1 to 3 of the Harbour Hopping in Southwest Cork ride (p134).

Glengarriff to Tralee

6 days, 360.9km

One of the highlights of cycling in Ireland is the peninsulas in west Cork and Kerry. The Ring of Kerry on the Iveragh Peninsula is the most famous; Beara is perhaps the most beautifully wild and rugged, with the added bonus of little traffic (but some strenuous sections). The best part of the Dingle Peninsula is west of Dingle town: here you'll find the greatest concentration of ancient sites in Kerry and the superb Blasket Centre at Dunquin, which reveals what life was like on the recently abandoned Blasket Islands. An extra day spent in this area is highly recommended.

The route largely follows parts of the Ring of Beara, Ring of Kerry and Dingle Peninsula rides. Additional days could also be spent to include Day 3 of the Ring of Kerry ride (p145) and riding the Gap of Dunloe (see Things to See & Do in Killarney, p148).

The terrain on all three peninsulas is relatively hilly: Beara has a few longer climbs and, on Day 2, a roller coaster of short, steep hills. From Kenmare is a relatively flat section, which becomes more hilly towards Waterville. The Ballaghisheen Pass between Waterville and Killarney is a tough 2.8km climb. Ireland's highest pass is the **Connor Pass** between Dingle and Tralee. It's 6.5km of steepish but relatively steady climbing.

Although traffic is very light on the Beara Peninsula, it's relatively constant on the Iveragh Peninsula between Kenmare and Waterville, and on the Dingle Peninsula, for the final 9km into Dingle town, and for the final 23km into Tralee.

From Glengarriff, follow the Ring of Beara ride (p141). Instead of taking the Healy Pass on Day 2, turn left at 46.8km onto the R573, following the coast road to Kenmare. Follow Days 2 and 4 of the Ring of Kerry ride (p145), then Days 1 and 3 of the Dingle Peninsula ride (p153).

Tralee to Galway

4 days, 245.5km

Heading from the gently undulating fields in the southern Shannon region to the tidal flats of Galway Bay, this stage begins in County Kerry, traverses County Clare and ends in County Galway. Highlights include the majestic Cliffs of Moher, traditional music at Milltown Malbay and Doolin, and the lunar landscape of the Burren.

Leaving the mountains behind, the terrain is more gentle than that of the previous section: mostly, it's flat to gently undulating. Traffic is light to moderate, but rarely intrusive.

From Tralee, follow the R551 to Tarbert, via the seaside towns of Ballyheigue and Ballybunion. At Tarbert (72km), take the car ferry (☎ 065-9053124, ⓦ www.shannon ferries.com) across the River Shannon to Killimer (€3, 20 minutes, hourly). The ferry sails from Tarbert on the half-hour; buy tickets on board.

Across the Shannon, the route follows the end of Day 1, then Days 3 and 4, of the Clare Circuit ride (p164).

Leave the Clare Circuit route at Kinvara; continue instead around Kinvarra Bay on the N67, which becomes the N18. At Clarinbridge (around 12km), turn left and follow minor roads around Galway Bay to Oranmore (at around 24km). Join the west-leading Coast Rd; it merges with the N6, which - after 8km or so - will bring you to into Galway city (p174).

Galway to Westport
3 days, 187.2km

The magical landscape of the Connemara region in County Galway is typified by lonely bogs, knobbly mountains and its characteristic loughs: tiny jewels sparkling in the bog, and long, dark pools brooding beneath glacier-smoothed mountainsides.

This stage leaves cosmopolitan Galway city and becomes progressively more lonely until it reaches Clifden, after which it blends mountain scenery with beaches, traces Ireland's only fjord Killary Harbour and passes the holy mountain Croagh Patrick on its way around island-adorned Clew Bay.

The terrain is surprisingly free of big hills: mostly gently undulating, it has some short climbs but nothing overly strenuous. Traffic is barely present except for the first 30km or so from Galway city and the final 20km from Louisburgh to Westport, both of which carry moderate flows.

The route follows Days 1, 3, 4 and 5 of the Connemara & Inishmór ride (p173), but excludes the Inishmór trip. At 95.6km the first day of this stage is the longest in the ride: it combines Days 1 and 3 of the Connemara & Inishmór ride. If this sounds too challenging the day could be broken at Rossaveal (38.6km) by a visit to Inishmór, the largest of the Aran Islands, as per Day 2 of the Connemara & Inishmór ride.

Westport to Sligo
4 days, 324.3km

Heading through northern County Mayo, the route takes the roads less travelled (at least by tourists), and goes from brilliant beaches to bleak bogs. Some wonderful weathered cliffs are featured, and you'll pass the Céide Fields, thought to be the oldest farm site in the world.

From Westport to Killala, the route follows Days 1 to 3 of the Beaches and Bogs ride (p185). Mostly undulating, the terrain becomes a little wilder on the Atlantic Drive section of Achill Island and is quite strenuous on the coastal stretch between Ballycastle and Killala. The N59 is relatively flat between the Achill Island turnoff and Bangor. Traffic can be busy on the N59 between Westport and the Achill turnoff and, on summer weekends, moderate on Achill itself. Other stretches that carry fast-moving traffic include Bangor to Belmullet and Killala to Ballina.

From Killala, take the R314 to Ballina, turn left onto the N59 and, at around 17km, go left on the R297. At around 45km, continue on the minor road that runs parallel to (and eventually joins) the N59 near Beltra (Béal Trá). Take the R292 and minor roads from Belladrihid to reach Sligo (p195) via the **Carrowmore Megalithic site**.

Budget travellers should note that no hostel accommodation exists in Belmullet or Killala. There's an excellent hostel at Pollatomish (see Day 3 of the Beaches & Bogs ride, p191); however, from Pollatomish to Sligo, the only budget accommodation is camping. An informal camping site exists near Killala; there's a camping ground near Ballina (see Places to Stay in Killala, p191), and another at Easky (almost halfway between Killala and Sligo).

Sligo to Derry
6 days, 409.3km

It's a long and thrilling haul from Sligo, famous for its associations with WB Yeats, through beautiful County Donegal to Derry. The terrain is rarely flat and includes some challenging long and steep climbs. The weather can change in an instant, and it pays to anticipate a few solid drenchings. But the stunning scenery, periods of isolation and easygoing people make this a memorable section.

From Sligo, take the N16 northeast towards Manorhamilton. At 15km, go left (signed 'to Yeats Country') and enjoy a leisurely pedal past Glencar Lake. Right turns at 20.6km (signposted 'to Glenvale B&B') and 27.8km will get you back onto the busy N15, all the while in the shadow of mighty Benbulben. Turn right off the main road at 30.4km and follow minor roads to

AROUND IRELAND

the turn into the **Gleniff Horseshoe** (around 40.7km); a trip around the Horseshoe adds about 10km to the day but should be considered mandatory – views out to Donegal Bay are outstanding. Continue on back roads to the R280 and go left (at 57.3km), through the town of Kinlough (61.3km) and then right (at 62.5km, signposted 'to River Drowse') to continue on back roads most of the way to Ballyshannon (p199) – you'll rejoin the N15 just south of Ballyshannon town centre.

From Ballyshannon to Derry, the route follows the Donegal to Derry ride (p199).

Inishowen Peninsula
3 days, 168.5km

Given that these three days begin and end in Derry, this section can legitimately be regarded as an option – albeit one you'd be mad to miss. Particularly if weather forecasts are favourable, Inishowen is a highlight of the far north. Undulating riding (excluding a very flat – and short – final day), spectacular views, quiet towns and a visit to Ireland's northernmost point at Malin Head are features.

From Derry the route follows the Inishowen Circuit ride (p211).

Derry to Belfast
3 days, 210.2km

Only wretched weather will prevent this from being the highlight of the Northern Ireland section, with two of its three days taking in the wonderful Antrim coast and glens. Views and attractions throughout are outstanding. Terrain is a mixed bag. There are protracted flat sections between Derry and Portstewart and again from Cushendall to Ballygalley. Between Ballycastle and Cushendun are some of the steepest climbs and descents in Northern Ireland.

To go from Derry to Portstewart, take the A2 northeast and turn onto the B69 (at around 25km) just before Limavady. Rejoin the A2 (at around 32km) just before Glebe and continue following it, hard on the coast, through Coleraine to Portstewart. A shorter alternative (involving some climbing) is to continue through Limavady (at around 26km) on the A2 then turn right (at around 29km) onto the B201. This will cut about 8km from the day's total, but will deny you the chance to see the coastline

around Downhill, which includes the well-known **Mussenden Temple**.

From Portstewart, the route follows the Antrim Coast ride (p236) all the way to Belfast.

Belfast to Carlingford
3 days, 189.7km

These are the last days in the North (the route crosses back into the South a few kilometres before Carlingford). After clearing Belfast and Newtownards, the route is rarely out of sight of the sea, passing along the Ards and Lecale Peninsulas, and skirting Dundrum Bay and the Mourne Mountains before hugging the shores of Carlingford Lough and the Newry River. Although most of this stage is on A roads, traffic isn't a major concern, especially if it is tackled midweek.

The route follows Day 1, and part of Day 3 of the Down South ride (p242) as far as Newcastle. From Portaferry catch the ferry (leaving every 30 minutes) to Strangford and pick up Day 3 of the Down South ride at the 13.4km (8.3 mile) mark (the turn onto the A2 in Strangford). From Newcastle (p248), follow the A2 to Kilkeel (21.3km) and continue onto minor roads south of town (the A2 turns west in the town centre) to visit Greencastle. Upon rejoining the A2 (around 31km), continue through Rostrevor and Warrenpoint to Newry, cross the river, then turn onto the B79 to Carlingford. Just before Omeath (Ó Méith; around 65km) the route crosses back into the South and the B road becomes the R173. It's just short of 8km from Omeath to Carlingford.

Carlingford
☎ 042

Carlingford (Cairlinn) sits handsomely on Carlingford Lough, in the shadow of 587m Slieve Foye, its narrow streets arranged around a collection of medieval ruins. This alluring town has history, a range of activities, accommodation and some fine places to eat.

Carlingford TIC (☎ 937 3033, Old Distillery Building, open daily from 10am) is on the R173 and can help with accommodation, activities and events. The TIC sells the *Medieval Town Trail of Carlingford* map, an essential starting point for explorations of the town's historic ruins. Most prominent is **King John's Castle**, built in the 11th and 12th centuries.

Places to Stay & Eat Book well ahead for beds in midsummer. Camp at *Táin Holiday Village (☎ 937 5385)* Tent sites €13-16 for two people. This place is about 6km west of Carlingford, near Omeath. At *Carlingford Adventure Centre (☎ 937 3100, Tholsel St)* dorm beds start at €14, singles with ensuite cost €23.

There is also a good selection of B&Bs. *Shalom (☎ 937 3151, Ghan Rd)*, where singles/doubles cost €33/49, is the best value close to town. *Ghan House (☎ 937 3682, Old Quay Lane)*, with singles €39 and doubles €102-140, offers an excellent dinner costing €34. Motel-style *Viewpoint (☎ 937 3149, Omeath Rd)* has comfortable singles/doubles costing €35/58, and great views. *McKevitt's Village Hotel (☎ 937 3116, Market Square)*, with B&B singles for €58-64 and doubles for €89-102, offers a big dinner for €30.

O'Hanlon's grocery store (Dundalk St) is open until at least 9pm. Nearby, *King John's Takeaway* does burgers and fries. There's good food at the *Oystercatcher Bistro (Market Square)* with starters for €5-9 and mains for €16-20. *Terrace Bistro (Newry St)* has starters for €3-7, mains for €8-16 and pastas for €11. *Jordan's (Newry St)* has bar food for €7-10.

Carlingford to Dublin
2 days, 150.6km

Lovely views and, in sections, busier roads characterise the remainder of the journey back to Dublin. From Carlingford, follow the R175, R174 and N1 into Dundalk (23.4km), then go left (at 24.9km) to Blackrock (29.3km). After a flat stretch on the R132 to Castlebellingham (37.8km), follow the R166 and minor roads through Annagassan, Dunany and Port to Clogherhead (Ceann Chlochair; 57.4km). From there, the R167 leads through Termonfeckin (Tearmann Feichín; 61.7km) and along the wide final reaches of the mighty River Boyne to Drogheda (Droichead Atha; 71.3km, p84).

The Drogheda to Dublin stage follows Day 8 of the Heart of Ireland Explorer ride (p85). Take particular care in traffic in parts where the route touches the N1.

AROUND IRELAND

Travel Facts

TOURIST OFFICES

Bord Fáilte (Irish Tourist Board; ☎ 01-602 4000, w www.ireland.travel.ie; Baggot St Bridge, Baggot St, Dublin 2) covers the Republic.

The Northern Ireland Tourist Board (NITB; ☎ 028-9024 6609, w www.discover northernireland.com; Belfast Welcome Centre, 47 Donegall Place, Belfast BT1 5AU) is the peak tourism body for the North.

See Business Hours (p262) for Bord Fáilte and NITB tourist information centre (TIC) opening hours.

Local Tourist Offices

Bord Fáilte TICs carry the free brochure *Ireland: Tourist Information Network*, which lists contact details and opening seasons and days for local TICs throughout the Republic and Northern Ireland. Many NITB publications include a list of local TICs.

A surprising amount of material in Bord Fáilte offices has a price tag (a by-product of self-funding requirements); NITB offices still have a lot of giveaway material.

Where possible rides in this book start and end at TICs, as they are usually central and a rich source of local information for cyclists.

Tourist Offices Abroad

Offices of Bord Fáilte include:

Australia (☎ 02-9299 6177, e itb@bigpond .com) 5th Floor, 36 Carrington St, Sydney, NSW 2000. It also has information on Northern Ireland.
France (☎ 01 70 20 00 20, e info@irlande-tour isme.fr) 33 rue de Miromesnil, 75008 Paris
Germany (☎ 069-6680 0950, e info@irish touristboard.de) Untermainanlage 7, D-60329 Frankfurt-am-Main 1
Japan (☎ 03-5275 1611, e bfejapan@oak.ocn .ne.jp) Ireland House 4f, 2-10-7 Kojimachi, Chiyoda-ku, Tokyo 102-0083
Netherlands (☎ 020-504 0689, e info@irish touristboard.nl) Spuistraat 104, 1012 VA Amsterdam
New Zealand (☎ 09-977 2255, e tourism@ire land.co.nz) 6th Floor, 18 Shortland St, Auckland 1
Northern Ireland (☎ 028-9032 7888, e info@ irishtouristboardni.com) 53 Castle St, Belfast BT1 1GH

South Africa (☎ 011-339 4865, e devprom@ global.co.za) c/o Development Promotions, Everite House, 7th Floor, De Korte St, Braam-fontein 2001, Johannesburg
UK (☎ 0800 0397 000, e info@irishtouristboard .co.uk) 1 Regent St, London SW1Y 4XT
USA (☎ 1800-223-6470, e info@irishtouristboard .com) 345 Park Ave, New York, NY 10154

Offices of the Northern Ireland Tourist Board include:

Canada (☎ 416-925 6368, e info@canada@ nitb.com) 2 Bloor St West, Suite 1501, Toronto, Ontario, M4W 3E2
England (☎ 020-7766 9920 or 08701 555 250, e infogb@nitb.com) 24 Haymarket, London, SW1 4DG
France (☎ 01 49 39 05 77) Centre PO 166, 23 rue Lecourbe, 77015 Paris
Germany (☎ 069-234 504, e nordirland@nitb .com) Westendstrasse 16–22, D-60325 Frankfurt
Ireland (☎ 01-679 1977, e infodublin@nitb.com) 16 Nassau St, Dublin 2
New Zealand (☎ 09-977 2255, e tourism@ ireland.co.nz) 6th Floor, 18 Shortland St, Auckland 1
Scotland (☎ 0141-572 4030, e infoglasgow@ nitb.com) 7th Floor, 98 West George St, Glasgow G2 1PJ
USA (☎ 212-922-0101, e infousa@nitb.com) Suite 701, 551 5th Ave, New York, NY 10176

VISAS & DOCUMENTS
Visas

Citizens of EU states and most Western countries, including Australia, Canada, New Zealand, South Africa and the USA, do not require a visa to visit either the Republic or Northern Ireland. Visas are required from citizens of India, Pakistan and some African states. EU nationals are allowed to stay indefinitely, while other visitors can usually remain for three to six months. If you're unsure of visa requirements and there's no Irish embassy or consulate in your country, contact the Consular Section, Department of Foreign Affairs (☎ 01-478 0822; 72–76 St Stephen's Green, Dublin 2).

Travel Insurance

It's essential to have a policy that covers you for medical expenses and luggage theft or loss, as well as cancellations or delays in your travel arrangements under certain circumstances (for instance falling ill before departure). There's a wide variety of policies; ensure that you stipulate to your travel agency that cycling will be your main mode of transport. Health and emergency medical cover is crucial; it's usually best to insure for the worst-case scenario, such as evacuation from a remote area, hospital treatment and a flight home. Some countries have reciprocal health agency agreements with Ireland and Britain; check with your national health authority or travel agency before leaving home and take along any necessary documentation.

Buy travel insurance as early as possible – when you book your flight is the logical time.

Other Documents

Make sure the validity of your passport extends for at least six months beyond your intended stay. Your home driving licence is valid for 12 months from the date you enter Ireland, provided you have held it for two years.

Membership of Hostelling International (HI) will give you access to An Óige hostels in the South and HINI hostels in the North (see Hostels, p33). You can become a member by joining your national Youth Hostel Association. There are also hundreds of independent hostels, which require no membership cards.

Other useful cards are the International Student Identity Card (ISIC) or, if you're under 26 but not a student, a European Youth Card (EYC). Both these cards provide discounts on transport, commercial goods and services, and admission to museums and sights. They are issued by hostelling organisations, student unions and student travel agencies.

Copies

All important documents (passport data page and visa page, credit cards, travel insurance policy, air/bus/train tickets, driving licence etc) should be photocopied before you leave home. Leave one copy with someone at home and keep another with you, separate from the originals.

Senior cyclists will generally only need to show proof of age to benefit from the many discounts available to them. These reductions include concession admission fees at museums and galleries, and free public transport. The minimum qualifying age is usually 55 to 65.

EMBASSIES & CONSULATES
Irish & UK Embassies & Consulates

Irish diplomatic offices overseas include:

Australia (☎ 02-6273 3022, e irishemb@cyberone.com.au) 20 Arkana St, Yarralumla, Canberra, ACT 2600

Canada (☎ 613-233 6281, e embassyofireland@rogers.com) Suite 1105, 130 Albert St, Ottawa, Ontario K1P 5G4

France (☎ 01 44 17 67 00, e irembparis@wanadoo.fr) 4 rue Rude, 75116 Paris

Germany (☎ 030-220 720) Friedrichstrasse 200, 10117 Berlin

Japan (☎ 03-3263 0695) Ireland House 5F, 2-10-7 Kojimachi, Chiyoda-Ku, Tokyo 102-0083

Netherlands (☎ 070-363 0993, e info@irish-embassy.demon.nl) Dr Kuyperstraat 9, 2514 BA The Hague

New Zealand (☎ 09-977 2252) 6th Floor, 18 Shortland St, Auckland 1

UK (☎ 020-7235 2171) 17 Grosvenor Place, London SW1X 7HR

USA (☎ 202-462-3939, e embirlus@aol.com) 2234 Massachusetts Ave NW, Washington, DC 20008–28490. There are also consulates in Boston, Chicago, New York and San Francisco.

UK (for Northern Ireland) diplomatic offices abroad include:

Australia (☎ 02-6270 6666, e bhc.canberra@uk.emb.gov.au) Commonwealth Ave, Yarralumla, Canberra, ACT 2600

Canada (☎ 613-237 1530) 80 Elgin St, Ottawa, Ontario K1P 5K7

France (☎ 01 44 51 31 00) 35 rue du Faubourg St Honoré, 75383 Paris

Germany (☎ 30-204 570) Wilhelmstrasse 70, 10117 Berlin

Netherlands (☎ 70-427 0427) Lange Voorhout 10, 2514 ED The Hague

New Zealand (☎ 04-924 2888, e PPA.Mailbox@fco.gov.uk) 44 Hill St, Wellington 1

USA (☎ 202-588-6500) 3100 Massachusetts Ave NW, Washington, DC 20008

Embassies in Ireland

Countries with diplomatic representation in Dublin include:

Australia (☎ 01-676 1517, ⎮e⎮ austemb.dublin@ dfat.gov.au) 2nd Floor, Fitzwilton House, Wilton Terrace, Dublin 2
Canada (☎ 01-478 1988) 4th Floor, 65–68 St Stephen's Green, Dublin 2
France (☎ 01-260 1666) 36 Ailesbury Rd, Dublin 4
Germany (☎ 01-269 3011) 31 Trimleston Ave, Booterstown, Blackrock, County Dublin
Japan (☎ 01-269 4244) Nutley Building, Merrion Centre, Nutley Lane, Dublin 4
Netherlands (☎ 01-269 3444, ⎮e⎮ nethemb@ indigo.ie) 160 Merrion Rd, Ballsbridge, Dublin 4
UK (☎ 01-205 3742, ⎮e⎮ passport.dubli@fco .gov.uk) 29 Merrion Rd, Dublin 4
USA (☎ 01-668 8777, ⎮e⎮ aedublin@indigo.ie) 42 Elgin Rd, Ballsbridge, Dublin 4

Countries with consular representation in Belfast include:

Netherlands (☎ 028-9077 9088) c/o All-Route Shipping (NI) Ltd, 14–16 West Bank Rd
USA (☎ 028-9032 8239) Queen's House, 14 Queen St

CUSTOMS

Travellers coming from outside the EU are allowed to import, duty free, €180/US$170 worth of goods – 200 cigarettes, 1L of spirits, or 2L of wine. Visitors from Britain and other EU countries can import increased amounts of goods, provided duty was paid somewhere in the EU and the goods are for personal consumption. Customs inspections at point of entry are for drugs and national security only.

MONEY
Currency

The Republic uses the euro, with coins (one, two, five, 10, 20 and 50 cents, plus €1 and €2) and notes (€5, €10, €20, €50, €100, €200 and €500).

Northern Ireland, as part of the UK, has not adopted the euro. The pound sterling (£) is used; its coins come in denominations of 1p ('p' for 'penny'), 2p, 5p, 10p, 20p, 50p, £1 and £2. Notes are printed in denominations of £5, £10, £20 and £50. You'll see both Northern Irish and British notes; Northern Irish notes are not readily accepted in Britain, but British banks will swap them for normal sterling notes.

Exchange Rates

A good currency converter is ⎮w⎮ www .oanda.com. At the time of going to print exchange rates were:

country	unit	euro	pound
Australia	A$1	€0.56	£0.38
Canada	C$1	€0.63	£0.43
UK	£1	€1.47	£1
USA	US$1	€0.93	£0.63

Exchanging Money

Banks offer the best exchange rates. Building societies often handle currency exchange and open longer hours than banks.

Exchange bureaus are usually open longer hours than banks, but offer poorer exchange rates and/or charge commission. Many post offices and some TICs in both the Republic and Northern Ireland have currency-exchange facilities. For banking hours see Business Hours (p262).

Cash In remote areas cash is essential and you're at more risk of losing it than having it stolen. It's a good idea to arrive in Ireland with some local currency, if only to tide you over until you find an exchange facility.

Travellers Cheques Most major currencies of travellers cheques are readily accepted in Ireland, and carrying them in euro is probably sensible if you're coming from, or travelling on to, other destinations in the euro zone.

American Express and Thomas Cook travellers cheques are widely recognised and you'll avoid paying commission if you cash cheques at the companies' offices. Keeping a record of the cheque numbers and the cheques you have cashed is vital in case of loss. Travellers cheques are rarely accepted outside banks and exchange facilities.

ATMs & Credit Cards Increasingly, travellers are eschewing travellers cheques in favour of debit and credit cards. They enable you to withdraw cash from selected banks and automatic teller machines (ATMs). Credit cards are also handy for large purchases. It's easy to find ATMs that are linked to international money systems such as Cirrus, Maestro or Plus. Ask your home bank about withdrawal limits and transaction fees – these can add up during an extended journey. ATMs have been known to swallow cards so if you travel exclusively on plastic make sure you have more than one card.

Credit cards such as Visa, MasterCard and Access are widely accepted although many small businesses in remote areas are still cash-only. While charge cards such as American Express and Diners Club don't have credit limits they may not be accepted by small businesses in out-of-the-way areas.

Security
There are few parts of Ireland where you'll go more than a day or two without seeing a bank so there's no need to carry large sums of cash. It's best to keep your money for the day in a jersey pocket (or perhaps a money belt) and spread the rest around your kit – handlebar bag, panniers and so on. It's not a bad idea to keep an emergency stash – something like €50 or £50 – in an almost-fail-safe place (a note covered in cling wrap fits nicely under a cycling-shoe footbed).

Costs
Ireland is a mixed bag budget-wise, expensive in some areas and for some services, fairly reasonable in others. Predictably, everything is more expensive in the cities than small towns. A typical daily budget might include:

item	euro	pound
youth hostel	€12.00	£9.00
camping ground	€10.00	£6.00
B&B	€25.00	£22.00
pint of milk	€0.45	£0.31
loaf of bread	€0.95	£0.70
pint of beer	€3.20	£2.10
litre unleaded petrol	€0.85	£0.75
newspaper	€1.30	£0.75

Tipping
Fancy hotels and restaurants usually add a 10% or 15% service charge; no additional tip is required. In simpler places, if you decide to tip, just round up the bill or add 10%. Tipping in bars isn't expected, but use common sense if you eat a meal in a pub restaurant.

Taxes & Refunds
Value-added tax (VAT) is a sales tax on most goods and services in Ireland. On large purchases to be taken outside the EU, non-EU visitors can claim back the VAT (minus an administration fee). You must be exporting your purchases within three months of the last day of the month in which they were bought.

Goods bought from stores displaying the sign 'Tax Free Shopping' or 'Cashback' come with a voucher that can be cashed at Dublin or Shannon airports. If you're not leaving Ireland from those airports, the voucher can be stamped at customs and mailed back for a refund; see **w** www.globalrefund.ie for more information.

In Northern Ireland, shops participating in the refund scheme will give you a form/invoice on request. This must be presented to customs with the goods and receipts when you leave. After customs has certified the form, it will be returned to the shop for a refund.

POST & COMMUNICATIONS
Post
From the Republic, postcards and airmail letters cost €0.41 to Britain, €0.44 to continental Europe and €0.57 to the rest of the world. A packet of five aerogrammes costs €2.80.

In the North postcards cost 28p to Britain, 38p to continental Europe and 46p to the rest of the world. The basic rate for 1st-/2nd-class letters to Britain is 20/28p; for airmail letters to Europe it's 38p and to the rest of the world 69p. A pack of six aerogrammes costs £2.20.

Mail to both the North and the Republic can be addressed to poste restante at post offices but is officially held for only two weeks. Writing 'hold for collection' on the envelope may have some effect.

For post office opening hours see Business Hours (p262).

Telephone
The international code for the Republic is ☎ 353, followed by the local area code (drop the initial zero). For Northern Ireland it's ☎ 44 28. To call Northern Ireland from Britain dial ☎ 028 followed by the number. To call Northern Ireland from the South use the ☎ 048 area code, then the number; the

Useful Phone Numbers

The Republic

Directory assistance within Ireland	☎ 11811
Directory assistance elsewhere	☎ 11818
Emergency	☎ 112 or ☎ 999
International access code	☎ 353
Operator	☎ 10

The North

Directory assistance within the UK	☎ 192
Directory assistance elsewhere	☎ 153
Emergency	☎ 999
International access code	☎ 44 28
Operator	☎ 100

☎ 028 area code will also work, but it's more expensive.

Payphones & Phonecards Most calls from payphones are timed and charged in three-minute units; minimum charges are €0.38 in the South and 20p in the North. International calls can be dialled direct from payphones; this costs more than using a private phone. Note that in isolated areas phones may only accept coins.

Phonecards come in several 'sizes' from €4/£5 up to about €15/£20. There are a lot of companies peddling phonecards; it's worth shopping around.

There's a wide range of international phonecards. Lonely Planet's ekno Communication Card, specifically aimed at travellers, provides competitive international calls (avoid using it for local calls), messaging services and free email. Visit w www .ekno.lonelyplanet.com for information about joining and using the service.

Mobile Phones Ireland uses GSM 900/ 1800, which is compatible with the rest of Europe and Australia, but not with North American GSM 1900 or the totally different system in Japan. There are three service providers in Ireland: Eircell, ESAT Digifone and Meteor. All three are linked with most international GSM providers, which will allow you to 'roam' onto a local service, but you will be charged at the highest possible rate. Mobile phone coverage in mountain areas is poor.

Email & Internet Access

Internet cafés are a common sight in all major centres and come and go from smaller towns. The local library is the best place to go if there's no Internet café in town.

If you plan to carry a notebook or palmtop computer, bring an AC adaptor to suit the standard Irish power supply voltage (220V). It may be easiest to buy this before you leave home. Email accounts are free with many of the local Internet service providers (ISPs), and you can usually set up over the phone.

TIME

The Republic and Northern Ireland are on Greenwich Mean Time (GMT). Without making allowances for daylight-saving time changes, when it's noon in Dublin, Belfast and London it's 7am in New York, 3am in Los Angeles or Vancouver, midnight in Auckland, 10pm in Sydney and 8pm in Singapore. Clocks are put forward by one hour from late March to the end of October.

ELECTRICITY

Electricity is 220V and plugs are usually flat three-pins, as in Britain. Many bathrooms have a two-pin 110V to 120V AC source for shavers.

WEIGHTS & MEASURES

The metric system is slowly replacing imperial weights and measures, but it's doubtful that the conversion will ever be total. On road signs distances are measured in miles and kilometres; vehicle speeds are always given in miles per hour. Food in shops is priced and weighed in metric; petrol is sold in litres but beer is served in pints. This book uses the metric system, although distances in Northern Ireland are also given in imperial. A conversion table is on the inside back cover.

LEGAL MATTERS

For legal assistance contact the Legal Aid Board (☎ 01-661 5811, St Stephen's Green House, Dublin 2). It has a number of local law centres that are listed in the phone book.

BUSINESS HOURS

Banks

In remote areas North and South some banks close for lunch (usually 12.30pm to 1.30pm) and some may open only two or three days (or two or three hours) a week.

Republic: Open 10am to 4pm on weekdays (till 5pm on Thursday or Friday)

Northern Ireland: Open 9.30am to 4.30pm on weekdays. Most stay open till 5pm on Thursday.

Post Offices

Republic: Open 9am to 5.30pm on weekdays and 9am to 5pm on Saturday. Most offices are closed for lunch (1pm to 2.15pm) on Saturday and smaller offices often close for lunch on weekdays.

Northern Ireland: Open 9am to 5.30pm on weekdays, and 9am to 1pm on Saturday.

Pubs

The only days when pubs definitely close are Christmas Day and Good Friday.

Republic: Open 10.30am to 11.30pm Monday to Saturday and 12.30pm to 11pm on Sunday. Most pubs stick to these hours throughout the warm months and may operate on reduced hours in winter.

Northern Ireland: Open 11.30am to 11pm Monday to Saturday and 12.30pm to 10pm on Sunday (pubs in Protestant areas may be closed on Sunday).

Shops Open 9am to 5.30pm or 6pm Monday to Saturday. Most larger centres have a seven-day supermarket with late-closing hours; often there'll be a late-closing night for all shops (usually Thursday and/or Friday). Small businesses (such as bike shops) often open and close at irregular hours and on a varied selection of days, depending to some degree on the owner's whim. Outside the cities, shops and businesses often close for one afternoon in the week. In small towns most shops are also likely to close for an hour or so at lunchtime. Most small towns have a late-closing supermarket or general store.

TICs and visitor centres Bord Fáilte and NITB offices are typically open 9am to 5pm Monday to Friday, and 9am to 1pm on Saturday, but the hours are often extended in summer and may include all or part of Sunday. Some offices are open seasonally only (from April, May or June to August or September) or for much shorter hours from October to April.

Tourist attractions Always check ahead to be certain; these may be closed for one or two weekdays. In the North they're often closed on Sunday morning.

PUBLIC HOLIDAYS

Public holidays in the Republic of Ireland (IR), Northern Ireland (NI) or both are:

New Year's Day 1 January
St Patrick's Day (IR) 17 March
Easter Monday March/April
May Holiday First Monday in May
Spring Bank Holiday (NI) Last Monday in May
June Holiday (IR) First Monday in June
Orangeman's Day (NI) 12 July
August Holiday (IR) First Monday in August
August Holiday (NI) last Monday in August
Summer Bank Holiday (NI) Last Monday in August
October Holiday (IR) Last Monday in October
Christmas Day 25 December
St Stephen's Day (Boxing Day) 26 December

If St Patrick's Day falls on a weekend the holiday is taken on the following Monday. In the South, banks and many shops, pubs and offices close on Good Friday even though it isn't an official public holiday. In the North, most shops open on Good Friday but close the following Tuesday.

Getting There & Away

It's easy to get to Ireland – take your pick from numerous airlines, and high-speed and not-so-fast ferries from several British and a couple of French ports.

AIR

Dublin is the Republic's major international airport; international flights also use Cork and Shannon. Some smaller airports, including Waterford and Knock, handle direct flights to the UK.

Warning

The information in this chapter is particularly vulnerable to change: prices for international travel are volatile, routes are introduced and cancelled, schedules change, special deals come and go, and rules and visa requirements are amended.

You should check directly with the airline or a travel agent to make sure you understand the conditions of your ticket. The details given in this chapter should be regarded as pointers and are not a substitute for your own careful, up-to-date research.

Packing for Air Travel

We've all heard the horror stories about smashed/lost luggage when flying, but a more real threat to cycle tourists is arriving in a country for a two-week tour and finding their bike with broken wheels or in little bits spread out around the baggage carousel. Fixing a damaged bike could take days, and the delay and frustration could ruin your holiday.

How do you avoid this? Err on the side of caution and box your bike. Trust airline baggage handlers if you want (we're told some people actually do) and give your bike to them 'as is' – turn the handlebars 90°, remove the pedals, cover the chain with a rag or bag (to protect other people's baggage) and deflate your tyres (partially, not all the way) – but is it worth the risk? If you want to take that sort of risk do it on your homeward flight, when you can get your favourite bike shop to fix any damage.

Some airlines sell bike boxes at the airport, but most bike shops give them away. Fitting your bike into a box requires a few simple steps and only takes about 15 minutes:

1 Loosen the stem bolt and turn the handlebars 90°; loosen the clamp bolt(s) and twist the handlebars as pictured.

2 Remove the pedals (use a 15mm spanner, turning each the opposite way to how you pedal), wheels and seat post and saddle (don't forget to mark its height before removing it).

3 Undo the rear derailleur bolt and tape it to the inside of the chainstay. There's no need to undo the derailleur cable. You can remove the chain (it will make reassembly easier) but it isn't necessary.

4 Cut up some spare cardboard and tape it beneath the chainwheel to prevent the teeth from penetrating the floor of the box and being damaged.

5 Remove the quick-release skewers from the wheels and wrap a rag (or two) around the cluster so it won't get damaged or damage anything else.

If you run your tyres at very high pressure (above 100psi), you should partially deflate them – on most bikes this won't be necessary.

6 Place the frame in the box, so it rests on the chainwheel and forks – you might want to place another couple of layers of cardboard underneath the forks.

Most boxes will be too short to allow the front pannier racks to remain on the bike; if so, remove them. The rear rack should fit while still on the bike, but may require the seat stay bolts to be undone and pushed forward.

Packing for Air Travel

Side View

ALL PHOTOGRAPHS BY JEFF CROW

7 Place the wheels beside the frame, on the side opposite the chainwheel. Keep the wheels and frame separate by inserting a piece of cardboard between them and tying the wheels to the frame (to stop them moving around and scratching the frame).

8 Slot the saddle and seat post, your helmet, tools and any other bits and pieces (eg, tent, sleeping bag) into the vacant areas. Wrap the skewers, chain and other loose bike bits in newspaper and place them in the box. Add cardboard or newspaper packing to any areas where metal is resting on metal.

9 Seal the box with tape and write your name, address and flight details on several sides.

Now all you need to do is strap your panniers together and either take them with you as carry-on luggage or check them in.

Top View

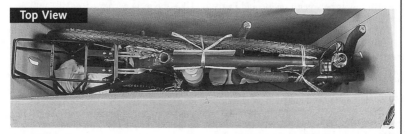

Bike Bags

If you're planning on travelling between regions via train, plane or bus then consider taking a bike bag. The simplest form of zippered bike bag has no padding built into it, is made of Cordura or nylon, and can be rolled up and put on your rear pannier rack and unfurled when you need to travel again.

Some of the smaller ones require you to remove both wheels, the front pannier racks, pedals and seat post to fit inside the bag. However, these make for (relatively) easy and inconspicuous train, plane or bus transfers so the extra effort is worthwhile.

Baggage Restrictions

Airlines impose tight restrictions on carry-on baggage. No sharp implements of any kind are allowed onto the plane, so pack items such as bicycle tools, pocket knives, camping cutlery and first-aid kits into your checked luggage.

If you're carrying a camping stove you should remember that airlines also ban liquid fuels and gas cartridges from all baggage, both check-through and carry-on. Empty all fuel bottles and buy what you need at your destination.

Most international flights to Northern Ireland land at Belfast airport, which is 30km (19 miles) northwest of the city; the more central Belfast City airport handles flights from some British regional airports. City of Derry airport takes flights from Britain and Dublin.

Departure Tax

An Irish government travel tax is built into the price of an air ticket and is also paid if you leave by ferry.

The UK

Direct flights leave London, Birmingham, Manchester and Glasgow for Dublin, Cork, Shannon, Kerry, Knock and Waterford in the Republic and Belfast in the North; there are also flights between London and Derry and Edinburgh and Belfast.

The main carriers are:

Aer Lingus (☎ 0845 084 4444, **w** www.aerlingus .com)
British Airways (☎ 0845 773 3377, **w** www .britishairways.com)
British Midland (☎ 0870 607 0555, **w** www .flybmi.com)
easyJet (☎ 0870 600 0000, **w** www.easyjet.com)
Ryanair (☎ 0870 156 9569, **w** www.ryanair.com)

Continental Europe

Direct flights leave Amsterdam, Paris, Frankfurt, Munich, Milan and Rome to Dublin, from Amsterdam, Frankfurt and Paris to Shannon and Cork and from Amsterdam to Belfast.

In addition to Aer Lingus, easyJet and Ryanair (see the UK), the main carriers are:

Air France (☎ 0820 820 820, **w** www.airfrance .com) 119 ave des Champs-Élysées, 75008 Paris, France
Alitalia (☎ 06-656 34951, **w** www.alitalia.it) Leonardo da Vinci Airport, Rome
Lufthansa (☎ 01803 803 803, **w** www.lufthansa.com) Von Gablenz Strasse 2-6, 50679 Köln, Germany

The USA & Canada

Direct flights leave New York, Boston, Baltimore, Chicago and Los Angeles for Shannon, Dublin and Belfast. There are no nonstop scheduled services from Canada to Ireland; the best plan is to connect to a transatlantic flight in the USA or fly to London and connect for Ireland there.

As well as Aer Lingus (see the UK), the main carriers are:

American Airlines (☎ 800 433 7300, **w** www .aa.com)
Continental (☎ 800 231 0856, **w** www.conti nental.com)
Delta (☎ 800 241 4141, **w** www.delta.com)

Australia & New Zealand

There are no direct scheduled flights from Australia or New Zealand to Ireland; generally it's cheapest to fly to London or Amsterdam for a connecting flight to Ireland. Round-the-World (RTW) tickets can be real bargains.

In addition to British Airways (see the UK), the main carrier is:

Qantas (☎ 02-9691 3636, **w** www.qantas.com) Qantas Centre, 203 Coward St, Mascot, NSW 2020, Australia

SEA

Ferries and catamarans provide a variety of services between Britain, France and Ireland. Special discounts and return fares compare favourably with cheaper air fares. If you're planning to drive around Ireland, it could be cheaper to put your vehicle on the ferry than to hire a car when you get there.

The UK

Numerous services link ports in England, Scotland, Wales and the Isle of Man to the Republic and the North. It's worth planning ahead because fares vary widely according to season, day of the week, time of day and length of stay. Return fares are usually good value and discounts may be available for ISIC cardholders, HI members and senior citizens.

The shipping lines are:

Irish Ferries (☎ 0870 517 1717, Ⓦ www.irishferries.com) Corn Exchange Building, Brunswick St, Liverpool L2 7TP. This company has ferry and fast boat services from Holyhead to Dublin, and ferry services from Pembroke to Rosslare.

Isle of Man Steam Packet Company (☎ 01624-661 661, Ⓦ www.steam-packet.com) Imperial Buildings, Douglas, Isle of Man, IM1 BY. This company offers seasonal ferry services from Douglas (Isle of Man) to Belfast and Dublin, as well as crossings from Heysham and Liverpool to Douglas. It is also linked with SeaCat.

Cycle-Friendly Airlines

Not too many airlines will carry a bike free of charge these days – at least according to their official policy. Most airlines regard the bike as part of your checked luggage. Carriers working the routes to Ireland from Europe, Asia and the Pacific usually allow 20kg (44 lbs) of checked luggage (excluding carry-on), so the weight of your bike and bags shouldn't exceed this. If you're over the limit, technically you're liable for excess-baggage charges.

Carriers flying routes to Ireland from or through North America use a different system. Passengers are generally allowed two pieces of luggage, each of which must not exceed 32kg (70 lbs). Excess baggage fees are charged for additional pieces, rather than for excess weight. On some airlines a bike may be counted as one of your two pieces; others charge a set fee for carrying a bike, which may then be carried in addition to your two other pieces. Check whether these fees are paid for the whole journey, each way or per leg.

Some airlines require you to box your bike, while others accept soft covers, or just ask that you turn the handlebars, remove the pedals and cover the chain. Check this policy before getting to the airport; only a few airlines sell sturdy boxes at the check-in counter.

When we looked into the policies of different carriers, we found that not only does the story sometimes change depending on who you talk to – and how familiar they are with the company's policy – but the official line is not necessarily adhered to at the check-in counter. If a company representative or agent reassures you that your bike travels for free, ask them to annotate your passenger file to that effect. If your flight is not too crowded, the check-in staff are often lenient with the excess charges, particularly with items such as bikes.

The times when you are most likely to incur excess baggage charges are on full flights and, of course, if you inconvenience the check-in staff. If you suspect you may be over the limit, increase your chances of avoiding charges by checking in early and being well organised, friendly and polite – a smile and a 'Thankyou' can go a long way!

If you're planning to fly with a discount carrier you need to be especially cautious; make sure you research all possible charges. One of the most popular discounters on routes between continental Europe and Ireland allows passengers just 15kg of checked baggage; additional weight incurs a hefty charge of €6 per kilogram. (And you can forget about the old lead-weight cabin-bag trick: this carrier allows a maximum of just 7kg for carry-on.) Before you've even started counting kilos, the carrier charges a flat €25 per flight per bike. To top it off, these charges are strictly non-negotiable – the carrier's website states that handling agents and staff are allowed no discretion in applying excess-baggage charges.

Norse Merchant Ferries (☎ 0870 600 4321, W www.norsemerchant.com) Canada Dock, Liverpool L20 1DQ. Norse has ferry services from Liverpool to Dublin and Belfast.

P&O Irish Sea (☎ 0870 242 4777, W www .poirishsea.com) Cairnryan DG9 8RF. P&O operates ferry and fast boat services from Cairnryan to Larne, and ferry services from Troon to Larne, Fleetwood to Larne, Liverpool and Mostyn to Dublin, and Cherbourg to Dublin and Rosslare.

SeaCat (☎ 0870 552 3523, W www.seacat.co.uk) SeaCat Terminal, Donegall Quay, Belfast BT1 3AL. SeaCat operates fast boat services from Heysham or Troon to Belfast and Liverpool to Dublin.

Stena Line (☎ 0870 570 7070, W www.stenaline .com) Charter House, Park St, Ashford, Kent TN24 8EX. Stena has ferry services from Holyhead to Dun Laoghaire, and Stranraer to Belfast, also fast boat services from Holyhead to Dublin, from Fishguard to Rosslare, and from Stranraer to Belfast.

Swansea Cork Ferries (☎ 01792-456 116, W www.swansea-cork.ie) Harbour Office, Kings Dock, Swansea SA1 1SF. This company has ferry services from Swansea to Cork.

France

Shipping lines operating between France and Ireland are:

Brittany Ferries (☎ 021-427 7801 in Ireland, ☎ 02 98 29 28 00 in France, W www.brittany-ferries .co.uk) Brittany operates a seasonal service between Roscoff and Cork.

Irish Ferries (☎ 01-638 3333 in Dublin, ☎ 053-33158 in Rosslare, ☎ 02 33 23 44 44 in Cherbourg, ☎ 02 98 61 17 17 in Roscoff, W www .irishferries.com) Irish Ferries operates services to Rosslare from Cherbourg and Roscoff. Eurail cardholders and Inter-Rail pass holders may be entitled to a substantial fare reduction; advance reservation is compulsory during July and August.

LAND & SEA

Bus Éireann (☎ 01-836 6111, W www.bus eireann.ie) and Britain's National Express (☎ 08705 808080, W www.gobycoach.com) operate Eurolines (W www.eurolines.ie) services direct from London and other British cities to Dublin and Belfast, with connections to regional towns and cities.

Ulsterbus (☎ 028-9066 6630, W www .translink.co.uk), with National Express and Scottish Citylink (W www.citylink.co.uk), has express services to major cities in Britain.

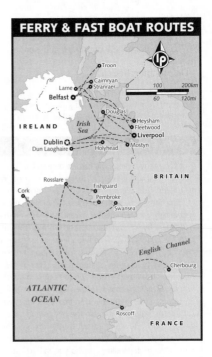

FERRY & FAST BOAT ROUTES

Getting Around

Despite an extensive network of roads and relatively short distances between towns, travelling around Ireland can be a complicated business. Direct road routes between even major centres are rare, and minor roads are devious and not designed for fast travel. Public transport, especially trains, can be expensive and/or infrequent, and is nonexistent in some areas.

AIR

Despite Ireland's small size there are several internal flights, which would be a quick although expensive way of getting around. Flights connect Dublin with Carrickfinn (County Donegal), Charlestown (County Mayo), Cork, Galway, Kerry, Shannon, Sligo and Derry.

Air Rianta (☎ 01-844 4900, W www.aer-rianta.com), the Republic's national airport authority, provides information about airport services and flight schedules, as well as arrivals and departures from Dublin, Cork and Shannon.

The main domestic airlines are:

Aer Arann Express (☎ 01-814 1058 for international callers, ☎ 1890 462726 in Ireland, **W** www.aerarannexpress.com)
Aer Lingus (☎ 0818 365 000, **W** www.aerlingus.com)
Ryanair (☎ 01-609 7800, **W** www.ryanair.com)

Carrying Your Bicycle
Aer Lingus carry bicycles as checked baggage, and you should notify it that you'll be bringing a bicycle when booking your flight. Check in one hour before departure with tyres deflated, pedals removed and handlebars and saddle lowered as far as possible; a large plastic bag will be provided to pack the bike in. It charges excess baggage rates (€1.20 per kilogram) if you're over the 20kg baggage allowance.

Aer Arann carries bicycles as checked baggage, with tyres deflated, pedals removed and handlebars turned and secured; see the boxed text 'Packing for Air Travel, (p264). It charges €2 per kilogram for bikes if you're over the 15kg baggage allowance.

BUS
The two main bus companies operating in Ireland are:

Bus Éireann (☎ 01-836 6111, **W** www.buseireann.ie) This company operates services throughout the South and to the North. Many services almost vanish outside the peak season (late June to the end of August). The Expressway Timetable includes details of discount fares and all provincial bus stations. It's available from major bus stations, larger bookshops and on the company's website, which also has an online booking service.
Ulsterbus (☎ 028-9066 6630, **W** www.translink.co.uk) Ulsterbus serves the North, and publishes four free regional timetables, available in Belfast at the Europa Buscentre in Glengall St and the Laganside Centre in Oxford St, and at larger regional bus stations. This information is also available online.

Bus Éireann carries bicycles on a 'space-available' basis (bookings are not accepted) and charges €9 per bike per journey. Unofficially, drivers appear to have a good deal of latitude, and unless you're cycling in a large group, you shouldn't encounter too much trouble getting a bike aboard. Always

check schedules in advance, and ask which services are least likely to be crowded.

Ulsterbus will carry bikes provided there's space; the charge is half the adult single fare.

Also operating in the South are private bus companies that compete with Bus Éireann on some routes, and provide services in areas not covered by the national company. The larger companies usually carry bikes free but you should always check in advance.

TRAIN
The operators of Ireland's rail networks are:

Iarnród Éireann (Irish Rail; ☎ 01-836 6222, **W** www.irishrail.ie) This company operates trains in the Republic on routes generally radiating from Dublin.
Northern Ireland Railways (NIR; ☎ 028-9066 6630, **W** www.translink.co.uk) NIR operates four routes from Belfast. One links with the system in the South via Newry to Dublin; the other three go east to Bangor, northeast to Larne and northwest to Derry via Coleraine. Printed timetables are available free from most stations.

Trains will get you to major regional centres faster than buses, and it's easier to load a bike aboard (generally they're plonked in the guard's van). However, in the Republic train travel is more expensive than using buses and the rail system isn't as extensive as the bus network.

Bicycles are allowed on almost all Iarnród Éireann intercity trains; check the website to see which services do *not* carry bikes. Bicycles aren't allowed on any Dublin Area Rapid Transit (DART) services or on Dublin suburban trains arriving in the city between 7am and 10.30am and leaving it between 4pm and 7.30pm. You must have a valid ticket for your bike before it's loaded onto the train; rates vary according to how far you are travelling.

Contrary to the situation in the South, train travel in the North is a cost-effective option. One-way fares on major rail routes (for instance Belfast to Derry) are comparable to the bus equivalent for passengers and cheaper for bikes (which travel for 25% of the standard fare).

Reservations
Reservations for Irish Rail can be made online, at most train stations or at Iarnród Éireann Travel Centres (35 Lower Abbey St,

Dublin 1 • 65 Patrick St, Cork). Tickets can also be booked by phone (☎ 01-703 4070, 021-504 888).

Reservations for NIR services can be made by phone (☎ 028-9066 6630).

CAR & MOTORCYCLE

Busy roads, parking difficulties and the cost of rental and fuel render cars all but useless for travel between rides (although a car may be useful for preride reconnaissance or for regional sightseeing). There is a good network of motorways in the North but in the Republic the comparatively few motorways are confined to the east and the Dublin ring road. Main roads (designated 'A' in the North, 'N' in the South) are generally good quality, although you'll find some alarming lapses in the west of the Republic. Most of the more recent N roads have a left side lane, marked with an orange dotted line, used by people walking, jogging, riding or hitching, and by slow vehicles. Minor roads ('B' in the North, 'R' in the South, and others without a designation) are generally narrow and often lined with high hedges; many in the Republic are in poor repair and have dangerous bends. Traffic can be chaotic in the towns, especially in the Republic, but is rarely busy elsewhere.

Safety belts must be worn by the driver and all passengers. Children under 12 years may not sit on the front seat. Motorcyclists and pillion passengers must wear helmets. For a discussion of driving laws particularly pertinent to cyclists see Road Rules (p45).

Speed limits are the same in the North and South: 70mi/h (112km/h) on motorways, 60mi/h (96km/h) on other roads and 30mi/h (48km/h) or as signposted in towns.

Metric and imperial measurements still appear in confusing coexistence. In the Republic, speed limits are in miles per hour (though in kilometres in some eastern areas). Green distance signs and new white ones are in kilometres, but older white signs, with raised black letters, show miles and the old route numbering system ('R' and 'T' roads). In the North, imperial measurements are still the norm. Printed copies of the road rules do exist; major post offices and perhaps TICs are the most likely sources.

Parking in cities and towns can be a problem; it's best to find designated, off-street parking areas for which you may have to pay. Roadside parking is fraught with regulations, and usually deepens the confusion.

Rental

Car rental in Ireland is expensive, so much so that it may be cheaper to hire a vehicle in Britain and take it across on a ferry. Or you may find a good package deal if you book in your home country. It's wise to book ahead in the high season (June to August). Off-season rates are considerably lower. Make sure that the price you are quoted includes insurance, Collision Damage Waiver (CDW) and VAT. If you plan to travel into the North from the Republic, check that your insurance covers this. There may be an additional charge for extra drivers, as well as an extra daily charge if you cross the border in either direction.

You must be at least 21 years old to hire a car; the majority of rental companies require drivers to be at least 23 and to have had a valid driving licence for no less than 12 months or even two years. Some companies will not rent to people over 70. In most cases you only need your own licence to arrange a hire for up to three months.

The international rental companies Avis, Budget, Hertz, Thrifty and the major local operators Murray's, Europcar, Dan Dooley and Malone have offices all over Ireland. There are many smaller and local operators. Motorcycles are not available for hire.

Remember that the smallest (and therefore least expensive) rental cars are unlikely to fit more than two riders with bikes and gear.

Automobile Clubs

The Automobile Association (AA; ☎ 028-9032 8924 in Belfast, ⓦ www.theaa.com • ☎ 01-617 9977 in Dublin, ⓦ www.aaireland.ie) operates across Ireland. The AA free-call breakdown number in the Republic is ☎ 1800 667 788 and in the North is ☎ 0800 085 2721.

In the North, members of the Royal Automobile Club (RAC; ☎ 028-9023 3640, ⓦ www.rac.co.uk) can call ☎ 0800 828 282 for breakdown service. In the South the number is ☎ 1800 535 005.

Glossary

Here you will find some of the more commonly encountered Irish words – including those used in place names on maps (in some cases followed by an anglicised version in brackets). Also included are Irish words frequently seen in public places and English terms that may not be familiar.

abhainn (ow, owen) – river, stream
achadh (agha, augh) – field
aill – cliff
aircin – creek, small stream
alt – height, high place
An Óige – Irish youth hostel association (literally 'The Youth')
arête – narrow ridge, particularly between glacial valleys

bachtai – turf banks
baile (bally) – village, settlement, town
bán (baun) – white
barr – top
beag (beg) – small
bealach (ballagh) – pass, col
beann (ben) – peak
bearna (barna) – gap
bia – food
binn – peak
Black and Tans – British soldiers recruited into the Royal Irish Constabulary soon after WWI
Blue Flag beach – EU-listed as clean and safe (usually patrolled and water-monitored)
Bó – cow
bodhrán – hand-held goatskin drum
bog – wet, spongy ground made from decomposing plant matter
booleying – traditional practice of moving herds to upland pastures in summer
boreen – old country lane or narrow road
bothar (boher) – road
boxty – potato griddle cakes
breac (brack) – speckled
buaille (booley) – summer cattle pasture
buí – yellow
bun – river mouth
burn – stream (Northern Ireland)

caishel (cashel) – prehistoric stone fort
calladh (callows) – lakeside or riverside grasslands prone to regular flooding

carn (cairn) – pile of stones
carraig (carrick) – rock
cathair (caher) – prehistoric stone fort; city
ceann (kin) – headland
ceilidh – session of traditional music and dancing
Celts – people who arrived in Ireland about 300 BC
ceol – music
cill (kil) – church, chapel
cillin (killeen) – children's graveyard
clint – natural cobblestone; slabs between the cracks (grikes) found in a natural limestone pavement
cloch – stone
clochain, clochán – beehive-shaped, drystone hut
cluain – meadow
cnoc (knock, crock) – rocky hill
coill (kil) – woodland
coire – corrie
col – low point or pass between two mountains
colcannon – potato and cabbage dish traditionally served on Halloween
cor – rounded hill
corrán (carraun) – serrated or crescent-shaped mountain
corrie – small, high, cup-shaped valley, often of glacial origin
crag – steep cliff
craic – fun, good times
crannog – ancient lake dwelling on a natural or artificial island
cruach, cruachan – steep hill
cuan – bay
cúm (coum) – hollow, corrie
curragh – rowing boat consisting of a wooden frame with tarred canvas as an outer skin

Dáil Éireann – Irish Assembly
dearg – red
dheas – south
doire (derry) – oakwood
doline – bowl-shaped depression down which water percolates in limestone country
dolmen – chamber of prehistoric tomb comprising huge supporting stones and a single large capstone
druim (drum) – ridge

drumlin – rounded or teardrop-shaped hill made up of debris left behind as a glacier retreated

dry stone – technique of building in stone without using mortar/cement

dubh (duff, doo) – black, dark

Dúchas – government department responsible for parks, monuments and gardens in the Republic

dumha (dooa) – mound

dún – fort, castle

eaglais – church

eas – waterfall

Éire – Irish name for the Republic of Ireland

escarpment – steep slope or cliff

esker – low ridge formed by glacial debris

fionn (fin) – white, clear

fir – men

fraoch (freagh) – heather

gabher (gower) – goat

Gaelige – Irish language

Gaeltacht – Irish-speaking area

gaoith (gwee) – wind

gap – mountain pass, col

garbh – rough

garda – Irish Republic police

glas – green

gleann (glen) – valley

gorm – blue

gort – tilled field

green road – old country route or road usually with a grassed surface rather than a bitumen or tarmac surface

grike – one of a network of semiregular cracks found in a natural limestone pavement

head ditch – wall separating summer pastures from the fields below

iarnród – railway

inbhear (inver) – river mouth

inis, inish – island

kil – church, chapel; woodland

killeen – children's graveyard

kin – headland

knock – rocky hill

lágh (law) – hill

leac – flat rock, flagstone

leataobh – lay-by (small roadside parking place)

leithreas – toilet

leitir (letter) – rough hillside

liath (lea) – grey

lios – fort or defended settlement

loch (lough) – lake or inlet

loughan – (small) tarn

lug, lag, log – hollow

machaire (maghera) – sandy plain or flat area near the sea

meall, maol (mweel) – bare hill

mám (maum) – pass

marriage stones – pair of stones with a hole through which marriage vows were made

mass path – walking path created by Catholics going to hidden places of worship during times of religious persecution

mná – women

móin, móna – turf

mór (more) – big

motte – substantial, flat-topped earth mound on which a timber tower was built

mullach – summit

NCN – National Cycle Network; a network of signposted cycling routes in the North

North, The – the political entity of Northern Ireland, not the northernmost part of Ireland

nunatak – mountain peak which pokes above an ice sheet and thus escapes the scouring action of glaciers

Ogham stones – marker stones engraved with a primitive form of writing

oifig an phoist – post office

oileán – island

ow, owen – river, stream

pairc – field

passage grave – Stone Age megalithic tomb contained in a large domed cairn, with the burial chamber reached by a narrow passage

peat – partly decomposed vegetable matter found in bogs and used as fuel

peat hags – area of bog where erosion or turf cutting has left peat exposed

pitched path – path laid with flat stones

plantation – the process of settling Protestants in Ireland in the 16th and 17th centuries

pobal – public

poll – hole, pond, small bay

radharc – view, scenery

raised bogs – mounds of peat covered with heather and moss

rath, ráth – fort or defended settlement
Republic, The – the 26 counties of the South (the Republic of Ireland)
riabhach – grey
ride – forest clearing, or way or road for riding horses through the woods
ring fort – term which covers rath, lios, dún and cashel – all roughly circular structures of stones and earth. They probably date from around 800–700 BC with some still used into the Middle Ages
rinn – headland
roisin – small promontory
ros – promontory
rothar (róhar) – bike
round tower – tall, tapering circular tower possibly used for centuries as a lookout or refuge
rua, ruadh – red

sceilig (skellig) – rock
sceir (sker, skerry) – rock, reef
scraith – topsoil
sea stack – coastal rock pinnacle
sean – old
sidh (shee) – fairy, fairy hill
sink hole – bowl-shaped depression down which water percolates in limestone country
sleán – traditional, long-bladed spade
slí – path
slí geill – yield right of way (road sign)
sliabh (slieve) – mountain
slidhe (slee) – road, track
souterrain – underground chamber, possibly of prehistoric origin but long in use, most likely for food storage
South, The – the Republic of Ireland

spate – flood
spinc – pinnacle
sráid – street
srón – noselike mountain feature
sruth, sruthán – stream
stuaic (stook) – pinnacle
suí, suidhe (see) – seat

Taoiseach – Irish prime minister
tarn – small mountain lake or pool
teach – house
teampall – church
theas – south
thiar – west
thoir – east
thuaidh – north
tir (teer) – land, territory
tobar – well
togher – ancient wooden trackways across peatlands
tombolo – narrow sand or shingle bars which link an island with the mainland or with another island
tor – tower-like rocks formed when frost shatters a nunatak
townland – traditional rural area (may be near a town of the same name)
trá – sandy beach
Travellers – modern-day itinerant people
trig point – survey marker found on some summits
tulach – small hill
turas – journey, pilgrimage
turlough, turlach – seasonal lake or pond found in limestone country

Way – marked long-distance trail

This Book

Countering unpredictable Irish weather with adventurous spirit inspired by this very special isle was a sterling crew of expert cycling authors. Ian Connellan was the coordinating author. He wrote the introductory, Northern Éire, Northern Ireland, Around Ireland and Travel Facts chapters. Nicky Crowther wrote the Dublin & the Northeast, and Southeast chapters. Nicola Wells wrote the Southwest and West chapters.

The Your Bicycle chapter was written by Darren Elder, with contributions by Nicola Wells, Neil Irvine and Sally Dillon; the Health & Safety chapter was written by Ian Connellan, Dr Isabelle Young and Kevin Tabotta. Material from Lonely Planet's *Ireland 5* and *Walking in Ireland 2* was used for parts of this book.

FROM THE PUBLISHER

At Lonely Planet's Melbourne office the coordinating editor was Marg Toohey. She was assisted by Sinéad Conlan, Melanie Dankel, Melissa Faulkner, Thalia Kalkipsakis, Craig MacKenzie, Anne Mulvaney and Tegan Murray. The coordinating cartographer was Andrew Smith. He was assisted by Tony Fankhauser, Kusnandar and Julie Sheridan. The layout designer was Sonya Brooke, who also compiled the colour pages. She was assisted by Vicki Beale, Yvonne Bischofberger and Indra Kilfoyle. Brendan Dempsey designed the cover and Simon Bracken prepared the artwork Illustrations were selected by Pepi Bluck and the images assembled by LPI. The project was managed through production by Glenn van der Knijff and Charles Rawlings-Way. Overseeing the entire process were commissioning editor Andrew Bain and series publishing manager Lindsay Brown.

Index

D

Bold indicates maps.

ABOUT LONELY PLANET GUIDEBOOKS

Lonely Planet published its first book in 1973 in response to the numerous 'How did you do it?' questions Maureen and Tony Wheeler were asked after driving, busing, hitching, sailing and railing their way from England to Australia.

Written at a kitchen table and hand collated, trimmed and stapled, *Across Asia on the Cheap* became an instant local bestseller, inspiring thoughts of another book.

Eighteen months in South-East Asia resulted in their second guide, *South-East Asia on a shoestring*, which they put together in a backstreet Chinese hotel in Singapore in 1975. The 'yellow bible', as it quickly became known to backpackers around the world, soon became the guide to the region. It has sold well over half a million copies and is now in its 10th edition.

Today an international company with offices in Melbourne (Australia), Oakland (USA), London (UK) and Paris (France), Lonely Planet has an ever-growing list of books and other products, including: travel guides, walking guides, city maps, travel atlases, phrasebooks, diving guides, wildlife guides, healthy travel guides, restaurant guides, world food guides, first time travel guides, condensed guides, travel literature, pictorial books and, of course, cycling guides. Many of these are also published in French and various other languages.

In addition to the books, there are also videos and Lonely Planet's award winning Web site.

Some things haven't changed. The main aim is still to help make it possible for adventurous travelers to get out there – to explore and better understand the world.

At Lonely Planet we believe travellers can make a positive contribution to the countries they visit – if they respect their host communities and spend their money wisely. Since 1986 a percentage of the income from each book has been donated to aid projects and human rights campaigns.

Lonely Planet gathers information for everyone who's curious about the planet – and especially for those who explore it first-hand. Through guidebooks, phrasebooks, activity guides, maps, literature, newsletters, image library, TV series and Web site we act as an information exchange for a worldwide community of travellers.

LONELY PLANET OFFICES

Australia
Locked Bag 1, Footscray, Victoria 3011
☎ 03 8379 8000 fax 03 8379 8111
e talk2us@lonelyplanet.com.au

UK
72 – 82 Rosebery Ave, London EC1R 4RW
☎ 020 7841 9000 fax 020 7841 9001
e go@lonelyplanet.co.uk

USA
150 Linden St, Oakland, CA 94607
☎ 510 893 8555 TOLL FREE: 800 275 8555
fax 510 893 8572
e info@lonelyplanet.com

France
1 rue du Dahomey, 75011 Paris
☎ 01 55 25 33 00 fax 01 55 25 33 01
e bip@lonelyplanet.fr
w www.lonelyplanet.fr

World Wide Web: www.lonelyplanet.com *or* AOL keyword: lp
Lonely Planet Images: www.lonelyplanetimages.com